W9-AJQ-389

ALSO BY JENNIFER HOMANS

Apollo's Angels

When the Facts Change: Essays, 1995–2010
(by Tony Judt, edited and introduced
by Jennifer Homans)

Mr. B

Mr. B

GEORGE BALANCHINE'S 20TH CENTURY

JENNIFER HOMANS

RANDOM HOUSE
NEW YORK

Published in the United States by Random House, an imprint and division of Penguin Random House LLC, New York.

Random House and the House colophon are registered trademarks of Penguin Random House LLC.

Text and image permissions begin on page 727.

Library of Congress Cataloging-in-Publication Data
Names: Homans, Jennifer, author.
Title: Mr. B : George Balanchine's 20th century / by Jennifer Homans.
Description: New York : Random House, 2022. |
Includes bibliographical references and index. |
Identifiers: LCCN 2022002681 (print) | LCCN 2022002682 (ebook) |
ISBN 9780812994308 (hardcover) | ISBN 9780812994315 (ebook)
Subjects: LCSH: Balanchine, George. | Ballet—History—20th century. |
Choreography—History—20th century. | Choreographers—United States—Biography.
Classification: LCC GV1785.B32 H66 2022 (print) | LCC GV1785.B32 (ebook) |
DDC 792.8/2092 [B]—dc23/eng/20220125
LC record available at https://lccn.loc.gov/2022002681
LC ebook record available at https://lccn.loc.gov/2022002682

Printed in the United States of America on acid-free paper

randomhousebooks.com

2 4 6 8 9 7 5 3 1

First Edition

Book design by Jo Anne Metsch
frontispiece: © St. Petersburg State Museum of Theatre and Music.
BALANCHINE is a trademark of The George Balanchine Trust.

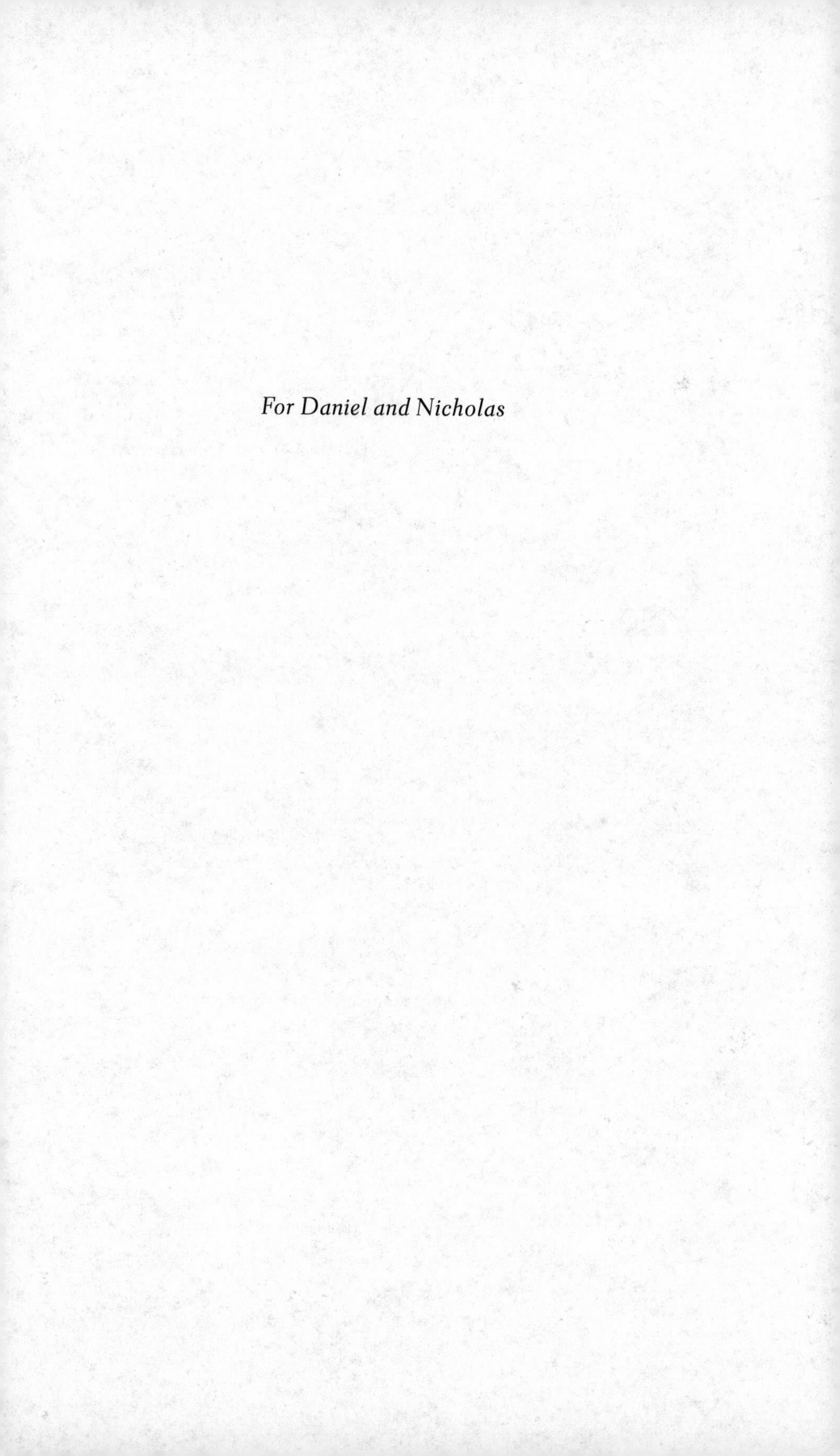

For Daniel and Nicholas

Why we use words? You know why? To communicate with somebody else, you see. The real life, the real reality . . . It's not on earth, it's what we cannot explain with words.

You would never abandon things on earth, so that's why you don't get anywhere. The portals are open for you, but the passage is narrow.

I believe in the moment. I believe in that moment, I believe what I see. The importance of the dance is the person. Choreographer doesn't exist. He suggests. Ballet belongs to a dancer that is now at this moment in front of you.

—GEORGE BALANCHINE[1]

CONTENTS

Mr. B

Introduction

DEAD SOULS

This: the suffering, the grit and hardship of everyday life, never once appeared in Balanchine's dances. It did not interest him—it was pedestrian, a degradation of the human body and spirit. Even the dead bodies in his ballets were set against a backdrop of eternity and had a sense of spirituality and redemption that elevated the body out of the ordinary—dead bodies, yes, but really dead souls. These were bodies purified and transfigured by the disciplined practices of ballet. And if loss was a theme in his dances, so were love and full-fleshed joy. He made many gorgeously costumed ballets that built to a crescendo with colorful kaleidoscope patterns of dancers synchronizing ever more complicated and demanding rhythms. These were fantastic entertainments that lifted audiences into the great good humor of being alive. He saw himself as a musician and theater man, a traveling ballet master, and he had worked in great opera houses and touring troupes, from the Russian czar's Mariinsky Theater of his training and youth to the Paris Opera, Broadway, Hollywood, and his own New York City Ballet (NYCB), which he cofounded in 1948. He said he was a showman, and like the old commedia dell'arte performers, he reinvented himself many times. He seemed ageless. For his dancers, even at the end of his life, "Mr. B" was a god and they surrendered their own young lives for a chance to dance his glorious ballets.

There was some part of him that did not think of himself as mortal at all. "I am not a *male*. . . . I am water and air and I am servant."[1] Or "I am a cloud in trousers," he said, a phrase borrowed from a poem he had learned early in life by the Russian poet Vladimir Mayakovsky. Some of the dancers who knew him best secretly called him "the breath," another word for spirit, really.[2] What this suggested, and it was a central theme of his life, was that he felt like a man with two bodies and he lived in them both simultaneously, with at times heartbreaking personal consequences. The first was the trousers—the earthly man delighted by sensual feelings and desires, who loved good food, fine wine, beautiful women. He devoted his life to dancing and everyone said that in rehearsals, even in his old age, he was more physically animated, expressive, and alive than any of his astonishingly athletic and youthful performers. The cloud or breath was something else, and he saw it as the source of his gift. It wasn't mind, exactly. It was more a physical inwardness, and at moments he could appear strangely detached, almost androgynous or asexual, like an angel who knows everything but feels nothing. A "servant" bearing dances to the gods. An airy floating spirit, elusive at times, even to himself.

He lived through his dancers. He was not like Mozart or Einstein or Picasso, working alone to change the way people hear or think or see. He needed dancers and a whole theatrical enterprise, but dancers above all. His gift didn't exist without them, and the most disoriented moments of his life were those when he found himself alone and unattached to dancers. He had to have them, and he gathered them and shaped them, making his own paints and pigments from their flesh and blood, meticulously reading and sculpting their minds and bodies. Making dances was personal, psychological, intimate even—they liked to say he knew them better than they knew themselves—and because women were his primary material, and because he was a man who loved women, sensuality and love were always a part of it.

For a genius, Balanchine felt small. "Maloross,"[3] he called himself because he felt undersized, and as a child in Russia they had called him "the rat" for his persistent facial tic, a kind of nervous sniffing and twitching under the right eye as he spoke, almost like a visual stutter. He sketched himself in childlike drawings at the end of letters he wrote to lovers as a tiny mouse in the company of a large female cat that he fed and nurtured. In his mind's eye, he was that man-mouse, "mighty mouse!"—a flourish at the bottom of the page, and he didn't imagine himself as particularly attractive, though women found him sexy. The mouse was like the cloud or the breath—something a bit secret in their midst—a watcher scurrying around in his mind preparing great delicacies for his dancers and audiences to enjoy.

In reality, he was not small at all but physically quite average: average height, average weight, average proportions. He had fine, dark features—"I am Georgian," he liked to say—and his Caucasian roots were visible in his dark, almond-shaped eyes, pensive and inward in portraits but lit and expressive in life. His forehead was high, and he had a delicate but large straightedge nose ("Bigger is better") that became his signature feature in the sketches of his face in profile that he used to sign letters. Only his hands were fleshy and muscular, perhaps from playing the piano, which he did almost daily for most of his life. He liked to work with his hands—cooking, but also carpentry and gardening. He could be found at the local market carefully touching and testing for firm cucumbers or the perfect tomato. Smells mattered, and once he could afford it, perfumes were a routine purchase for the women dancers he admired (a different scent for each).

Appearances mattered too and he had a dandy's interest in clothing and dress. Pictures from his St. Petersburg youth show him with a dramatic flair, hair slicked back in a Byronesque sweep with dark eye makeup to emphasize the point. Later, in Europe, he favored Italian suits and bow ties or colorful foulards, and he loved his American Western-style shirts with string ties and a turquoise flourish. In the studio it was a simple shirt, neat slacks, and flexible jazz or street shoes, and everyone remembers how he would roll up his sleeves as he entered the room, a sign that the work was about to begin. He took a personal interest in costume design and could be seen bent lovingly over a swath of fabric or absorbed in adjusting a headdress, and he always insisted on the finest materials for his dancers.

These sensual delights came against a backdrop of hardship and privation. He had experienced cold and starvation as a child in revolutionary Russia, his skin covered with pus-filled boils from malnutrition. The fear of gnawing hunger and the acrid smell of dead bodies piled in the streets in those early years never really left him. He had a weakened constitution. He was struck with tuberculosis (TB) as a young man, and soon after his arrival in the United States in 1933, he suffered mysterious epileptic-like fits and recurrences of TB, leaving him with a collapsed lung and narrowing left chest. Hardly a year passed when he was not suffering or seeking medical help for some real or imagined ailment—another source, perhaps, of his feeling small and vulnerable, but also part of his enormous stamina and determination to enjoy life's pleasures and, above all, to make his dancers perform to their very fullest. "What's the matter with now?" he would say. "You might be dead tomorrow!"

But really, it was all something of a secret. How Balanchine made his extraordinary dances and how the New York City Ballet had come to be—nobody quite knew and nobody could quite say. In the early 1960s, Balanchine wrote an unusually terse letter to his associate Betty Cage asking her to please turn down a request to write his biography by a journalist he didn't particularly like. If he "wants to know about my inspiration, or who is my Muse," Balanchine wrote, "then he will never know that. Because I won't tell him, and it is not going to be written enywhere, for anybody to know."[4] There was something urgent in the secrecy, and Balanchine built walls around his gift and walls around his company, as if there were some kind of magic spell that might be broken by exposure. By the time he died, the company was not just a company; it was a kind of secret society, a utopian community with its own elaborate rituals and taboos, and they were all members, monks and angels, mute scribes and devotees of Balanchine's art. Family secrets were never divulged, not because they were ugly or incriminating, though some were, but because the secret was part of the power, it was part of what they were all doing there together. If they knew, he once said, they would think I was crazy. Other than the dancers, Lincoln Kirstein—brilliant, huge, troubled, mad, loyal Lincoln—was the only one who understood, and they didn't talk about it either.

Americans like to see Balanchine in their own twentieth-century light. Wasn't he making ballet modern, abstract, twelve-tone, and progressive, and weren't his dances icons of speed and urban accomplishment, ornaments to freedom and innovation? The State Department sent the company out on Cold War tours, and Balanchine went—"I am an American"—but the sight of Communism sickened him more than they could imagine. Russia was probably the deepest disappointment he had ever known. He had seen and suffered the way Communism could turn words and reason to wood, and he had set his own path away from the materialist Bolshevik Revolution that had violently interrupted his childhood and seduced his native land. And so there he was in New York City, quietly building a village of angels and erecting a music-filled monument to faith and unreason, to body and beauty. It was his own counterrevolutionary world of the spirit, an alternate vision of the twentieth century.

Balanchine himself was a kind of secret too. Restraint and civility were his natural disposition, and he was a deeply private man. The mask came naturally, at birth perhaps, but was fixed over years of history and experience. As he built the NYCB up around himself, he withdrew more and more inside. No drama, no tempers, no pretense, a simple craftsman at work daily. Even his use of language was secretive. He was a sophisticated linguist and spoke Russian, German, French, and English. He loved wordplay and puns and wrote limericks (many of them erotic) and romantic song lyrics. Yet although he lived in the United States for fifty years, he spoke a strange pidgin English that was extremely expressive but impossible to pin down in its winding syntax. It was brilliant but eccentric, hidden, foreign, part of the mask, and also a way of still being Russian—not *Soviet* but his own Russia, of his own making. He wasn't an intellectual, W. H. Auden had rightly observed, but something more—"a man who understands everything."[5] "I have been alive for a long time," Balanchine would later say, and he did know a lot, read a lot, but he held all of that to himself and dispensed it patiently in thin streams to reporters or dancers or curious outsiders who blankly ignored his digressions into the finer points of fairies or the afterlife. He conserved: energy, temper, ideas—concentrated them in an increasingly dense and secret inner world that had fewer and fewer outlets as he aged. By the end the only real problem he faced was the one he and his dancers had made together: how to live in the real world when the unreal world of the stage was so much more alive?

He didn't think about it much. He focused on music, the grounding and “floor” of his life and dances. He read books. He played the piano. He absorbed. He cooked. He gardened. He liked carpentry. He ironed his own shirts and could be seen through the window of his apartment in the early morning hours with a towel around his waist, ironing alone. He washed cars. And he made ballets. The rest was left unspoken. It is all in the dances, he said. But it wasn’t, quite.

RUSSIA

Chapter 1

HAPPY FAMILIES

When Georgi was born one cold January day in 1904, he was his mother's first illegitimate son. It was official: he was number 160 on the list of newborns at the Church of the Nativity on the Sands in St. Petersburg, where Maria Nikolaevna Vasil'eva had dutifully registered his arrival. On this critical document establishing Balanchine's existence in the eyes of God and the Russian state, his father was absent, and his mother, the authorities noted in a neat hand, was Orthodox but "unwed." The problem was not only that Balanchine came into the world in a half-fallen bastard state, somehow discredited from the start; it was also that without a father, Georgi had no patronymic, and without a patronymic his entire genealogy was in doubt. Who was he, even?

His older sister, Tamara, born two years earlier, was illegitimate too. Ditto his brother, Andrei, who came a year after Georgi, in 1905. On Tamara's document, "ILLEGITIMATE" was even scrawled like a scarlet letter in bold capitals under her name. Had Maria's children been born in Western Europe, they might have held some rights through their mother, but this was Russia, and children automatically took the legal status of their father. The sad fact was that without a paterfamilias none of them had any legal standing at all. They hardly existed. There was only one way back into the social and political fold: in special cases, usually with influence and money changing hands, a child might be legitimized ex post facto by imperial consent and the word of the czar himself.

A cramped note in new ink amending Tamara's, Georgi's, and Andrei's birth documents tells us that this is exactly what happened. On March 18, 1906, the district court legitimized the birth of each of Maria's three children, and on September 23, the Church recognized this change in status too. It was all verified, for anyone who cared to look, in document no. 13025. When Georgi was later asked for his birth certificate, he was able to present an official dictum—Birth Certificate no. 5055—grandly stating that by imperial decree at the St. Petersburg County Court of the Seventh District and acting on a decision from March 18, 1906, it was hereby affirmed that Georgi Melitonovich Balanchivadze had in fact been born to legally wedded parents, both of the Orthodox Christian faith and both married for the first time. His father, it was proclaimed, was the "Hereditary Honorable Citizen Meliton Antonovich Balanchivadze." Stamps, signatures, office duties paid.[1]

This administrative sleight of hand may have normalized Balanchine's birth, but it did nothing to change the facts. If Georgi's parents ever did formally marry—no record has been found—it was not, at least in Meliton's case, for the first time. When Georgi and his siblings were born, Meliton had a whole other family: a wife and two children back in his native Georgia. Many years later, Balanchine would wistfully tell his first biographer that this unnamed and faceless first wife, whom he never met, had died and that his father had been a widower—but she hadn't, and he wasn't.[2]

The matter was serious, if not unusual. There were growing numbers of illegitimate children in St. Petersburg in these years, as peasant women, scarves wrapped tightly around their heads and carrying their belongings, fled their villages for new opportunities in nearby urban centers. Marital traditions loosened their hold on these and other urban mothers—townswomen, craftswomen, women filling jobs in businesses and factories, Georgi's mother perhaps among them, who found themselves at once independent and vulnerable in new ways. Official shelters, called "angel factories," even paid two rubles per head for abandoned babies in an effort to absorb the increase in children left by their often struggling and unwed mothers. Even for those with the advantages of rank or wealth, the consequences could be serious: illegitimacy precluded the inheritance of family wealth—Pierre's problem in the early pages of Tolstoy's *War and Peace*; Alexander Herzen's problem in life. Wealth was not a Balanchivadze problem, at least for now, and nobility was out of the question. "If you are noble," Balanchine later said, "you always want to find out where you come from, my French so and so, my mother was so and so. . . . But they were simple people, nothing, not important."[3]

And so at the moment of birth, there were already complications, uncertainties, revisions, and pasts that would never quite reveal themselves fully or that later took on the aura of secrets and blank spaces in his mind. Balanchine may not have cared that he was officially illegitimate or known that his parents later maneuvered to "correct" the record, but it was a fact of his parents' lives, and children always absorb their parents' facts. Balanchine never had the confidence of his past, and when he looked back down the long corridor of his life to that distant point where it all began, he saw only shadows and vague outlines. "I don't know, I don't know," he would say when pressed, winding his voice around the question and trying to find something to fill the hole in his mind. Thus emerged the first truth of his life: the bedrock was sand.

Meliton Antonovich Balanchivadze came from a clan of state peasants in the rural enclave of Banoja, just outside the small town of Kutaisi in western Georgia.[4] You can go there today and meet the Balanchivadze descendants still living there and see the sprawling graveyard of Balanchivadze ancestors buried in fenced outdoor plots, each like a miniature home complete with a small graveside table to make visitors comfortable, since talking with the dead was part of life. You can read in the church records going back into the nineteenth century that Khosia was the father of Otia, who was the father of a monk and his brother Kaikhosro, who married Tula, and together they bore Balanchine's grandfather Amiran.

The family were peasants, but they were rising, and this very Amiran pulled himself up from the unglamorous business of soil and dirt in one of the only ways possible at the time: the Russian Orthodox Church. He managed to attend seminary in Kutaisi and become a parish priest, a deacon, even, and part of the white clergy, so he changed the Georgian Amiran to the more Russian-sounding Anton. Others in the family joined the more ascetic black clergy of celibate monks—the ancestral monk, to begin with, and later an uncle whose investiture Balanchine would witness as a child. Anton married a local peasant girl, and together they produced Meliton—the first of several children, only four of whom would survive. Meanwhile, Anton was becoming something of a local leader, and his parishioners were apparently so partial to him that they built in his honor the small gray stone church of St. George, which sits high on a hill overlooking the cemetery and the village. Meliton was raised down the hill and across the dirt road, in the shadow of St. George and at the center of what was then a small and impoverished farming community.[5]

It mattered that it was St. George, who would be little Georgi's patron saint too, and this modest church is the only firm structure that ties Balanchine to that dusty place in his family's past. St. George, whose image Balanchine would keep near him in icons all his life, lost his mother at age ten and devoted himself to brave military feats in the name of God. In his martyrdom he was Christlike and is said to have suffered tortures including a caustic lime pit, iron hooks, and being crushed by stone, broken on a wheel, and burned with a torch. An angel often protected him. St. George famously appeared in paintings and icons riding a white horse and radiating light as he speared an evil dragon worshipped by terrified pagans and saved the beautiful maiden they had offered in sacrifice to this vicious beast. The maiden then led the dying dragon to the town center, where St. George slew it for all to see, a performance that freed the damsel and her people and brought them to the Christian faith.

The village of Banoja sits in the narrow valley of the Rioni River near the town of Kutaisi and some 143 miles west of Tbilisi, at the foot of the Greater Caucasus Mountains. The Caucasus are the highest range in Europe and stretch from the Black Sea to the Caspian Sea, setting Kutaisi, Tbilisi, and the whole of Georgia dramatically (at times violently) apart from Russia and its capital of St. Petersburg, where Balanchine would be born and raised. Some thought of Georgia as Russia's "southern Siberia,"[6] since the only way in from the north was over a perilous military highway with hairpin curves through a rocky and beautiful wooded mountain pass, a region romanced in tales by Pushkin and Lermontov.

Since the early nineteenth century, the entire region had been forcibly incorporated into Russia and its diverse, fractured, and at times warring regions ruled by the vast and byzantine administrative structures of the czar. From the imperial point of view, there was no such thing as "Georgia," and the censors forbade even the use of the word, at least in Russian. Education was in Russian, not Georgian (which has its own beautifully ornate alphabet), and the Church was the Russian Orthodox Church, not the far more ancient Georgian Orthodox Church, with its deep pagan influences and ties to antiquity.[7]

This was the Georgia that Meliton was born to, and as a child, he naturally began walking his father's path. He had been baptized in the nearby Kutaisi Cathedral, and like his father, he was educated at the Kutaisi seminary (his grades in all subjects—Russian, Latin, Greek, arithmetic, and spiritual history—were low), and although he went on to the more prestigious Tiflis Theological Seminary in Georgia's capital city at the age of fourteen, he soon dropped out and returned to Kutaisi to marry Gayane Eristavi, a local girl from an old but impoverished noble family. The couple had two children, Nino and Apollon, and for a moment, Meliton appeared set to continue on the family path through a life that would end in the little Banoja cemetery under the Church of St. George with his ancestors all around.

As it turned out, however, this was only Meliton's first family. Balanchine belonged to Meliton's second, Russian, family and a whole new life. Nino and Apollon were Balanchine's distant half-sister and half-brother, a fact that Balanchine barely knew. He never met Nino, but as a young child he would briefly meet Apollon—who was twenty-two years older—in St. Petersburg, though Balanchine later rarely mentioned him. Friends and dancers close to Balanchine in the American years of his life were shocked to meet this unexpected relation, who appeared at his side during the NYCB's 1962 tour to Tbilisi. "This is my brother," Balanchine blankly noted as he presented this forgotten man, who had been wasted from years in a Soviet political prison before taking up the family mantle of priest.[8]

It was history and an ample dose of wanderlust that broke Meliton's family and set him on a new path. Meliton had been born a year after the watershed liberation of the serfs across Russia in 1861, an event as momentous (and flawed) as the end of slavery in the United States. He came of age with the resulting "back to the people" movement of artists and writers drawn to peasant traditions of music, dance, and art. At the same time, the Russian authorities in Georgia were trying forcibly to erase these traditions in the name of a unified Russian homeland. Tension mounted as loyalty to the Russian language and to a host of increasingly rigid political and cultural practices dictated from distant offices in St. Petersburg became more and more difficult for local Georgians to sustain—even for those like Meliton and his family, who were loyal to the czar and to their own advancement in the Russian state apparatus. Complicating matters, industrialization, railways, and urbanization were fast changing the landscape, and Meliton was part of a larger flow of poor and displaced peasants and people of various ranks in search of opportunity moving into Kutaisi, Tiflis (later Tbilisi), and other rapidly growing towns and urban centers. The seminaries at Kutaisi and especially Tiflis were known as stepping-stones to higher position and stature in the Russian system, but by the time Meliton arrived, the Tiflis seminary in particular was also becoming a breeding ground for a growing Georgian nationalist *ressentiment*.

The seminary had been especially harshly Russianized—Georgian icons stripped from church walls and destroyed, Georgian history summarily banished from the syllabus. Life inside the walls of the "Stone Sack," as the students none too fondly called the massive neoclassical building, was strict. Students were occupied from dawn until late in the evening with classes and rehearsals, and Sundays were spent standing for hours in long Orthodox services. Meliton joined the seminary choir and took up chanting—one of Georgia's oldest musical and religious traditions—at the ancient Sioni Cathedral, not far from the seminary. None of this rigor or religiosity prevented a growing dissent: secret reading circles, urgent cultural and political meetings, and heated debates multiplied as resistance to the repressive Russian state hardened. A few years after Meliton left, the seminary would become the intellectual training ground for another poor peasant boy recently arrived from the neighboring town of Gori: Joseph Stalin.[9]

Meliton fell under the influence of the work of the poets Akaki Tsereteli and Ilia Chavchavadze, leading figures in the growing Georgian national awakening. Music was his greatest talent, so Meliton abandoned any aspirations to a life in the clergy and instead busily devoted himself to a flurry of Georgian musical pursuits that would come to characterize his life. With his young family stationed in Kutaisi, he took up work in opera and organized his own touring ethnographic choir that performed in traditional Georgian dress—pictures show him handsomely posed in a dapper European suit and tie (a sign of social stature, no matter Georgian national sentiment) amid his swarthy black-booted, belted, and sabered all-male choir of Georgian musicians. Meanwhile, like so many composers of his generation, Meliton was traversing the countryside collecting and transcribing folk songs, but in a sign of his simultaneous admiration for more Westernized Russian musical traditions, he also sometimes doctored these local compositions by turning "wildly" dissonant Georgian trichords into more "civilized" Western classical triads. He even wrote his own songs—Balanchine would too—and set to music the poetry of Tsereteli and Chavchavadze. Georgia and Georgian music became his life.[10]

It was a restless and ambitious time, and Meliton soon wanted to go to St. Petersburg to further his musical studies. His younger brother Vaso was already there studying painting with the renowned Ilya Repin, another leader in the "back to the people" movement. To pay for his trip, Meliton tirelessly raised money by putting on shows with friends, and in 1889, at the age of twenty-seven, he left his Georgian wife and two small children, ages three and five, crossed the forbidding Caucasus Mountains, and made his way to the capital of Alexander III's imperial Russia.

He moved in with Vaso and politely petitioned as "the son of a Priest" to enroll in a composition class at the St. Petersburg Conservatory of Music with Nikolay Rimsky-Korsakov—drawn no doubt by the composer's works based on folk and fairy tales.[11] Rimsky-Korsakov had been a founding member of the "Mighty Little Heap" of Russian composers fully trained in Western musical traditions but devoted to developing a distinctly national musical style rooted in the ancient cultures of the Asian steppe, the Caucasus, and points east. He had just premiered his colorful *Scheherazade*.[12]

Alexander III was setting his own neonationalist tone in the capital city and turning "his" Russia sharply against the Europeanizing instincts of St. Petersburg and his more cultivated father, who had been assassinated by anarchists in 1881. The son was burly, awkward, carelessly educated (his brother had been the heir apparent but had suddenly died), and he despised the French-inspired etiquette and what he called the "endless cotillion" of the St. Petersburg elite. He proudly declared himself a Muscovite and thought of himself as a "true Russian": Slavic, Orthodox, and committed above all to the sanctity of his own autocratic rule.

He set about changing the look of the country, in part by building new churches, new monasteries, and new convents, including the garish onion-domed Church of the Savior on the Spilled Blood in St. Petersburg, erected on the site of his father's murder and a deliberate affront to the city's otherwise elegantly restrained European architectural style. Balls at the Winter Palace took on Muscovite themes, and officers and members of his guards were even encouraged to grow bushy beards, eschewing the long-standing Petrine regulations mandating a clean-shaven "Western" look. Epaulets, sabers, armor were out; caftans, Russian caps, and jackboots were in. Icons and crosses were added to flagstaffs, and Alexander doted like a proud father on the children of his great empire. His coronation ceremonies included Russia's nationalities: Georgians, Finns, Cossacks, Poles, and others performing their own native dances in traditional costumes around a beautiful central woman: Rus.[13]

Meliton was in his element. Impatient with the rigors of a conservatory education, he eventually abandoned his musical studies and instead threw himself headlong into re-creating his Georgian musical life: Georgian evenings, Georgian singing groups, theater, opera, dinners, parties. He started work on "the first Georgian opera," *Wily Tamara*, from an epic poem by Tsereteli about Georgia's beloved medieval Imereti queen: the seductive and strong ruler of Georgia at its cultural peak. Always short of money, Meliton managed to win support from Prince K. I. Bagration-Mukharinsky, of the Georgian royal family and a dynastic relation to the mythic Tamara.[14] He did not complete the opera until much later but got far enough to stage an excerpt at the prestigious Hall of Nobles in 1897. It was a formal affair, just the kind he liked, with champagne and endless toasts, elegant food, and couples in colorful national costume—a Georgian version of the Russian balls so fashionable at the time, in which guests set their Parisian finery aside and arrayed themselves instead in traditional Russian dress of the past, embroidered and brightly colored. For all its claims to Georgianness, however, Meliton's opera, like so much of his St. Petersburg life, was performed in Russian. Balanchine remembered his father this way: "He didn't *do* anything, not serious, he was a good speaker, always invited as guest to speak at parties, for flowery speech, beautiful, things like that."[15]

In the course of it all, Meliton managed to achieve a certain social stature. As an artist he was awarded the title of Hereditary Honorable Citizen, even though he officially belonged to the *Raznochintsy*, or "People of Various Ranks," a catchall administrative category for accomplished freemen who were not quite socially elevated enough to make it onto Peter the Great's all-important Table of Ranks. The table, which had been invented in the early eighteenth century and would endure until the revolution abolished it, established a hierarchy of civil and military ranks that formed the backbone of the Russian political order. It was a way of controlling the elite by destabilizing its members: power and upward mobility, and especially the coveted titles of nobility (along with valuable privileges, such as exemption from military service or the capitation tax), depended on loyalty to the state and the personal favor of the czar rather than on birth alone. And while the highest ranks were largely occupied by the hereditary nobility, it was possible to step into the lower ranks—and to climb. At least in theory, Meliton—little peasant-boy Meliton, the lowly son of a parish priest from Banoja—had half a chance.

But only half. The People of Various Ranks were also seen as outsiders—dismissed by many above them as upstarts—and the most anxious and unstable category in an already unstable order. Everyone knew that these were people who might one day rise, but they were far more likely to tumble down the social and economic ladder into the dreaded "dark masses" below. They constituted a precarious middling social group—part of Russia's notoriously undeveloped middle class—that included non-noble civil servants, scholars, townspeople, merchants, and artists. The "Hereditary" prefix in Hereditary Honorable Citizen was important since it made it clear that Meliton's children, assuming they were legitimate, would inherit his status, which was not always the case with the "Honorable Citizen" category. It made Meliton marginally more secure—a small rung up and a sign of his ambition and respectable standing.

We don't know how Meliton met Balanchine's mother, Maria Nikolaevna Vasil'eva, a fragile, porcelain-looking woman with a remote demeanor and shy, inwardly focused eyes. Nor do we know much about her, except that she loved music and was deeply religious. Meliton affectionately called her Gogosha, bridging his worlds by mixing the Georgian word for "girl" with the Russian diminutive.[16] She was eleven years his junior, but Balanchine thought the gap was twenty-five years, and he pictured his father as perennially "old" and his mother as warm and delicate: "blond, small nose, very kind, small, soft woman, very nice . . . No, no, she was absolutely calm and soft and did not ask anybody to do anything." Later, his brother gave him photos, which show her fine features and gentle frame and her solidly bourgeois self-presentation: ribbons and cinched crinoline, stiff bows, delicate lace or a patterned blouse, high collars, and wispy blond hair pulled softly back. "Like people in a Chekhov play," Balanchine recalled, implying dress but also an underlying melancholy.[17]

According to her children's birth certificates, Maria was a former craftswoman and the daughter of a merchant of the Tsarkosel'skaia Second Merchant's Guild in the well-heeled Tsarskoye Selo area of St. Petersburg. The guild generally included men in retail trade, shop owners, small-factory owners, and anyone of professional standing who could afford the steep fees, which meant that she too belonged to the striving social universe of the People of Various Ranks, notoriously susceptible to rank-mania and acutely aware of the symbols and trappings of status—clothing, education, wealth, the right address, the right church, the right society. Maria told her children that her father was one Baron Nicholas von Almedingen, a German businessman who abandoned his Russian family and returned to Germany, at which point her mother, she said, gave Maria *her* name, Vasil'eva. Maybe it was true or partly true or not true at all: the records of Maria's birth and ancestry are nowhere to be found, in spite of diligent scholarly research in the vast Russian archives, and although it is true that the Almedingens, a notable family of writers, officials, and military men, do later appear in Balanchivadze letters and lives, there seems to be no mention of Maria in *their* recorded history.[18]

Whatever her lineage, Maria had sisters, at least one by a different father. They appear as constant fixtures in the few recovered family letters and memories: Aunt Nadezda, Aunt Anya, Aunt Milia, Aunt Sofia—who *was* a documented daughter of an Almedingen and a close companion to Maria, especially in her later years. These sisters were the closest family Maria seems to have had, although among them Balanchine only really remembered Nadezda: "Her family name, same my mother Vasil'eva . . . same mothers, two daughters . . . two different fathers, they were sisters but different names one called Maria Nikolaevna, the other Nadiera Vasil'eva." Nadezda attended the Oldenberg Institute, a primary technical school (to age thirteen) for children of all classes, founded by the duke and duchess Alexander of Oldenberg, who also sponsored hospitals, orphan asylums, and other charitable institutions. These were disciplined, hierarchical, and insular places—much like Meliton's seminary or the ballet school Maria would later choose for her son—emphasizing obedience and fine manners. Nadezda's name appears on the student lists and family lore says Maria went there too, but she is missing from the school's official ranks, which may account for her childish hand and uncertain spelling and grammar. The literacy rate of urban women, including aristocrats, still hovered around 38 percent just before the turn of the century.[19]

We are left a shadowy and unstable world. Balanchine had none of the certainties of the aristocratic Nabokovs, Stravinskys, and other well-to-do White Russian artists he would later know, who grew up on well-appointed estates and were given a thorough education in Western literature, languages, and art, not to mention a strong sense of their own permanence in time and space—illusory, it would turn out, but powerful nonetheless. His was a more far-flung heritage, uprooted and unstable but also dynamic and full of surprises and unexpected turns, and one of the most unexpected came in 1901, just before Tamara, Georgi, and Andrei were born.

That year, Maria Nikolaevna Vasil'eva won the state lottery. Suddenly, they were rich. The prize was significant: an astonishing two hundred thousand rubles.[20] It was a shocking piece of luck, especially since the lottery was talked about by everyone but almost no one actually won. It had been created by the state in the 1860s to attract small investors to purchase moderately priced bonds, with the calculation that a very occasional large win would inspire people of modest means, such as Maria and Meliton, to gamble on the chance.[21] It worked, and by the 1890s the lottery had become a source of feverish gossip and giddy fantasies of instant wealth and happiness, although Chekhov warned, in his story "The Lottery Ticket," that such fantasies could also be ruinous.[22] The annual drawing at the State Bank was a much-anticipated social event, with its large rotating drums churning bits of cardboard, each printed with a name and serial number, until the winning tickets were finally drawn and the winners' lives dramatically changed.

Maria's unexpected winnings meant that her three children were not only illegitimate but born into a world of fairy-tale wealth and giddy expectations. The money, it seems, belonged to Maria, who eventually included Meliton by power of attorney.[23] Property and wealth were the only things a woman in Russia could own outright without the permission or oversight of a father or husband. As a woman, Maria otherwise had little independence: women had no right to travel, reside alone, enroll in education, or take a job without a father's or husband's approval. But even married women could own and manage their own property, including cash assets. And besides, at this point Maria was technically single and, by all accounts, on her own. Rumors still cut through the family: did Meliton, as his Georgian family lore would have it (even to the present day), rush to see a priest to erase his marriage to his Georgian wife and marry the now-rich Maria instead? We don't really know, but probably not, since Gayane is later on record saying that Meliton sent support over the years and even paid for her to visit health spas.[24]

We do know that whatever the complications of their formal relations, Maria and Meliton wasted no time in spending the windfall. First there was real estate, and the couple moved several times to various fancy addresses near the Smolny Cathedral, in the northeast corner of the city, before they finally settled, when the children were toddlers, in a large twelve-room apartment in an art-deco building located on the wide, neatly cobblestoned Suvorovsky Prospekt, named after the heroic general of the 1812 war. They were not far from the Nikolaevskaia Military Academy and the Suvorovsky garden, formerly on the Suvorov family estate. "To coachman we would say Suvorovsky Prospekt near the Academy," Balanchine said of one of his few clear memories of these early childhood years.[25]

Next came the dacha. In 1906 Maria purchased a plot of land in fashionable Lounatjoki, a forested region dotted with clear lakes on the Karelian peninsula in Russian-occupied Finland. It was some three hours by steam train from St. Petersburg's Finlyandsky Station, along the coast about halfway to Vyborg. Lounatjoki was a popular region for summer homes among the St. Petersburg elite, and the little town boasted a modest station house where travelers could connect to a small steam tram that carried people to various destinations deep in the woods. The necessaries were within reach: there was a domed Orthodox monastery with a bell tower surrounded by a neat white picket fence, an old barn for summer theater, a post office, and a small bakery. "Little Pinewoods," the plot was quaintly called, and in 1908 Maria added a second plot to the expanding family holdings.[26] On the property, they built a large, rambling, two-story log house in a classic dacha style, with generous porches for long afternoons over the samovar and a cozy rustic feel that evoked the warm Russian interiors and country life immortalized in *War and Peace* with Natasha's famous dance.[27]

The rest followed. In St. Petersburg there was a staff of cooks and maids and wet nurses for the children—a professionally shot baby photograph shows Georgi lying in the ample lap of his wet nurse, a large young woman dressed in traditional Russian *sarafan* with strings of pearls and an elaborate headdress, her milk thought to be a vital source of Russian soul. There was a German governess, another coveted attribute of stature and a bow to Maria's supposed distinguished family roots. Meliton acquired a fancy gleaming coach and a handsome white horse—St. George!—to complete their fairytale life, except that it turned out to be a circus animal trained to rear onto its hind legs and prance to music, a trick that one afternoon toppled and wrecked this proud family chariot. The white horse mysteriously vanished.

There were photographs of the three children taken at the tony R. Charles Studio (with branches on Nevsky Prospekt and Vasilievsky Island). We can see them posed in freshly ironed sailor suits or white Cossack shirts or elaborate harlequin costumes with bobble hats and long curling hair. At home there were feasts, parties, and celebrations, and Meliton used some of the money to finance his Georgian musical soirees, along with a Georgian chorus. He even paid to have a friend and ethnomusicologist collect and edit the letters of Mikhail Glinka for the occasion of the fiftieth anniversary of the composer's death. Like Meliton, Glinka was fully versed in Western musical forms, and he too had incorporated folk themes into his compositions and organized (in his case, serf) choirs and orchestras. Soon after Georgi's birth, Meliton's brother Ivan, who was in the army, arrived with his Polish wife and lived with them for a time. Apollon—the lost Georgian half-brother Georgi barely knew—was pursuing a military career and visited too.[28]

There were constant guests, and the company Meliton and Maria kept seems to have been a mix of artists and musicians, but also political figures, churchmen, and well-placed government officials. Georgi's godparents included very high-ranking men indeed: Konstantin Konstantinovich Stefanovich, fourth rank and a former vice-governor of Georgia who later joined the Interior Ministry and in 1908 served on Pyotr Stolypin's agricultural-reform commission; his father was dean of the imposing Kazan Cathedral off the Nevsky Prospekt. Or Vasily Lvovich Velichko, fifth rank, who was Tamara's godfather; when *he* died his cousin stepped in as Georgi's godfather.[29] Velichko was a Ukrainian-born nobleman and a poet and essayist who had worked with Meliton on an opera libretto. He had been the leader of a Russian-nationalist literary group in the 1880s and 1890s that included the philosopher and mystic Vladimir Soloviev, a key influence on artists and intellectuals fighting for a spiritual revolution. Velichko was also a founding member of the darkly extremist Russian Assembly, which later shaded into the murderous Black Hundreds.

We don't know if Meliton sympathized with Velichko's virulently racist and anti-Semitic rhetoric, but we do know that—Velichko aside—Meliton had many Socialist friends, most of them doomed to tragic political fates. Balanchine later recalled his father's admiration for Irakli Tsereteli, a Georgian Social Democrat who would serve in Alexander Kerensky's government and become a key player, with Meliton, in the short-lived Georgian Menshevik republic in 1918 before fleeing to the West as the Bolsheviks swept their Menshevik cousins brutally aside. Or Nikolai Chkheidze, another Georgian

Menshevik active in Petrograd and later in Tbilisi; he too would escape to Europe, where he committed suicide. Andrei also recalled long dinners and his father's friendship with the Georgian revolutionaries Mamia Orakhelashvili and Shalva Eliava, who would hold important positions in the Bolshevik government when it came to power in Tiflis—both were arrested and executed during Stalin's Terror in 1937, just weeks before Meliton himself died there. It was a full and expansive house, and Meliton, on the rise, wasn't the kind of man to discriminate politically.[30]

Befitting a man of his newly assumed wealth and stature, Meliton began foolishly styling himself a businessman. He started by setting up a business importing Kakheiti Georgian wines on the prosperous Liteiny Prospekt, a commercial street busy with tramlines, carriages, and customers browsing shop fronts decorated with colorful pictures of the goods available inside. Further cementing his position, he joined the board of the Fourth St. Petersburg Mutual Credit Association, a lending organization for entrepreneurs, and set about building a portfolio of financial investments, throwing himself headlong into Russia's chaotically industrializing economy.

By the fall of 1910, he was in trouble, as his desperate letters to Maria prove. Anguished and writing from business trips in far-flung locations, Meliton nervously assured his wife that things would work out. He might be able to sell some land in Yalta, and that roof-tile factory in Moscow would be okay, and the necessary graphite and sand would arrive in only ten days, and the money should be guaranteed. This time, he promised, he would spend it only on a factory to manufacture foundry vats (of all things), and it was possible there would be more money from Georgi's godfather Stephanovich in Minsk. Meliton swears he will then come home and return to his music and everything will be all right, but he knows it won't. "I feel like I am throwing away my most precious thing—my family."[31] He was playing the odds, gambling really, and the luck that had won them the lottery in the first place never returned.

And so the wealth that Georgi and his siblings had been born into quietly vanished. Maria and Meliton let their prize St. Petersburg apartment go and around 1910 moved the family permanently to the simpler Finland dacha. Maria sold a second plot of land there too. But it was not enough: Meliton's mounting debts caught up with him, and he was taken under house arrest (says Andrei) or sent to debtor's prison (says Balanchine). Balanchine later imagined a dark Soviet-style plot, saying his father was betrayed by friends who gave evidence against him and landed him at the dreaded Kresty Prison, a cruel and ironically cross-shaped facility in St. Petersburg later immortalized by Anna Akhmatova, who stood for "three hundred long hours" at the "hard doors" to hear word of her son, arrested by Stalin's henchmen.[32]

Wherever Meliton was confined, his sudden disappearance had an air of eerie secrecy. Maria told Georgi his father was collecting folk songs in the countryside, the kind of well-intentioned lie no child believes, and the whole episode was so confusing that Balanchine later thought his father had been gone for two years, even though it was probably a matter of months. Indeed, not long after his desperate letters to Maria, the irrepressible Meliton seems to have been back in Georgia celebrating his fiftieth birthday, drinking wine and delivering flowery toasts with friends and family in Kutaisi. Balanchine recalled his father's return from debtor's prison quite differently. In a gilded memory, he saw his handsome father walking slowly up the path to the porch of their home in Lounatjoki to his children and beautiful waiting wife. He was carrying a single red rose—a story Andrei flatly denied.[33]

Chapter 2

ICONS OF CHILDHOOD

Sand was building on sand, and his childish memories, including things Balanchine saw but didn't know he saw, piled on top of what we know, or think we know, about what really happened. In his mind, everything about his distant past later pooled into a single sentence: "Oh yes, we were very happy," he quietly said of his childhood, and he had lots of rose-colored memories to prove it.[1]

In St. Petersburg, he remembered Christmas and a church plunged in total darkness until the choir sang and candles shone on the magnificently bejeweled priests and altar boys in their glittering brocade vestments. He remembered how he wore velvet to the annual Christmas party in the Grand Hall of Nobles, and never forgot the city's enormous and fantastically decorated tree and how the children all played games such as leapfrog and *rucheyok*, a scene he would later reproduce in *The Nutcracker*. He remembered how at home there was a glorious tree too, with the smell of pine and candle wax, decorated with gold paper angels and stars, silver tinsel "rain," and fat glass pears that didn't break if they fell.[2]

There were trips to Eliseyev's vast emporium on the corner of Nevsky Prospekt, a palatial art-deco building with stained-glass panels, bronze statuary, and lavish window displays of delicious candies and fruits. Inside, there were vaulting ceilings and chandeliers, and sawdust-covered floors that muffled the footfall of customers as they browsed the delicacies imported from around the world. Eliseyev, a successful wine merchant, had even built a small theater with tall windows and a modest stage for operettas on the second floor. And, of course, there were Meliton's shining white horse and carriage, "Suvorovsky near the Academy," and walks he was told he took as a boy with his governess in the beautifully cultivated formal gardens nearby. It was said that he sat on a bench on the neatly groomed park path close to a man who waited patiently until the small boy had played and gone before he threw his concealed bomb, killing a nearby target.

The bomb was an example of the things Balanchine didn't notice or remember, except as something vaguely ominous. He didn't recall the overcrowding and filth in the streets, the sewage dumped into cesspools in back alleyways, and the rickety wooden carts that arrived by night to collect the rotting and stinking refuse. Or the large signs in menacing red letters in public places warning against the drinking water, as cholera and TB outbreaks routinely swept the city. He was too young to fully register the mounting unrest and violence, the strikes and protests, the seemingly random attacks—bombs, assassination attempts, gunshots—launched by anarchists, Black Hundreds, and extremist factions on the left and right, some in the pay of the czar's secret police. And he couldn't have known about the weakening, languishing power of the great czar himself in a Russia that had faced humiliating defeat at war with Japan, immediately followed by the suicidal events of Bloody Sunday in 1905, when His Majesty ordered his troops to fire on his very own people—priests, families, women, children—as they marched peacefully from strategic points across the city to the Winter Palace, floating Orthodox flags and singing hymns to their "Czar-father."

Balanchine may not have known, but children absorb their surroundings, and the deteriorating atmosphere of St. Petersburg was silently imprinted like a menacing drumbeat onto his "Oh yes, we were very happy" early years. And as he separated the memories out over the course of his life, like wheat from chaff, all that was good and warm and childhood seemed to slide onto the imperial side of the ledger, and all that was violent, anguished, and upsetting piled up in a heap around the dark incidents that eventually led to the most inescapable disruptions of all: war and revolution. But his light-suffused memories stayed with him; they were the jewels he would sew into the hem of his mind and carry with him out of Russia. He had to remember them because no one else would. He took no family with him, and he had no relations to tell him the stories of his life, so he developed the habit of holding it all inside. And if these memories, so carefully and balletically constructed in his mind, have a whiff of romance and untruth, what matter? He was building his repertory, and who else was there to say otherwise?

At home it took only two chairs set side by side to make a church altar. Balanchine remembered playing the priest in imaginary robes with his siblings, blessing parishioners and reciting whole portions of the service word for word by heart. He stood for hours with his mother and aunt in stone churches on Sundays and especially for the long Easter midnight services. Year after year he watched the mysterious cloth imprinted with the image of Christ laid in the center of the church on an altar or table of flowers. He delighted in the merriment when the cloth was lifted and the lights flooded, and he walked by his mother's side as people hugged each other and joyfully processed and sang "Christ is risen!" He recalled his awe too at a special service in the cavernous Kazan Cathedral for the tonsure of a Georgian relative, who prostrated himself dramatically on the hard floor with a black cloak thrown over his body; "already he was out of this world," Balanchine later recalled.[3] The cloak was then ritually pulled from the inert man who rose and became—magically—a monk or bishop. Georgi himself eventually became an altar boy, eligible finally for the coveted brocade vestments. He remembered too the little church in Finland and the walk to the "tiny" tram down the road from their house that took the family to worship on Sundays.

And so the Orthodox faith, with its ritual beauty and music, took its given place in his mind. Belief was not a choice, it was a fact of his life from the moment his name was recorded in the church registry. Images and icons, especially, were there from his earliest years right up to his last moments—set in the high corners of Russian houses or later in portable frames propped up on tables in the various apartments he occupied in New York. When he died, his assistant found a small, carefully mounted bishop's staff on his bedside table, along with icons of St. George and St. Nicholas, and a blessing crucifix. Balanchine's relationship to the organized Orthodox Church was occasional, and his spiritual beliefs often took a mystical turn. But still, the practices of the Church, its liturgy and aesthetic, were among the greatest legacies of his childhood—part of the architecture of his imagination.[4]

And if we think of Balanchine's childhood as the formation of a mind as well as an accumulation of experiences, icons in particular were key. They gave him one of his first visual languages, a way to *see*. Icons are flat and two-dimensional. They show us images of saints and other venerated figures, or biblical scenes, but they have none of the seductive emotional drama and storytelling of Catholic art—there are no bodies bent in anguish, no bloodied and burdened Christ, no faces clenched in mourning. Instead, these figures are bloodless and eternal, impassive and immobile. Flatness indicates immateriality, and everything about the flesh and the carnal state is excluded, giving the iconic figure the weightlessness of shades or angels—or dancers. They have bodies, but they are transfigured—the purified and illuminated corporeality of the divine. Icons have no source of light, which means no shadows, just as there are no shadows in the Kingdom of God. The light emanates from *within*, and iconographers like to say that the background of an icon is light itself. All of this immateriality, even though an icon is itself a material object to approach, touch, look at, see.

Moreover, icons use "inverse perspective." Western traditions of perspective bring the viewer into a painting by guiding the eye from the picture's surface to a distant horizon, but icons do the reverse. The horizon is turned back onto the worshipper, and the icon is designed to *reach out* and pull him into its midst, to cross over into the divine. Mary or Christ or St. George is not experienced as narrative—everyone already knows their stories—but instead as a nonlogical and nonverbal visual experience. In the image, everything unfolds *at once* in its immensity, and practitioners yearning to cross to the other side come up close to an icon, face-to-face, leaning, forehead on the image, kissing it, concentrating on it, seeing it even with closed eyes. It is not the image itself that is the focus, but the realer-than-real figure or world accessed through the window or lens of the icon. The experience is sensual and total rather than intellectual or chronological. Icons that have been especially prayed before are considered a more effective gateway because you are united not only with heaven but with all those who have stood and offered their prayers before this image.

Also, icons are never signed. Iconographers, like priests, are in service to God, and the whole process of making an icon, the discipline and obedience to a prescribed set of rules and rituals, is designed to remove the I from the experience. Icons are never self-expression, nor are they original—what man could presume to create the divine? And even though iconographers work from past images, and are bound by tradition and witness, an icon is not a copy of a past icon: the hand of man on paint, oil, resin, is admitted and recognized, even if the I of the ego is not. Each has its own integrity, and like a Greek chorus, icons are part of life. They watch, they judge, they see, and they can elicit good and exact vengeance. Couples cover them when they have sex. Icons were part of Balanchine's inner life, and they bring to mind many things he would later say of his dances and how he made them.[5]

But Finland. In many ways Finland, where the family ended up when the wealth had faded, was Balanchine's best childhood of all. Lounatjoki was a midsummer-night forest of towering pine and birch, with willow trees, mosses, and dozens of varieties of mushrooms—his mother taught him a song to distinguish the poisonous types, and he set out to hunt and dig in the woods, which tinkled with the bells that mothers attached to their children to know they could always be found. There were plump yellow "pineapple" strawberries and large black huckleberries made into sweet jams and pies. He recalled planting in the sprawling garden with the chickens and a pig who became a companion ("very intelligent") until it was finally killed and served to him at a dinner he refused to eat. There were arduous walks to the lakes several miles away, and long summer white nights. In winter there was deep snow and a sleigh and bells and skis to carry you over the heaping fifteen-foot drifts. There was a shaggy white dog to put on the sleigh and a brother, a sister, a German nanny, and a mustached university student in a black cap and coat who tutored the children and played croquet in the garden. Books did not figure much, but his mother did read them fairy tales. There was a sauna he hated—he ran from the heat and steam—and a piano he loved.

Georgi played four-handed pieces with Andrei, and his mother played too; the children organized shows and concerts—just as the families of Tchaikovsky, Nabokov, Tolstoy, and Stravinsky did on their summer estates in the timeless world of Russian aristocratic country life. Tamara created costumes and sets while Georgi and Andrei designed musical programs: "What would you like to hear?" When his father was home, but also back in St. Petersburg before the money was gone, they all played and sang Georgian folk songs, including the spiritual "You Are a Vineyard." And when guests came, as they often did, especially when Meliton was present, there were traditional table songs to accompany the lengthy and impassioned Georgian toasts. Or all those gathered sang urban songs from Kutaisi and Tiflis that sounded a bit like opera, and sometimes the family played gramophone records of old Italian singers. If there was dancing, as there was at Christmas, Andrei remembered Zholia, as he fondly called Georgi, hanging back, shy and watchful, or hiding in a corner to avoid being asked to perform. He kicked and flailed his arms at anyone who disturbed his anonymity.[6]

The children learned three-part singing, polyphony, and the competitive improvisation typical of Georgian folk music, with singers—and children—vying to outdo one another. In this tradition, there was little unison or solo singing, and a song would be performed instead by three voices, usually male and of solo caliber. Repetition was avoided and innovation prized, so that performances of a known song were rarely the same. The singers were considered the author, and the composers of folk songs were anonymous or lost to time. The three voices generally moved in close musical proximity, and improvisation, the children quickly learned, was not freestyle. There were strict musical rules and conventions, and the three-part voice structure naturally limited individual freedom—you can't go far when two others depend on you. Besides, the performers were there to *serve* the text, which (a bit like icons or Balanchine's dances) required a restrained and unemotional approach, even to highly emotional music. Don't act, just sing or play the music well, and the rest will follow. All of this would later serve Balanchine in his dances.[7]

These convivial and brightly lit memories stalled against the everyday fact that Meliton was often gone: "Not around very much, *I don't know,* on business, I don't know where he went, little bit with us, sometimes he goes away, I don't know, trying to find a job, I don't know," and finally: "Father didn't live with us."[8] So it was a home of women and children, which made his mother sad, he said, but she was okay, maybe, and in any case she ran the busy household herself with the help of an occasional aunt. She was like that: a woman who, in spite of her eggshell appearance, seems to have possessed the necessary inner strength to manage her maternal duties, her wayward husband, her staff and children, and her own peculiar fate—a once rich little poor girl, everything now squandered, alone in the absence of any evident parents of her own.

Meliton was forgiven. Forgiven his absences and poor financial judgment, forgiven his flighty headlong preoccupation with whatever was next in his line of business or musical pursuits. He left his son Georgi with one lasting gift: Georgia. It was a difficult gift—imaginary really—since Balanchine was only ever there briefly on State Department tours in 1962 and 1972, long after his father and mother were gone. The facts sometimes blurred in his telling, but people close to him—including one of his wives—later swore he told them he was born and raised in Georgia. "My tribe," he liked to say as he aged, turning the pages of a large old Georgian book he kept in his small eclectic library on the shelves of his office at the New York State Theater.[9] He once sketched himself in traditional Georgian dress, saber drawn, fiercely baring his teeth and performing a lezginka, or perhaps a warrior dance.[10]

What Balanchine gained from the idea of Georgia and the fact of Lounatjoki was a point on the map where he could locate himself that was *not* Russia. It was an outsider stance, passive, and a way of belonging nowhere, since he would never really have Georgia and would soon lose Lounatjoki. Meliton was Georgian, and Georgia was truly his home, but his son was a Petersburger by birth and by fate, and St. Petersburg's open "window on the West" offered him a European orientation, another imagined place on the map and in his mind opposed to the Russian, become Soviet, behemoth. He was sunk into the imperial world and into its illusions and sights, smells, and sounds—the sensual recall of which was all the more intense for being ephemeral.

Gogl-mogl: 6 egg yolks, 6 tablespoons sugar, ½ teaspoon vanilla, cooked to a froth, chilled, and served in spoonfuls to her three children in the evenings. It was a comfort-food custard thought to have medicinal qualities, originating in the Caucasus and among Central European Jews. Georgi loved it. And Maria's summer garden of potatoes, carrots, cabbage, cucumbers fed them into the winter as they salted the cabbages and made sauerkraut with caraway and stored it underground until it was translucent, Balanchine remembered, "like immense beige, tissue-paper roses."[11] There were pickled cucumbers and mushrooms placed in a large barrel with salt, pepper, bay leaf, and onion—all left to cure. When the vegetables were ready, the children would scoop a large mushroom, add a dollop of sour cream, and eat it. There were eggs that Balanchine later prepared "like mama used to" at his own little Lounatjoki-like dacha in Weston, Connecticut: buttered pieces of pumpernickel mixed with eggs, salt, pepper, and dill; cheese on top; cooked until they set and the cheese melted. There were blinis and on rare occasions caviar ("Mamenka, mamenka, caviar, caviar!") and candies carefully locked in cupboards, distributed to deserving children—or trips to St. Petersburg, where Eliseyev's carried chocolate, rope, flour, wax, soap, sugar, coffee, candy, and they all shopped together with Maria, who didn't buy too much sugar because it was so dear.[12]

Was it true, as Balanchine later told one dancer, that he liked to take a small Georgian dagger and hide it in a book or a shoe and when he was scolded go secretly to his mother's Persian rug and cut out the elaborate patterns with the knife but leave them carefully in place—so that when the rug was taken up to be beaten and aired, the pieces all suddenly fell out, to his delight?[13] Or that his nanny taught him a little too much about sex, like one of Stravinsky's governesses who was fired for wanting to gaze too intently upon the children in the bath? Or that as an adult he felt forever guilty for never thanking his mother for the wristwatch she had once given him at great sacrifice to her ever tightening budget?[14]

This one he remembered clearly. One afternoon he walked to the little nearby barn-theater, where the children were sometimes taken to local performances. When he arrived, it was closed, but he somehow found a way to scramble underneath and by chance he reached a crawl space and managed to push his way up through what turned out to be the trapdoor. He emerged, like a wily character in a play, and found himself standing alone center stage staring into the theater. It was deserted, so he paused to take in the space, which stood expectantly before him. As he moved through the building, he came upon the dressing rooms and the perfumed scent of powder and fresh makeup. When he was later telling this story, his mind traveled at the same moment to how as a child he liked to dress up in girls' clothing. "Absolutely, and now you could think that it could be probably perverse, like sissy, but probably I liked girls and wanted to put dress on me—probably something screwy about that too, that Freud would analyze," he mischievously said.[15] And then his mind moved to how he and his brother would sit in bed at night in their shared bedroom—Tamara had her own—talking about the great seductive beauty of the local woman dentist.

"Happy" may be the wrong word. Alone, a bit secretive, content perhaps with his own inner world and the pleasures of food and nature that his mother and the countryside provided. Quiet, "closed in and dry," Andrei said. A watcher. Even photographs show something silent and removed in Georgi's upright childish demeanor. He had Maria's distant eyes and slightly pursed lips, and the long, bald, high forehead of his father, but slightly lifted, which made him seem to look down on everything from a summit. It was a quality people who knew him would remark upon his whole life. He was simple, charming, but remote and deeply reserved, except at the theater, where he was open and animated, like his voice when he tells of coming up through the trapdoor into the feeling of an empty stage and the smells of powder and makeup. These are the moments he cares about. The rest was fine, okay, monotone, we were happy, I suppose. Family life.

Early one morning in August 1913, Maria took Tamara, age eleven, and Georgi, age nine, to St. Petersburg. Andrei was only seven and may have tagged along. The first stop was the Imperial Cadet Corps, the czar's elite officer-training school and one of the few imperial institutions that allowed entry to children of lower social standing and promised almost certain advancement. Meliton and Maria were still trying to rise and wanted Georgi to have a place, but he failed to be admitted that day.

Next, Tamara was scheduled to audition to become a dancer at the Imperial Theater School—another sure path to social advancement since students at the school were in immediate service to the court and the czar. It was her second year trying, and Balanchine later defensively explained in some detail and with residual anger that Tamara simply did not have the necessary "protection" in high places to help her through the grueling audition process in which as many as a hundred little girls vied for a few precious spots. Meliton had been working behind the scenes for a year trying to use his connections to secure his daughter a place, begging closely placed people he knew to "have a word" with the director on his daughter's behalf, but he did not succeed. Tamara too failed to be admitted that day.[16]

While she was failing, Georgi was blindsided. The moment the school administrators saw him—a boy!—they added him to the examination pool. And so he joined the children gathered in the large waiting area, where they were soon paired off and lined up to go to the infirmary. Each was asked to undress completely to be examined alone by a doctor. Georgi was carefully checked for a strong heart, good eyes (essential to navigating a brightly lit stage in a pre-contact lens era), straight spine, and strong legs, not bowed or knock-kneed. Immunizations were scrutinized, and a note signed by Dr. Y. Ivashkevich and added to Georgi Balanchivadze's file referred to the two scars on his left shoulder, proof of smallpox vaccination.[17]

Those who failed any part of the medical exam were sent home. Those who remained, Georgi among them, filed in pairs into a large dance studio for the next part of the examination. A panel of artists from the Imperial Theater, elegantly dressed and seated facing the children behind a large imposing table, greeted them. The prospective students were called upon to walk, run, and skip past the judges, who might stop one or another child to examine his natural grace or physical proportions. Some were asked to place their heels together to affirm once again that the legs and knees were straight and in correct anatomical order. Georgi's demeanor apparently stood out, and he was asked to walk across the room by himself. His slight physique, straight posture, and calm exterior made him a natural candidate; he was just the kind of blank physical slate they were looking for. Finally, there were basic tests in reading, writing, and arithmetic.[18]

When it was all over, Georgi Melitonovich Balanchivadze was accepted on the spot. A few days later, on August 13, Meliton wrote officially to the inspector of the school with the necessary "humble" petition for entrance, enclosing the required birth certificate, passport, and record of smallpox vaccination.[19] By then Georgi was already in the hands of the imperial court. Immediately following his successful audition, he was taken to have his hair cut to regulation length, uniform fitted, and bed assigned. His mother, sister, and brother left that same day, and Andrei recalled his brother's bitter tears as they departed. Georgi went to sleep alone in the large dormitory room in the boys' wing, with its neat rows of beds occupied by strangers. It was an anguished and empty moment for a small child, and he could never quite make sense of it emotionally. The ground had shifted too abruptly one day to the next, and Lounatjoki and his mother, which had seemed so timeless, were suddenly gone. It felt like a betrayal but perhaps, above all, a humiliation. *How could they?* Fifty years later he was still angry and hurt, even though his entrance to the Imperial Theater School that day had by then proven to be the gateway to an astonishing subsequent life and career.

"They just *left* me there . . . like you take a dog and leave it."[20]

Chapter 3

WAR AND PEACE

He was only nine, but when Georgi arrived at the Imperial Theater School on that warm August day in 1913, his first childhood ended and a second began. "Like a dog" was less the rage of a powerless boy against the will of a mother than a way of saying just how fast and far he had been dropped out of one life and into another. Everything had been traded: mother for minder, hearth for school, Russian country life for the discipline and routines of a Europeanized imperial court art. There were simply no continuities, except the sense he would make of it all inside.

The world and the profession Georgi was now entering were governed by two imposing facts that would reveal themselves to him over time: the first was the imperial court, and the second was the war. The court was the blueprint for Russian ballet, and anyone who grew up in its midst was silently initiated into its strange past. It had all begun with Peter the Great's ambitious Europeanizing project that had brought French and Italian ballet to Russia in the first place. This was not a mere matter of cultural borrowing—it was a human-engineering project on a mass scale, unrivaled in scope and ambition until the Bolshevik Revolution that finally overthrew it: making Russians into Europeans. Under Peter and his successors, uniforms, ranks, and St. Petersburg's architectural style, food, gestures, etiquette, and language were all foreign and European. Czars from that point forth customarily married foreign princesses, and it was no accident that Nicholas II's wife was both German and a granddaughter of Queen Victoria, or that French was the lingua franca at court right up to the revolution. Ballet was part of this project. With its Italian and French origins, it provided essential training in the etiquette, comportment, and gestures of the European nobility.

Russianness didn't go away. Even the most palatial Europeanized homes, filled with imported marble, fine art, and crystal chandeliers, often had inner Russian sanctuaries with a warm fire, a samovar, and comfortable rugs. Some said the Russian psyche was similarly split—the "real" inner Russian soul hidden behind the external facade of European man. Becoming European was thus a highly theatrical enterprise: there were roles to practice and enact, lines to learn, and steps to memorize. The ballets and spectacles that ensued on the Russian stage were ritualized performances of this central premise of court life, one of the many ways that Russians rehearsed over and again the fantasy of foreignness governing their lives.

Behind the court, or at its core, lay a deeper and colder historical fact that Georgi would have to absorb too: serfdom and the peculiar institution of the "serf ballerina." When Catherine the Great released the nobility from their duties at court in the late eighteenth century, many retreated to their often-lavish country estates and set about making their own personal theatrical replicas of court hierarchies and the drama of acting European. On these estates, the masters played the czar and cast their serfs as their courtiers. They went to great lengths to train these serfs for their new and unfamiliar roles, importing European ballet masters, singing instructors, musicians, and poets to teach young serf girls, in particular, to act the role of courtiers to their kings. These serf ballerinas were even trained to attend balls and ceremonial functions, ornaments on the arms of their masters.

The line between art and sex was predictably thin, and serf ballerinas, many of whom were highly trained and sensitive artists, often also doubled as concubines or staffed private harems, displaying themselves or performing in the nude or scantily clad, whips as occasional props. Humiliation and self-erasure were among the requisite skills of any dancer. By the mid-nineteenth century, the fiscal structures supporting this feudal indulgence had collapsed, and many of these dancing serfs were subsequently sold to the Imperial Theaters. There they won their freedom, but at the cost of a new kind of service, this time to the czar himself: the imperial court decided their professions (this one for theater, that one for dance), and they typically owed a decade of service in exchange for their training. Nor were they free to leave the city or to marry without permission, and sexual exploitation remained commonplace. Years before Georgi arrived at the Theater School, serfdom and these residual practices had formally ended, but many of the students and staff at the Theater School were still from low or former serf backgrounds, and the Imperial Theaters were still run, in part, by high-ranking former serf-owners and their descendants. The ballet's leading dancer at the time, Matilda Kschessinskaya—Golden Matilda, as she was popularly known—was only the most recent and notorious example of the continuities: the lowly daughter of a Polish character dancer, she had been lavishly kept by the heir apparent, Nicholas himself, with a mansion, jewels, objets d'art, and vacations on the Riviera. When he married and became czar, she moved on to a grand duke.

All of this was silently present within the thick stone walls of the Imperial Theater School, which had its own part in the story too. Its origins stretched back to the early years of the court, when Empress Anna invited a French ballet master to teach the sons and daughters of her palace servants, whose etiquette and comportment were essential to their role at court. At the same time, Anna asked the ballet master to teach the young boys at the Imperial Cadet Corps—the very same elite military training school to which Georgi had just been refused entry. It was another practice related to ballet; from its earliest French and Italian beginnings, ballet had grown up side by side with the military arts, and this pairing also became a central feature of life at the imperial court. And so, when the czar's architects designed Rossi Street in the early nineteenth century and worked to map the court onto the city in stone, they positioned the Imperial Theater School directly across the street from the Vorontsov Palace, home to the czar's elite military academy. The military and the dance: the arts of war and peace, close historical cousins with shared steps and methods of training, facing each other in mutual dedication to discipline, rank, and the spectacle of autocracy. This was Georgi's new home.

He had arrived at a difficult moment. The court that had given ballet its life was in crisis, and the czar and his men were busy building ever thicker walls around the court to block out the mounting signs of imperial collapse. Strikes, assassinations, bombings, famine, and peasant uprisings were all met from the Winter Palace with the full force of repressive state violence, and Nicholas II seemed increasingly ill-equipped for the role history and his own cumulative ineptitude were thrusting upon him. In spite of formal appearances at the lavish celebrations of three hundred years of Romanov rule, including a spectacular ballet performance, it was difficult not to find the czar increasingly cut off from "the people" he purported so passionately to represent. He was retreating—into the inner sanctum of his wife's Victorian domesticity, with its overstuffed furniture, green wreaths, pink ribbons, lilac blossoms, quaint English chintzes, and walls hung with glittering icons. Into Feodorov village, a toylike Russian town he built near the Alexander Palace in Tsarskoye Selo, his preferred family residence, where he could attend a specially designed neonationalist cathedral and a private "cave church" dug below. The village was a perfect theatrical fantasy of past grandeur, manned by soldiers reassuringly dressed in seventeenth-century-style costumes: even the train station was a stage set with Muscovite tent roofs reminiscent of early Russian palaces. Not least, Nicholas and the court were retreating into the Imperial Theaters and the ballet, which seemed to many to represent, as one old aide-de-camp put it to the bewildered French ambassador on the eve of Russia's collapse, "a very close picture of what Russian society was, and ought to be. Order, punctiliousness, symmetry, work well done everywhere."[1]

As he retreated, Nicholas was also inadvertently undercutting his own divine aura, in the name of the same misguided nationalism and "his" people. You could see it in small things. For the first time ever, the czar's face was reproduced on postal stamps circulated—and routinely canceled—across the realm. To the discomfort of his censors, he even allowed his image to appear on kitschy souvenirs, such as trays, china, candy boxes, and scarves (the line was firmly drawn at handkerchiefs). And in a strange mirror of the traditions of the serf ballerina, Nicholas permitted mere actors to play His Royal Highness on the stage, representing his full majesty in their own lowly image.[2]

As Georgi stood on that warm August day in 1913, freshly shorn and uniformed and anxiously awaiting instruction on how to begin his new life, none of them knew just how little time was left. Only a year later, the czar would stand stoically on the balcony of the Winter Palace, facing a sea of his people on their knees holding icons and religious banners, to announce that Russia was at war; only four years later Lenin would stand on another balcony, this time at the palatial home of the ballerina Kschessinskaya, before an angry crowd, to proclaim the revolution. Lenin would take the notorious and by then sacked residence of Golden Matilda as his headquarters, a symbolic strike at the heart of the court and the world to which little Georgi Balanchivadze now belonged.

Inside the school, nothing ever seemed to change or move. Georgi wore the same uniform daily for years, even after the war began to take its depressing toll—neatly creased military-style black pants, trim white shirt, light-blue jacket with the lyre emblem on the collar, and a round, hard-rimmed, cadet-style cap—the kind of uniform designed to make a boy stand tall and move with precision. That was for everyday life. For dancing, the boys stripped to a more minimal and revealing (knees visible) costume of shorts with an anonymous, plain fitted shirt, socks, and white ballet shoes, tools of the trade. The girls, who lived separately on the first floor, wore long cornflower-blue dresses, demure white pelerines, and black aprons, with pressed white aprons saved for Sundays. Day students wore a motley brown. Younger girls had one braid down their backs and called their elders "goddesses"; older girls were allowed two braids and further marked their stature by folding their shawls in large triangles thrown nonchalantly over their backs. For dancing, girls were given modest gray knee-length frocks with petticoats in the lower divisions, pink for the higher, and the coveted pure-white frocks for the few girls who reached the top of their class. Purer and purer, a hierarchy of virtue. They all wore clean pink cotton stockings held up at the hips with an elastic band, hair tied neatly back in a low bun, and ballet shoes with ribbons wound twice or thrice around the ankle and tucked neatly, in the style of Grecian sandals.

The regulations for courtiers were at least as strict and detailed as they were for young dancers. Everyone wore uniforms at court or at least dressed meticulously according to rank: patterns of embroidery, length of dress and train, cut, fabric, color were all rigorously prescribed. A change in rank mandated a change in uniform, and like the children of Theater Street who emulated them, courtiers advanced by color, in their case from white to black trousers, red to blue ribbons, silver to gold thread. Nicholas II even decreed separate military and ball uniforms for men, weapons tastefully removed for dancing. And it was not just dress: gesture, language, seating, place in the hierarchy of official occasions were all carefully mapped and choreographed.

Georgi's day began with a call to order. A school minder marched through the dorm rooms at the crack of dawn ringing a loud bell. Then came a cold-water wash in a large brass communal sink, then dressing followed by a second bell signaling inspection: two straight lines, heads up, arms down, slight bow of the head (curtsy for the girls), and "good morning." Then prayers. Breakfast was tea and bread with an egg at 8 A.M. (butter rations could be cut in half and exchanged for pastries twice weekly) followed by lessons at 9 A.M. and ballet class from 10 A.M. to 12 P.M. Lunch consisted of meat, pasta, and vegetables, after which they all took a walk in the garden or around the block—strictly supervised by adult minders, with special care taken over the older girls lest they be spied upon by interested gentlemen.

Academic classes were held in small classrooms with slanted wooden desks and chalkboards, and Georgi learned French (to address the czar), history, geography, arithmetic, Russian language and literature, aesthetics, theatrical makeup, geometry, and catechism (his best subject). The education was serious and had been upgraded after the turn of the century to match *Realschule* (modeled on the German example). Dinner, with dessert, was at 4:30 P.M. sharp in the boys' dining hall at long tables with white tablecloths and a school official seated at the head of each. Younger children were formally corrected on etiquette by their elders in an intimidating and ritualized pecking order. And watching over them all was the inevitable icon, this one with a bold red candle behind glass, lodged in the high corner near the ceiling, where icons always sit. As if the day would never end, they then took a second dance class—pantomime, fencing, and, for the older boys, ballroom dance (a rare chance to meet the girls). Finally, they practiced music—piano for Georgi—and did homework, supped modestly on plain brown kasha, and went to bed exhausted at 9 P.M. Georgi somehow found a little light to read his favorite Max and Moritz, Jules Verne, or Sherlock Holmes stories into the night. Steam baths in the bathhouse happened once a week, or to scrub a child clean upon return from a trip to the filthy city outside.[3]

It was a highly regulated life. No sports, ice skating, biking, or playing ball, at risk of damaging valuable limbs. Visitors admitted only at set times in a single room under observation. Trips home carefully planned and monitored. When the boys did play, it was Robin Hood or war, but no swords or sabers were allowed. There was actually little need to venture outside the stone box of their compound since everything the children required was on site, including an infirmary and a small but elegant chapel with a beautifully ornate and bejeweled iconostasis, located at the top of the building, down the hall on the right. The priest was the fastidious but kindly Wassily Faustovich Pigulevsky, who lived in the school with his wife and nine children and loved cards and wine as much as he did God. He had been there since the 1880s and had designed the catechism courses, which included Old and New Testament, Slavic paganism, and Western religions. He took confession. "Little fool" or "idiot," he would chide the students as they enumerated their sins. When Georgi's turn came to serve the Communion wine at Lent, he whispered to a new student, who looked especially pale and wan: "You can drink it, it tastes good. Don't worry, I'll pour some more."[4]

True to their serf-ballerina past, the students were a motley collection of orphans, children of former serfs, and children of dancers, ushers, costume ladies, seamstresses, and composers; many had no father that anyone could speak of, and a few came from military families or—rarely—the more privileged classes. They were all under the care of strict imperial minders, men and women such as the inspectress Varvara Ivanovna Likhosherstova, who by the time Georgi arrived had been at the school for as long as anyone could remember. A relic of the impoverished nobility and the daughter of a major general, she was formerly of the august Smolny Convent and had her own sad life: unbeknownst to the children, she had married an officer who died, leaving her alone with two sons and in need of an income. Rigid and difficult and known for her mean temper, she looked a bit like a priest herself with her black robes hung to the floor, mannish square jaw, high white collar fastened with a brooch, and shocks of severe white hair. She carried a lorgnette, the better to examine every aspect of her young students' lives.[5]

For anyone who broke the rules, as the children all did, the punishments were clear: time standing alone under the large clock in the corridor, where the other children passed by and meanly pointed or whispered; or no sweets; or no visits home on Saturday; or—worst of all—Sunday grounding. Georgi received his share of these reprimands, dutifully logged in the record book for childhood sins such as yelling, hitting, lying, or making excuses to avoid chores and duties. On many weekends he escaped this regimented life and went to his aunt's apartment nearby, and sometimes he made the trip home by train to Lounatjoki. At Christmas his first year, his father even hosted a party for all the boys, which meant that one weekend a group of staff, teachers, and students bundled onto the train with Georgi and made their way to the Finnish countryside for the day's festivities. It was the kind of party Meliton loved, but that Georgi spent in a corner, shyly watching.[6]

But often Georgi stayed at school and spent the empty Sunday afternoons alone in the music room, a large dance studio hung with heavy gilt-framed portraits of the czar and other dignitaries. He didn't seem to mind that the room was haunted by an old monk or singing teacher called Ruch or Ricci, who was said to have hanged himself there, to the squeamish delight of children who made a game of seeking out his spirit. In the corner near the ballet barres sat a beautiful and ornate grand piano (sometimes two), and Georgi could stay practicing and improvising for hours in the melancholy company of himself, the czar, and the monkish ghost. Or, in another studio, he could gaze upon the portrait of the darkly mysterious Istomina, a soulful dancer Pushkin had loved and courted and written about nearly a century before. Pushkin's fellow writer Alexander Griboyedov also knew and admired Istomina, who became the cause of a double duel that took the life of an admirer and cost Griboyedov his left hand. Pushkin later planned to write about these dramatic events, but before he could do so, he was himself tragically killed in another duel. In the close atmosphere of the school, all of this could seem very near, especially to a boy who could recite both Pushkin and Griboyedov by heart.

Better still, Georgi could peer through the small keyhole in the door to the dance studio where the artists of the Mariinsky Theater rehearsed. It was a secret view, like coming up through the trapdoor of the old deserted theater in Lounatjoki or being hidden behind the lens of a camera. He saw but couldn't be seen as he peered at the dancers while they worked, spying on the beautiful young women in practice clothes and toe shoes, hair pinned back, with wool warmers on their slim legs, and maybe a tutu or skirt and a colorful shawl or thin sweater. The other students called him "rat" because he was small—the youngest in the boys' hall—but also because he developed around this time his characteristic sniffing tic, like a rat seeking or busily foraging for shiny tokens in the trash. It was a tic that would endure for most of his life, the first of many masks he would hide behind and a sign of his nerves and appetite for traveling unnoticed through the worlds he found himself in, collecting scraps and gems to be stored in his mind and later extracted for use in art.

Still, even the thick walls and timeless routines of the school and the court could not keep the outside world fully at bay. In the months after the war began in 1914, there was suddenly less sugar. The children went without once a week, a small sign of the terrible sacrifice the war was already exacting on the soldiers and the people outside. Soon the authorities asked to use the school infirmary to care for wounded men, but court officials politely refused. Instead, there were bandages, all types, in need of sorting for easier use when they reached the injured or maimed, and the children were put to work on the large piles in their spare time. The landscape outside began to change too. On their brief excursions and carriage rides to the theater, they glimpsed the czar's army recruits, hundreds upon hundreds of them in full military dress engaged in drills and exercises in the palatial squares nearby. Soon refugees, the wounded, street children, and orphans of the war arrived as the dispossessed reached the city on trains, on foot, and in makeshift carts and carriages. Dead bodies began to appear too, dull unannounced facts piled in the streets or on pyres or laboriously removed to the city's overburdened morgues.[7]

Trips home became less frequent. Georgi's family was naturally preoccupied. Soon after the war began, Maria's passport tells us she was living at least partly in Petrograd (as St. Petersburg was now called) at various addresses, and an attached photo shows her peering tensely into the camera, her crinoline and lace replaced by a simple workmanlike dark wool coat with an unadorned and battered flat-brimmed hat, lips stoically pursed, looking childlike and vulnerable in spite of her forty-three years. Another portrait from the time shows her working with the wounded, and we can see her stiffly posed in civilian dress with a group of Red Cross nurses and uniformed soldiers wrapped for warmth in long gray coats and wearing caps emblazoned with the czar's insignia.[8] The rest of the family had dispersed: Tamara was finally admitted to and spent a year at the Theater School in 1914 but was not talented enough to be invited back, and she was sent instead to Meliton's brother Ivan's family in a far-off town and then to Kasimov, where Ivan was deployed. Andrei ended up in Petrograd for school too, and he and Georgi were together for a while with Aunt Nadia. Meliton was shuttling between them all, working to keep the ever-troubled family interests intact.[9]

At the theater the timeless regimes of artistic life were disrupted, and the adults were naturally tense and preoccupied. Even the glamorous and seemingly untouchable Kschessinskaya was soon presiding over a twenty-bed hospital for the wounded in her mansion and making capricious trips to the front with grand dukes she knew. Olga Preobrazhenskaya, another prominent but more down-to-earth ballerina, organized performances for the troops and nursed the wounded with her own hands in a makeshift hospital in the courtyard of her home. Other dancers took nurses' training and disappeared to join the war effort.[10]

As for the children, life at the school carried on. In spite of these intrusions from the war and the world outside, they were still students, and they still studied and took dance classes. They still went to the theater and danced child roles, even though the whole atmosphere was changed. Now French, English, Belgian, and Russian anthems played before every performance, and there were benefit nights to raise money for war orphans and the destitute. But the house was still full, if anything oversubscribed, as audiences took comfort in the habits and luxuries of an increasingly threatened past.

Ballet class began daily at 10 A.M. sharp. Class trained the mind and body, and it was Georgi's formation, the first and most important formal schooling he ever had. And if the bloodline of Russian ballet originated in part with serfdom, its tradition passed through children. Fragile, unformed bodies with still-malleable muscles and bones could be purposefully pressed and honed against nature to become symmetrical and aligned, balanced and poised. A body *made* graceful. The routines of class were so engrossing that the students hardly noticed the increasingly unbearable irony of striving for grace as war crippled and maimed the men fighting outside. This was not a practice of the mind, after all, nor was it a tradition of inquiry. It was more like a religion or a language inculcated through required physical habits introduced at a young age that last a lifetime. Knowing what the rituals and movements mean at the moment of mastery is unimportant; that comes later, if it comes at all.

So there he was every morning, with the other boys in neat shorts and shoes lined up at the barre, single file, moving in unison to music from a piano sitting in the far corner of the studio. The steps follow a prescribed, centuries-old order. First position, heels together, toes open, hand on the barre to steady the unbalanced body, arms down, back straight up through the spine, shoulders relaxed and wide, belly button pulled to the vertebrae, bones aligned. Release the excess, muscles wrapped around flesh, simplify, simplify, simplify. It is basic: Find the axis. Drop a plumbline from the top of the head down through the spine into the heels in first position, divide the body down this center, right from left. Turn out the legs, turn out the feet, turn out the hips, turn out the spine. Open them up, pry them open; mostly in life we stay closed and protected.

Practice alignment, precise angles, directions—front, side, back, 30°, 45°, 90°, do it again, again, again. Back to first. Back to home. Find the axis. Find the center. Add more, move more, legs higher, arms circling, legs traveling front, side, back in increasingly complicated patterns and rhythms, to the beat, in time. All together, stay together, keep the time. Push, move, travel. Don't think, do. Imitate, obey, repeat, again, again, again until the body does it alone and the mind is still. Do it without the words, no words, the teacher keeps the words, just imitate, don't think, don't ask why. Balanchine later said it: "Dancers are like animals—when dogs bark, they understand each other."

"We spent a year, I think," he later recalled, "learning how the foot touches the floor" when landing from a jump. Just that—the foot coming down and making the first point of contact with the floor. "It is like a bird landing. We have a Russian word for it, and we grew up with that."[11] And with pain, because even young bodies break. Consider what it means to land from that jump, the full weight of the body coming down to the floor through a single pointed foot, the substantial vertical and centrifugal force of the leap passing through the small metatarsal bones and into a thin ankle, reverberating up into the calf, knee, thigh, hip, spine, as the energy exits out through the limbs or the top of the head. Repeat. Repeat. Repeat. A year of repetition of this one small movement, at least. Eight to ten years of strenuous training, at least. The ankle, ligaments, or bones can give way in a split second or over the duration, but give they do, and studiously ignoring hurt and aching limbs is part of the training too. People call it discipline, but really it is renunciation: of pain, but above all of physical frailty. Dancers learn to treat their bodies as not quite their own. Just keep going.

Hierarchy is the organizing principle of the whole enterprise. The advance from one level to the next through strict mastery of physical feats is the obvious exterior criteria. Ballet is measurable, like math: either you can do the required steps in the required way and move on, or you can't. But there were other more-hidden hierarchies too, stacked like Russian dolls for young dancers to discover. The Apollonian body was the highest, an ideal of classical proportion and the measure of man, dressed up with the noble etiquette and gestures of the Europeanized aristocracy. Other kinds of bodies were considered less elevated but equally necessary: from the middling medium height and build—that was Georgi—to the short and thick peasant stock. Steps and combinations were similarly ranked. Highest were the controlled adagio dances slowly showing off the admired noble gestures and proportions, like Greek statuary in motion. Lowest were the quick-paced bumptious jumps and comic capers of the heavily muscular common folk—although by Georgi's time, high jumps and turns had been absorbed into the vocabulary of the vaunted danseur noble, thanks to the slow erosion of noble ideals ever since the French Revolution. Like the serf ballerinas before them, the dancers learned to span the social spectrum and play peasants, villagers, townsfolk, courtiers, commanders, princesses, czarinas, and czars.

However, there was a chink in the armor of this rarefied court art. Standing at the barre in the studio every morning, the children were all equal before the steps. With effort and practice, any child—any body type—could master the movements. In class, the boys (in this case) all wore the same anonymous shorts and shoes, practiced the same steps, received the same instruction, and could be forgiven for feeling at moments that they were part of a strictly meritocratic system. Autocratic, but meritocratic. In this simple fact lay the radical secret at the heart of the historically hierarchical forms Georgi was inheriting. Remove the idea of the body as an expression of the social and political order, and you are left with the body as a blank slate. Or, taken further, the body as machine. The bows, gestures, and etiquette of aristocratic life, after all, were vestiges—vestiges of the French nobility, vestiges of serfdom, vestiges of a European past. The tension, the problem, lay in the thin line between free will—possible but not encouraged—and the rote movements of the automaton. The solutions for that would come later. For now, boys like Georgi, age nine or ten or eleven, faced simpler questions. Can you hit the ceiling with your hand at the height of a jump? Can you turn three or four or five or six times? How much can you do physically—just how fast and far can you move and what does it take to break free?

Georgi was learning steps, but he was also learning how to learn. Dancers do not work from texts because there are no texts. Dances are passed from person to person—from one dancer's body to another. Nothing is written down and little or less is said. Children learn instead through imitation. Monkey see, monkey do, except not quite. Dancing is more than mere copying and requires a talent and physical intelligence evident in a young dancer from the start. It involves an instinctive eye-body coordination that some people "just have," while others are blocked at the barrier of the mind—they see but cannot translate what they see onto their own bodies. Nothing happens physically. Or something happens, but it is flat and uninteresting, too literal. Imitation is like the talent of the jester, the mime, the clown whose animation illuminates the play. Or the translator animating a foreign text. It takes erasing—erasing the ego but not the hand, the touch, the body, the thing that animates. Balanchine had this physical instinct in abundance. He was never a refined dancer, but he was a wicked mimic (he later mercilessly aped Trotsky) and could immediately catch the essence of any person, step, or gesture in his own body.

Learning to instantly reproduce and recall long, intricate sequences of movement and gesture is something more mysterious. It has to do with music and memory. Dancers' bodies are like the memory palaces of antiquity. The idea of the memory palace, after all, was always physical. As ancient sources tell us, there was once a banquet at which the ceiling collapsed and the guests at the table were instantly killed and their bodies mangled beyond recognition. A poet, however, had stepped out of the room just in time and survived. At first, he was unable to identify the bodies or to recall who exactly had been at the dinner, but finally he was able to name each guest by going around the table in his mind and recalling where each had been seated. Memory depended on physical location—on the seating chart in the poet's mind. From there came the idea of a palace with many rooms and many tables, with closets and drawers to put things in.

For dancers, music is that kind of palace. Every piece of music has a structure, and dancers become intimately acquainted with its rooms and corridors. They know where to find the steps and gestures because they are ordered by the music, located in space and time. Once a dancer physically enters the music—which is different from dancing externally *to* or *with* the music—and internalizes the rhythm, the basic pulse or beat, the steps take on that necessary order and sequence. Great dancers can match their own inner pulse—their very own heart rate—to the musical pulse, which is a way of taking the music inside the body. Eating the music, eating the steps. At that moment, the steps become fixed to the music in the body of the dancer. The dancer knows them both "by heart."

Begin at the beginning—you don't remember? Go back, run it again, take it from the top. If you start from the beginning, the rest will follow, like the seating chart at the table or the rooms in the palace. But trained dancers do more. They don't have to start at the beginning or at the head of the table to recall the sequence: they can enter midstream, get into the palace through any door. Drop the needle in the middle of a piece of music and a trained dancer will know where she is. She can enter time at any point in a sequence. In this sense, dance training is not about rote memorization at all; it is about time. The passage of time and moving around in time, precisely.

The memory of a dance can last longer and run deeper than the memory of poetry or an actor's lines, perhaps because (akin to physical trauma) the body was *there*. If years later a dancer hears the music for a dance she once knew—really physically knew—her legs and arms will automatically start to do the steps, even if she has long since forgotten them. It is Proust's madeleine for the body: suddenly you are there.

Ballet keeps children children. It works against growing up and aging, halts the process by suspending the mind. "Don't think, just do"—Balanchine's later mantra, implicit in his early training—is a way of prolonging youth. Physically, of course, dancing keeps the body young by honing its natural beauty, and dancers often look young long after they are. This is because they were once so fit, perhaps, but also because ballet begins with androgyny. The childish body is androgynous, angelic even, and ballet preserves that lithe, nymphlike flexibility, especially in girls, whose bodies are more malleable and naturally slight. Men and women will later train differently to their strengths, but that childishness never quite disappears, and dancers naturally return to a moment of seemingly limitless physical capacity. Ask any old dancer trained from childhood to perform a ballet, and in the split second of her movement you will see in her aged body the astonishing return of her youth. Teachers rely on this uncanny experience: in the seventy-year-old former ballerina, you can immediately detect, and imitate, the seventeen-year-old girl.

Georgi's main teacher was Samuil Andrianov, a tall, slim, elegant dancer who was still young—barely thirty and actively performing. He taught in his street clothes, and his dapper but modest image and devotion to his students left a deep impression. He was married to one of Georgi's favorite ballerinas and teachers, Elizaveta Gerdt. Gerdt was pure, clean, cool, although some critics (Balanchine later explained) called her "a vegetarian-vegetarian dancer" and saw her as icy, without blood. They wanted a hot dancer, he said, but he thought she was wonderful, "like crystal."[12] Her father, Pavel Gerdt, a tall dancer with an elegant physique from an old Russianized German family, had taught her. And so it went: dancer begat dancer begat dancer in a long chain reaching back in living memory deep into the nineteenth century. Pavel Gerdt had worked directly with Marius Petipa and Pyotr Tchaikovsky.

. . .

On Sundays and Wednesdays, ballet nights at the theater even during the war, a horse-drawn carriage would arrive at the school entrance to fetch the children, Georgi among them, to perform child roles in the evening's ballets. They called it Noah's Ark, and in the winter it was a sleigh with uniformed footmen and they went wrapped in furs. The carriage transported the children through the narrow streets and up over the cobblestones of the wide-open plaza in front of the theater, past the trolley, past the lampposts, past the ticket queues of students and workers who couldn't afford subscriptions that wound around the palatial Mariinsky Theater; now past the soldiers and the wounded too, and the ragged homeless children about their age in thin-soled shoes. The theater had been named by Czar Alexander II after his German wife, Empress Marie, although when the war came its name became Petrograd, like the city itself, a reminder that Germany was now an enemy force. The theater's flat dome and elegant portico entrance, and its seemingly endless proliferating quarters added over the years to the main building in the style of the nearby Winter Palace, made the building look grand and imposing, a spectacle unto itself. The students climbed from the carriage and slipped into the side entrance, reserved for orchestra members and children of the school, and mounted the six flights up to their dressing rooms.

Remember that theaters do not have windows. They are closed off, worlds apart with their own sources of light and darkness—more closed, even, than the stone school. This one was a sprawling territory of sewing rooms and costume workshops with massive stone pillars and long serviceable wooden tables strewn with silk, gold, tulle, bright ribbons. Whole wings were devoted to costume painting, and there were prop shops and several enormous hangar-like workshops for developing sets and decor. There were also large and small dressing rooms (women to one side of the stage, men to the other), photography studios, a dedicated shoe room, and vast spaces where costumes were stored, not to mention dance studios and music practice rooms along with manifold offices full of people noisily attending to the business of art.

In the front of the house, the main cloakroom had efficient school-like cubbies and tables for packages and umbrellas and orderly rows of hanging space. There were elegant enclaves for royal dinners and events, chandeliered and tucked off the main halls with small tables laid with fine linen and china. A large open foyer with cold floors and high ceilings welcomed the public. The greenroom was located in the no-man's-land between the public and the backstage. During intermissions the imperial family and other dignitaries, dressed in full regalia, could go there to smoke and enjoy the company of costumed ballerinas stretching their limbs and warming up for their parts.

The inner sanctum of the theater itself was soft and feminine, a boudoir almost, powder blue, gold, curved and ornamented, with plush chairs for spectators. On ballet nights, the house was packed with members of the court in full evening dress, although during the war a more sober look eventually took hold. High officials, military men, and Imperial Guards traditionally occupied the front orchestra, and in the "diamond row" one could find "officers with spurs and remarkable moustaches, ladies with bare, snow-white bosoms, diamonds, perfume, lace." The front row of the stalls was reserved for balletomanes, a strange breed of male spectator (later despised by Balanchine) obsessively in love with this dancer or that, gossips, fans, who were temperamentally (the theater's director sourly noted) "monarchists, adherents of olden times, of fictitious traditions—essentially, of routines." Once upon a time, they cooked, carved, and ate the old ballet shoes of the legendary dancer Marie Taglioni. The gallery, upper tiers, and loges were packed with a full array of Russian society: students, women and families, clerks, lackeys, servants, valets, and artisans. Everyone came.[13]

The czar had his own large and impressively lavish box facing the stage, framed by its own proscenium arch. To Balanchine as a child, it seemed "like a colossal apartment" with blue walls, although Nicholas II sometimes chose instead to sit in the corner box next to the stage, where he could look out over the entire house of his people. Various other Romanovs occupied the boxes in the tier above. The ushers wore tailcoats with the czar's double-headed eagles, and the deep royal-blue stage curtain was emblazoned with the same eagles, signaling his power and domination over his assembled realm. Above the proscenium, a large ornate clock lovingly supported by two golden cupids marked the time as the orchestra played below.[14] On special days the children of the Theater School might be escorted ceremonially to the czar, where they were introduced one by one—"This is Balanchivadze"—as they each bent to kiss the hand of Nicholas II. The great czar, who was in fact small, of slight build, effeminate, would then bestow upon each appropriately awestruck child a large gold box of fancy chocolates bearing the imperial insignia. Balanchine later recalled the thrill, "Like army meets general, you know, they stand waiting and general comes in, and it was like that."[15]

Discipline was paramount, and indeed the leading positions in court ministries were often recruited from high military echelons. The director of all Russia's Imperial Theaters at the time was one Vladimir Arkadevich Telyakovsky, officer of the Horse Guards, Academy of the General Staff, with the rank of colonel. He ran ten theater buildings, seven troupes, seven string orchestras, two brass bands, two choruses, two theater schools, a library, a photography department, two medical facilities, a carriage department, four electricity-generating stations, a publications department, and other technical-support departments. It was a sprawling administrative empire on an openly autocratic model that Balanchine would later emulate: authority ran to Telyakovsky and directly to the czar himself.[16]

Georgi learned the theater's every aspect as he hurried through its long corridors on performance days. He grew accustomed to life backstage, with dancers and ballerinas milling about, half-dressed, made-up, gossiping, adjusting bodices, tights, tulle, ribbons, silk, jewelry, costumes, shoes—all crowded into the half-lit wings awaiting a cue. Stagehands were there pulling sets and attending to lights; conductors and musicians who weren't yet in the pit loitered among the stage managers, costumers, prop men, and hairdressers. The air was thick with the smells of makeup, fabric, sweat, paint, light, oils, resin, perfume. Like dancers everywhere, Georgi pulled up his tights and put on his shoes, tight slippers with elastics to secure the arch, and dipped his feet into the box of sticky amber rosin crystals, crunched to smithereens by imposing ballerinas in hard toe shoes. Someone sprinkled the slippery and sharply raked wooden stage with water from gray tin cans, like watering a garden, for still better grip. One bell for half-hour, two bells for fifteen minutes, and three bells calling the dancers immediately to the stage. Electric lights, still relatively novel, could be blinding, and there were plentiful enchanting stage effects too, engineered with real fire, water, and animals. On stage Georgi witnessed fountains running colored water, burning buildings, lilac bushes that magically grew, live horses, and rotating floors that seemed to carry the dancers across space and time.[17]

"Monkey: a student," the program noted. "That was me"—Balanchine, proud of the anonymity, later told a friend. He was a monkey in the lavish court spectacle *Le Talisman,* with the perfumed and bejeweled Golden Matilda in the lead role. He performed child roles across the imperial repertory, mostly in ballets of Marius Petipa: a small Saracen in *Raymonda,* where he climbed over the parapet to see a Crusader killing a man whose head ran with blood; a toy soldier in *The Fairy Doll*; a Spanish boy in *Don Quixote*; a child in the Garden Dance in *The Sleeping Beauty*; an Egyptian in *Daughter of Pharaoh*; a soldier, a mouse, and eventually the athletic leaping candy cane in *The Nutcracker*; he danced a mazurka too, in bright white tights and military tunics in *Paquita,* a mirror image of the military parades the children could see on the plazas outside.[18] He watched: Bekefi, a Hungarian dancer, for example, in a czardas or a polonaise and mazurka the dancers had learned from the Polish dancer Kschessinsky (Matilda's father, who enriched himself by instructing aristocratic families to perform their own mazurkas at fancy-dress balls). He saw Pierre Vladimirov, the company's rising danseur noble—better than the great Nijinsky, it was whispered, although at the time, Georgi didn't much like the dancers everyone else admired.[19] Danseurs nobles seemed to him stiff and too clean, far from the dashing Turks and Cossacks that filled his boyish imagination, but he was nonetheless taking it all in, and he would later hire Vladimirov to teach in his American school.[20]

As Georgi took his place in the wings and scrambled onto the stage, he was playing his role as servant to the czar, part of a self-conscious display of the imperial social order paraded across the stage inside the theater, just as outside it was beginning to collapse. He watched the dancers form themselves like soldiers in perfectly straight lines moving with precision in strictly measured time. He watched the hierarchy and the order. He watched the older dancers playing peasants, villagers, townsfolk, courtiers, commanders, princesses, czarinas, and czars, but looking back, you could see that Georgi had arrived at a moment of disorientation and loss. The theater and the ballet, the walled world within the walled court, were in the midst of their own crisis too.

To begin with, Marius Petipa was dead. Petipa had been the reigning ballet master of the czar's imperial ballet for some fifty years, from his arrival from Paris in 1847 until his retirement in 1903, and his ballets still made up the greater part of the company repertory: these were the dances Georgi grew up with, and Petipa was everywhere in his life. The old ballet master had died in 1910, but his rehearsal chair was still sitting—empty—in one of the main dance studios; the students believed that if you sat on it, you might meet his ghost. One evening, creeping to the spot secretly in the dark, Georgi and a friend tried.[21] "Petipa died when I was about six years old," Balanchine later remembered, "but Tchaikovsky and Petipa were alive for me. And people around me talked about them as if they were alive."[22] In his young mind, they *were* alive, and over the years, Petipa would even seem at moments to inhabit him. Like Russians becoming European, Georgi was imitating, ingesting, and swallowing whole, and he would eventually freely borrow steps and patterns, but also music, from this man he never met. He even took on, or shared, Petipa's practice of watching performances tucked quietly into his first-wing post.[23]

Tchaikovsky was dead too. Everyone knew of his passing, and the uncertain causes of his untimely death in 1893, and of his legendary funeral service, organized by the directorate of the Imperial Theaters with a full orchestra at the Kazan Cathedral, with sixty thousand people gathered for six thousand places.[24] Tchaikovsky and Petipa had changed ballet forever, just as Balanchine would later revolutionize the art with Stravinsky. Tchaikovsky's music was floating everywhere in the dancers' lives, in ballets, in class, in music lessons, and Balanchine never shied from this vast childhood resource. He spoke freely to anyone willing to listen of his conversations with the dead but close Tchaikovsky and looked to the composer constantly across the mortal divide for advice and guidance as he made his own ballets to the composer's music. "He helped me, or else he would say don't!"[25]

Meanwhile, Petipa had complained bitterly when he was old and infirm that his ballets without him were fraying: not my dances. It was true that the courtly life Petipa's ballets expressed was fading and that he was no longer there to keep alive his own legacy and the record of the world he and his dancers had celebrated. Without his personal presence, endless squabbles erupted over the details of his languishing steps. Factions formed, and in a premonition of the drama that would follow Balanchine's death, a fight for power over the ballets and their future ensued. But dancers still had to dance, and Petipa's embattled ballets mostly settled into a stolidly classical mold, embalmed for the benefit of future generations. By the time Georgi encountered them, they were even more conservative than they had been in the first place. That was part of the tradition too.

A new and revolutionary generation meanwhile came and went, and Georgi and his friends missed it. It all started before he was born but came to a head in the wake of the upheavals of Bloody Sunday in 1905. Sympathy strikes, meetings, and protests erupted across St. Petersburg, and Rimsky-Korsakov—Meliton's teacher—sided with the strikers and was dismissed from the prestigious Conservatory of Music. Glazunov angrily followed in protest (though both later returned to their duties). When the czar issued his concessionary but short-lived October Manifesto, riots erupted at the opera ("Down with autocracy!"), and the dancers at the Mariinsky organized their own strike. A group of young dancers led by Michel Fokine, Anna Pavlova, and Tamara Karsavina held secret meetings, and the students at the Theater School, Vaslav Nijinsky among them, staged protests. They were a new breed: They read and paid attention to politics, and some of them were radicalized. They went to work for "the people," and they wanted a greater say in the running of the theater and the future of their art. And although the strike was subsequently peacefully resolved, those who had taken part in the meetings were never quite the same. The long-established bond joining them obediently to the czar had been severed.[26]

In 1909 many from this new generation abruptly left St. Petersburg to perform in Paris with the young impresario Sergei Diaghilev. By 1911 most had cut their ties to the Imperial Theaters and moved to Europe to dance with his new and renegade Ballets Russes. And although some returned home briefly when World War I erupted, this youthful and radical life force of dance had largely moved abroad—leaving the ballet Georgi entered as a boy bereft of its most innovative energy and spirit. But institutions, like people, can live parallel lives, and word of the glamorous Parisian seasons of these riotous breakaway dancers filtered back through letters, tales, and fragments whispered in classrooms and hallways. The mere fact of their existence set a precedent.

The year Georgi arrived at the school, 1913, age nine, was also the premiere in Paris of Nijinsky and Stravinsky's *Sacre du Printemps*. Georgi didn't know, but he found out.

Meanwhile, Petipa's ghost continued to rule their small lives. Every time the dancers went on stage in one of his many ballets, they encountered the old ballet-master's mind. Even in child roles, they entered into the structure of his dances, like walking through an old still-furnished house recently deserted by its owner. The composition and construction, the way the steps make the body move, the patterns of people, the narrative frame: all of that was still there, no matter the fraying. Night after night, year after year, Georgi and his friends climbed into the skin of Petipa's art. No wonder Balanchine later insisted that his own dancers learn the same rules, feel the same music, and repeat the dances until they were fully incorporated, a permanent part of the person. Petipa was like an anchor dropped into the body of this small boy.

It is easy to feel sick before performing one of Petipa's variations. They are too physically demanding, too mentally intricate, and you know before you start that a moment's lapse can shatter everything and leave even the most skilled dancer stumbling, panting, in fragments. With success, it is like being inside a great idea, full of the energy that comes at the instant of insight, legs strong, incisive, slicing through the rhythms. Yet the legs that seem to control it all: you can't even see them. These are tutu dances, and that odd pancake costume strung around the waist with a hint of the baroque cuts the dancer off from her own feet and legs, as if from her own past. A body divided. You can't check; you have to trust, and the rules are strict. The slightest false move or cheat—a leg straying off-center or a step out of line—immediately throws the whole body into disarray, like a poem poorly scanned.

The patterns across the stage are mirrored in the body: front, back, diagonal. Threes repeat almost superstitiously: three steps, three times, three directions—three like beginning, middle, end; three like the Trinity; three like Pythagoras's theorem. Ballets never say what they are about, but one way to discover their motives is to keep counting, and dancers are constantly counting, marking time. Just go, just go, don't stop, just go, the teacher would say, pushing the dancer from behind—push a bit ahead, just a hair, so the body doesn't lose track. Equilibrium is forever perilous, and the stage floor at the

Mariinsky was dangerously raked, slanted at a sharp angle so that audiences could better see the whole. Dancers learned to calibrate their balance and weight on this disorienting incline, like dancing on the deck of a ship tilting to sink.

But Petipa presented a problem too. In his dances, the only way forward was back into enchanted worlds like the hundred-year dream of *The Sleeping Beauty*, with its princes and fairies and courtly rituals of birth, love, and marriage. Petipa was the cloistered enclave that ballet and the court had become, and by the end of 1916, the world outside and the ravages of the war that Russia was losing were becoming impossible to ignore. Food was increasingly scarce and fuel in dangerously short supply. It was cold. Dancers were performing without heat or proper nutrition, their thinning limbs wrapped in wool and down, if they could find it. As they danced, their breath froze in a white mist midair. Outside, inflation was spiraling out of control. Who could find or afford sugar now? The streets were thicker and thicker with dead and crippled bodies, and the stench of decay and disease could be overwhelming. Politically and militarily the situation was dire: the czar had lost touch almost completely, and faced with crisis upon crisis, he burrowed deeper and deeper into the sterile and fatalistic dogma of autocracy and his own divine right. That frigid December day, when Georgi was escorted into the czar's box at the theater and felt he was meeting a general, anyone watching might have wondered: general of what? The czar's armies, largely composed of peasants and the children of serfs who had been freed, were dying in his streets and fields. Georgi, a friend noted around this time, looked thin and pale, "almost transparent."[27] He was twelve.

Chapter 4

A CLOUD IN TROUSERS

They started to shoot. People were running, shouting, firing from windows and rooftops, and there were police, soldiers, and bodies falling dead in the wide imperial streets. At barely fourteen and still slight of build, Georgi was running too in those early revolutionary days, crouching in doorways and darting down side streets to avoid the gunfire. The Imperial Theater School and the Cadet Corps across the road were natural targets, and one afternoon a bullet tore through the school window, shattering glass as the children dropped to the floor. Armed men later broke into the building and held one of the school minders at gunpoint as they searched the premises for "monarchists," but finding only children and dancers, they abruptly departed. Another day several hundred armed and frozen soldiers from the 137th Infantry Division took over the premises as a shelter, and ballet classes were suspended until the authorities eventually moved the soldiers along, fearful that the floors wouldn't hold their weight. Nothing felt safe, and even as the children slept in neat rows in their dormitory beds, or later moved to the tighter quarters of the infirmary for warmth, there was always the chance of being awakened by the sound of executions taking place in the streets below. The walls of their lives had finally been breached.

As the havoc of the revolution took hold, basic supplies grew scarce. The school struggled to care for the children until finally it couldn't. It closed. Then it reopened to day students only. With thinning faculty and students fleeing to their families, they were a rump group, and closures were intermittent. By the fall of 1918, in an unlikely turn of events, the school managed to reopen for good—this time, in the name of the workers and the new Socialist state. Meanwhile, Georgi was back and forth between this beleaguered imperial institution and his worried mother and aunt on Bolshaya Moskovskaya, but mainly, like most of the city, he was living in the streets.[1]

The streets of the czar's once orderly town were occupied by workers, peasants, soldiers, revolutionaries. There were protests, processions, military bands, speeches, funerals, and thousands upon thousands of men in dark coats and caps and women with scarves wrapped tightly around their heads, gathered carrying banners, red flags, icons, coffins. Disruption became a fact of life, as sabotage, requisitions, and long queues for food vied with intermittent fighting between reds, whites, greens, blacks (anarchists), nationalists. It was a chaos of civil war and terror unfolding in their lives, and in these extreme and unpredictable conditions, shops were boarded up, transport suspended, and streetlights out due to cuts in electricity. Even horses, the only power left standing, were gnawing on wood or being shot or sold for a pittance. Who could afford to feed them?

As people struggled to survive, the injured and maimed continued to arrive and could be seen sitting listless and uncared for in alleyways and stations. Bands of orphaned or abandoned children joined them, camping in the streets, under boats and bridges, inside barrels or garbage cans and even among the dead in cemetery vaults, anything to escape the icy winter winds. Soon after Lenin's arrival in Petrograd, Georgi found himself standing in one of these crowds, this time at the ballerina Kschessinskaya's old mansion, which had long since been ransacked and occupied by revolutionaries, who lounged, dirty from fighting, on the settees and grand staircases of her silk and gilt imperial splendor. Lenin was using her home as his headquarters at the time, where from the balcony one day, he furiously expounded his April Theses. Europe too is on the eve of revolution, he shouted down at the restless crowd, and on May Day that year, the children of the school (which reopened for a moment) participated in a mass outdoor demonstration and revolutionary spectacle with an engulfing cast of thousands.[2]

Georgi was hungry. His mother sent him to the store where he used to buy bread, he recalled, "and it's enormous and there's no bread and . . . they make fun, 'Oh there's no bread today,' and the next place there's no bread and the next day there's no bread. Then it is terrifying." His life rolled into one urgent pursuit: get food, somehow. "Maybe if person has a pinch of salt or gives you matches, and finally you go around on the street and you try to see if a person has a piece of bread or potato peels—sometimes people have potato peels—and you say, I have matches do you have potato peels? They say yes and you give the matches and they give the potato peels. Or somebody with salt—pinch of salt—and you get coffee grinds, used already, but you eat them . . . or someone makes a coffee-grind cake. Awful, nothing, no bread, nothing; when I say awful, I know because I didn't eat for *days and days.*" Or sometimes, rarely, the city or the government had food. "You find out, next week on Friday giving away some bread. And you have to register and some kind of ticket, then you get into the big line, which you stay: night, day, and the next night . . . and they give you piece of bread, or some days it was soup. Red Cross . . . gives you wonderful stuff: it was warm dirty water, with little thrown in cucumber peels, I don't know where the cucumbers went, but was cucumber peels and potato peels sometimes you find in it. That's what it was, gray water and you have your own little thing like that—[tin] cup—and they give you that. . . . It was *everyone* like that, it was *starving, starving.*"

Or you eat cats, if you can—but more often "there was no pussy cat on the street because people would grab them and eat them." One time a horse fell dead in its tracks from disease, and he watched as people rushed with knives to "cut pieces" and carve whatever was left on the starved beast's bones, an image scarred onto his brain for life. Sometimes he even went to the black basement of the theater, where boys with quick, terrified fingers could catch rats for eating. He stole things. "The army—or something like that—would have a barge with dry fish or something, and near Fontaka River, for army—Red Army. We used to go . . . myself and others and go and run and grab this fish, sometimes a live fish, and one friend grab a live fish and he is running" with the fish thumping against his chest. Or they would find the "small dry, not a carp, dry, dry, dry fish" he later saw in Jewish delis in New York, salted and piled in great mounds by old women on the streets to be sold. If you were careful, you could snatch a handful and fly away through the streets and gobble the fish to expunge, momentarily, the terrible fear that hunger brings.

He worked where he could—anything for food—and later remembered sewing leather saddles and bridles and reins for an old saddler: "You work and work and . . . he has a little money and he give you—[but] money doesn't mean anything, like a million dollars might be five cents—or soup or something if he has prepared it, or coffee grinds." Another job meant walking through the dark streets late at night, hovering in doorways for safety, to "an awful dreary small movie house." He played piano there for silent pictures, "most dreariest thing, small movie far away in the dark, and I used to walk there, took hours, no street cars, in the dark, small screen, elongated room, almost like Luna Park, Max Linder mostly." He stayed for hours bent over the piano improvising waltzes, marches, little songs, anything he knew. Sometimes they gave him something in return, but more often they sent him away empty-handed—"Get the hell out of here!"—and he made his way back through the cold streets with their gleaming black puddles of melted dirty snow. As the months went on, he developed painful welts on his skin from malnutrition—at one point, a friend counted thirty of these oozing boils to her five. Eventually a cough came too, the first signs of the TB infection that would plague and weaken him for years to come.[3]

The stench as they moved through the city in the warmer months could be unbearable as rotting corpses quickly overwhelmed the old St. Petersburg smells of leather, sheepskin coats, cabbage soup, and sunflower oil. Bodies were everywhere: piled in the streets, spilling from overcrowded morgues, and stacked at cemetery gates. There was a shortage of coffins, and people took to wrapping their dead in mats or stowing them in borrowed coffins (marked "please return") and dragging the growing multitude of forsaken bodies on wooden sledges to be dumped at mortuary doors. Sometimes the dead were killed again: sacred bodies previously embalmed by the Church ("dolls," the revolutionaries called them) were exhumed and defiled to prove the end of God and religious practice. Rasputin's decaying corpse was dug up, soaked in gasoline, and set ablaze, and the black smoke and vile odor of this hated imperial relic poured over the city for hours, like a kind of incense of the revolution. Adding to the haze were the ad hoc cremations, desperate exceptions to the still-prevailing burial practices of Orthodoxy—a gruesome thought in a faith that takes the body to be inextricable from the soul. Cholera, influenza, typhus, and TB swept the town. Funeral rites and mass graves dug in the streets were commonplace, with coffins laid row upon row and the inevitable grim crowd peering in from above. By 1920 two-thirds of the population of Petrograd would be dead.[4]

Georgi's father had gone again, this time for good. As the czar's government fell, Meliton rushed to play his part in the political and musical life of his beloved Georgia. He wrote to Maria in his breathless way that his welcome home had been grand and that he was busy establishing a music school, mounting operas, and working to define the musical life of his little embattled nation. He was happy to report that his Georgian family had embraced him. His grandson was getting married, and he was seeing his sister. He had been to Boromi and Kutaisi and Tiflis. "Come, we will all live together," he wrote to Maria, who was still in Petrograd. And then after the October Revolution: "How are you in this terrible time? We are reading about the unbelievable barbarism of people gone wild. It would have been so good if you got out of that cursed city when I wrote to you. Because I foresaw all of this. Now it will of course be hard to leave Petrograd, but it would be good if it somehow did happen. Nothing similar can happen here, because Tiflis and Kutaisi are protected by our regiments. . . . When you decide to leave, telegraph me. I will transfer the money." Georgia was by then in the hands of the more moderate Mensheviks and would for a moment become an independent republic—before the Red Army swept the entire region into the Bolshevik fold.

Meanwhile, the house in Lounatjoki was lost. The peninsula too was overtaken by civil war and the fight for Finnish independence as the Russian state collapsed and the Germans advanced. And although a friend would much later send Maria an old dried flower from her beloved lottery-won property, none of the Balanchivadzes would ever see the place again. For the moment, Maria stayed in Petrograd with Georgi and Andrei; Tamara was in school near Moscow and would soon join her father in Georgia. They were still a family trying to reach each other across distant political crises. "Dear

Dad!" wrote Georgi and Andrei, and they reported in Georgi's childish hand that the dance teacher Andrianov had died of consumption in Crimea, and they had seen *The Demon* at the Mariinsky. Milk was 150 kopeks a bottle, they said, but there was none; bread was 28 kopeks a pound, butter 2 rubles and 60 kopeks—but there was none of that either. They were hoping to come to the Caucasus after Christmas, they said. Andrei finally went, but it was a harrowing trip with family friends by train, truck, and cart. He made it, barely alive. Tamara finally got there too. And in the fall of 1918, Maria, who was working as a clerk at the Petrograd district Soviet of Deputies, applied for and received a passport to leave for Tiflis with Georgi. The permit allowed them to go for a year and to travel through the Orsha or Kursk border crossing, a daunting prospect in the midst of the violence. They never went. Andrei wrote to his mother from Tiflis in 1921, pleading, don't worry about us, take care of yourself and Georgik, and he asked that she please deliver a special letter to Georgik directly "into his own hands," but no one remembers what it said. Finally, sometime in 1922, Maria left Petrograd too and joined Meliton, Andrei, and Tamara in the Georgian capital, while Georgi stayed in Petrograd, alone. The letters ceased.[5]

His father was gone and his mother was fading from view, like she did in photographs, her skin so translucent and pale and her look so remote that she seems barely to exist. Her application for a passport for the two of them was evidence enough of her devotion and desire—desperation really—to keep her son with her. But by then Georgi's life was already being absorbed into the revolution, and it could be said that these were the years when he became a generation. He was too young to belong to the generation at the revolution's forefront and too old to belong to those of its aftermath. He came of age flush with its brutal events and utopian aspirations, and it emptied him out and filled him up. He almost died—he should have died—he wasn't one of the strong ones and knew it, and that fragility was something he carried with him the rest of his life. It was part of his occasionally brittle poise. What happened to him next, as his family receded and his life at the school resumed, was a kind of coming-of-age by extremes: the gross brutality of deprivations and physical lows accompanied by a thrilling exposure to new ideas, theater, literature, and art. Hunger and revelation.

. . .

None of it should have been possible. The Imperial Theaters, after all, were under attack, and the revolution should have spelled the end of ballet and wiped Georgi's designated career off any list of possible future lives. And, indeed, immediately following the initial uprisings in February 1917, the former Mariinsky Theater was covered in red flags and supplied with a stump box for political speeches as crowds gathered in the wide-open spaces of the plaza outside. Inside, the imperial blue and white decor and glinting chandelier were all that remained of the old order: the golden eagles crowning the boxes had been torn out of the wall, leaving gaping holes, and other imperial insignia had been covered in thick red cloth. The ushers soon exchanged their gold-braid-trimmed courtly uniforms for plain gray trousers and jackets, and where the czar's courtiers had once sat came soldiers and workers in dark overcoats and plain-clad women with short hair and high-cut woolen blouses. They were joined by party officials and haggard men and women recently released from imperial jails or returned from Siberia, unless they had scalped their free tickets to the highest bidder.[6] The czar's coat of arms was gone from the program books too, replaced by the simple image of the lyre. And if there was any doubt over the finality of these changes, the impressive royal-blue curtain with its ornate imperial insignia was replaced with the gauzy white Grecian curtain that the radical theater director Vsevolod Meyerhold had made for *Orpheus and Eurydice*. "The Marseillaise," sung in full-throated Russian, opened performances as a new (if temporary) anthem.

Dancing was harder than ever. There was little or no heat and water froze in glasses, and the orchestra sounded sharp as the instruments squeaked eerily in the frozen air. Sometimes radiators burst, covering the floor with glassy sheets of perilous ice. The dancers stood in the wings, clad in fur hats and heavy coats, with woolen tights, sweaters, or whatever they could find thrown over their thin costumes. They slid out from under these layers for a few moments as they went on stage to dance before quickly covering themselves again. As they performed, their breath was steam. And in the constant effort to keep warm, they drank endless cups of carrot tea and ate potato-peel cakes with a bit of molasses, if there was some. On a good day, during intermissions, members of the audience might appear backstage with offerings of bread or a bottle of sunflower oil, humbly taken from their own meager rations. The dancers were all so thin and tired, and adding to their load, they were also performing at workers' clubs, in factories, and for the army. Once the school resumed classes, Georgi was there with the other students, and they arrived on foot, dodging through the streets in terror of stray gunshot or on rickety wooden sleds repurposed to replace the glittering Noah's Ark carriages that had once carried them to the theater. They danced the old repertory, mainly, in the old costumes with the old sets—what else was there? But as the months went by, and the struggle for control over the theater and its repertory unfolded, an astonishing fact emerged: ballet would not only survive, it would take its place as a prominent cultural institution and anchor of the Bolshevik state.[7]

One reason was Anatole Lunacharsky. Lunacharsky was Lenin's commissar of education in charge of cultural affairs, and he saw himself as the "poet of the revolution." A playwright and passionate orator, he was a self-proclaimed "God-builder" who believed that the revolution had to happen in the Russian soul and spirit as well as in the material conditions and political arrangements of society. The arts could help. He talked about the revolutionary necessity of "an infinite higher force" and insisted with a kind of missionary zeal that "God is not yet born, but being built."[8] To become this new utopian man, the proletariat would need an education, and Lunacharsky's taste was decidedly Old World European. Some years earlier he had led a Communist Party school in Europe, which included a barely disguised grand tour to Italian museums to study Renaissance painting. He was also the author of a two-volume study titled *Religion and Socialism*, which argued that Karl Marx was not only the prophet of rational scientific Socialism but also a great humanist and moral philosopher. In keeping with these ideas, he was certain that it would be ideologically shortsighted to discard classical music, dance, and art in favor of "The Internationale"—as many were suggesting at the time. On the contrary, he said, the proletariat should build on the aristocratic and bourgeois culture that was now theirs by right of Revolution and History. As Balanchine later put it, more cynically, Lunacharsky "was intelligent man, and he wanted to preserve, but he had to convince them it would bring people for [party] meetings." Lenin was skeptical. He harbored a deep suspicion of the "pure landlord culture" and "pompous court style" of the Imperial Theaters and accused Lunacharsky of "scientific mysticism." Nonetheless, Lenin eventually relented, and Lunacharsky wasted no time establishing the former Imperial Theaters and classical ballet as part of the spiritual foundation of the newly emerging Socialist state. When the doors of the Theater School reopened to students on October 12, 1918, Lunacharsky delivered the welcoming address. Georgi was there.[9]

Among Lunacharsky's closest advisors in the early days of the revolution were the poets Alexander Blok and Vladimir Mayakovsky and the theater director Vsevolod Meyerhold. For a time these artists were his triumvirate, and in many ways, they became Balanchine's too. They had already made a strong cultural mark. Like Lunacharsky, they gave themselves fully to the revolution—and would eventually be destroyed by it. It was true that Blok would die in 1921, and Mayakovsky and Meyerhold would eventually split from Lunacharsky, unwilling to abide his "classic generals" and state academies of art.[10] They eventually threw their artistic lot wholly to the street and a kind of cultural anarchism, which Georgi would follow too. But even in the midst of fierce debates and political realignments, this triumvirate belonged to a forefront—there were many—and Blok and Mayakovsky, at least, would always believe in the "third" spiritual way that lay at the heart of Lunacharsky's vision of revolution.

Georgi had been watching Meyerhold since he was a child. He had been part of Meyerhold and Fokine's 1916 revival of *Orpheus and Eurydice* set to music by Gluck, a score he would return to, which featured some two hundred near-dead bodies on stage, frozen in unnatural poses, hanging off cliffs, and falling into Hades through trapdoors or crawling and squirming as if through slime across the length of the stage. He had been a gnome too in Meyerhold's production of Lermontov's *Masquerade,* with music by Glazunov based on Glinka's Valse-Fantaisie in B-Minor—another score Balanchine later choreographed himself. *Masquerade* was a massive, deliberately decadent production, with some four thousand costumes and set designs, elaborate masks, lush eighteenth-century gowns, and a magnificent ball featuring more than 150 dancers. The actors performed stylized, rhythmic movements, giving the production a nervous, carnivalesque fatality, "on the border of delirium and hallucination" as Meyerhold put it. The house lights were left up and large mirrors broke the fourth wall by reflecting audience and actors back onto each other, a startling effect to those who were present on the opening night, as the first shots of the revolution were heard outside.[11]

Georgi also understudied Meyerhold's 1918 production of Igor Stravinsky's opera *The Nightingale*, which he would later stage himself, and although he was barely fourteen, he remembered how Meyerhold relegated the singers to a bench on the side while dancers pantomimed the action on stage. More radical still, that same year Meyerhold worked with Mayakovsky and Kazimir Malevich on *Mystery-Bouffe* in celebration of the first anniversary of the revolution. The actors at the Imperial Theaters refused to perform such a daring piece, so the play was recast and moved to a small experimental theater nearby. Audiences—Balanchine thought he was there—witnessed a tidal wave destroying the world and leaving only seven pure (workers) and seven impure (bourgeois) couples on the Ark; the pure finally fooled the impure, threw them overboard, and made their way to a promised land of rainbows, cars, trains, and the exotica of modern industrial life. Mayakovsky himself played the role of the Commonest of All Men. No one much liked it, but Lunacharsky was pleased, and Georgi and his friends delighted in reciting Mayakovsky's verse from the scene in which the actors gleefully tear up posters from the Imperial Theaters, chanting:

> We are tired of heavenly sweets
> We are tired of paper passions. . . .
>
> We want space!
> Today
>
> Over the dust of the theater
> Our slogan will catch fire:
> All is new!
> Stop and marvel![12]

Meyerhold wanted a more and more radical theater free of stale conventions and "Uncle Vanyas whimpering on the settee," as Mayakovsky snidely put it.[13] Meyerhold talked of dismantling the footlights and bringing the street to the stage, and eventually of "denuding the theater" of fancy costumes and sets in favor of something more direct and austere. He also imagined a kind of contemporary commedia dell'arte of wandering mimes and circus performers, and he incorporated popular forms such as masks and acrobatics. At one point he even broadcast breaking radio news bulletins onto the stage as part of a performance.[14] Dance was key, and, working with a doctor involved in physical culture who had also trained Red Army commanders, Meyerhold eventually turned his ideas about movement into a system he called biomechanics: bodily positions anatomically designed to touch "points of excitability" and to train the body like a machine. Forget inner motives in acting, he said in a pointed reference to Konstantin Stanislavsky and his prevailing psychological method, actors need to work from the outside in. Don't conjure the reason to shout, just shout; or as Balanchine later transposed it, "Don't think, just dance." Meyerhold was after a kind of bodily plastique—an acrobatic, dynamic, almost sculptural kind of dance, bodies bent in extreme shapes and poses, or moving in rhythmic patterns, drilled to machinelike precision. Emotion would follow—or not.[15]

In the fall of 1919, Lunacharsky appointed Andrei Aleksandrovich Oblakov to head the school. It was a decisive moment for them all. Tall and thin with a haggard physique, Oblakov was shy and receding, a former dancer who had nonetheless taken a stand among the rebels at the theater in 1905. He had traveled Europe with Diaghilev and was a curious, well-read man, who liked to invite the students to his book-lined apartment on the first floor of the school to discuss poetry, politics, and art. He regaled them with stories of Fokine, Pavlova, Karsavina, Alexander Benois, Léon Bakst, and the ideas animating Diaghilev's World of Art. His sister was sometimes there, boldly playing Stravinsky or Debussy on the piano. But above all, he encouraged Georgi—who was now becoming a more adult George—and his friends to read the poetry of Blok, Mayakovsky, Akhmatova, Sergei Yesenin; George's reputation as a "walking almanac" of Mayakovsky's verse grew stronger by the day. One night Oblakov read aloud Blok's *The Twelve*, which George would soon stage as a dance. There were outings too, and Lunacharsky arranged for the students to attend a screening of D. W. Griffith's epic film *Intolerance* at the Splendide Palace movie theater on Karavannaia Street. After the show they reenacted scenes from the film in the bathroom, with George in the starring role of the princely lover.[16]

As for Blok, a living beacon for them all, he longed for what he called the "Beautiful Lady," who revealed herself to him in a vision and found her way into his poetry and his life. He married Liubov Dmitrievna Mendeleeva (daughter of the renowned scientist), who went on to write a history of ballet, and they aspired to a celibate marriage in a small house lined with roses, but Blok ended up drinking and in brothels and in a tormented ménage à trois with the writer Andrei Bely, a Theosophist engaged in occult fantasies, who was in love with Liubov too. Meanwhile, Blok wrote passionate odes to his Beautiful Lady, and when the revolution came, he defended it, telling friends that his sacked country estate deserved it and that he could hear the "roar of the collapse of the old world" in his head. "I see angels' wings behind the shoulders of every Red Guardsman," he said, and then he wrote his epic if deeply ambivalent revolutionary poem, *The Twelve*—and went to work for Lunacharsky.[17]

The common enemy, as Mayakovsky put it, was *byt* (a Russian word describing the stultifying, crippling stagnation of everydayness and the stuck bourgeois routines of ordinary life). "Byt is motionless . . . like a horse that can't be spurred and stands still" and "slits of byt are filled with fat and coagulate," he said, barely able to contain his disgust. Byt kills the human spirit, drives away love and eroticism, and feasts on laziness and boredom. People "sleepwalk" through life and need to "wake up!" The only solution was an almost violent awakening—a revolution of the spirit so profound that it would interrupt and overcome not only byt but Nietzsche's eternal recurrence (in the air at the time) or Buddhist reincarnation or whatever seemingly inescapable cycle of life and death people found themselves in. The goal was not an eternal afterlife of the spirit, but an Elysian Field that would be physical and fully embodied. An eternal now. Mayakovsky put it this way: "Soon there will be no more death, and the dead will be resurrected," and he was clear that this meant the flesh-and-blood body too, for "how can bodiless beings have a heart? / . . . My eyes fixed earthward . . . / this herd of the bodiless, / how they / bore me!"[18]

Many of these artists were (more or less) taken with Theosophy and the writings of the Russian psychic Madame Blavatsky and her disciples, including Rudolf Steiner, P. D. Ouspensky (Balanchine's favorite), and G. I. Gurdjieff (Lincoln Kirstein would be for a time obsessed). These cult-like figures were interested variously in seances, automatic writing, dance, and physical exercise as transcendent Dionysian theatrical experiences. They also looked to earlier Russian philosophers, such as Vladimir Soloviev (1853–1900)—Blok admiringly called him a "knightly monk"—with his lifelong pursuit of the "Divine Sophia," a mystical woman with azure eyes and a radiant aura, who appeared before him in a Moscow church and then in the reading room of the British Museum and finally on a trip to Cairo. She was seductively androgynous, he said, a Platonic unification of male and female, material and spiritual, human and divine, and he became obsessed with her presence. Soloviev defended erotic love as a joining of the material and the divine, but he renounced sex—in theory and (very imperfectly) in his own life. Unrequited desire could be harnessed as energy, he thought, and he imagined a great collective abstinence that would finally end death in a phantasmagorical transfiguration of mankind and all of Holy Rus. The idea of the Divine Sophia also drew on early Orthodoxy, in which the spirit was feminine. The Church later anxiously masculinized references to spirit—even the pronouns were changed—to shift the feminization of God and make the Father, Son, and Holy Ghost male. These were the ideas flowing around Balanchine. He was so young, and the moment was so dense. He absorbed what came his way, in snatches and pieces, and he already had a strong internal sense of what interested and amused him and what did not.[19]

"Dear boy, die!" their teacher G. G. Isaenko liked to say in his loud tenor voice to poor unsuspecting students as they passed in the hallway, a strange recognition of the death all around them. Everyone knew the cue: fall immediately to the floor and lie there until he shouts, "Dear boy, get up and go about your bloody business!" Sometimes Isaenko disappeared, leaving a boy "dead" for twenty minutes or more before rescuing him with the "get up" cry.

When it was George's turn, he looked at Isaenko and coolly noted, "I would rather die than be humiliated," and they became friends. Isaenko was old and crooked and had a puffy face, watery eyes, and a bloated stomach that preceded him into any room as he entered. He had spent nearly three decades at the school as a lowly boys' caretaker, and he was now second in command and an avowed Communist and admirer of Lunacharsky. His apartment, which the students visited often, was darkly lit and filled with fancy old rosewood furniture covered with leftover bits of dried-up food and layers of grime he refused to clean. But he could be festive too, and threw a school New Year's party with truth or dare and charades and George at the piano playing waltzes. He took George under his protection, and George even lived in Isaenko's apartment for a moment with another student—some whispered that the old man was in love with him. Isaenko kindly gave his fragile student extra food when he could and talked and gossiped with him at length about theater, poetry, and ideas. George took it all in and later amused his friends with wicked imitations of the strange and fond Isaenko.[20]

It was like a charivari. The old school porter, a diminutive man with bowed legs, was now suddenly deputy director of administration—and a key figure in wringing extra rations for the children from the authorities. The black-clad minder Varvara was still there too, but she was no longer quite in charge. She scolded and scorned as she always had, but the moment she left the classroom, the children liked to flip her desk on its back, attach it to their ankles, and drag it triumphantly through the halls. For her part, Varvara took to defiantly carrying an open umbrella, even in the sunshine. Who knows what she was going through inside? Father Pigulevsky, still an influence on George but priest no more under the new anti-God regime, busied himself rewriting his beloved Catechism classes as "morals and customs," or the history of cults and worshipping rituals. In addition, he put himself in charge of a "brigade" of boys, including George, who went out into the city equipped with a large carving saw and a coarse sack to forage for fuel and sustenance. They cut wood from fences, houses, and window frames and did odd jobs for cash or scraps of food, such as shoveling the deep eternal banks of snow. Once they found a stash of chocolate bars from the fancy St. Petersburg confectioner Georg-Borman, along with some Japanese sugar that tasted like halva, in an old abandoned basement. They brought it excitedly back to the school late at night and, eager to share these rare prerevolutionary treats with the girls, broke noisily into their quarters and together they all feasted. Varvara slept through the revels, and her stern investigation the following morning into the boys' alleged misconduct was waved aside by Isaenko, who thoroughly approved of such adventures. They almost felt warm and enclosed, thanks again to Father Pigulevsky, who managed to find some iron pipes that he used to make small heaters, rigged to funnel the smoke through the broken windows, so they could toast their frostbitten fingers and faces.[21]

Who cooked for them? They did, and it could even be said that in the things that mattered most, the students were in charge. There were meetings to air grievances and agree on procedures governing their lives, and a committee of boys was elected by the student body: the Uchenicheskyi Komitet, they proudly called it, or UchKom for short. George won a spot. UchKom was responsible for the delicate task of rationing the daily bread, and every night the committee met to cut the coveted loaves into equal pieces, one-eighth of a pound for each student. They developed a special method of slicing that accounted for every crumb. And when efficient American Red Cross ladies finally appeared in 1921 as famine overtook the country, UchKom happily kept score of the plentiful provisions they delivered, including condensed milk, hot chocolate, and corn porridge. Any remaining rations were dutifully offered to the drama students lodged upstairs, and like all good Communist organizations, UchKom even took it upon themselves to organize social events for their little community, such as ballroom dancing, games, musical soirees, and plays they rehearsed and performed themselves. They also took it upon themselves to purge their own ranks, and in a final ironic turn not long before George graduated, the students voted to expel poor Isaenko for alleged cruelty to the children. He was out but continued to share his rations with George and those who would have him.

There were new friends. Yuri Slonimsky was a drama student who took to the ballet, and George, who was by then thin and pale, with hair parted down the middle and sad eyes, daringly snuck Slonimsky into the theater, past the guards, for performances.[22] Tuka, as everyone called him, lived with his family nearby and often invited the grateful and hungry George to his home for meals and Jewish holidays. Slonimsky's sister was at the music academy, and when George enrolled there too, they played together. Tuka also brought into their little circle Volodia Dmitriev and Boris (Boria) Erbstein, students from the Academy of Art who had worked with Meyerhold. Dmitriev had designed the sets for Meyerhold's 1920 production of Emile Verhaeren's *The Dawn* in a cubist, metallic-looking industrial style—"theater as mass meeting," Meyerhold called it.[23] Dmitriev was a self-professed philosopher obsessed with Rudolf Steiner and his Swiss *Goetheanum*, a cathedral to art and spirit, named after Goethe and built on occult principles. Erbstein was a student of the artist Petrov-Vodkin, who used icons and inverted perspective to disarmingly erotic effect. Boria, as his friends called him, was Jewish but soon converted to Russian Orthodoxy. He spewed anti-Semitic epithets and ritually burned any money his well-to-do father, a successful laryngologist, kindly provided. In keeping with this self-consciously eccentric image, he wore a fur-lined leather cap with drooping ears, even in the summer, along with sailor's shirts and bell-bottom pants, since he had taught the Baltic Naval Fleet. Rounding out this bizarre picture, he shared a flat with a mad old woman who covered herself in kerosene once a week to rid herself of fleas, perhaps because their large room with two beds and a potbellied stove also contained a shockingly tall pile of garbage that Boria refused to remove as a matter of principle. It was like the shitty life they were all leading, he said.

There were others in their odd group, orphans of a past that was disappearing in plain sight. The eccentric A. V. Shiryaev, a Petipa loyalist, left when the old master bitterly retired, spent time in Europe, and returned to the school in 1918 to teach. He amused the students with his escapist world of puppetry and objects he liked to build, such as an aquarium full of glossy fake seaweed and goldfish. He kept a collection of stage masks, costumes, theater posters, dolls, and musical instruments, and he was preoccupied with an early film contraption he had contrived to record dances, a kind of advanced flip-book animation of sketches and puppets that he ran frame by frame through a makeshift projector—it is from these flip-books that we know of the original *Nutcracker* Hoop Dance, danced by Shiryaev and eventually by Balanchine. Pavel Pavelovich Akorchev was a teacher who played four-hands with Balanchine and coached his talent. Or the ballerina Olga Preobrazhenskaya, formidable as ever, who choreographed her own free-form solos in a Grecian tunic on an empty stage and once asked George to perform with her—she was like a cardinal, he remembered, and it also gave him a chance to dance with the frail and moving Olga Spessivtseva, who was herself a bit mad.[24]

Ivan Ivanovich Sollertinsky, who became a friend too, arrived to teach one afternoon in a soldier's overcoat and barely looked at the students as he set *The Song of Roland* on the table in front of him and began reciting the text by heart, lisping as he went. He had come from Mikhail Bakhtin's philosophical circle in Vitebsk and was in Petrograd to complete a doctorate in Spanish literature and philology when Oblakov invited him to lecture at the school. A scholar of prodigious memory, Sollertinsky spoke many languages and was an accomplished musician with an endearing habit of conducting the various orchestral scores he had committed to memory while walking down the street, eyes averted, wrist pumping an imaginary baton. He carried an old knapsack and scribbled notes to himself in Portuguese so that the authorities could not decipher his thoughts.[25]

Through it all, George was at the piano, and in 1920 he managed to formally enroll at the still prestigious Conservatory of Music next door. He practiced constantly, wearing gloves cut at the fingers to ward off the cold, and friends remembered Beethoven, Bach, Chopin, Schumann, Tchaikovsky, Weber pouring into the hallways as he sat in an empty classroom playing for hours. He wrote his own compositions, practiced four-hands with anyone who would, and set Blok and Nikolay Gumilev's poetry to music, improvising his way through the verse until he was satisfied. And he started to make dances. Oblakov encouraged them all, the girls included, to choreograph, and he assigned music for the purpose—Schumann, Saint-Saëns, Mendelssohn.

Night: a woman arched with one leg high in arabesque, supported by leaning into a kiss.[26] It was a yearning pas de deux to Anton Rubenstein's Romance in E-flat Major, and George named it after Pushkin's impassioned love poem.[27] He danced the opening performances himself with Olga Mungalova—blond, wispy, remote, a dancer he admired. He was also working with his friend Lidia Ivanova on her *Valse Triste* to music by Sibelius about a blind girl and death. At one point she opened her mouth in an agonized silent scream, like Munch's "loud unending" scream or the "huge orifice" scream of

Bely's iconoclastic novel *St. Petersburg*, which they were all reading.[28] Solicitous of George's obvious talent, Oblakov guarded the doors to the studio against interruption as George worked, and stood nearby in the first wings of their little theater during George's performances for teachers and students.

A few of them even took the time to restage *The Magic Flute*, a lighthearted old ballet by Lev Ivanov, with George and Lidia in the leading roles and new sets and costumes by Dmitriev and Erbstein. Half a century later, when Balanchine was sick and dying, he would assign this forgotten minor work to a young choreographer (Peter Martins) and a bewildered group of American dancers at his own New York school, like some nostalgic rite of passage to which they had no access.[29] Who knew that back in the summer of 1920, George and his friends had danced *The Magic Flute* in Tsarskoye Selo amid the czar's former palaces and grounds, reclaimed for children's groups after the revolution? The girls stayed in the elegant Yusupov summer palace, and the boys were lodged in the nearby mansion of an old imperial colonel. They performed outdoors with a grand piano at the end of a terrace stage, made their entrances and exits through the rose gardens, and changed in the gazebo nearby. Still chronically underfed, they were momentarily content as they inhabited this old imperial haunt in their wide-brimmed hats, their costumes wrapped in bedsheets and slung over their shoulders, accompanied by the eccentric Oblakov and Isaenko, with Varvara and her open umbrella parading in the long white nights. Erbstein and Dmitriev were there too and slept in the garden, and no one quite remembered where Tuka stayed. In a private moment, the girls gleefully ran naked through the grass.[30]

Still, it was not the idyllic *Magic Flute* but *The Storming of the Winter Palace* that seemed to sum up this moment in their young lives. This epic revolutionary festival was designed to commemorate and reenact the revolution on its third anniversary, with a cast of eight thousand and an audience of more than one hundred thousand—far more than had attended the revolution itself. The dancers of the school and the theater were recruited to the cast. Palace Square, which George had walked across countless times over the years, was brightly lit, and a large production team stationed on elevated platforms coordinated this theatrical reenactment like a military deployment. At the appointed moment, the square was plunged into darkness and the directors mobilized trucks, bayonets, machine guns, and signaled the requisite shot from the cruiser *Aurora* stationed nearby. They cued searchlights, a five-hundred-piece orchestra, and a large chorus, as the action unfolded on white and red stages set against an impressive Red City of factories rising in their midst. The final battle took place inside the Winter Palace itself and was a pièce d'occasion all its own: the windows of the palace were lit from behind, and audiences watched the pantomimed combat enacted in silhouette, like a silent film of their newly memorialized lives. The whole event clocked in at under two hours, and when it was all over, the exhausted actors and dancers made their way home through the darkened streets and boarded-up buildings.[31]

In 1921 Lenin proclaimed the New Economic Policy (NEP), and George graduated from the school and met the woman who would become his first wife. Tamara Zheverzeva (soon to be Tamara Geva) was a beautiful and aspiring, if not yet successful, dancer, age sixteen, who came to the school for night classes when George was teaching. He walked her home. There were awkward teas in her family salon, and he shyly asked to be with her alone, but instead of the anticipated kiss, he wanted to try out some steps in her living room. He asked her to perform the erotically tinged *Night* with him. It was seduction through dancing, she said, bodies moving and entwined. It was also the beginning, for him, of a Pygmalion-like desire to make a woman into something beautiful, his own kind of Divine Sophia.

Tamara's father, Levko Zheverzev, was charmed. He was half-Turk, half-Tatar, from a Muslim family that manufactured gold lamé, chalices, and miters—anything in gold, gold leaf, or precious stones—for the Orthodox Church. He had supplied the imperial family with heavy funeral clothes sewn with golden thread. Zheverzev was deeply cultivated and a well-known patron of avant-garde art. Meyerhold had performed at the little theater in his home, and Mayakovsky was a friend. And although Zheverzev was arrested during the revolution and his factory closed and collections partially confiscated, a petition of artists—Mayakovsky in the lead—won his release, and he was allowed to keep his home. Balanchine never forgot the vast library, and it was through Tamara and her father that he once briefly met Mayakovsky. George played their grand piano, and he and Zheverzev talked about Mahler and Wagner.

Tamara's mother was hardly there. Wild and glamorous, an uneducated music-hall singer whom her father had kept for years in a separate apartment before finally bringing her and the children into his family home (after his disapproving father's death), she was prone to dramatic love affairs and fond of lacy lingerie and sealskin coats. Tamara hated her, loved her, had it all in her too, and it was not hard to see that George was part of Tamara's impossible flight from her mother's mauve boudoir into the more serious precincts of her father's art—or that George was drawn to both. The fact was, George reminded her of her father. They had the same dark features and were both quiet with long black hair that fell over one eye—though George sometimes also applied a dash of eyeliner for effect. Her father, who mattered almost as much as his daughter in this three-way liaison, liked George and saw in him a new talent in his lifelong pursuit of the avant-garde.

Did they marry in the chapel of the Theater School with the old priest Pigulevsky presiding? Priests were being summarily shot, but many Russians still followed the Orthodox faith, so why not them too? But did Tamara wear a pale-blue crepe dress with a short veil made from a piece of fabric she found somewhere, and were there makeshift earrings crafted from orange blossoms, old shoes too small for her feet, and a fancy turban spun around her head from some leftover crepe? No one seems to have witnessed George standing next to his bride in a suit and tails borrowed from the theater's wardrobe department. And what about George's father and brother? No one thought they really came from Tiflis for the celebrations; Meliton noted that he visited the following year, but said nothing about George or a marriage, reporting instead that his prized Andrei had become a musician "blessed by God." Tamara promised it had all happened, but none of George's other friends or colleagues recalled this fantastical event. Alexandra (Choura) Danilova, who was close with George and would soon become his second (common-law) wife, was thoroughly miffed at his mawkish secrecy, if such a ceremony had even taken place. It was nonetheless soon official. On October 24, 1922, someone registered George and Tamara's marriage at the Petrograd Central District office. By then George had already moved in with Tamara's family, and the couple would soon find their own apartment near the Moika canal. Were they in love? Does it matter? He was eighteen, she was seventeen, and they were trying to make ballet progressive in revolutionary Petrograd.[32]

George was by then a reasonably good dancer in a demi-caractère style, with a middling thirteenth-grade rank at the former Mariinsky Theater and a salary of 2.745 rubles (exempt from income and property tax). His graduation solo in 1921 had been a dagger-thrusting Georgian lezginka, and he excelled in roles full of jumps and tricks, such as the Hoop Dance in *The Nutcracker*. "I wanted to be a dashing kind of a man on stage, leaping and turning, and something like that . . . more like a glorified restaurant, dashing Turks, Cossacks, sabers," he later explained, amused at his own bad taste.[33] Outside the theater, as *Night* had shown, his work was quite different, and as Lenin's NEP introduced private enterprise and loosened state controls on industry and culture, the pace of life in the city changed dramatically. Nightclubs, cinemas, cabarets, and restaurants popped up overnight in a giddy show of pent-up desire. There was food in the shops again, but only the party elite and newly well-to-do NEP men and profiteers seemed able to afford it. George and his friends were making ends meet by performing dances in as many of the burgeoning venues as would have them. Gigs were stacked like vaudeville acts, and George and Tamara often rushed in a single evening from one cabaret stage, coats thrown over costumes, to the next. He and a friend even made an orchestra with pots and pans and piano.[34]

They were seeing things too. Lunacharsky invited Isadora Duncan, the iconoclastic American freestyle dancer inspired by ancient Greek themes, to build a Socialist dance school, and although she was by then aging and overweight, she still delivered her famous dance sermon to the strains of "The Internationale"—red cloak wrapped dramatically around her fleshy and free-flowing body. George later scoffed and denied any influence, but he was too close to know just how deeply Duncan had shaped the landscape he grew up in. Nikolai Foregger's *Machine Dances* was inspired by Mayakovsky, who was moving ever further into anarchism and poster-board art. And Foregger's show—we were impressed, a friend of George's remembered—was a music-hall review portraying the body as a machine, with dancers enacting pistons and gears to musical noise from the factory floor.[35]

In the fall of 1922, George plunged into this giddy artistic society. He worked with the Factory of the Eccentric Actor, started by Grigory Kozintsev and Leonid Trauberg, Ukrainian Jews and future Soviet filmmakers recently arrived in Petrograd. With backgrounds in painting and theater, they too were deeply influenced by Meyerhold and Mayakovsky and interested in "Americanization," film, circus, jazz, boxing, and acrobatics (to "desanctify" theater, as Foregger put it). They all adored Charlie Chaplin. Their group included clowns and jugglers, and the young Sergei Eisenstein was a close collaborator. They invited George to work with them on a new production of Nikolay Gogol's *The Marriage* titled *The Marriage, Not According to Gogol*—which meant that not a word of Gogol's text was uttered. Instead, this was to be a "rhythmical battering of the nerves," and the show featured actors playing Chaplin, Einstein, and Gogol (scolding them ironically for taking such liberties with his play). There were robots on roller skates playing mechanical parts: a Steam Bridegroom, an Electric Bridegroom, a Radioactive Bridegroom, with flashing lights, and fragments of horns, bells, and whistles throughout. The pace was relentless, as if speed were a way to escape from time, and Eisenstein sat in rehearsals watching intently and muttering impatiently, "Slow! Too slow!"[36]

George performed in *Dance Symphony: The Magnificence of the Universe*, choreographed by Fedor Lopokov, Lunacharsky's newly appointed director of the ballet at the former Mariinsky Theater. Lopokov came from a theatrical family; his father had been chief usher at one of the Imperial Theaters, and his sister Lydia was in Europe dancing with Diaghilev (and would soon marry John Maynard Keynes). *Dance Symphony* was self-consciously experimental, and Lopokov rehearsed at night with a group of young dancers, including George and several of his friends, who goaded the choreographer with their Mayakovsky slogans: "Not like before!"[37] Set to Beethoven's Fourth Symphony, *Dance Symphony* had no story, no plot, no narrative device. It began simply with a chain of men walking across the front of the stage, one arm raised with the palm of the hand shielding the eyes, the other extended forward into the darkness ahead, another gesture George would later borrow. The dances that followed bore grandiose titles, such as "The Birth of the Sun" and "Thermal Energy," and Lopokov said he hoped to harness what he called "cosmic forces" in a surging, rhythmic spectacle, but George was particularly entranced by Lopokov's musical skills and excitedly showed the dancers how Lopokov had used musical devices in movement, such as parallel voices or counterpoint. He had the idea, which Balanchine took, that a movement could *look like* a sound—not people dancing *to* music, but people dancing *the* music, a visual image of a musical idea. Major and minor keys in music, he thought, for example, corresponded to movements made in "inside" and "outside" directions (en dedans and en dehors). One critic likened the performance to Malevich's *Black Square*, and Balanchine later recalled that they were aiming for a kind of "Suprematism" in dance.[38]

Black Square, first shown in 1915 at the *Last Futurist Exhibition of Painting 0.10* in Moscow, was one of the first abstract paintings. It was also unabashedly apocalyptic: "0.10" marked the "zero hour" of the end of the old world, and the ten artists that would begin anew. With the simple image of a flat black square, Malevich hoped to free art from the material world, including the human figure. The idea was spiritual, and to make the point, he hung the painting high in a top corner of the gallery, like an icon. This was not Malevich's first black square. He had made another, even earlier rendition in the suprematist production *Victory over the Sun* in 1913—with financial support from Tamara's father, Levko Zheverzev. It was an attack on the "sun" of rationality and the characters spoke an invented shamanistic (and utterly incomprehensible) "transrational" language they called Zaum, or "beyond the mind." There was an equally disorienting score and fractured cubist-style sets, with actors in gas-mask-like headpieces, and blinding lights turned onto the audience. "We have shot the past," they proclaimed.[39]

Malevich later explained his desire to make paintings that do "not belong solely to the earth. The earth has been abandoned like a house. . . . Man feels a great yearning for space, an impulse to break free from the globe of the earth." He was fascinated with space, technology, science, and the possibility of ending death. When Lenin finally died in 1924, Malevich was a leading figure on the official Immortalization Commission to save the great man's body. It is no accident that Lenin was preserved in a large Malevich-designed cube or that images of black squares were freely distributed to the party elite in the interest of their collective salvation—not from sin but from death itself.[40]

Lopokov talked this way too. Ballet, he said, should be unmoored from sets, costumes, and stage effects and stripped to its basics—the human body moving in space. But there was a practical problem with transferring suprematist ideas to dance. How could the dancer, a concrete, life-and-blood material figure, be made abstract? Lopokov's answer was music. He wanted to make the dancers a pure representation of a musical score. Not beautiful women or flirtatious ballerinas in elaborate dramas or wedding-cake spectacles, but starkly impersonal beings, shapes, and forms—black squares of dance. Some attacked *Dance Symphony* for being obscure, but George sprang to Lopokov's defense in a rare critical essay published in *Theatre Magazine*. In a sign of his growing notoriety, that month George's picture also appeared on the cover.[41]

Nothing mattered more in this array of new experiences than the dances of the Moscow choreographer Kasyan Goleizovsky. When George and his friends attended a performance of Goleizovsky's small troupe in Petrograd, they stayed up all night feverishly discussing and debating what they had seen. Here was a self-proclaimed leftist ballet master set against the dead academicism and decadence of classical dance. Goleizovsky had left the Imperial Theaters to form his own company, and although he preferred to work with highly trained classical dancers, there were no fairy-tale plots or decorative tutus in sight. His ballets were essays on eroticism and spirituality, nervous and acrobatic, and part of a burgeoning Moscow scene in experimental forms of "new dance" and plastique, including dances performed nude, or near-nude. In Goleizovsky's *Dance of the Seven Veils*, which George later planned to stage in the same way, Salomé stood on a raised platform in radiant light, while men gathered all around reached to touch her as she shed her veils and the moon shone on her almost naked body.[42] If this was not enough, Goleizovsky's *Funeral March* (to Nikolai Medtner's score) ended with bodies clad in black lying on the floor in the shape of a cross, which then breathed to macabre effect—another image George would lift directly into one of the last dances he ever made. Some dismissed Goleizovsky as kitsch or merely pornographic, but Balanchine and his friends were obsessed. Goleizovsky apparently admired the young choreographer too. When he proposed to establish a workshop in Petrograd, George was asked to teach choreographic improvisation.[43]

With his star rising, and encouraged by Dmitriev, George gathered their group of friends and suggested that they start their own troupe. They would call it the Young Ballet, founded with the express purpose of "[moving] ballet from its dead point," as one of the dancers later noted. Not surprisingly, they failed to win official approval for this venture from the theater or from anyone else, but they went ahead anyway. Principles were established: they would be a collective of equals with no stars or rankings, and no one would be paid. Any money they made would go toward costumes, pianists, rehearsal space, and dancers who were sick or in need. They would perform works by a range of choreographers, but Balanchivadze's work would hold a special place, and an early program announced their lineage: "From Petipa, through Fokine, towards Balanchivadze."[44]

A threshold had been crossed. In their contained and chaotic world, George was becoming a leader of sorts: a watcher still and ever involved in his own inner life of music and poetry, but also a young man calling attention to himself. People noticed. They were picking him out and asking him to make dances or to fix dances that weren't working. He was available, quick, unobtrusive. Could he add something, please? He didn't mind, because at least when he was making dances, he seemed to know what to do. But there was more to it than efficacy. He had internalized the driving revolutionary ambition that was all around him. He wanted to make ballet "progressive," and it upset him when artists he liked saw it as a remnant of a dying imperial world. That wasn't him. The former Mariinsky was the "dead point," and *he* at least was pushing on and situating himself in the lively world of experimental dance exploding under the NEP. The goal was clear: to elevate dance and himself into the ranks of the revolutionary artists he so admired.

On June 1, 1923, at 1 P.M., the Young Ballet had its premiere at the hall of the former city Duma on Nevsky—now October—Prospekt. It was an early-nineteenth-century red-brick building with a pentagonal tower known to Petersburgers for its launch of colored balloons warning of city flooding, and more recently as a gathering place. The provenance was excellent, since Lunacharsky, Mayakovsky, and Ouspensky had all spoken there. To announce the performance of the Young Ballet, Erbstein made a futurist-style poster thickly scrawled with screaming red writing. The program would begin with familiar classical dances—the past—but it was the final dance that signaled their bold departure, Balanchivadze's own *Funeral March* with sets and costumes designed by Dmitriev and Erbstein to Chopin's sorrowful dirge.[45]

Funeral March was danced by the entire troupe. They rehearsed and also sewed and painted together, using old fabric they found somewhere to make short gray tunics with black and silver geometric shapes and tight, mournful hoods of embroidered black and silver lace. The dance has been lost and forgotten, but descriptions from the time tell us that it was more liturgical than balletic. The performance began with a procession of six women walking onto the stage on pointe, single file, heads bent, arms crossed as in death. There were four men carrying a girl lying flat on her back, lifted high overhead like a coffin. Tamara recalled "changing from the mourners into the dead . . . our bodies twisting into arches and crosses."[46] Toward the end, the dead girl was finally lifted horizontally once again and carried off the stage. The women followed spirit-like on pointe behind, like a chorus with faces uplifted (a study for Balanchine's later *Serenade*). When the dance ended, silence fell over the house. No one moved, and the dancers waited anxiously until the applause finally came. There was so much applause that they repeated the dance. *Funeral March* was a company hit.[47]

In the weeks that followed, the Young Ballet performed all over the city: from Pavlovsk Train Station to Sestroretsk near the Gulf of Finland. They danced for whoever would have them. George was a consummate showman, and he was careful to produce light, entertaining dances along with darker, more romantic-sounding ballets bearing titles such as *Enigma, Elegy, Étude,* and *Extase* to music by Anton Arensky, Sergey Rachmaninoff, Alexander Scriabin (another occultist), and himself. All these dances are gone, but a photo shows him with Tamara, barefooted and bare-legged in ragged Grecian tunics. She is thrown over his shoulder, sprawled on her back, legs bent around him in a twisted embrace. Not everyone liked these unorthodox movements and a sharp volley of criticism attacked George for his perceived heresies: "a solid evening of theatrical vulgarity," Akim Volynsky announced. Accentuating the disagreement, a caricature of George appeared in the press with Mayakovsky's motto: "All is new! Stop and marvel!"[48]

Meanwhile, George was in demand. He was hired by the former Mikhailovsky Theater to work on plays, including Ernst Toller's *Eugene the Unfortunate* directed by Sergey Radlov, another Meyerhold disciple. The sets and costumes were by Dmitriev and the poet Mikhail Kuzmin, who called the play a kind of expressionist "scream-drama" full of exaggeration and pain. George's dance took place in a second-floor window lit in silhouette, like the final scene of the revolutionary reenactment of *The Storming of the Winter Palace*. He choreographed invalids on crutches moving against a background of mechanical ballerinas mindlessly repeating their irrelevant exercises.[49]

The Twelve, based on Blok's epic poem and first performed in the fall of 1923, was a direct reckoning with the revolution. The performance took place at the Institute of the Living Word, yet another Lunacharsky-supported project. Founded in 1918 by professors of linguistics, theater, and classics, it was a school devoted to developing the nonverbal skills necessary for the full expression of a new Socialist life, including an experimental theater focused on improvisation and the contemporary revival of ancient choral dance (inspired in part by Isadora Duncan). It drew together performers, physiologists, phoneticians, literary scholars, dancers, and speech therapists and focused especially on live speech as a mass art—part of a new revolutionary culture that would include gesture and a study of the ways in which words affected the body, and the spirit. The poet Gumilev had been involved, before he was shot by Lenin's Cheka in 1921, just two days before Blok himself died—or was allowed to die by deliberate bureaucratic neglect preventing him from seeking necessary treatment. The two events seemed related in the minds of many in the city's literary world, and it was in this darkening climate that *The Twelve* came to be.

We don't know if George chose Blok's poem or if it was chosen for him, but we do know that the head of the institute worked with him to plan a dance to words. Instead of music, a chorus of fifty chanted the poem while the dancers performed steps based on old Russian folk dances: not ballet, not legs twisted in erotic embrace, not ironic futurist antics. George needed a different vocabulary for this poem, and he found it in a return to the people. He worked hard on the difficult folk rhythms, counting them out for the dancers, beat by beat, over and over again. Blok's poetic rhythm had come in part from popular songs, or chastushka, mixed with intonations from liturgy, political slogans, and sharp rounds of rifle fire. George answered his depiction of the energy, vulgarity, and violence of the revolution with the deepest of the Russian deep: incantation and the peasantry.

In the poem, twelve Red Guards are marching with their rifles through a blizzard of frozen snow and crippling wind. They are shooting and shouting like hooligans at God and women and the world. One of them finally slits the throat of Kate, the woman he loves: "Kate, are you satisfied? Lost your tongue? / Lie in the snowdrift then, like dung!" The language and pace of the poem are staccato and ugly. At the end the hungry mongrel dog of the old world is limping behind the twelve Guards as they see a fleeting figure in the back streets: "Come out, comrade, or you'll regret / it." They start shooting, but the elusive figure won't fall in their fire. Suddenly, as if from nowhere, this figure is out in front leading them all, carrying a blood-red flag and crowned with a diadem of frost. The Twelve are the apostles, and he is Jesus Christ. When George's dance ended—and we don't know what he did to depict this ragged and icy Christ—the reaction was sharp and immediate: enthusiastic cheers and angry recriminations, "Bravo!" mixed with "Away with the ballet master!" Some left; others rose from their seats to applaud.[50]

Was anyone surprised when around this time an official announcement went up on the dancers' call board at the former Mariinsky Theater? It stated clearly that any dancer who worked with the young Balanchivadze would be immediately dismissed.[51] It was a warning: he had not been fired, yet, but his activities were formally disapproved of and would be noted. He was already engrossed in a new dance to Stravinsky's *Pulcinella*—the conductor Vladimir Dranishnikov had surreptitiously given him the score—and he also wanted to work on *Le Sacre du Printemps*, but when he approached the authorities, permission was firmly denied.[52] The Young Ballet, like all ad hoc groups, was open to suspicion of possible political aims—now more than ever. Lenin's precipitously declining health and the power struggle that was already under way made the ground they were all standing on dangerously unstable. In light of widespread and increasing persecution, including show trials and arrests, forced exile, and point-blank executions, this posting on the wall of the state theater could hardly have been reassuring.

On April 4, 1924, George and several of his dancers, including Tamara (now performing as Tamara Geva), Danilova, Ivanova, and Nicholas Efimov, signed a contract to dance abroad on a summer tour (just months before Moscow formally closed all studios and companies practicing plastique or "new dance" forms, sending its advocates, including Goleizovsky, scurrying underground).[53] George and his friends planned, they said, to leave the day the former Mariinsky season ended in June and to return that September for the start of the new season. The tour would be managed—and paid for in gold—by one Vladimir Dmitriev.[54] Dmitriev was an opera singer who had lost his voice and spent the NEP years as a casino croupier. He knew the dancers from the opera, and their initial plan, discussed into the night at George and Tamara's kitchen table, was to go to the Far East, but when that fell through, they thought they might travel to Sweden, Norway, Denmark, and across Europe. At one point Lidia Ivanova hesitated: a psychic at a party had dropped Lidia's ring into a glass of wine and seen a vision of a boat and Lidia drowned. Maybe it would be better if she didn't take the steamer they were planning to board to Germany, she told Choura. Maybe it would be better if she didn't go at all. On June 15 the ballet season ended but they still didn't have exit visas, so they kept performing. On June 16 Lidia Ivanova drowned.[55]

No one quite knows what happened. That night, Choura and Lidia had been scheduled to dance in a variety show at the former palace of the dowager empress, now a public garden. George and Tamara were in the audience, and when the show skipped their friends' dance, they went backstage and found Choura but no Lidia. Lidia had gone boating with some friends that afternoon, Choura said, and had failed to appear for the performance. After that, the facts blur, but the fear and confusion stayed with them all for life. Tamara remembered a man in a dark trench coat with a pocked face, who informed them coldly that Lidia had been killed in a boating accident, and warned them not to get involved. There was a long white night spent searching the piers for any sign of the boat or of their poor lost companion. They finally found the gashed ruins of the boat and even managed to track down the gnarled Finnish captain who had rescued the survivors. Over cold coffee in his shack nearby in the early hours of the morning, he admitted to the friends that there had been a crash with a large ferry and three men had been pulled onto this boat with ropes, but the girl . . . She must have been sucked under the propellers.

They all knew, or thought they knew, that Lidia socialized a bit too freely with the party elite and members of the GPU, Lenin's secret police, and there were whispers that she knew things she shouldn't have known. She was beloved as a dancer, and as the news of her mysterious death spread through the press and across the city, there were warm tributes but also dark insinuations that this beautiful young artist had been cruelly sacrificed. Some said the body had been found underwater with a bullet through the head; others believed Lidia had been raped, murdered, and thrown into the sea. Or was it all a brutal ballet-world intrigue of jealousy and retribution? The three men who had escorted Lidia on the boat and survived (another died with her) were said to have been seen the very next day drinking and laughing in a local restaurant. Lidia's murder was never proven, but in the minds of George and the dancers who knew and loved her, it didn't need to be. Who *didn't* believe that Lidia had been killed by the Socialist state? The very next day, the small touring troupe received their exit visas. Early on the morning of July 4, they met at the Nevsky Embankment to board the ship for Stettin.

Did they know that the *Preussen*, the German ship that would carry them away that morning, was one of the so-called Philosophy Steamers that had also carried some of Russia's greatest minds into forced exile two years earlier? Lenin had planned it personally: philosophers, writers, historians, economists, and mathematicians, many of them interested in Orthodoxy and mysticism and the inner worlds of mind and spirit, were rounded up with their families and sent off. They were on the wrong side of the revolution, Lenin said, and he wanted them gone. Many of them ended up in Western Europe or America and devoted their lives to the counterrevolution of the spirit that Lenin had killed.[56]

When George and his group arrived that morning, it was cold and wet with a freezing drizzle. They waited for a long time before their baggage was finally taken from them, searched, and loaded onto the ship. They didn't have much. Choura wore her best dress and packed a change of clothes, some family photographs, and an icon. Finally, they were shown into a dingy room with a table covered with passports and visas, where a man sat glumly scrutinizing them. Dmitriev nervously talked too much as the men were taken behind a partition and body-searched. The women were next, and every hem, lining, and pocket was examined for smuggled goods. Armed guards then escorted their small party past the modest gathering of family and friends, including Tamara's beleaguered father, who stood stoically shivering in the icy rain. No hugs or touching allowed, just get on. The gangplank pulled up, and the ship pushed out.[57]

The *Preussen* was already another shore. Small but luxurious, with elegant salons, clean, well-appointed cabins, full bathrooms, and a modern wireless telegraph, it comfortably accommodated seventy-five passengers for the three-day journey. The German staff was polite and efficient, and Balanchine especially remembered the food: "beautiful bread, just sitting there like that, so casually, with nobody guarding it." The day they arrived in Stettin, they revised their little pledge to one another, copying it out by hand and noting that its new terms could be extended by mutual agreement past the initially envisioned September return date. It was a recognition that they needed to stick together, and that there might not be a return passage.[58]

Looking back, there was something finite and discrete about this Russian part of Balanchine's life. It was sealed, like the train that had carried Lenin into Petrograd and the German boat that carried George out. Tamara Geva remembered him being calm as they left, which she attributed to his faith in God, but he was always calm in other people's estimation. A better explanation may be temperament. In those tumultuous years, his already secluded nature had been burst open and forced shut at the same time. It was not that he revealed or withdrew himself. Instead, he had the detachment of a survivor, an ability to sweep away feelings when they overwhelmed him and to start over—or keep going. And if privacy was one of the revolution's most notorious costs, Balanchine paid it too. He faced the world, which had threatened to eat him alive, with uncanny composure.

His family was left behind. They were all in Georgia. He somehow didn't belong—to them or to Georgia or to Russia or even to his own youth. The geography and axis of his life were shifting. It is not that Balanchine had grown up too fast—lots of people do—but that he had come of age surrounded by trauma and violence on an epic scale. Perhaps more troublingly still, the destruction and death that engulfed his city and his life came with, and even in part caused, an artistic vitality that was central to everything he went on to do. The revolution had ruined his childhood and provided, in no small measure, the sources of his genius. It was an impossible equation. Later he had nostalgia, memories, and yearning for an idea of the imperial Russia he thought he had lost, but the revolution was inside him too, and if in history and memory they were opposed, this may have been more a sign of pain than forgetting. In him they coexisted.

In the years to come, he still quoted Mayakovsky, but not the Mayakovsky of "All is new! Stop and marvel!" The phrase that lodged itself even deeper inside and became a kind of self-portrait was a different one. "I am a cloud in trousers," he liked to say, especially to women he loved but could not quite have. Anyone who knew Mayakovsky's agonizing and bombastic poem—which none of the women did—could see that the "cloud in trousers" was not at all calm or the spirit-man that the phrase might imply. Balanchine was telling them something else entirely. Mayakovsky had originally called his poem "The Thirteenth Apostle" and first recited it aloud at Osip and Lily Brik's home in 1915. He read it without moving. His large handsome frame barely contained his raging and mocking voice. Maksim Gorky later said he had only ever read such a conversation with God in the book of Job. The poem was inspired by an elusive woman Mayakovsky had just met—"La Gioconda," he longingly called her. In the poem we see him in pain, broken, defiant, angry, grandiose, at odds with "Mister God," and anguished because finding his poetic voice in the scorching world he lives in depends on a woman and the love she can't or won't surrender. When she tells him she is getting married, he steels himself. Oh yes, he says, "I'll be strong. / See how calm I am! / Like a dead man's / Pulse." Maybe, he finally admits, exhausted by the wrenching performance of his own life, he is "nothing more" than "the thirteenth apostle / in the most ordinary of Gospels." But still he raves at the sleeping universe and its cruel deceptions, "an enormous ear riddled with stars for ticks." It was the scream of a man wrung out by his times and his own insides. "Down with your love, down with your art, down with your system, down with your religion," he later summarized.[59] Mayakovsky's anxious and brutalized voice was not Balanchine's, but "A Cloud in Trousers" (as the poem was renamed) was a veiled sign for anyone who knew it of just how much they had all been through in those years and of how narrowly George had escaped.

Mayakovsky mattered to Balanchine too because they were both Georgian. The poet was born in a small village near Meliton's Kutaisi, to a family of impoverished aristocrats, which meant they had similar origins. And Mayakovsky was young, just eleven years older than George, almost his generation but not quite. They also shared an illusion—a woman holds the key to an artist's gift—and Mayakovsky's intense longing and the torment of unrequited passions cast a long shadow forward onto Balanchine's life. In the end, however, their ways parted. Balanchine left, while Mayakovsky stuck with Russia and stayed the Soviet course until he could no longer bear it. On April 4, 1930, he shot himself through the heart. His suicide note included a simple and heartbroken plea to the woman he had loved most: "Lilli—love me." In the painful ménage à trois that had ruled his life, she had eluded him, and the lines that followed became a kind of epigraph for the disappointments of a generation.

> As they say—
>   "The game is over"
> love's boat
> has smashed against the reef of the everyday.
> I'm quits with life

Mayakovsky was by then famous, and Stalin rewarded this dead and disenchanted poet with a state funeral. Lunacharsky was there, and Mayakovsky's bloodied body had been cleaned and placed in an open coffin, resting on a red square.[60]

When Balanchine called himself "a cloud in trousers," he was nodding, consciously or otherwise, to the poet and the past, and hinting at the effect of those fated years on his own inner life. He may not have known it at the time, but as he sailed out of the port that day, Georgi Balanchivadze had everything he needed to wage his own counterrevolution of spirit and art. And if he didn't yet know all that was inside him, and all that he was taking with him on the ship that cold, wet morning, that was okay. Emigrants don't always know their own secrets. Their problem is different, and George was facing it. What now?

RUSSIA ABROAD

As the Austro-Hungarian, Ottoman, and Russian empires weakened and collapsed and dozens of new states were created in their wake, millions of people found themselves stateless and in flight from the places they had once thought of as home. Russians, Armenians, Georgians, Poles, Ukrainians, Romanians, Hungarians, Germans, Greeks, Turks were leaving: on foot and skis; by cart, train, and boat; over clogging roads and railway tracks; and through shipyards ill-equipped to handle the bloated volume of these newly dispossessed masses. The numbers were alarming. In the years during and just after the war, more than one million Russians fled the newly emerging Bolshevik state; hundreds of thousands of Greeks fled Asia Minor; Poles, Balts, and Germans moved from and within war-torn Eastern Europe; at least 350,000 desperate Armenians rushed to escape the genocide perpetrated on them by the Turks; and some 100,000 Romanian Jews found themselves suddenly stateless. Many of these refugees were moving west: to Berlin, Prague, Paris.

For Russians fleeing the Great War, revolution, and civil wars, the situation was dire. People jammed into overcrowded trains and boats through the Crimea to Istanbul, Greece, Bulgaria, and Serbia; or they walked overland or across frozen water into Finland or to Poland and then into Germany. In the east, after the fall of Vladivostok, they made their way somehow to Harbin or Shanghai. Ports and train stations were desperate places, overflowing with refugees, worn, disoriented, and terrified. Families were separated in the chaos.

All of this on top of the devastating war losses that had left few untouched. The Great War caused some twenty million military and civilian deaths (from starvation, disease, massacres, casualties) and left twenty-one million injured or maimed; if you include the typhus epidemic that spread in the war's wake, the number of dead and afflicted rises still higher. As refugees across the Continent fought their way out, death was everywhere and survival nowhere certain.

Balanchine's future lay with these fleeing refugees. It was not just that he was among them. Many of the artists who would become his closest collaborators and friends, and their families, were escaping too, including: Nicolas Nabokov, Boris Kochno, Nathan Milstein, Vladimir Dukelsky, Varvara Karinska, Pavel Tchelitchew, Olga Preobrazhenskaya, André Eglevsky, Nicholas "Kolya" Kopeikine, Felia Doubrovska, Pierre Vladimirov, Anatole Obukhov, Florentine Karp (née Liepetz), Balanchine's physician Dr. Lewithin, Mikhail Arshansky, Eugenie Ouroussow, Nathalie Gleboff, Natasha Molostwoff (Armenian), Rouben Ter-Arutunian (Armenian), Lucia Davidova (Armenian). Others were the sons and daughters of émigrés, or the children of earlier escapees (many of them Jews). When the dancer John Clifford confessed to Balanchine in the 1970s after years of working together, You know, Mr. B, I am not English—my real last name is Povailitis; it is the Greek spelling of a Lithuanian name (Clifford was his father's stage name), Balanchine responded: "You know dear, I always knew."[1]

Looking down from above at the chaotic human landscape of these war-torn lands and populations in flight, we can see the people who would be important to Balanchine converging on Europe from all directions. Many would eventually make their way to the United States, but for the moment, this was where history dropped them, and it is worth noting just how much everything that happened to Balanchine subsequently began here, with the dissolution of empires.

He arrived in Europe just in time. Berlin and Paris, the two artistic centers that would affect him most, were exploding with new ideas and art, in part because of these displaced arrivals. He departed just in time too, as the Europe that now lay before him stood ready, once again and for the second time in his still youthful life, to commit political suicide. He seemed to have this kind of timing. He had entered Russian imperial and revolutionary culture in time to absorb its most crucial ideas and art, and was gone before Stalin took power and destroyed it all. Now he was poised to inherit something of twentieth-century European culture as he came of age a second time before moving on once again, this time to America, before Hitler and his collaborators swept it all away once more. He had a knack for swallowing dying civilizations whole and getting out.[2]

When he arrived, Balanchine was Russian. When he left, he was also European, and although he would spend more time in these interwar years in Paris, London, and Monte Carlo, it was Germany that made the first mark.

Chapter 5

WEIMAR CULTURE

They traveled to Berlin's Stettiner Bahnhof by train. No one met them at the station, and they found themselves confronted with Berlin's intimidatingly cold, bustling order and clipped pace. George had a smattering of German, but none of them spoke well enough to feel at ease. "Berlin is freezing even when it is sixty degrees," the writer Joseph Roth noted at the time, and it was true that the city could be outwardly standoffish and remote. They found their way to a cheap boarding house on Potsdamer Platz, a large plaza known for its bright marquees and crowded cafés and cabarets, a panoply of Weimar cultural life. Tamara Geva recalled learning right off that an apricot-colored shirt on a man meant he was selling sex. In those first days, she arranged with a wigmaker to have her hair cut into a neat bob in the style of the "new woman"—corset-less, independent, boyishly slim—in exchange for her silken locks. Then she and Choura bought fashionable wide-brimmed hats with long veils that they draped ineptly, like inadvertent mourning garb.[1]

Berlin, so recently defeated in war and beset with partisan violence, nonetheless had the energy and appearance of a thriving social and economic life. Even the haggard men pulling cartloads of worthless deutsche marks, victims of the devastating hyperinflation that just months before had wiped the life savings of a nation off the ledger, seemed to have disappeared into the nooks and crannies of this hardened and chaotically striving town. The war-wounded and maimed, begging in the streets or sitting aimlessly at intersections, had become just another feature on a landscape otherwise teeming with human industry. It was a city enamored of its own mechanical and commercial achievements: trains, trolleys, and cars; factories and machines; shops full of produce, baked goods, and meats—sights that still shocked the half-starved Russians. In the mornings you could see grizzled old men ritually washing the sidewalks with pails of steaming water, and Old World babushkas alongside young war widows carrying baskets of bread to market, or pass by colorful shop windows and stands full of illustrated magazines with seductive advertisements flashing images from the new medium of photography. Films celebrating the city liked to highlight its purposeful men, women, and children with neat satchels tucked under their arms or lunch pails in hand striding to factories, schools, and offices, as if nothing had ever disrupted their ordered lives. By the summer of 1924, the economy had stabilized, and the moderate statesman Gustav Stresemann was at the helm. For the moment, at least on the surface, Germany seemed intact.[2]

There were other reasons to feel at home. In the years immediately following the war and revolution, Berlin had become, as Ilya Ehrenburg put it, a "Russian Refugee Republic." Some half-million Russians fleeing their homeland had congregated in Charlottenburg, or "Charlottograd," as it was locally known, or in Wilmersdorf or one of the smaller Russian enclaves in the city. They were guests of German *ressentiment*. The Germans, angered at the Allies' unrelenting demands for crippling reparations, had embraced their old Russian foes and in 1922 formally reestablished relations at Rapallo. And so Russians of all kinds—monarchists, White Russians, Mensheviks, Jews, Russian Germans, and the Orthodox—flooded in and set about re-creating their lives on this new German shore. There were Russian theaters, bookstores, doctors' offices, law practices, hairdressers, restaurants, cafés, newspapers, and refugee centers. The Russian avant-garde also arrived in force: Mayakovsky, Malevich, Meyerhold, Wassily Kandinsky, Vladimir Tatlin, Naum Gabo, and Antoine Pevsner, among others, visited or stayed. This vibrant émigré culture, however, depended precariously on the weak German mark, which had made life blissfully cheap. When inflation hit in 1922–23, the Russian community faltered, which meant that by the time Balanchine and his friends arrived, the center of Russia Abroad was already shifting to more affordable ground, this time in Paris and Prague.[3]

No one in this shrinking émigré society seemed much interested in a bedraggled troupe of Soviet—they were Soviet—ballet "stars," as they were billing themselves. Dmitriev managed to arrange a concert in a small, poorly lit hall with an old out-of-tune upright piano pushed unceremoniously into the corner of the stage, but almost no one came. Uncertain of how they would ever support themselves, he reached farther afield and secured a tour of Rhineland spa towns: they would be an act in Weimar's popular variety and cabaret shows, performing alongside clowns, dogs, horses, jugglers, marching bands, acrobats, and the "serial souls" of "Girl Revues" and kick lines. It was work, but the rupture with their old lives could be jarring and dispiriting. George later recalled his excitement at going to hear his fellow émigré Sergey Rachmaninoff perform in Vienna and presenting himself backstage to suggest that they do a ballet together, but Rachmaninoff, a White Russian whose family had been forced off their country estate in 1917, haughtily dismissed this untitled Russian dancer, a stinging humiliation Balanchine never forgot—or forgave.

Geva claimed they also performed in the prison holding the leftist playwright Ernst Toller, arrested after his participation in the Munich uprising in 1919. If so, it was another link to their past, since George had choreographed Toller's *Eugene the Unfortunate* in Petrograd, but nothing apparently came of this connection either. At least there was plentiful bread, which they instinctively wrapped in white linen napkins and snuck back to their rooms in small, clean hotels, just in case. They cruised along the Rhine, noting from the ship's deck the castles and lush greenery already grown over the wartime blight: Wiesbaden, Ems, Mosel.

Looking back, these first months were a bit of a blank. Or maybe he was a bit of a blank. In Leningrad (as Petrograd had been renamed in 1924), Balanchivadze had been known—he had a name and a community, a context. In Europe, at least now, at the beginning, he was nobody but a hired theater-man with a little traveling troupe hustling odd jobs on the road. We lose track of him in these years for the same reason that he lost track of himself. He was one of those millions dropped off the map into exile. Tracing him through Weimar is a bit like reading a photographic negative that will fully reveal itself only in the chemical bath of a later environment. We know what he absorbed in those years from his later dances, but we know less of his life at the time.

Still, he later said that Weimar culture formed him: "My first influences were in the twenties and they were German. German cabaret performers, German films with stars like Conrad Veidt—you know, elegant and decadent."[4] He was a watcher, and as difficult as those first months were, Weimar was also an opportunity. "I knew nothing, *nothing*!" he later recalled, and that was another blank: Europe. His formal schooling had been interrupted by the revolution when he was just thirteen years old, and now, at twenty, a slim young man in a loose-fitting suit, with hair combed neatly back, he was still the "Tiflis pixie," as a friend put it, and it was true that he knew "nothing, *nothing*" about European culture and art. The revolution had been his greatest education, and if he later forgot or failed to say much about what he saw in his first months in Germany, it was because he owed too much, absorbed too much, took it all so deeply inside that the debt disappeared and what he learned became fully part of him and flowed out into his dances. To understand what he absorbed, we need to know what he saw.[5]

Entertainment in the Weimar Republic was virtually unregulated, and sex was everywhere: in cabaret, but also in "meat shows" and striptease acts, with kitschy titles like "What Sailors Dream Of" and "Berlin without a Blouse"; in decorative erotic tableaux, featuring lesbians, homosexuals, transvestites; and in sultry dances staged in upscale salons, with young ladies wearing silky scarves and long strings of pearls—and nothing else. There were more efficient "Girl Revues," named after the review of soldiers by inspecting officers and featuring precision kick lines and military formations (with guns as a favored prop): the Admiral Girls, the Paris Mannequins, the Tiller Girls, the Hoffmann Girls, the Jackson Girls. These athletic "girl machines" typically traveled with chaperons and pastors, adding, as Joseph Roth noted, to their "provocative moral purity . . . their nudity does not serve lust, but rather anatomy: the development of feminine musculature as visually instructive experiments."[6] The émigré Russian critic André Levinson called them an "army of modern Eve, the anonymous sportswoman, the impersonal beauty, the serial-soul."[7] This kind of cold detachment, sex without sex, and lines of ponytailed serial souls would find their way into Balanchine's dances; he would also later encounter it, in a watered-down form, in London music halls and in Hollywood. When he got a chance in London in 1931, he immediately tried it on in his own revue, "Balanchine's Girls."[8] The idea behind all of this was not only an unleashed male fantasy but also the new women with lives and loves, as well as sexual desires, of their own—women who might not marry, women who might be lesbians, women who were sexually self-possessed and, at least in some imagining, *free*.

In another key, there were new forms of experimental and expressionist dance, which Balanchine would later copy and use, but also set himself against; "not Bodenwieser, dear," he later said, dripping sarcasm at a grimacing dancer. Bodenwieser was Gertrud Bodenwieser (1890–1959), a *very* serious Austrian dancer with a small touring company in the 1920s. Classically trained but influenced by expressionistic forms, she made dances with heavy moral and political messages and titles such as "The Pilgrimage of Truth" and "The Demon Machine" (against the perils of industrialization).[9] Ditto Valeska Gert, who performed, for example, *Der Tod* (Death) by standing before her audience and "dying" for three excruciating minutes—in silence, eyes flung convulsively back in their sockets, body spasming in pain. Or Anita Berber, who made a spectacle of her own drug-addicted and wildly sexualized life. Trained in ballet, she mixed classical steps and gestures with macabre cabaret grimaces, exaggerated physical plastique, flagrant nudity, and intoxicated ravings. As Salomé, she dipped her body in blood, undressed, and executed graceful steps with gruesome red globs dripping from her arms and hands.[10]

Rudolf Laban (1879–1958), another character on Balanchine's expanding landscape, was a painter, dancer, and pioneer of *Freitanz* ("free dance"). He spent his youth in Munich and Paris studying art and taken up with cabaret, gambling, and pornography. Later, like so many artists at the time, he was changed by the Russian artist Vasily Kandinsky's writings and art. In 1911 Kandinsky had published *Concerning the Spiritual in Art* and simultaneously shown the abstract painting *Composition V*. Like Malevich, and so many of Balanchine's contemporaries and predecessors, Kandinsky was deeply influenced by the practices of Theosophy, and he wrote of Madame Blavatsky in a chapter titled "Spiritual Revolution." He too was disenchanted with the everyday external world in which he lived—and with the conventions of painting in reproducing this world: stories, perspective, and the depiction of real life and objects, including fantasies about this external life. He felt sure that art was at a threshold. Spirituality and an otherworldly abstraction, he wrote, might finally prevail over the old materialist art.

The idea of abstraction was rooted in the word itself, which implied at its origins something that was removed or isolated from the real world, and Kandinsky envisioned an ideal "kingdom of the abstract."[11] In *Composition V*, he had thus eliminated all traces of objects, people, and nature—"real" life as it is lived externally—in favor of line, color, rhythm, and pure form. Like Balanchine, Kandinsky was a trained musician and admired Bach, and he had been influenced by Arnold Schoenberg's experiments in prewar Vienna with the erosion of traditional musical tonality and the "emancipation of dissonance," as Schoenberg put it. The twelve-tone system, which was more fully worked out by 1924, just as Balanchine was arriving on the scene, replaced older musical hierarchies with a "democracy of tones" that both expressed and—crucially—newly *ordered* music around dissonance and chromaticism. It was an upheaval that Balanchine would later return to in some of his most radical dances to music written around this time by Schoenberg, Anton Webern, Paul Hindemith, and Stravinsky. For Kandinsky, the link to painting was direct. If the composer could remove tonality and the conventions that had governed Western music for centuries, why couldn't the painter remove the conventions and objects that had governed painting? He was also drawn to poetry and wrote a volume of poems titled *Klänge* (*Sounds*), which contained an instruction to repeat a word until it became senseless and disconnected from the conventions of language: "simulating aphasia." Only then, in this disassociated state, could words regain their power to strike directly at the human heart.[12]

Ballet was especially difficult, Kandinsky wrote, because of its origins in the highly external and physical worlds of sexual and religious practice. It was too tied to beauty and stories, and to the human figure, which was by definition its subject. Taking abstraction to its most extreme point raised vexing questions. How could dance eliminate the human figure without eliminating itself? Kandinsky tried in his own 1909 abstract ballet, "Yellow Sound," using geometric figures and colors (not people or dancers) moving to an original musical score. Later, he became interested in Gret Palucca, a young, boyishly built, reddish-blond dancer trained in ballet, and he sketched her at the height of a jump and drew the arc of her bodily line. But Kandinsky was also naturally drawn to the body and to the senses as a possible pathway into a spiritual life, bypassing language, reason, and the intellect—no words. The critic Wilhelm Worringer identified this impulse as early as 1908 as "the will to abstraction," an anxious desire to purify, isolate, or abstract an object or art from a world that could not otherwise be fully ordered or controlled. In this sense, abstraction was another way of confronting overwhelming emotions. Expressionism spilled them out, while abstraction removed them into line and shadow, or as Kandinsky put it, "the visible trace of the invisible."[13]

In 1913 Laban used these and other ideas to found a school of dance at the renowned Swiss utopian colony of Monte Verità—known for its health cures, vegetarianism, sunbathing, and spirituality. There, for example, he led a two-day-long outdoor Sun Festival and brought together his adherents in improvisatory "movement choirs." These choirs, with their mesmerizing circle dances and ecstatic celebration of nature and strong, youthful bodies, eventually joined with a larger and growing German nationalist preoccupation with *Korperculture* that the Nazis would harness to their racialist enterprise. But for the moment, Laban's work culminated in *Freitanz*, which took like the wind in the 1920s as schools teaching "free" expressive movement sprang up across the country, part of a widespread interest in group gymnastics performed outdoors in the nude. His own interests eventually took him back to Kandinsky and research into space, time, and the breakdown of movement into an abstract dance notation (which Balanchine would later try and reject)—"trace forms," as he put it, "in the land of silence."[14]

Mary Wigman, whose innovations Balanchine would both internalize and reject, was a student of Laban, and her style of expressive movement, or *Ausdruckstanz,* also widely influenced American modern dance. Wigman joined Laban at Monte Verità, where she improvised her *Hexentanz* (witch dance) on a rock on the side of a mountain and participated in the colony's communal rites. (She later widely performed the *Hexentanz,* in varying, usually improvised and incantatory forms.) She got involved in Dada and its Zurich-based "art is shit" cabaret culture protesting the barbarism of war and the senselessness and depressing collapse of meaning left in its wake. One performance had George Grosz (discharged from the army after a breakdown) on a sewing machine and Walter Mehring on a typewriter, accompanied by a stuffed effigy of a German officer with a pig's head. Kandinsky's poems were read aloud and seemed to catch what one artist called the "nullity of appearances and reason" haunting them all.[15]

After the war Wigman had a breakdown. Afflicted with TB and distraught at the return of her brother maimed in combat, she went to a Swiss sanatorium, where she performed for shell-shocked veterans and psychiatric patients. Influenced by expressionist painting and her own ongoing engagement with Kandinsky's mysticism, she developed movement that was barefoot and weighted, from the gut and back. Her concern was not abstraction at all; hers was a full-blown expressionist cry. The real world was too full of pain to ignore or "isolate," and her solo dances had titles such as *Death* and *Sacrifice.*[16] As her fame and influence grew in the 1920s and 1930s, she toured Europe and America and acquired disciples and followers, but not everyone appreciated her primal dances. Lincoln Kirstein, who saw her perform in New York in 1931, "decided instantly to dislike" her, noting in his diary that she pompously billed herself as "not a dancer but a priestess." Her subject, he complained, was "ecstasy, bliss, despair, etc., consequently the only possible climax is always exhaustion . . . [and] an unsatisfactory system of gestures proving conclusively the great superiority of the ballet technique over hers."[17] Balanchine would be more instrumental about it. Over the years, he would abstract the gut-driven and free-form physical vocabulary, strip out the piety, and ignore the rest.

Another figure on his landscape was Walter Gropius, who during the war had been buried for three days under a building destroyed by artillery shells, a terrifying experience that convinced him that something new would be required of artists when the war ended.[18] In 1919 he founded the Bauhaus. Inspired in part by the great medieval cathedrals built by master craftsmen from all trades, Gropius saw art as a craft—Balanchine later did too—and he looked to ancient artisanal skills and modern industrial technologies to design buildings, furniture, and clothing—art to remake the way people live in an age of mass production. The aesthetic was simple, white, open, functional, attractively spare, and stripped of unnecessary decorative effect. "We felt that we were literally building a new world," one of its practitioners later recalled.[19] Kandinsky, who had left and just returned from witnessing the war and revolution in his native Russia, became a key player, as did Paul Klee (who taught abstract painting, but also weaving), Joan Miró, and Josef Albers. Palucca, who had by then embarked on her own solo dancing career, was a frequent visitor, and Stravinsky and Hindemith, crucial figures for Balanchine, were among the many invited speakers.

Gropius's theatrical division was headed by the painter Oskar Schlemmer, who wrote at length about the *Tänzermensch*, a new kind of dancer who could be both abstract and artificial—a puppet or a mannequin, an automaton or a mechanized doll—all themes that would fascinate Balanchine. She could be double limbed, broken limbed, multiple headed, metaphysical. Schlemmer's *Triadic Ballet*, first performed in 1912 and later (in full) in 1922 and 1923, became famous for its geometric dancers and circus-like figures with bodies "built" into cones, circles, or triangles with padded cloth, papier-mâché, or even metallic or colored paint applied directly to the body. His scenarios included Salvador Dalí-like instructions such as "bodies look for heads, which are moving in the opposite direction across the stage." It was another kind of "kingdom" of pure forms—and Schlemmer's ideas, like Kandinsky's and the Bauhaus itself, were utopian. With advancing technology, the body could be disassembled and rebuilt into anything, with no anatomical limits.[20] Not a bad description of Balanchine's own eventual aspirations.

Balanchine owned a painting by Max Beckmann, probably given to him by the painter himself, and he later wanted Beckmann to do sets for a restaging of his 1933 production, with Bertolt Brecht and Kurt Weill, of *The Seven Deadly Sins* (it didn't work out). Beckmann too was drawn to Theosophy and ideas of spirituality and otherworldliness. "What I want to show in my work," he once said, "is the idea which hides itself behind so-called reality. I am seeking for the bridge which leads from the visible to the invisible." The war had changed him. Beckmann had been in East Prussia and Belgium and had written home from a field hospital in Flanders, marveling at the "half-clothed me streaming with blood, being bandaged in white down below the half-light. Huge pain. New Ideas of the flagellation of Christ."[21] After he was discharged in 1915 for a nervous breakdown, his work took an apocalyptic turn in paintings such as *Resurrection* (1916) and *The Night* (1918–19). He envisioned more violent, crooked scenes in *Dance in Baden-Baden* (1923), with its shut-eyed, impassive Weimar women in crude and twisted poses, trapped in an off-kilter *Cabinet of Caligari*–like room. In these years he was moving from expressionism to a more detached and emotionally removed depiction of the war and its consequences, part of the "new objectivity" and focus on cold, hard social facts: a rational description of the irrationality flooding their lives.

One night Balanchine saw a Max Reinhardt production with a spectacular mechanized stage that turned as the dancers waltzed, and Reinhardt joined the growing panoply of influences in Balanchine's life. A Viennese Jew born in the 1880s, Reinhardt (né Goldmann) was known for founding the Salzburg Festival with Hugo von Hofmannsthal and Richard Strauss in 1920. But Reinhardt is perhaps best known for his grandiose modern mystery plays mixing reality, dreams, dance, music, and fantasy with a kind of Catholic religious pageantry. *The Miracle*, for instance, commissioned in 1911 by the British music-hall magnate Charles B. Cochran (Balanchine would work with him too) had choreography by Gertrud Bodenwieser and featured two thousand actors, a choir of five hundred, and a two-hundred-piece orchestra including an organ. Reinhardt refitted the eight-thousand-seat theater as a cathedral with the audience as the congregation. His productions also explored the new technological possibilities of the cyclorama, an infinity of bright blue light as backdrop that would become a Balanchine staple. Balanchine knew Reinhardt and probably saw *The Miracle*, which was revived many times and toured Europe and America for over a decade. He also later drew directly on the Hollywood film of Reinhardt's fanciful *Midsummer Night's Dream* for his own ballet and film of Shakespeare's play, and he was delighted when one of his young dancers asked if he should play Puck like Reinhardt's Puck: "You know about Reinhardt?!"[22]

It would take a lifetime to spin out all that he saw and heard in the Weimar Republic in his own dances. In the coming years, Balanchine would renounce many things, but not Weimar. What he saw there was part of his life and part of his range. And in the logic that seemed to rule his newly itinerant life, many of the artists he admired there would soon end up, like him, on a ship to America, in their case fleeing the Nazis. Looking back, we can see a kind of republic of art taking shape out of the war-wrung lives of artists and refugees, and the ideas and impulses that came of their experiences. Of particular importance to Balanchine would be the tension between the violence of expressionism and the remove of the concrete "new objectivity" and the "will to abstraction," along with the desire to build a counterutopia of spirit—what Kandinsky had called a "kingdom of the abstract." It was all in the air they breathed.

On a more immediate and practical level, however, Weimar was proving impossible. Their little troupe struggled to find work, and when the enterprising Dmitriev finally managed to arrange a music-hall gig in London, they packed up and went. When they got there, they found a friend. Lydia Lopokova—small, animated, a free spirit with unkempt hair and no makeup—appeared in their dressing rooms one night after a show. She was the sister of the choreographer Fedor Lopokov, who had staged the *Dance Symphony* that had so affected Balanchine back in Petrograd. She had come to Paris with Diaghilev before the war and had married, in 1925, the economist John Maynard Keynes, himself deeply involved in extricating Europe from the war and, as he put it, the perilous consequences of the peace. The troupe fell into a deep conversation with Lydia that would continue for years to come. They told her about her besieged brother back home, and how he was still living in one room, how there was not enough to eat, and how they had all fought to stay alive. Meanwhile, they were finding it difficult to keep up with London's demanding commercial pace. Their hand-sewn imperial costumes had tiny, finely stitched buttons that took so long to fasten that the dancers were missing entrances and the troupe was soon fired. On November 3, just months after their departure from Russia, they paused once more to rewrite by hand their contract to one another, extending their collective obligations to April 5, 1925. It was another anxious sign of just how alone they were and how much they felt they still needed one another. By then their red Soviet passports were no longer valid, and they found themselves stateless, unemployed, and running out of money.

In Paris, Sergei Diaghilev, whose Ballets Russes was another kind of Russia Abroad, had heard that a talented young choreographer by the name of Georgi Balanchivadze had recently arrived from Leningrad. In need of new Russian talent, Diaghilev immediately sent his trusted cousin to find Balanchivadze. The cousin missed the troupe in Berlin, but using Diaghilev's wide-ranging contacts, he telegraphed to London to find Balanchivadze and requested a meeting in Paris. That was one account of it. Another said that the troupe made its own way to France, one of the few countries that would take a bunch of stateless entertainers, and received Diaghilev's summons from a smelly hotel near the fish market in Les Halles, just as they were considering hocking George's only suit in order to eat.[23] In any case, a date was set, and Diaghilev and Balanchivadze prepared to meet. Diaghilev was fifty-two and already a legend. George was twenty and had never met him.

Chapter 6

BIG SERGE

Sergei Diaghilev belonged to the cultivated world of the old imperial elite. Born in 1872 in the provincial Russian city of Perm, a thousand miles from St. Petersburg, he received a typically European-style upbringing—though without his mother, who died in childbirth. His family home had French Second Empire furnishing, original paintings by Rembrandt and Raphael, and a fairy-tale ballroom with parquet floors and a grand chandelier. Diaghilev spoke French and German and played the piano, and the family hosted literary evenings and musical gatherings. They were politically progressive: his grandfather (a vodka distiller) had worked to end serfdom, and his aunt was a feminist involved in reform-minded circles. He knew Tchaikovsky ("Uncle Petia") and later attended the composer's concerts in St. Petersburg. He even met Tolstoy and stayed at his estate in Yasnaya Polyana. As if plotting his future, Diaghilev traveled widely in Europe, and met the composers Gounod, Saint-Saëns, Brahms, and Verdi, and, perhaps most important of all, heard Wagner's complete "Ring" cycle at Bayreuth. He deeply admired the composer's idea of *Gesamtkunstwerk:* poetry, art, and music fusing to create a complete and absorbing theatrical world on stage—an inspiration for the future Ballets Russes.[1]

As a young man, Diaghilev was restless. He moved to St. Petersburg and attended law school; he wanted to be an artist and studied painting; he thought he might be a composer and studied music; he started an avant-garde journal, *The World of Art*, with friends and wrote criticism; he mounted exhibitions and curated art. Above all, he loved ballet. He aspired to a high position at court and the Imperial Theaters, but in spite (or perhaps because) of his connections in high places, his efforts to establish himself at the Mariinsky were struck down by court intrigue, and Diaghilev was humiliatingly barred from the civil service and forced to settle for a minor post.

In a sign of his ambition and visionary mind, he turned elsewhere and in 1905 mounted what turned out to be a prophetic exhibition in St. Petersburg: more than three thousand portraits of Russian aristocrats from the time of Peter the Great to the present. The exhibition opened soon after Bloody Sunday, and in a speech at a Moscow banquet, Diaghilev explained that he had traveled across Russia to collect paintings and artifacts and had seen a dying world: "remote estates boarded up, palaces terrifying in their dead splendor . . . Here it is not people who are ending their days, but a way of life. . . . We are the witnesses," he went on, "of a great historical moment of reckoning and ending in the name of a new, unknown culture—a culture which has arisen through us but which will sweep us aside." He lifted a glass to the "ruined walls of the beautiful palaces" and the culture—his own—whose certain death he had just pronounced. He hoped the "new aesthetics," whatever they were, would come without too much pain.[2] Then, with little hope of a future at the imperial court, he set himself the task of showing Russia—the Russia that he felt sure was ending—to Europe.

He began in 1906 with a sweeping exhibition of Russian art and music in Paris in a quasi-diplomatic venture financed by a combination of Russian and French private and state monies, a sign of his astonishing ability to galvanize people and resources. In 1908 he arranged a season of Russian opera and hoped to repeat his success the following season, but when he ran into financial difficulties, he turned to a much less costly option: ballet. "Bringing brilliant ballet company eighty strong, best soloists," he cabled to his Paris presenter, "start big publicity."[3] The czar granted him permission to borrow dancers from the Imperial Theaters, and in the spring of 1909 some of Russia's greatest performers, including Fokine, Pavlova, Karsavina, and Nijinsky, boarded the train to Paris. By 1911 many had cut their formal ties to the Mariinsky and transferred their loyalty to Diaghilev, and the Ballets Russes was officially born. It would perform across Europe and the Americas, but never in Russia itself.[4]

In the coming years, Diaghilev reimagined ballet through the sheer force of his own personality and drive. He was an entrepreneur, a producer, and above all an avatar of the new: "Astonish me," he liked to say. His taste was as wide-ranging as his knowledge of culture and art, and he boldly lifted ballet out of its prim, courtly isolation and into the expansive and vital world of contemporary Russian and European music and art. He presided czar-like over his productions, working tirelessly to raise money; rally collaborators, dancers, stagehands, and press; monitor rehearsals; book theaters and tours; negotiate contracts; resolve strikes; generate publicity; hound artists; and somehow bring a performance to the stage. The energy he expended was almost superhuman: his passport contained a bewildering array of stamps, and his notes and voluminous correspondence attest to his close attention to the artistic, intellectual, and practical minutia of his theatrical enterprise. He was like a one-man Mariinsky, except that the Ballets Russes eventually succeeded without significant state support. "You can't imagine what it's like," Henri Matisse later confided to a friend after working with the company. "There's absolutely no fooling about here—it's an organization where no one thinks of anything but his or her work." And: "Diaghilev is Louis XIV."[5]

One of Diaghilev's greatest early accomplishments was to turn ballet into an image of Russia. Not the imperial Russia he rightly saw as dying but an imagined Slavic ur-Russia, exotic, primitive, modern—and self-consciously styled, as the artist Alexander Benois put it, "for export to the West."[6] *The Firebird* (1910), one of the Ballets Russes's first great successes, had a story culled from Russian folklore, modified, and embellished by Diaghilev and his friends. For the music, the impresario commissioned the young Igor Stravinsky (1882–1971), a student of Rimsky-Korsakov's, and while composing the ballet, Stravinsky pored over ethnographic studies of native songs and the long "back to the people" musical tradition (which had so entranced Balanchine's father). The choreographer was Fokine, who had his own interest in peasant songs and dances. The costumes and decor for the ballet, created by Léon Bakst and Alexander Golovin in a vibrant style, were similarly ornamented and oriental and inspired by peasant art.

Other "Russian" dances followed, among them *Scheherazade* (1910), an ersatz Arabian Nights story adapted from an extant score by Rimsky-Korsakov, with sensationally colorful decor, costumes by Bakst, and choreography again by Fokine. It featured the gorgeously full-bodied Ida Rubinstein in alluring oriental attire, with Nijinsky as a scantily clad slave and, as Fokine gleefully put it, "a mass slaughter of lovers and faithless wives" fully enacted on stage.[7] *Petrouchka* (1911) was another Stravinsky-Fokine dance, this time a nostalgic tribute to a beloved puppet character of the makeshift wooden theaters (*balagani*) traditionally erected during holidays in the main square at the Winter Palace.

In his almost giddy drive to establish new fronts for the avant-garde using old Russian forms, Diaghilev soon turned for choreography to Nijinsky, his lover and star dancer. In 1913 Nijinsky staged *Le Sacre du Printemps* to a new score by Stravinsky. Drawing once again on what they and the designer Nicholas Roerich took to be the Scythian and peasant roots of Russian culture, they conceived the new ballet as a ritual reenactment of an imagined pagan sacrifice of a young maiden to the god of fertility and the sun: a rite of spring. But this was not the lush orientalism of *The Firebird:* the decor depicted instead an eerily barren landscape strewn with votive skins and antler heads, and Stravinsky's loud, static, and dissonant chords, driving syncopation, and haunting melodies reaching into extreme registers sounded to many brutal and disorienting. The choreography was shocking: there were stomping tribal dances with hunched figures and awkward pigeon-toed poses, and a ritual abduction of the "chosen maiden" followed by a solemn procession led by a white-bearded High Priest culminating in the girl's agonizing dance of death. All of this was delivered in cold blood, with clinical detachment. The riot that accompanied the first performance was another Diaghilev coup. The theater, it was said, was "shaken like an earthquake," and the noise in the audience was so loud that the dancers could barely hear Nijinsky standing in the first wing on a chair shouting out the difficult counts. Critics called it the "*massacre du printemps*," and as events pushed the Continent closer to war, *Sacre* was increasingly understood as an ominous prelude. Back in Russia, Balanchine was nine, and never saw it.[8]

Soon after *Sacre,* Nijinsky and Diaghilev's partnership unraveled. Nijinsky impulsively married a Hungarian woman whom he hardly knew, and in a fit of jealous rage Diaghilev fired him. Nijinsky tried to make it on his own but was woefully incapable of managing his affairs. His last solo, performed in 1919 in the first stages of the madness that would overtake him, saw him Christlike at the head of a cross laid out on the floor before him as he announced to a small audience: "Now I will dance the war . . . the war which you did not prevent and are also responsible for."[9] Finally, ill-health, artistic frustration, and his growing obsession with Tolstoyan religious dogmas and the horror of the war unfolding in their midst resulted in his physical and financial collapse.[10] With schizophrenia closing in on him, Nijinsky was committed to an asylum in Switzerland in 1919 and would never recover his mind. Balanchine was fifteen.

Meanwhile, with Nijinsky gone, Diaghilev made what turned out to be his last-ever trip to Russia to find another young protégé. This time, it was Léonide Massine (1896–1979), a dark, handsome character dancer from the Bolshoi Theater, who would later become Balanchine's nemesis. Massine soon stepped into Nijinsky's former life: he became Diaghilev's lover and the chief choreographer for the Ballets Russes. The outbreak of war and the Russian Revolution, however, threw the company into disarray. The difficulties of arranging papers and crossing borders, securing engagements, and raising money to pay dancers and keep himself afloat made Diaghilev's enterprise unstable at best.[11] By 1918 less than half his reassembled troupe was Russian: Poles, Italians, and English (with charmingly Russified names) filled out the ranks, and the Russians who did stay were soon stateless.

Diaghilev himself was cut off. He closely followed events back home, and like many displaced Russians, he at first supported the revolution. Stravinsky, who watched its events from Europe, was swept up too, and enthusiastically orchestrated the popular Russian folk song "The Volga Boatmen" to serve as a new national anthem. Diaghilev had the tune played before all his shows—but when the Bolsheviks took over and the country lapsed into bloody civil war, they both stepped back. With little access to the young Russian artists who had always fed his enterprise, Diaghilev turned instead to the European avant-garde and produced lighter, often ironic entertainments with Picasso, Matisse, Jean Cocteau, Erik Satie, and Darius Milhaud, among others.

At the same time, and this is where Balanchine would find him, Diaghilev was haunted by his homeland. He began collecting Russian books and icons, scavenging through shops for precious documents of the pre-Bolshevik past. His library was carted in crates across Europe along with the Ballets Russes sets and costumes, like cherished family relics.[12] He threw himself at reckless expense into the one ballet that seemed to hold a complete picture of a lost imperial world—Tchaikovsky's *Sleeping Beauty*, first performed in St. Petersburg in 1890. Diaghilev's revival premiered in London in 1921 at the Alhambra Theatre, a music hall that took on *Beauty* as a pantomime—retitled *The Sleeping Princess*. Diaghilev lavished his attention on every detail and recruited as many old Russian dancers and designers as he could find in his quest to capture the grandeur of the original; Stravinsky worked on the music and became the ballet's greatest advocate; Nijinsky's sister, Bronislava Nijinska, who had spent the war making experimental dances in the heated artistic environment of Moscow and Kyiv, returned just in time to help. The English cared little for Diaghilev's flight of Russian nostalgia, however, and the production was a commercial disaster and forced to fold. Diaghilev was shocked, emotionally devastated, and faced with financial ruin.

Boldly, and perhaps a bit nostalgically, he turned to Stravinsky and Nijinska, and together with the designer Natalya Goncharova, they produced in 1923 one of Diaghilev's greatest and final "Russian" ballets: *Les Noces* (*The Wedding*), which Balanchine would soon perform. Stravinsky first had the idea for the music while he was composing *Sacre*, and the score, written intermittently through the war in Switzerland and not fully completed until 1923, recalled Russian folk songs and the Orthodox liturgy. It had the percussive drive of *Sacre*—there were four grand pianos on stage—but it was more lyrical and religious in tone, especially in its choral parts. Nijinska's dances were radically austere but emotionally powerful, and she worked with Goncharova to create plain brown and white costumes and a stark constructivist set with flat, steely blue geometric shapes—wedges, arcs, rectangles—and hard benches arranged in a formal and static design. The steps of the dance were classical but stony and archaic: "automatized motions," as one critic put it, which looked like "machinery: mechanical, utilitarian, industrial," but these harsh images were cut with women endlessly braiding ropes of hair or heads piled one on top of another in tragic communal pyramids, like a drawing by Käthe Kollwitz. The women performed on pointe, drilling their toes into the floor, but there was another, more soulful purpose to the shoes too: Nijinska hoped to elongate the dancers' bodies to "resemble the saints in Byzantine mosaics."[13] Automatized and mechanical, tragic and Byzantine: another confluence that would make its mark on Balanchine. He was nineteen.

After *Les Noces*, Nijinska and Diaghilev appeared to give up on Russia and move instead to a then-fashionable European style, in which Nijinska again overturned convention without forgoing classical form: *Les Biches* (*The Darlings*) (1924), to music by Francis Poulenc with sets by Marie Laurencin, saw women in pink flapper dresses, with Chanel pearls and cigarette holders, along with athletes in shorts, in a choreography that played openly with ideas of androgyny and same-sex desire. *Le Train Bleu* (1924) with music by Milhaud, a libretto by Cocteau (who wanted the ballet to be "an article of fashion . . . a monument to frivolity"), and a festive curtain by Picasso (who had by then married a Ballets Russes dancer). Coco Chanel designed the costumes from her latest collection of leisurewear for the tennis-playing elite. *Le Train Bleu*—set "on a beach in 1924"—was named after the train that carried wealthy Parisians to their champagne vacations in Monte Carlo; in the ballet, they could see—themselves! It was a success with the public, but critics were divided, and backstage the more serious and talented Nijinska had clashed badly with Cocteau and others on Diaghilev's team.[14]

That year, Diaghilev made one final attempt to return to his homeland, just as George was leaving it. He met with Mayakovsky in Berlin to discuss plans to bring the Ballets Russes to Russia. He wanted to meet Goleizovsky and was interested in working with Meyerhold. The signs were initially encouraging: Mayakovsky was in touch with Lunacharsky, and plans proceeded, but even though Diaghilev's visa came through, he suddenly grew cautious. He was hearing ugly stories about the political situation that gave him pause. When he found out that his then lover Boris Kochno was being refused a return passage, Diaghilev canceled their trip. He would never go back, but his situation in Europe was growing serious. It was one thing for the Ballets Russes to work with European designers and even composers, but this was a Russian company, and Diaghilev's enterprise rested on his ability to bring fresh choreographic talent from the homeland, which now seemed definitively blocked. Nijinska, meanwhile, was increasingly frustrated and wanted out; by the end of 1924, she had decided to leave the company, and it was in this context and troubled state of mind that Diaghilev arranged to meet the young Georgi Balanchivadze.[15] This time, perhaps, Russia was coming to him.

The meeting, which was really an audition, took place at the elegant duplex apartment of Misia Sert, a patron and close Diaghilev friend. She was Polish and Jewish, born Marie Sophie Olga Zenaide Godebska in St. Petersburg to a prominent artistic family; she married often and well—the Spanish painter José-Maria Sert was her third husband. Voluptuous, with dark eyes and a small but expressive mouth, she greeted the young dancers in an elegant red gown and invited them upstairs into her lavishly furnished living room, where they met Diaghilev and were served tea on fine china.[16]

Diaghilev was a large man—Lopokova and Keynes called him "Big Serge" or "the Buddha"—but by the time Balanchine met him, he was already a bit heavy and showing signs of aging. His enormous, majestic head (he ordered special wide-girth hats) sat a bit too heavily on his softening and slightly bent shoulders, an external sign of his weakening internal constitution. Beset with diabetes and other ailments, his health was becoming a constant problem. He took care with his appearance, although he increasingly refused to look in the mirror or to have his portrait painted, fearful, Dorian Gray-like, of seeing himself grow old. It was rumored that he owned only one suit and one hat, a myth that appealed to the parsimonious George, but it was obvious on first glance that his dark suits were expensive and tailored, and he came scented and adorned with a monocle and ivory-tipped cane. At the time, Balanchine couldn't help wondering if the impresario's coal-black hair, with its legendary gray streak painted just above the right temple, wasn't a lie. Surely the coal black and not the gray was dyed, a fact attested to by lovers who noted the oily dark smudges on his pillows. In states of deep concentration, he could be caught chewing his tongue.[17]

Diaghilev welcomed them with his soft and alluring voice, sharpened by a habit of dropping unaccented syllables of long Russian words, which gave his often foulmouthed speech a melodious gait. First, he eagerly plied the young dancers with questions on the state of life and art in the new Soviet Union. After tea, he wanted to see them dance. They pushed back the furniture and in stocking feet with shirt open to the waist, George took Tamara and they performed one of his more acrobatic pas de deux, humming the music as they went. Diaghilev was impressed. Could Balanchivadze also choreograph opera? Yes. Could he work quickly? Of course. Diaghilev turned to Choura, who had grown plump from her enthusiasm for Europe's plentiful supply of bread. How much do you weigh? She was not amused: What are you buying, a horse—maybe you'd like to see my teeth? They were hired on the spot. Like Diaghilev's previous protégés, George had at least two roles: he would dance and make dances.[18]

Their contract didn't begin immediately (they hocked Balanchine's suit to help keep them until they began), but soon they were provided by Diaghilev with Nansen passports.[19] For those lucky enough to get one, a Nansen passport was a kind of miracle. Invented just two years before and named after Fridtjof Nansen, high commissioner for refugee affairs at the League of Nations, they were part of a collective European response to the overwhelming volume of refugees pouring in from Russia, Armenia, and points east, and could be used to travel and to petition for residency abroad. Above all, a Nansen passport protected the holder from the dreaded possibility of deportation. A few months later, Diaghilev also presented Georgi Balanchivadze with a new and very French name. He was now Georges Balanchin (soon to be George Balanchine). Around this time, back in Leningrad (and unbeknownst to him), Georgi Balanchivadze had been formally fired from the Imperial Theaters, and his expired passport made him stateless.[20] On that day in Misia Sert's living room, Balanchine got more than a new name and a new job. He got a new Russia: the one that Diaghilev had invented.

He got to know it firsthand. One of his tasks as a dancer was to step into

Diaghilev's glory-days Russian ballets, many of which were still bread-and-butter staples of the company repertory. And because he was a great mime and not a great dance technician, Balanchine was often assigned secondary character or dramatic roles, which gave him a familiar vantage point: watcher. In the coming years, he performed an old man in *Petrouchka*, the wicked sorcerer Kastchei in *The Firebird*, a "Negro" in *Scheherazade*, and a member of the ensemble in *Les Noces*, *Le Sacre du Printemps* (Massine's), *Le Train Bleu*, and *The Sleeping Princess*, now retitled *Aurora's Wedding*. He couldn't help but notice that many of these dances seemed, like Diaghilev himself, a bit old and "*déraciné*" (uprooted),[21] as one observer put it, and it was also true that the English and other dancers stepping into the roles once occupied by Karsavina, Nijinsky, and Pavlova simply weren't possessed of the same belief in these ballets, and their effect was naturally muted.

For Balanchine, the problem went deeper. He had experienced the traumatic events of the war and revolution at home, firsthand—on the filthy ground, not from the snowy heights of the Swiss Alps—and it was hard to see this old exoticism and imperial nostalgia as anything but quaint. Even the memory of these dances broke along the fault lines of war and revolution. When Diaghilev had tried to revive Nijinsky's *Sacre du Printemps* in 1920, no one could remember the steps, and he had to ask Massine to make an entirely new ballet. Balanchine danced in Massine's restaging, later noting that it was hard to be shocked by this once-shocking ballet after you had heard the barrage of German guns.[22]

Dances, George began saying, were as ephemeral as butterflies and should never be repeated or revived. We should be wary, however, of taking his word for it. "Butterflies" was a mantra and a myth that he was already taking on—a way of erasing a past he had in fact inherited. For Balanchine, denial and forgetting were a necessary housecleaning. The old Russia could be suffocating, and he didn't want or need its weighty past. And if Nijinsky and Nijinska in particular were obvious artistic predecessors in their ties to Stravinsky and in their move toward a "cold" and more abstracted style, he ignored the debt. Diaghilev's Russian dances were as much of a "dead point" as the old imperial ballets back in St. Petersburg, and Balanchine was as eager as ever to do his job and move on. "All is new!"[23]

He found a partner in Stravinsky. Balanchine later charmingly recalled his awe at their first encounter: "It was like meeting a cardinal. You're not nervous—I was nervous when I met Ginger Rogers—but here I wanted the truth. Stravinsky was the greatest comfort I ever had."[24] The composer, who was a generation older and already a giant in his field, would be a mentor and friend, and the only father figure George ever really had. There was no one George respected more, and it would be hard to overemphasize the importance of Stravinsky in his life. Revealingly, however, and in spite of his initial interest, Balanchine never staged *Le Sacre du Printemps*, and he would leave *Les Noces* and *Petrouchka* to others. Nijinsky and Debussy's *Afternoon of a Faun* was not his territory either. Rimsky-Korsakov's *Scheherazade* he would stage once in Hollywood—as farce. Balanchine would meet Stravinsky on other ground, but he showed little affinity then or later for the Slavophilia that Diaghilev and his friends had invented and now bequeathed to him. *That* was not his Russia.

All of this made it hard for Balanchine to be Diaghilev's last protégé. Recognizing the talent of his latest recruit, Diaghilev lavished attention on George—just as he had on Nijinsky and Massine and continued to lavish now on his next protégés (and lovers), including his secretary and collaborator Boris Kochno and the dancer Serge Lifar. Diaghilev took Lifar to Florence, Venice, Siena, Assisi, Ravenna, and Rome and—Baedeker in hand—showed him museums, the Vatican, churches, Pompeii, and Herculaneum. Diaghilev gave Lifar a list of things to see and memorize, please, and George remembered seeing them too: paintings by Raphael, Botticelli, Mantegna (*The Lamentation of Christ*), Piero della Francesca, Donatello, Lippi, Francia, Masaccio, Michelangelo, and "our" Milanese, Luini.[25] One afternoon Diaghilev deposited George in a chair in a small chapel in front of a painting by Perugino with the instruction "Look!" while he went to lunch—a ploy Balanchine initially resented but then appreciated as he sat staring and finally better seeing the painting's beauty and detail. On another afternoon they sat in an Italian village square watching commedia dell'arte and street performers. Back in Paris, George spent time at the Louvre and studied *The Lady and the Unicorn* tapestries. And his work on Diaghilev's new ballets was its own vast education in music and art; he would also meet and work with (among others) Milhaud, Rieti, Satie, Picasso, Matisse, Derain, and Cocteau.

But disciple? No. He was not the kind of person who could be taken under wing, and he and Diaghilev both knew that George had no interest in the homosexual closeness that generally came with the position. He avoided too the snarled relationship Diaghilev had with Stravinsky and others, full of dramatic breaks and reconciliations, usually over contracts and money, which simply didn't interest George. He and Diaghilev had dinner together maybe three times in all of the years Balanchine was there—the first time, George nervously overcooked everything, and Diaghilev took one look at the mushy meal: "What's this, kasha and more kasha?" Diaghilev was a force, like a storm that could overtake you, and Balanchine naturally positioned himself in the calm eye of any turbulence. What Diaghilev gave him was something different: a chance. A chance and a place to work. "If it wouldn't be for him, I wouldn't be here," Balanchine later admitted.[26] In this sense, they saved each other. Choreographers can't practice or exist without dancers, composers, designers, and the machinery of a theatrical enterprise. Diaghilev gave him it all. And if this gift came with some old ballets, like Russia in ruins around him, George didn't mind. He was at a low point and needed a place to work. Diaghilev was at a low point too. He needed new Russian ballets, and he was right that he would find them in Balanchine.

During his first season with the Ballets Russes, Balanchine made dances for some twelve new productions of opera and ballet in the course of a two-month run in Monte Carlo—a new production every five days, on average, in addition to his hours of rehearsals as a dancer learning the standard Ballets Russes repertory and moonlighting at small seaside resorts. His ability to produce quickly and well, without tantrums or fuss, was immediately seized upon by Diaghilev, who gave him more and more to do. It was an apprenticeship by volume, and George was like a machine: he could turn out a completed dance in a matter of hours, without losing track of his other duties. Opera was important, and he immersed himself in the scores that came his way, ingesting music and experience he would draw on for the rest of his life, in staging opera—which he continued to do—but also in his ballets. He later noted, for example, that he learned from Verdi, whose compositions have built-in stops to let the singers rest, "and he makes these rests part of [the] composition, think of that . . . silence becomes also fantastic" because you need a measured amount.[27]

The demands on his time and stamina were enormous. Daily company class began promptly at 10 A.M. and was a mandatory and exhausting drill of classical technique; fines were issued to anyone who missed it. At first it was taught by Enrico Cecchetti, old and bent, a veteran Italian ballet master who had worked for years in Russia. He liked to have the dancers stand in alphabetical order at the barre and move "up" one spot every day so that he could scrutinize each one. Balanchine found these ancient habits and the movements Cecchetti gave small and mousy, and he preferred the more generous Russian technique classes offered by his old compatriots, such as Nikolai Legat, a dancer from the Imperial Theaters resettled in London who also taught for a time at the Ballets Russes, or Olga Preobrazhenskaya or Lubov Egorova, both emigrated and settled in Paris. Even Golden Matilda, who had long since fled the revolution and settled with a grand duke, now gave her own classes and was often seen in Monte Carlo, where she liked to gamble with the other dancers.

Class was followed by rehearsals and performance or more rehearsals. Exhaustion, injuries, arguments, and emotional breakdowns were a constant feature of company life, and as the months went by, Balanchine increasingly managed a lot of that too. This one had mumps and couldn't perform; that one tore his tendon after colliding with Lifar in the wings; another sprained an ankle. And what about the dancer who tried to hang himself because his girlfriend left him? Or the ubiquitous diet pills and women too weak to rehearse well? George angrily threw Tamara's and then Danilova's pills away and told them to eat salad and sweat more instead. Most annoying of all were the petty rivalries—nasty whispers or giggling at rehearsals to slight another dancer (she's mocking me!), who would then storm out. These childish scenarios infuriated George, who complained bitterly that this kind of stupid behavior was costing him valuable rehearsal time.[28]

He was not shy and immediately set out to import dancers from Leningrad and his Young Ballet. He wrote letters, sent telegrams, asked friends and colleagues, and reported to Diaghilev (in Russian): "Mungalova does not want to leave, Kostrovitskaia married one (incidentally) very talented artist . . . and she would leave only with him."[29] Stulkolkina, Arkhipova, and Mikhailov were ready to leave now, he said, if Diaghilev could only secure the necessary papers. There were others already in Germany, one in Riga (send word soon, she is out of money and can't wait). George pressed for action: our performances will be "more interesting" with these dancers, he said, if only Diaghilev could get them (he didn't).

Balanchine worked on all fronts to find dancers he liked. That first season, for example, he met Diaghilev in London at the studio of Serafina Astafieva, an old Ballets Russes dancer (and grandniece of Tolstoy).They found her in her usual white silk stockings, black bloomers, and skirt with a wool scarf wrapped turban-like around her carrot-orange wig. She wore pearls and carried a thin black-and-gold stick, which she used to prod her students' legs and feet. Under her auspices Diaghilev discovered an unlikely prospect: Alicia Marks, a waiflike fourteen-year-old girl from an Orthodox Jewish family, whose father had died suddenly, leaving her mother destitute. Alicia was petite, with dark hair and fine features; she had knock-knees, fallen arches, and thin and undeveloped legs "as fragile as Venetian glass," another dancer recalled, but behind this frail exterior lay "the kick of a horse," and the girl easily and naturally performed the difficult acrobatic steps Balanchine gave her. Diaghilev Russified her name to Markova (she memorized it in Cyrillic to read the casting sheets, which were always in Russian), and she (and her mother) joined the Ballets Russes.[30]

George set to work with Markova on a restaging of Stravinsky's *Le Chant du Rossignol*, a good example of the kind of assignments Diaghilev was giving him and how he worked. Stravinsky had written the opera, a kind of Russian chinoiserie, during the war and had adapted it for Diaghilev as a ballet in 1919 with choreography by Massine and bright costumes and sets by Matisse. It was a score George already knew from Meyerhold's production in Petrograd, so he was able to work efficiently. Stravinsky was in and out of rehearsals, at the piano playing four-hands with the pianist, insisting on tempo and gently coaching the bewildered Alicia through the complicated counts and rhythmic structures. They worked at times with a pianola, and Markova recalled how she and George would rehearse into the night, with Diaghilev and Kochno stopping by, after dinner, around 11 P.M. to see what progress had been made. On one of these evenings, Diaghilev corrected the tempos Stravinsky had set. George dutifully adjusted the movement, but when Stravinsky saw it, he was furious—a lesson George didn't forget.

There were long sessions too at Vera Soudekina's costume shop, with Diaghilev, Stravinsky (Vera was his mistress and eventually his wife), Balanchine, and Matisse standing over Markova's small body, scrutinizing every detail of her dress. Matisse had conceived the magical bird who saves an emperor's life as an androgynous white creature in clinging silk tights and top with a tight white chiffon cap hiding her feminine hair. There is no record of George's reaction to Matisse, but when Alicia fell ill one evening, George squeezed himself into the white silk, crammed his too-large body into her tiny birdcage, and pranced gleefully through her variation—a comic and bawdy performance that delighted the cast and the audience. It was the kind of hammy, irreverent clowning he relished, and whenever he was thrown into a new part, the dancers all waited to see what he would come up with. In *Petrouchka* he went on one night as an old man with an obscenely long penis for a nose.[31]

As for competitors, there was only one who gnawed at his mind, and that was Léonide Massine. Balanchine ingested Fokine, Nijinsky, and Nijinska in gulps by dancing their ballets, but Massine was different. He had been banished by the time Balanchine arrived, but Diaghilev brought him back in moments of need, and Massine still had a magnetic hold on his former lover. George watched as Diaghilev sat glumly in rehearsals refusing to speak to Léonide or angrily sending Kochno to sit next to him instead. Massine was Balanchine's opposite: moody, dark, self-involved, and notoriously vain. He had heavy-lidded eyes and wore blousy crepe-de-chine shirts and black alpaca pants stitched with elastics inside to straighten the line of his otherwise badly bowed legs. Physically he was small but arresting, with a heavy dose of machismo.

Making dances was for Massine a tortuous experience involving a heavy burden of study, and he would arrive at the studio with his thick black book of notes and diagrams and labor for hours over his choreography. It was like "dancing for the Grand Inquisitor," Danilova said, and Lopokova noted that

Massine's nature was "always twisted in the wrong direction."[32] Massine haughtily ignored Balanchine from the start—except that he forbade George to watch certain rehearsals, lest he steal ideas. When Massine finally complained to Diaghilev that he had already "thought" of a step George composed, Diaghilev just said, "If it is so easy to steal your thought, better stop thinking."[33]

No matter: Massine was the biggest name in the business, and his dances were not only widely admired and critically acclaimed but truly innovative. And although Balanchine never admitted it, he borrowed freely from Massine's plastique and tableaux of draped and entwined figures. He would live for decades in Massine's shadow, and everything about the man galled him. They rarely met, but Massine seemed to dog him at each juncture, and it didn't help that women fell in love with Massine's dark good looks and melancholy temperament, among them Vera Zorina, who would later marry George—while she was still languishing after Massine.

As for where to live, it had been enough that there was cold running water from a tap in every room at the pension George and Tamara first stayed at on the rue du Pont Neuf in Paris and even at the whorehouse that gave them rooms near Pigalle. But now that they were paid members of the Ballets Russes, they settled in a small flat at 5, rue Gavarni, off the shop-filled rue de Passy in the 16th arrondissement. It was a modest, attractively art-deco building, a bit cramped in the style of a low-end pension, and their apartment was up a narrow winding staircase and off a small hallway. They were not often there. The company also had a base in Monte Carlo, thanks to generous funding from the municipality, and they took a room at the Hôtel du Prince, or some other affordable establishment, along with the other dancers.

Monte Carlo might have been more of a home. It had long since been a vacation resort for the imperial elite and was now teeming with dispossessed grand dukes and aristocrats—mere mention of the delicious piroshki at Filippov's in St. Petersburg would bring an enthusiastic comment from a stranger standing nearby who had been there too. Its palm trees and glorious coastline, along with its lavish baroque-style opera house and equally sumptuous casino, presented an image of a White Russian retreat that George never had. If you looked closely, however, you could see the signs of a darker life in the gardens nearby. Small black crosses drawn onto the pathway marked the spots where patrons distraught from gambling losses had shot themselves. More practically, a surgery facility for those who survived was conveniently located up a lift and through the glass doors at the top of a building and doubled as a treatment center for injured dancers.[34]

Diaghilev stayed at the fancy Hôtel des Bains and an adjacent brasserie served as his office. The dancers rehearsed in a dingy basement studio nearby, and Balanchine sometimes ended rehearsal early to escape into the bright summer air, a practice that Diaghilev strictly policed and punished. Or Balanchine would have lunch with Stravinsky, who had a home with his wife and children in Nice. Stravinsky's son Soulima remembered trying to get into a concert by Ignacy Paderewski one evening, but it was packed and oversold. Balanchine just said, come with me, and he took Soulima into the bowels of the theater, winding down dark corridors to the lower level under the stage, and they sat there, in the pitch dark, on crates, and listened for the footsteps of the conductor above them, then the applause, as the entire concert played above them.[35] Still, for all of its allure, Monte Carlo was never a home. The Ballets Russes was a touring company, and they were nomads who lived in whatever theater or dance studio they found themselves in. Pictures show them all perpetually in stations, elegantly dressed in suits, dresses, and hats and patiently waiting to board the next train: London, Berlin, Madrid, Lisbon.[36]

As George became more and more engrossed in his work, Tamara grew increasingly disoriented. She was never going to be a great dancer, and she was jealous of his attention to other dancers. She gained weight and began dieting and looking for other work. Sensing the change and at a loss to repair it even if he had wanted to, George fell in love with Choura Danilova—who *was* a great dancer. By the time Geva walked out of their marriage, he was already gone in the one area that mattered most to them both: dancing. He wrote to Diaghilev sarcastically announcing his wife's departure, "[Tamara] will not work this year. Due to her stupid methods of losing weight she has reached a situation in which her doctor has forbidden her to dance. She has joined Baliyev [a Russian nightclub act] and will sing in a gypsy chorus and clap her hands."[37]

Still formally married and unable to obtain a divorce without the proper papers, George had nothing to propose to Choura but a common-law marriage, so they moved to an apartment in the passage Doisy in the fashionable 17th arrondissement, full of Russian émigrés and not far from the Russian Orthodox Church. Dmitriev moved in with them. He aimed to start a photography studio to produce society portraits for the wealthy, but it never took, and he was still living on Balanchine's and Danilova's salaries. Bossy and intrusive, Dmitriev had latched on to George. The dancers referred to him as Balanchine's Rasputin; a Svengali, Danilova said, and his friends darkly joked that it was as if Balanchine and Dmitriev had murdered a man and Dmitriev threatened to tell.[38] Dmitriev claimed his strange hold over George was loyalty because he had gotten them out of Russia, but there seemed to be something more in their bond, born of shared secrets and the conspiracies of survival. Balanchine disliked him but needed him and kept him around. Dmitriev was the first in a series of male friends or helpers to whom Balanchine would attach himself over the years, not lovers necessarily, more like devoted servants or sycophants.[39]

George could be aloof, or shy, and his friends thought of him as a loner and "a rather placid homebody."[40] He had no interest in the fancy parties and *le tout Paris* that surrounded Diaghilev and the ballet. He preferred instead to dine informally at a café with a few musicians or dancers he knew or to cook for them himself at home (his French concierge was teaching him how).[41] He had a smattering of French and even less English, but his world was Russian. He liked to tell stories and act out all the parts, and he and his friends could sit for hours at the Café de Paris in Monte Carlo with a fifty-centime cup of coffee or at Giardino's in Paris over a plate of boiled beef.[42] When they could afford it, he went to Chez Korniloff, a Russian restaurant with icy vodka and plentiful caviar frequented by the likes of Feodor Chaliapin and Prince Yusupov (Rasputin's murderer).[43]

It was in these years that George met the composer Nicolas Nabokov (nephew of Vladimir), the pianist Nicholas Kopeikine (who had escaped Russia by train hidden in a pile of shit), the composer Vladimir Dukelsky (later known as Vernon Duke), and the painter Pavel Tchelitchew.[44] If George did go to parties, he stuck close to the piano and could be seen bent over the keys in concentration as he played into the night, or boisterously playing four-hands with Dukelsky. If there was no piano, he might sing from the few show tunes or songs he had memorized: "Everybohdy lohves my bohdy, but my bohdy lohves nobohdy but me."[45]

He preferred to stay home. In Monte Carlo, Geva—who loved nightlife—would go out with Dukelsky, who was in love with her and welcomed a chance to sweep her off to a club or bar. George grumpily relinquished her but preferred to sit in his bathrobe reading or strumming his guitar and singing to himself sotto voce.[46] He later farmed Choura out to his neighbor, the pianist Vladimir Horowitz, who took her dancing while George relaxed alone at the hotel. In Paris, when he finally had a piano at home, he could spend hours immersed in Bach—pure music, he said. Skip Scriabin, he told Choura when she begged for a change; Bach was a genius.[47] Or he liked to write humorous and erotic limericks, which he later gleefully shared with friends, a lifelong pastime. He also composed his own sentimental songs, such as "Valse Pestchinka," which he then critiqued in red ink in the margins: "Ok" or "Play this slower or eliminate."[48] He read: books but also scores, and he could be seen comfortably propped on pillows in bed, reading music the way most people read a novel before sleep. He could walk into the studio to make a new dance empty-handed, without papers, plans, notes, or any apparent preparation, and whole ballets seemed to pour out of him unsolicited, but this was only because he had labored at home for weeks, sometimes years, often transcribing a score by hand to know its intricacies better still. Confident of his own gift, he was, as a friend put it, "supremely unconcerned with worldly success, merely intent on doing a good job."[49]

George genuinely didn't care about wealth and freely gave away what money he had or treated it like a toy. Choura wanted a dress or a hat? He bought three. His generosity was known and taken advantage of by dancers forever short of cash, and as ballet master his salary of 2,500 francs was higher than theirs.[50] He gave what he had without thinking and sometimes found himself suddenly broke. He had to plead with Diaghilev in 1925 for an advance of 1,500 francs—he couldn't afford food, much less hotels, doctors, or massage therapists, he said.[51] Once in Monte Carlo he had given so much away that he didn't have enough to pay his own hotel bill, so he made a rare trip to the casino, bet what little was left all on a single number and won, paid his bill, and walked out. He didn't particularly like rich people and resented being drafted as the entertainment for patrons' parties, where he and the dancers were trotted out to dance in living rooms and fed buffet dinners in the kitchen with the house staff before making their way home on foot, too poor to afford a taxi. Once he was hired to stage an entrée for a lady patron to perform at Claridge's Hotel, but when he arrived at her home at midnight in his work clothes to rehearse as planned, he was refused entrance and deposited in the mud like a tramp by two policemen outside.[52]

He did go to orchestral concerts and to shows and was especially taken with the American dancer Josephine Baker, part of his growing fascination with black American culture. Baker, the granddaughter of a tobacco-plantation slave, was raised in the slums of East St. Louis. She got to Paris via vaudeville and the Harlem Renaissance, and her show *La Revue Nègre* at the Théâtre des Champs-Élysées in 1925 made her a star. It was a variety act featuring tap, spirituals, skits, and dancing, but above all a self-consciously eroticized and exoticized Josephine. She once made her entrance entirely nude, sprawled upside down in a split on the shoulder of "a black giant," and she danced with cross-eyed frenzy, legs flying, puppetlike, critics said, and body shuddering. They called her the black Venus or an African Eros; a Salomé, George said. Her powerful sexuality, ironic grasp of race, and skillful manipulation of her role as celebrity entertainer—to largely white audiences—impressed him deeply. (And that was before she worked for the French Resistance or adopted her "rainbow tribe" of multiracial children.) One afternoon, she invited George to lunch at her lavish château-like home in Le Vésinet, just outside Paris. He put on a proper suit, took the train, and in one of those tongue-in-cheek stories he liked to tell, Josephine met him at the door stark naked with a dusting of white flour and holding a bouquet of three flowers. The surrealists were also riveted by Josephine's sexuality; Cocteau designed sets for her, Fernand Léger made her part of his society, Matisse made her into a cutout, and Alexander Calder turned her (several times) into a wire sculpture.[53]

The dances George made with Diaghilev in the 1920s are, with rare exceptions, lost and forgotten, but pictures and contemporary accounts tell us just how deeply George dove into Dada, surrealism, Bauhaus, and constructivism. He worked with artists who, like him, were picking through the devastation of the war in their minds and obsessed with broken limbs and severed parts, mannequins, puppets, and the body as machine. It is worth recalling that surrealism too had origins in the experience of war. Two of its earliest French leaders, André Breton and Louis Aragon, met in 1917 as medics at a psychiatric ward of a military hospital, where they observed soldiers' compulsive, morbid visions. Nor would surrealism be a passing phase for Balanchine (he had no interest in its flirtations with Communism). He would return to Derain (again) and Tchelitchew (a lot) and move on to Esteban Francés, Kurt Seligmann, and Dorothea Tanning, all of whom shared a "lost generation" disenchantment with reason and the visible world. George later knew and was "grimly fascinated," as a friend put it, with Dalí.[54]

Jack in the Box (1926), for example, had a score by Satie that Diaghilev was rumored to have lifted from the dying composer's pockets but more likely fished out from behind Satie's broken piano in his shockingly decrepit apartment, covered in filth and littered with faded newsprint and scraps of ideas. Satie had started as a cabaret pianist and liked to tinker with ironic wordplay and mocking concepts, such as "furniture music" ("Don't listen! Keep talking!"). He had already composed a score filled with noise and street sounds for Diaghilev's *Parade*, in 1917, in collaboration with Cocteau, Massine, and Picasso. Satie was also involved in *Relâche* (1924), a Dadaist production for a rival company in Paris, which included a surreal film by René Clair and a nonsense text by one of Dada's leading lights, Francis Picabia. George was given the task of making dances for a life-size puppet that performed with Danilova, blacked up in face and body (and photographed by Man Ray, the Russian-born Emmanuel Radnitzky), while mimes moved Derain's cardboard clouds, like his whimsical Pierrots, around the stage.[55]

What to say about blackface, an all too common theatrical trope that Balanchine was trying out at the time? A mark of contemporary prejudices, certainly, but also a sign of his keen and enduring interest in and admiration for black American theater and dance, which he had encountered most recently in Josephine, but also in London music halls and in film and popular culture. In a Ballets Russes production at London's Lyceum Theatre in 1926, he made dances for a ditty with music by Lord Berners called *The Triumph of Neptune*, including a blackface dance for a drunk character named Snowball that clearly fascinated him. George himself still performed, and a series of informal photographs taken on the rooftop of the theater show him in tattered clothes and full blackface, with grotesque lips and facial features, posing with lanky, slumped disjointedness.[56]

La Chatte (1927) had music by Henri Sauguet, another Satie-inspired composer, and "kinetic constructions" by the Russian émigré artists (and brothers) Naum Gabo and Antoine Pevsner, who had worked with Kandinsky and Malevich and were also involved with Gropius and the Bauhaus. Gabo and Pevsner devised costumes and sets consisting of abstract, industrial-looking tubes, circles, segments, ellipses, and cones in mica and steel, with tutus layered in gelatin or isinglass. It was Schlemmer all over again: the body as machine or industrial gadget, and although Balanchine obliged with biomechanical-like dances of interlocking limbs, the dancers were really there to show off the tubes and cones of mica and steel.[57]

Nothing compared to the bodily disarray of *Le Bal* (1929), in which the Italian surrealist Giorgio de Chirico, who had recently proclaimed his return to classicism and antiquity, scattered the stage with fragments of statuary and plaster body parts, along with human figures made of columns and bricks, the body and city in ruins. The dancers chafed in their white body powder and grating wool gloves, designed to make their hands look like marble, and the body stockings painted with bones were tight and constraining, making it hard to move. The matching score by Rieti was a burlesque of musical styles, and George answered with "stone guests" at an ill-fated ball performing grotesque jigs, foxtrots, military marches, and angular, acrobatic steps. One critic complained that Balanchine had abused the classical dance "by literally putting it to torture . . . with a type of sadistic satisfaction," which, of course, was the point.[58]

It could be said—and was—that in ballets such as these, Diaghilev was giving up or giving in to the decadent "roaring" parties and fashionable high jinks of the artistic worlds of Paris and Monte Carlo, besotted with money, drugs (plenty of opium), and the antics of whatever latest artistic craze attracted a *scandale*. But this would be a misreading. In fact, by bringing these artists together, Diaghilev had his finger directly on the pulse. If the work sometimes seemed silly or offhand ("awful," Balanchine later recalled), it was meant to be. Nonchalance was its own kind of nihilism. The problem, which Balanchine faced, was that by depicting the human form as a puppet or mannequin encased in industrial gear—or reduced to columns, bricks, and skeletal bones—these ballets were choking the body off from itself. They were for him a dead end. He had been dropped into Diaghilev's world, played in Diaghilev's theater, tried many things, and learned enough for a lifetime, but he had lost, or not quite found, his own voice.

Balanchine's state of mind came out in a Dalí-like self-portrait he probably made around this time and later stashed in an old notebook. It was a pencil sketch, and he called it the "Adler" (German for eagle). The eagle could be

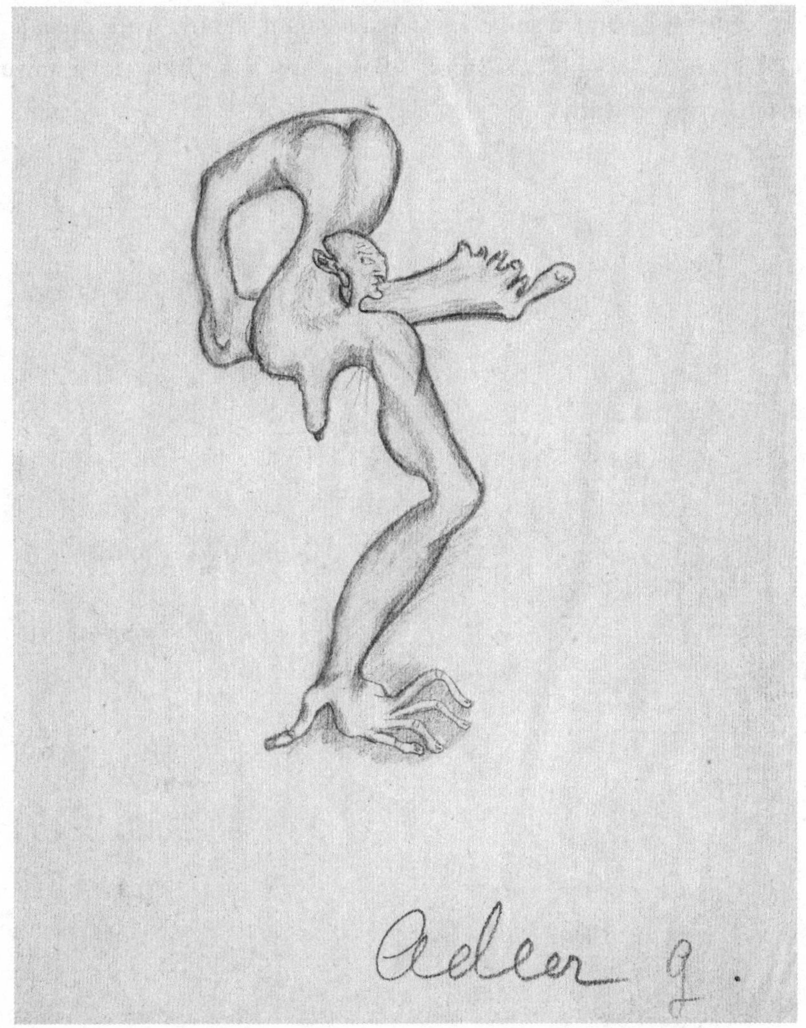

many things: an imperial insignia, a good-luck charm, even Zeus's bird of prey in the seduction of Ganymede. Balanchine drew himself as a man who is not really a man: his body doesn't exist. Instead, he is one long phallic limb twisting around itself. A small penis-like protrusion sticks out of one part of this grotesque limb, and a tiny head—his—sticks out of another. It is George, in his signature profile, with large nose, high forehead, big ear. He is standing on that single serpent-like limb, which coils into a large hand planted in the ground with too many long spindly witch-like fingers. This contorted body has a muscular power and unmistakable direction—a big toe attached at the top of the twisting limb points urgently ahead. But there is no wingspan, no flight. This "eagle" is grounded and constrained, focused, almost beady eyed, and entrapped in its own grotesque form.[59] Balanchine was looking for a way up and out. It was Stravinsky who provided it.

Chapter 7

APOLLO

In April 1926 Stravinsky returned, after a long lapse, to the Orthodox Church. He confessed, took Communion, and devoted himself anew to the practices of his childhood faith. In the weeks and months to come, he collected icons and became actively involved in the church near his home in Nice. He even wrote a heartfelt repentant letter to Diaghilev, with whom he had fought bitterly over money and contractual rights. The reasons for Stravinsky's sudden reconversion are difficult to fully isolate, but they had to do with his growing sense of crisis in many aspects of his life: guilt over his long and openly passionate affair with Vera Soudekina and his long absences from his sickly and pious wife as she raised their four young children, but also a deep disillusionment with Soviet Russia, which was pushing him, along with others in the émigré community, into the arms of Orthodoxy. Musically, he was moving away from the Russified musical language of *Le Sacre du Printemps* and even *Les Noces*—and toward Bach and a pristine, spiritually pure, and neoclassical sound. To the astonishment of many, Stravinsky seemed to be engaged in a full-scale renunciation: of his homeland and his own musical past, a renunciation closely tied to his returning faith. *Apollon Musagète*, a new ballet whose choreography Diaghilev assigned to Balanchine, was part of this awakening.

In these months, Stravinsky grew close to Jacques Maritain, a Catholic neo-Thomist philosopher, and his wife Raïssa Umantseva, a Russian Jew who converted to Catholicism. Maritain's work and Sunday-afternoon gatherings at his home in Meudon, which he and Raïssa shared with her Russian mother and sister, drew several other artists around Diaghilev, including Cocteau, Georges Auric, Georges Rouault, Nicolas Nabokov, and Stravinsky's close friend at the time, the Russian critic Arthur Lourié (another Jew converted to Catholicism). They were all there to be saved. Cocteau had lost his lover to a sudden death and retreated into despair and an opium haze. Nabokov was the victim of seizures that could plunge him into bouts of drinking, brawls, and suicidal despair. Maritain became a close spiritual influence and advisor. Stravinsky too found solace in Maritain's ideas and through him entered a Catholic intellectual tradition that became an important element in his approach to music and art. It was an approach that filtered back to the more reclusive George.[1]

Maritain argued against the Romantic view of boundless self-expression and the inspired artist and insisted instead on the craftsman and "maker" (homo faber) engaged in the "honest labor" of technique, simplicity, truth, and limits. He argued for an impersonal and detached aesthetic and a return to classical ideals, by which he meant not a slavish adherence to antiquity but a modern revision—like skyscrapers, Diaghilev said. They all admired Pushkin, who saw himself as a cobbler selling his wares for the best price and producing clean and disciplined prose, free of what he called "shabby ornaments."[2] Cocteau argued for "a music for every day, a music I can live in like a house," and Maritain pointed to the anonymous cathedral-builders of the Middle Ages, noting that artists should see themselves as humble servants of God and the divine order—icon makers, every one.[3]

In July 1927, Stravinsky began work on *Apollon Musagète*. The star of the Ballets Russes production was to be Diaghilev's lover, Serge Lifar, a man with a beautiful physique but poor training and a hard, manipulative soul. Balanchine's friends called him the "fake Ukrainian" for his self-promoting airs, but Diaghilev didn't care, and George set about teaching "the kid" the finer points of dancing.[4] When Stravinsky played the completed score for the impresario in Nice, Diaghilev wrote to Lifar excitedly about the tremendous role his new muse was about to be given. The music, Diaghilev said, was a "filigree counterpoint around transparent, clear-cut themes all in the major key: somehow music not of this world, but from somewhere above . . . without any intentional Russianizing."[5] Balanchine later called it "white music, in places as white on white," a comment bringing to mind Malevich and his spiritual path to abstraction.[6] It was this music, Balanchine said, that first taught him that he too could "eliminate."

Stravinsky wanted de Chirico for the design, but Diaghilev settled on André Bauchant, who produced a decorative affair with flowers, Grecian tunics, laced sandals, and a horse-drawn chariot. Diaghilev moved quickly to change it, and the next year Coco Chanel dressed Apollo in crimson silk with gilt enamel hair and the muses in white tunics cinched at the waist with fashionable Charvet ties. She covered their hair with tight white caps, giving them an otherworldly, androgynous look. When Balanchine began work on the dances, Diaghilev turned to Derain as they watched one afternoon in the studio: "What he is doing is magnificent. It is pure classicism, such as we have not seen since Petipa."[7]

Stravinsky too talked of his new ballet as part of a return to classicism. It was a tribute, he said, to Jean-Baptiste Lully and the French seventeenth century, to the court of Louis XIV and the birthplace of classical ballet. Stravinsky spoke of versification and how he had folded the strict rhythmic patterns of alexandrines by the French poets Boileau-Despréaux and Racine into his musical structure. He drew too, he noted, on Bach, and on his beloved Tchaikovsky, whose own use of classical forms Stravinsky had long admired. With his typical attention to detail, he mapped the story of the ballet in the music. It would show the birth of Apollo and his education at the hands of the muses Calliope (poetry), Polyhymnia (mime), and Terpsichore (dance). They would dance for the god, and he would choose Terpsichore. In an allegorical pas de deux, music and dance—freed from mime and words—would join in sublime alliance. Stravinsky had traveled about as far as he could go from the Russian steppes of *Le Sacre du Printemps*, and in a sign of this ongoing musical and intellectual shift toward Europe and the West, he said that he hoped that his new dance would "remain in the aural memory as a pure fresco in the manner of Poussin."[8]

Ballet, Stravinsky further explained, echoing Maritain (and Nietzsche), represented to him "the triumph of studied conception over vagueness, of the rule over the haphazard," and he saw in it a way to come

> face to face with the eternal conflict in art between the Apollonian and the Dionysian principles. The latter assumes ecstasy to be the final goal—that is to say, the losing of oneself—whereas art demands above all the full consciousness of the artist. . . . And if I appreciate so highly the value of classical ballet, it is not simply a matter of taste on my part but because I see exactly in it the perfect expression of the Apollonian principle.[9]

He was looking to the trained balletic body to clarify whatever "vagueness" he so dreaded.[10] And so Stravinsky, with Diaghilev, turned to Balanchine to reestablish an Apollonian still point that might reanchor their artistic lives. What they got was something quite different.

In his notebook, Balanchine sketched ideas for the opening scene of *Apollon Musagète*. He drew a commanding woman, legs split wide and crotch open to the audience, seated high on a platform. She towers over the small, crouched figure of the unborn god below, who is surrounded by a crowd of huddled, anonymous faces, like masks or eyes peering out into the night. In another sketch, the woman is a cross-legged, Buddha-like deity, and this time she is sitting on the erect leg of a man standing on his head, as his leg pierces her vagina. Around them all, we see temple worshippers, some prostrate in prayer. Beneath these eroticized images of power and submission, George practiced signing his new name in a large, curling script: "Balanchine."[11]

Apollon Musagète opens on an island: a platform raised high on a darkened stage that seems to float in a single spotlight. On it sits the pregnant Leto, alone. She is the lover of Zeus and has been banished by his jealous wife, Hera. No one in the Olympian realm dares to house Leto in her hour of maternal need. Finally, she is allowed onto a small craggy island—which is really her sister cruelly turned to stone by Zeus for refusing his advances. This

is where we find Leto, alone and about to give birth to Apollo. Her labor is painful and prolonged.

Balanchine pictures her in that moment, just as he did in his notebook. She sits sweeping her body in circles of pain and rhythmically clutching her stomach in sharp contractions, legs splitting open to the audience and closing again as she resumes her labor. Physically, she is anguished, more Wigman-like than any idealized image of classical statuary. But Balanchine stops short of a full-throated expressionistic cry. He steps back, and there is something profoundly impersonal, and even formal, in her agonies. This is not only a return to classical forms but also a reliance on the distance and detachment of ritual, in which only rote acts, not self-expression, are required.

Next we see Apollo, a swaddled man fallen from Leto's womb onto the ground below. Then the unwrapping of lineaments, not unlike the tight swaddling customary for Russian newborns and thought to straighten the legs and calm the interior. Then the ceremonial presentation of the lyre. Apollo is the god of music and will lead the muses in song and dance. Still, Balanchine concedes nothing to Stravinsky's classical form. His Apollo staggers and lurches wildly around the stage, a novice who has not yet found his balance and footing. Apollo, Balanchine said, was not a god at all but a regular guy, and he told Lifar to think of himself as a soccer player. Even in his first solo, in which the young god is beginning to master graceful steps to the strains of a stately violin solo in the style of Bach, there comes unexpected awkwardness and pain. The young god falters and stumbles midstream; his chest caves, and he falls to his knees, physically exhausted.

In the course of the ballet, this moody god will reject Calliope, muse of poetry, who arrives with her tablet and stylus but, seeing Apollo's displeasure with her literary skills—words!—shrinks like an injured animal into the wings; he will also turn away from the beautiful Polyhymnia, muse of mime, who fails to express herself without opening her mouth wide and blurting out—more words!—before fleeing bent in humiliation from the stage. Terpsichore, danced by Balanchine's own Choura Danilova, is the only one who offers herself fully and without words: head and body thrown into a deep backbend before the god, who finally succumbs.

In a kind of consummation, Apollo poses as Adam in Michelangelo's Sistine Chapel image of the Creation of Adam, and Terpsichore steps into the place of God and joins her finger to Apollo's. Suddenly, we have crossed from antiquity into Genesis and the biblical origins of mankind. In this mixed pagan and Christian moment, Balanchine gives us a striking reversal: God is a woman, a muse of the dance, and it is a woman who is giving life—and art—to this godly man. Their dance together is tender and intimate, as she leads him, shows him, and teaches him, until finally he leads her too. They are themselves: not gods at all, but a mere man and woman practicing the life-giving art of love. There are almost no steps, only walking and simple gestures between them, elaborated in dance, and all of Apollo's instinctive and childish thrashing falls away. They invent: she will sit on his knees and wrap his arm into hers; he will lower himself and balance her on the back of his neck and she will seem to swim freely in the air; and they will end with her body flush against his back in embrace as they bend together in a long arch, arms open to the sky.

The vanquished muses return, and they all join in celebratory unison, but as we reach the end of the ballet, the music abruptly departs from the purity of Bach and Lully and moves into a darker register. We are in Stravinsky's "vagueness," and there is something yearning and almost fatalistic in these final phrases; Stravinsky called them tragic, which is what we feel as the muses solemnly follow Apollo single file and he mounts a platform to stand where his mother, Leto, once lay in agony and perdition to give him life. In the final moments, he reaches upward (or later stands with the muses arrayed on his back like a sunburst); there are horses, a chariot, and a distant vision of Mount Olympus. He has grown from boy to god—become an artist in the arms of women—and the moment is weighted with time and fate, as he leaves youth and stands poised to ascend. They are together but deeply alone.[12]

Some critics were distraught. Where was the dignity and repose of this famously controlled god? One called it a parody, and Balanchine liked to tell of another who sharply questioned him: "When have you ever seen Apollo on his knees?" To which the ballet master coolly responded, "When have you ever seen Apollo?" This wasn't the Greek or Apollonian classicism they—or Diaghilev—expected, and what Balanchine achieved in *Apollon Musagète* had little to do with the ornamental and aristocratic gestures of Petipa or the French seventeenth century; nor did it rely on the fashionable costumes or decor surrounding the dance. Indeed, Balanchine would eventually strip the sets entirely and perform the ballet in simple white practice clothes on an empty stage. Instead, the impulse was to wipe it all away—he too could eliminate—and in response to Stravinsky's pristine score, Balanchine found his own blank slate. The language he invented was spare and elemental, in part because it placed dance in the realm of formal poetic gesture and painting reaching back to the Renaissance, beginning with Michelangelo's touch. In this new compositional frame, narrative did not depend on traditional pantomime. Words, and gestures mimicking words, flew away. If anything, Balanchine's uncluttered dances, free of past styles of ballet or folk forms, were a search for Malevich's "zero hour" for the human body, a kind of *White Square* (1918) for dance that would "not belong solely to this earth."

Apollon Musagète was Balanchine's own kind of renunciation: of Diaghilev, of Weimar, and even of his own Russian past. He had lived in all those worlds, grown up in Petipa's imperial dances, come of age with the revolution, stood on the Scythian plains of the Ballets Russes, and inhabited Diaghilev's interwar experiments. He had taken and ingested all he could of

European culture and art. He had spent these years chipping away at the body, breaking it down and contorting or destroying its tonal center, and now, finally, he had found a way of demolishing all that he knew by using what he knew. "Not since Petipa" was a way of identifying *Apollon Musagète*'s elemental simplicity, but by stripping the body of Petipa's intricate and ornamental physical logic, Balanchine had also erased Petipa, or part of him. Renunciation didn't mean denial. It was all inside him, including the urgent press to move on.

His relationship to the world at that point was both disoriented and acutely sensual. *Apollon Musagète* wasn't first person or third person, or even second person. It wasn't a dialogue or a monologue. It was mute, like the watcher. Mute meant that words, narrative, and explication were not his main currency. Words were not his way in the world. The deed, the act, the gesture, was all. The gesture, but abstracted. Not the story of feelings, but feelings themselves.

On a more practical level, Balanchine was ready to live under his own rule. He was tired of Diaghilev's constant maneuvering. When the impresario tried to replace Danilova with Alice Nikitina, a dancer Balanchine didn't particularly like or care for, he was furious. The company was being supported at the time by the wealthy Lord Rothermere, scion of the *Daily Mail* in London, who was in love with Nikitina and wanted her to dance the role. Ever mindful of the company purse, Diaghilev acquiesced, and Balanchine finally compromised by giving Nikitina some but not all the performances. Diaghilev then fitfully decided he did not like the Terpsichore variation anyway and cut it. When Stravinsky finally found out, he calmly threatened to pull the music altogether—at which point the variation, and Danilova, were restored. Adding to Balanchine's restlessness, that year his knee gave way when he was dancing, and he was rushed into immediate surgery at the Russo-French hospital in Villejuif with one Dr. Aleksinsky, a renowned Russian émigré surgeon.[13] The procedure left him with painful and stiffly limited motion, a fact that came as something of a relief. Finally, he could stop performing and apply himself fully to making ballets.

• • •

By this time, Diaghilev was slowly dying. He had developed infectious boils on his skin and Kochno was draining them daily and bandaging the painful open sores. This annoyance, compounded with his more strenuous struggle with diabetes, left the impresario feeling old and besieged. It didn't help that he had recently discovered that his half-brother in Russia had been arrested by the secret police and disappeared. When Diaghilev tried to investigate, his inquiries through the French authorities were met by the Soviets with stony silence.[14] Meanwhile, he hadn't given up on Russian artists. He was in negotiations with Meyerhold and hoped that he could present a joint season with the Moscow Art Theater. Above all, he was pouring whatever he had left into a new ballet with music by Sergey Prokofiev: *Prodigal Son*. Diaghilev wanted Matisse to design the sets but settled instead on Georges Rouault, one of the few modernist and religious painters working at the time. Diaghilev and Kochno wrote the scenario, which truncated the biblical parable into a tale of exile and redemption: the prodigal son and his repentant return into his father's arms.[15]

Balanchine, who was assigned the choreography, didn't particularly like Prokofiev or his music. Prokofiev had recently composed for the Ballets Russes *Le Pas d'Acier*, a "Bolshevist" ballet with dancers wielding hammers busily building the new Socialist paradise, and in another sign of just how far his musical affinities were from Balanchine's, he had complained disdainfully in letters to Mayakovsky of *Apollon Musagète*'s "Bachiness."[16] Rouault, who was French and an old friend of Jacques and Raïssa Maritain, was a more natural collaborator. Shaped by the turn-of-the-century revival of Byzantine art, Rouault had apprenticed himself to a glazier's workshop and helped to restore the medieval stained-glass windows at Chartres Cathedral. The sets he came up with were both stark and expressionistic: a rectangular wooden slab, which—turned every which way—served as table of drunken feasting, ship of captivity, and finally the pillar on which Balanchine pinioned the ruined and naked son, Christlike, on the cross. This simple table, ship, cross was the prodigal's life: home, sin, repentance, return.[17]

Prokofiev and Balanchine clashed on just about everything. When Prokofiev saw Balanchine's dances, he was appalled. A practicing Christian Scientist, he found the eroticized steps for the temptress Siren and the sinning son wildly "indecent" and offensive in a Gospel parable.[18] He complained to Diaghilev, who stood firmly by his choreographer and told Prokofiev he knew nothing about dances and should be quiet. Prokofiev also disapproved of the vulgar depiction of the conspiring, and eerily bald, blue-green "goons," who corrupt the son and steal everything he has, leaving him alone and nearly naked on the stage. Balanchine later explained that he had made the goons into subhuman "protoplasm" with skittering movements and sinister shaved heads. "There's no sex to them, you know—they're insects . . . disgusting looking." Balanchine was annoyed at Prokofiev too: "[He] wanted a real garden and real wine and real mustaches and all that," he later explained dismissively. "He wanted the *Prodigal* to look like *Rigoletto*."[19]

Instead, Balanchine's dances were wild and disorienting, and critics once again noted their "inhuman contortions" and "strained acrobatical feats." The choreographer and writer Agnes de Mille, who was there, described the goons as gargoyles and abnormal, undeveloped creatures and wrote of the Prodigal Son's shrunken loathing as he "thrashes in the dust and draws himself into a knot, kicks free, turns feverishly over and around and back again."[20] Suffering was not acted out but *shown* in coldly "abstracted," feverish turns.

Icons were key. Even the Siren—overpowering, inscrutable, a seductress who entrances the son by coiling him into her serpent legs—was an icon. Her movement was flat and stylized, never sensually seductive, and Felia Doubrovska noted that the steps were "not ballet at all" but something else entirely. She wore a form-fitting bright-red bodice, short skirt, and long crimson cape, and every night she painted her long and exposed legs with Rouault's black serpentine lines, as if her body were stained glass. With her erect posture, high-priestess headdress, and heavy bejeweled necklace, she was an overwhelming erotic force. Her movement was hieratic and ceremonial. "Byzantine icons, Byzantine icons," Balanchine repeated over and again, and he told her to be cold and impersonal, like a snake.[21]

Nor was the emotional encounter between father and son the central dramatic moment in the ballet. Instead that privilege was given to the son's long journey home, an excruciatingly drawn-out passage in Prokofiev's score. Balanchine worried about how he would fill these long pages of music, which clocked in at well over two minutes. His answer was to strip the stage of everything and make Lifar—on his knees and barely alive—claw and pull himself with his staff, slowly, inch by painful inch, across a dark and empty horizon, like refugees everywhere. For what seems like an eternity, this is all we see. "Lifar on his knees made the ballet,"[22] Balanchine later admitted, and he drew a sketch of Lifar at this moment in the dance, signed, dated, and dedicated to the dancer.[23]

In a final twist, when this lost son finally arrives home, he is not met by the compassionate father figure so powerfully depicted in the Gospel. Instead, Balanchine made the father cold and formal, more priest or icon than man. His movements are stylized replicas of priestly gestures, and for later productions of the ballet, Balanchine even brought images of icons to the theater to guide the father's makeup design. In the original production, the father was danced by the émigré Michel Fedorov; later, Balanchine liked to step into the role himself.[24]

At the final moment of forgiveness, instead of stretching out his open arms to his supplicating child, this father steps stiffly back and makes the son hoist himself onto his father's chest, pulling himself up by the priestly vestments and curling his broken body into a fetal position, where he hangs like dead fruit on an inert trunk until finally—finally—the father wraps his cloak around his son as the curtain falls.[25] The father is stern because life is stern, or it has been for this son who finds himself not in the bosom of family love but in the arms of an icon. And although the ballet had wide appeal to audiences, it was not an ecumenical or universal conversation across oceans or faiths. Balanchine had made it a strictly Orthodox affair. If we understand the Russian Revolution to be one of the great episodes of iconoclasm, these icon-filled dances also stood as a riposte: to Prokofiev, but above all to the Bolsheviks who stole their world away.

The ballet was well received by the public, but Balanchine and Prokofiev both left the experience with bitter feelings toward the production and each other. When it was all over, Balanchine politely requested a share of the royalties. Prokofiev rudely refused. Kochno went to court for his and won; Balanchine let it go but bore a grudge. He would never again work with Prokofiev, who in any case would soon move back to the USSR and compose music for Socialist Realist dances under Stalin's watchful eye.[26]

. . .

That summer, the Ballets Russes dispersed for a break. Balanchine was in London working with Lydia Lopokova on a dance for the film *Dark Red Roses*, a kitschy early British talkie. He was staying with Lydia and Maynard Keynes at their Tilton home, rehearsing on a grand piano they had borrowed for the purpose and having rambling conversations with Keynes about everything from politics and economics to music and ballet. On the afternoon of August 19, they were all at the film studio in Wembley sitting around in costume and makeup waiting to shoot their scene when the evening newspaper arrived with headline news: Diaghilev was dead. Keynes wrote to his mother describing the ensuing "extraordinary scene," as the dancers fell into a tight huddle crouched on the floor, oblivious to the noise and film machinery, actors, and crowds of supers noisily milling about them. They sat there, stooped and circled, for several hours telling stories of "Big Serge" and all they remembered of his momentous life. For Balanchine, Diaghilev's influence had been huge.[27]

Diaghilev had died in Venice at the Grand Hotel surrounded by the only family he now had: Misia Sert, Kochno, and Lifar. As he lost consciousness, he sang from Tchaikovsky's requiem *Pathétique* Symphony, which he had heard as a young man in St. Petersburg, a score Balanchine would also later use for his own memorial dance. A priest delivered the *Panikhida* by Diaghilev's bedside, and the funeral took place shortly thereafter, a final performance organized by Misia and paid for by Coco Chanel, who had missed the death but rushed back for the burial services. A black and gold gondola with gilded angels and a deep-red cross carried the coffin to the steps of the Greek Orthodox church of San Giorgio dei Greci. It was a well-chosen theater for this final rite, built by Greek exiles during the Renaissance and dedicated to St. George. The coffin was lifted through the church's elegant Palladian arches and into the modest sanctuary, where it rested beneath a high dome, painted under the supervision of Tintoretto in rich blues, reds, and golds, showing the floating dance of saints and apostles.[28]

As their small group gathered, an onlooker stumbled unknowingly onto the scene with a friend. He was a tall, bulky man, but he had a way of disappearing into his own mass, and he watched quietly from the side, hidden amid the gleaming icons, as beadles in cocked hats bearing wreaths lifted the flower-laden bier and laid the dead Diaghilev before the magnificent Byzantine iconostasis. The Orthodox service for the dead began. When it was over, the catafalque was once again lifted onto the funeral gondola, bound this time for the burial ground on the remote island of San Michele.[29]

The chance onlooker was Lincoln Kirstein, a young American on his own Diaghilev-like pilgrimage to see culture and art. He didn't know until later that the man being laid to rest that day was the great impresario whose life's work had already largely inspired his own. And as these two men—one young, Jewish, and American, the other dead, Orthodox, and Russian—encountered each other across the mortal divide, it was possible to believe that Diaghilev had produced his own double at the very moment of his passing.[30] Fate building on fate, the torch was passed in this elegant Venetian church dedicated to Balanchine's own St. George.

Chapter 8

MAGIC MOUNTAIN

Less than two months after Diaghilev's passing, Balanchine collapsed. He had taken a job at the Paris Opera to choreograph a new ballet to Beethoven's *The Creatures of Prometheus*, with Serge Lifar in the leading role, and soon after they began work, Balanchine passed out in rehearsal.[1] He was immediately treated for pneumonia with "cupping," a burning of the flesh to draw out inflammation, but he kept working. Then came pleurisy, which put him in bed. Finally, he was coughing blood, and it was clear that his childhood TB had returned in force. He consulted Dr. Édouard Rist, a French expert in this deadly disease, who had recently published an important study of possible cures. The news was not encouraging. According to Rist, Balanchine fell into a high-risk category, and everyone knew that the "white plague," as it was known, was a common cause of death, especially among young men. Rist brushed aside homespun remedies. Forget about raw meat, fake drugs, charlatan potions. There was only one chance of survival, he said: sanatorium. It was urgent that George get away from the polluting and exhausting demands of Paris, and Rist recommended an immediate treatment of complete rest high in the mountains with plenty of cold, clean air.[2]

Balanchine panicked. In one of the few notebooks we have, he tried to compose a letter to his English producer explaining that he was ill and could not come to London, but after multiple cross-outs and rewrites, he abandoned his dangling sentences and turned to Kochno, a loyal friend, for help. Kochno wrote a clear missive on the next page to "Mon Cher Ami," explaining that Balanchine had to leave immediately for Switzerland and would be gone for at least a month. He begged the producer to please advance any money owed to Balanchine to help defray the costs of his precipitous departure. Balanchine left it to Lifar to make his own dance and boarded a train for Mont Blanc, high in the French Alps. In a trick of memory, perhaps, Choura Danilova later claimed that she accompanied him, but there is no sign of her there, and Balanchine didn't mention it and only said that he felt very alone.[3]

The Grand Hôtel du Mont Blanc in the Haute-Savoie was a newly built sanatorium subsidized in part by philanthropists and the French state. The idea was to provide affordable care for intellectuals, artists, and others who could not necessarily bear the burdensome expense of a rest cure at a place such as Davos, already made famous by Thomas Mann's *The Magic Mountain.* (Balanchine had never heard of it.) This was not only a good-will measure. TB was contagious and easily spread through tiny droplets in the breath, and it was reaching epidemic proportions. In the public imagination, it was still associated with poverty, sexual licentiousness, and personal hygiene, and seen by many as yet another sign of the degeneration of the French state. The sanatorium movement, which gained momentum after the war, was a way of isolating the sick in the hopes of once and for all eradicating this scourge from the body politic.

The hotel was built into the side of a mountain. As he approached, Balanchine would have seen the rows of covered verandas where the "horizontals" lay taking in the sun and air, wrapped in wool blankets carefully folded under their feet. Physicians in regulation white or black coats supervised the patients, whose lives were governed by pulse counts, weighings, X-rays, temperature checks, spit cups and spittoons, and above all by doing strictly nothing. George soon learned that reading had to be light, talking was discouraged, and even the exertion of hair brushing was prohibited. Bedpans were preferred to the effort of rising to walk to the toilet. Exercise was out of the question until a patient improved: even a brief walk could leave a tubercular wheezing for air. The only thing that was not discouraged was plentiful food to boost a patient's weakened constitution, and trips to the dining room were among the great events of the day. Balanchine dutifully ingested a quarter pound of butter every morning "which tries to get out of me through my nose," he reported to Kochno, but he had gained four kilos in just twelve days. Still, even in these supposed ideal conditions, the chances of surviving TB were poor. It was hard not to notice the large cemeteries discreetly tucked into the nearby hillsides of most sanatoriums.

The symptoms of the disease could be terrifying, and George had them. Coughing bloody sputum, of course, but also ghostly pallor and a feverish red "hectic glow" of the cheeks, racing heart and inexplicable torpor, and above all an almost eerie air-starved lightness of being. This was a wasting disease, and those who suffered from it watched their flesh consume itself and the mortal body wither as the spirit took its delirious hold. It was like becoming transparent—or all spirit, a fact that made some people think of TB as a voyage into otherworldly bliss or saintliness. The model for Botticelli's pale Venus was tubercular. There was disgust too, especially in the ways that the dematerializing body seemed to drown in its own fluids: phlegm, mucus, blood, sputum. Meanwhile, nails and hair, already dead, grew blithely on. And sex!—the dying man's salve and the consumptive's rage often pushed its way boldly to the fore, and the sense of longing welling up inside the afflicted flesh could be overwhelming. Some doctors even prescribed sex as an antidote. Not George's, apparently, but George did write to Kochno of the heightened thoughts of "future GIRLS" besieging him as he lay in the pure and icy air.[4]

The doctors had a cure they thought he should try. His thigh, which was infected, could be splinted and immobilized. But the lungs, they said, must rest too, and they recommended a treatment that could temporarily deflate a lung and allow it complete rest. Artificial pneumothorax (AP), or "gas refills," as it was called, was a new therapy in which the negative pressure of the pleural cavity surrounding a single lung was pierced with a small needle and the cavity filled with gas. In this newly pressurized environment, a lung would naturally collapse and "rest." This state wouldn't last, but "refills"—that is, deflations—were readily available until the lung had taken sufficient repose. The risks were well known: pleural shock, faintness, infection, even death. Still, AP was widely thought to be a patient's best chance, and Balanchine's doctors pressed their case. He said no. He had seen men all around him die from that. Like Franz Kafka (who had recently died of the disease), George preferred to eat and endure.[5]

Lying there high on a mountain far from his life and in the grips of a wasting disease, it was hard not to become a bit detached from his body. We might even say abstracted—removed, isolated. It was a known process, part of the way TB could take hold of a man's character along with his body, making its victims a bit dry or cold inside, the heat of sexuality raised in compensation for the loss. These crevices of cold bespoke an essential mistrust, like scars or little warts grown in the heart. At the moment of their forming, it is only natural that a man would in some deep interior part of himself pull away, and Balanchine did too.

His life there, he told Kochno, was "rather sad," but he was reading the Russian historian Vasily Klyuchevski (purchased in Paris in a Soviet edition for sixty francs), the Bible, Dostoyevsky, and Pushkin, and he was "famous" there as a pianist and played for his fellow tuberculars in the evenings. "I want to buy the *Rite of Spring* record," he said, "with God himself as conductor." He had hope, he said in another letter, that his "old friends" (including "the kid" Lifar) would visit soon. It wasn't gay at the Grand Hôtel du Mont Blanc, but the view was "pure Picasso." And when Kochno came, could he please bring the white ointment in the drawer of Balanchine's night table? His lips, he explained, were cracked, and he was obliged to use butter to soften them. Then he drew arrows pointing to the hotel pictured on the stationery and wrote, "Here lies the body of Balanchine." He signed off with a few bars of music and an affectionate kiss. The friends never made it to Mont Blanc. There was no sign of Danilova either. He had only one companion: the wife of his knee surgeon, "a very nice and a rather intelligent lady," who was also a patient at Mont Blanc, and as they both improved, they walked together in the woods.[6] Ill and alone, George wrote to his mother and was saddened to receive nothing in return.

Finally, he made his way back down the mountain to Paris, healed enough and plump, to a different kind of bad news. When he presented himself at the stage door of the Paris Opera to resume his work there, he was refused entry by a guard. Lifar had since gotten himself appointed ballet master, and in a preemptive strike against George's greater talent, he had summarily barred him from the theater. Apparently, no one (including George) cared enough to object to this abject double cross. That was that, and George moved on.[7] Ever practical, and in need of money, he returned to the London music hall and finally accepted a job in Copenhagen setting old Ballets Russes dances for the Royal Danish Ballet. Faced with the iconic dances of Fokine and Massine—*Scheherazade, The Legend of Joseph, La Boutique Fantasque, The Three-Cornered Hat*—Balanchine rechoreographed them all: one way of getting past them. He was done with Diaghilev, he wrote to Kochno: "I did not plan on any continuation of the Diaghilev business. It is over for me."

Meanwhile, he disliked the orderly Danes and the quaint orthodoxies of the Danish Golden Age, and he immediately declared to the press that he had never heard of their revered ballet master, Mr. August Bournonville. In return, they declared that they had little interest in what they took to be the new-fangled plastique of his dances, including *Apollon Musagète*. "The people here are shit," he wrote to Kochno. "Nobody understands anything. Their heads are up their asses unless they see something resembling a sandwich." He did find a friend in Kjeld Abell, a young Danish set designer and director, interested in Meyerhold and Reinhardt. They had first met in Paris, and pictures show them suited with cigarettes in hand. His only other consolation was to buy himself a lime-green Willys-Knight sports car. "It's delightful and has a marvelous engine," he reported to Kochno, and George took the car with him when he returned to London for another music-hall gig.[8]

He was still intermittently sick, and although the TB had retreated, he apparently remained an active carrier and was not supposed to kiss or breathe too close to anyone. To make matters worse, he ended up back in the hospital in London with painful and mysterious boils on his back and found himself under the treatment of Diaghilev's old doctor. "I'm reading Anderson's fairy tales and cry, and pray to Botticelli hanging on my wall," he wrote to Kochno, adding, in an essential aspect of his character, "I don't take my temperature, instead I choreograph new dances." Once his health returned, he thought he might stay in England. "I'm very happy living in London," he reported, saying that he was going to the cinema a lot, listening to the "barbaric" English language (he finally enrolled in a beginner Berlitz course), and admiring the local girls.[9] Maynard Keynes was already involved in trying to bring Lydia's brother from Russia and hoped he might also secure papers for George, but he failed.[10] So George eventually took the Willys-Knight and bought himself passage on a boat back to France. When he arrived at the border, he was stopped and faced with heavy import fees. He didn't have the cash, and his Nansen passport (and poor grasp of English) made him a natural target for questioning, which triggered his fear of police and deportation. Without hesitation, he handed the car and keys *gratuit* to a surprised bystander and boarded the ship alone.

Hearing this story upon his return, Danilova angrily rejected the gift of lapis lazuli earrings he presented to her. In Russia, she coldly noted, lapis lazuli was a building material and had nothing to do with the kinds of jewelry she desired. Danilova could be haughty and icy, but she was also worried about her future. They had been through so much, and he kept throwing it all to the wind. He wasn't cold, exactly, but it was becoming clear that his heart did not translate love into the more usual ways that occupy a life. He had a different path that was not really a choice. He gave himself to women by making love to them in dances. It was in this sense a secondhand heart, or at least a heart once removed from the source. For a dancer, it was irresistible. For a woman, it was not quite enough.

Another thing: it turns out that it is possible to have a brilliant mind and a simple, almost childish heart. A bereft heart. The kind of heart that hides from the mind and really just wants to be left alone to love in a simple, detached way, without the pain or complication of insight. There was some of that in Balanchine's love for Danilova. Leave me alone; let me work. Keep your distance. I promise to send roses. But Danilova wanted to be taken care of, reassured, and pampered with beautiful things—the right beautiful things—and she thought she knew what they were. Expensive things that the deprivations and trying circumstances of childhood and youth had snatched away. I wanted security, she later sighed, and it was true that he didn't care. He didn't have an eye or a heart or even a stomach for those things. Or did he know very well that she would take the earrings and the car as a slight? He also had that—the capacity for quiet inner resentment—and he could be vengeful. The car was almost too revealing; he just wanted to drive away, to get away, but there was nowhere to get away to, and when the car became a burden, he simply left it. He and Choura had in any case grown apart when he was in the sanatorium. She didn't want another brush with death, and, besides, he was down, and who knew if he would be a successful artist again. So the fragile threads of childhood and exile that had brought them together dissolved. They didn't exactly split up; they just went their own itinerant ways. She sent him a letter, half-hoping he would step into the breach like a white knight and sweep her back. Instead, he waited, and then said stiffly that he agreed. In the end, they were more alike than they perhaps knew at the time: emotional orchids who preferred the thin air of their own inner environments. It was a strength, of sorts.[11]

George wanted to work on his own, but without money and resources, he was thrown back on the old Diaghilev networks, this time René Blum. Blum was tall, kind, and cultivated and probably the best chance anyone had to carry forward the work that Diaghilev had so abruptly abandoned. Raised in a large and prominent French Jewish family, Blum had deep ties to leftist politics and Parisian culture—his brother was Léon Blum, soon to be the first Socialist leader of France. René had defended the falsely accused Captain Alfred Dreyfus in the Dreyfus affair and been awarded the Croix de Guerre for his courage fighting at the Somme and for rescuing artworks before the bombing of Amiens Cathedral. He was involved in literature (including the early publication of Proust) and in cinema, theater, opera, and ballet. Since 1924 he had worked with Diaghilev in Monte Carlo staging dance and opera and producing theater, so when Diaghilev died, Blum was already in situ, and he moved quickly to secure funds for a new ballet company. By 1932 he was finally ready and hiring back key players from Diaghilev's old enterprise, including André Derain, Christian Bérard, Boris Kochno—and George Balanchine.[12]

George began as he always began: with the dancers. He told Choura, a bit cruelly, that at twenty-seven she was too old, much too old, for the company he had in mind. It was an old lover's slight, perhaps, but not really. The geology of her body—layered with Russia and all the events and theatrical airs she had absorbed since—was too complex. George wanted a clearer and cleaner horizon, trained but untried bodies, the younger and blanker the better. So he made the pilgrimage to his former colleague's large studio on the top floor of the old Olympia Music Hall, and greeting Madame Preobrazhenskaya warmly, he pulled up a chair in front of the mirrors to watch her advanced ballet class; he scouted too at the Chauve-Souris and other venues.

He eventually found three young dancers: Tamara Toumanova and Irina Baronova, both age thirteen, and Tatiana Riabouchinska, age fifteen. They were girls, really, but beautiful, even voluptuous, and as it turned out, not blank at all. They were the children of White Russian émigrés, and although they were still "babies," as the press liked to say, they too carried the strain of war and revolution inside them. Their stories were familiar: full of high-ranking imperial families, brothers and fathers who were shot, harrowing escapes made by cattle wagon or smuggled across borders into Romania, Shanghai, and finally Paris. Ballet was the old world they had lost, and it ordered their (and their mothers') broken lives.[13]

The dances Balanchine made for these "baby ballerinas," as the press dubbed them, are lost but seem to have been a curious mix of technical feats—the three gleefully spinning out bravura turns—and limpid poses showing them "bent sadly," as one recalled, like weeping willows draped across the stage, heads fallen in hands. "A ghostly assembly, going about its ghostly business away from the comprehension of men," as one critic put it. Balanchine's melancholy movements hung easily on their young bodies, and like little Alicia Marks before them, they were innocent of their own expressive capacities. They were not slim or boyish, after the Chanel-like fashion of the day, and Toumanova in particular had a full, womanly body and awkward grace. Balanchine knew how to exploit their weaknesses as well as their strengths—how to show the soft gullies of a body, a place or access point to feelings not fully conscious or in control. He had an instinct, gently, for the jugular. They just did what they were told, and he was careful not to spoil their effect by telling them anything more.

Instead, he pampered them like the children they were: Had they slept and eaten (he recommended horsemeat to their mothers)? Did they have the proper clothes? He rewarded them all with pastries when they rehearsed well, and Toumanova, whom he was a bit in love with, recalled receiving cherry chocolates from Pasquet and a jeweled Cartier watch. Balanchine gave her private lessons in a rented studio where scenery was stored, near the Terminus Hotel, and when she and her mother went to his apartment for lunch, he liked to make tomato juice—that's what they drink in America, he said. He liked her father too, and gave him beautiful editions of Pushkin as a gift. George even took Tamara to a ball, instructing her not to talk too much, especially about her pet rabbit. Kochno noted that it all felt a bit like a kindergarten, but on stage the girls were poignant and spectacular, beautiful women with childish minds.[14]

It was with Blum that George also first met and worked with the costume designer Barbara Karinska, who would become an intimate collaborator. Born Varvara Andryevna Zmoudsky in Kharkiv, Ukraine, Karinska was a solidly built woman with a square face tapered with a thin chin. She wore dark Chanel suits only and was partial to pillbox hats and large jewelry made of amethysts or religious tokens. Her father had been a wealthy textile merchant, and she had married a Socialist who died in the typhus epidemic after the war, leaving her with a small child. She later married the lawyer Nicholas Karinsky, but they lost each other in the chaos of the war and revolution. Slated somehow to become commissar of museums under the Bolsheviks, she fled instead in the 1920s with her daughter to Europe. She met Balanchine in a restaurant and was taken on by Blum to make costumes for (among others) the "baby ballerinas." She learned on the job, cutting through reams of tarlatan and working long hours in the basement "cave" of the Monte Carlo opera house as she taught herself her trade.[15]

Blum was not as authoritarian—or as visionary—as Diaghilev had been, and he made the serious mistake of partnering with Colonel Vassily de Basil, a charming but hardened Russian Cossack with a sketchy and largely invented past. Almost immediately, the "Gangster Colonel," as Blum came to call him, peremptorily invited Massine to replace Balanchine.[16] Blum was upset and loyal to Balanchine, but not strong enough to right the situation, and he in any case recognized Massine's superior reputation, not to mention the fact that Massine came with rights to some of Diaghilev's old sets and costumes. It was the Paris Opera and Lifar in another key, and Balanchine's reaction was the same. He avoided the confrontation and left. That was that, except that de Basil then turned around and tried to sue him for breach of contract, gnarling him in an unwanted legal dispute—another reason for wanting to be his own boss.

Unemployed again, he wrote to Kochno, who had left Blum too, sarcastically imitating Cocteau's notorious announcements for his parties with lavish decor and real lions: "Dear-you-who-hang-about-the-streets-of-Toulon-at-night-and-go-to-bullfights-instead-of-getting-to-work-creating-new-ballets-of-genius-Boris." George reported conspiratorially that he and Dmitriev were now sure that there was no future with Blum and de Basil, who in any case seemed set on resurrecting dead Russian ballets. "Now is the moment to start work in earnest. Return to Paris as soon as possible and I will follow you soon. . . . Then we'll start looking for work together."[17] With Kochno, he immediately set about raising money from Diaghilev's old clan—Misia Sert, Coco Chanel, and Cole Porter (who had a crush on Kochno), among others—and soon pulled together a small troupe of artists and dancers who were willing to work for almost nothing, many of them Diaghilev loyalists, including Derain, Bérard (who was by then Kochno's lover), Sauguet, Milhaud, the still "baby ballerina" Toumanova, and a few others.[18]

Balanchine was in his element and working hard in the studio every day, but in their enthusiasm, they quickly burned through what money they had and found themselves on the brink of bankruptcy before they had even had a chance to perform. Derain only half-jokingly suggested that they get a truck and perform outdoors like a commedia dell'arte troupe. Instead, someone brought Mr. Edward James to rehearsal. James was an eccentric and wealthy English dilettante, age twenty-four, with a taste for surrealism, and he impulsively agreed to take on the whole project and cover all its costs, including generous salaries for the artists. He wrote them a large check (more would follow) with one condition: that George make James's wife, the actress Tilly Losch, the star of the show.[19]

Tilly Losch was a Viennese dancer, the daughter of Russian Jews, and a strikingly sensual and charismatic performer. She had studied with Wigman and worked closely with Max Reinhardt in his epic baroque spectacles, most recently in the lead role of the Nun in the 1932 London revival of *The Miracle*. Balanchine had already worked with her in the London music halls, and while he resented James's amateurish artistic meddling, they were all grateful for his patronage, so he conceded. Kochno and James also approached Kurt Weill, who had already been in talks with Diaghilev and whose recent *Threepenny Opera* with the singer Lotte Lenya had been a runaway success in Paris.

Weill hesitated, but after Hitler took power in January 1933, he soon changed his mind. He had long been a target for the Nazis, who quickly moved to shut down his performances by official edict. Friends warned that he was high on the Gestapo's arrest list, and in March he drove to the French border, parked his car, and walked across on foot, carefully avoiding the German border guards. Lenya, his then wife, left the country too. Finding himself unexpectedly in Paris and in need of money, Weill gratefully accepted James's generous commission for a new ballet, *The Seven Deadly Sins*.

Already Balanchine was losing control. Weill wanted Cocteau to write the scenario, but when Cocteau refused, Weill convinced Bertolt Brecht to join. Brecht had also just fled Germany and wanted the libretto to compare Göring and the Reichstag fire to Nero and the burning of Rome, but he was overruled. The conductor Maurice Abravanel, a Sephardic Jew from a distinguished family of rabbinical scholars, had also recently left Berlin, and he too joined their venture. Weill's old collaborator Casper Neher arrived to create the sets and costumes. Balanchine's little troupe was beginning to look like a different kind of refugee entourage.[20]

Aiming high, James booked the company at Théâtre des Champs-Élysées, where Nijinsky's *Sacre du Printemps* had premiered, and notified the elegant Savoy Theatre that a London season would follow. To conform to the rules of the English theatrical unions, Balanchine hired several English dancers, who joined their ever-expanding troupe, Les Ballets 1933, in Paris for rehearsals. Even so, the troupe was small: just over a dozen dancers, and Balanchine had only a few months to assemble a tour de force of new ballets. The company worked long hours at the "black hole of Calcutta," as they called it, a sweltering, darkly lit studio in Paris with a linoleum floor and no ventilation (they later moved). George arrived every morning in neatly pressed black trousers and a white shirt and nodded as he sat down at the upright piano in the corner to begin class. He played jazz, classical, improvisation, and jumped up to give them steps and corrections. The barre was grueling, with unheard-of repetitions and physical demands. Fifty high-kicking grands battements on both (right and left) sides instead of the usual twelve was only one example of the paces he put them through as he pounded away at the piano. Toumanova wore rubber wraps, which supposedly took off water weight in sweat; after class she would stand in a large enamel basin, and they all watched as she unwrapped herself and the sweat poured off her body in rivers.[21]

The primary challenge, though, was *The Seven Deadly Sins*. In spite of their gratitude for work and escape from Hitler's rise, no one seemed to be on good terms. Brecht and Weill were already at odds and barely speaking, and Lenya and Weill were in the middle of a rancorous divorce. Neher was a bit too sympathetic with the Nazis for anyone's taste and spent his time complaining that Brecht's libretto was "literary trash." Losch and James had long since been at odds and the "gift" of Les Ballets 1933 was doing little to save their marriage (she would later accuse him of homosexuality; he would sue her for adultery with a Russian prince). Then there were artistic differences. Weill wrote to Brecht in June: "It's the usual chaos. Of course, a small clique has developed out of the devotees of the old Ballets Russes, for whom ours isn't 'ballet' enough, not enough 'pure choreography.' Because of that there have been tremendous fights for the past few days, and . . . though Balanchine is swaying between two factions, he's worked well and has found a style of performance that is very 'balletic' but still realistic enough."[22]

The Seven Deadly Sins began with a single image: two women, strangers but twins, weak, vulnerable, huddled together like outcasts under a single hooded cloak. A "double Tanagra," Balanchine said, referring to the ancient figurines of anonymous women wrapped in shawls and often buried with their owners.[23] The girls were Tilly and Lotte, who looked uncannily alike, and Balanchine saw them as alter egos: Anna 1 would be mute and a dancer, and Anna 2 would speak and sing for them both. What followed was an allegorical tale of the fall of Weimar, set in Louisiana, as the two Annas became embroiled in a twisted frenzy of greed, envy, lust, gluttony, and the rest. Weill's music was satirical and drew heavily on popular song and dance forms that jolted the action forward with propulsive rhythms, tense dissonance, and abrupt shifts between major and minor keys. For Balanchine, working with Tilly and Lotte—one Austrian, one German, both Jewish and deeply informed by Weimar musical and theatrical life—was a return to Berlin and the first months of his own émigré life. He naturally reached for cabaret, mannequin-like poses, and those Weimar "girl machines" with their "serial souls."[24] Kirstein found it "wiry but intense like a nightmare," with "a deliberate, shabby elegance, very German."[25]

The other new works Balanchine made for Les Ballets 1933—even the lightest—were dark. *Les Songes,* with a jazzy score by Milhaud and boxy costumes by Derain (difficult to move in), was the story of a nightmare; *Les Fastes*—more Derain, this time with a score by Sauguet—was inspired by the Etruscan festival of Lupercalia and featured pagan dances with buffoons and acrobats in huge body masks and a priest in a three-way headdress showing youth, maturity, and old age. There was an orgy and an "unpleasant and biting" undercurrent (Kirstein) inspired by funeral rites and the Tomb of the Triclinium in Tuscany. *L'Errante,* to Franz Schubert's *The Wanderer,* was about a woman in the last ten seconds of life—wearing a clinging green satin gown designed by Edward Molyneux (who dressed Greta Garbo and Marlene Dietrich), her feet tangled in it as she moved through memories until two and a half miles of white silk fell from the sky and swept her away. *Mozartiana,* to music by Tchaikovsky, was another funeral march—two men in black shouldering a pyre draped with a girl in white. The company also took on Nicolas Nabokov's *Job,* an ambitious oratorio with a libretto by Jacques Maritain and choreography by Massine.[26] In the program notes, Balanchine wrote that Les Ballets 1933 was not a theory or movement of art; it existed only to capture something of that particular year in their lives. And so it did.

Which did not make it a success. Reviews for Balanchine's new enterprise were mixed, and the reception of *The Seven Deadly Sins* in particular was difficult. Florentine Karp, a young Russian émigré who would later become Balanchine's doctor and a close friend, was there one night and recalled pro-Nazi demonstrators protesting the performance and shouting "Vive Hitler!" and "En bas les Juifs!"[27] In London the ballet was retitled "Anna-Anna" because the lord chamberlain didn't approve of a religious title for such a licentious work. Walter Gropius was in the audience and came backstage with disturbing reports of the situation in Germany.[28]

Meanwhile, competition was fierce: Blum and de Basil's company, featuring new dances by Massine, was in season too, and so was Lifar's Paris Opera Ballet. It was a kind of post-Diaghilev showdown—Lifar, Massine, and Balanchine—and Lincoln Kirstein was following it all and running excitedly back and forth between theaters, gossiping with anyone who knew anything about the ballet. He summed it up as "Les Ballets 1933 progressive, Monte Carlo, reactionary"; apparently Lifar didn't really figure. In the swirl of it all, Kirstein, who was still under the influence of the mystical Romola Nijinska, wrote in his diary, "We agreed that Balanchine was much less serious than Massine," whose ballets, he said, sent him into "ecstasy."[29] The writer Janet Flanner, who was reporting on the performances, told him that "Balanchine was down with his notebook at the Chatelet, right after [Massine's] *Presages.*"[30] Kirstein worried that Les Ballets 1933 had "too much choreography by one man," Balanchine, who was "no Fokine." "But," he continued, "it is where we want most to be; it does happen; it has a kind of brilliance."[31]

Balanchine's troupe couldn't keep up, and by the time the Savoy opening came, James was busing in workers from his country estate to paper the otherwise sparsely sold house. With Romola, Kirstein met Balanchine briefly one night and thought he looked exhausted and a bit ill. James insisted they bring in "stars" to boost sales, an idea that Balanchine hated. Suddenly, to Balanchine's intense annoyance, Lifar was there brandishing (as Kirstein put it) "his magnificent instrument and his lousy conceit."[32] But even that wasn't enough. Finally, after the company played for several nights to near-empty houses, James pulled out. On July 15, Les Ballets 1933 folded.

The next day, Balanchine put on a fresh gray-flannel suit and went to lunch with Kirstein. They had seen each other a few days before at a party at Kirk and Constance Askew's (Kirk had studied art at Harvard, and their bohemian salons in London and New York drew artists and the literati). Balanchine had arrived with the dancer Diana Gould and the young choreographer Frederick Ashton, and he and Kirstein settled into a long conversation (in French) about the state of ballet and the possibility of an American company. Balanchine had been "charming," but also forthcoming and intense about his own ambition, and it was this conversation they now continued over lunch.

Balanchine only wanted to do new work, he explained, aspirating through his teeth as he spoke, and he emphasized that one must never revive anything. Dancing is like butterflies, a breath, a memory, then gone. *L'Errante* was already dead, he said, and *Prodigal Son*, even Lifar's stunning entrance on his knees, was vieux jeu now. Petipa was "intolerable," and the nineteenth-century legend Marie Taglioni would look ridiculous to the modern eye. Striking out his only competitor, he assured Kirstein that Massine's dance to Tchaikovsky's Fifth Symphony was unmusical and shouldn't be done; besides, Massine was old (nearly forty!) and didn't have good dancers. Kirstein was enchanted and noted that Balanchine did not possess a single photo or clipping of anything he had ever done. The past was for him dead. Kirstein asked if dance notation was useful, but Balanchine said: "Not really." It was all memory. "Nijinsky notated *Le Sacre*, but couldn't remember it the next week." Balanchine said he had learned the Stepanov notation method in school, but he could only compose with flesh and blood before him like a sculptor with clay, putting off here, taking on there. As for technique, "An American girl in Montmartre could do 200 fouettés, but what of it?" James and Losch, for their part, were "hysterical" and de Basil was a disaster—dishonest, cooking the books, a "voleur Russe" who was ridiculously suing him for having left the company—and now he was being sued again, this time by the hysterical James.

He was moving on and was planning to join Stravinsky and André Gide to make a new *Persephone* with sixty boys' voices for Ida Rubinstein, a wealthy Russian émigré dancer who had built a company around—herself. He also had an idea for a big new erotic ballet, he said. He had perhaps strayed too far choreographically with Diaghilev, he reflected, and he also wanted to return to "the uninterrupted melodic line of folk-song, Tchaikovsky ballets, and eighteenth century music." He missed the refinement and simplicity of classical form, the "elimination" of *Apollon Musagète*, and the ways that a more distant past could help to wipe the slate clean and start anew.

True, Balanchine was consumptive, as his aspirating lisp alarmingly conveyed, and a friend warned Kirstein that Balanchine had only a couple of years to live. But Kirstein thought that might be enough to make a "real start." He saw in Balanchine a man "brought up during the Revolution [who had] been so sick that . . . one has the feeling about him of a desperate, unhurried but terribly compacted, directed activity." Kirstein suggested Hartford, where his friend Chick Austin was opening a new museum for modern art. The museum could be a home, Kirstein told Balanchine, and he excitedly pulled out a map of the United States and pointed to the spot. Ignoring the details—Balanchine had no idea what "Hartford" even meant—Balanchine said he could bring Toumanova and her partner and of course her mother, who could cook for them all. He could do wonders, he said, with twenty girls and five men: "Americans have great potential . . . and must be made to love the music and love the dancing. . . . They have spirit and could be touched off into fire." He wanted to come to America, he said; it had been his life dream. Europe was over.[33]

It was a crucial moment. Consider the counterfactuals: Balanchine could have pushed for the Paris Opera job instead of letting Lifar have it, but he let it go. He could have pushed back when de Basil fired him, but he let that go too. And when Kirstein suggested Hartford, Balanchine might very well have dismissed the whole idea as a crazy American adventure with uncertain backing in a small town he had never heard of—which is exactly what it was. He could have stayed in Europe, where he finally had a name and a French carte d'identité and could at least find work.[34] But he didn't. We could say that he got lucky, that he was given a ticket out just in time, that he had an instinct for countries and continents in collapse, that it was the hand of fate or God, or that for once he was not caught in the jaws of history. A better explanation might be personality. He watched, he waited, he let things happen to him. He didn't push, and he didn't encumber himself. He was always ready to walk away and move on. Besides, his body wasn't promising a long life. He already "should have died" once in Russia and again at the Mont Blanc sanatorium. So when the time came, he went. He may have thought he was finally going to America, but really he was entering a new world: Lincoln.

AMERICA

Chapter 9

LINCOLN

The difficulty of living inside his own body had begun shockingly early. Lincoln Kirstein came into the world with a botched circumcision, which led with terrifying speed to septicemia, emergency surgery, and near death. This "unholy inheritance," as he later put it, and his mother's subsequent fearful overprotectiveness, accentuated his already ingrown sense of physical vulnerability.[1] In a rash moment at the age of twelve, as if to be finally done with this difficult start, he took his mother's nail scissors and cut off a last offending lock of flesh or scar tissue crowding his groin. It was a grueling episode he later recorded with characteristic deadpan.[2] The imposing six-feet-three-inch, 250-pound body (all bone) that grew up around him in the years to come surrounded him like a fortress. On top, his brilliant, brooding mind weighed so heavily that his neck and spine seemed eventually to curve and hump under the burden. A "child ogre," an acquaintance called him, and it was undeniable that there was something heaped and rocky about this outer shell.[3] He couldn't quite get comfortable inside. It was in part a desire to free himself from his own physical form that drew Lincoln to dance.

His mind was craggy too. He was brilliant, almost too brilliant, and his intellect was steep and fast-moving but rarely elegant. Even at school, his instructors noted that his thoughts raced alarmingly and recommended an atmosphere of discipline and drilling to tame his veering imagination.[4] Later, bristling with opinions and judgments, he did not suffer fools and was famous for his "widows"—friends suddenly abandoned for months or years for no apparent reason other than that Lincoln was bored or they had lost their usefulness. The trivia of everyday life didn't have much place in his heated mind, and he was known to abruptly stand up and walk out in the middle of a lunch, leaving his mystified guest at the table to finish his meal alone. It was not that Lincoln was socially unaware—he knew how to move in the polite and monied circles that were his habitat from birth, and his intensity had a certain charm. But his mind, like his body, could be disturbingly erratic, leaving him at the mercy of the manic-depressive cycles and bouts of mental illness that periodically afflicted him (Lincoln's "crazies," Balanchine called them),[5] leading at times to complete physical breakdown, institutionalization, straitjackets, electric shock therapy, the body and brain gone badly awry. He craved authority and submission—even humiliation—anything to subdue his febrile inner states. Ballet provided relief. It was everything that he was not—beautiful, graceful, ordered, harmonious—but also many things he very much was, or yearned for: erotic, sensual, pure artifice.

Even at a young age, Lincoln found dancing more than an escape; it seemed to offer another way of life. The life he had been given, a bit like the body he lived in, did not quite fit. Born in 1907, he had German and Jewish roots, and his parents were the children of émigrés—a tailor, a lens grinder, a wet nurse. His father, Louis, had a scrappy start, but after a string of failed enterprises, he had finally gone into business in Boston with the Filene brothers at the new Filene's Department Store, a venture which made him a wealthy man. He took his place as a prominent figure in the local Jewish community and in the city's wider political life, although as a Jew he was never fully accepted by its blue-blood elite. During World War I, when Lincoln was a child, Louis's influence and ambition expanded further still. He proudly served at a high government level procuring uniforms for the army and later involved himself in federal policy to restore European industry. He made sure he was well-connected: close to Louis Brandeis and Felix Frankfurter, friendly with Calvin Coolidge, and later privileged with a direct line to Franklin

D. Roosevelt, all of which would matter greatly for Lincoln and George's ballet enterprise.

The family home was formal in a high-bourgeois Victorian style, and Lincoln spent his early years surrounded by the lavish material evidence of his father's success: blue velvet curtains, gold wallpaper, black-and-gold lacquer furniture, vermilion satin, bronze busts posed on ample dark wood bookcases. There was a silver Rolls-Royce chauffeured by Dante, the son of Nicola Sacco of "Sacco and Vanzetti" (the Italian American anarchists convicted and executed after an unfair trial during the "Red Scare"), whose cause Louis had championed. Lincoln dutifully attended Saturday school and high holidays with Louis at Temple Israel, the local Reform synagogue; though more affecting to him, especially after the Nazis, were his grandmother's Hebrew prayer books and German Bible readings, her love of Heine and Goethe, her Old World marzipan and twisted pretzels. His mother was uninterested in her Jewish roots and dismissive of religion generally; "it's all theater," she liked to say.[6] So, in a way, was their household: the stagy decor and draped interiors, Louis's set-piece Anglophilia and penchant for military parades, the spectacle and requirements of his hard-won respectability and high public life—all of which Lincoln would both moodily reject and reproduce in his own extravagant, theatrical style. In keeping with the family scenario, his education was gold-plate: Exeter and Harvard, except that he flunked out of Exeter (where he took to reminding himself every morning that he would die that day, or that if he forgot to remember this sobering fact, he would surely expire; bored, he pasted a picture of Freud on his mirror and told his schoolboy friends that this white-bearded gentleman was his Austrian grandfather, a stunt that did not go over well with the authorities).[7] As for Harvard, Lincoln failed the entrance exam twice before finally securing a place.[8]

The Ballets Russes was one of the forbidden luxuries of his youth and a sign of a more unleashed physical world outside his family's formal purview. The company's performances in Boston just after World War I had been strictly prohibited by his mother: too licentious. She was not alone. Ballet, with its open sensuality, did not integrate easily into a puritan New England landscape, but finally, a permitting, probably gay uncle took Lincoln to see Anna Pavlova in New York, five nights in a row. In these memorable performances, he joined the ranks of audiences astounded by this small, birdlike woman, who had the mysterious capacity to send an entire theater into a trancelike ecstasy (when she died in 1931, scores of young women reportedly fell spontaneously into a state of hysteria). He saw Isadora Duncan—another cult figure—and although he liked her less, the free-form and rhythmic dances he learned at Camp Timanous in his youth lifted him, he said, into a kind of "rapture."[9] Vaslav Nijinsky, whose dancing he never witnessed, became a lifelong artistic and erotic passion, one of many homosexual loves, and Lincoln pored over lush images of the great dancer in books and magazines and would later compose his own lavishly illustrated monograph on this beloved object of desire.

Diaghilev became an obsession. Even before Lincoln stumbled onto the impresario's funeral cortege in Venice in 1929, his own life, consciously or otherwise, began uncannily to track this ghostly twin. He would later pay tribute to Diaghilev's constant, almost haunting presence in his life by permanently placing the impresario's visiting card in a dish in the foyer of his own home. Like Diaghilev, Lincoln wanted to be and do everything. He thought he might be a craftsman and apprenticed himself to a stained-glass-window painter; he attempted a novel and published poetry; he painted; he took up dancing and even considered, for a brief deluded moment, becoming a dancer.[10] At Harvard as an undergraduate in 1927, he poured himself into founding, with Varian Fry (thanks to Louis's generous financial support), the literary journal *Hound and Horn,* devoted to bringing the next new generation of poets, writers, and critics to the fore—just as Diaghilev, as a young man, had founded *The World of Art*.

Hound and Horn was inspired in part by the writings of T. S. Eliot, and in those years, Lincoln and Varian were "living" *The Waste Land*. The poet's essay "Tradition and the Individual Talent" became for Lincoln a kind of "breviary,"[11] and Eliot's argument against art as mere individual self-expression (me and my feelings) and for a depersonalized and classically based art (a submission of "me" to tradition and a higher authority) seemed to articulate everything Lincoln believed in—and to lead him naturally by his own path to Diaghilev and dance. *Hound and Horn*'s roster, a sign of Lincoln's wide-ranging taste and inspired by a potent mix of intellectual and sexual desire, would include James Agee, Walker Evans, Edmund Wilson, Glenway Wescott, Paul Valéry, Sergei Eisenstein, James Joyce, Gertrude Stein, John Dos Passos, John Cheever, William Carlos Williams, e. e. cummings, Wallace Stevens, Roger Sessions, Ezra Pound (when he and Lincoln fell out, Pound dubbed the magazine "Ditch and Bugle")—and Lincoln himself.[12]

Finally, like Diaghilev, but for reasons of his own, Lincoln came to ballet through art. At Harvard he studied art history and was working on a thesis on the ecstatic paintings of El Greco. Lincoln also had a serious interest in modern art, but rather than simply studying or enjoying this interest, he felt a compulsion to do something. In 1928, during a dinner at the elegant Shady Hill mansion near Cambridge of the art historian Paul Joseph Sachs, Lincoln and two undergraduate friends proposed a new museum: the Harvard Society for Contemporary Art.

The friends were John Walker II and Eddie Warburg. Walker, the scion of a wealthy Pittsburgh family, had been paralyzed from a childhood illness and spent his youth in a wheelchair roaming the Metropolitan Museum of Art—not far from his doctors. When Lincoln heard that Walker's rooms at Harvard were covered in reproductions of Picasso, Vlaminck, and Grant, he introduced himself. Eddie, soon to be a lynchpin in Lincoln's life, was the son of Felix Warburg of the immensely rich and civic-minded Jewish banking family from Hamburg. Felix was a founder of the Kuhn, Loeb & Co. investment bank in New York, and Eddie had grown up in the palatial family mansion on Fifth Avenue (now the Jewish Museum). Unlike his practical and ambitious father, however, Eddie was scattered and emotionally fragile and had no idea what he wanted to do with his life—not to mention his tremendous wealth. He had a taste for modern art (against family advice, he had purchased Picasso's *Blue Boy*) and attached himself to Lincoln, who possessed an abundance of the intellectual energy and confidence Eddie himself lacked.

Lincoln's idea for a new museum found enough support that the friends rented rooms at Harvard and opened in 1929 with an impressive series of exhibitions: Alexander Calder's *Circus,* Buckminster Fuller's Dymaxion House, Chaim Soutine, Isamu Noguchi, Giorgio de Chirico, Max Beckmann, George Grosz, Paul Klee, Oskar Kokoschka. Diaghilev had almost single-handedly brought Russian art to Paris; Lincoln set out to almost single-handedly import modern European art to America. The Harvard Society's activities depended on his tireless Diaghilev-like backstage maneuvering—letters, telegrams, visits, phone calls, crisis management—as he, Warburg, and Walker mined their considerable contacts and became adept at shipping paintings via the Railway Express Agency or stowing canvases from various private collections in the back of Warburg's coupe and driving them back to Cambridge, to be hung on the gallery walls by night.

Their Harvard teacher Paul Sachs (of the prominent German Jewish banking family of Goldman-Sachs) taught a seminal "museum course" aimed at training a new generation of curators, and his students also included Alfred H. Barr Jr., founding director of the new Museum of Modern Art (MoMA) in New York in 1929; Charles Everett "Chick" Austin, who took over Hartford's Wadsworth Athenaeum Museum of Art in 1927 and soon turned it into a leading house of modernism; Julian Levy, who would open his influential gallery in Manhattan in 1931; and the architect Philip Johnson. Walker would later direct the National Gallery of Art in Washington; and Warburg would soon join the Junior Advisory Committee of the newly founded MoMA and become an important patron. It was a formidable group, many of whom would become key supporters of Balanchine.[13]

Soon after Diaghilev died in Venice, Lincoln published an astounding and providential essay in *Hound and Horn*: "The Diaghilev Period." It was an assessment, but also an announcement, as if the death of this man he had never met released his own pent-up ambition and desire. Lincoln called Diaghilev a great "synthesizer" and "catalyst," who had helped dancers and choreographers capture "that living, tremendous exuberance of human divinity" that could also be found in artists such as El Greco, Mozart, Racine, and Bernini. Lincoln now brushed aside Massine as a "clever" satirist and predicted that the future of dance lay instead with the "revivified, purer, cleaner classicism" of George Balanchine, whose work Lincoln had by then seen on summer visits to Europe. By this he did not mean an old or outdated nineteenth-century style of classical ballet. Nor did he have in mind what he later called the "ritual suicides" of ballerinas in Romantic ballets such as *Giselle*.[14] Rather, he said, Balanchine was using ballet's "rigid idiom" not to uphold its "Catholic absolute dogma" but precisely in order to "flout it." He found George's dances spare, remote, and at times tragic in ways, he said, "which can only be described as Attic."[15] The future of dancing, he felt, was threatened by the "reforms" of modern dancers (by which he seemed to mean everything from Wigman to Martha Graham) prone to a subjective and "aimless emotional vacuity, the appalling facility of loose gesture under the guise of free dancing." What the world needed, he concluded, was "a new Diaghilev" who might "save dancing . . . from a facile oblivion." What the world needed, in other words, was Lincoln Kirstein.[16]

By then he was writing everything down.[17] Lincoln kept diaries intermittently from the time he was a teenager, but in the years between 1930 and 1937, he dramatically intensified his efforts to record the details of his life. He clearly thought that at least some of what he was doing would matter, and he seemed to know—and he was right—that what he wrote would be the best account we have of this period in Balanchine's life and his own. The diaries are large black books, covered edge-to-edge on every page in Lincoln's tight, black-ink script, no paragraph breaks, as dense and imposing as the man himself. They stand as testimony to the impressive and exhausting pace of his activities in these years, and to the driven and anxious state of his mind as he tried to find a way to make dance his life. It is worth recalling that as he wrote from day to day, Lincoln had no idea what in the world would come of it all.

The first page of each book begins with a dramatic proviso: "To be destroyed unread in case of death." It was a warning of his candidness, especially perhaps about his explicitly articulated homosexual activities, but also concerning Balanchine's difficult early American years. He was telling secrets to himself, and maybe (as diaries do) to us, but not yet. He excerpted—and freely embellished—sections of his diaries in his own subsequent writings, but he withheld the unexpurgated black books for a long time: until Balanchine was dead. Then Lincoln handed them to the critic Richard Buckle, who was embarking on a biography of the choreographer. He intended it as a corrective: he wanted Buckle, and the world, to know that there had not been a grand plan, and no "blinding Pauline dream" had led him to Balanchine. Instead, "it was one step at a time all the way. I was no visionary, but merely a sly fellow playing at an exciting game."[18]

A decade later, as he himself was nearing death, he deposited the diaries at the New York Public Library, for all to see. It was another corrective, but also an admission. He had a powerful inner compulsion to make a mark. "Make your own comment," he once bluntly told a young dancer taking a new role,[19] and one of his marks and purposes in life, beginning with the diaries that he made sure did not go "unread," was to provide a text and a story for Balanchine and the ephemeral art of dancing, which otherwise had none. Balanchine left almost nothing. He was a disappearing act; Lincoln was his self-appointed scribe. In the years to come, he would devote himself in countless essays, articles, and books—beginning with the diaries themselves—to explaining to anyone who would listen what Balanchine was doing, why ballet mattered, and how it all came to be. His role as scribe, as he must have appreciated, also gave him the last word.

Becoming a "new Diaghilev" required study and self-application, and Lincoln energetically applied himself—and chronicled it all, from the grandeur of his vast and chaotic ambition to the depths of his craterous loneliness and chronic self-doubt. On his summer tours to Europe in the late 1920s and early 1930s, de rigueur for his social set, he packed his days with ballet and pursued everyone he could think of who had anything to do with dancing: Maynard Keynes and Lydia Lopokova, Duncan Grant, Leonard Woolf from the Bloomsbury set, Serge Lifar (a "small dark, slightly oily and compact" man, who received Lincoln while lounging in bed in a red bathing suit; he "pulled a corner of a yellow puff up, out of modesty, to his chin. . . . I found he would be of no use to me at all"),[20] Christian "Bebé" Bérard (fat, queer, coarse, Wildean and humorous, who also received visitors from bed, dressed in black pajamas, traces of opium all around), Tamara Toumanova (and her inevitable *maman*), Kochno ("disdainful, getting bald; in a way horrid"[21] but close to Diaghilev, Massine, and Balanchine), Stravinsky (a "lizard-rat"),[22] Benois, Derain, Berman, Tchelitchew, Brancusi, Genet, and Dalí (who "used to sleep with crumbs under his foreskin to induce dreams").[23] Lincoln debated ballet, art, and literature with Philip Johnson, Alfred H. Barr, Virgil Thomson, and e. e. cummings. They were all interested in dance, but not the way he was. They saw and talked; he pushed himself deeper and deeper, hunting out dance archives and libraries across Europe, stuffing himself with facts, figures, history, gossip, anything he could find that might illuminate this ephemeral art. His search was intentional, fanatical almost, but also lonely and far-fetched, and there was something haphazard and wandering in these long and impatient European days. We often find him back at his hotel, depressed and exhausted: worries, bad food ("dined miserably . . . on putrid pork sausage . . . worried about the ballet"),[24] shifty nights, terrible dreams. He had the minor but telling habit of cutting his toenails painfully short, a kind of punishing compulsion that seemed to encompass his feelings of smallness and self-doubt; that great heavy hulk of a man sitting alone on the edge of a bed lamenting to his diary at the end of a taxing day in which he had done more than most people would consider humanly possible, "as usual cut my toenails too short, so my little toes hurt."[25]

His mind spun in these years—in all years—from dance to sex to art, parallel tracks running through his brain. He slept early on with his brother George, an event that filled him with ambivalence, competition, delight, and disgust, and he devoted himself from a young age to cruising, slumming, sailors, and dancers. A long line of lustful homoerotic infatuations and often achingly unrequited relationships occupied his fantasy, and his wide-ranging circle of homosexual and bisexual artists, writers, composers, and dancers set a pattern for his life. He was primarily gay, but he also had intimate relationships with women, and in 1941 he would embark on a lifelong and complicated marriage with the depressive and long-suffering painter Fidelma Cadmus, sister of Paul Cadmus—one of Lincoln's gay friends and an artist whose homoerotic paintings he collected and admired. She was his one and only wife—his fond letters to her show that he did love and depend deeply on her, but there was plenty of misery too, as she somehow abided his ongoing affairs and the ways he brought his male lovers home and into their troubled life.

Lincoln would never stop falling in love with dancers. He would even later claim that he owed his decision to commit his life to ballet to his overwhelming erotic infatuation with the dancer Lew Christensen, a blond Apollonian beauty. His correspondence, like his diaries, is full of dirty fantasies and insinuations, and he liked to sign off with intimacies such as "horror pants," "naughtykins," "miss pussy," or "nasty pants." The record of his shame, however, is at least as revealing as the details of his desires. "In the middle of the night," he wrote in 1932, "I could not sleep. . . . I boiled with the shame of my wastes and losses in a violent mental & spiritual pain, promising the torturing gods to lead a life of unique density. . . . No more nights of cruising around, learn to box, write my book all over and finally wrestling with the angels, slept."[26] He knew, of course, that his homosexuality placed him in a distinguished lineage, stretching from antiquity right through to (pre-Lydia) Maynard Keynes and the "higher sodomy" of the Bloomsbury set—not to mention the notorious sex life of Nijinsky's once-lover and his own mentor, Serge Diaghilev. Desire and dance were part of the same life force—greater than I—that swept all before it, and the homosexual culture around Lincoln would prove a vital force in the company's culture and success. It was all part of the "life of unique density" that he aspired to, and sex was to him primary, secretive, and ephemeral, apart from his work in the world but also something that drove it. Everything—and nothing at all.

Lincoln was drawn to art, eroticism, and ballet the way he was drawn to priests, magic, mystery plays, and High Church spectacle—anything that might satisfy his craving, as a friend put it, for "immersion or revelation."[27] His father tried to ground him and leveled pointed reminders that he would always be a "Jew-boy," a fact affirmed by the rampant anti-Semitism all around him—not least in his "Fascist friend" Phil Johnson, whose homoerotically tinged sympathies for Hitler and the brownshirts angered and appalled Lincoln.[28] He would never be not-Jewish, but he also made an art of posing, as he put it, as "a sort of false gentile."[29] Partly this was instrumental—he knew what it took to get around in elite Waspy circles—but Lincoln's ambivalence also ran deeper. He later explained, "The God in whom I believe is neither Jewish nor Christian; all a Jewish God means to me is the fact that He chose a people to be His people. I cannot think He chose one over another. That they were elected to suffer seems to have been true, but it seems to me that salvation is possible to all, even outside the Greek Orthodox or the Roman Church. Otherwise the question of the Jewish vs. the Christian God: c'est de la literature."[30] Which meant he was a kind of "heretic," he said, and his Jewishness seemed to function in his mind like a good wife, who stayed quietly at home while he roamed promiscuously through what he later called "all my religious periods."[31]

All his religious periods started early: his undergraduate thesis at Harvard was on the ecstatic paintings of El Greco, with their Orthodox Byzantine iconography and emanation of divine light. In the coming years, Lincoln would immerse himself in Islamic Sufism, Zen Buddhism, Theosophy, and above all, the teachings of the Russian spiritualist G. I. Gurdjieff—a major influence in his life. He was strongly attracted to Roman Catholicism and would convert for a time. He even considered Orthodoxy, and his enduring interest in theology and the occult was another bridge to Balanchine, who also ranged widely from his Orthodox base. It was Lincoln, for instance, who would later introduce George to Sufi poetry.

Gurdjieff was a shady figure of deliberately misty origins. He was Armenian Greek, maybe, and a self-appointed guru of spiritualism who had taught in Moscow, where his students included P. D. Ouspensky—another spiritualist, much admired by Balanchine. Gurdjieff belonged to the world of Soloviev and Blok and to the Theosophy, Rosicrucianism, Kabbalah, Gnosticism, and Madame Blavatsky that had filled Balanchine's youth. Like them, Gurdjieff was obsessed with the fourth dimension, eternal recurrence, sex, immortality, and how to "wake up" sleepwalking people from the numbing routines of daily life.[32] He had fled Russia during the revolution, dragging his followers into the chaotic flow of émigrés by a familiar path: Crimea, Constantinople, Tiflis, Berlin, and finally Paris, where in 1922, near Fontainebleau, he established the Institute for the Harmonious Development of Man.

Guests at this strange retreat, Lincoln among them, were immersed in a lavish oriental decor and submitted to a punishing course of fasting, sleep deprivation, manual labor (carpentry, farming, chores)—and, above all, rhythmic movement exercises and performances that were the heart of Gurdjieff's spiritual practice. These were a mix of supposed devotional movements derived from Christian monks, whirling dervishes, village work dances, gymnastic exercises performed in the caves in Kafiristan, and whatever else Gurdjieff had to hand and memory, constituting a body of practices later known simply as the "Movements." Gurdjieff called himself a dancer and had a cultlike following among White Russians and Americans living in interwar France—including the writers Upton Sinclair, Gertrude Stein, Ezra Pound, and Katherine Mansfield. Diaghilev, who also knew Gurdjieff, even briefly considered staging some of his dances. There was a strong New York following too, and Kirstein knew he had been marked as a "rich boy" (one of Gurdjieff's notorious "sheep to be shorn"), but there was something about the sexualized theatricality of Gurdjieff's enterprise, and the genuinely demanding physicality of the dances, that seduced him. Similarly, in discussing religion with a friend entering the rabbinate, he noted that "I have literally no concept of a religious experience . . . although I daresay if what is called 'aesthetic perception' was investigated, it might ultimately come to what he calls 'religion.'" And although Lincoln eventually rejected Gurdjieff as too nihilistic, the experience marked him, and took him into the Russian strains of thought that had also formed George Balanchine.[33]

In New York, where he settled after Harvard, he continued his pursuit of the dance. To the astonishment of family and friends, who couldn't quite fathom his ballet obsession, he sought out Michel Fokine and spent hours questioning and talking to the old, disenchanted ballet master. Offering himself as an unlikely disciple, he climbed the narrow staircase to Fokine's grungy dance studio on Riverside Drive to find himself the only man in a dance class full of glamorous chorus girls and ancient overly made-up ballerinas. ("You have a lot of nerve!" one remarked admiringly.)[34] Baffled by the complicated routines and unable to string the steps together in his awkward and untrained body, he nonetheless persisted. "Dancing," he confessed to his diary, "makes me feel marvelous."[35] He spent hours interviewing Fokine and (in 1934) produced a book about him. Picking still further through the remains of Diaghilev's world, he was writing a book about Nijinsky ("so drunk on the Nijinsky idea couldn't stop talking about it")[36] and spending untold hours helping the scheming and unstable Romola Nijinska, who was writing her own version of her husband's life and was herself lost in mysticism. He attended performances by just about everyone in Depression-era New York, including Kurt Jooss, Massine, Wigman, and the German dancer Herold Kreutzberg ("all hysteria, madness, post-war German expressionism, or else arrogantly and too elegantly homosexual—a tulip tied with a baby blue ribbon to his forehead").[37]

Meanwhile, he was also curating shows at MoMA and carefully negotiating his leftist taste, for example, in *The Post War World*, his 1932 mural show of American artists, which several members of the board found offensively "Communistic."[38] Lincoln valiantly defended the artists, but he was careful not to compromise his relationships with money and power. He blustered, threatened, backed down, and shuttled between the angry artists and MoMA committees, Barr, the board, and lawyers until Nelson Rockefeller finally worked things out.

He was also involved in the uproar over the Diego Rivera mural in the atrium of the new Rockefeller Center the following year. When Rivera placed a large image of Lenin at the center of the mural, the Rockefellers asked him kindly to remove it. He refused. Lincoln worked hard to reconcile the warring parties until Nelson finally ordered in the bulldozers and had the mural destroyed. Seeing that the fight had been lost, Lincoln fell back to Nelson, "the question being; how much chance do I think I have to use his resources."[39] He was becoming single-minded: "I wd use anything to hand as a weapon to get the ballet," he told a colleague at MoMA in the fall of 1932.[40]

His sensibility, even in art, revolved around "the human body in action," which both defined and deformed his aesthetic judgment.[41] In these years, he personally supported (and pressed Barr and MoMA to collect) art from such a bewildering range of artists, from the minor homoerotic paintings of Paul Cadmus or sculptures of Gaston Lachaise ("the glorification and revivification of the human body," Lincoln rhapsodized)[42] to Pavel Tchelitchew's surrealist paintings of exposed innards and bloodied veins and Elie Nadelman's fine Tanagra-like figurines and folk art. Lincoln was also seriously involved with film, and even there, the body was all. He tried hard (and failed) to save Sergei Eisenstein's *Que Viva Mexico!* when its funders abruptly withdrew. He admired the filmmaker for many reasons, but especially because "Eisenstein above all others," he wrote of his footage of ritualized native dances, "understands the moving human body in its stylized lyricism."[43] When Barr invited Lincoln to preside over the creation of a film department at MoMA in 1932, Lincoln plotted to bring all the arts together under a single roof—the museum as total theater: Eisenstein to head film, music under Leopold Stokowski, drama under he wasn't sure who, and dance under Balanchine—or "me."[44]

Or "me" was a clue to Lincoln's heart. He envisioned a new kind of ballet with American artists and themes, with himself as that American Diaghilev curating and commissioning new work. He wanted a ballet of *Uncle Tom's Cabin*, for example, and asked e. e. cummings to write a scenario and Virgil Thomson a score. He imagined dances about Custer's Last Stand, *Moby-*

Dick, Pocahontas, and the defense of Richmond.[45] To bring these ideas to the stage, he had tried and failed to get Nelson Rockefeller to house a ballet company at Rockefeller Center. He had schemed unsuccessfully to place it at Radio City Music Hall.[46] He continued to press MoMA, but Barr was skeptical. He got a more sympathetic response from Chick Austin in Hartford. Chick loved the Ballets Russes—"the most intense emotional experience of my life"—and (like Lincoln) thought a museum should be a palace of the arts.[47] Chick had the added flair of being a skilled magician, and he mixed serious exhibitions with Gatsby-style parties and art extravaganzas held in the museum's galleries. (He later ran a circus.) Wadsworth already had impressive programs in contemporary film and music. Maybe Chick would like to add ballet?[48]

When Balanchine said yes to the idea of a new American ballet in the summer of 1933 at his meeting with Lincoln in London, Lincoln knew he had arrived, and every muscle and nerve in his being suddenly focused on a single goal. What followed was more like a conversion than a decision. He returned to his hotel that evening and wrote, in his tight and urgent hand, what can only be described as a prophetic sixteen-page letter. At this crucial moment, he did not reach for Barr or Rockefeller or even (for the moment) Warburg. ("[He] is being psychoanalyzed and feels I got too much out of him for Lachaise etc.," he confided to Muriel Draper; "I can't get this from Dad on acct. of the H and H. Would Alice de la Mar [DeLamar] be interested? Would Stokowski?")[49] He aimed lower and surer, reaching for the man who might help him most: Chick Austin.

> Batts Hotel
> Dover Street, W1
> July 16, 1933
>
> Dear Chick:
>
> This will be the most important letter I will ever write you. . . . My pen burns my hand as I write: words will not flow into the ink fast enough. We have a real chance to have an American ballet within 3 yrs. time. . . .

> Do you know Georges Balanchine? If not he is a Georgian called Georgi Balanchavidze. He is, personally, enchanting—dark, very slight.... He is 28 yrs old—a product of the Imperial schools. He has split from the Prince de Monaco as he wants to proceed, with new ideas and young dancers instead of going on with the decadence of the Diaghilev troupe, which I assure you, although it possesses many good if frightfully overworked dancers, is completely worn out in artistic-commercial....
>
> Balanchine is socially adorable—but he hates the atmosphere both of society as such (Lifar loves it) and the professional Broadway Theatre. For the first he would take 4 white girls and 4 white boys—about sixteen yrs old and 8 of the same, negros. They would be firmly taught in the classical Idiom—not only from exercises but he would start composing ballets at once so that they would actually learn by doing. As time went on he would get younger children from 8 yrs. on.... He could start producing within 3 months. Now, if you could work it he could use your small theatre: a department of the museum as school of dancing could be started.... Balanchine is willing to devote all his time to this for 5 yrs. He believes the future of Ballet lies in America as do I. I see a great chance for you to do a hell of a lot here.

"This school," Lincoln tumbled on,

> can be the basis of a national culture as intense as the great Russian Renaissance of Diaghilev. We must start small. But imagine it—we are exactly as if we were in 1910, offered... a maître de ballet as good as Fokine—who would also be delighted to cooperate. It will not be easy. It will be hard to get good young dancers willing to stand or fall by the company. No first dancers. No stars. A perfect esprit de corps.

As a *museum* enterprise, Lincoln continued, pitch rising, it would become a "government art theater" protected from the crass commercialism of Broadway. Chick's museum would become a home for art, theater, film, and ballet, and he and Chick would find themselves at the origins of a new American renaissance. It would not cost much to get started—just $6,000, and "we have both done harder things than to raise $6000." He begged Chick to join him in throwing everything he had behind Balanchine:

> He is an honest man, a serious artist and I'd stake my life on his talent. . . . He could achieve a miracle—and right under our eyes: I feel this chance is too serious to be denied. It will mean a life work to all of us—incredible power in a few years. . . . Please, Please, Chick if you have any love for anything we do both adore—rack your brains and try to make this all come true. . . . Please wire me, give me some inkling as to how you will receive this letter. If not I can't sleep. I won't be able to hear from you for a week—but I won't sleep till I do. Just say Proceed or Impossible. If Impossible, I will try to think of something else—but as I see it—Hartford is perfect. It will involve no personal loss. The $6000 is just a guarantee—for poor Balanchine. . . . He's been tricked so often.
>
> We have the future in our hands. For christ's sweet sake let us honor it.
>
> Yours devotedly,
> Lincoln.

When Chick read this letter in Hartford, he cried out: "My God! You just don't *know* what this *is,* what it *means,* the *possibilities*!" He raced out of the museum and "ran, really ran" to the trustee he needed to convince in order to proceed. Telegrams flew; money was hastily raised, mostly from the old Harvard gang: Phil Johnson, Eddie Warburg, Kirk and Constance Askew (all students of Sachs's museum course). Lincoln himself pledged $2,000 and upon his return from Europe went directly to Eddie Warburg, who committed $5,000 (more than $100,000 today) on the spot. He had never even seen a ballet.[50]

By early September, they had managed through high government contacts to secure State Department approval for the arrival of George—"St. Balanchini," as a clerk charmingly designated their charge[51]—along with his manager, the inevitable Dmitriev. ("What does Dmitriev DO anyway? Is he essential?" Lincoln cabled; the answer from Balanchine was swift: yes, essential.)[52] They had soon confirmed contractual arrangements, including Balanchine's return passage to Europe from New York—in case Kirstein turned out to be another Edward James, Balanchine said. Rights to perform Balanchine ballets were secured from Derain, Bérard, and Tchelitchew, and Lincoln sent a last-minute note asking George to stuff whatever costumes he could find into his luggage. Finally, Lincoln sent money and they formally incorporated their new company as "The American Ballet," with Austin, Warburg, and Kirstein heading the board. In Paris, Balanchine and Dmitriev arranged passports and booked passage on the White Star Line. Balanchine wrote to Kirstein with one final detail: might he please inform Tamara Geva (who had made her own way to America a few years earlier and found success on Broadway) of George's imminent arrival?[53]

Lincoln worried. "Extremely tired; nervous . . . will I ever settle down? Will the ballet ever come across? What about money?"[54] And what about Chick—was he steady? "DONT GET COLD FEET," Lincoln anxiously cabled.[55] The Great Depression haunted him, though not at this moment for its devastating social effects: Would it wipe out museum trusts and the possibility of developing art in America? Would it destroy his ballet?[56] And Balanchine, what about Balanchine? Would he be "poisoned" by the influence of Geva and others and sidetracked into Hollywood or Broadway?[57] Would his chronic ill-health mean he might up and die? Three days before the great arrival, Lincoln confided to his diary: "Hoped all day I won't die, or Chick Austin or Eddie Warburg won't before we get the ballet."[58]

Chapter 10

NEW YORK

On October 17, 1933, the *Olympia,* sister ship to the *Titanic,* docked safely in New York Harbor. Austin, Kirstein, Warburg, and a reporter and photographer from the local Hartford daily were there to meet Balanchine and Dmitriev. At first, immigration officials refused to let them disembark. There was a discrepancy in their visa arrangements, they were told, and they would have to make their case to the authorities back on Ellis Island. At this point, Eddie made his way on board and used his father's good name to climb the chain of command until the captain finally discharged the Russians to Eddie's authority.[1] Lincoln whisked the dazed guests through the gray Depression-era streets to the fancy Barbizon-Plaza Hotel, where he had booked a two-bedroom suite on the thirty-fourth floor with suitably stunning views of Central Park. They dined at the hotel—in French—and Balanchine practiced the few words he knew in English: "Okay kid," "scram," or (referring to Eddie) "one swell guy." Please, no visits to cathedrals, he said. Lincoln, already assuming a paternal stance, worried about Balanchine's health: he looked a bit too ruddy and had coughing attacks, especially when he smoked, which was all the time. The next day they toured Grand Central Station and the Chrysler and Daily News buildings and visited Tamara

Geva—Balanchine took roses—while Lincoln met with the dance critic of *The New York Times* and angled for a Sunday feature. The following morning, they ate at the Horn & Hardart Automat, which delighted Balanchine, and made the long drive to Hartford.[2]

Then came the rude awakening. In Hartford, Balanchine requested an eighteenth-century apartment and had to be told that such a thing did not exist in this modest American town. They toured the museum and were greeted by a posse of angry local ballet teachers incensed that a foreigner—a Russian, no less—had taken this choice American job. Balanchine grandly told the assembled locals (in French) that he would be creating a "cathedral of ballet" in their midst.[3] It was an inauspicious beginning, and early the next morning Dmitriev informed Lincoln that Hartford was impossible. Lincoln, depressed and demoralized ("Slept fitfully feeling it all absolutely at an end. I feared this end for a long time. . . . Now it was here"),[4] nonetheless girded himself and whisked the two Russians off to his sister Mina's home in Ashfield, Massachusetts. They pored tensely over budgets and plans, and George immersed himself in recordings of Negro spirituals and the songs of Gilbert and Sullivan. Ever "sex-starved," he suggested that perhaps inviting some women would help, and Mina obligingly called some pretty young friends to lunch.[5] They were all tired, and Lincoln plied George with so many questions about Russia that George, annoyed, finally dryly responded that "in Russia" they used half-pumpkins in the water to decoy ducks. Or they didn't, but one could.[6] As for Hartford, it was no use, and less than two weeks after Balanchine's much anticipated arrival, Lincoln found himself guiltily abandoning Chick Austin and running after "my Russians" back to New York and an uncertain future.

They built the School of American Ballet (SAB). Fast. It opened its doors on January 1, 1934, less than three months later.[7] It is difficult to convey the compression and chaos of these weeks and Lincoln's vital role in making it all happen. He had been rehearsing for this moment all his life, and when it came, he charged. It was Lincoln (with Eddie's cash) who made sure that "Bal and Dim," as he called his two charges in his diaries, were housed and fed. It was Lincoln who arranged for renewal of their soon-to-expire visas (without which their deportation was certain)—a task involving letters, phone calls, trips to D.C., consultations with Bill Bullitt at the State Department, and months of bureaucratic runaround, until finally his father's friend Charles Wyzanski at Labor pushed things through. Documents had to be collected and signed: medical certificate, police certificate, declaration of moral character (attested by Kirstein and Warburg), affidavit in lieu of birth certificate, proof of assets. It was Lincoln who personally escorted the pair to a U.S. consular agency in Canada the following April, put them up at a hotel, and dealt with the authorities on location so that they could reenter the country from Montreal with freshly minted documents under the by then strict U.S. immigration quota.[8]

Meanwhile, Lincoln worked to tame his Russians' sometimes wild expectations of America's vast wealth and commercial possibilities as they planned the school over long lunches at the Automat, at the Russian Tea Room (where the head waiter Anatole, formerly of the czar's army, presided),[9] or in meetings at Lincoln's apartment or Eddie's home. Lincoln scoured the city for real estate; signed the lease; consulted with lawyers; incorporated the school; hired (and fired) contractors and publicity agents; lost sleep over the wall obstructing the dance studio and whether it was foundational or could be moved (it could); arranged for the linoleum floor; negotiated with the tailor in the space next door, who had to be relocated; and got Phil Johnson to help and to later design the foyer. It was Lincoln who ordered the furniture and mirrors, fixed the barres when they were installed backward, and polished the mirrors. And it was Lincoln who used his contacts to drum up press coverage—and guiltily fielded Bal and Dim's rage when the press was mostly about . . . Lincoln.

Not to mention: lunch upon lunch and letter upon letter that Lincoln wrote to wealthy and influential friends, beating the drum for the school. It still wasn't an easy sell. Alfred Barr thought the whole idea was crazily utopian, and others failed to see the point. A ballet school at the height of the Depression? Why? Lincoln drained his personal bank account and anxiously begged for more money from his father, who still controlled his cash flow and was reluctant for his son to invest too much in this fanciful obsession. In response, Lincoln plotted to give up *Hound and Horn* to focus on the school and prepared himself to ask his father to please shift his support from the journal to the ballet. He was determined, but he felt the strain: "Wondering if I was finally having that breakdown everybody anticipates for me. Could I indefinitely support the strain of Balanchine's infinitely delicate tenuosity . . . and the strain of money[?]"[10] What with "keeping Lachaise, Laskey, Craig, Dollar, Loring, Hawkins and incidentally, myself," he felt spread thin. Plan after plan, shifty nights, and the perennial "cut my toenails too short out of my nervousing."[11]

Above all, Lincoln courted Eddie Warburg, who was ever anguished about his homosexual impulses and lack of purpose, and Lincoln spent hours with his angst-ridden friend analyzing Eddie's daily analysis with the Russian émigré doctor Gregory Zilboorg, a kind of Freudian Gurdjieff who fleeced his famous clients of everything from cash and fur coats to sex, and now had his claws dug deep into Eddie. Eddie tried to get Lincoln to sign up too, but Lincoln sensed a scam—"Typical bushy-lipped analyst; interest in the arts. I am suspicious of anyone I can flatter that easily. . . . Nasty man."[12] He was in any case far too busy searching for "ways and means for parting Eddie Warburg from his useless thousands, for the sake of the Museum of Modern Art. An American Bauhaus if it is ever built. An American Ballet—if I ever get it."[13] Finally, he succeeded in convincing his rich friend to lead, and bankroll, their whole enterprise. Balanchine, present at one of these meetings, dryly summed it up: "Eddie be just like the president of France; the name, title and nothing to do."[14]

Balanchine, meanwhile, was busy re-creating his Parisian-émigré world. Nicky Nabokov was teaching at the Barnes Foundation in Philadelphia, and George enlisted him to help refine his musical skills in counterpoint and harmony (he liked to call Nicky on the phone: "Alo, this is President Roosevelt").[15] A copy of their exercises together includes intervals, chord inversions, species counterpoint, four-part harmonization, dissonance resolution, analysis of nonharmonic tones, cadential writing, modulation, and orchestration.[16] Vladimir Dukelsky was in New York too, and Nicholas Kopeikine was a constant companion. The Russian Tea Room was a frequent destination (thanks to Eddie's tab), and George even freely wandered into the kitchen to prepare his own favorite dishes.[17] Tamara Geva was there, and although he thought they might resume their marriage, she had by then married Kapa Davidov, the ex-husband of Lucia Davidova.[18]

The eccentric Lucia was becoming one of George's closest and lifelong friends. Petite with pale skin and jet-black hair, she had a deep voice and impenetrable patent-leather eyes.[19] She dressed immaculately in dark dresses or skirts with cashmere sweaters, hair pulled tightly back in a severe bun (not a wisp), high penciled eyebrows, and red lipstick, with three strings of pearls adorning her neck. She had that special skin that makes pearls mature, and it was said that she was paid to wear them. Her large, crooked smile was not warm, and she was the kind of woman who as she aged received guests only, Blanche Dubois–like, after 4 P.M. when the light had dimmed. Armenian-born around the turn of the century, she had a background as mysterious as her appearance. Her papers say she came from Constantinople, but she may also have lived in, or passed through, Transcaucasia, no one quite knows. She spoke, apparently, elevated Russian and seems to have fled in the years around the Armenian genocide and eventually made her way somehow to Europe and then to the United States—where she arrived as an "actress" with husband in tow in 1922 on the SS *Lapland* (part of the Red Star Line, which sailed under the British flag from Antwerp via Southampton to New York). She was naturalized in 1927.

Lucia was a personage. She was a regular at White Russian society events in New York and had an affair with the Russian-émigré aviator Igor Sikorsky. He taught her to pilot planes, and she flew the Atlantic (in London in the 1930s, she was an active member of the Aeroplane Club). In the 1940s and 1950s she would live for a time in Hollywood and could be seen in photos keeping company with stars such as Greta Garbo and Lauren Bacall. She was the longtime lesbian lover of the wealthy American railroad heiress Alice DeLamar, who owned large country estates in Weston, Connecticut, and Palm Beach, Florida, where Lucia wintered and George liked to go. Lucia had a dark force field and was a self-styled mystic and seer. She was probably partly in love with George, but she was more like a brothel madam, as a friend later recalled,[20] someone with a hint of vulgarity who quietly elicited confidences, and she was one of the few people George would turn to with his troubled love life.[21] Their fates were already enjoined since, in the tangled and incestuous circles of émigré life, she had married Kapa Davidov, also Armenian and a high-end tailor (Prince Serge Obolensky was a regular customer) and, he claimed, former captain in the Russian Imperial Cavalry.[22] When they divorced, Kapa married, in 1931, and four years later divorced, Tamara Geva.

Lincoln and George were together a lot. They saw Lifar and his troupe, Massine's company, and Kurt Jooss ("Nothing is as painful to me as bad dancing," Lincoln groaned),[23] along with movies, theater, and art. They went slumming in Harlem, and George crudely suggested that "it would be fine to do a classical ballet with negresses in tutus of gold and silver palettes and white bodices."[24] He asked if Lincoln had ever "screwed a negress." "I said no, but had always wanted to." "Alors," he said blithely, "nous irons ensemble."[25] Lincoln eventually tried with difficulty to explain that in "ce pays," for him at least, things were different. It is hard to say whose humor was more adolescent. Lincoln indulged his "nastypants" asides to gay friends, while George delighted in making obscene sketches of erect penises, in the sand at the beach;[26] or in a restaurant, out of matches, featuring the hated Edward James (beer down, cock up);[27] or more sketches at dinner with Eddie Warburg (who prudishly destroyed the evidence).[28]

Then, just three weeks after his arrival and in the midst of trying to get the school up and running, Balanchine's temperature spiked. Lincoln, fearing the worst, took him to see the Warburg family physician, the well-known endocrinologist Dr. Henry Rawle Geyelin. Tests showed an active tuberculous spot (Lincoln drew a little stick figure in his diary: *x* marks the spot). George could not expect to live for more than ten years, the doctor proclaimed, and should be immediately hospitalized to control this recent flare. George said he was too tired to go to a hospital and would rather die in the street. Maybe a Russian "potion" would be better. A Russian drugstore was called, and a midwife arrived and said it was pneumonia—not TB at all. She cupped Balanchine, who turned green. Lincoln was by then pacing the long, carpeted corridors outside George's little apartment, certain that his choreographer was going to die and that this was the end of his American Ballet. Dmitriev was saying it would be too costly for George to live forever in a sanitorium. Lifar arrived and called the Grand Duchess Marie and Misia Sert, who urgently sent their own Odessa-born doctor, Miron Silberstein. Silberstein arrived and pressed his way through the growing throng surrounding George. Geva and her ex-husband Kapa Davidov arrived. Pierre Vladimirov arrived. It was starting to feel like the railway-car scene in the Marx Brothers' *Night at the Opera*, but by then George was calmly listening to Bruno Walter in a performance of Tchaikovsky's *Francesca da Rimini* on his broken radio, which never fully turned off unless Lincoln buried it in a Turkish towel.[29]

Silberstein said maybe the hospital after all, so Balanchine went, irritably complaining that all he wanted to do was work and blaming everything on Dmitriev. It was Mont Blanc all over again, but this time without the views and fresh air. He glumly distracted himself with Bach and imagining new dances. Or fell into feverish nocturnal diatribes against Fokine and Massine and the Russian émigré critic André Levinson, whose essays on the old Diaghilev days Lincoln had recently given him.[30] When George was finally released from the hospital, Lincoln took him immediately by train to Ashfield and Mina, where, though he was "plagued," Lincoln reported, with nightmares and wet dreams, he was "quiet, well-behaved and he eats." On one of these off-kilter nights, George dreamt that he was walking in a deserted place and found a fallen angel. She was speechless. He married her, and she learned to talk, but he couldn't understand anything she said. He later composed a piece of music for Lincoln, which he inscribed: "To Lincoln, Ashfield's Nights. Remembrance of Things Past. George."[31]

Balanchine was out sick for over a month and didn't return to New York until late December, just before the school's opening. Still weak, he threw himself into teaching. The school was located on the fourth floor of the Tuxedo Building at 634 Madison Avenue at Fifty-ninth Street, with large studios, wood floors, and huge picture windows looking out over the street. Isadora Duncan had once had her studio there too, and their neighbors in the building included the Tuxedo Ballroom, Cooperman Furs, a few painter's lofts, and the (competing) Yakovleff School of Ballet. Sammy's Delicatessen on the ground floor made thick hot pastrami sandwiches with mustard, and the dancers could also go to the corner drugstore for a quick "pep cocktail" of orange juice blended with a raw egg for fifteen cents.[32]

One afternoon, Eugenie Ouroussow, an elegant woman, small at five feet two but with an imposing carriage and a quiet, restrained manner, appeared at the school. Lincoln and Dmitriev hired her immediately to help run things. She was a Russian princess, the daughter of Prince and Princess Sergei Ouroussow, a family of diplomats and wealthy industrial magnates (glassmaking, crystal), and her family had deep literary roots; her grandmother's salon in Paris on the rue d'Alm was frequented by Guy de Maupassant, André Gide, Oscar Wilde, and Henry James. Eugenie had fled revolutionary Russia as a child with her parents through the Crimea to Paris, where she studied philosophy and letters before emigrating to New York in 1930. When she heard about Balanchine's new school, through Russian friends, she was working at Macy's. She knew of his work and naturally gravitated to this new venture. Engaged to Dmitry Lehovich, a Russian who had served in the White Army of General Denikin and later wrote a scholarly book about him, she was herself writing a book about Boris Pasternak and the Russian symbolists and was a serious student of the work of Soloviev, Blok, the Neoplatonists and Christian mysticism, eroticism, icons, and the Divine Sophia. Her manuscript, completed over the years she was working at the school, quoted Soloviev: "The final task of the perfect art is to realize the absolute ideal not in imagination only but in the very deed—to spiritualize and transfigure our actual life."

Fluent in Italian, English, French, and Russian, Ouroussow later became close to Edmund Wilson, who sent her work to Isaiah Berlin at Oxford University and encouraged her literary aspirations.[33] But her life was with Lincoln and George. She was an anchor and would stay at the school until her death from cancer in 1975. Her relationship to Lincoln was deeply loyal; with George, background served all. He bowed to her superior social stature, and she fondly—but not jokingly—called him a "peasant" and devoted herself to his enterprise.[34]

Ouroussow was one of the "Three Fates," as they were known, strict ladies who would preside over the school for decades in their simple but tastefully tailored skirts and efficient low heels. Ouroussow was soon joined, in 1938, by Natasha Molostwoff, or "Molo" or "Black Natasha," as she was called for her dark glamour and mysterious origins (probably Armenian). She had a wild streak and a house on Fire Island, a kind of free-spirited bohemia on Long Island Sound, where everyone camped on the floor in one large room, including George, who often joined them.[35] Sandra Loris-Melikov, the third fate, was the granddaughter of a minister to Czar Alexander II, but she got multiple sclerosis and was eventually replaced by Nathalie Gleboff, who arrived in 1959. Gleboff was the daughter of a Russian White Army doctor. Born in Romania on the way out of Russia, she and her family ended up in Paris, where she would earn a degree in philosophy from the Sorbonne (and work with Simone de Beauvoir and Jean-Paul Sartre). She joined the French Resistance during World War II, and finally came to New York as a GI wife, thanks to her Russian émigré husband, who fought for the Allies as an American citizen before moving on to a career at the United Nations.[36] These Fates or Graces—the Gleb, the Mole, the Kangaroussoff, as a friend later fondly called them[37]—were the unsung soul of the School of American Ballet. They had been part of its Russian story before any of them ever met.

The dancers were American teenagers. Or were they? In a pattern that would repeat in the decades to come, many among them were the children of Russian and European émigrés. Kirstein formally noted the trend and put the number at about eighty percent in 1934.[38] Annabelle Lyon, from Memphis, was the daughter of first-generation Russian émigrés. Ruthanna Boris came from a family of Viennese and Georgian Jews; her grandfather had been master of the Spanish Riding School under Emperor Franz Josef, and her father's family was from the Caucasus. Leda Anchutina was born in Siberia. Marie-Jeanne Pelus was the child of a French milliner and an Italian chef. Barbara Weisberger, who at age eight hid under the piano watching Balanchine work, came from a family of Ukrainian Jews from the Pale of Settlement. Daphne Vane was really Virginia Pappé, daughter of a St. Louis steel-mill worker from a family with Catholic French-Alsatian roots; Heidi Vosseler's parents were Swiss and German. Edward Caton was born in St. Petersburg, where his father oversaw the czar's stables—and fled the revolution. Others were American, and George was especially taken with Holly Howard, Virginia-born to a proud military family, who came to New York with her divorced mother and her twin brother and ended up at SAB. Another favorite was Kathryn Mullowny, decorous, polite, a bit wild, and the daughter of a criminal-court judge in Washington, D.C. She came to New York escorted by her mother and grandmother (and later married a navy man). Lew Christensen, shy and quiet, tall and blond, with a perfectly proportioned physique, was from a lapsed Mormon family in Utah, distanced from the church when his dancer-father's too-successful theatrical pavilion won the disapproval of church elders. He and his brother William were a vaudeville team, and he ended up at SAB in 1934 and later became Balanchine's first American Apollo—and one of Lincoln's greatest love objects.[39]

Balanchine found many of his new dancers through the Philadelphia school of Catherine Littlefield, which he mined ruthlessly for talent. She was a feisty, chain-smoking, cussing dancer from an old theatrical family, who established one of the earliest ballet companies in America. Her school offered ballet, folk, acrobatics, and tap, and recruited male dancers—Littlefield called them "athletes" to avoid homosexual stereotyping—from dockworkers, bricklayers, milkmen, and boxers. Balanchine gratefully accepted several of her unevenly trained dancers, and her sister Dorothie, "a big bouncing field-hockey girl" (according to Eddie Warburg),[40] was invited to teach beginners at SAB.[41]

Felia Doubrovska arrived with her husband, Pierre Vladimirov, former "prince" of the Mariinsky, tall and perfumed, with wide Slavic features, flowery hands, and a powerful classical technique, to teach the more advanced ballet classes. (Vladimirov told his students that he entered the theater walking on his heels as an ordinary man, but went on stage on the balls of his feet, as a prince; "let others be stuck on earth.")[42] They were soon joined by other Russians: the Moscow-trained Kyra Blanc (Dmitriev's wife); Anatole Vilzak, who had known George when they were children at the Theater School in St. Petersburg; and the former Mariinsky luminary Anatole Obukhov, grand but humble, a man who hid his stuttered speech in peppermint Life Savers, which he also pressed into the palms of the deserving, and who liked to snap his fingers dangerously close to students' faces to make them wake up and listen. Muriel Stuart was English but a Pavlova protégée who had also worked with Martha Graham and specialized in plastique. Wafting lilac scent, she taught in a bathing costume, barefooted, pulling pins from her cascading hair as she showed students how to "go to the floor" and use their backs in contractions and other modern-dance movements.[43] Balanchine also taught "character" dance and demonstrated the vigorous Russian, Hungarian, and Polish stomping rhythms, high kicks, and whirling partner dances with abandon.[44] Janet Collins, a black modern dancer, taught too. To train the students' minds, Kirstein gave weekly lectures on the history and aesthetics of dance from Rome to the present.[45] Dmitriev taught stage makeup, and Ariadna (Roumanova) Mikeshina, a composer and concert pianist from the St. Petersburg Conservatory of Music, married to a high naval officer in the czar's army, played for classes and rehearsals.[46] It really was St. Petersburg on the Hudson.

The atmosphere was professional and rigorous. The students were young, mostly teenagers with no experience or any idea what it meant to study dance. Whatever they had learned before, George changed. They had to learn or relearn the etiquette of training, beginning with how to dress: Ruthanna Boris, who had danced at the Met with the Old World Italian teacher Madame Galli, came to her first class wearing a fanciful long flowing pink practice dress and had to be politely told that Balanchine would like her, please, to cut it to uniform length: short so he could see and properly correct her hips and legs. Elise Reiman was gently instructed to set aside her Hollywood-style gold Grecian sandals, in favor of more sober ballet slippers.[47] As a teacher, Balanchine was demanding and could be harsh—sadistic, Dmitriev said—in pushing the dancers relentlessly, through exhaustion and tears. "Your feet are like sausages." "Be born again," he said to one poor girl.[48] One day he spent an hour trying to teach a boy to glissade—a hopeless task that left George morose and foul-tempered; on another day he was so discouraged he gave the dancers a combination ending in a sustained attitude on one leg—and when they got to this precarious pose, he left the room and went home.[49]

They had fun too: the Christmas party in 1934 saw George at the piano or performing wittily sarcastic imitations of the artist and dancer Angna Enters, whose fashionable mime acts did not impress him. There was wild dancing, especially by Holly Howard in her "Apache number," and Kopeikine belted scenes from tragic operas in high coloratura. Mikeshina sang soulful peasant songs in Yiddish, Russian, and Georgian, with Balanchine accompanying, until she finally broke into the last bars of "The Internationale," and Kyra Blanc sang the revolutionary lyrics at top voice. The dancers playfully presented George with a ballet-girl doll and a clever limerick about how he loved and deserted his successive girls. (Lincoln got a rare book of nursery rhymes.) Awkward as ever, Lincoln sweated frightfully, lost his watch, sprained his foot, and finally got to bed around three.[50] None of this allayed his underlying giddy doubts and despair, and he ended his 1934 diary with a sigh: "It's not Irish whiskey tonight: why use liquor when I'm this way drunk or sober: [*illegible*] If so I'd just better stop tonight; goodnight; Darling Lincoln."[51]

Balanchine was busy, but lonely. At this moment in the early 1930s, he had no family, few friends, and—by all accounts—little time to live. His bout of ill-health had if anything intensified his sexual appetite, and his natural charisma and dark Georgian melancholy made him a magnet to women. He worried that his TB was contagious, but when his doctor finally assured him, a bit oddly, that he could have sex as long as he avoided kissing, he began courting various of his beautiful young dancers. Women, he said, soothed him.

Heidi Vosseler, one of his greatest loves at the time, was Miss Adelaide Ida Vosseler of Germantown, Pennsylvania, a community settled by Quakers and Mennonites near Philadelphia. Her father was a Swiss mechanical dentist from Zurich—he made teeth. Her mother was Bertha Tamm: a stout and very wide German, who was always fully corseted and wore dark high-collared dresses edged in black lace. She had sex, she told her daughter, through a hole in the sheet (not uncommon at the time). This good lady sent her daughter to Dorothie Littlefield's dancing school and from there to New York to work with Balanchine. Heidi roomed with the equally glamorous Daphne Vane, another love object, who had fled her strict Catholic upbringing in St. Louis to dance at Radio City Music Hall and model for *Vogue* before finding her way to Balanchine. According to Lincoln's diary, there was also the "little ash blond," Miss Elmore, who seems to have been George's fiancée for a brief moment before she disappeared from the record, and there were others.[52] These were exceptionally beautiful and adventurous, very young women full of the sexual misconceptions of their upbringing: when Heidi got her period, she thought she was bleeding to death, and she was sure that the mere kiss of a man would make her pregnant. How did she feel when George Balanchine chose *her* to be the lead figure in his dances—and in his life? In a sweet note he sent her before one of her performances, he called himself her "little Georgian husband" and intimated that he was "hoping to find a shady nook for my sinful head." And although their love affair eventually faded and she married another dancer, Heidi secretly kept George's letters, carefully hidden from her husband and children, for the rest of her life.[53]

How ironic that George, raised on a steady diet of Blok, Soloviev, and erotic mysticism, and come of age in revolutionary St. Petersburg and the sexual revolutions of jazz-age Weimar and Paris, had ended up in puritan Depression-era America—on the outer cusp of the genuinely promiscuous bohemia of New York in the "roaring" 1920s. The Jewish families of Lincoln and Eddie were of stolidly bourgeois German descent, inheritors of equally restrictive sexual mores, and the physical freedom of George's dances, it turned out, was a bond between them all. Eddie was drawn to Balanchine, he said, not because Eddie liked ballet—he didn't—but for the open sensuality of the dances.[54] His father, Felix Warburg, took one look at the school, with its dancers in revealing tights and leotards, and noted disapprovingly that it had something of the air of a brothel to it; but even he admitted that a rehearsal of Balanchine's *Serenade* inexplicably moved him to tears.[55]

Balanchine hadn't made a new dance since he arrived—too sick, too busy. He was full of ideas, mostly on religious and mythological themes, which he shared enthusiastically with Lincoln. Maybe something on the Song of Songs[56] or the story of Ruth. Or a "Jewish ballet" with liturgical music and Hebrew words spoken in chorus.[57] Or maybe a dance about two lovers who die when they touch.[58] And what about Ovid's Orpheus and Eurydice or Diana and Actaeon?[59] Even Lincoln's pet idea for a balletic *Uncle Tom's Cabin* eventually piqued George's interest, although not for the racial politics Lincoln had in mind. George, who had read the book, imagined the characters nude and masked or, at the end of the ballet, dressed in Louis XIV finery for a heavenly dance of celestial planets with a boy's voice as God reciting "certain words" from the Bible.[60]

The search for music was constant, and Lincoln routinely hunted out musical scores and delivered them to Balanchine. One day Lincoln brought him Schumann, Schubert, and Mussorgsky from the library. On another he suggested Gottschalk, "we took it and played it, but it sounded too silly." Balanchine was interested in Weber's overtures, but they seemed impractical, and for some reason Mendelssohn was a no-go too. Balanchine was interested in Richard Strauss's Five Piano Pieces, op. 3, but nothing came of that either. Finally, he settled on Tchaikovsky's Serenade for Strings, op. 48, a score he knew well from his childhood and from Michel Fokine's ballet *Eros* (1916), which he had seen in Russia in his youth.[61]

Tchaikovsky had composed his *Serenade* in four movements: "Sonatina," "Waltz," "Elegy," and "Tema Russo," a vigorous Russian folk-themed finale. The dance Balanchine imagined, however, was tragic, and he began by setting aside Tchaikovsky's upbeat "Tema Russo" entirely and ending his ballet instead with the poignant third-movement "Elegy." He would later add the Russian-themed finale back into the ballet until Tchaikovsky's complete score was finally fully represented—but he would still crucially flip the last two movements and end his ballet with the "Elegy." Balanchine called his dance *Serenade*, and on March 14, 1934, he began work with students at the school on this new dance.

At the end of his morning ballet class, he climbed onto a bench at the front of the room to survey the dancers who had come that day. He asked them to take a short break and then return to the studio. Lincoln reported that he complained that his head was "a blank," and asked if Lincoln might pray for him.[62] His gift, he reminded himself, might at any point desert him.[63] As the dancers stood expectantly waiting, he started to talk. In pidgin English, he told them how he was a child at the Imperial Theater School when World War I began and only thirteen when the revolution erupted three years later. The memories still haunted him: gunfire in the streets, scavenging for food, killing and eating cats, and freezing in subzero temperatures. He told them about the small dance company he had started, and about leaving for Berlin and Paris and working with Diaghilev. He talked anxiously about Germany and the "awful" Hitler, much on everybody's mind in 1934, and about the *Heil* salute. And he showed his young American dancers how to stand facing front and to raise their right arms straight up, but then to break this harsh pose by turning their arms and heads softly to the side, gazing up at their hands, which shielded their eyes from the light of the moon.[64]

This is one account. Later generations of dancers knew nothing of Nazis or war or revolution; some thought that this story of *Serenade*'s first day was apocryphal, and Balanchine even liked to joke about it sometimes—"give it a

Heil Hitler," he said in the 1960s to a startled Karin von Aroldingen, whose father had been in the Wehrmacht.[65] Lincoln reported in his diary on that March day in 1934 that Balanchine was composing "a hymn to ward off the sun," and Kirstein can perhaps be forgiven for later transcribing his own tight handwriting in thick black ink to read "a hymn to ward off sin."[66] In later accounts and for most dancers, *Serenade* was simpler than all of that. It was a serenade, after all, and it naturally began with women in the moonlight, hands raised to shield their eyes from the rays of light beaming in from downstage right. It was the light of God, Balanchine also said, too bright for human eyes to bear, or he said nothing.[67]

He began by quietly approaching each dancer, taking her courteously by the arm, as was his natural manner, and escorting her to a spot on the floor. There happened to be seventeen women present that day, so he placed them in a pattern for seventeen: two perfect diamonds of eight, with a single dancer at the point joining the two formations. From the front, every dancer could be seen—like an orange grove in California, he later liked to say.[68] Another day only nine came to rehearsal, so he made a dance of nine; then six, so six; then one was late—and so in the dance, a girl arrived late and found her way through the other sixteen like a woman lost in a forest of trees. Another day a girl fell, and her fall became a key dramatic moment in the choreography too. Then there was one man, so the ballet had one man. Accident and fate were a theme of the dance, and Balanchine also used them in its making. Chance was the greatest tool he had been given in life; no wonder he used it in art. In less than two weeks, like one long breath, the dance was done.

Getting it to the stage was harder. Money was short, and George had an offer from Hollywood to make a film about Anna Pavlova and planned to take it. Lincoln felt his "weakness grow apace," and the future of "ballet in America as such" seemed to him increasingly grim and "exhaustingly precarious."[69] They finally arranged with Eddie for *Serenade* to have its first performances at the Warburg family estate in Woodlands, New York, for a group of some 250 invited guests in celebration of Eddie's twenty-sixth birthday. It was just the kind of society affair Balanchine despised, and as Lincoln quibbled with Warburg over money and logistics, George went out and bought himself a Dodge.[70]

They scrambled for costumes. None of the costumes worked out, and Lincoln spent hours "more or less fruitlessly with Bal. at Bloomingdales, while he tried to make up his mind about costumes for the Boys." He complained that "Bal" had "a spoiled boy's vanity which makes him at once refuse any given suggestion. One must approach him always from behind. Even this [is] no cinch as there are always more than two alternatives." With no solution in sight, Lincoln scoured the racks at Abercrombie's alone and chose some basic shirts; the women would wear practice tunics. Lincoln noted nervously that the ballet was still not firmly set: "Bal. changes things all the time right up to the end."[71]

On the appointed day in June, Lincoln, George, Dmitriev, Kopeikine, Mikeshina, and the dancers all drove to Woodlands for the opening-night performance. They arrived to rain and busied themselves mopping and re-mopping the soaked and slick outdoor stage and installing the necessary rudimentary lights. Balanchine was furious that there was so little food and drove off to find more as Lincoln studied the forecast and pondered on whether they should cancel. "God's will be done," Balanchine calmly intoned upon his return. The audience arrived for the party and drank too much, and the performance finally went ahead. The dancers got through the first two ballets, but as they took their places for *Serenade*, the skies opened, and they were forced to abandon the stage. The drunken guests retired to the mansion for a raucous feast, while Balanchine and the dancers were shunted to a damp garage for a cold poor-man's repast. Ouroussow said, a bit dramatically, that it reminded her of sitting shivering and hungry on boxes in harbors during the Russian civil wars, but the point was taken. They tried again the next day, bringing their own sandwiches this time. More rain, and although Mikeshina and Kopeikine could barely play the damp and sticky piano keys, the show went up, and the dancers finally performed Balanchine's ode to transcendence under a drizzle.[72]

Serenade opens with music. The audience listens to the opening phrases of Tchaikovsky's score, which is profoundly lyrical—he had written it, he said, "from an inward impulse," and he described it as "heartfelt."[73] The seventeen dancers are also listening, hands raised to the light. They do not move, but they sense one another, and when the time comes, they begin simply and quietly in unison to the slow ascending notes of Tchaikovsky's opening theme. First, the wrist breaks—only the wrist—and the raised arm slowly falls to the brow and folds across the chest in a pose of half-death—a fleeting thought—head and eyes averted. It is a simple but profound gesture, amplified seventeen times. The feet turn out into ballet's first position, the beginning pose of their daily training. From there, the dancers, still moving in choral synchrony, open legs and arms sideways to second position and fold their feet into ballet's "home" fifth position, sweeping their arms open and wide, palms up, chests and faces raised to the skies. Everything suspends for a moment over this spiritual image in the half-light. Then the beat falls, and they begin to dance. It is often said that this opening sequence is symbolic: women becoming dancers. But in practice it feels more like dancers becoming spirits—and witnesses to their own transformation in the dance to come.

The ballet has no story or narrative. It is internal—inward, like the music, and more of a prayer or ritual than a theatrical spectacle. It is a dance of women—a man appears briefly as a love object, but these women are its main subject, and they dance together and break apart, recombine in twos, threes, sixes, eights, nines, and sixteens, as if blown by a strong wind in swirling patterns that seem to carry them through the dance: "We ran and ran and ran."[74] They rarely lose sight of one another and move seemingly effortlessly, arms enlaced or around waists, hands offered and taken, moments of call and response. Even when a woman dances alone, she is still "one of us" and folds back again into the ensemble. There was neither hierarchy nor royalty in the little society that Balanchine assembled in *Serenade*. To some this made the ballet seem democratic—a republic of women—or, perhaps, a republic of spirits.

The dances have very few traditional steps—"I was just trying . . . to make a ballet that wouldn't show how badly they danced," Balanchine later remarked of his poorly trained hodgepodge of students.[75] But the stamina and full-bodied sensuality that the ballet requires pushed his young dancers to their limits and remain unmatched in the dance repertory. The running, swirling, off-balance, nonlinear, and circular movements that swing the body with centrifugal force into a kind of bent space were anything but classical. The point was never symmetry or control. It was, instead, a kind of relentless space-devouring momentum. "What are you saving it for, you might be dead tomorrow."

There is no plot, but there is a drama that builds until the "Elegy" begins and the girl who fell (Heidi Vosseler) lies in a heap or (in some renditions) corpse-like on her back in a corner of the stage, as if stricken. A man who seems to love her enters from the far corner with a "dark angel" (Kathryn Mullowny) wrapped around him from behind, their bodies flush, like destiny on his back, George said.[76] Her hand reaches around him and covers his eyes, blinding him. (Balanchine joked that the man was nearsighted and needed help.)[77] His arm extends to find his way, but it is her step that literally pushes and guides his feet forward. They walk like this together on a long diagonal toward the fallen woman. When they reach her, they stop, and the angel removes her hand from the man's eyes. He sees. They bend gently over the fallen girl, and raise her up, and the three of them together form a pose taken directly from Antonio Canova's sculpture *Psyche Revived by Cupid's Kiss,* in which the winged Cupid bends compassionately and erotically over his beloved Psyche.

The Dark Angel is an angel of fate. Angels in the Catholic and Orthodox faiths are a way of showing the presence of God among men—of making the invisible visible. They are also witnesses and messengers like the choruses of antiquity, "clear and spotless mirrors," who can tell a tragic story without themselves suffering.[78] Pure of mind and spirit, bodiless and sexless, angels do not typically eat or feel emotion or make love (except in Milton), and they are a constant unseen presence in human life. They watch, intervene, and move unseen in our midst; "You are his eyes," Balanchine told one dancer who performed the angel, endowing her with powers verging on the occult.[79] Angel and man are two bodies as one, and her strong arms become eagle-like wings that wrap forcefully around him and cover his eyes in a clear gesture of possession. He is hers, and fate is a woman.

Yet it is not fate and the angel who prevail in the end; it is love and the fallen girl. In Balanchine's translation of Canova's *Psyche Revived by Cupid's Kiss,* the fallen girl is Psyche, who has betrayed her promises to her lover Cupid (by looking into his forbidden face) and to his mother Venus (by smelling the vapors of beauty brought from the underworld). At the moment depicted in the sculpture and brought to life in *Serenade,* the beautiful Psyche—our fallen Heidi—has erred by looking into Cupid's forbidden face. She lies in a deathly sleep. Cupid bends lovingly to revive her, raising her up in his arms in a near-kiss as he embraces her breasts and she circles her arms softly around his neck, and his wings rise behind him in a sign of both virility and immortality. We know how the myth ends. The gods, moved by Cupid's love for this lost girl, give Psyche ambrosia, and she too is immortalized. In Greek her name means both "soul" and "butterfly," and the butterfly is the symbol of the immortality of the soul.

In *Serenade,* Balanchine made Cupid not one but two people. He is man and angel, and it is man and angel who together bend over and revive the still-mortal fallen girl. What happens next in the ballet is revealing: man and angel separate, and the angel walks deliberately in front of the man, and the fallen girl, and steps into a stately arabesque, posed on one leg on pointe, barely touching the earth. The man sits beneath her on the ground, workmanlike, and reaches across the fallen girl to hold the angel's single supporting leg and steady her precarious balance. Then he holds and rotates her leg as if he is the axle and motor in a music box, making the ballerina spin. She may be his eyes, but he will have his say! In the first productions, costumed in short tunics, he was a visible engine, and the audience could see him turning her leg to spin her body. She controls his fate, but he has devised her.

They all three rise and dance together, until the girl is lying inert again in a pile on the floor with the man standing over her. The Dark Angel shadows him still, and now she flaps her arms like powerful wings purposefully behind him, and her hand sweeps across his face to cover his eyes. Blind once more, he extends his arm forward and they move on, exiting the stage. This simple gesture of blinded walking turned the wing of the stage into the edge of the earth, marking the interminable voyage of a man with no home.

The fallen girl is left alone in a heap in the corner. But love—not the man, but love itself—has transformed her, and somehow she has the strength to rise and run to a group of women gathered across the stage. She embraces one—"the mother," Balanchine once explained[80]—before she turns slowly away, as three blank-faced men enter, like pallbearers. She waits, facing the back corner of the stage on a diagonal. They lift her straight up by her feet so that she is standing upright, not supine, high above them all, in another stratosphere. A bright light streams in from the high distant corner—the place in Russian homes where religious icons live. By now there is a small society of women in formation below her, and she is carried ceremoniously away. As she goes, the women below rise onto pointe and they all float slowly together, opening their arms, chests lifted as they were in the opening ritual, going into the light that once made them shield their eyes.

This is the dance that came out of Balanchine in those early weeks of March, in the studio on Madison Avenue, and was finally performed on the Warburg estate. It had the arc of a life: from the innocence of first steps to the experience of a final procession into the unknown. There was tragedy woven through—not a cathartic Attic tragedy but a more melancholy and Romantic evocation of loves that cannot last, endings that must come. The spiritual and religious themes that had preoccupied George ever since his youth were present too: blindness and seeing, love and fate, death and submission. There was passion but no melodrama. Watching *Serenade* is like being in a dream or a memory: we don't *feel* emotion; we *see* it. And what we see above all is yearning and loneliness, missed love, and the fragility of it all. Nothing lasts; you must move on.

The only respite seemed to lie with music and dancing, and *Serenade* had both. Even at its most melancholy moments, it offers the solace of glorious dancing; no one cries in the face of such beauty. It was far away from traditions of spectacle or court dance and belonged instead to a lineage of painters and poets taken up with eros and the feminine form. George had that power: he could give women—and it was women who mattered—a way of moving that, like the loves that *Serenade* depicts, was a kind of revelation. It was a ballet made from the chance events of their collective lives, woven into a structure that allowed them (and generations of women to come) choices and spontaneity. In those moments of dancing, they could be themselves. If anything, this was his first American theme, and it was not directed at his audience but at the women, his dancers. *Serenade* belonged to them, but Balanchine was their maker. As for the fated man in their midst, Balanchine was unsparing. He is left alone with the Dark Angel, who covers his eyes and makes him walk on.[81]

What was less clear was what these women should wear, and what their setting should be. The many changes in the costumes and sets in these early years were a sign of Balanchine's uncertainty. He wasn't yet sure who these women were and how they should look. There were various Grecian tunics (with chic gloves and hats in Paris) alluding to antiquity and the nude. (A rejected version in the fall of 1934 was made of pink latex that tore easily and was finally scrapped. "Great row as to whose fault it was—Balanchine's or Oakie's," said Lincoln, referring to William B. Okie Jr., the costume designer.)[82] The practice clothes and tunics, it turned out, were a kind of placeholder, and Balanchine wasn't satisfied until 1952, when the costumes were completely redone by Karinska in a way that enhanced the ballet's spirituality. From that moment on, the women wore a version of long light-blue tulle skirts, recalling the otherworldly dead spirits of past Romantic ballets such as *Giselle*. As for the sets, there were several versions in the early years, mostly by artists Lincoln knew, but Balanchine disliked them all. They were soon dispensed with entirely, and the dance was performed on an empty stage in a carefully invented blue light: illuminating, pure, celestial.[83]

When the first performance at Warburg's estate was all over, it could be said that Lincoln's crowd had been there. Mina, e. e. cummings, Chick Austin, Nelson Rockefeller, Alfred Barr, and Julian Levi were among the guests who witnessed this great work danced on a cold damp night in what amounted to an elaborate school recital at a rich man's country castle. The ballet's official premiere the following year in New York, under the baton of émigré Hungarian conductor Sandor Harmati, passed relatively unnoticed.

A month later, Balanchine collapsed.

Chapter 11

TIME OF TROUBLES

He was driving with Lincoln near Ashfield when suddenly his body went rigid. He gripped Lincoln's arm, slavered, stiffened. Lincoln stalled the car as George seemed to go mad, his body lashing out wildly, legs kicking, tongue sputtering. George's foot smashed into the emergency brake and split it as he crushed Lincoln's glasses in another thrashing move. Lincoln fought to pin him down with his belt. A maid from a nearby house saw what was happening and called the state troopers, who arrived to find Balanchine on his knees in the dirt at the side of the road. He no longer recognized Lincoln, and he could not speak. A doctor arrived and quickly administered morphine as George swung one last punch, causing the needle to break off in his arm, before falling unconscious. They got him into a nearby house until an ambulance came and delivered him to Northern Westchester Hospital in Mount Kisco.[1]

Doctors, tests, X-rays of the skull and chest. The diagnosis was uncertain: brain disorder, brain tumor, meningitis, TB, TB of the brain, toxemia, perhaps induced by injections of parathyroid adrenaline given by the gland specialist Dr. Louis Berman—George's latest health fad to strengthen his intermittently consumptive body.[2] As it turned out, George explained in a letter from the hospital to his "darling" Heidi Vosseler, these were "poison injections."[3] Lucia Davidova heard the news and immediately called Dr. Berman, whom they both knew. ("He is not only a good doctor, but an excellent chef, honey instead of sugar," George had told Lincoln.) Berman indignantly said that this wasn't possible, and it must be epilepsy due either to George's starving during the Russian Revolution or to TB, and sure enough George spat blood, and newly active lesions were found. In the days to come, Lincoln took George through a round of experts including Eddie's Dr. Geyelin, who wanted to treat any possible TB by putting air in George's spinal cord and doing a full pneumothorax treatment. George, having regained his senses, point-blank refused, saying he'd seen people at Mont Blanc die of it.[4]

He wrote again to Heidi, in that way he had: intimate, open, deeply lonely, even insecure. "My Darling," he began in his almost childish hand, saying he didn't want "eny" help with the writing and that he preferred privacy to accuracy. He thanked her for her postcard—"it rilly happies thing in my life"—and explained that he wasn't well but hoped to be "all rite" soon. "I hope you'l understend something frome this letter," he wrote, "I am alwayse hopping to come in Philad. And see you it's only my whishe," and he encouraged her to be a "good girl. Good Carmen and good Aida," referring to the dances she was performing at the time. He hoped she would write again. "Good bay Darling, Your G. Bal."[5] What he really wanted, he told Lincoln, was a wife to take care of him. Instead, he agreed to a prolonged eight-week rest at a local health farm.

Lincoln found one that would take a patient with active TB. Cranker's Health Camp in Mount Kisco was part spa, part recuperation facility. Recently opened by William H. Cranker, an ex-policeman become physical trainer, and his Swiss wife, it boasted lawns, gardens, a golf course, bowling, billiards, and a phalanx of attending physicians and nurses. Cranker later worked with Eleanor Roosevelt to treat polio patients, among others, but at the time his new "camp" was just beginning. Lincoln noted the run-down gentility: iron bedsteads with "grimy" mattresses and not entirely clean facilities. There was a piano, but even that didn't work. The other guests, George's only companions, included a fat and kindly Jewish woman and would-be poet; a child-man in his thirties who behaved like a ten-year-old; a disgruntled assistant New York State prosecutor; and an old madwoman who said she had once written a book about God. George remarked when it was all over that if he were Chekhov or Gogol, he could write a magnificent, sad book about the whole experience.[6]

He wrote again to his "Darling litle Heidi Chopin," a pet name he had for her, in receipt of her letter to him. He told her about the piano that wouldn't play and the dog that smiled and the chickens that sat on his leg and ate from his hands but would nonetheless be killed and eaten tomorrow ("Dog not yet," he added reassuringly). In another letter, he told her he was enjoying "her friend" Goethe. "It is very difficult to read, but . . . take first part of Faust and read slowly. Bedaid [besides] the politikol idea and philosophical there is a magnificent poetry. Ecscuse my speling. In thirty years will be better. Good bye now angel—1000 ki . . . s, Yours oncle Tom." He enclosed a sketch of himself sitting alone on a bench outside the Cranker house, haggard and bent over an accordion. In his last letter to her, he said sadly that he had tried to call his family but couldn't get through, noting that probably the authorities were afraid of people trying to "come here." The truth: "Now I am alone." He wondered if his Heidi would come to New York, and he invited her to stay with him for a few days. "My love to you always," and he signed off as he always did to her—not as her lover "Georgi" or even "George" but more formally as her choreographer: "G. Balanchine."[7]

Meanwhile, he monitored his body, waiting for his hand to go numb—a sure sign of an oncoming fit. The doctors said he might have to have fluid drained from his brain. He kept luminol, an antiseizure drug that calmed him, close to hand. Word was out, Lincoln told him, that Balanchine had gone mad like Nijinsky and been put away. At least—unlike the sad Mont Blanc days—friends, such as they were, did visit: Kopeikine, Vladimirov, Kirstein, Warburg. No Heidi, at least that we know of. Finally, six weeks later, Lincoln collected George from the Cranker camp and left him with Kopeikine. That night, luminol in hand and not wanting to be by himself, he climbed into bed next to his loyal pianist.[8]

That was August 1934. In November, he had another bout of coughing and saw another TB specialist, Dr. Ornstein this time, an émigré Romanian Jew who knew Dr. Rist, his old TB doctor from Paris. More rest. Three months later, more TB appeared. More rest prescribed. Even when he was feeling well, he was fearful. Would it return? Would he live? Lincoln, ever fraught, felt their project was on hold, and like a worried parent, he existed in a state of constant alert to George's every cough or sniffle. In April of the following year, Balanchine decided to get an injection against TB, probably the vaccine, which was only preventative, not curative, but what did he have to lose? Attacks of coughing—it didn't help that he was still smoking—continued intermittently for at least two years. Once he woke screaming in the night, saying that death was coming to take him.[9] Few among us could sustain the physical regime and demands Balanchine faced daily, but his sense of his own inner fragility—of death at the door and a stolen life pulled each time from the brink—this was a feeling that never left him, even as the TB somehow gradually subsided. He never forgot that he was one of a very few who escaped.

Ideas for ballets he might stage for their fledgling but still-existing American Ballet company kept coming. George was moving ever further from "ballet-ballet,"[10] as Lincoln called it, and what he increasingly envisioned, Lincoln thought, was a kind of choreodrama of dance, drama, and maybe even spoken word or choral song.[11] Dmitriev complained that the classical training they were offering at SAB was useless—that Balanchine cared only about music and plastique and pantomime—and he scoffed impatiently that George was a philosophical anarchist with no interest in the traditional balletic repertory, which was true. Vladimirov disliked George's unorthodox choreography too, but Pavel Tchelitchew was pushing for something more radical still. He told Lincoln that he was interested only in revolutionary art, that he admired Bosch, Breughel (the Elder), and El Greco. He believed in Balanchine, but warned Lincoln, a bit self-servingly, that "without a guide or check Bal is lost. He's been in NY a year and more—who are his friends, that foul vulgar whore Davidova, that bastard Dukelsky, Volodin a crazy nice Russian, Kopeikine, Soudeikine. That's all. He lives on flattery: it will be his undoing."[12] They nonetheless saw a lot of each other, and Balanchine saw Tchelitchew as a real Russian, deeply religious, a man who believed in God and fatality, but also in Marx—which George saw as bad and also passé.[13]

Lincoln, meanwhile, had his own ideas for dances. He pressed George to make a dance about "something without L'amour as the subject-matter." "I told him he only had one subject matter, love, and that had been worked out."[14] What about *Medea* in a huge leftist, Soviet-style production, he suggested, astoundingly insensitive to George's past. George sniffed and said okay but that Medea's dead body would have to be executed by the troops. Lincoln didn't give up. What about a Communist-style "Red Hydra" spectacle? Balanchine sniffed again and said it could only be done in Russia, with masses of people, and anyway how did Lincoln know that the Fascists were any worse than the Communists? Lincoln told him. Avoiding confrontation, and evidently annoyed at these naïve and intrusive suggestions, George said okay, let's do a ballet about two revolutionary parties and let the audience choose. At the end there would be a white flag, and people could splash it with the winning color. Lincoln, missing the irony, insisted that the end must be red. By then George was barely listening: "Pourquoi pas?"[15]

Lincoln was finding out what he already feared: that he was no Diaghilev and that George didn't want or need a Diaghilev. It was painful. He wanted nothing more than to collaborate with George, and he never stopped proposing ballets, designers, and composers and pursuing plans that Balanchine often matter-of-factly squelched: "Bal said no." It was a kind of humiliation that curled him up inside, especially when George, rubbing salt in the wound, suggested that perhaps Lincoln was just rich, "another Eddie James." "This cursed me for the rest of the day. I felt cheated out of it, vengeful and sorry for myself . . . knowing he was quite right and that he has a righteous fear of dilettantism. . . . My place in the picture of school and company is increasingly remote."[16] Humiliation became part of the emotional currency between them as George nonchalantly took what he liked from Lincoln's riches, but also from his deep and erratic intellectual and artistic holdings, and waved the rest aside. Lincoln admitted that he hadn't really thought it through: "As a matter of fact I thought hardly at all of what I'd do, imagining only consecutive and charming collaboration. . . . Irritation, resentment at my own ego and laziness, nervousness." He settled for the back door, the servant's entrance—and this is where he would eventually stay, whispering ideas, dropping a pile of books on George's desk, suggesting a thing or two and then stepping back: "I also know Balanchine can be abley and efficiently influenced, if it is sufficiently indirect, flattering and if the suggestions are validly imaginative."[17]

At the moment, George was obsessed with the idea of a courtroom pantomime where the condemned faced a three-headed judge, with a whole crime scene reproduced with evidence, "like Hauptmann's ladder" from the famous Lindbergh baby kidnapping much in the news at the time. It could be like Dostoyevsky, George excitedly explained to a baffled Lincoln.[18] One afternoon Lincoln found George at home reading the complete works of Goethe in Russian, and George said he wanted to do a dance based on the second part of *Faust,* and he had an idea too for a Gershwin ballet about New York City (that would happen in 1969, although Massine got there first, in 1940, with a dance he called *The New Yorker*). He wanted to do a dance with Hindemith on Breughel's fantasy utopia *The Land of Cockaigne* (Massine got there first again, although the project fell through when he suggested Dalí as a designer and Hindemith, astonished at this poor taste, pulled out.)[19] George had written to the composer William Boyce, requesting a score.[20] He had an idea too for a work on the twelfth-century Igor epic, already the basis of Borodin's opera *Prince Igor* and later translated by Vladimir Nabokov as "Song of Igor's Campaign." He wrote a scenario (since lost) for a Pushkin-themed Romantic ballet.[21] As for love, George wasn't done with it yet: "L'homme est une insecte sexuelle; everything is sex," he told Lincoln. Or, rather, the "act of love itself was nothing, it was the imagination and perversity clothing it that was exciting."[22]

Getting his ideas to the stage was another matter. Even the prospect of a small touring company seemed almost impossible to achieve, and so far all they had were a few occasional bookings (New York's Adelphi Theater, Lewisohn Stadium). Finally, in April 1935, thanks in large measure to Lincoln, Eddie, and more Harvard connections, Balanchine was named ballet master at the celebrated Metropolitan Opera, with the American Ballet in residence. They had arrived! The Met would be Balanchine's American Mariinsky, his Paris Opera, the perfect home for the national ballet company George and Lincoln had envisioned all along. To celebrate, they had lunch together at the Rainbow Room atop Rockefeller Center.[23]

The idea was grand. The American Ballet would split its time between the Met and national touring. The company even had a new manager, the St. Petersburg–born impresario Alexander Merovitch, who had worked with prominent émigré musicians, many of them Balanchine's friends and acquaintances, including Horowitz, Stravinsky, Nathan Milstein, and Gregor Piatigorsky. There was new money too, as Merovitch brought on another wealthy Russian clan: the Manischewitz family of Cincinnati, who had just opened a new matzo factory in New Jersey (Lincoln called Manischewitz the "Matzoh-King").[24] This unlikely team of Russians and Jews—Merovitch, Manischewitz, Balanchine, Warburg, and Kirstein—booked the American Ballet on an ambitious transcontinental tour. Half of the dancers would stay in New York to begin work at the Met, and the other half would go on the road, with Balanchine shuttling back and forth between them. The tour would blanket the country, taking the company to some sixty towns and cities from New Haven to Princeton, Cleveland, Chicago, St. Louis, Omaha, Tulsa, Dallas, Los Angeles, Seattle, Vancouver, and points between. They departed in high spirits on buses from Rockefeller Center on October 15, 1935: photos show Balanchine and his dancers (mothers in tow) all neatly dressed in pleated skirts and matching cardigans, carting large black theater trunks labeled in bold: *AMERICAN BALLET TRANSCONTINENTAL TOUR*. The Russian wardrobe mistress Dounia Mironova, once in service to the legendary Anna Pavlova, shouted orders to them all in Russian. Balanchine played the press in his charmingly Russian English, joking tongue in cheek that *Alma Mater*, a silly dance he had recently made at Eddie's insistence about the Yale-Harvard football match, might in certain Ivy League towns prove artistically scandalous.[25]

Less than two weeks later, this ambitious enterprise ended in farce. Merovitch, it turned out, was both dishonest and psychologically unstable, and early in the tour he began threatening to use the two pistols he possessed to kill Balanchine and Warburg. Red-faced and shouting uncontrollably in whatever town they found themselves in, he said he was everyone and everywhere, and that he would seek out the enemy and destroy all spies. He even appointed one of the frightened young dancers as his deputy. As Warburg tried to cope with this sudden descent into madness, Balanchine began to feel ill again. Finally, in the small mining town of Scranton, Pennsylvania, the company ran out of money and Merovitch disappeared. Back in New York, Lincoln was fielding frantic calls from Eddie, who couldn't reach the

"Matzoh-King" or Merovitch, but once it became clear that the company had been swindled and was bankrupt, Eddie's lawyers moved in to clean up the mess. Lincoln got on a train to Scranton, and George, Lincoln, and Eddie gathered the startled company at the empty theater and told them the tour had been officially canceled. Get back on the bus to New York, George instructed the dancers, and come to class at the school as usual in the morning. Eddie left immediately for Mexico, on the advice of his analyst, to recover from the "psychic shock" of this wild defeat.[26]

The Met engagement soured too. Balanchine was controversial, and he was frustrated and growing desperate. He rashly threatened to return to Russia, where his friends and family, he said, were now in important positions, which was only sort of true.[27] His direction of Gluck's *Orpheus and Eurydice* in the spring of 1936 pushed things over the edge. It was an opera he knew well. As a child, he had danced in Meyerhold, Fokine, and Golovin's spectacle featuring Hades as a ghastly field of frozen half-dead bodies hanging from cliffs and sinking through trapdoors.[28] Now, working with Tchelitchew, he put the singers in the pit (as Meyerhold had) and staged Hades as a forced labor camp, with barbed chicken wire, dead branches, and bodies covered in cheesecloth in an eerie, unnatural light.[29] Tchelitchew insisted that ballet was old and dead, and it was up to Balanchine to do something "wholly boiling in the new,"[30] and the movements, more pantomime than dance, were ugly, angular, grotesque; the dancers writhed on the floor and plunged from the sky on wires with pitchforks. You are in hell; you must *see* torture, he said.[31]

Alarmed members of the Met board objected and wanted Tchelitchew removed from the project. Balanchine threatened to walk out. By then he had somewhere to go: he was running back and forth to Broadway, successfully staging dances for the Ziegfeld Follies, and working with Rodgers and Hart on a new musical, *On Your Toes* (1936), a satirical send-up of a Russian ballet company—featuring a gunslinging Merovitch-like mafioso and starring Ray Bolger and Tamara Geva. When the scathing reviews of *Orpheus* came in a few weeks later ("Travesty"; "Elysian Fields resemble Flanders battlefield"; dancers twisted "in the usual Balanchine knots"), Balanchine knew it was only a matter of time. The strain of work and failure took its toll. He was coughing again and feeling feverish and exhausted.[32]

Meliton Antonovich Balanchivadze, Georgi's father, who was born in the Georgian peasant village of Banoja, was a composer, a bon vivant, and a failed businessman.

Meliton, sitting center-right in Western attire, with his traveling Georgian choir in traditional dress. They toured Georgia performing peasant and folk music, both before his departure for St. Petersburg and after his return to his native land following the revolution.

Georgi's mother, the delicate but strong Maria Nikolaevna Vasil'eva, seated with dog. The other two stolid women may be Georgi's aunts.

Georgi Melitonovich Balanchivadze, top left, with his brother, Andrei, and his sister, Tamara, professionally photographed in St. Petersburg during the family's wealthy lottery-winning days.

The family's country hou in Lounatjoki, Finland, purchased with their lott winnings. It was a short tr ride from St. Petersburg, when the money dried up the family moved there permanently. The childre were tutored and spent lo days roaming the country

Georgi in Lounatjoki during his happiest childhood years, neatly shorn and simply dressed, with his characteristically reserved demeanor.

The Imperial Theater School in St. Petersburg, where Georgi lived as a student from the age of nine. He often spent weekends alone playing the piano, surrounded by portraits like these of Russian dignitaries.

The Russian Orthodox chapel at the school. Religion was Georgi's best subject, and he grew up with icons and religious music and ceremony, all of which exerted a strong influence on his art.

Alexandra Danilova, a fellow dancer at the school, would later leave Russia with Georgi and become one of his lead dancers and his common-law wife.

Lidia Ivanova, another talented fellow dancer who worked with Georgi. (Note her delicate and restrained imperial style.) Lidia later drowned mysteriously in a boating accident shortly before her planned departure from Russia with their small troupe. Georgi and his friends were sure she had become too friendly with security agents and that her death was a state-sponsored murder.

The 1917 Bolshevik Revolution: a demonstration at the grand manor of the ballerina (and once mistress to the heir apparent) Matilda Kschessinskaya. The manor was taken over by Lenin, who used it for a time as his headquarters and delivered speeches from the balcony—a strike at ballet was a symbolic strike at the heart of the czar's imperial order.

The former Mariinsky Theater in 1919. The theater had been stripped of czarist insignias and the old "diamond row" of royalty and the elite replaced by a new audience of workers.

Imperial Theater School graduation 1921: Mikhail Mikhailov, Georgi Balanchivadze, D. K. Kirsanov, and Nicholas Efimov, with fashionably slicked hair and uniform dress.

A poster for Balanchivadze's Young Ballet in May 1921, in a radical poster-art style typical of revolutionary artists at the time.

Erotic Fantasy: Two Embracing Nudes, by Kasyan Goleizovsky, a choreographer whose work captivated the imagination of Balanchivadze and his friends. Moscow and St. Petersburg were teeming with experimental choreography inspired by machines, speed, eroticism, nudity, biomechanics, the absurd.

Balanchivadze and his first wife, Tamara Geva, danci
his *Étude* (1923), barefoot and entwined, the year be
their departure for Berlin.

Balanchine in Paris in 1927, during his Diaghilev days. In a sign of his playfulness and lifelong interest in science, he inscribed the back of this photo or calling card with Newton's first law of motion.

Serge Diaghilev ("Big Serge") with Léonide Massine, who came from the Bolshoi and was Diaghilev's protégé and, for a time, his lover. Massine was Balanchine's rival as a choreographer and later for Vera's heart.

Balanchine as Kastchei in Michel Fokine's *The Firebird* (1926), one of several character roles he took on with the Ballets Russes. He was a good but not great classical dancer, and Diaghilev immediately saw his value as an expressive actor and mime.

La Chatte (1927), inspired by an Aesop fable, had music by Henri Sauguet and "kinetic constructions" by the Russian-émigré artists Naum Gabo and Antoine Pevsner consisting of abstract industrial tubes, circles, and cones in mica and steel, as well as tutus layered in gelatin. Balanchine made biomechanical dances of interlocking limbs, especially for the seven featured men, shown here.

Alexandra Danilova in full-body blackface for *Jack in the Box* (1926), with music by Erik Satie and costumes by André Derain, in a photo taken by another Russian émigré, Man Ray.

Lubov Tchernicheva, Alice Nikitina, Alexandra Danilova, Felia Doubrovsk and Serge Lifar in a staged photo for *Apollon Musagète* (1928). To Balancl annoyance, Nikitina, the mistress of a donor, doubled in Danilova's role as Terpsichore. The costumes were by C Chanel, who was close to Diaghilev.

L'Errante (1933), to Schubert's *The Wanderer*, was first made for Balanchine's Les Ballets 1933 in Paris. It was about a woman in the last ten seconds of her life. This photo shows the American production a few years later, which reproduced the long gown in which the woman entangles herself as she wanders through her memories.

Mozartiana, for Les Ballets 1933, shown here in its American production, had music by Tchaikovsky. It was another dance about death, as seen in this image. Balanchine would return to *Mozartiana* in an entirely new dance for Suzanne Farrell near the end of his life.

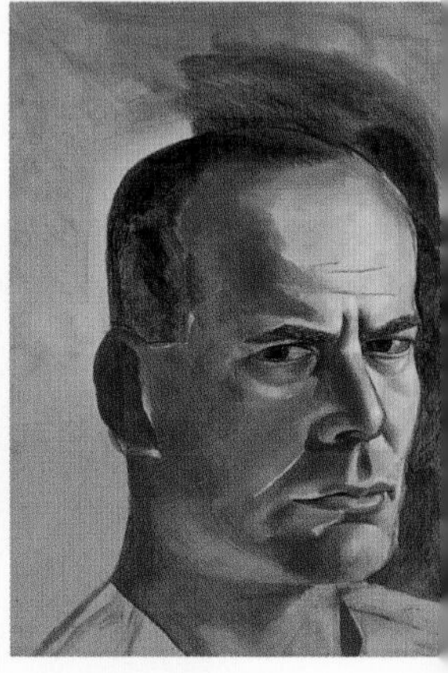

Lincoln Kirstein came from a wealthy Jewish émigré family i Boston. He was a force in the v of literature, art, and theater, b was obsessed with ballet—and Balanchine. This 1950 portrai Lucian Freud captures Kirstei monumentality and vulnerabil his seriousness and anguish.

Kirstein and Balanchine in animated conversation at Kirstein's eccentrically decorated home on Gramercy Square. 'hey met in 1933 and stayed together until Balanchine's death in 1983. They were a ıd of odd couple: the physically enormous and awkward Lincoln and the small and poised George.

ɜalanchine teaching at the School of American Ballet soon after its founding in 1934. Located ·n the fourth floor of the Tuxedo Building at 634 Madison Avenue, the school was supported in ırge measure by Lincoln's wealthy friend Eddie Warburg—who, when he signed on, had never een a ballet.

Balanchine correcting a dancer at the School of American Ballet. He is demonstrating the linear geometry of classical form, which was the foundation of his most radical departures. The photo is by Henri Cartier-Bresson.

Balanchine's first America
ballet was *Serenade* (1935
had its unofficial premiere
outdoors on the Warburg
in Woodlands, New York,
invited guests in celebrati
Eddie's twenty-sixth birth
1934. The dancers were
students, the costumes we
improvised, and Tchaikov
score was played on a dan
piano.

Eugenie Ouroussow was a White Russian princess and one of the "Three Fates" who presided over the school. She arrived in 1934 and stayed until her death in 1976. Her family had fled the revolution, and she was Paris-educated in philosophy and literature. In addition to her duties at the school, Ouroussow wrote about Pasternak, the Russian symbolists, and Christian mysticism.

The mysterious Armenian-born, Russian-speaking Lucia Davidova was Balanchine's closest confidante. She had that special skin that makes pearls mature, and it was said that she was paid to wear them. She married and lived with men but was also the longtime lesbian lover of the wealthy railroad heiress Alice DeLamar.

Balanchine and Eva Brigitta Hartwig (stage name Vera Zorina), in a seemingly relaxe moment in their otherwise difficult relationship. They married in 1938. She was his third wife.

Vera Zorina in *The Goldwyn Follies* (1938), a Hollywood film Balanchine choreographed for her. She was glamorous but not a great dancer, and their unhappy relationship spanned his Broadway and Hollywood years. These "commercial dances," he let her know as his heart broke, had nothing to do with the "eternal" dances that were his lifeblood.

Balanchine and Zorina rehearsing Rodgers and Hart's *I Married an Angel* (1938). He worked very physically, trying things out, demonstrating, pushing technique and possibilities to the limits, as we see in this flying leap.

A postcard of Balanchine with Todd Duncan, Katherine Dunham, and Dooley Wilson on the set of the all-black musical *Cabin in the Sky* (1940). Balanchine directed and put his own money into the production. He learned a lot from Dunham and her dancers, who fondly called him "Bally."

The Nicholas Brothers were ›ther influence on Balanchine, who reproduced in his own ˈcal idiom the freedom and off-balance torque apparent in this ıage, one example of the many ays that black American music nd dance shaped Balanchine's choreographic style.

Balanchine with Nicholas Magallanes and Marie-Jeanne Pelus, around the time he made *Concerto Barocco* (1941) for Marie-Jeanne. Balanchine was interested in revealing the human form. These staged erotic photos juxtaposing full nudity and full dress were fashionable at the time; this one is by George Platt Lynes, who took many erotic and homoerotic photographs of Balanchine and his dancers.

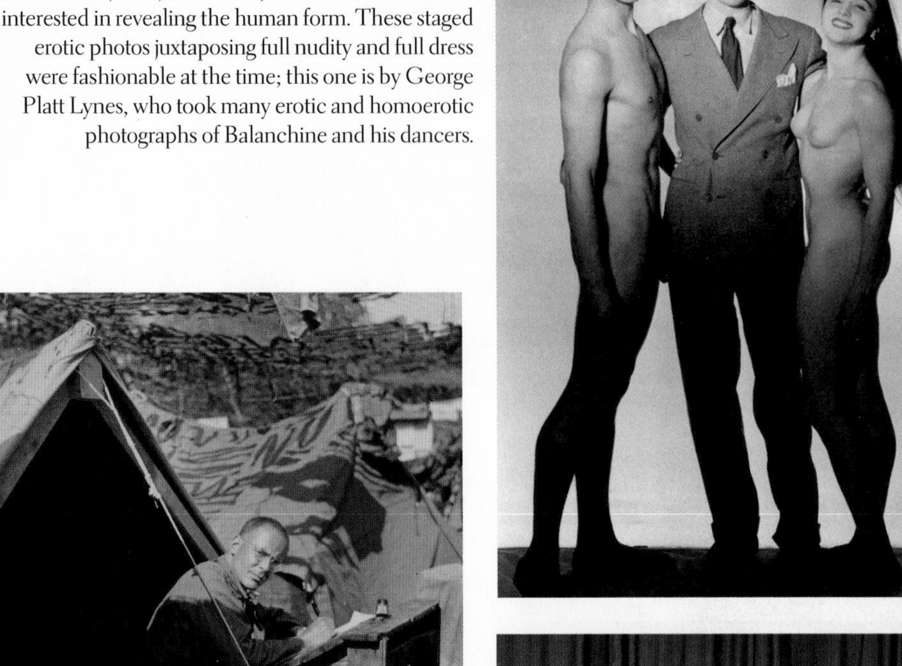

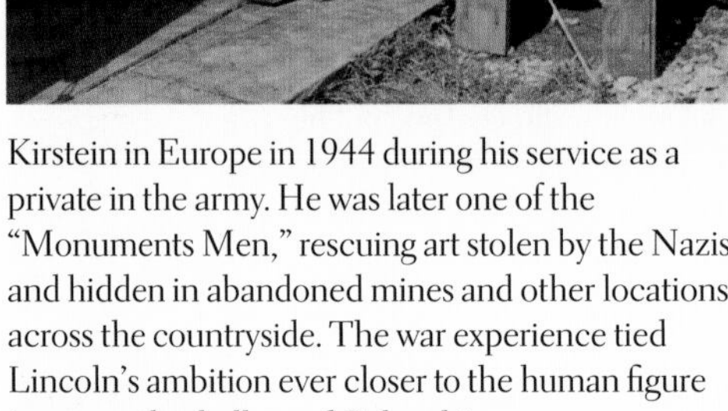

Kirstein in Europe in 1944 during his service as a private in the army. He was later one of the "Monuments Men," rescuing art stolen by the Nazis and hidden in abandoned mines and other locations across the countryside. The war experience tied Lincoln's ambition ever closer to the human figure in art—and to ballet and Balanchine.

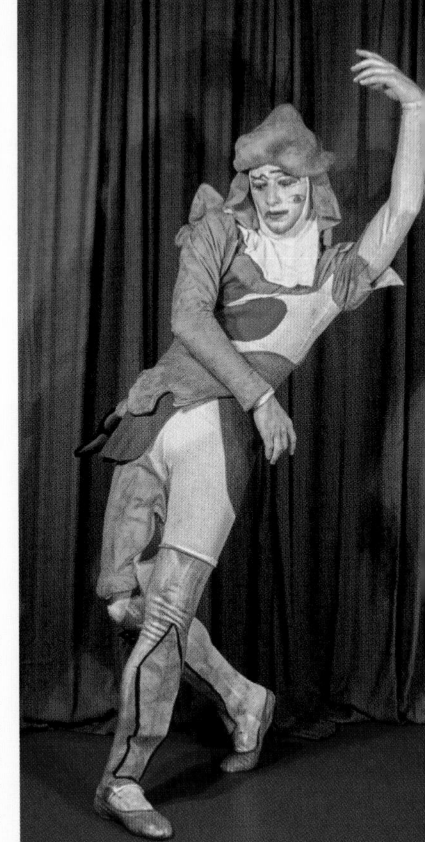

The rubbery Todd Bolender as Phlegmatic in the original production of *The Four Temperaments* in 1946. Balanchine immediately took scissors to Kurt Seligmann's elaborate costumes and eventually stripped the ballet to black-and-white practice clothes.

chine in 1946 marrying Maria
ief, his Native American princess
ar bride. She was his fourth wife.

Tallchief as Eurydice with Nicholas Magallanes in the title role of *Orpheus* (1948) at the moment when Orpheus is returning from the underworld, just before he looks back and she dies.

uil Le Clercq as the leader
Bacchantes in *Orpheus*.
imbed and daring, she was a
hrough dancer in Balanchine's
d would soon become his fifth
t wife.

Tallchief in *Firebird* (1949), which was a box-office hit and saved the NYCB from one of its chronic fiscal crises.

Balanchine was a serious musician and often made his own piano reductions of a score. "I don't *listen* to the music, I *read* it," he said. He wore glasses only in private moments.

Balanchine conducting *Symphony in C* at City Center in He liked to step up to the podium whenever he could. On a joke, he appeared dressed as Toscanini.

Betty Cage talking with Balanchine's European agent, Leon Leonidoff, another Russian émigré. Betty ran the NYCB administratively for decades from "headquarters" at City Center. She was a black woman and a practicing white witch, who also read palms and tarot cards and gave impromptu tai chi classes to the dancers.

In 1953, when she was barely twenty, Barb Horgan ("Horgie" to the dancers) joined B Cage and stayed at the NYCB for the rest life. She was later Balanchine's personal assistant, companion, and, after his death, executor of his estate. They are seen here i 1960s attending a gala performance.

Barbara Karinska (born Varvara Andryevna Zmoudsky in Kharkiv, Ukraine), another émigrée, worked with Balanchine in Paris in the 1920s and at the NYCB for the rest of her life. Known for her use of the finest materials and attention to detail, she sometimes sewed secret hearts or personal signs into the hems of dresses. Balanchine worked closely with her and involved himself in every aspect of costuming his dancers.

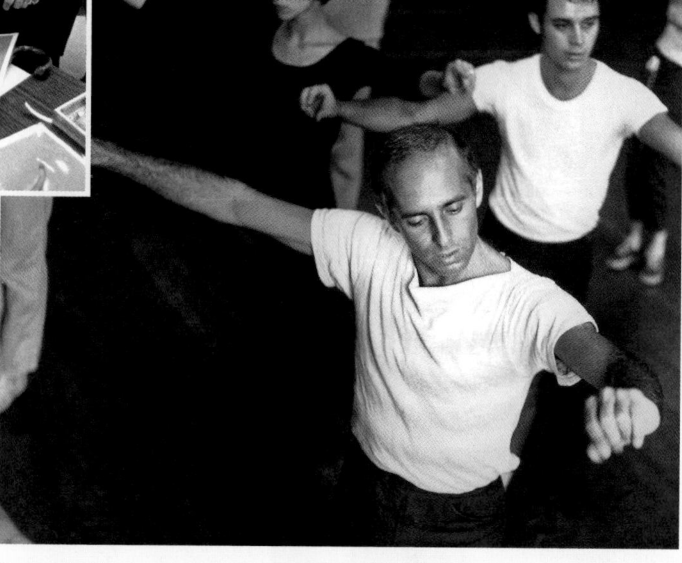

Jerome Robbins was already a big name on Broadway when he joined the NYCB in 1949. He called his youthful, colloquial dances "ballet in dungarees," and he stayed with the company, with interludes elsewhere, until after Balanchine's death. He was one of the only living choreographers Balanchine respected, and for Jerry, Balanchine was "a God."

Robbins and Tanaquil Le Clercq were soulmates. Tanny would marry Balanchine in 1952, but her relationship with Jerry was lifelong, and their correspondence was lengthy, passionate, and witty; he called her "Lucy," and she called him "Charlie Brown." This photo, taken by Tanny, points to Jerry's split and at times tormented character, especially about his Jewishness and his homosexuality.

Tanny being seduced by Death, danced by Francisco Moncion, in Balanchine's *La Valse* (1951). The ballet ends with her corpse lifted on high in a ritualistic circle dance.

Tanny and George in a publicity shot for *Metamorphoses* (1952), based loosely on Kafka's story, with music by Paul Hindemith. Tanny was the object of the cockroach's desire.

Tanny, George, and Natasha Molostwoff at Molostwoff's bohemian Fire Island retreat. "Molo" or "Black Natasha," as she was called for her dark glamour and unknown origins (probably Armenian), joined Balanchine and Kirstein in 1938 and was one of the "Three Fates" who ran the school for decades to come.

To make matters worse, according to Lincoln, the dancer Holly Howard, who was by then George's girlfriend of over a year, had what was rumored to be her fourth or fifth abortion, an illegal and potentially dangerous procedure, especially for a girl who was barely of age. Holly's furious mother was blaming George for ruining her young daughter and threatening to have him deported, which was not out of the question, given the emphasis in the 1930s on deportation as moral cleansing. According to Lincoln, the accusations against him also included syphilis and homosexual predilections, and that fall an immigration agent came to question George, sending him into a rare panic. Lincoln consulted a lawyer, just in case.[33]

What to do with these troubling facts? Even if we assume the abortions were true—and "Bal" certainly comes out of Lincoln's diary at this moment looking callous and frightened—we don't really know what happened. Rumors flew in all directions, then and afterward, and at least two dancers later repeated Lincoln's accounts. John Taras later spoke of "they say" rumors that there were several dancers who were "gaga" over George and would wait for him on the doorstep, like squeamish fans. Or that Holly became a whore—no evidence—and it was George's fault. A fellow dancer at the time inscribed a photograph of Holly as "Balanchine's 1st major 15yr old sweetheart"—although records show that Holly was born in 1918, putting her at eighteen or just under in 1936, but we don't really know how long the two had been involved or what age she gave to herself or her friends. Holly's family says that there were love letters she kept which are now lost (or withheld), and the members of her family that are willing to talk knew of the rumored affair and abortions, but not from Holly herself. They speak of her as lively and unconventional, a wayward woman who lived a fast life of drink and parties, taught ballet, never married, and died young of cancer; but this could also read as a description of an independent woman (and mother) who was looking to escape the restrictive bourgeois world she had been given, the tail end of the 1920s bohemia, or a description of one of the more ubiquitous flappers, young women drawn to New York and "sexual revolution" and above all determined to make a new and freer life.

What we do know is that Holly Howard was from a proud military family with a pedigree that included Oliver O. Howard, who ran the Freedmen's

Bureau after the Civil War; Howard College was named after him. Her father was a general (West Point with Patton and Eisenhower), and she grew up wherever he was stationed, which was mostly in the Philippines. Her mother, Lois, was from a military family too, and when she divorced (a humiliating event in military circles, though perhaps a relief to her), she gathered Holly and her twin brother and moved to New York, a bold move, where Holly ended up at Balanchine's school (her brother became an army physicist). Her family says Lois was independent-minded, and later became a socialite who traveled the world. Holly was like so many of the women who came into ballet: a beauty with a spirit of adventure, a poor education, and a divorced mother, except that her background was more distinguished—and more "fallen," at least in its own terms—than most.

Lincoln's diaries indicate that Lois was Holly's escort, and thus spent time with George too, and that she loved the glamour of theater and Hollywood. But we have no idea what her role was in her daughter's romance. George was of course immensely attractive—accomplished, famous, handsome, foreign, charming, and self-possessed—but also lonely, sickly, and needy. Whatever happened between Holly and George, she was pretty and talented, and he had a strong and unchecked (socially or inwardly) appetite for pretty and talented—as we know, there were others. Not to mention *her* sexuality, love, ambition, adventurousness, shame, mother, father, brother, past, who knows what, and in what combination.[34]

As for abortion, it was all too often used as a form of birth control, a fact which is difficult to digest given the inevitable trauma it must have produced. There were good clinics at the time, and the procedure could be relatively safe. Did Lincoln supply the necessary connections, or did Holly have them already—or not? Or did she abort through potions, pots of steam, excessive exercise, or any number of "folk" remedies in use at the time? Four is a lot and we don't know what she, or he, went through, except that it all seems finally to have led to a crisis for them both that, in the way of things, affected her far more than it affected him. She had the abortions; he was not deported, and moved on.

The denouement to the Met debacle was brief and disappointing. George stayed on to mount a successful Stravinsky Festival in 1937, including a new dance in collaboration with Stravinsky on the old Russian theme of gambling and the capriciousness of fate: *Card Party*, not a major work, but at least Stravinsky conducted the premiere. The Met had by then written George off and refused to support anything he touched—Eddie Warburg paid for it all. The following year, in the spring of 1938, Balanchine was finally fired and the American Ballet sent packing. He wrote a strongly worded statement to the Met, along with an angry letter to the press noting that ballet at this supposed house of high culture was simply "bad ballet" and that working there was like "being in prison."[35]

Everything he had been working for all those years since his arrival in 1933 was unraveling, and it was all happening at once. Lincoln, chafing to have his own artistic voice, had organized his own little touring company, Ballet Caravan, where—without George—he could finally do what he had always really wanted to do: commission American dances by American choreographers and artists on American themes. In the Caravan's short and exhausting life from 1936 to 1940, it toured the country presenting such dances as *Pocahontas, Filling Station, Yankee Clipper,* and *Billy the Kid.* Lincoln enlisted James Agee, Paul Cadmus, Virgil Thomson, Elliott Carter, and Walker Evans (who photographed the dancers),[36] among others. George contributed a few ballets and felt annoyed, but let it go.

Eddie Warburg was moving on too. He had finally lost patience with the constant debacles and financial sinkhole of the ballet, and when his father died in 1937, leaving him in charge of a vast family estate, Eddie washed his hands of the whole enterprise and was gone. Only SAB was left standing—barely—as Lincoln begged his father for help to continue without Eddie. Thanks to Lincoln and the endless patience of his father, the school survived, even with George often away and on the road. In 1938 Lincoln bought Dmitriev out of his shares, and Dmitriev left (Florida!). George continued to send him money when he could; Dmitriev, he said in refrain, had gotten him out of Russia—"I would not be alive if it weren't for Dmitriev!"[37] That year, in a naïve attempt to make it on his own, George set up a new ballet company and issued shares, but records show that George Balanchine Inc. had only one registered buyer: George.[38] In the fall of 1939, the dancer and heiress Lucia Chase delivered the final blow. With the designer Oliver Smith, she founded

Ballet Theatre (soon to be American Ballet Theatre): here was the company that George and Lincoln had aspired to, seemingly snatched out from under them by a wealthy amateur. George was invited to join, but he turned the offer down.[39] He still wanted a ballet company, but he wanted it on his own terms.

It was a "God's will be done" moment, and he followed the path that presented itself to him now. By then he had a new agent, the savvy Milton "Doc" Bender (a dentist who met Hart of "Rodgers and Hart" while cleaning his teeth and promptly switched professions), who had Balanchine choreographing on Broadway and in Hollywood and making more money than he imagined possible. He was teaching less, but he still drew on dancers from the school and the old defunct American Ballet when he could, featuring them in shows and movies as his commercial career accelerated. By 1937 he was busy working with Rodgers and Hart on *Babes in Arms*, and that summer he boarded a train with Kopeikine, bound for Hollywood to make his first film with Sam Goldwyn and George Gershwin: *The Goldwyn Follies*. Commercial theater and film, as Lincoln later put it, took better care of Balanchine than he and Warburg ever had.[40]

Here was a bright new beginning, maybe. Money, success, glamour, fame; it was an American dream, and Balanchine seemed to have it at hand. He was successful at commercial theater—efficient, direct, easy to work with—and he could wheel out excellent dances on demand. He liked it too, and in the coming years, from 1936 to 1945, he would choreograph more than a dozen Broadway shows, five Hollywood films, and an impressive stream of operas, operettas, and ballets. He worked with Rodgers and Hart, Irving Berlin, Frederick Loewe, George Abbott, Frank Loesser, and Truman Capote. He didn't let his theatrical work go and still found time to make ballets for Ballet Theatre and Sergei Denham's Ballets Russes. He was moving constantly, from hotels and apartments to other hotels and apartments, traveling the continent by train, car, and plane from New York to Los Angeles to Boston to Cape Cod (where he worked with Larry Hart) to Weston, Connecticut (where Vernon Duke had a house), to South America (on tour with his own pickup ballet companies twice, and a third time in 1945).

It was the life of a traveling showman, and Balanchine knew it like the back of his hand; this was his father's old game, and he had practiced it in Petrograd and in interwar Berlin, London, and Paris. He allowed himself to be managed by agents and impresarios, which was fine, and he signed on the dotted line, but with his own ballets—the work that really mattered to him and the most valuable property he thought he possessed—he took meticulous care, expertly and often personally negotiating conditions, royalties, and rights with whoever wanted his dances. He hated contracts and avoided them at all costs: he had already been sued back in Europe, he explained to one frustrated manager, and was a "free man" with no desire to obligate himself to anyone. His preference: please send check. Or he simply gave his ballets away for no charge. What did he care? He was making plenty of money on Broadway.[41]

Hollywood was its own game, and when Balanchine got off the train in Los Angeles, met by photographers and the press, he thought he had entered paradise. The West Coast sun, color, and bright light, along with its exotic foliage, vast open spaces, and plentiful fresh fruit loaded into wheelbarrows at open-air markets, delighted him. This was surely what his father's native Georgia was like, he said, and he was certain that the warm, dry climate would have a curative effect on his lingering TB. For once, things were easy. He had a house in Beverly Hills, a car, a salary, and he was living the kind of celebrity life he had first glimpsed in grainy silent films back in Petrograd during the dark and starving days of the revolution.[42] He dubbed Hollywood, and America generally, a "land of lovely bodies" and was known to make a U-turn just to gaze at an attractive woman—he playfully called them "tsoupoulias," a word he invented from the Russian for young chick.

It was an exile society, and he fit right in with the Russian, Austrian, Hungarian, and German émigrés who passed through or stayed, including Igor Stravinsky (in 1940), Arnold Schoenberg, Dimitri Tiomkin (who later told George that his score for *High Noon* was just Russian folk music, slowed down: "A *steppe* is a *steppe* is a *steppe*. . . . The problems of the cowboy and the Cossack are very similar"),[43] Fritz Lang, Otto Preminger, Billy Wilder, Josef von Sternberg, Rouben Mamoulian, Anatole Litvak, Fred Zinneman, Ernst Lubitsch, Lewis Milestone (Milstein), Gregory Ratoff, Thomas Mann,

Bertolt Brecht, and Franz Werfel, among others. He even met his fantasy idol, Ginger Rogers—it was like being introduced to the Statue of Liberty, he said, but he fled when she began spouting Christian Science aphorisms.[44]

By all outward appearances, Balanchine was succeeding mightily. Inwardly, though, things were different, and in retrospect we can see that he was entering a kind of Faustian moment, a brightly lit life that was really a dark disenchantment, an outgrowth of the upheavals and ill-health that had plagued him for so long. The backdrop was Broadway and Hollywood, and he played his role in musicals and films with the consummate professionalism he brought to all his work. The money was part of the fantasy, and he would spend it freely—on jewelry, cars, pianos, an American dream home—although Doc Bender was right that really it was all wasted on George, who didn't seem to care a whit for material gain. Underneath, or at the same time, there was something else going on, and this other sadder story began with two events that coincided with the unraveling of the American Ballet, the Met, Eddie, and all the big plans and ambitions that had brought him to America in the first place: the death of his father and a rending marriage that nearly destroyed him.

Chapter 12

ZORINA

One afternoon in the fall of 1937, Lincoln Kirstein walked into the studio where Balanchine was working, put a telegram on the piano, and left the room. Balanchine finished his rehearsal, read the telegram, placed it back on the piano, and abruptly disappeared without a word. The telegram was from his brother, Andrei, notifying him of his father's death. He wrote sadly in Russian to his mother in Tbilisi: "Devastated by this loss. My tender kisses to all, Georges."[1] He hadn't seen his "pepenka" since before the revolution, when he was a boy, and their correspondence since had been thin and impersonal. "Heartfelt congratulations dearest Dad for the jubilee," George had dutifully cabled from New York when Meliton was fêted for his fiftieth-anniversary jubilee in 1934.[2] And Meliton himself had written the year before his death, proudly announcing to Georgi that his Georgian opera, which he never seemed to finish, was finally being performed at the Bolshoi Theater in Moscow, "the mecca of art." He made no mention—censorship was strict and inevitable—of the horrors being inflicted on family and friends at the time by Stalin and Beria's Great Terror.[3]

Balanchine saved almost nothing, but he saved his father's and mother's letters, tidily folded in their envelopes, and for years he kept a picture of his kindly-looking father—neatly groomed in a Western suit and bow tie, clipped beard, and carefully tapered mustache—on his bedside table, a talisman for a man he had hardly known but whose life occupied a large place in his memory.

The death of a father is the end of any childhood, but it was especially so for Balanchine, who had to grieve alone. He was by then a traitor in the eyes of the Soviet state, the son and brother who had deserted to the West, and a curtain of fear had fallen between him and his family. Fear, in his mind, of deportation or recrimination (the KGB broke legs and bodies for far less); in theirs, of association and disappearing into a Soviet night. (Unbeknownst to George, although he suspected as much, Andrei was picked up around this time in a black car, taken to a secret location, and asked by the party to denounce his brother, a clear warning in Stalinist times.) George sent money but said little, wrote less, and didn't offer a return address. It was a peculiar fact of exile and the Cold War that in order to care for his family, he couldn't know them. The only protection they all had was silence—its own kind of family tie.

Instead, he wrote to Vera Zorina, a glamorous young dancer, age nineteen, with whom he was falling passionately in love. He wrote by hand, in his still-broken English: "I have received telegram from Russia that my father die. this is awful news for me because I loved my father. Now I have no father any more. excuse me for telling you my trubles." And later: "I did not have my parents since I was a boy of eight which I was given to the school. We where poor at the time. And so from my childhood I have the habit to keep everything in myself."[4] Something had shifted inside. It was one more pillar down, a pillar he wasn't much aware of until it was gone, and he found himself, unknowingly perhaps, more vulnerable than ever to his own loneliness and fragilities, just as Zorina was entering his life.

They had met in 1936 at the opening-night party for *On Your Toes,* and she belonged squarely to his newly burgeoning Broadway and Hollywood life. She also belonged to his past. Zorina was European, born Eva Brigitta Hartwig in pre-Weimar Berlin, and marked by her own story of loss and emotional disrepair. When she was a child, her mother had abruptly left her father for another man, who then refused to divorce his wife, leaving Brigitta's lovelorn mother stranded alone with her little girl. Soon after, her father accidentally drowned. She and her mother wandered, and her mother became seriously ill and almost died. Brigitta dealt with this perpetually upheaved childhood in part by devoting herself to ballet, which at least ordered her body and mind. She worked with Max Reinhardt, and in 1934 she joined the Ballets Russes de Monte Carlo, led by Massine at the time, and was given a new, suitably glittering Russian name: Vera Zorina. By then she was a voluptuous young woman, blond, remote, and alluring, with soft, wide features and an hourglass figure—a mesmerizing beauty but a mediocre dancer. Massine began their affair immediately.

He was nearly forty and married; she was seventeen and fatherless. He sent her a mink coat and jewelry from Cartier and arranged for the two of them to meet secretly in distant hotels and resorts. He wrote love letters on tiny, tightly wound scrolls of paper, which he stuck like miniature prayers in the cracks of walls and doors and under mats, instructing her at what place and hour they might next meet. Following their trysts, he sent torrid letters declaring undying love. Above all, he romanced her with glamorous lore of Diaghilev, hinting at the career that awaited her in his capable artistic hands. It was a cruel situation, and she was lost: so lost that she helplessly agreed to join him with his wife on vacations, where alarm clocks signaled the end of Brigitta's time with her lover, and he left Brigitta isolated in her room to return to his domestic life.[5] She even accompanied the marital couple on tour and traveled in their homey trailer, which—hooked to a Lincoln town car—carried their ménage à trois (and a Lithuanian cook) across the United States. The other dancers took the train. There was talk of a Mexican divorce, lawyers, unmet promises, until finally one night in a Florida hotel on tour, Zorina slit her wrists. Massine took a new lover.[6]

This was almost but not quite the state that Balanchine found her in. Soon before they met, Brigitta had chanced upon another figure from George's past: the hated Mr. Edward James. James invited Brigitta and her mother on an Italian tour ending with a stay at the Ritz in Paris. As if by design, he introduced her to George's old friends: Tchelitchew, Rieti, Dalí, the Serts (post-Misia). The following year, Zorina took on Tamara Geva's old role in the London production of *On Your Toes*. It was a small step from there into Balanchine's life. Thanks to Massine, she had even learned a smattering of Russian along the way.

The Massine problem, and it was a problem, was another thing they shared. Massine, whom Balanchine considered a lesser talent, had always been ahead. When George had arrived from Russia, Massine had been top in Diaghilev's mind; when George was fired from Blum's Monte Carlo company after Diaghilev's death, it was Massine who had replaced him; and as George struggled with his health and failed to establish a viable American company, Massine was being hailed across the country and around Europe as the reigning king of dance, the "master choreographer of today," as the eminent critic Edwin Denby put it.[7] Even Lincoln had been taken with the choreographer's epic symphonic ballets (although he later called them "silly").[8] By the time George met Zorina, Massine was successfully producing dances with many of George's most coveted collaborators—including Tchelitchew and Karinska—to scores by Hindemith, Tchaikovsky, and Gershwin. And now, of all the women George could have chosen, he had fallen in love with Massine's forsaken mistress.

George's romance with Brigitta got serious on the Hollywood set of *Goldwyn Follies* in the fall of 1937, around the time of his father's death. She was the star of the show, and he had imported a group of dancers from his American Ballet too. He was supposed to be working with George Gershwin on the music, but the composer had fallen suddenly ill and abruptly died of an undiagnosed brain tumor. George's old friend Vernon Duke had taken his place, and with Kopeikine at the piano, George set about glorifying Zorina's beauty—a feat that met with no resistance since Goldwyn was not-so-secretly infatuated with Zorina too (he provided her with an apartment and every amenity and was known to trail her home to glimpse her from his car a block away). George made a Busby Berkeley–style water-nymph ballet, in which she rose dripping wet through lily pads from a pond, clad in sheer gold lamé that clung seductively to her body. Or he posed her dramatically in a quasi-surrealist setting on a large white statue of a horse (de Chirico, he said), amid Greek columns (Palladio, he noted), as an airplane-engine wind machine blew off her dress.

When he tried to offset these kitschy scenes with a dark depiction of the Spanish Civil War—set to Gershwin's "An American in Paris" no less—Goldwyn took one look and said no thank you. George was furious. Goldwyn, who annoyingly called him "Georgie," also refused to follow George's meticulously planned camera shots.[9] The cameraman on the film was Gregg Toland (known several years later for his innovative cinematography in Orson Welles's *Citizen Kane*), and Balanchine and Toland were experimenting with huge klieg lights placed in trenches dug into the floor (Balanchine's idea) and flooding up into a face (Zorina's). Toland was a master of artifice, using light, camera angles, and timing to make fictional worlds, and photos show George in shirtsleeves and intensely engaged, crouching behind the camera next to Toland or arranging Zorina's limbs, mannequin-like, at just the right angle for a shot. "That's where camera vill be shott!" he excitedly told Goldwyn. He later wrote to his mother back in Georgia, telling her that in the *Follies* he had figured out a new way to put dance on the screen.[10] Goldwyn was unimpressed and finally hauled "Georgie" into his office and told him that his newfangled dances were too "artistic." Miners in Harrisburg would not get them. To which Balanchine reportedly responded: "Mr. Goldwyn, I'm not President Roosevelt, what do I care about the miners in Harrisburg? Besides, there are no miners in Harrisburg: I know because I've been there!" and walked off the set. He was planning to return to New York immediately, but Duke and the art director on the production, who had fallen in love with one of George's dancers (and would soon leave his wife and five children to marry her), patched things up with Goldwyn so that they could all finish the movie.[11]

Goldwyn couldn't take from Balanchine all he had learned, and his fascination with film would never leave him. It was just the kind of complicated visual problem he loved: How can you fit a square stage production into a triangular camera field? How can three dimensions become a flat two-dimensional surface—without losing depth and kinetic life? Film allowed him to guide the viewer's eye through the editing of shots; whereas theater was more like a painting, in which composition guides the eye. Years later he explained: "I have to make your eyes follow from here to there, I am thinking of that all the time, that's what it is to make [the] public to see. And if you dance everywhere like Massine did, he called that contrapuntal—but first of all we do that anyway the legs are always doing that. . . . But he misunderstood so it is a mess. You have to point public . . . force public to see."[12] It was a thrilling new power, and on set, George was constantly behind the camera, editing the shots in his mind. As with every artistic technique that interested him, he grabbed what he could from the movies, and the idea of guiding the viewer's eye made a lasting impression.

Zorina—and her pushy mother—joined George's Russian entourage over long dinners with Kopeikine, Antoine Volodine, the Nabokovs, and Vernon Duke. There were five-pound tins of caviar with black bread, sweet butter, and vodka, but Zorina was always dieting and taking diet pills—not too many, George cautioned, and he later warned: "110 pound is ridiculous for your tipe of girl"; "eat more otherways you will loos your beautiful bust."[13] She was working hard to become the dancer that she would never be, and in her mind that meant a slim figure. George doted on her, fed her, dressed her, and fretted over every aspect of her costume, hair, and wardrobe. He shopped with her, sent her to his friend the Russian designer Valentina, and gave her expensive gifts, including earrings from Cartier ("like a gesture from a Duke of Russia") and—less appreciated—her very own phonograph. The more he gave, the more he loved, and everything he did in Hollywood and much of his Broadway work would be for Zorina, as he tried to win her (and her ambitious mother) with the gift of his talent.[14]

Zorina saved a trove of George's love letters to her from their years together, heartfelt outpourings in his broken English expressing his innermost thoughts on the nature of love and what was happening between them.[15] Whatever the charms of their initial encounter, George knew from the very beginning that Zorina didn't love him as much as he loved her and that her heart was still with Massine. This humiliating fact made him pour out his feelings even more strongly, as if to unseat the competition: "My Darling Angel . . . Last night when I heard your voice I trumbled." His declarations of love alternated with self-loathing as a pernicious jealousy entered into their relationship: "I now [know] you think that I am cold, with no feling, and . . . Maybe you dont care much. I am afraid that your remark about Leonid [Massine] is not a joke. I see you stil want him." George was right; she did still want Massine, but rather than leaving her, George pursued harder. He never worried about his career, he confided, except now so "that you will like me more," and he yearningly hopes she "will love someone who will make you very happy and that someone will be G. I wish you would be here now. I am so lonsom. I am sorry darling forgive me."[16]

"Forgive me." He loved too much, too tragically, too suffocatingly, she later complained, and she wasn't the last to say that his love could be overwhelming. "I bless every minute from the moment I have met you but I often wonder why I am so lucky why God gave me such a tresure. . . . I exist only the time I read your letter."[17] Or: "I am happy now, like I never was before in my life. Just to think, that I have something wonderful wich belongs to me alone. Some thing wich moves around, has a most beautiful haven blue eyes and Angels heart. One thing I am sad about is, that I would never be able to tell you how I feel. Maybe I could do it on the stage." The stage: the only showcase of his heart, but she—she!—was not fully up to it, emotionally or as a dancer. Instead, he asked Tchelitchew to paint her portrait so that he could put "her" in his apartment; he bought himself a watch at Cartier, he wrote to her, so that he could hear "her" ticking on his arm, always.[18] It was not only that he idealized her—that would be too simple. It was that he loved her for who she might be; she retaliated with who she might have been: Massine's wife.

Back in New York in 1938 they were working together on Zorina's Broadway debut in Rodgers and Hart's *I Married an Angel*, a title that recalled George's old dream about the angel he married only to find he could not speak her language. When they were not in rehearsal, George was working secretly on a surprise: making Zorina's dressing room into a cozy abode with colorful curtains and fresh paint.[19] She found him remote and called him priestlike, her "Prince Myshkin," after Dostoyevsky's troubled mystic, pulled between the life of the spirit and tawdry everyday reality—which was not far off. When George proposed marriage during the show's run, she hesitated, saying she needed more time. He became depressed, consumed with jealousy, and friends thought he was losing weight. She was meanwhile busy falling in love with Orson Welles, who sent her passionate letters at every hour of the day, or flirting with the debonair Douglas Fairbanks Jr. At the opening-night party for *I Married an Angel*, George watched miserably as Fairbanks charmed the room in his elegant smoking jacket, while George himself felt diminished and small, standing awkwardly aside in his favorite Russian shirt, which he now hated. Still, he persisted: "Why don't you fly [to] Hamburg and spend few days with me at hotel as my guest. Love Balanchine."[20] When she finally agreed to marry him, the news went out over the tabloid press that Fairbanks had been jilted and George had won. A Pyrrhic victory, as it would turn out.

They were married on December 20, 1938, at the elegant art deco Borough Hall in St. George, Staten Island.[21] St. George: his Russian name day and another sign or symbol of his effort to bring her to him. They inquired about a religious ceremony, but when the Catholic priest they found learned that George had been married in the USSR and had no divorce papers, he turned them coldly away.[22] That Christmas Eve, George gave Zorina another surprise in celebration of their vows: a large box containing a cheap Woolworth's raincoat, except that concealed inside the plastic coat lay a dreamy, pure-white ermine fur. He sent a picture of this happy Hollywood couple—Zorina wrapped in ermine, George in tux and tails—to his poor, languishing mother in Tbilisi, soon after Meliton's death (and unaware that she was living through Stalin's atrocities), proudly asking her blessing.[23] Still suffering from bouts of homesickness and his father's death, George drove himself from Hollywood to New York with a detour through the American state of Georgia—just to see what it was like.[24] But with his marriage, he was captivated: "My own darling wife[,] my god is in you," he wrote; "You are my life. . . . Yours forever gogi."[25]

Another surprise: George secretly bought twenty-six acres of land in Fort Salonga, near Northport in Long Island. He—still secretly—hired a team of architects and poured himself into designing and building an American home for his beautiful, newly wed wife. It was a pink dream house fully furnished down to the last detail with colonial American maple furniture and wallpaper from Macy's. There were rocking chairs and bookcases enclosed in glass, a hand-painted Swedish dining table with matching benches, and prints in the bedroom of nineteenth-century ballerinas: Marie Taglioni, Fanny Elssler, and Lucile Grahn. He called it "Balrina," fusing his name with Zorina's to sound like "ballerina." Did he realize he was echoing the white-picket-fenced home that Alexander Blok had once presented to his own idealized wife and

"Divine Sophia"? Or was this more like Chaplin in *Modern Times* (1936), the tramp playing house with the orphaned Paulette Goddard, wrapping her in ermine and dreaming of a home to house their love? When George finally drove Zorina out to Long Island to present her with this glorious surprise, accompanied by Kopeikine, Volodine, and her mother, who came to bless their new home with bread and salt in the Russian tradition, there was only one problem: George had quite forgotten to give his perfect pink house a front door.[26]

Back in real life, George, Zorina, Zorina's mother, their German shepherd, Wingoff, and a German housekeeper were all living in a small apartment in Lucia Davidova's brownstone at 11 East Seventy-seventh Street, where Lucia had settled (thanks to Alice DeLamar). Davidova was by then a steady confidante, and George came and went freely from her formal and heavily curtained home, seeking her solace and advice in matters of love. This time she had a front-row seat. Zorina cruelly placed pictures of Massine around their apartment, and so Léonide formally joined their chaotic household, as Zorina gave to George the experience that Massine had given to her: unrequited love. She was "mercenary," Davidova said, and George was "dog-devoted."[27]

Not entirely. George waged his emotional battle on the only ground he knew he had: dancing. He and Zorina worked together a lot, but always on Broadway and in Hollywood; he withheld from her his more serious dances, the ones she truly coveted, which is to say his real inner life. He simply closed the door to her on this part of his mind. Worse, he cast other women in these dances, placing their pictures in his mind's eye. It was a revenge, of sorts. But it was also a return to his own real life: whatever his love for Zorina, and however much he gained on Broadway, it could not allay the feeling that he was cut off from his own most vital source: serious music.

In the fall of 1940, as their relationship was sinking, he returned to *Serenade*. He expanded it for the dancer Marie-Jeanne Pelus, one of the first to be trained at his school. She was the kind of dancer Zorina could never become. Physically small, she was fast and full-figured and had muscular legs and feet and an astonishing technical facility. For her—with her—George restored to Tchaikovsky's score the Russian theme ("Tema Russo") with its soulful and joyful melodies derived from Russian folk songs. Marie-Jeanne's "Russian dance" began slowly and intimately and then opened and built into a fantastic outward kaleidoscope of patterns, the stage filled with women and beautiful dancing. It was a respite, an affirmation, a reaching out, and it was no accident that he and Marie-Jeanne would soon be romantically involved. Above all, it was a return to Tchaikovsky, a Russian musical home. *Serenade* was like that: a ballet Balanchine kept at his side and made and remade at key moments in his life with dancers he cared for, or needed, and admired. And at the time, he needed Marie-Jeanne, a dancer who could go with him into the deeper side of his imagination. Zorina did not have the physical or inner resources for this kind of dancing. She could not be made; Marie-Jeanne could and was.

As his marriage collapsed, George retreated, and his unfailing ability to immerse himself in making dances was one of the saving facts of his emotional life. He could make those leaps: from dark nights to brightly lit days, and the studio was the respite it had always been. No one could touch him there. Commercial work kept him occupied and amused, but in spite of his desire to escape it, it did more than that. American musical theater, movies, and popular culture, from Chaplin to ragtime and jazz, had been a preoccupation since his youth in Russian avant-garde circles, and he enthusiastically took it all on and turned it to his own purposes. *On Your Toes* included a wickedly satirical rendition of an old Diaghilev chestnut, *Scheherazade*.[28] He was famously easy to work with, and Richard Rodgers (another son of Russian émigrés) later recalled playing the music for "Slaughter on Tenth Avenue," the big dance number in the show, in a two-piano arrangement at a friend's apartment for George. When Rodgers came to the end, George was silent and turned abruptly to leave. Rodgers stopped him and "went into the pidgin English I used with him then, 'you don't like? You don't say anything.'" George responded, "Am too busy staging. I love," and they were off to the races.[29] He set himself challenges: for the pas de deux for Ray Bolger and Zorina, he made a sexy duet with one rule: no touching. Balanchine was learning from the dancers too, and Bolger recalled him setting the structure and a few key sequences in one of his solos and then leaving the studio: you have sixty-four counts, do something. His fascination with tap was apparent: in another number he juxtaposed tap and classical dancers like a dance-off: "shagging" versus pirouettes. As for telling a story in dance, he once asked Duke for a Russian translation of a show they were doing together, and when he heard the plot, he just said, "Stupid. Glad I didn't read it," and went off to make his dances.[30]

For *I Married an Angel*, based on a Hungarian play, George and Larry Hart, who was by then a friend, had gleefully concocted a spoof on Radio City Music Hall and the paintings of Salvador Dalí (George's idea) in the form of a "surrealist ballet." "You can't keep writing about old Budapest all night," Hart explained to the worried producer as the rehearsal stretched into the night. George sent out for a large black cloth and dozens of red gloves. He cut holes in the cloth, hung it, and had the dancers stick their red hands through the holes while another dancer sat on a bicycle suspended from the sky and a beheaded man sauntered about with his head tucked under his arm. As a final touch to Zorina's costume, he bought twenty-four toothbrushes and strung them around her neck. Hart finally explained to the befuddled producer that the point of the ballet was quite simply to let Balanchine "fry Dalí's ass."[31] The following year, in 1939, Balanchine worked with Dalí himself planning a " 'musical to end all musicals' based on Aristophanes's *Clouds*, which they planned to call something like 'For crying out Cloud.' "[32] It never happened.

What did happen were his own songs, simple show tunes composed at the piano—something he had always done, but this time he wrote lyrics in English. These songs, undated and scrawled or scored in his own hand, were sentimental love songs, probably to women he loved, that tapped into a welling emotion otherwise hidden from sight. They were simple. Simple songs to simple music: this is what he liked about Broadway and Hollywood. It was direct, clever, clear, no pretense, and he had serious and enduring admiration for Rodgers and Hart, the Gershwins, and Cole Porter. Their workmanlike approach was his approach too: just work, no drama, no fuss. For a man who drew from such deep emotional wells, he had remarkably little angst in the studio. There, he was unencumbered. His songs were that way too. Happy imitations of sad thoughts and feelings. Some scanned, others didn't, depending perhaps on the state of his English:

There was chaos before God made a woman
and then theos for spite created few man they all ate apples god
knows why
all went to Hades but not J.
Cause
she is not like all other girls
that are much finer than ocean pearls—abundant
treasures of golden curls and lips are so alarming-charming
They wait for you all day and night
To take you on theirs nightly
Flight and dwel in heaven and
Love in hell you'll smell and when
You standing near they make
You tremble instead of saying
I love—you mumble-shamble
No she's not like these girls at all
That are so gorgeous and so divine
She is the fairest one of all
Cause she is mine.

Or "Last Night I Dreamt":

Last Night I Dreamt
that you and I
why did you come
to make me cry
how come and why we ever met
for now I'm lost and can't forget

Or a constant Balanchine refrain:

Why not I? When you were passing by
Why not you? When I was passing through.[33]

But what Balanchine really wanted from the American musical theater was to figure out how black people danced. He had been fascinated with jazz, tap, and other forms of black dance ever since Russia and since he had worked with Josephine Baker in Paris, as well as with, among others, the legendary American tap and jazz man Buddy Bradley in the London music halls. In 1926, Balanchine had made his dance for Danilova in blackface and had "corked up" himself to perform a drunk in a music-hall act, following in the long and unhappy tradition of blackface, minstrelsy, and white men imitating "negros"—a sign nonetheless of his ongoing fascination with black dance and dancers.

His ventures with Lincoln slumming in Harlem clubs and bars were no mere diversion. Artistically, he was constantly watching, studying, and trying things out—a self-conscious process of absorption that his work on Broadway and Hollywood deepened. In the *Ziegfeld Follies of 1936*, he made a dance for Josephine Baker, who was in town from Paris (and prohibited by America's separatist racial laws and practices from entering her hotel through the front door even though she was a star, a fact she did not hesitate to take to the press). "Five A.M." had music and lyrics by Vernon Duke and Ira Gershwin and featured Baker in an all too common trope, far less sophisticated than those she came up with herself: dressed in a skimpy costume and surrounded by a group of elegantly dressed white men. For *On Your Toes*, George was "assisted" by the impressive (and unrecognized) black tap dancer Herbert Harper, and he worked closely with the eccentric Ray Bolger, an innovative tapper of Irish Catholic descent. During rehearsals, George glued taps onto his jazz shoes and asked Bolger to teach him.[34] For *Babes in Arms* (1937), he personally recruited the acrobatic Nicholas Brothers, of Mobile, Alabama, who had made it big in Harlem and in films such as the short *An All-Colored Vaudeville Show* (1935). They did their act downtown with George and then raced up to the Cotton Club to perform the midnight and 2 A.M. shows.[35]

In the simple fact of trying out steps, stealing some and inventing others, beginning with "corking up" himself, Balanchine was stepping, knowingly or otherwise, into the complicated and vexed history of American slavery. Theater was still segregated across the country, but when Balanchine arrived on Broadway and in Hollywood, black dance, in all its great variation, was also in the midst of an intensely creative moment coming out of the Harlem Renaissance, the Jazz Age, and new talkie films: ragtime, Dixie, blues, and big bands; Duke Ellington, Count Basie, Cab Calloway, Benny Goodman, Glenn Miller, Buck and Bubbles, Bill "Bojangles" Robinson, Charles "Honi" Coles, the Nicholas Brothers, Fred Astaire, and Chaplin. The crossing lines of multiple traditions, all tensely bound to the issue of race in America, were exposed: white and black minstrelsy, white and black blackface, whites imitating blacks and blacks imitating whites—it was all there. And Balanchine was part of a long migration of white artists to black art in search of renewal—artistic, emotional, and cultural. Tap dance, but also gospel, ring shouts, swing, Lindy hop, challenge dances, flash and splits, flips, stunts (picked up in part from the vaudeville circuit), and jive—which meant the easy stuff, doled out to white dancers who couldn't handle a too-complex rhythm—were wildly popular.[36] Balanchine was watching, trying it out, and taking it in as fast as he could.

He later said that Fred Astaire was the greatest American dancer of all. "He is terribly rare. He is like Bach, who in his time had a great concentration of ability, essence, knowledge, a spread of music. Astaire has that same concentration of genius; there is so much of the dance in him that it has been distilled."[37] In a way, Balanchine was like Astaire: a white man reinventing black dance in his own image. Astaire had started in vaudeville and was there in Harlem too, and he begged, borrowed and stole and invented, honed, and refined whatever he found useful in the making of his own self-described "outlaw style," a fusion of black-white, them-him, past-present, all tinged with an Old World elegance and attention to balletic line and form. He did it in films such as *Swing Time* (1936), with its "Bojangles of Harlem" number featuring Astaire himself in blackface, and *Shall We Dance* (1937) with Ginger Rogers; his best films were made in the same years Balanchine was working on Broadway and in Hollywood. Then there was the cherished matter of artifice and illusion. Astaire personally dubbed his own taps (Rogers did not—her taps are Hermes Pan) and was closely involved in the exacting art of rhythmic postsynchronization. Astaire once called his sound editor on a Sunday to microshift the timing of a step: in a twenty-four-frame-per-second segment of film, there are four sprockets, and Astaire asked the editor to shift the timing by one sprocket hole—or 1⁄96th of a second.[38]

All of this, and tap dance in particular, presented Balanchine with a vast new vocabulary and ways of moving and thinking about dance that naturally flowed into his own: tap was fiercely competitive and inventive, improvisational, and a kind of dancing that saw the body as a musical instrument, not only in the sound of taps but in the complicated and syncopated cross-rhythms unleashed through the body: arms, legs, hips, ribs, torso, head—all moving in a kind of physical counterpoint.[39] George did more than borrow. He immediately began to incorporate moves, styles, techniques, syncopation, and other rhythmic patterns drawn from black dancers into the DNA, the inner physical and musical structures, of his own balletic art.

Cabin in the Sky (1940) was his deepest plunge yet into black traditions and dances. He directed, choreographed, and sank his own money into this all-black musical, inspired by Gershwin's *Porgy and Bess* (1935), and based on a story by Lynn Root called "Little Joe," on a biblical theme. The black cast was directed by White Russians: Dukelsky wrote the music; Boris Aronson, a Russian-Jewish émigré artist, designed the sets; Balanchine did the rest. He wanted to get the Roach sisters and Cab Calloway (as the Devil), but they were too expensive, so instead they hired Jules Wilson and (eventually) Ethel Waters. For the dances, Balanchine recruited Katherine Dunham and her company of black dancers, and cast Dunham herself in a lead role. Dunham was a dancer, but she was also, unusually, a trained anthropologist with a doctorate from the University of Chicago who had studied performance and ritual from the Caribbean, Latin America, and Africa. Her dancers were versed in ragtime, blues, boogie-woogie, honky-tonk, Lindy hop, rhumba, and even plantation and minstrel dances. When Balanchine hired her, she was coming off the huge success of her own shows, based on her research, retooled for Broadway, at the Windsor Theater in New York: *Tropics* (1937) and *Le Jazz Hot* (1938).[40]

For her part, Dunham felt a special kinship with Russians. She had studied ballet with the émigré Bolshoi dancer Ludmilla Speranzeva in Chicago. Ballet was all but closed to blacks at the time, but Speranzeva didn't care and welcomed Dunham into her classes. Dunham saw parallels between soulful

Russian dirges and gospel-choir spirituals, and so did Balanchine. He wanted to open the show with a Russian (or Georgian) lament, but Ethel Waters refused, so he settled instead for "Wade in the Water." As they worked, the Russians argued at top voice in Russian, and the "Negros," as Duke called them, asked "Bally," as they fondly called Balanchine, what it was all about. Balanchine quickly picked up their steps and style and even, to their amused delight, a few black-English linguistic turns. He gave the dancers free rein, working with Dunham to incorporate their dances into his own. He was especially attentive to moves they did goofing around during breaks, and it is fair to say that Dunham, a formidable figure in American dance, was a vital influence on Balanchine.

Martin Beck, who owned the theater they were working in and had become a producer on the show, didn't like what Balanchine and Dunham were doing. He found the dances too sexualized and wanted some old-fashioned tap and hoofing instead. When Balanchine stood by Dunham and refused to change a single step, Beck lost his temper: "To make it short Mr. Ball-an-chain, you either fix these silly dances of yours or you get out of my theater!" Balanchine had been here before and played the cue: "It's my theater—I am director! You get out!" and he and the Russians all walked out of Beck's office and back to work on stage with Dunham and the dancers. That was that. Success was its own victory and the opening-night reviews for *Cabin in the Sky* that October were glowing, especially for the dances. To celebrate this success, Balanchine went with Duke and Zorina to the fancy 21 Club and drank Pommery Greno champagne late into the night—a gesture that did nothing to change the fact that his marriage was an ongoing source of pain and difficulty. He and Vernon then left together immediately for a vacation in Cuba—sans Zorina. On the ship, George happened to meet a psychiatrist and spent hours holed up in a cabin with him, pouring out his romantic woes and seeking advice.[41]

When he got back to New York in December 1940, he did something he never publicly admitted to doing: he left Zorina. Walked out. He liked to say that she had left him (she said it too), but it wasn't so. And when she tried to make amends, he wrote sharply, hitting her where it hurt most:

Dear Brigitta,

You were not sincere when you asked me to come back. Are you sincere with yourself? Unfortunately you began to be flat. Everything helps you on this way, that can kill a woman and an artist.

Pity.

George.[42]

Shocked, she cornered him after a ballet class and, like a little student, approached him to say that she had no pride and needed an explanation. He answered in another letter, assuring her that she did have pride, and he respected it because it was a "substantially feminine" impulse to protect and defend something so important—their love. When they first met, he explained, he saw her as "a poor littel girl which is born with a good heart, not so good helth and certenely with inspiration of art." Poor because of her sad family life; poor because she had been misled by Massine into confusing "what you thought was a big love" for what was in "reality a passion, jealousy, constant alarm, nerves[,] and this . . . brought the open vein." She slit her wrists, he said, for "false" love, and he thought that his "creative love" might repair her and make her into "the real Brigitte." He would take happiness in that. But, he went on, she saw his love instead as "weakness," and this idea she had "about my weekness became a real obsession" for her—and for him too. This time, he says, she is not slitting her veins but instead becoming "flat" and "killing" the woman and the artist inside her. And yet! "I still want very much to have a wife, but tell me please have you yourself?! . . . You told me you love me, so please, read this letter through this love if it is a sincere one and give me <u>all your objections</u> and I promiss you if your love is sincere not to fail in my pride to protect and defend also my love. Your George."[43]

Next, she tells him (he writes) that she wants a husband she admires who will advise and guide her artistically. Please, he cautions: admiration is not love. And when she explains that her first love is art, he firmly disagrees. "How can you speak about love for art when the deep conception of love in itself you eliminate?" "Your university of art," he sarcastically notes, "is only the spectacular side of some ones spiritualy poor life." He reminds her that "the first subject of art was the love for God," which became human love, since "we are God's creations." He does not want a marriage based on "interest," he says. He wants a woman, and he is hurt that she does not want all of him and strikes back (again) by telling her that she is merely a "spectacular" Hollywood dancer and not an "eternal" artist at all. "Don't forget, that I have some experience in matter of art and not only spectacular art what is mostly yours but also in the creative inspiration of art what is an ethernal art."[44]

Is it really a sign of weakness, he persists, that he sits around the house in his dressing gown all morning instead of being out in the world? He tells her a long story of a play he once saw in which a housewife complains bitterly that her inventor husband just sits around all day on the couch until finally the husband defends himself: "I am thinking!" He then invents the washing machine, and they become millionaires. "Well, Darling, everything that you told about my work, and my dressing gown, is perfectly true, but don't you see there some similarity when it is a question of creation?" Then, a rare statement of ambition: "But I promise myself to be a producer, and I am on the way, and I will be."[45] He has made it hard for her, he admits. He has idealized her, burdened her with his vision of her, and lost "himself" in the process. So now he is going to "run backward to Balanchine . . . he is a good boy!" "After all Darling, Balanchine was always a creative man and much more [now] than before I need to have myself for my work and for my art which is also my love. Specialy now." His art, he says, slipping into an old Russian theme, "will be so different than the ordinary life."[46] A scrap note to himself (that ended up in Zorina's papers) showed something of his struggle to regain himself: "Mind produces all action. Your true course is to destroy fear and leave the field to God, Life, Truth and Love, remembering that God and his ideals alone are real and harmonious."[47]

Three months later, in March 1941, Zorina is sending him roses and calling him on the phone. He is thanking her for the roses and begging her, please, "don't call me. Don't meet me." "You make me only suffer."[48] He is sad but also angry: "You tell me about your love—which one? The last one? A new one? . . . I had a wonderful conception of love. I should love to keep it. Good night my Darling. G."[49] Yet he is also pulled back in, tormented, and quickly arrives again at the full bloom of his obsession. He begs her to go with him to see a doctor he has met, Dr. Yourgi, who could be a neutral listener, who could help them if only she would agree, if only she could get past her "revulsion" for seeing this Dr. Yourgi. Doesn't she love George enough to do that small thing, he asks? She will not. He cuts back to the open wound of Massine: "I prefer to tell everything to the third person a doctor then to have a third person in my home who was your lover."[50]

He admits, beseeching her, that he has been for some time at "the end of all my physical and moral forces" and that staying with her is too "dangerous for me." He is still seeing a doctor, a different one now—Dr. Shwartzer—and "having lots of treatments." He no longer wants her "sacrifices," he wearily says, and he announces once and for all that he has lost all faith in her and her supposed love. "What, after . . . all I told you, can I expect from your love?" But, but: why, why, why does she refuse their last chance, their Dr. Yourgi chance, when "I [w]ould do for you everything!"[51]

Their separation cut him down. He spent Christmas that year "ghosting" (sneaking in without paying) on the couch in a hotel room in Texas with Danilova and another dancer. His spirit emptied, he passed hours bent over a coffee table with glue and scissors making miniature Christmas ornaments for their tree, just as he had done as a boy back home: thin braids of pink-pearl cotton painted green and looped to tinfoil wrappings on Hershey's Kisses; toothpicks and matches cut up and made into a tiny sleigh with tiny Santas and silver angels. It was like the pink house, the dressing room, the fur coats, and gifts—a lovingly built stage set. And when Danilova went off with another male dancer, he suffered stomach tension and cramps and gratefully accepted hot tea and a tummy rub from a sympathetic dancer, fondly calling her his "Mamouchka."[52]

In New York, friends saw him standing mournfully in front of Zorina's building, looking up at the windows in misery, or alone crying on a park bench, and he commiserated openly and broke into tears over bottles of red wine in restaurants with anyone who would listen. Adding to his troubles, his ample earnings had slipped through his fingers. He was stone broke and had to borrow money from Larry Hart.[53] Davidova thought he was suicidal. When a fire swept through the halls of the school while George was teaching one afternoon, he rushed to get the students out but lingered himself in the smoke and was one of the last to leave the building. "I wouldn't have minded if it destroyed me," he glumly told Natasha Molostwoff.[54] Ironically, he and Lincoln were by then engaged in (eventually failed) negotiations with the ubiquitous Massine over a possible plan to merge the nominally surviving American Ballet and Massine's Ballet Russe de Monte Carlo. There were rumors that Balanchine might replace Massine. He didn't, and the whole thing fell through.[55]

Five years of lingering love letters ensued as George's relationship with Zorina hung on by the few threads that had always bound them: her career and his desire. They would continue to work together here and there, but their marriage diminished into an intermittent affair, laced with resentment and without the common life and wife George had so hoped to make of his little Brigitta. In 1942 he wrote to her, "Milaia Moia Britittoushka this is a few word from lonsom man. I think of you all the time—during the day and see you in my dreams at night. After all this five years together I feel like if I just met you. Why Hollywood is not in New York?"[56] In a way it was. He had just featured Zorina at Madison Square Garden in a dance for elephants at the Ringling Bros. and Barnum & Bailey circus, which he and Stravinsky had taken on for extra cash: fifty elephants, fifty girls in pink, and Zorina in skimpy dress perched on top of a huge beast.[57] Still, a year later: "I am thinking of you all the time and in diferent ways and positions, most of all, don't be insulted. I want you very much in my bed at night, afternoon and morning. I love you my darling and kiss you all over. Your g."[58] A year after that, in 1944: why, why, why, he wrote with an anger born of hurt, did she refuse to come to him *as his wife?*[59] Zorina later admitted, "If George had said to me 'The hell with Hollywood! Come and dance with me,' our lives might have been very different."[60] But he never did. Not that. He loved her as a woman, but not as a dancer. She loved him for his dances, but not as a man.

Jump ahead to January 1946, when all was finally dead and done between them. Zorina made the trip to Reno to formalize their divorce. The divorce papers record an embittered ending. Her lawyers accused George of "extreme cruelty of a mental nature" causing Zorina intense anguish and impaired health.[61] If so, she never admitted it. His side of the story was different, and he was later angry: "It was dirty, she didn't love me. She only married me because Massine married another woman and she was going to show him she could get another choreographer. . . . I wasn't good enough for her, and certainly not glamorous enough for her ambitious mother." In any case, they had already divided the property months before, and in a final ironic gesture, George gave Zorina the pink house with no front door.[62]

As it turned out, his emotional collapse in 1941, which was the real end of their intense and beleaguered life together, saved him. He was not artistically derailed by bad times. It was the good times—sunny Hollywood, bountiful Broadway, pink house, beautiful wife—that threatened his gift, and somehow he never let them last. Like an injured animal, he moved on and smelled out another woman, another situation, another way to make dances. Rupture was painful, but not destructive. He had an instinct for his own genius, and loss and unattainable or unrequited love seemed to stand at its heart. In Zorina, and the drama with Massine, George had ferreted out a perfect match: loss seeks loss. He didn't plan it that way; he didn't even say or perhaps even know it was so, but it was true. We know it from the facts. And the fact was that in the dark midst, or maybe in the clearing, of his breaking marriage to Zorina, he turned to Bach's Concerto in D Minor for Two Violins and made *Concerto Barocco,* one of his most "eternal" ballets.[63] It came when the trance of their love was being dispelled and his mind was turning to Bach and to Marie-Jeanne. It came with Lincoln's return and a new project that took him to South America, about as far as he could get from Zorina. It came with the growing crisis of war in Europe.

Chapter 13

BALANCHINE'S WAR

He began as he always did, with the dancers he had in the studio that day: they were ten. No, eleven, but the eleventh was a man who was almost invisible in the ballet. *Concerto Barocco* began in the spring of 1941 as an exercise in "stage practice," a course Balanchine taught to his most advanced students.[1] The structure was clear. The music was Bach's Concerto in D Minor for Two Violins: Marie-Jeanne danced the first violin, and Mary-Jane Shae was the second. The man was William Dollar, an able partner for Marie-Jeanne. The eight women were the orchestra.

He had been listening to the music for several years on an old phonograph, especially the recording performed in Paris in the early 1930s by the Romanian conductor and composer George Enescu and his young prodigy Yehudi Menuhin. Menuhin later married an English dancer who had worked with Balanchine in Les Ballets 1933, and George sometimes dined with them when he was in London. Several years earlier, Lincoln had urged him to make a ballet to this same Bach concerto for the tap dancer Paul Draper, the son of Lincoln's friend Muriel Draper, and although it never happened, the idea of "swinging" Bach with the rhythms and techniques of American tap and jazz dance stuck in his mind.[2]

The decor, which was soon added, was not clear: the dancers were costumed in annoyingly sticky rubberized fabric, netting, and leaves, and the ballet was set against a backdrop of arches and water, all designed by Eugene Berman. Soon all of this would go, and *Barocco* would be danced in practice clothes against a blue cyclorama. This was not initially an artistic decision: the ballet was first stripped to these basics in New York four years after its premiere, when Berman fussily pulled the sets and costumes, saying they hadn't been properly constructed.[3] Leotards and tights would have to suffice. But an extraordinary photograph taken at the time indicates that in some part of his mind, Balanchine was already moving in this direction. He just hadn't found a way to get there yet.

The photo shows Marie-Jeanne standing stark naked, long hair flowing down her white back. The dancer Nicholas Magallanes is standing with her, also fully naked and expressionless. They are posed in a slight profile, genitals hidden in contrapposto modesty, like a modern Adam and Eve. Standing between them, we find Balanchine, fully dressed in suit and tie, with an arm around each of their naked bodies. This picture was taken by George Platt Lynes, a fashion photographer and one of Lincoln's circle, who had a taste for erotic and especially homoerotic photography (he would later work with Kinsey documenting American sexual practices). In the late 1930s, Lincoln and George hired Lynes to take publicity shots of their dancers. His photography studio was not far from the School of American Ballet, and it was there that—stripped to the waist and cooled by large fans and huge blocks of ice in the summer heat—he took dozens of photographs of dances and dancers—portraits but also multiframe sequences from ballets, often with George's help, with the dancers almost or fully naked. ("Should I wear pasties?" one dancer asked, and Balanchine replied, "If you feel uncomfortable, but no.")[4] They look naked—caught off guard among the clothed—but they also look like the idealized nudes of painting and sculpture. Naked and nude: they were both, or something in between.

This photo, and the later chance costume revision, revealed *Barocco* for what it was: pure abstraction. "No sex story, no period angle, no violence," as the critic Edwin Denby put it. No words, and no clothes. The simple fact of the human body, idealized and abstracted—removed or detached. He was searching for a kind of costume that would not make Marie-Jeanne "act" or look like someone else, but instead amplify her—not in an "express yourself" way, not Marie-Jeanne, but *Marie-Jeanneness*. He wanted to *see* the person through the clothes. In her photographic nudity, and later white marble Grecian tunic, she would not be a theatrical character, but a kind of icon of the person she already was. She would be sufficient unto herself, in a dance that was sufficient unto itself, with music that was sufficient unto itself. Balanchine combined all of these "sufficient unto itself" arts into a plotless dance greater than any of its parts.[5]

All of this required an intense emotional distancing, and Marie-Jeanne did not smile, seduce, or seek to please when she danced, but instead disappeared behind the mask of her wide sculpted face and high cheekbones into an internal world of her own making. The ballet was like that too: it did "not seem to be trying to win your interest," Denby wrote, "but before you know it, it has absorbed your attention and doesn't let it go."[6] That year, Balanchine gave a radio interview in English in which he read a text on the origins of dance in religious rite and Greek tragedy and at the end talked extemporaneously about his work. *His* ballets, he said, were not about the usual nineteenth-century balletic stories at all. They were about music and *time*.[7]

Barocco is about time. Dancing it is nonstop math: numbers, rhythm, syncopation. Keeping pace with its interlocking music and steps is like following the logic of an intricate mathematical equation. With math comes pattern, and long unfolding geometries of line and circle, with bodies braiding in and through one another. Pattern in the body too, and movements so anatomically calibrated to music that they seem to share the same source. It is a living picture of the Neoplatonic idea of the harmony of the spheres so beloved by Bach and Balanchine both: math as god, and dancers as a choir of angels. The corps de ballet was crucial. The two soloists come and go, but the eight women, like the orchestra itself, never leave the stage. They travel the ballet together, live its full arc, define its inner world. There is reverence—when they bow gently to one another at the beginning of the lyrical second movement, it is like being in a church. None of this was pious. The ballet, as one dancer recalled, was also full of the influences Balanchine was taking from black

American dance forms: jazzy steps, jutting hips, witty, syncopated moves, along with his own sly and insinuated "kinky details."[8]

Musically, *Barocco* was complex, and as the scholar Kara Yoo Leaman has shown, Balanchine deftly threaded the movement through and against Bach, creating a related "jazzy" syncopated dance score of his own. He amplified Bach's syncopation, for example, by misaligning visual and musical accents—the dancers and the music emphasizing different notes, thus creating a kind of tension that finally mathematically resolves as music and movement fall into realignment. Or, at one point, the dancers count 5555552 for the music's thirty-two eighth-note pulses arranged in four measures of 2/2 meter. It all adds to 32, but the accents along the way are different for musician and dancer—which explains why Balanchine didn't mind that the dancers counted "their way" against the correct musical counts. He was taking these techniques in part from his work with Dunham, Bradley, and other black dancers and from tap, Lindy hop, ragtime, and jazz, and Leaman points out that musically setting fives against a duple meter, with a "hiccup" to right the math, was like adding danced "doo-wahs" to Bach. He was not alone in this kind of playfulness. He saw and admired, for example, the black pianist Hazel Scott, who was known for "swinging" European classical music in hit recordings such as the 1940s "Bach to Boogie." In another technique, he created visual and emotional echoes by binding a particular combination of movement to a particular musical phrase and then later repeating the movement combination to a different musical phrase. Dancers and audiences didn't often know the formal mechanisms behind these effects, but they did feel the kinesthetic response, as Balanchine worked to "swing" classical ballet.[9]

To dance this way, you have to take everything off. Expression, persona, personality—your very *self* must go. The mathematical concentration requires pure mind and pure body—no distraction. This is not easily done. How do you take *yourself* off? How do you escape Marie-Jeanne to arrive at *Marie-Jeanneness*? Balanchine achieved this in part by pushing his dancers to physical extremes, and Marie-Jeanne's cramping and aching limbs as they worked were a sign of the limits and sheer exhaustion that generations of dancers would encounter in moving as fully and precisely as this ballet required. He was accessing inner resources: physical and musical powers that lay otherwise dormant inside muscle and bone. It was pure technique, but the opposite of abstinence. "Marie-Jeanne had an animal and sexual response to Bach. . . . She was not a metronome, it was so lush, so sensual," one of the dancers who saw her noted.[10] There is a disarming intimacy in this kind of emotional and physical distancing and de-robing. In *Concerto Barocco,* Balanchine was asking all his dancers to take off their clothes emotionally. He never did—never had to: they revealed him themselves.

After an open dress rehearsal in New York, the ballet formally premiered on June 27, 1941, in Buenos Aires during a long and grueling tour to South America arranged by Lincoln soon after George's break with Zorina. After Lincoln's exhausting attempt to run his own company, he realized he needed George, and this new tour was another one of his schemes, this time tied to the war.[11] As the situation in Europe worsened, Nelson Rockefeller had found his way into Roosevelt's administration as coordinator of inter-American affairs. He had a small budget to develop business and cultural relations across South America as part of an effort to measure and quell the growing pro-Nazi sentiment in the region. Lincoln organized the dance tour and was also discreetly charged with reporting on the political effectiveness of local U.S. embassies—and was provided for the purpose with a guide and undercover "nurse," who traveled with them too (a fact that, in addition, earned him FBI surveillance).[12] Before their departure, Lincoln composed a letter to the dancers warning the "kids" that this would be no "normal ballet tour" and more like "an army expedition." Conditions would be "rude" and "rigorously extreme," and they should expect difficult changes of altitude, poor accommodations, and uncertain access to food and water. He attached a long list of required vaccinations.[13] The itinerary was ambitious: Argentina, Uruguay, Brazil, Colombia, Peru, Venezuela, Panama, then on to Trinidad, Puerto Rico, Cuba, and Mexico, if we can get the vessels, Lincoln said.

They traveled by cattle boat and military-transport plane, including an earsplitting nine-hour flight over the Andes when a blizzard shut down trains and boats. As forewarned, there were wartime shortages of food and water, and long gaps in payment as Lincoln struggled to transfer money from the United States, leaving the dancers penniless and with few provisions. They were plagued by sickness from exhaustion and food poisoning, and Lincoln kept his usual frantic schedule and worried about everything from "nasty Germans" and Nazi sympathizers ("there are *V*s for 'Vichy' everywhere [in Uruguay] and the Nazi papers say it stands for Vengeance, Vice, Versailles")[14] to the logistics of contacting and hiring the local artists and commissioning set designs for the ballets. He felt burdened: "I don't ever want to have a company again," he confided to a friend, "I hate the running of it, travel lousy[,] worry abt money. . . . I will do ballets but for other people. . . . Only for . . . the REAL dance lovers or Dance Haters. I am a dance hater."[15] Balanchine, on the other hand, seemed to sail through it all, "patient and calm." This was nothing compared to past privations he had endured, and it was a relief to be far from the drama of Zorina. "We really owe him everything," Lincoln wrote to his father. "He gets $100 a week and he's worth $2000."[16]

George was by then, briefly, romantically involved with Marie-Jeanne and feeding her steaks to keep her thin and strong. She needed her fortitude. Along with *Barocco,* he had made *Ballet Imperial* to Tchaikovsky's Piano Concerto no. 2 in G Major—although the score was abridged, rewritten, and rearranged by the Russian pianist and conductor Alexander Siloti, another émigré. It was a technically demanding tribute to Petipa and the imperial St. Petersburg of George's childhood, with a fanciful blue-gold decor by the designer Mstislav Dobuzhinskiĭ, offering a nostalgic view onto the Neva. And so these ragtag Americans danced Balanchine's imperial elegy in South America in the summer of 1941—as the Germans invaded the USSR.

His family had fallen silent. He had no idea where or how they all were. The duress and expense of the war eventually caught up with their little tour too, and that November they all returned home, and the company dispersed. George settled into a new apartment on Central Park South and Lincoln, still mindful of his charge, arranged to have it furnished with pieces by the designer Alvar Aalto left over from a recent MoMA exhibition.[17] One month later the Japanese bombed Pearl Harbor, and the United States entered the war. Lincoln was preoccupied with MoMA and other projects. George was busy too—never without work, as his assignments on Broadway, in opera, in operetta, and in Hollywood mounted, including *The Lady Comes Across* (1942), *Rosalinda* (1942), *The Merry Widow* (1943), and *What's Up* (1943).

He did his best to help with the war effort. In May 1942 he made a dance to benefit Russian war relief for an event Lincoln organized, and he organized another dance for a performance at the USO headquarters in New York. He said yes to the Joint Anti-Fascist Refugee Committee to use his name to raise money for Spanish refugees and yes to helping the Committee of 100 arrange performances of "various types of Negro music" performed by "Negro musicians and artists," including Marian Anderson. "Negros" were serving too, and civil rights was to the fore. He donated the Dobuzhinskiĭ designs for *Ballet Imperial* to MoMA, to help with wartime needs and programs for art in army camps.[18] He also sent money to the Tolstoy Foundation and other relief agencies to aid Russians in France with "Happiness" parcels of milk, sugar, butter, coffee, and other necessities, asking that his old colleagues Benois, Egorova, and Preobrazhenskaya be added to the lists of the needy. In Hollywood he made dances for Zorina in the B-grade patriotic movie *Star Spangled Rhythm* (1942) and, later, to entertain the troops, *Follow the Boys* (1944).[19] He registered for the Selective Service, and in 1943 received his notice of classification: too old (at thirty-nine).[20] Lincoln had registered too. He was not too old, and when his deferment ended in February 1943, he enlisted in the army and was gone.[21]

At this point, our story divides: Lincoln's war in Europe and Balanchine's war at home. Two fronts, two men who separated at this moment but finally came together again at the end of the conflict, each for his own reasons—each for his own war. They might have finally simply parted and gone their own ways: they had already been drifting apart for some time, and there was nothing inevitable about their old ballet project. The war and Lincoln's departure, coinciding as it did with George's commercial success, would have been a natural fork in the road. But that's not what happened. Instead, neither of them lost sight of ballet or of each other. Looking back on it all, we can see that the whole struggle—their struggle—between 1933 and 1945 was a kind of interregnum in each of their lives. It was a time of opportunity but also of troubles: the Depression and the rise of Hitler; their umpteen failed companies;

George's ill-health and self-inflicted marriage; and the war, the genocide, the decimation of Russia, and the end of a European life they each knew and loved. The war divided their lives and set their mutual course. But in the early days of 1943, when Lincoln departed for the army, neither of them knew how the war would end or whether they would ever work together again. Nothing was certain, and as they stood at that juncture, looking ahead into the black hole of a war they might lose, the answer would have been: who knows.

This was George's second war—third if you count the Russian Revolution—and by all accounts, it worried and devastated him. He was physically safe this time, but he knew the dangers firsthand. And because it also coincided with his painful break with Zorina, it is perhaps not surprising that he was living a kind of double life. It was the "cloud in trousers": the man in trousers was in the external world, busy, working, contributing, teaching, and getting shows to the stage, and his everyday schedule was full and demanding. But internally, in the cloud part that was harder to know and follow, something else was going on that revealed itself in his work, which showed a mind firmly set on Bach and God. It had started with *Barocco*, but it didn't stop there. Instead, it went deeper, he went deeper, and Bach and God became the theme of his war.

In the spring of 1943, as Lincoln departed for the army, George began work on another war-charity production, this time with Stokowski (a Scotsman of Polish heritage) and the designer Robert Edmund Jones. They were staging *The Crucifixion of Christ*, based on Bach's vast St. Matthew Passion, at the Metropolitan Opera as a benefit for the Quaker American Friends Service Committee.[22] Supported by a roster of international luminaries, it was for and by children—to help starving children around the world—and performed by students from Columbia, Juilliard, the High School of Music and Art, and the School of American Ballet. The program included drawings of abandoned waifs by Tchelitchew and Bérard, along with photographs, recently exhibited at MoMA, by the war photographer Thérèse Bonney, known for her images of broken families in the embattled Russian-Finnish borderlands—the site of George's own childhood dacha, destroyed in an earlier war. Not so long ago, George had been one of those ragged and hungry children too.[23]

Stokowski and Balanchine conceived the production as a modern miracle play, recalling Reinhardt's spectacular interwar mystery plays, with their casts of thousands. George had been circling the St. Matthew Passion ever since he had heard Stokowski conduct it soon after his arrival in New York: "C'était ciel: tout simple," he told Lincoln at the time. Their production, Stokowski wrote, would be a kind of sacred dance enacting Church liturgy in the form of an ancient Greek drama, with two large choruses singing against and across each other: an angry mob and those loyal to Christ, along with the chorales sung by everyone. They cut Bach's (over three-hour) score to almost half its length, but they still took their audience, following Bach, through the harrowing story of Christ's passion: from Mary Magdalene anointing the Savior's head, to the Last Supper, Judas's betrayal, Pilate, Golgotha, and the Crucifixion, ending with a scene in which "the veil of the temple is torn."[24]

The roles of Peter, Judas, Pilate, and Mary Magdalene were performed by hooded and masked mimes moving like living sculptures over ramps and platforms that joined audience to actors in a common liturgy. Christ appeared only as a beam of golden light—he could not be given human form, Balanchine insisted. Mary, played by Lillian Gish, washed Christ's feet by stroking the light shaft with her hair. George had seen Gish in *The Birth of a Nation* when he was a child, in a cold theater during the harsh days of the revolution, but she was known more recently for her starring role in the popular anti-Nazi war film *Commandos Strike at Dawn.* "The Star-Spangled Banner" opened the show.

It was a pièce d'occasion, and nothing about the production was saved or ever revived, but even the fact of its performance and its scanty remains provide a window onto George's mind. *The Crucifixion of Christ* was one culmination of his ambition to bring episodes from the Bible to life on the stage, just as Bach had brought them to his Lutheran congregations in dramatic musical form, and he envisioned a kind of living, moving painting, on the scale of Tintoretto, Veronese, and the Renaissance artists he so admired. Musically, it is worth noting that Balanchine made only two dances, ever, to the music of Bach, and that he made them back-to-back during the war: *Concerto Barocco* and *The Crucifixion of Christ.*

God was on Balanchine's mind in other ways too. The following year, he was writing down his ideas about choreography on notecards and scraps of paper for an article for *Dance Index*, a journal Lincoln had founded in 1942, in part as a response to the war ("Dancing has survived every disaster the Western world has known," Lincoln said in an introductory essay. "It seems to exist instinctively in response to some blind necessity, which in an almost preposterous sense, ignores all the frightening facts of human survival").[25] In his absence, Lincoln had put his friend the writer Donald Windham in charge, and he hammered poor Don with detailed letters on how to run the magazine, what to publish, whom to see, and where to sell it. In an issue from 1945, Balanchine laid out his thinking on his elusive art in an article published under his name. Windham worked with him to turn his scribbled fragments and notes in broken English into solid prose, reporting to a friend that he found Balanchine at home on East Fifty-second Street: "He is supposed to be sick but there were hordes of people there. Krassovska, Danilova, Marie-Jeanne, Mary Ellen, all lounging on the fur covered bed in which he lay so that it looked like a Harem. And he was drinking coffee and eating pastry. The bedroom walls are decorated with female nudes (drawings) by Rodin. . . . He checked the article with a few suggestions for changes."[26] In the end, though, Windham's version lost the force of Balanchine's imagination and the intense, if disorderly, metaphysical dilemmas preoccupying his thoughts at the time. George's original piecemeal notes, neatly filed and never published, are the only surviving evidence we have in his own hand of how he thought about making dances. They show a self-consciously analytic and philosophical, if idiosyncratic and religious, mind and a man engrossed in the relationship between dance, time, and God.

By then George's Orthodox practice, if not his faith, was increasingly unconventional. He had already married twice outside the Church, and he rarely attended services. It wasn't even clear he was entirely welcome: not only had he erred in the crucial matter of matrimony, he also belonged to a profession dismissed by the Church as an illicit and sinful display of the human body. Ballet was strictly off-limits for most self-respecting priests, but in George's mind, dancing was not sinful at all; it was a spiritual endeavor with reasons and roots the Church could not fully provide. Now, with civilization as they all knew it in collapse and Bach, religious spectacle, and the seventeenth century on his mind, we find him searching for a way to place dance, and his own life's pursuit, in a divine order.

Spinoza might seem an unlikely place to begin. This seventeenth-century Sephardic Jew, philosopher, and lens grinder exiled from his own Jewish community in Amsterdam at the age of twenty-four, in part for introducing radical—some said atheistic—ways of understanding God, was a far reach from George's Russian Orthodox upbringing. But Spinoza had already been an unlikely precursor for Goethe and the German Romantics and for Nietzsche and others in the pantheon of influences George was gathering around him. Besides, as Lincoln pointed out, George was a kind of "amateur theologian" who scavenged unsystematically across a range of religious, philosophical, and literary texts, taking what he needed and ignoring the rest.[27] At the moment, he was looking to Spinoza.

One fragment: "Spinoza: the infinitude is within itself has also its notion within itself. Its notion is its being and its being is in its notion"—a reference, in George's clumsy English, to Spinoza's *Deus sive Natura*, "God or Nature." This was not the personal Judeo-Christian God, the divine creator who made the world and presided over it. In Spinoza's view, laid out in the *Ethics*, there exists only one single substance from which everything flows. "God or Nature" is that single substance: self-causing, self-sustaining, eternal, "an infinitude," as George noted, and worthy of contemplation and love.[28] This pantheistic view was important for George because it was a way of elevating and spiritualizing matter—including the human body.

In Spinoza's thought, the Cartesian mind-body split ceases to exist, and the body is not relegated to the lower, earthly rungs of the Christian Great Chain of Being. Mind and body are identical—the same—and body is as much an aspect or "mode" of God as mind is. The mind can conceive of itself only through the idea and experience of the body. And although the body as a whole will eventually die, its essence, like the essence of the mind, exists eternally. Mind and body are thus not hierarchically ranked: mind is not "higher" than body, and it is natural for God to exist in a multitude of ways. So Spinoza gave Balanchine a way to spiritualize the body and to elevate it. The body was now more than a vessel of the spirit; it was spiritual itself—if the dancer could bring it to that state. We can glimpse this idea in Balanchine's answer, a few years later, to an interviewer from a Christian Orthodox journal questioning his allegiance to such a sinful art: "We do not sin by dancing, we use our bodies like flowers in the field, which are growing and beautiful. . . . The body can and should do the same thing."[29] *Deus sive Natura.*

Reading on, we find that Balanchine is especially preoccupied with the paradoxical question of how this corporeal art, and the body itself, can be made spiritual. What is the "can and should" that dancers must *do* to "use [their] bodies like flowers in the field"? One fragment tells us:

> Before we start to move at all, a choreographer has to realize one very important mat[t]er. Our body has to free itself from the earthly heaviness, our brain has to achieve a certain freedom from naturalistic material. It has to be transformed into spiritual lightness of our body. This particular feeling of unearthliness or elevation is just beginning or first position, a point of start.

It was the beginning of an answer that would end with training. You have to remake the body, and the way to remake it is to train it. Here was George, drawn to "eternal dances" but faced from day to day with the sticks and bones of making dancers and dances. How you get from the physical to the metaphysical in this deeply physical art has something to do with how you do pliés and tendus.

He is similarly preoccupied with questions of eternity and time. How do you get from eternity, which is a kind of not-time, to dancing, which is fundamentally "about time"? There are differences, he wrote, drawing loosely (and at times confusedly) on Spinoza, between eternity, duration, and time. Eternity is forever and unbroken—without past, present, or future—an infinite and impersonal flow. Duration is the passage or flow of time that we experience. And time (like Spinoza's *tempus*) is the ways people invent to measure this flow by breaking it up into small parts. For Balanchine, music and dance were two ways to measure and divide up time, and he moved easily from there to Goethe and an idea (George's own) of dance itself as something, as he had put it to Zorina, "eternal"—by which he seems to have meant a feeling of time suspended or stopped—a feeling most performers would recognize. An eternal present or, as he puts it, "You are divine."

> First we have to understand... eternal time which fills our existence.... [It] can never be stopped[.] Even Goethe in his *Faust* said "[the] instant [the music] stops, you are divine." He meant this long eternal time which is everywhere forever one with its beauty, happiness and sorrow. The instant which Goethe meant was [a] small part of eternity. If we would be able to feel it would not be necessary to divide time in different artificial parts.

He goes on:

> We are trying to prolong our time by dividing [it] in small parts, we say this minute and we think... it is one [w]hole but it is not because [each] minute has past, present and future [within it].... [T]his life [is] invisible untouchable and [it] seem[s] like nothing is there but it is there and we [k]now that and to make our selfs to understand better we divided it in different pieces of time with artificial elements like metronome.... Time as a whole exists only for particular purpose for choreographer who has to [e]ngrave his practical ideas on three dimensional spaice.

The task of measuring time can be accomplished with a clock or a metronome, but also with music and dance. Dance was thus a way of *showing* both time and the passage of time. The choreographer's role was to catch the "fundamental rhythm" of time—the bass-line beat—even as it was being divided and measured into musical notes and the steps of a dance.

Every dancer who has studied with a competent teacher for, say, an average of ten years possesses a fairly impressive vocabulary of movements, familiarly known as steps. But these steps when separate are devoid of meaning and acquire value only when they are coordinated in time and space and, most important of all, when they obey the only eternal and fundamental rhythm, irrespective of the different existing ways of dividing it. Moving the body in time, on time—*dancing*—thus becomes a way of expressing "God or Nature"—a way to catch the beat, the pattern and rhythm, of the universe. Music sets the pulse; dancers catch it in their steps—another way in which dancing reaches the divine.

Ideas and theories from his own experience spooled through his mind. Making a ballet, he said, drawing on Eisenstein and on his Hollywood years, was like making a film. A film might *seem* to tell a story, but it is in fact made up of discrete images or frames, and the viewer's mind is left to fill in the empty gaps. We see an actor seated; next we see him standing outside; we "fill in" that he stood up and walked there. Similarly, a dance may *seem* to flow fluidly from a dancer's body, but it is in fact made up of discrete steps, which the eye and the memory reassemble in the brain as a flowing dance. Like film, dance is a fantasy or illusion governed by montage. In a dance, it is up to a choreographer to choose the steps (assign the shots) and then to edit the sequences to arrive at the desired effect of the dance:

> Ballet is a visual art. It reaches the audience through their eyes. . . . Scientists have discovered that the eye actually does not see movement. The mind remembers each static position and creates the illusion of seeing action, but actually the eyes see only positions as static . . . [like] the individual frames of a motion picture film. A man without memory could not see a ballet, for he could see only positions, and the ballet is created by the memory of the relation of the last position to the next position in which the dancer is poised.

Balanchine then explained the "materials," as he put it, that go into a dance. First, a choreographer must collect in his own mind and body what Balanchine called a "kaleidoscope" of "abstract memories of forms," a collection of gestures, physical states, and bodily images that live in his "mind or mental fluids" and can be set in time. These images might be moving, but they might also be still.

> Silence, plasticity and immobility are the greatest forces, they are as impressive even more, then, rage, delirium and ecstasy. When the body stays and remains in immobility, every part of it should be invisibly tense.... Every preceding diferent movement has to be in contrast to next.... This stratification of attitudes lives constantly in [the] coreographers mind. He uses them whenever he needs it, [or] he leaves them out. But they are not ready combination and not set to any time or meter. They are—abstract memories of forms.... This calaidoscope of movement lives in a choreographer's mind like microbes live in a drop of water. With one exception—that they remain in the mind or mental fluids.

To emphasize the abstract nature of these materials, and how it felt to have all these images swimming in his mind, George mimicked Spinoza's use of Euclidean mathematical forms, which recalled his own musical training and the deep connection between the mathematical and musical arts, so fully expressed in *Barocco*. He noted that the "infinite combination" and "endless chain of those combination[s]" of steps and gestures that occupy a choreographer's mind might be written as "$n + u$." But he was careful to point out that these "abstract memories of forms" come from concrete experiences. They come from life:

> Movement as an important visual sensation is quite different from movement which people employ for purely ordinary functional purposes. People who walk on the street are moving not for the purpose of producing beautiful activity, but because they have to cover a certain distance. Nobody cares whether or not he produces beauty of movement from rolling barrels or handling trains or elevators. However, in all of those movement one can find some important visual dynamic if one will try. It may take some time and patience, but it can be done. For instance, very few people notice the tops of buildings. It has always been very hard for me to discover why some people have the necessity to investigate things, and others never see anything, even though they have eyes to do so.... But those who care to see and remember that they have seen could easily try to observe more things at once. They

> could try to cultivate their visual senses. Because movement is in itself a very important element of our vision if one pays attention.[30]

"If one pays attention": Balanchine was consciously *seeing* things that most people wander past. He was absorbing into his own mind and body the look and pace, the "dynamics" and timing, of everything from rolling barrels and elevators to trains and the tops of buildings. Music, sculpture, and painting famously grounded Balanchine's dances, but here was an indication of the ways in which he also incorporated everyday life, registering in his "mental fluids" the "visual dynamic" of the world around him. He had always been that watcher, quietly observing and absorbing life from a corner of the room.

A choreographer's primary "material," however, is human. It is dancers. For without the physical presence of dancers, he insisted, a dance does not and cannot *exist*.

> A choreographer is different from a writer in a mechanical way. A writer sits in a room alone with paper and pencil and what comes out is himself. It represents him. but a choreographer works with living muscles, with dancers who are all individual people. The dancer's health, attitudes, personality (his own things) are involved. The result is not me. Another person is involved in the result. He has melted himself into it like sugar in coffee. It can never be separated out.
>
> The material of choreography is dancers, all trained in a certain discipline, but all different. If you take away a specific dancer, the step remains, but performed by someone else it may be nothing.... Choreography... exists after it has been suggested to the dancers and the muscles have the urge to move. [It] is the mechanical help to move, a suggestion from one person to another. When the dancer begins to move[,] something exists. If you say it doesn't matter which dancer dances, you deny the reality of the original existence.[31]

The dance comes, in other words, from a physical encounter between two people. That was the simple start of a dance, just as it was the simple start of "the original existence."

As for Goethe, whose Faust owed so much to Spinoza, he was on Balanchine's mind too. Not only was Balanchine reading Goethe in these years; he also staged the Walpurgisnacht bacchanalia from Gounod's opera in Mexico City in June 1945, just as the war was ending and soon after he had written his "Notes on Choreography and Teaching." What's more, he had told Lincoln he wanted to stage the second part of *Faust* too. He was no doubt drawn by Gounod's score, but it was also Goethe's writing that amazed and delighted him, and *Faust*, alongside the Bible, *A Midsummer Night's Dream*, and *Don Quixote*, was already a key text.

We need especially to look at the second part of *Faust*, the part Balanchine told Lincoln he wanted to stage, because it is this second part that leads back to Spinoza and the moment when "the music stops."[32] Part two is narratively unhinged, wild and fragmentary, seemingly without boundaries, borders, or any conventions of unity in time, space, and action. It ranges across genres from satire, allegory, tragedy, and comedy to opera, medieval pageantry, masquerade, and courtly love and romance; it suspends time and place, whisking us from ancient Greece to the death of Byron. If we move directly to the moment in the story when "the music stops," we find ourselves with Helen, Troy's abducted beauty, conjured as a shimmering image of loveliness, a phantom that both seduces and eludes Faust. They are in love, but when death calls her and the enchantment must end, the stage direction instructs: "The music stops." In the presumed silence that follows, Faust takes this glorious woman into his embrace, but "her body vanishes," leaving him desolate and alone, grasping her emptied clothing. A moment later, her "garments dissolve into clouds which envelop Faust; carry him upwards, and drift away with him." The moment heralds what Goethe had long since foreshadowed. Erotic love—"Eros: first cause of it all"—would cost Faust his soul.[33] In his wager with the Devil, Faust has given up bookish knowledge (Zorina's "university of art") and mortgaged his soul for an eternal life of experience and sensuality: "In the beginning was the deed," not the word at all.[34] Faust will die and forfeit his "immortal part" only—only—if he has an experience that makes him want to "end" time and say, "Beautiful moment, do not pass away."[35] That time-stopping, eternal present is Helen.

But astonishingly, at the end of the tale, when Faust dies and the Devil comes to collect his due, Goethe abruptly changes course. In the final scenes, God, the Angels, Mater Gloriosa, a Chorus Mysticus, and a whole host of Christian figures sweep down to save Faust's soul, and his "immortal part" miraculously escapes and flies up into the heavens. He is saved! It is a redemptive and religious finale, but we can also see these last scenes, with their Bach-like harkening choral song, flight of angels, and rich magnificence, in theatrical as well as theological terms. God and the angels are the characters, the final phantasmagorical creatures, that Goethe needs to rescue his protagonist. Even Spinoza recognized the possible human desire to imagine Christian figures and storied acts.

And so: grace. Faust is saved by this inexplicable and unearned gift delivered by the hand of God. A new spell is cast, and suddenly the wager is off, its terms obsolete.[36] The Mater Gloriosa even enlists the help of a Penitent, "once known as Gretchen": "Come! into higher spheres / outreach him! / He must sense you to find the way." In the concluding stanzas, the Chorus Mysticus sounds Goethe's lasting themes, which were already Balanchine's too:

> All that must disappear
> Is but a parable;
> What lay beyond us, here
> All is made visible,
> Here deeds have understood
> Words they were darkened by;
> Eternal Womanhood
> Draws us on high.[37]

As if to underscore his own preoccupation with these themes, Balanchine also staged, in the early 1940s, Shakespeare's *The Tempest* (for the ever-lingering Zorina) and *A Midsummer Night's Dream*. *Don Quixote* was not far behind, and he and Nicky Nabokov were already discussing it as a full-length ballet. All these works, with their illusory and disappearing worlds of seeming and image, in touch for a moment with profound and ephemeral truths that lie beyond words and then are gone, had a natural appeal for Balanchine. Through the looking glass of his own mind, they found perfect expression as: dance.

The trail doesn't end here. With Balanchine's notes touching on Spinoza, Goethe, and choreography, we arrive back, by a long path, to George's youth and the ideas that had preoccupied him for so long: to Blok, Mayakovsky, and Nietzsche; to the revolution and the Bolsheviks' desire to conquer mortality—stop the music or end time and become divine. Some Bolsheviks thought they could do it by creating a materialist paradise on earth. Some White Russians aimed instead for an Orthodox spiritual revolution culminating in a millennial apocalyptic transfiguration. Balanchine was slowly coming to a more modest solution of his own. The solution, perhaps, was not material or millennial at all. It could be, maybe, theatrical—it could be a dance. Not just any dance, but an "eternal" dance "about time." Such a dance could be an alternate universe or ideal world. It could summon for an instant the divine in a present-tense physical and earthly moment. A staged paradise, more real than the real.

Why did all of this matter to him? Why did he need to know that dances were in some way divine? He needed to know because it wasn't enough for a dance to be beautiful or entertaining. He was looking for a way to ground his art—and his life. Music was that ground. As he already knew and his dances to Bach suggested, music was not only a divine art; it was also a metaphysics and, more concretely, a place. It was a place he could live, a place that took him out of himself, an escape from the intense dislocation of exile and loneliness that were his constant companions. It was a ground he could stand on, a foundation he could build dances on, like the chalky-white grounding of an artist's canvas. But to build, he would need a company of dancers, trained dancers. This need would repeat mantra-like in his life through the 1940s because he couldn't quite seem to get there. A company would be a ground, but also, if he could just get there, a home.

For the moment, he was left with a powerful fantasy—and nothing solid to hold on to. At a similar moment in *Faust,* Goethe had reached for God, and Balanchine did too. In a heartrending postscript to the searching and at times confusing philosophical musings of his "Notes on Choreography and Teaching," we find a single pristine page, filed at the end, perhaps by chance: a careful copy in his own hand of the Russian Orthodox Prayer to the Holy Cross of the Lord. He wrote it in the midst of his thinking about Spinoza and Goethe,

Bach, the war, and Zorina and his own unrequited "eternal love." He transcribed the prayer by hand in Russian, though not in Cyrillic, in black ink, and we can only imagine what he was feeling as he wrote, probably from memory, this supplication. It was a plea, a port of call, and he wrote it in his best hand.

Prayer to the Holy Cross of the Lord

> May God raise, and His enemies dissipate, and may those who hate Him flee from His face. As smoke disappears, let them disappear; as wax melts away in the face of fire, so will the demons perish at the face of those who love God and bless themselves with the sign of the cross, and in the joy of those who say: Rejoice, Most Honorable and Life-giving Cross of the Lord, drive out demons by the power of the crucified our Lord Jesus Christ upon you, who descended to hell and stomped out the power of the devil, and bestowed upon us Your Holy Cross to drive away every foe. O Honorable and Life-giving Cross of the Lord! Help me together with the Holy Virgin Lady the Mother of God, and with all the saints forever. Amen.[38]

It was a comfort, a solace he was not finding at the moment in women, or the world. It is worth noting too that in Russian Orthodoxy, the Madonna is less virginal than a figure of motherhood, mercy, and intercession, spiritually connected to Mother Russia.

As the war ended, Balanchine found himself involved in a last war effort and prophetic episode of Faustian fate. It began innocently enough in January 1946 with a wartime benefit performance, this time for the National Foundation for Infantile Paralysis.[39] Polio was the new TB, and veterans returning home from Europe and North Africa were bringing it with them. The disease had been present in the United States at least since the turn of the century, but it seemed now to swell to epidemic proportions. It was not an epidemic, but it felt that way because polio attacked, maimed, and killed children disproportionately and without warning, turning its victims into cripples overnight and sending the worst-afflicted into isolation and iron lungs in a desperate effort to save them from a terrifying death by suffocation. Like TB, polio brought intense fear, a feeling Balanchine knew all too well, and parents were told to keep their children away from open drains, crowds, pools, and camps, which seemed to be the source of this mysterious and evil infection. As the country returned to a peacetime footing, authorities anxiously let the public know that this was the new threat to the nation.

The National Foundation for Infantile Paralysis, or the "March of Dimes," so-called after *The March of Time* newsreels that reported the war in cinemas across the country, had been founded by President Roosevelt, polio's most famous American victim. Paralyzed since the early 1920s, Roosevelt had made frequent trips to a remote health spa with thermal baths in Warm Springs, Georgia. Eventually he had purchased the spa and run it as part of the March of Dimes. In the weeks before VE (Victory in Europe) Day, Roosevelt died at Warm Springs—fondly known by then as his "little White House"—and Balanchine's ballet was part of the annual "Birthday Balls" to benefit the March of Dimes held in cities across the country on the occasion of the late president's birthday. Dimes, imprinted that year with Roosevelt's face, poured in.[40]

Balanchine called his dance *Resurgence* and cast in the lead role a young and exceptionally talented student at the school: Tanaquil Le Clercq, thin and fragile, beautiful but childlike at age sixteen—and perfect for the part of a young dancer struck by this cruel disease. Balanchine, darkly clad, danced the ominous role of polio himself, and when he touched Tanny, as everyone called her, she fell to the floor paralyzed. The next scene found her confined to a wheelchair, and she could move only by waving her arms. At the end of the ballet, showered with dimes, she rose miraculously and danced joyously with her fully healed body.[41] The music Balanchine chose was Mozart: the Quintet in G Minor, K. 516, an unusually unsettling chromatic piece with a dark pathos, composed by Mozart as his father was dying. The foundation wrote to him personally thanking him for the performance, but it was a dance he would later deeply regret.

That same month, January 1946, as Balanchine's divorce from Zorina finally came through, he took steps to settle himself. In August he married Maria Tallchief, a striking, exotic-looking dancer with Native American origins, half his age and his fourth wife. They had met in 1944 when he was staging an operetta, and it would be fair to see her as a war bride. She had grown up on the Osage Reservation in Fairfax, Oklahoma, which wasn't as far from Balanchine as it might at first seem. Her father was a full-blooded Osage made wealthy when the tribe struck oil; he lived on his oil checks, drank too much, and fought with greedy interlopers over headrights as his culture imploded before his eyes. Her mother was an outsider from Kansas, of Catholic and Scotch Irish roots, and Maria had taken refuge with her strong-willed grandmother, a keeper of Osage traditions and rituals, who (with her father) took her to secret forbidden ceremonial events with music and dancing held in hidden locations around the reservation. When Maria was ten, her parents escaped to Los Angeles and a more bourgeois life, where she studied piano seriously—she had perfect pitch and considered a concert career, but she also took ballet with Bronislava Nijinska, and in 1938, at age thirteen, joined the Ballet Russe de Monte Carlo. She worked with Massine and Danilova, and several years later, Balanchine was there setting work and cast her in *Songs of Norway*.[42]

By then he was forty, and she was nineteen. Her diaries, written in childish round script, announced their first encounter, "I guess I surprised him by my not succumbing to his charms. (ha! ha!) He is very nice—but I'm afraid he's a little too old for me and—ah well!"[43] By then she was a beauty: dark olive pallor with a broad, sculptural face and jet-black hair. She was disarmingly strong but fragile, large-boned, with a wide back, long torso and arms, and short but shapely legs. He noted her talent, promoted her career, and after his divorce came through, he picked her up after a performance and abruptly proposed marriage. It was matter-of-fact, and he delivered his offer in the MG before they left the parking spot. She had nothing to lose, he said; they could work together, and if it didn't last, she could move on. She hesitated: she still called him Mr. Balanchine. (The idea was so outlandish that when she told Vida Brown, a dancer friend, that "George" had proposed to her, Vida said, "George who?") He persisted and took her to dinner at the Stravinskys' (she sat quietly while they conversed in Russian) or to Romanoff's Russian restaurant and cuddled and kissed her in a horse-drawn carriage in New York, "Vozmee minye, Mashka, ya tvoi"—Take me, Maria, I'm yours.[44]

On August 16, 1946, George Balanchine married Elizabeth Marie Tallchief at Manhattan's county courthouse. He wore a gray suit with peaked lapels and a bow tie, and she came elegantly turned out in a beige jacket and white silk shirt. Her parents strongly disapproved and refused to attend the ceremony—George was too old, too foreign, too divorced. He didn't care. For him, Maria was perfect—gorgeous, a wonderful dancer, and an echt American. He even liked to say that he was John Smith to her Pocahontas, and she took him to meet her grandmother in Fairfax, Oklahoma, who greeted them at the door to her small home with her hair in a single long braid down her back with a tribal blanket thrown over her shoulders. She showed George her collection of Native relics and a portrait of Maria's grandfather, Chief Bigheart. She offered to bead him a belt and bestowed the gift of a turquoise bracelet, which he wore right up to his death. Maria romanticized her Tall Chief image too, perhaps in part because of Balanchine's fascination with it, and pictures from the time show her posed in her own colorful traditional blanket, beaded headdress, and feathered bouquet.[45] He loved Westerns and started wearing cowboy shirts and string ties, a Wild West look he would keep long after they parted. It was a fantasy, but she made him feel very American, another way of settling.[46]

On September 25, 1945, Lincoln returned from Europe. He immediately found George, and they began working again. By the spring of 1946, they had plans for yet another new ballet company, but this time, things were different than they had been all those failed companies ago. They were different in part because Lincoln was different. The intervening two and a half years, since his departure for Fort Dix in 1943, had been like another life. Lincoln had lived through his own war, and it had changed him in ways that would have consequences for them both.

Chapter 14

LINCOLN'S WAR

Lincoln's war began with his father's death. Louis Kirstein died unexpectedly of pneumonia on December 10, 1942, two months before Lincoln was scheduled to report for duty at Fort Dix. The memorial service at his childhood Temple Israel was attended by more than a thousand admirers, including luminaries from the local and national political elite. Lincoln, who wrote so much about so many things, said nothing.[1] But as he prepared himself for the war, he did not forget that his own death in battle might follow, and he was careful to write to Eugenie Ouroussow, who promised her loyalty, entrusting her with the fate of his precious SAB and promising to align his estate to help her sustain it in the event of his own untimely passing. In a touching last wish, he noted that if Balanchine died from ill-health, still a likely outcome in his hyperalert mind, she might appoint in his place Lew Christensen, a dancer Lincoln continued to love and admire. ("He is not imaginative but has been poor, and hence has a sound instinct for survival. Who else do you want around? Anyone? There is no need as far as I am concerned.")[2]

The war pitted Lincoln against his ever-inconsolable body. When he enlisted, he applied for counterintelligence, but, like many Jews and homosexuals, he was turned down for this sensitive role ("I am being investigated and the more I think about my irresponsible past, the less I think that military intelligence will much care to have me irritate them") and instead enlisted as a private.[3] He was thirty-six years old, and basic training made him feel "both ancient (my bones) and infantile (my dexterity)."[4] The work was so hard that some nights he just cried and cried. His young tent mates, who generally lacked his age and education, targeted him for pranks "like turning the bed over or throwing coal all over my tent."[5] "I will never make a good soldier," he wrote to a friend; "I cleaned my mess kit so well I took all the skin off my finger-tips with lye-soap,"[6] he reported to another, and he was thankful that his corporal was an art lover who assigned him to entertainment and bandshell decor. At Fort Belvoir he studied to become a combat engineer but also managed to spend time curating an album and exhibition of battle paintings and sculpture, with showings scheduled at the National Gallery of Art, the Library of Congress, and MoMA. With his usual energy, Lincoln was planning to open a war museum in D.C. or at West Point and preparing a book on the subject. Soon after he shipped off to England in 1944, and then to the Continent, the army finally found a way to better use his vast intellect and expertise. As the war was ending, he was assigned to the Monuments, Fine Arts, and Archives section under Patton's Third Army. Their mandate was to recover Europe's stolen art, which the Nazis had stripped from churches, museums, and private collections and hidden in mines, basements, and storage depots across Germany and Austria.[7]

The "Monuments Men," as they became known (Lincoln called them "medics of culture"),[8] were headed by George L. Stout, formerly of Harvard's Fogg Museum, and included art historians from Yale, Princeton, and Harvard, some of whom Lincoln already knew. Stout had been his teacher at Harvard, and his direct superior was Captain Robert Posey, a New York architect he had met.[9] If this seemed familiar ground, nothing prepared Lincoln for what he saw when they entered defeated Germany amid intermittent last-ditch fire (two on their team were killed). As they moved by jeep into former Nazi territory, past dazed soldiers, displaced persons, and frightened locals, the remnants of Europe's murdered Jewry lay before them. Lincoln found himself attending High Holiday services in a damaged synagogue in a ruined village where only four of two thousand Jews remained. In the town of Hungen, he and Posey discovered eight large buildings packed with papers and archives collected for a planned Nazi racial-studies institute and containing artifacts "weighing five hundred years and a thousand pities," he wrote, from "all the Jewish congregations in Europe." In Nuremberg he sat in the bombed-out offices of *Der Stürmer* surrounded by a vast library of valuable ancient Jewish texts (some with bookplates identifying their murdered Jewish owners) and religious objects, including a silver circumcision plate and vellum rolls from Prague and Amsterdam.[10] He wrote to his sister on the personal stationery of the paper's publisher, Julius Streicher, describing the despicable local Germans who feign innocence or resistance: "Hitler was what they wanted, they made him, and everything else is simply eye-wash. They voted openly for him in 1933 and all things being equal they would vote for him tomorrow morning at eight oclock."[11] Lincoln entered Göring's lavish estate, decorated with stolen French Gobelin tapestries, Gothic carved-wood saints, and graceful Tanagra figurines. The Nazi general's uniform still hung pressed and ready to wear in the closet.

Finding the stashes of Nazi war booty required sleuthing and the awkward task of ferreting out dark secrets from reluctant German locals. The discovery of Jan and Hubert van Eyck's *Adoration of the Mystic Lamb,* known as the Ghent Altarpiece, for example, began with a chance lead from a local dentist treating Posey for a toothache. The dentist led Posey and Lincoln to his son-in-law, a German scholar of medieval art who before the war had worked in Paris with Harvard's own Kingsley Porter, before becoming an SS officer and associate of Göring. In a long interview over cognac in a book-lined home deep in the remote German countryside, this wary and defeated SS man divulged the painting's hiding place in the Altaussee salt mine near Salzburg. Not long after, he shot himself, his wife, and his child. Lincoln, Posey, and their team rushed to follow this lead and soon found the altarpiece stashed in flimsy cartons wrapped in cotton lying on the damp dirt floor of the mine, which was packed with thousands of objets d'art, including masterworks by Michelangelo, Fragonard, Watteau, Vermeer, and, as Lincoln exclaimed, "Christ knows what not." The Germans had arranged to dynamite the mine in the event of Allied victory, and its walls were still dangerously fused, although local anti-Hitler miners had earlier risked their lives to secretly remove as many of the explosives as possible and hide them under bushes and branches on a nearby road, which made it possible for Lincoln, Posey, and their team to enter. This was only the most spectacular of many such discoveries, and Lincoln was understandably obsessed. It was heartbreaking work: salvaging the remnants of a past that millions of war dead would never inherit.

It was art but also architecture, and they came upon palaces, churches, cathedrals, fantastic Renaissance and baroque monuments, and Gothic civic and domestic structures—many reduced to rubble "bricked up high" as "unwelcome tourists like ourselves try to figure out where was what, the last time we were here." He was haunted by memories of childhood visits to this ancestral home and found "where Ma and George and I were 20 years ago" now "efficiently strafed and richly ruined."[12] Trier, Cologne, Mainz, Frankfurt, and "the beautiful breathing memories of the greatest epoch of pure Germanic culture, of Kaiser Maximilian and Cranach and Durer are gone, *spurlos veraekt,*" he reported to a friend. It amounted to nothing less, he quietly noted, than "the destruction of the monumental face of urban Germany . . . and that's too much elegance to remove from the surface of the earth."[13]

In a final strange and disorienting event before he returned home depressed and exhausted, Lincoln accidentally ran into Lew Christensen. This quiet, mild-mannered dancer had fought with the 254th Infantry Division and spent the war doing the gruesome work of gathering the dead and mutilated bodies of his comrades from the field of battle. As the fighting ended, he had been assigned the task of administering a German town. When he and Lincoln met, somewhere near Trier, they were deeply moved to see each other—so much had happened since their innocent ballet days—but there was little to say. "No point in reminiscence," Lincoln later wrote, recalling their encounter, "the last ten years seem ploughed under."[14]

When Lincoln arrived back in New York in September 1945, he already knew that the war had been the most important experience of his life. The destruction of Europe's Jewry and an entire civilization, and his experience salvaging works by the old European masters from the war rubble, focused him in new ways on the central project of his life: the human figure. As he reflected on his service, the great problem facing art in the postwar world increasingly took hold in his mind: figuration or abstraction, the body or the erasure of the body? Both were understandable reactions to the war—the two world wars—that had so cruelly desecrated, mutilated, and slaughtered millions of men, women, and children, leaving seas of broken and dead bodies in its wake. How could art depict—or ignore—*that*?

Ballet, with its devotion to making beautiful bodies, was a living artistic link to a devastated European past. Lincoln still didn't much care for "ballet-ballet," but in George's new kind of dancing he saw the possibility of restoring figuration in Western art. A few years later, Lincoln published a book with Muriel Stuart on ballet technique and put Leonardo's Vitruvian man on the cover, noting that "the academic dance is a fortress of [the body's] familiar if forgotten dignity. . . . Future painters and sculptors may one day return [to it] for instruction in its wide plastic use."[15] West Point became another favorite model. He did not hate the army at all, and there was something in the comradery, the instant society these unlikely companions had made together, cooking fried ham and pineapple tarts for their whole company, that appealed to his lonely soul.[16] He even admired the training. Like the School of American Ballet, he said, military training was not designed to make "well-rounded humanists"; it was making officers, just as he and Balanchine were making dancers. In 1946 SAB was recognized under the G.I. Bill of Rights, and its enrollment, which had grown to more than four hundred students, included some fifty war veterans.[17] "It's very lean, it's stoic, and it's laconic and it's cloistered," he later explained, emphasizing the connection. George, he felt, had a similar interest in adapting "for civil uses, situations that were essentially military."[18] It was a warding off of chaos. They had both lived through a war now.

Lincoln and George founded Ballet Society in the spring of 1946. "Now, with the close of the second world war," Lincoln wrote in a formal announcement, "broader directions are possible and desirable. The safe use of ballet-subjects merely nostalgic or charming . . . is essentially a mediocre pastiche," and he left behind his own quaint ambition for an American folk art and committed himself to a new and "adventurous taste." It is a "BIG enterprise," he told the composer Virgil Thomson, and constituted his best take on "what is possible for me to do in the ballet-field." He would contribute half the money himself and hoped to raise the rest through subscriptions. Balanchine would be the artistic director; Lincoln assigned himself the modest title of executive secretary. Ballet Society, he noted, would not be like any other arts organization: it would finally realize his utopian scheme to bring together all the arts in a single enterprise. Ballet Society was to be just that: a whole *society* of art that would include theater, ballet, ballet-opera, chamber opera, books, records, fellowships for dancers, films on dance, and new ballets and dances from around the world—including, for example, "native dances filmed by the US signal Corps in Japan, Thibet, and China."[19] It would also, for the moment, be an exclusive "society" affair: a subscription-only club, a gimmick they invented to attract support and hopefully stay solvent.

The first performances of this new troupe were scheduled for November 20, 1946, and Lincoln booked the small auditorium at the recently established Central High School of Needle Trades in an old garment workers loft on West Twenty-sixth Street. It was one of Roosevelt's Work Projects Administration (WPA) projects, newly redesigned in an art-deco style to house a vocational school for fashion and theatrical design, and the program featured, among other works, an important new dance to music by Paul Hindemith: *The Four Temperaments.*

The Four Temperaments was Balanchine's own summation and moving on. It spanned the war. He had commissioned the music himself from Hindemith in 1940 and had worked on the ballet on and off for years. Hindemith was from the Weimar world: he had fought in the trenches in World War I, composed music in an expressionistic style while working with artists such as Kokoschka, and was subsequently part of the Neue Sachlichkeit (New Objectivity) and a move toward a sparer and more dispassionate sound, although he never surrendered his commitment to tonality. His music was soon banned by the Nazis as "cultural Bolshevism," and when his efforts to accommodate the regime failed, he emigrated to Switzerland and, in 1940, to the United States, where he settled at Yale University. George had approached the composer as early as 1937, but Massine got there first, and George backed away. In 1939 he tried again with a ballet titled *The Children's Crusade*, to the composer's Symphonic Dances, based on the story of French and German peasant children who, during the Crusades, set out to reconquer Jerusalem and reclaim the True Cross of Christ.[20] George already had a piano reduction in hand when performance funding fell through and the project was canceled. Hindemith finally broke with Massine in 1940, finding him an "uncultured non-artist" working in an "atmosphere of ass-art and evil conniving," which helped clear the way, and that fall, Balanchine asked Hindemith for a new dance and put "his $250 'bucks' on the table," as Hindemith put it, to have him compose it.[21]

By October 1940 George had his own handwritten copy of *The Four Temperaments* with "BALANCHINE" neatly inscribed in bold letters on the binding. At his apartment on East Fifty-second Street, he gathered Milstein, Kopeikine, the violinist Samuel Dushkin, the cellists Raya Gárbuzova and Gregor Piatigorsky, and the conductor Léon Barzin to play it, and he and Maria went to Yale to hear Hindemith conduct the score.[22] His idea was to preview the ballet in New York that summer, with Hindemith at the podium, and then take it on the South American tour—"I am supposed to conduct," Hindemith wrote to his agent, "but as always with these ballet things you will not know until five minutes before the performance," and sure enough, that plan fell through too.[23] In South America, George kept working, and the ballet morphed for a moment into something more surreal, called *Cave of Sleep*, with designs by Tchelitchew, which Hindemith apparently axed: gruesome blood-red images of flayed bodies revealing innards and arteries with labels such as "Nervous System, The Muscle System."[24]

Finally, Lincoln brought in the Swiss émigré artist Kurt Seligmann, a surrealist painter interested in magic and alchemy, and in the fall of 1946, Balanchine completed the ballet. Seligmann's elaborate costumes were difficult to move in: he made the dancers into trees or seashell-like creatures wrapped in bandages with Ping-Pong balls, little fans, or other medieval-looking props hanging from their limbs. There were bonnets glittering with tears, bright red "pumpkin hats," and heavy suede helmets. Melancholic had a purple face. When Balanchine saw his dancers festooned in these elaborate constructions, he immediately climbed onto the stage with a large pair of scissors and began cutting (Tchelitchew, who may have recommended Seligmann, standing resentfully at the back of the theater, said, "You know what that is? . . . It's a long piece of shit").[25] Later, Todd Bolender, perhaps at Balanchine's instigation (we do not know), went one step further. He shed his hot and heavy Phlegmatic dress and performed his role nearly nude (wearing only white underwear and socks) at the photography studio of Lynes, who immortalized it in a series of freeze-frame images.[26] It was a premonition, or perhaps even the shadow of a plan. In 1951 Balanchine would discard Seligmann's costumes entirely in favor of simple black and white practice clothes, a uniform to bare the ballet's inner workings and its dancers.

The Four Temperaments was a clinical dissection of the human body. It referred to the Hippocratic and Galenic medical model, prevalent from the Periclean age through the seventeenth century, in which the body and emotions were thought to be governed by inner "humors" or bodily fluids—rather than ruled from the outside (as earlier thinkers speculated) by demons, spirits, or sorcery. According to this new science, there were four such humors: blood, phlegm, black bile, and yellow bile, and each was associated with a mood or emotion. Blood (a primal substance different from the red blood flowing through arteries) brought sensuality and optimism. Phlegm made a person feel old, sluggish, and lethargic. Black bile caused melancholia—and even madness, but also creativity. Yellow bile was its opposite: the source of choler, giddy high spirits, envy, and temper. A person's mental and physical health, the theory went, depended on keeping these precarious humors in balance. Balanchine and Hindemith's ballet described each humor in its pure, unadulterated state—that is, the sick body, not the balanced body. It was a physical and musical portrait of extreme emotional states, bodies in a state of anxiety and pain. None of this would be conveyed externally through acting or facial expression; the dancers wore blank faces (masks of a sort) and the temperaments were shown as Balanchine, like Hippocrates, imagined them. By body alone.[27]

The body dismantled like a machine. A once-strong supporting leg bent and broken like a warped metal pipe. A man pivoting a woman like he is screwing a twisted nail into the floor. A woman thrusting her hips jarringly off-kilter and swinging into a gyrating arabesque that her partner can barely control. There is sex, but it is mechanical: a woman's legs split wide to the audience; a man's thigh jutting phallically between her legs as their bodies interlock. They do not melt or romantically join, but instead assemble like industrial parts.

Dancers climb in and out of their own movements, squatting, skittering, backs humped with effort, and at times they appear dismembered, joints broken. There is no easy flow, and the steps and phrases unfold like the montage of static images in Balanchine's choreographic notes: a man without a memory cannot see a dance.

Melancholic and Phlegmatic, internal and vulnerable states, are danced by men. Sanguinic and Choleric, powerful, almost fury-like, are danced by women. Psychology is irrelevant. When Phlegmatic, danced by the rubbery, modern dance–trained Bolender, doubles over in pain with jerky, clutching movements, it is not because someone has done something to him. No one has done anything. Nor is he reacting to bad news or sad thoughts that we know of. It is more like watching an inner world of unstable fluids ungoverned by the bony spine of anatomical and classical form. Balanchine, moreover, found a way of moving that looked like the music—not a translation or a copy or an enactment but a formal and physically external visualization of music and insides. He showed Bolender the "kind of violent passion" it would take to break through, even momentarily, the "terrifying lethargy" of the body—"an explosion of passion from lethargy back to lethargy."[28]

And when Melancholic plunges himself backward into a deep arch, as if in full surrender, we have no idea why. All we know is that his head is thrown behind him and that in this impossibly back-bent, blinded, and vulnerable position, he edges himself backward, face-first, into the wings. The causes of his inner state are inaccessible, hidden in humors lodged in the crevices of bone and sinew or coursing through flesh. All we know, all we can see, is the melancholy that is physically and musically upon him. The emotion is powerful, but since it has no obvious origin or explanation, the dancers perform the dislocated movements with cold detachment, as if they are watching themselves from the outside. One looks at his hand as if it were not his own.

Balanchine kept changing the ending and couldn't seem to get it right. Finally, he settled on the "atomic bomb" finale, as the dancers called it, in which William Dollar as Melancholic was repeatedly thrown up into the air like a corpse from the center of an amoeba-like circle of dancers, until finally the circle closed over him, burying his body beneath.[29] A few years later, Balanchine excised this too-literal image and replaced it with something more abstract. In the new and enduring version, to the final ominous and careening phrases of the music, Melancholic and Phlegmatic carry Sanguinic and Choleric in weighted low-flying lifts, legs split, against a horizon of dancers, men and women, in a straight military-style kick line, throwing their legs aggressively at the audience as they advance, hips jutting, and perform rote poses in unison semaphore. On the final inexorable stroke of the music, the soloists fly down this runway and exit the stage, legs split and heads thrown back, as the curtain falls.[30]

The Four Temperaments was a threshold. It was a different kind of dance than Balanchine had ever made before. There was no hint of narrative or romance or spirituality or surrealism. The lush expressiveness of *Serenade*, situated at the beginning of his American years, was gone. The physical language, like the musical score, was instead fragmented and sparse, heartless even, but also tense and careening—as close to neurotic as he ever came. The result was a dance that was clinical in its exterior look and disarmingly intimate in its microscopic examination of the outward appearances of physical and musical facts.

Abstraction in dance begins here: not in removing the human figure, but in drawing it ever closer. The point was not to feel but to show—as if the body one inhabited were not one's own. These bodies—these dancers, these people—appeared strange, foreign, and indifferent. Removed, like Kandinsky's "kingdom of the abstract," except, and this was the key, these foreign objects were still full-blooded human beings. The toxic humors, the body sickened by too much bile or blood or phlegm, was not a distant Hippocratic theory or lost ancient world. It was these dancers, here and now, and they were gripped by forces they could not control, the grasp of fluids and the fight with bone. And when Balanchine changed the final "atomic bomb" image, the distance between *Serenade* and *The Four Temperaments*, Tchaikovsky and Hindemith, 1934 and 1946, fully clarified. This was not a god-filled world where people live and die; it was a taut geometric and scientific universe of his own making—and unmaking.

All of this gave *The Four Temperaments* a gray heart. It was shadowed the way a heart can become when it has been through too much. You can breathe fine, feel fine, but there is something leached, drawn down, pulled unnaturally away from the inner flow of blood into the weaker regions of the outer limbs—consumed by temperament, perhaps, or maybe just a bit hidden. It was a sign of the ways that Balanchine could live, and make us live, on other people's intimacies, of the ways that other people could be our insides. The effect of *The Four Temperaments* involved a strange negative-image approach: the audience felt the feelings that the dancers did not express.

It was a threshold for Balanchine too. Something had ended, and unbeknownst perhaps even to himself, he was finding a new direction, away from mysticism and God and toward the full weight of man. His new dances in the years to come would have plenty of Olympian gods, but fewer spiritual worlds and biblical deserts to cross—not until *Noah and the Flood* in 1962, the year of his momentous return visit to Russia, and then Suzanne Farrell and *Don Quixote* in 1965 (its own special circumstance) and, after that, not again until he reached the last years of his life. He would never do another ballet to Bach's music again. He was not giving up on divinity. *Barocco* had shown and *The Four Temperaments* elaborated a central theme: that the body could itself be *made* divine, not through magic or the touch of the gods but through work—rhythm, harmony, and dissonance; joint, muscle, flesh, and clay in hand.

After the premiere, Lincoln wrote to Lucia Chase in a rare moment of equanimity: "What Balanchine has done with Hindemith is miraculous. It is insanely difficult to dance, and I am sure many people will think it is hideous, but the only justification I have is to enable him to do exactly what he wants to do in the way he wants to do it."[31] A clear announcement of resolve, even if it did not always hold, to serve Balanchine. "I've been looking for authority all my life," Lincoln admitted, and "Balanchine had it to the nth degree."[32]

Did he? In his work, perhaps, but in his life—and love—authority was more elusive. George and Maria were living on the road, its own kind of home, and had already moved out of the apartment he had been renting from the Pecci-Blunt family, wealthy Italian patrons of the arts, and moved into the Hotel Woodward on West Fifty-fifth Street. George carted around a few belongings, including the old photo of his father, along with the usual icons, which sat on whatever bedside table he had, a reminder of a past not so easily settled or escaped. Even these comforting images could not ward off the ghosts haunting his sleep, and he would sometimes wake in terror, screaming and babbling in Russian, and have to quiet himself somehow. In an effort to settle further, but never quite, he even bought property, this time with no house, in a growing informal artists' colony in Weston, Connecticut, from Davidova's wealthy friend Alice DeLamar, who offered it at a discount.

His marriage was governed by dancing. They worked grueling eighteen-hour days, and rehearsals began as early as 7 A.M. and often lasted late into the night. On the way home in the evenings, they liked to stop at Sammy's Delicatessen to pick up a meal, but, like most of his dancers, Maria was chronically exhausted, limbs aching, dead on her feet. And although Davidova and others said George had married Maria because he was obsessed with sleeping with her, and she was a good Catholic girl and had refused, once that was over, they retreated to separate beds. Maria later confided that she wasn't even sure she had seen George fully naked, and she admitted he was too preoccupied with dancing to be much of a lover. He was so excruciatingly private that when they visited friends, he didn't even like to ask to use the bathroom, preferring to wait, childlike, until they got home rather than reveal this embarrassing bodily need.[33]

They played house as best they could. He cooked and left her instructions: "Dear Mashka! Please look in the oven every 20 minutes and baiste it and put some about two spoons of wine. . . . General coock," with a cheerful drawing of himself in a chef's hat. The night that Stravinsky and W. H. Auden came for dinner, she was so frazzled that she sent a full pot of potatoes rolling on the floor, which Stravinsky kindly helped her retrieve: "No one will know." She grew accustomed to socializing with Milstein, Tchelitchew, Rieti, Berman, and Horowitz (who shared George's interest in painting), although when the Russians started talking about food, she fled to bed, knowing they would go on for hours. Dinners at the Milsteins' were especially notorious. Milstein's wife was Romanian and made sure they all knew that *she* was a *real* aristocrat (her father was murdered by the Iron Guard when he refused to convert his silk factories to munitions) and the cook, Lisl, was German; "Oh lordy, George is cooking tonight!" she would exclaim good-naturedly when George arrived, knowing he would throw her kitchen into disarray with his preparation of homemade piroshki, blinis, and borscht, served piping hot on fine china—with heated bowls and a spoon in each so as not to crack the china—and there was plenty of wine, whiskey, and black tea in glasses sweetened with spoonfuls of Georgian jam.[34] Alexander and Tatiana Lieberman, Horowitz, Toscanini, and Nicky Nabokov, variously, came to these spirited dinners. Other times, George and Maria drove out to the country to see Volodine, or to Natasha Molostwoff's crowded bohemia on Fire Island, although Maria preferred to stay home playing poker into the night with her dancer friends, relegating George to a cot in the hallway.[35]

Her strict domesticity and contradictory nature annoyed George intensely, and he complained to Davidova that his gorgeous young wife washed out her leotards in the sink at night, sewed her own clothing from patterns bought at Bloomingdale's, and mopped the floors and laid newspapers, bossily instructing, "Don't walk there!"[36] "I don't need a housewife," he confided bitterly, "I need a nymph who fills the bedroom and floats out."[37] She was just as fastidious at the theater, and girlish too. Maria's corner of the dressing room was pink—pink placemat, pink tissue box, pink pincushion—and had piles of Life Savers and gum, which she chewed constantly. She kept a whole lemon on hand, and on performance days, she cut it and carefully placed the open halves in the first wing, wadded with Kleenex: lemon for saliva control; Kleenex to wipe sweat from her face.[38]

As a dancer, she was a star. She had tremendous stage presence, along with an already strong Russian training from her years with Nijinska. From there, George carefully, patiently, methodically molded her body and restructured her technique in classes, rehearsals, and the informal private lessons that filled their days off.[39] Every waking hour was ballet. When they drove George's black Mercury convertible to California, with Nicky Magallanes and composer Remi Gassmann, one summer for vacation, George immediately arranged to spend the days giving Tallchief and Magallanes, her dance partner, an intensive training course with himself at the piano. It was more of a working relationship than a marriage, and it would not last.

The future of Ballet Society was uncertain too, and the following year, in 1947, George took up an invitation from the Paris Opera and left for five months to stage his work there. Paris still had enormous allure. The Paris Opera, after all, was still the only house that could rival the Mariinsky, and the likelihood that their little Ballet Society would even survive was dim. George wrote to Lincoln saying that he was sure he would be asked to stay in Paris but that he didn't really want to. He found the city grim. There were shortages, and he asked Maria, who followed him there, if she could please bring Nescafé, milk, and soap.[40] The Grand Hotel, where they were living, had no heat and plenty of mice, and he took to hanging food in baskets from the ceiling.[41]

Worse, the theater was still fighting its own war, roiled by pro- and anti-Lifar factions. Lifar had led the Opera through the Occupation and had collaborated shamelessly with the Nazis.[42] A well-established anti-Semite in the 1930s, he had fawningly given Hitler a personal tour of the Opera, knew Goebbels, and socialized with Otto Abetz, Hitler's ambassador to France, assuring the authorities in obsequious letters that he was "pure Aryan." After the war, as part of the epuration and trials against collaborators taking place across French society, Lifar had been purged and exiled from the Opera (he would soon return, unscathed), but his supporters continued to rally, and protests and strikes by the theater's anti-Lifar machinists and corps de ballet were evidence of the ongoing struggle. Balanchine had long since turned against Lifar (he told Lincoln in 1935 that Lifar was little more than a "masturbator").[43] The situation was awkward since Balanchine had been invited in Lifar's absence to restore the Paris Opera Ballet's broken morale—an impossible job, and he could not escape the infighting and was alternately celebrated and vilified, an exhausting drama that discouraged and alienated him.[44]

He complained to Lincoln through Maria, who took dictation and tidied up his poor English:

> We gave *Apollo* for the second time last Wednesday, and though the public received it very well—there are those critics (friends of Lifar) who are not so warm towards it. Have even heard that they have gone so far as to intimate that every step was stolen from Lifar's ballets. Of course all this doesn't bother me in the least—as I don't have the time to listen to or read such petty "stuff."

But he did read it, and it did irritate him. And although "Tall-Chief" was a sensation, he was frustrated with Toumanova: "She is no longer the same person she used to be," he wrote to Lincoln. "She is primarily interested in making money and glorifying Toumanova. I personally don't want to ask her please don't discuss this with anybody—as when I return I shall tell you about the whole matter in detail." He consoled himself by taking Maria to the House of Guerlain to find "her" scent (L'Heure Bleu) and to the House of Dior for "New Look" dresses (she left with two in black). He also met with the Italian composer Luigi Dallapiccola, who "played me his music for chorus a cappela [*sic*]—and [I] think it might be a good idea to put that together on the same program with Rieti. I found it very interesting—and am sure you would like it," he assured Lincoln.

As for the Paris Opera, the company had no talented choreographers, he said, and a lazy work ethic dictated by long lunch breaks and "le restaurant." He managed to make a new work, *Le Palais de Cristal*, to a recently discovered nineteenth-century score by Georges Bizet. It was a fiendishly difficult ode to joy for a large cast, as if to say to these war-plagued dancers: just dance! But the experience of working with them left him cold. "To tell you the truth," he confided to Lincoln, "from now on I would like to devote all my time towards making a good American company." It was 1933 all over again, and once again Balanchine was turning his back on Europe, and away from more secure American opportunities too: he didn't want to work on Broadway or join with Lucia Chase or anyone, he said; he didn't even want his ballets performed by Ballet Theatre's "mythical ballerinas." Wouldn't it be better, he beseeched Lincoln, for *their* little company "to be independent or die?" He pressed the point, "Are we going to exist?"[45]

Sure enough, soon after George's return from Paris, things were tipping toward the usual precipice. *The Four Temperaments* had cost close to $10,000, a vast sum at the time, and they knew from the outset that at best they would only recoup half through the box office.[46] Money was running out. There was no security, no horizon, and they found themselves, once again, on the verge of collapse. By now Lincoln didn't have much margin: he had already poured $60,000 (nearly $1 million today) of his own money into Ballet Society to keep it from folding, and he estimated that he had personally spent nearly a quarter of a million dollars on the ballet since he started. That fall, his brother George sent him an accounting of his assets, reminding him that he simply wasn't that rich, and advising him strongly against pouring more into the ballet sinkhole.[47] "I am having a very hard time about money for Ballet Society," Lincoln confided to Virgil; "actually, nobody cares what we do; it has no chic and I don't know whether to try to get a 'Committee' of people or not."[48] Worried, Lincoln did what he always did: he mobilized. He wrote letters to wealthy friends; he tried to drum up press interest and support; he organized an exhibition at MoMA, *Stage Design for Ballet Society;* he commissioned the ballets George wanted to make, including one by Rieti and one by Stravinsky; and he rented yet another space, for yet another series of performances, this time at the City Center of Music and Drama, an old Shriners temple recently refurbished by the city as a theater.[49]

Balanchine immediately set *Le Palais de Cristal* on his more meager Ballet Society dancers. In Paris he had had forty-eight highly trained dancers, each cast in one of the four movements of Bizet's symphony; in New York he could not rustle up (or pay) more than thirty-five, so he reduced the size of the corps de ballet and doubled up the dancers. In Paris each movement had a different color, and the dancers had been costumed in brightly tinted tutus; in New York this was a problem because the doubling up would scramble the color scheme. The solution: white. Balanchine painted his colorful Parisian celebration white and took away the fairy-tale title in favor of Bizet's: *Symphony in C.*

The casting told its own story. The confident first movement was led by his commanding and steely wife, but the ballet's greatest pas de deux, to the yearning second-movement adagio, was performed by the company's new, elegant, and long-limbed beauty, Tanaquil Le Clercq—a "colt-angel" Lincoln called her, for her lanky athletic body and disarming luminosity. *Symphony in C* was such a success that Lincoln and George decided to open a few of their subscription-only Ballet Society performances to the general public, who came—and "shrieked" their approval, as Lincoln happily put it, with more than a dozen ovations.[50]

Two weeks later, on April 28, 1948, they presented *Orpheus,* a subject that had preoccupied Balanchine since his humiliating Metropolitan Opera defeat. It was a theme long since coveted by Russian symbolists and devotees of Theosophy, the occult, Wagner, and Nietzsche and *The Birth of Tragedy from the Spirit of Music*, and Orpheus had inspired modern works by Rainer Maria Rilke, Jean Cocteau, Jean Anouilh, and Max Beckmann, among others. Balanchine's brand-new *Orpheus* was made in close collaboration with Stravinsky. Lincoln saw it as a natural next step: Orpheus, protégé of Apollo and son of Calliope (muse of song), would be the second ballet in a Greek trilogy he already had in mind: *Apollo, Orpheus*—and something else to come.

Stravinsky and Balanchine had begun work on the ballet in the spring of 1946 at Stravinsky's Beverly Hills home, where they pored over Ovid and a classical dictionary to outline a scenario, surrounded by Stravinsky's impressive collection of clocks and metronomes. Balanchine later delightedly described their workmanlike meetings, saying that when he told the composer that he would like to begin the ballet with Orpheus alone on an empty stage, standing hunched over Eurydice's grave with his back to the audience, Stravinsky calmly asked:

> "How long would you like him to stand without dancing, without moving? A sad person stands for a while, you know." "Well," I said, "maybe at least a minute," so he wrote down "minute." "And then," I said, "his friends come in and bring something and leave." "How long?" asked Stravinsky. I calculated it by walking. "That will take about two minutes." He wrote it down, and it went on like that.[51]

Stravinsky was also present for many of the rehearsals, where he continued this practical approach, pressing George to be precise about time. When they arrived at the point where Eurydice dies, Stravinsky interrupted, "Maria, how long will it take you to die?" Tallchief slumped to the floor, and Stravinsky counted, snapping his fingers. Four counts. He added four counts of silence to the music, "Now you are dead."[52] And it went on like that: another ballet "about time."[53] Stravinsky, who conducted the premiere, described it as "a long sustained, slow chant."[54]

For the design, Lincoln (with George's approval) brought in Isamu Noguchi, a young Japanese American artist who had created sets for Martha Graham and more recently for another dance presented by Ballet Society: Merce Cunningham and John Cage's *The Seasons* (1947). Lincoln had known Noguchi since the days of the Harvard Society for Contemporary Art, and Noguchi had studied with Brancusi in Paris and was close to Arshile Gorki, Nicholas Roerich (the designer for Nijinsky's *Sacre du Printemps*), Willem de Kooning, and others from the emerging New York School of abstract expressionists, many of whom were also interested in myth and ritual. After Pearl Harbor, Noguchi had protested the U.S. internment camps by committing himself for seven months to a camp on a Native American reservation in the Arizona desert (which he naïvely hoped to convert with government support into a collective utopian community). After Hiroshima he spent more time in Japan, where he had lived as a child, and *Orpheus* reminded him of ancient Japanese myth.

For the ballet's decor, Noguchi studiously avoided ethnic Greek themes and designed instead an abstract set using primal, universal, mythic materials—wood, stone, bone. The stage landscape was barren, recalling *Le Sacre du Printemps*, with three large stones that sometimes rose and floated. There was a simple burial mound, and Orpheus's lyre was made of balsa wood, as light and lasting as his song. Balanchine's only addition was a white China silk curtain (like the one he used in *L'Errante*) that would fall from above to mark the filmy boundary to the underworld and could be mysteriously billowed from behind, conveying unrest. When Lincoln told him that they simply could not afford this $1,000 silken prop, George disappeared from rehearsal and returned with a pile of white material, cut from parachute. He refused to say where he had found it or how he had paid, but Maria suspected he had raided his own funds or borrowed from his accountant against future earnings.[55]

The lighting was a key too. Lincoln brought on Jean Rosenthal, who had also worked with Graham, and at John Houseman's WPA Federal Theater, Project 891. She was used to working with no money and few sets and was interested in patterns and "pools of light" that could emphasize movement and emotion. Rosenthal's stage composition, with its deep chiaroscuro and shafts of diagonal light or low horizontals beamed straight from the wings, created the illusion of dancers moving in an elevated plane of light, giving the ballet the look of a living painting.[56]

Orpheus begins and ends at a grave: first Eurydice's, then Orpheus's own. Musically, it begins and ends with the harp, the soothing sound of Orpheus's lyre. The two images are superimposed: death and the eternal power of music. In between, Balanchine and Stravinsky followed Ovid's account of both Orpheus's descent into the underworld past the furies ("the Gestapo of Hell" Stravinsky called them)[57] to beg for his beloved Eurydice's life, and Pluto's assent on condition that Orpheus not look back at Eurydice until they have left the underworld. To Ovid's account, they added an Angel of Death or Fate, a male Hermes-like escort who could lead the lovers between worlds, but who also mirrored Eurydice.[58] The angel performed a poignant pas de deux with Orpheus as they set out for Hades in search of Eurydice, curling his snakelike body around the mournful Orpheus, just as Eurydice coiled her body, this time agonizingly, around her lover's body as they set out to return to earth and life. At the crucial moment, with one foot out of Hades, Orpheus looks back, and Eurydice falls dead to the ground. He gathers her into his arms, but she is sucked under the white silk curtain back to Hades, leaving him, Faust-like, "clasping nothing but empty air."[59]

To Ovid's account of the ferocious Bacchants, who dismember and decapitate Orpheus, leaving only the gruesome image of his bloodied but still-singing head, Balanchine and Stravinsky added their own prettified apotheosis. At the end of the ballet, Apollo appears carrying Orpheus's head, which is now a large lyre-like mask. The mask is Orpheus's image, his face, his eyes and blinded sight; it is his lyric instrument, but also the evidence of his tragic inability to return his beloved Eurydice to life. Apollo sadly strums this lyre-like mask—the unbloodied face of his dead son—and finally places it in Orpheus's grave. Then comes the less than convincing deus ex machina: the lyre is resurrected—lifted to heaven in a divine spotlight, still "singing" as the sound of the harp returns. The effect, Stravinsky said, was meant to be less redemptive than compulsive. At the end of the ballet, he purposefully and repeatedly "cut off the fugue with a pair of scissors" and inserted the harp, to show the song of Orpheus returning like a "compulsion, like something unable to stop. Orpheus is dead, the song is gone, but the accompaniment goes on."[60]

In this *Orpheus*, the real ending comes earlier, when the Bacchants, that sisterhood of terrifying furies, tear Orpheus to pieces (in revenge, Ovid says, for Orpheus's retreat into homosexual devotions, but this goes unmentioned in the ballet, except perhaps in the angel). These fearsome creatures, in skin-tight unitards with long, ecstatically frizzed red or gold hair, assault Orpheus with knifelike high kicks, legs split, bodies in gut-hollowing contractions flung off balance, pointe shoes hammering into the ground. They attack but stop short of a physical strike. Instead, they menace poor Orpheus, defenseless without his lyre, gradually forcing him to his grave mound as he opens his arms Christlike until, at the crucial moment of death and decapitation, they pile over him and bury him in their midst—recalling the "atomic bomb" burial of *The Four Temperaments*. In later versions, they mark the execution with a sharp severing gesture as they throw him backward into his grave. The bloody dismemberment deed is done behind the protective wall of their bodies, and the rising lyre is a harmonious Apollonian finish that does little to soften the Dionysian compulsion, as Stravinsky put it, of the inexpressibly murderous rituals that killed Orpheus—but not his song.

As for love and Eurydice, Balanchine's Orpheus presents an anomaly. Orpheus looks back not because he fears Eurydice is not following or has lost her way, as the story typically suggests. He knows she is there because she climbs onto his back, wraps herself around his body, and winds her limbs seductively through his, as he blindly partners her and studiously averts his eyes. For Balanchine, their love is a kind of suicide neither can prevent: in order to become herself, she must *be seen* by this man who loves her, and her seduction is driven as much by anxiety as by sexual desire. For him the compulsion is different: in order to be Orpheus, poet and musician, he must *see her*. Being seen is nothing to him; everything to her. But when he looks and beholds her, she dissolves in his arms—and the music stops.

Orpheus could also be taken, and was, as a kind of mourning ritual: the lonely burials and winding journey to the underworld, the blind and suffering pas de deux "in the dark" with the Angel of Death, and the image of resurrection and an afterlife signaled in the simple and purifying notes of a harp and the vision of the rising lyre. There was something elegiac about this dance and the ways that it invoked the universal story they were all still witnessing as lines of refugees crawled their way from somewhere across the postwar landscape, as well as the ways that Balanchine and Stravinsky had tried—and failed—to plow under the hellish powers that were the ballet's most lasting image.

Orpheus was a public and critical success. Lincoln was so nervous that he left the theater before it was over and missed the ovation, but at the last performance of the ballet that season, when Balanchine, Stravinsky, and Noguchi took the stage for the final bow, the cheering, Lincoln said, was like that for "Babe Ruth at Yankee stadium." *Life* and *Time* were planning stories, he wrote excitedly to Mina, and there were movie and TV possibilities. Davidova gave an elegant dinner after the first show, and on the last night, Lincoln hosted a party at what he wryly called the "kosher-baroque room" of the Great Northern Hotel, where they all did the rumba and jitterbugged into the night. It had been a gamble: "insanely expensive," Lincoln noted, "but we have come out way on top as the leading organization of its kind, and it is on our own terms." Even Balanchine agreed that it was exactly the production they had needed to stay alive.[61] The truth, as they both knew, was a bit less varnished. The theater during their 1948 season was never more than a third full, and they had racked up a large deficit with almost nothing in reserve to pay it. They survived only because Lincoln managed to pull from his usual resources: in his father's absence, his mother stepped in to help, and Nelson Rockefeller finally wrote a check for $5,000 to carry them through. Another close call.[62]

Soon after the premiere of *Orpheus,* Lincoln Kirstein received a visit from Morton Baum, chairman of the executive committee of City Center. Baum had not been to much dance in his life, but he was a serious amateur musician, and *Orpheus* and *Symphony in C* had moved him deeply. A tax lawyer by profession, Baum was from a poor émigré Jewish family, and he had made it to Harvard Law School and served under Governor Dewey and Mayor La Guardia, who in 1943 brought him on to help convert the old Mecca Temple on Fifty-fifth Street into a theater. La Guardia was another immigrant son, this time Italian, and he had lived and worked in Budapest, Trieste, and

Fiume. He spoke several languages, including Italian, German, French, and Yiddish (his mother was Jewish), and he had a lifelong interest in music. La Guardia wanted New York to have theaters like those of the great European cities—but not like the elite, Old World Met, with its Waspy board and prohibitively expensive tickets. The City Center of Music and Drama was to be an affordable theater, offering music, opera, and ballet to the city's working people from all of New York's boroughs, including war workers, members of the armed services, students, and the middle and lower classes. The city would provide cheap rent and a small subsidy; the rest was up to ticket sales, and Baum was in charge of finances. A public-minded civil servant, Baum was an upstanding member of his Reform synagogue, and his practical, business-like manner, and "rabbinical instruction"—"Yes, yes," he would counsel Lincoln, "it's all very well to hate 'em, but is it worth your energy?"—naturally reminded Lincoln of his own father. When they met that afternoon in the fall of 1948, they recognized each other immediately.[63]

Baum found Kirstein in an irritable mood and was surprised to hear this large young man launch into a bitter tirade about the whole ballet venture, complaining that Ballet Society was exhausted and would have to fold. Baum wanted a resident troupe, and Lucia Chase's Ballet Theatre and Sergei Denham's Ballet Russe, both of which had performed at City Center, were in the running, but Baum was interested in Ballet Society. As Lincoln railed "against the entire ballet field," Baum began to feel that this was one of the strangest meetings he had ever had. "Mr. Kirstein," he finally interrupted, cutting to the business at hand, "how would you like the idea of Ballet Society becoming the New York City Ballet?" Lincoln paused. "If you do that for us, I will give us in three years the finest ballet company in America."

Had he finally stumbled upon a match? A new and scrappy improvised home for a new and scrappy improvised company; two Jews, one Russian, all with émigré pasts, a shared love of music, and a proven willingness to improvise with no guarantees. Baum immediately called another meeting, this time with Kirstein and Balanchine, and the details were speedily worked out. To the question "Are we going to exist?" Lincoln finally had an answer: yes. On October 11, 1948, the company gave its first performance as the New York

City Ballet at the City Center of Music and Drama. The program was *Concerto Barocco, Orpheus,* and *Symphony in C*.[64] The company logo would be Orpheus's lyre, which had been stitched on Georgi's uniform at the Imperial Theater School.

Still, the NYCB was not the panacea that it would later seem. Baum and City Center took over running expenses and deficits, but they would not fund new work, nor would they pay Balanchine (or Kirstein) a salary outside the usual royalties, although it was not clear Balanchine, who was allergic to contracts, even wanted one. When Betty Cage went out of her way a few years later to press for a $10,000 annual fee, George rejected it: "I don't want agreement drawn up. I don't want any contract with City Center. And more so, I don't want $10,000 from Baum, and that's definite."[65] The dancers got by on very little, and in the months and years to come, the company would run heavy deficits and there would be plenty of opportunities for the whole venture to collapse.[66] Already, in January 1949, Lincoln was writing to Mina that "the theatre feeds one's normal anxiety to such a degree that it is terrifying. I am only holding on to it long enough to get George established at the City Center, and I will gracefully retire and go abroad myself for a year, with Fido to Italy to look at pictures. But I cannot do this until June 1950, at the earliest." It was an anxious refrain repeated over the years: "This morning I would like to abandon the ballet forever" crossed with "My decision as of yesterday to leave the ballet forever is not valid." Or, more realistically, "There is nothing to do abt the ballet but endure it."[67]

He never left, and if the story of the company's founding, and the lucky appearance of Baum, have the whiff of myth, there was truth to it too. Ironically, though, the greatest truth had nothing to do with Baum. It had to do with George and Lincoln. *They* were the fact that the war had finally established. They were both, each for his own reasons, and in spite of constant threats and plans on both sides to leave, there to stay.

People later said, and Lincoln said it too, that Balanchine never really needed Kirstein (or anyone really); that his talent was too great to fail and he would have accomplished it all on his own. They said that Lincoln and George were not close, and it was true that they were not friends and didn't share the same taste or the same politics or the same society. They didn't necessarily like or dislike each other—what would have been the point of that? Their relationship was practical: Lincoln occupied himself with money and management so that George could make dances. But even that wasn't true. "It is not your nature to be involved in money and commercial things," George gently counseled Lincoln a few years later; "maybe you could be an advisor."[68]

But it was not true that George didn't need Lincoln. He did need him, or, rather, he had him. His wives, he liked to say, all left him. Lincoln, for better and worse, stayed anchored to the spot. He had stamina, and by now they had a past. Lincoln would be the most lasting relationship of Balanchine's life. He sunk his teeth in hard and didn't let go. Dmitriev had saved Balanchine from the USSR; Lincoln had saved him from Europe. And George depended on Lincoln's doggedness in that quiet, airy way he had, as if nothing could touch him. But it could: revolution, hunger, exile, and chronic illness were proof enough of his vulnerability and exposure to the harsh elements of fate. Lincoln never lost the habit of walking into a room and just standing there, which is what he did in George's life. He could be comforting, maddening, annoying, crazy, indispensable, superfluous, but he was always there, and he always had ideas. In the years to come, they were like two trees planted side by side, each surrounded by his own weather. You can see them in countless photographs, Lincoln next to George in the studio, in the wings of the theater, on the stage. Often, they are not even talking or looking at each other; they are both just there, the airy "cloud in trousers" and the heavy, knit-browed "navy suit." Baum later noted that he found himself in the odd position of playing Sancho Panza to George and Lincoln's two Quixotes. Between them, he said, George was the more practical.[69]

Timing was essential and finally it was on their side. Ballet Society was morphing into the NYCB just as the war was morphing into the Cold War. Events outside the theater were moving quickly: Stalin's speech before the Central Committee in Moscow, in 1946, drawing a hard ideological line between the USSR and the West; the consolidation of territory in the Soviet bloc; the Iron Curtain speeches of Winston Churchill and John Foster Dulles, also in 1946; the Marshall Plan announcement in 1947; the Berlin blockade of 1948; the Greek civil war; and the formation of NATO in 1949.[70] The Cold War was beginning, and the NYCB would play a role. To do so, George would need a company of first-rank dancers. The task he faced was the task he had always faced, except that now it was also the problem facing postwar Europe and America: build.

Chapter 15

COMPANY

"Headquarters" was Betty Cage's cramped office at City Center. From there, she had a direct line to Lincoln, George, Morton Baum, and the dancers. She could be tough and ran the company with a combination of Machiavellian precision and softly sardonic wit, deftly maneuvering budgets, debts, payments, people, travel, and troubles of all kinds, not to mention taking in young, unhoused dancers—her "instant children," she called them—until they settled. Lincoln summed up her responsibilities as "at once labor negotiator, certified public accountant, legal expert, mother superior, confessor, psychiatrist, and practicing witch (white)." It was true that she was a witch. The dancers called her "the psychic," and she read their palms or tarot cards and helped them with life decisions by throwing the I Ching. Her Monday-night dinners were known for their séances and Ouija boards, a fashion in artistic circles at the time, and with her husband, the writer Edward Maisel, she wrote a book about tai chi—which she practiced avidly and taught to the dancers.[1]

Betty was black, a fact which nobody in the company so much as commented on, then or since. She had a fulsome body, generous, not stern, with thick curly hair and warm sunken eyes, offset by darkened eyebrows pruned to a skeptical arch. Her skin was so light she easily passed as white, and she had been passing all her life. Her parents were both black and working class; her father had worked the levees in Louisiana and eventually took a job as a meat inspector, and Betty was raised in Buffalo, New York, during the Depression. The census reported that they were the only "Negro" family on the white blocks they lived on, which also housed German, Russian, Hungarian, and Polish émigrés.[2] Educated at the local teacher's college, she had made her way to New York City and the surrealist journal *The View*, where Lincoln found her in 1947 and scooped her up to help with the company. She had just turned thirty and never left.

Running the company was no small task, and in 1953 she got help. Barbara Horgan—"Horgie," as the dancers called her—was of Irish and German descent, and she had a dour but wry demeanor and stoic endurance that suited her for the job. Her parents were second-generation émigrés who had done well in real estate. Her mother was a Kroger, of a successful grocery-store chain, and there was some money there, which her father, whose family came from breweries and coal, made ample use of in his many, usually failed, ventures. Barbara, an only child, attended the exclusive Nightingale School in New York, which gave her a confident finishing-school polish, although she was restless and dyslexic and wanted to be in theater. She got a job at Sam Goody's record store and was studying acting and modern dance (using rubber bands on her wrists to signal left and right). One afternoon, she strayed, with a few of the NYCB dancers she had come to know, into headquarters, and as they collected their pay (small bills crammed into bulging envelopes), Betty surveyed Barbara, asked a few questions, and hired her on the spot: fifty-five dollars a week; performances for free. Barbara was twenty and never left.

Together they did everything, from payroll to schedules to helping get the entire company onto buses, planes, trains, and into hotels; they accompanied them on long European tours, where they set up makeshift headquarters with a small portable typewriter in hotel rooms across the Continent. From there, or from the office at City Center, they dealt with composers, set and lighting designers, budgets, shortfalls, injuries, replacements, costumes, shoes, and salaries, not to mention various tantrums, Lincoln's "crazies," and Balanchine's escalating life. George called Barbara "my humpbacked horse," after the magical horse in a Russian tale that helps vanquish the obstacles placed before a young prince so that he can win the princess and become the czar.[3]

Balanchine also had Eddie Bigelow, an Adonis-like man with a muscular body, a chiseled face, and the rough-hewn appeal of a misplaced New Englander. He had danced for Balanchine in the 1930s, but his career had been interrupted by the war, which left him with the hardened muscles and worn feet of a soldier. Balanchine took him back, first as a dancer, then as his new Dmitriev—this time, for life. Eddie was loyal, stoic, controlled, a man who could steer his way through any situation and didn't mind running errands, delivering messages, escorting dancers, dealing with mothers, lost tickets, stray luggage, and missing costumes, no task too menial. It was a role he had been practicing for all his life. His father, a journalist who abandoned his family, had left Eddie and his brother to fend and care for themselves and their sister—and their mother, a strict Christian Scientist with Victorian morals, crippled by polio. During the war, Eddie was a conscientious objector but nonetheless volunteered to drive an ambulance in Burma, a harrowing job that exposed him to "wounded men . . . the sight of burned villages, bodies broken, lying all askew." He kept forever his British Empire Medal, civil division, which documented that Volunteer Bigelow had rescued the wounded under fire many times. He had had his war too.

Underneath there was something deeply unsettled in Eddie's person that politics and alcohol could rouse and rile. He read *The Nation* and *Mother Jones* and could launch into tirades about corporate greed and the plight of the working class, drinking and chain-smoking as he went. He was compulsive and collected stuff: cigarette wrappers, Buddhas from Burma, and old bits of wood from various moments in his life, not to mention books on poetry, politics, and history. It steadied him to steady others, and he was a reliable handyman with rock-solid loyalty to Balanchine. Lincoln, who was capable of jealousy, complained that Eddie's "eyes are like oysters staring up at you from the bottom of a urinal." The dancers called him Balanchine's saint and acolyte, or his sycophant and slave. George just called him Eddie "Big and low."[4]

The dancers who joined the company in these early years were often outsiders, eccentrics, men and women with minimal education, a streak of bohemia, and an intense physical desire to dance. Foremost among them was Jerome Robbins, who came on as a dancer but also as associate artistic director in 1949—a crucial foundation stone to the company George was building. Like Robbins, many were the children of Russian or Central European émigrés or in some way fatherless; others were adventurous souls from rural areas in the South or out West. These were not seasoned professionals, usually; they were "kids" as Betty called them, young teenagers or starting out, and Balanchine gave them their education. The NYCB was a dance company, but it was also a family, they said, a tribe, a clan, eventually a dynasty, and Balanchine was the father, the husband, the lover, the boss, the patriarch—but rarely the friend. Their bodies and souls were his tools and his livelihood, and he scrutinized who they were and where they came from like a painter or sculptor concerned with the provenance of his oils or clay. Their personalities and pasts mattered—that was clay too—and no one was a more avid gossip than Balanchine, who made it his business to know about their lives and exploits.[5]

It would take a tome to know them, but here are a few examples from the varied and complicated people he chose, and who chose him:

Barbara Walczak, small, with an analytic mind, was the child of Polish Catholic (converted Jews) painters, actors, and writers, who sent Barbara to SAB at thirteen. She spoke Polish at home, a fact that interested Balanchine. She had a short, stocky body made crooked by childhood polio. Balanchine once told her that if she were an animal, she would be half-cat, half-mink, half-mushroom. Not a compliment, but she was smart, hardworking, and a reliable foot soldier, so he kept her—until someone younger and better came along.[6]

Barbara Millberg grew up in Brooklyn in a family of émigré Jews from a shtetl in Odessa. Her father had come to the United States as a teenager, served in World War I, made it through medical school, and became a dentist. Her mother, from an Orthodox background, was his hygienist. They were Communists and atheists, and they spoke Yiddish at home, although her father spoke Russian to Balanchine. Barbara was a sickly child and given ballet lessons with "Miss Selma" to strengthen her body and eventually sent on to SAB. She joined Ballet Society in 1947 at age fifteen.[7]

Pat McBride (later Lousada) was Irish and Italian. Her father was a coal miner and later an electrician and janitor at a hotel in Bronxville; her mother, who grew up on a tenant farm in Piedmont (her grandfather was the church organist), emigrated with a wave of impoverished Italians and worked as a seamstress. She liked to say she was French to seem more elevated, and she enrolled her daughter at SAB, which she saw as "a place to come up in the world, a place for outsiders to come in, a company of adventurous types." Pat was in Tanny's class and danced with Ballet Society and then NYCB. She left for an unhappy marriage that ended in divorce to a man who disapproved of her dancing.[8]

Una Kai grew up in a Danish Lutheran family in New Jersey. Her father was a chemical engineer; her mother, a nurse. Upright, passive, independent, with a tight, orderly mind, and sensually long blond hair (someone once made a ballet for her hair). She had a hidden streak of adventure and made her way to New York and SAB and NYCB. She was married to Eddie Bigelow for a time and was close to Tanny—from across a room, you might mistake them. She saw a lot of Balanchine and was embarrassed by his "earthiness" and "vulgarity," although she later claimed to have had an intermittent affair with him. She wasn't a great dancer, but she could memorize whole dances, so Balanchine moved her to the role of ballet mistress and sent her across Europe to stage his dances.[9] He had an uncanny instinct for where each dancer might later (or sooner) fit into the growing institution he was building.

Janet Reed, cute, comic, spirited, was born in 1916 in rural Oregon and raised by her grandparents in an old stagecoach inn with no heat or electricity. Her grandmother could wring a chicken's neck and kill a snake with a stick, and Janet attended a one-room schoolhouse until her mother, a beautician, kidnapped her after a nasty custody battle. She eventually made her way to New York, joined Ballet Theatre in 1943, and toured the country on trains filled with army troops—the troops ate first; the dancers got the leftovers. In hotels the dancers played the "army game": two register for a room; four share it. George told her she should be an actress; she asked how, and he replied,

"Read Shakespeare." But in 1949 he needed dancers, and she joined the NYCB.[10]

Yvonne Mounsey was born on a farm near Pretoria, South Africa, and danced in Britain and with various Ballets Russes spin-off companies. Tall and glamorous, with a womanly figure and a wide red-lipstick smile, she traveled the world dancing and worked briefly with Balanchine in New York. He found her again in Mexico City in 1945 working as a nightclub dancer and in 1949, pulling from everywhere, he invited her to join the NYCB as a lead dancer.

Patricia Wilde, née White, was one of the company's few daredevil, bravura dancers in the 1950s—she would try anything. Her stage name was Balanchine's idea and a reference to Oscar Wilde. Pat grew up on a farm with sheep, horses, and a big orchard, outside Ottawa. The youngest of five, she was raised in hard times by her divorced mother and siblings. Used to caring for herself, she traveled to a two-room schoolhouse over backroads on skis, finding her way by memorizing certain trees and fences, and Balanchine loved that she knew about plants and vegetables and that she went mushroom hunting and sold what she found at the local market. She studied dance locally with émigré Russians and began performing professionally at age thirteen. By eighteen she was in the NYCB.[11]

Melissa "Milly" Hayden was born Mildred Herman, to a large family of Orthodox Jews from Kyiv, resettled in a close-knit community in Toronto. Her grandfather was a scholar, and her father sold fruit wholesale. She attended Hebrew school and studied ballet with Russian émigrés, and in 1942 she moved to New York, alone, and danced at Radio City Music Hall and Ballet Theatre, with a brief stint in pre-Castro Cuba with Alicia Alonso. By the time she settled with Balanchine, she was an international star. Moody and dramatic, and whip smart, she had dark features, short skinny legs, a huge rib cage, and commanding shoulders. Balanchine didn't love her theatricality or her star quality—she wasn't putty in his hands—but he counted on her. When the others were out with illness or injury, "Mighty Milly" (Balanchine called her "old iron-sides")[12] was always there, stocked with a colorful array of "vitamins" to bolster energy and a portable mirror to set up backstage.[13] She was vivacious, deep, raunchy, a woman of risk—when dancing with her,

Jacques d'Amboise liked to run and touch the back wall of the theater before he raced on stage to catch her in a turn, a thrilling stunt that kept them both on the edge they loved. When a complicated partnering maneuver during a performance once left her breathless and unconscious on stage with broken ribs, for example, she brushed aside the cold packs in the wings and tore back on stage, barely sentient, to finish the ballet. She retired from the NYCB at age fifty in 1973.

Diana Adams was her opposite: tall, pale, cold, a Southern belle born in Staunton, Virginia, to divorced parents from Georgia. Diana had a regal beauty—elegant long legs, arms as thin and fragile as glass, and an anxious, breakable personality. Her hands were always cold and a little bit wet, and she spoke with self-consciously perfect diction. She started dancing on Broadway and in the 1940s found her way to Ballet Theatre and briefly married Hugh Laing, a fellow dancer who was gay, or bisexual (she called him Hubby Hugh), but anguish soon followed; Laing admits he was violent and later begged her forgiveness, but she simply left. Her letters show a woman locked inside herself, and she could disappear, driving her father to threaten a police search if she failed to answer his letters. Balanchine fell in love immediately with this broken-winged woman. He called her his "alabaster princess," after the hard, smooth exterior that covered over her pained and intensely private emotional life, and she would rank as one of his great dancers and most desperate and failed loves.[14]

Tanaquil Le Clercq was his first homegrown American dancer, fully trained from childhood by him and his teachers at his school, and she had danced with Balanchine since she was a teenager. Born in Paris in 1929, she was the daughter of Jacques Georges Clemenceau Le Clercq, of half-French, half-German ancestry (the French head of state Clemenceau was his godfather), who taught French literature and wrote poetry under the pen name of Paul Tanaquil—her namesake. He was also a serious alcoholic, whose drinking eventually destroyed their family. Her mother was Edith Whittemore, a St. Louis socialite who made her daughter her life and was present at every turn, knitting bouclé suits, darning toe shoes, making countless egg-salad sandwiches, and escorting her glamorous girl everywhere. Even so, Tanny was fiercely independent (Diana addressed her in letters as "Dear Fearless") and an avid reader with a wickedly sardonic wit. Blessed with fine features and a long, slender, flexible, and lanky body, she looked and moved differently than Balanchine's other dancers, a fact that drew him to her as a dancer—and a wife.[15]

Behind her came Allegra Kent (née Iris Margo Cohen), a dispossessed Jewish girl from Texas, California, Florida, and a childhood spent on the road fleeing poverty and her absent father—a Texas oil wildcat, amateur boxer, crook, and traveling salesman. Her mother, who controlled her life, was the child of poor Polish-Jewish émigrés on New York's Lower East Side, a lost woman and an obsessive adherent of Christian Science. The name change from "Cohen" to "Kent" was her anguished grasp at social respectability; "Allegra" was little Iris's own longing after Longfellow's daughter in *The Children's Hour*. Allegra grew up imprisoned by her mother's Christian Science edicts: no possessions (her precious dolls, toys, and books were routinely destroyed), pain doesn't exist (she stuck herself with pins to test the proposition), ambition is illusion, and sex is deception. Ballet was perhaps the only real "nonreal" world that her mother would allow, and she studied with Nijinska in Los Angeles in the 1940s, competing with muscular GIs who proved to her that ballet didn't have to be pretty or quaint. She was fashion-spread gorgeous, but there was something of a "mountain goat" in her dancing, she said, and she was troubled, internal, and wild, with a glamour that bewildered and bewitched her. She arrived in New York to study at SAB with only one possession: an avocado plant. Balanchine immediately took her into the company in 1952, age fifteen.[16]

The men were their own ramshackle lot. There was no established professional route for a man in the 1940s or 1950s to become a ballet dancer, and the "sissy" stigma ran high. The war had further decimated the ranks, and many of Balanchine's early male dancers were a bit older and out of central casting: men who "looked like dancers," as he put it, even if they had limited or no technique. Some were drawn to ballet because they were gay, and the fluid sexual world of dance offered a relatively free society, or because they stumbled on it through show business or on the G.I. Bill.

Bobby Barnett, for example, was from a family of homesteaders—Scotch Irish, French, and Pennsylvania Dutch—and grew up in a small farm town in rural Washington State with no electricity or running water. He discovered dance through Saturday-night movies of Astaire and Rogers and through his entertainment detail during his service in the navy. After the war he trained with Nijinska on the G.I. Bill, and when he got to New York and showed up at an open-call audition at the NYCB, Jerome Robbins took one look at his able body and said, "Get dressed, you have rehearsal upstairs right now."[17]

Billy Weslow came from out West too, this time Seattle, where he had been in the Coast Guard and arrived on the G.I. Bill in a uniform with a loaded pistol, some fishing tackle, and a notoriously foul mouth. Balanchine tried to wrestle his body into a shape—literally thrusting his knee in Weslow's spine to pull back his shoulders. Weslow wasn't a great dancer, but he stayed.[18]

Francisco Moncion, dark-skinned and handsome, was from the Dominican Republic and came to the company through Pavel Tchelitchew, who saw him working out at the gym in the local YMCA. George called him "my Islander," which Moncion grew to hate, and made him the company Othello—black but not too black, forceful, dramatic, and striking; he was Death in *La Valse* and the Angel of Death in *Orpheus*, and he stayed for nearly forty years, until after Balanchine's death. The company's other leading man in these early years was the Mexican-born Nicholas Magallanes. He had been "found" by Lincoln through gay circles and trained at SAB. He eventually joined the company, and his movie-star good looks and serviceable technique made him a reliable partner for Maria and Tanny. He was part of the "royal family" of dancers personally close to Balanchine and would stay with the company for the rest of his life.[19]

The other men tended to divide: they were either classical or expressive, and few had the range to incorporate both. Todd Bolender, Ohio-born, had a rubbery, flexible body, poor classical technique, and a Wigman-inspired style that made him a key figure in many of Balanchine's most original dances.[20] Jonathan Watts was raised on army bases by his stepmother and divorced military father ("If he had known I would be a dancer and gay, he would have taken a gun and killed me"). He had a solid classical technique and wanted to be a prince, a prospect that didn't much interest Balanchine, so Watts eventually left.[21] André Eglevsky was the only prince Balanchine needed: Russian,

Bolshoi-trained, and necessary in the early years as a model and for bravura roles—who else could perform them?

Jacques d'Amboise would eventually be Eglevsky's replacement and one of Balanchine's most trusted and extraordinary dancers: a street kid from New York, his father was Boston Irish (Ahearn), and his mother ("the Boss") was French Canadian (d'Amboise)—it was she who shifted the family name to the more "aristocratic" d'Amboise when Jacques started dancing. He grew up mainly in Washington Heights, where his father worked as an elevator man for Columbia Presbyterian Medical Center. He went to Catholic school, hung out on gang-ruled streets, and ended up in his sister's ballet classes. Tall, strong, elegantly built, with a radiant smile and brimming with energy, he had an intense physicality, evident from childhood. At age nine, he wanted to fly—and believed the nuns when they told him that a strictly observed nine-week novena would make his wish come true. So he did the novena and jumped off a six-story building in his Three Musketeers costume. He was lucky to land with a sprained ankle on an adjacent building two stories down. In 1942 his dance teacher sent him to the School of American Ballet, and he soon dropped out of school and joined Ballet Society and then the NYCB, age fifteen, at its founding. He would stay until after Balanchine's death. The dancers called him "Daisy" for his youthful optimism, but for Balanchine, Jacques was a kind of surrogate, and he recognized in him his own roaming ambition—and worship of women. "He's like me," he would explain to Betty when she objected to his special treatment.[22]

Arthur Mitchell was born in New York, but his parents were from Georgia. His father worked as a janitor in their building at 536 West 143rd Street in Harlem, and his mother checked coats at the fancy 21 Club. The family attended the Convent Avenue Baptist Church down the street, where Arthur sang in the choir. He went to the High School of Performing Arts, and in 1952 Lincoln saw his graduation performance, a dance he called "Wail," and offered him a scholarship to SAB. Arthur also studied ballet with Karel Shook, a white man determined to break the color line in ballet, who had also taught at Katherine Dunham's school.

The following year Arthur's father confessed to and was convicted and incarcerated for the gruesome murder, in a gambling dispute, of a white man, whose body was found decapitated and dismembered.[23] The toll this horrific event took on the family and Arthur's inner life is difficult to gauge—he didn't talk much about it—but it left him more than fatherless. He and his four siblings helped to cover the janitorial duties and worked part-time jobs to sustain the family. In 1954, Mitchell worked with Balanchine as a dancer in the musical *House of Flowers*,[24] and the following year, Balanchine and Kirstein both took Mitchell under wing; he later said they were "like surrogate dads, you know what I mean."[25]

For Mitchell's company debut, Balanchine asked him to dance in *Western Symphony* with Tanaquil Le Clercq, who was very pale and by then his wife, prompting someone in the audience to cry out, "My God, they've got a Nigger!"[26] When parents called the school protesting, "I don't want my daughter to dance with the Negro," Balanchine just said: then take your daughter out. In 1958 he would cast Mitchell in *The Nutcracker* as one of the princely cavaliers to Diana Adams's Sugar Plum Fairy in a performance that was broadcast on national TV. In rehearsal, as Mitchell offered his black hand to her white one, Balanchine glanced up at them both and said, "I hope Governor Faubus is watching," referring to the violently racist governor of Alabama during the recent Little Rock crisis. When the TV producers objected that a white woman dancing with a black man would destroy their ratings across the South—Balanchine said, he's a member of the company, and we must have him.[27] By then he knew Arthur well. He had met his mother, and they had talked about their families. Arthur invited George to parties with James Baldwin and others, and George became an important spiritual guide, telling this new charge, "I always have two angels at the bottom of my bed protecting me."[28] Arthur, he implied, might need an army.

These dancers are only a few of the many who danced with the NYCB in its early years. Their modest team also included the conductor Léon Barzin, son of a musician and a professional ballet dancer as well as a protégé of Arturo Toscanini. Barzin had already had a big career as a violinist, violist, and then conductor in Europe and America, and he had joined Balanchine and Kirstein in the Ballet Society years. Barzin talked about the "third dimension" in conducting, by which he meant the way music came from the body.

Schoenberg fondly described him as being "of the crouch and tiptoe school . . . He would not only crouch for pianissimos and get on tiptoe for fortes. He also would dance to the music—his beat was all curves." Barzin was largely responsible for the high quality of orchestral playing in these early years, and he could be tough with the dancers too. He once stopped the orchestra in the middle of a performance to scold them, "You weren't listening to me."[29] But Barzin was busy and incurred Balanchine's wrath one evening when he allowed an assistant conductor to perform Bizet without asking permission. The botched tempos made George "angrier than I have ever seen him," Betty reported to Lincoln, and although Barzin quickly stepped in for the final movement, the poor assistant was "mud in George's book." Balanchine was already nurturing Hugo Fiorato, a Barzin protégé, who had joined Ballet Society as concert master and stayed for life. Balanchine fondly called him "ego furioso," after Ariosto's sixteenth-century chivalric poem *Orlando Furioso*.

The lighting designer Jean Rosenthal was born Eugenie Rosenthal in 1912 to Romanian Jewish émigrés from a family of tailors. Her parents made good as doctors, and she attended Yale's drama school and worked with Martha Graham and in theater; Lincoln brought her to Ballet Society, and she continued to work for the company. Small, wiry, round-faced, and intense, she called her crews "honey" and darling," ate at local drugstores, and lived alone. She and Balanchine sat at the lighting board in the middle of the theater and came up with new ways to light dance. "Less is possible," he would say.

Theater has solid, material sets—a couch or table—and slow-moving action that can be mapped in advance and separated into lit quadrants, but dancers moved quickly and were everywhere on stage. As Balanchine stripped scenery, lighting dance meant lighting the air. Air has particles that catch light, and dancers move through air *into* the light, making calculations of intensity, tone, timing, and color delicate, depending on the desired effect. Balanchine wanted lighting that didn't draw attention to itself, that was organic, not an effect, and Rosenthal gave it to him. For all her innovation and stature, however, she didn't last. Sometime in 1956, Lincoln brought in Ronnie Bates, the brother of a friend, to help with stage managing and lighting, and Jean didn't like it. Ronnie was a kid from Arkansas who had served in the navy, drank too much, and was a bit lost. He was nobody, and Rosenthal *was* lighting in the city and based at the NYCB, or so it seemed, until she made the fatal error of giving Balanchine an ultimatum: Ronnie or me. If there was one thing Balanchine couldn't abide, it was a direct challenge to his artistic authority—he immediately chose Ronnie. Rosenthal wrote him a crestfallen note hoping that he would change his mind, but he didn't. In fact, as far as we know, he didn't even bother to respond.[30]

Ronnie Bates was just what Balanchine needed, another orphan-like man who knew that George Balanchine had saved him and given him his life. Ronnie was loyal to the core and would stay at the NYCB until after Balanchine's death. The fact that he would soon marry Diana Adams only tied him more deeply to Balanchine, who brought Ronnie along and let him make his own mistakes as they worked together side by side, "maybe little more blue; let's try; maybe not, dear." Balanchine would sometimes appear at the lighting board during a show, and the crew later developed a warning system to notify the backstage that he was on his way, so that someone could be there to shift a color or tone midperformance. Ronnie was tough talking, loved women and drink, and had a bawdy sense of humor, and Balanchine also saw that he could handle the macho crew of Local 1—which mattered if they were to get anything done. The crew would go to the wall for Balanchine.

All told, they were an odd bunch of theater people who fell in love with George. They were in love with his dances, but they were also in love with his cause. He had a kind of inverse charisma, a quiet inner certainty that anchored them all in what was already the most exciting theatrical and emotional experience of their lives. He knew what to do. And what he was doing was larger than himself, larger than any of them.[31] They felt it, and he opened the doors to anyone with enough smarts and talent to get the job done. He didn't micromanage them; no one did. They just took control, pitched in, invented their jobs, and built up the company as they went. He would rein them in when needed—even Lincoln could be corralled. They were part of a new cosmology, with George in the God spot.

Chapter 16

DISCIPLINING THE BODY

It was a closed world. The first rule was secrecy. What went on behind company walls stayed behind company walls. The astonishing thing was just how quickly the walls grew up around them and how enduring and fortresslike they became. Without anyone quite knowing how it happened, George made them the wardens of their collective secrets. It was a way of circling them around and demarcating the boundaries of loyalty to one another and the dance. The second rule was devotion—to the work they were doing through him. Anything else was a distraction. The task they were facing was enormous, and he demanded their full attention. His job was to make them into dancers, which was not merely a matter of teaching them how to better perform balletic steps and poses. It was a matter of sculpting, with them, a whole person—mind, body, and soul—and it began with training and the ritual daily class. The idea was to make their ordinary "civilian bodies," as one dancer put it, into something extraordinary.[1]

In the early 1950s, George gathered a small group of dancers and returned to first principles. With them, he systematically reimagined the ballet lexicon. He did it without music—he wanted to get away from the trite tunes typical of ballet classes, which automatically sent the dancers into the static poses and saccharine prettiness he was trying to abolish. Instead, he talked—a lot. To illustrate a point, he told involved stories (as their muscles grew cold) about animals (spider monkeys, cats, cheetahs) and from literature (Ovid, Gogol, Ouspensky), used phrases from TV commercials (when they were lazy, he asked for the full "99 beans of coffee" or "More Park sausages, Mom!"), and loved to give them images of food (Can't you "be like" baked ham with marshmallows?; "Tanny, your legs look like asparagus—cooked asparagus!"). To correct a dancer's grand plié, he turned to Pat Wilde—"What's that vegetable that you grind up, and it is hot?" She told him. "Ah yes, you look like horseradish."[2]

He imitated their dull, effortful movement—"Do you speak that way?" he would say in a droning monotone. "Don't be zombies, wake up." He tried everything to make them understand: "When you speak, you accent certain syllables. A sentence will have different meanings, depending on where you place the accent. For example, *how* do you feel? How *do* you feel? How do *you* feel? How do you *feel*." Or when a dancer extended her leg, nonchalantly, high over her head, he said, "You must participate and present it like it's your leg, the rattlesnake's head is fifty feet away from his tail, but he knows that his tail is shaking."

"Doing" a step is performative: it reaches outward to the audience and says, Look at me, watch me, see what I can do. "Being" a step is a way of inhabiting it fully and pulling the audience into you. It is internal, a state of being almost like dancing alone—the audience is free to watch, if they like, but the dancer is in her self-made world, an enticing state all its own. It is a kind of interiority that can be achieved in many ways: through blank execution of the steps with no facial expression, or through an unleashing—the dancer as a wild animal tearing past himself through space. Or the dancer as a glorious cat: look if you like, I couldn't care less. "All of the rest of us, who thought we had to perform, and smile," a corps de ballet dancer later reflected, "we didn't understand that 'performing' was the opposite of what he wanted."[3]

He told stories and parables. One day he said he had a dream about eating a marvelous yogurt that was in front of him, but he could not eat it because he didn't have a spoon. So the next night, he fell asleep holding a spoon in his hand. Unfortunately, he never dreamed again about the yogurt![4] Or "Do you know what an artichoke looks like?" he said on another day. "In California they are not male or female. That is a dancer!"[5] His voice was calm, quiet, rarely angry, and full of rhythmic enthusiasms—"Pow! Bam! Move! More!"—and he kept time by tapping the beat with his foot, snapping his fingers, or thumping his body. Occasionally Kolya Kopeikine appeared, or George would sit at the piano himself and regale them with what he called "Roumanian tearoom music," or some funny and unexpected show tune to make them relax.[6]

One day they worked on pliés. Only pliés. For several hours they practiced at the barre this simple bend of the knees that begins every dancer's daily practice. They did them very fast and excruciatingly slow, with varying physical dynamics. He emphasized full-body breath and timing, and they practiced moving their arms to catch the exhale and sweep them into a movement. The next day, it was tendus. This simple extension of the foot and leg from fifth position was agonizingly difficult, and they did it in all directions, front, side, back, in multiple iterations (four, eight, sixteen, thirty-two, sixty-four repetitions) at impossible speeds and with tricky timing. How about sixty-four ronds de jambe in varying speeds and accents? Maybe sixteen cabrioles in arabesque to grand plié—an impossible feat. Or what about thirty-two entrechat—six to grand plié? It was relentless, and he could be mean. "You have done eight grand battements today," he told one dancer, "and six of them were bad." He then calculated how many, at that rate, would be wasted in a week, month, year. "That's a lot of wasted time!" he said, as he moved on. Another day he worked on arms, and the next morning he stood next to a dancer as she failed to do what he had taught the day before. "You know what it's like? Like Borzoi. You know what Borzoi is? It's a huge, beautiful Russian wolfhound. Teeny, weeny little brain. They are so stupid that they only let them out on the open plains. If they let them go near trees, they run into them."[7]

To increase turnout and precision, he placed a twenty-dollar bill between their thighs to make them squeeze their inner legs tightly together while moving the leg in and out of a perfect fifth position. If it fell to the floor, it was his; if their thighs held it, they got it. To build strength, he asked the women to wear old toe shoes with the inflexible shank or sole along the bottom of the foot still in place—not the more comfortable slippers typical of most ballet classes. This forced them to develop the muscles to roll up through their metatarsals onto their toes, rather than hop or spring up to pointe, as most teachers instructed. He wanted them to feel "at home" in this stiff apparel so that their feet would have the pliability of gloved hands, the suction of an elephant's trunk holding the floor. Dancers who perform on pointe inhabit two worlds: the flat-foot earth and the elevated airy atmosphere of on pointe. Usually these worlds are distinct—the dancer "hops" between them and is either up or down, heaven or earth. George was training them to "roll" seamlessly between them.

One day he excitedly told them that he had learned a new English word: "mobility." That's what he wanted from them, he said—to move: faster, farther, higher, and more precisely, with wider range, greater extension, more turnout of the hips and feet, and space-devouring energy. How far could the body be pushed and distorted without fully abandoning balletic form? He was tuning their bodies to the speed and transmission of the car, the train, the plane; shearing the traditional symmetries and alignments of classicism and the Vitruvian man into the curved, spherical, and off-balance space of Einstein and an imagined fourth dimension—which he talked about constantly. To get there required plunging into their own flesh, and there was something almost sexual about the deep access it took to turn the body out through the hips and legs, up through the shoulders and spine. Getting there meant seeing art and other kinds of dance—he sometimes sent them to take class, for example, at Katherine Dunham's school. Even for those with a natural facility, the work could be extreme and painful, violent almost in the torque and strain on joints and ligaments. There were days when they cried with hurt and frustration, and as George expanded this small group to the full company, many took to warming up thoroughly in advance of his classes to avoid sore or damaged muscles. Others didn't show up at all—their bodies couldn't take it.

After class, those who came often carried on the analysis over lunch or dinner, and George elaborated on the technical details he was after. He drew sketches, such as the one Tanny saved—in red—of bare feet in fifth position with the heels slightly raised and little arrows pointing to the exact spot where the dancer's weight should fall: on the balls of the feet, not sitting in the heels.[8]

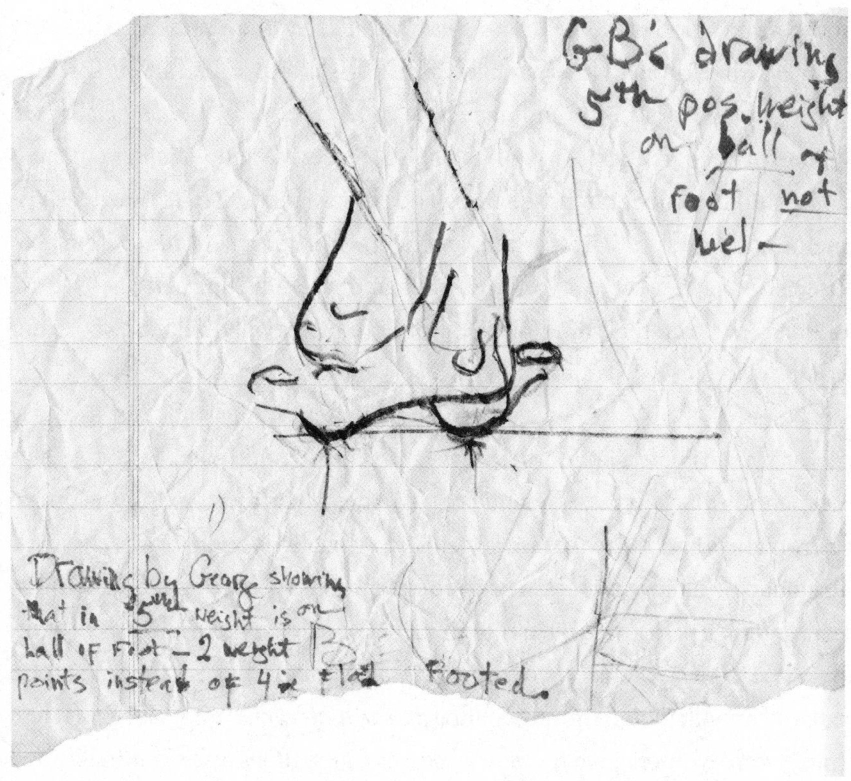

This was no minor technical point. Pushing the weight forward from the heels to the balls of the feet readies the body. It is a position of high alert, fight or flight, readiness to instantly pounce catlike in any direction. Most of us live in the past and the future—in memories of yesterday and plans for tomorrow—but the weight on the balls of the feet places the dancer in a physical and temporal now. She is not hanging back, nor is she is rushing forward; she exists in a hyperfocused present, with a touch of anticipation. "Ballet is not tomorrow or next week," he liked to say, "it is now."[9]

Their bodies were an object of concern. He wanted to reveal the beauty of the female form, and he paid close attention to the shape and contour of their figures. He was not against costume: he lovingly designed many lavish dresses and tutus with Karinska, but he wanted above all to show their bodies. Fat or too much flesh was an obstruction. It got in the way of *seeing*, he said, and he wanted his dancers to wear their muscles with only the thinnest coat of flesh. If they got too heavy, he would take them out of ballets until they slimmed down again—"too fat dear." To be clear, he tacked a blunt notice to the company board, written in his own hand: "BEFORE YOU GET YOUR PAY—YOU MUST WEIGH!" and signed it with a flourish: "*G. Balanchine*."[10] He later explained to a dancer who had gained excess weight: "You are in a cocoon, and the cocoon must go away and then we can *see* you down to ligaments and bones."[11] The dancers laughed off this stringent requisite with a childish song they set to a Viennese waltz and gleefully sang on tour: "We are on our new diets still / Swallowing pill after reducing pill / Balanchivadze envisions with glee / A ske-le-ton NYCB."[12]

None of this was new. Dancers' contracts typically included a clause about weight and keeping their instruments in sound repair. Aesthetically, women way back in the Romantic era of dancing fairies and sylphs had been known to live on rose water to lighten and purify their bodies to a pale spirit-like state. Ideas of excess flesh even echoed back to centuries of Christian ascetic practice performed by saintly women who starved themselves as virtuous penance to bring themselves closer to the angels and God. Or the pale tubercular beauty depicted in Botticelli's *The Birth of Venus*, for example. These transparent women were thought to possess miraculous inner spirituality and magical powers—their ethereal bodies touched by the divine.

This was not yet fully bound up in the medical pathology of anorexia nervosa, a condition with deep roots that would take its full-blown form and ravage young women, especially of the American upper middle classes, including dancers, in coming years. Balanchine never wanted his dancers rake thin, and his chosen ballerinas were often voluptuous and womanly, even in their most slender states. He would fire women who were too thin—the work was too demanding to accommodate the truly faint or "sk-el-at-al." But the controlling idea of "seeing" through flesh exerted a powerful and often destructive hold on their minds. It got inside them, like a vigilant eye tracking their shape and appetites. For many, Balanchine was an inner eye molding their bodies to an idealized image they desired but didn't necessarily possess or even fully understand. He objectified them, and they objectified themselves. This was not Narcissus drowning in his own image; it was more Pygmalion carving his beloved statue, which comes to warm life under his passionate lover's touch, blessed by the goddess Venus. The result was a kind of inner detachment, the body—their own bodies—as alabaster or marble.[13] "Sculptors use wood or marble and chisels. I use dancers and steps," he said. Except that he handed the mirror—and the chisels—to them.[14]

It was akin to Plato's counsel to lovers to never stop chipping away and honing the stone of the body to reveal its true beauty and form—"working on their statues," as the Neoplatonist philosopher Plotinus put it, to carve away excess flesh and to polish and make smooth their bodies until they had become "wholly [themselves], nothing but true light." It was a kind of mystical thinking, in which the fallenness of the body was seen as thickened with unrefined matter—Balanchine's "fat." The real body was the inner luminous body of pure light. Even light had a shape, and the goal of carving away or shedding the thickened exterior was to reveal this inner light-body. What was revealed was not, as Balanchine saw it, some abstract idea of pure soul, or even an idealized "perfect" form, but a clear and sharpened sensuality. This luminous body was a refined human instrument. It could see, smell, hear, touch, and taste more, and more acutely.[15]

Dancing pared the body, honed the musculature, subtly shifted bones. Training was transformation, and working with Balanchine involved a kind of metamorphosis entangled with pain, self-destruction, and shame, but also with desire and joy.[16] External form could even harmonize a fractured inner life, at least in the moment of dancing. It didn't erase a person's faults or dull her anxieties, but it did hold out the promise of a more ordered soul. At peak the dancer felt fluid and strong, integrated, coordinated, and above all clarified. Less mass and less food clogging the system (more blood to muscles) added to the feeling of the body as "true light" and a well-lubricated machine. Even the salty sweat purged through the ritual exercise of daily class felt like an unburdening, a purification that set a dancer apart from her unholy and civilian self. She was a different creature, part of a tribe, a chosen member of art.

In practice, it could be cultish, and the dangers were obvious. These were young women whose bodies were filling out, and "working on your statue" could be an assault on natural biological processes. Dieting, pills, weight loss, excess exercise, long exhausting hours, and too little sleep could become a rite of self-punishment or a pattern of privation that could lead to illness—but also to heightened or altered states, especially under the bright lights and adrenaline highs of performance. Add to this the erotically charged atmosphere of the theater with practically naked young bodies working long hours and living in close quarters—George could be found during breaks sitting in a dressing room with Tanny and Diana in their bras and panties, smoking cigarettes.[17] It was all ignition, part of the fuel that animated their bodies and lives.

George could be crude, or "raunchy," and his civility and chivalrous manners were matched by his almost Shakespearean delight in bawdy jokes and insinuations. When the dancers stood in class wearing minimal practice clothes with legs lifted high, crotches exposed, he might slyly say, "Very important ladies, this is your social position." At a rehearsal for *Orpheus*, he chose a princess from among the gathered dancers by asking, "Which of you is virgin?" and plucked the youngest from the group. He even goaded the "three Barbaras" in the corps de ballet to recite a dirty dressing-room limerick they had composed as entertainment at a fancy dinner for wealthy donors—a feat met with stony disapproval from the assembled patrons as George sat laughing like a schoolboy on the side (Lincoln, who worked hard to wring money from these stones, was not amused). He told jokes: "What's the difference between a circus performer and a ballet dancer? Circus performers have cunning stunts, and ballet dancers have stunning cunts." He told stories (delighting especially in the discomfort of rich patrons) about starving in Russia and "eating pussy" cats. They all amused themselves by making up limericks, and George kept a small notebook in which he composed his own naughty verses about the dancers. ("There was little man from the—West / Who offered his sex for a—test / He was Tudor's madam / But changed in to Adam / And now he's doing his—best" (Hugh Laing).[18] And there was plenty of locker-room talk with stagehands and other male dancers. It was not that he was sleeping around, necessarily. As one dancer put it, "Everything was sexual, very little was sex."[19]

At some point, he made a drawing titled "spaghetti," playing on his own possessiveness. A dancer who later sat gazing at this sketch, only commented smilingly, "So Balanchine," and it was.[20]

They did not complain, not then, not later. They weren't looking for consistency or high moral character. They didn't expect the man to live up to his

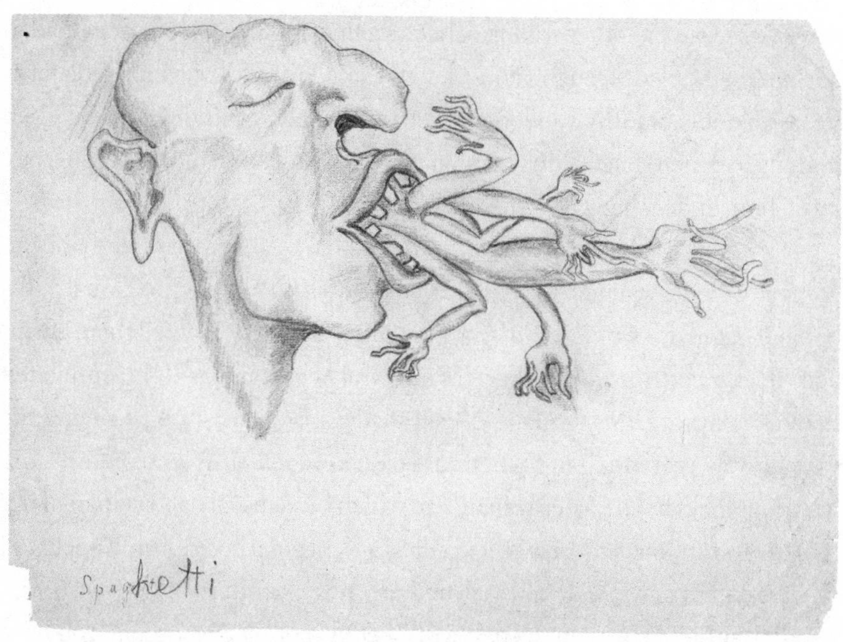

art; and they didn't ask him to be as beautiful, sad, joyous, erotic, or strange as his dances; didn't assume that because he dealt with matters of the soul, his own soul would be clear or settled. The question didn't arise in part because they—at least the ones who lasted—were ruthless too. Had to be. At some level, they accepted it all, which is perhaps why even those who were most hurt overwhelmingly defend him. Working with him and dancing his ballets was quite simply the most powerful experience of their lives. "I realized," one dancer later reflected, "that this was a man whose tools were human beings, and this was a man who did not want to compromise. All right: as human beings, perhaps he treated us badly at times. But he had to decide where his artistic integrity lay. . . . I think he had every right as an artist to walk away from a dancer when she was no longer the look he wanted; perhaps he had a right to destroy Marie-Jeanne; perhaps he had a right to destroy all of us when he felt he could no longer use us."[21] What many intuited too was the price he paid. His whole being and purpose was bound up with them and their bodies. He was at their mercy. If they changed their bodies, went off with boyfriends, couldn't get the steps, or refused to love him or "work on their statues," his ballets would not be seen or heard. It was true that they were dispensable—

there was always another willing dancer waiting in the wings—but she had to be trained, molded, brought along, known, and loved, all of which took time. It was a double bind. Without them, he was silenced. Without him, they had nothing to dance. They didn't complain because in the end it was simple: they loved him, and he had given them their lives.

How they looked in public mattered to him. As representatives of the company, they should dress well, he said—skirts and blouses, no casual pants or (later) jeans, for women. No beards for men, please, he wanted them clean-cut. Beards were for Muscovite peasants, and like Nicholas II, he prohibited hairy displays in his company of self-made aristocrats. Long hair for the women was preferred, and when Janet Reed rebelliously chopped off her luxurious locks before a performance in which her sensual hair was part of her role, he was furious.[22] Worse, when Allegra Kent got a nose job and appeared in class with a newly botched face and tiny nose, courtesy of her self-hating Jewish mother, he was enraged. It was a betrayal of the first order. "You have lost all character in your face," he said, and he punished her by immediately revoking her solo parts.[23]

Casting was his most powerful lever. They wanted to dance, and he held the keys to the kingdom. It is difficult to express the depth of their desire. Dancing his ballets *felt* wonderful. It was an overwhelming experience, everything at once—music, light, feeling, sensuality, intellect, order, and soul-giving release. When it all worked, it could be transcendent and sensual at the same time, sex without sex (one said), and an entry point into another "realer than real" world. They wanted to live there. But they were also young women, as Diana once explained, and most didn't care as much about dancing as he did. In Europe, Diana and Tanny were forever trying to slip out of class early to sit in cafés, eat good food, sightsee, and enjoy life.[24] He had to counter *that* too.

Casting kept them on edge, and he bestowed or withdrew coveted roles at a moment's notice with no explanation or a curt "too fat, dear." Losing a role was a serious matter: not dancing was a physical deprivation and a sign of his displeasure, but it was also a loss of face in the community. He could be cruel. To a dancer who tried and tried but couldn't get the timing he wanted, he finally just said, "Why don't you just stop? You will never do it right."[25] Still, they longed for his favor. They wanted to be chosen and everyone knew that in dancing at least there would be a next bride. They (and their mothers) anxiously watched and read the tea leaves of his emerging interests, while he remained deliberately aloof. Dancers were invited to join the company in mysterious and offhand ways, often through Betty or another emissary mentioning that "Mr. Balanchine" would like them to come on tour or that they had rehearsal later that day—leaving them scrambling to find out where and when they should appear. He rarely met with any of them privately—exchanges between them over roles, time off, or whatever was on their mind mostly happened in hallways and elevators; he hated confrontation, and this way he could naturally move away and end the encounter. He didn't even call the dancers by their names, which he knew very well. Instead, he lumped them into a single anonymous appellation—to him, they were all "dear." Along the way, he would ask a few he truly loved or desired to "please call me Georgi," but most wouldn't and instinctively distanced themselves from him too. They were "dear," and he was "Mr. B."

He was jealous. Jealous of their bodies but also of their boyfriends. Boyfriends were distracting and could become husbands. They threatened to rob him of his finest dancers, and it was true that a woman on whom he had lavished years of time and training could disappear in a moment to matrimony and motherhood. He made it known that he didn't want boyfriends around the theater, and the dancers kept their romantic lives secret or discreetly arranged to meet suitors at some distance from the stage door. One dancer who married received a gift from Mr. B. It was a case of red wine labeled *Nuit Saint George*, and the accompanying note said simply, "Remember me." Some, like Ruth Sobotka, didn't care. The daughter of prominent Viennese Jews, she possessed a confidence others lacked, and her boyfriend appeared nightly and stood silently in the wings in his tattered overcoat and frayed beard. The dancers called him "el Stinko," but really he was Stanley Kubrick, and Ruth married him—and left the company.[26]

Balanchine didn't want to lose his dancers, but he also, truly, didn't want them to lose themselves. He made his case: marry and you will become "Mrs. Him," he said, darning socks and doing dishes at home. Stay with me, and I will give to you your very best self in dancing—which was true. It was a feminist position, in its way. In the 1950s these young dancers had a level of professional independence and a possibility of self-fulfillment that the typical middle-class "home and hearth" suburban housewife could only imagine. He was training them, urging them, teaching them how to avoid living an average life in a pedestrian world. He wanted them for his other, more-real-than-real stage world. It was an alternative, a choice they would have to make. He later told one dancer who wanted to take a leave from the company the story about twelve women waiting for God to come; six brought oil for lamps, but the other six didn't have enough oil and left to get more—but they didn't make it back in time to go to heaven. "Ballet is artifice," he said to one of the many dancers he lost to another man; "marriage is reality."[27]

With the few who did marry and keep dancing, he fought to maintain his authority. When Pat Wilde got married in 1953, she did it quietly. The morning she took her vows, she appeared at the theater and asked the ballet mistress to break the news to Balanchine. He said something like "how nice" and immediately scheduled a rehearsal. He would need Pat that night—her wedding night—from 7 to 9 P.M. to work with him on a difficult dance. It was a showdown, and as she saw it, they fought it out over steps in the studio. She appeared at the appointed hour, and he gave her more and more difficult things to do, worked her to the bone, and kept her overtime until 10 P.M. Enraged and determined not to be outdone, she danced herself ragged, but even she knew the battle had already been won. Balanchine was the boss, and ballet came first. Even male dancers felt the pull. When Jacques d'Amboise married the dancer Carolyn George in 1956, Balanchine knew he would lose Carolyn (he did; she quit to have children), but this time his primary focus was on the immensely talented Jacques. The marriage took place between matinee and evening performances, and Balanchine made a point of casting them both in the evening show. A joke—and yet.[28]

Pregnancy was an obvious obstacle to dancing, and he hoped they wouldn't, but some did. ("All babies look like Eisenhower to me," he quipped, or "It's easier to make a baby than a loaf of French bread.")[29] Melissa Hayden had a son in 1954—and left the company temporarily to attend to this maternal event in her life. Babies were not welcome at the theater, and the few dancers who had them kept them quietly at home.[30] Because Balanchine was never in love with Milly and because he knew she was a theatrical animal and he would never lose her as a dancer, he took the inconvenience in stride. But he did love Diana Adams and he did love Allegra Kent, both of whom would disappear intermittently into unhappy marriages, pregnancies, and prolonged departures, triggering in George his own series of personal and artistic crises. Still, he didn't fire them and would keep Allegra in particular on full salary through long absences. With dancers he cared about, he had infinite patience, and he pushed, prodded, and maneuvered over years to draw them into his vision of their lives. None of this was blunt coercion. He was asking for something deeper, a willful relinquishing of will. In order to make them great dancers, he had to fully have them. It was a kind of possession, and only a few ever surrendered unconditionally.

Carolyn George explained it this way in her diary in 1946:

> Balanchine was our God. It's not so easy to explain. We didn't pray to him. We asked him for help with our dancing because he was all knowing, all seeing, you believed with all your heart that what he saw in your dancing was absolutely true, and right.... What a luxury—a God, a leader, you believe without doubt, and can follow in blind faith. You can accomplish 100% more because you don't have to question every move you make ... just follow.... This was America and his dream of America was BIG-BOLD-FREE and in some cases RAUNCHY.[31]

"It felt like a religion" was a common expression of what it was like to dance for Balanchine. Jacques d'Amboise and others had secretly nicknamed him "the breath," by which they meant God breathing "the essence of life into his dancers."[32] Others referred to him as the "great white father" because of the power he held over their lives.[33] Balanchine talked about them as angels because they were trained to be "clear and spotless mirrors" reflecting the divinity of dance; because they were messengers from God; because they were physical beings who were paradoxically all spirit, creatures who, "when they relate a tragic situation, do not themselves suffer."[34] These were not the haloed cherubs or virginal women of religious paintings. The point was not purity but detachment. They were complicated fallen people like any others—nomads, soldiers, exiles, plain corn-fed American girls—but in dancing they were striving for something more. None of this was some grandiose plan, his or theirs. To the contrary, the performance was won by myriad individual impulses and a collective spirit that seemed to emanate from Balanchine. They were an odd little society, a terpsichorean order built on discipline, hierarchy, and revelation—a counter-Enlightenment way of life. He taught us, they all said, how to live.

They didn't ask questions. That's not what they were trained to do. Their art was mute, but it was deeper than that. When Lincoln suggested sending a dancer to Auden to expand his literary education, George quipped, only half-joking, "If he learns to think, he won't be able to jump."[35] It was not that he didn't want them to learn; he encouraged many of them to read—Tolstoy, Gogol, Chekhov, Cervantes, Shakespeare, the Bible—and sent them to museums across Europe and in New York (Forget about my ballet, you are in Rome! What have you seen?).[36] But he was also ambivalent. Strictly speaking, they didn't need any of that to do his ballets, and he didn't want ideas, acting, or philosophizing on stage. "Don't think, just dance," a company mantra ascribed to George and repeated by generations of dancers, was less a prescription for rote obedience than an approach to art. It was part of the doctrine of now. Being fully present required emptying the mind of its own commentary. George said it many times in many ways: "Horses don't think, they just go." Or "Dancers like to do what they are doing. It is as much a part of life to them as breathing or eating. They can't be anything else. A potato cannot be a rose and a rose cannot be a potato."[37]

As for politics: leave it outside. In 1948, for instance, he asked the left-wing contingent among them to please leave their Henry Wallace buttons at the door. They just didn't understand the evils of Communism, he explained, and to illustrate the point he launched into an impromptu and comic pantomime backstage enacting his departure from Russia and playing all the parts: the fat apparatchik who stalled over their papers before letting them through the checkpoint, the posturing authorities, himself as a terrified young man. It was like watching a play by Kafka—or Gogol—one dancer recalled.[38]

Perfection was the enemy, its own kind of deadening inner commentary, and Balanchine kept them alive and in the moment by routinely throwing them into ballets they hardly knew at the last minute. There was no money or time to over-rehearse, but he was also deliberately playing for spontaneity. When they worried that they were ill-prepared or didn't know the steps or wouldn't do it right, he just said, "Don't worry dear, I am the only one who will know." Or (to the overly cautious Diana Adams): "Why are you so boring? I don't care what steps you do, just do something!"[39] When another dancer asked him how she should do a role, he quietly said, "Do it any way you want to; this is our theater, and we can do whatever we want." He tried to shave the edge off their anxiety: "If you don't know the right road, then you can take the detours."[40]

Fun was another way of disarming them. One night as the curtain went up, the dancers looked to the conductor and found George at the podium, baton raised, elaborately made up and costumed as Toscanini. Another night, he went into a role in a comic ballet on an impulse and played it like Groucho Marx, to the delight of the dancers stacked in the wings laughing. In Italy he got himself a Vespa and raced like a cowboy alongside the trains that carried them from city to capital city.[41]

Touring bound them closer: in 1952, 1953, 1955, and 1956 they were all together in Europe traveling from town to town for several months of the year. For many of them, it was their first trip to Europe, and "headquarters" had to manage them all. Betty could go for a long time, parsing problems and firing off letters and missives with a kind of war-weary wit. ("Do you think we could make it a misdemeanor for any dancer to speak to the press?" Or, to Lincoln: "George says this is a wonderful opportunity for the dancers and if they don't like it, they can go to hell. He himself is tired and underpaid and he wants to stay in Europe and be the director of La Scala. He says tell AGMA [the union] and Baum that.") But she could drink too much, and at her mind's limit, she would shut down and lock herself in a room or train compartment for hours, even days, before emerging to pick up once again where she left off.[42]

Keeping the dancers focused was essential: Balanchine still needed them in peak condition, and the hours were long and exhausting. They were dancing on heavily raked stages, which required a complete physical reorientation, and Balanchine could be nervous and demanding. The conditions in these immediate postwar years were difficult. In Franco's Barcelona, they faced freezing dressing rooms, no running water, and military guards, and the dancers had food poisoning and fleabites from their cheap hotels. In Berlin, still a bomb site, there was no hot water until 5 P.M.; in London they were given ration books to pay for food.

Wherever they were, the studio was the studio—four walls that blocked out everything else. It was work—even a coffee cup placed on the piano was quietly removed by Balanchine; it didn't belong there. In rehearsals, his mind was tightly focused on the dancers, but also on the music. As preparation, sometimes years in advance, he studied the music and liked to make his own piano transcriptions, meticulously copied out by hand from whatever orchestral score Barbara or Betty managed to locate. By the time he arrived at rehearsal, he knew the music by sight as much as by sound: "I don't *listen* to the score," he later said, "I *read* it," and he knew the score as a conductor does.[43] The score sat like a diagram in his mind's eye, and as he worked with the dancers, he consulted closely with the pianist—often Kolya in those days—to clarify a phrase or a musical problem.

The point was not to mimic or paint the music with movement but to range through it, matching, contradicting, displacing, anticipating musical motifs and themes in unexpected ways. He was building a counterscore, intricately bound to the original. As Hugo Fiorato put it: "He had the faculty of not just interpreting the music or putting steps on top of the score. He added another dimension. It's as though he added contrapuntal rhythms, phrasing, lines, that made the score more attractive, interesting, and exciting, and clarified the intent of the composer." The dance "went with the music but was another part that became integral to that score."[44] Musicologists now better understand the sophistication of this achievement, and we have learned how Balanchine employed techniques ranging from simply starting a dance phrase before a musical phrase to mapping pitch to the spatial height of steps and using pre-imitations and metrical displacements—the dance comes in advance of the sound; rhythms are seen before they are heard.[45] Adding to this understanding, neurologists are discovering through the study of mirror neurons and kinesthetics, for example, what audiences know from experience: that when we *see* a dance, we mimic its movement and sound in our own bodies. We *feel* it, and in some sense *do* it, even if we haven't lifted a finger. By making intricate links between what we see and what we hear, Balanchine made us feel it more and more acutely.[46] His dances brought a sensory and intellectual expansion, without revealing the source of the effect.

Music was perhaps Balanchine's greatest secret. He told the dancers nothing, did that part without them, and didn't show them or teach them or make music a serious part of their education. "See?" he once said to Jacques in the wings. "The rhythms of the steps for the corps de ballet—syncopated—and the patterns they move in, are playing with the harmonies in the music. It is so interesting." But Jacques just "nodded, smiled, and acted as if I knew what he was talking about."[47] Why did Balanchine keep all of this to himself, and why did he keep them in the dark? One reason, as every dancer knows, was that they had their own ways of counting, which made sense of Balanchine's dance score, even if their "dancer counts" ran counter to the musical counts. So really, they knew exactly what they needed to know. Besides, for most dancers, music is sensual and instinctive: not words or plans or analysis but the touch of bodies, the smell of sweat and perfume, the immediate physical problem of working out steps and timing. Analysis is like words—it can get in the way of spontaneity and *just dancing*. The experience of physically interlocking with or lacing through music in ways that invigorate and quicken the body and spirit makes a dancer *feel* more alive.

A deeper reason for his secrecy had to do with code. Balanchine held the code to his dances. He was the only one who held all the parts in his mind, and what seemed to "pour out of him" was in fact a complicated mental and physical assemblage of moving parts: people, personalities, heights, shapes, steps, sounds, and musical structures, not to mention costumes, lights, and set designs—all of which he ultimately controlled. "Sometimes it seemed as if the company were flowing out of his veins," one dancer noted.[48] None of it was "creative," he insisted. "God creates, I assemble." There was a lot to assemble. To the dancers it seemed like magic, or a gift; he did not burden them with his labor.

All of this meant that when the curtain went up on a Balanchine ballet, audiences did not "see a ballet"; they witnessed a group of dancers making their way through a living, shifting labyrinth of split-second choices, calculations, mistakes, regrets, adjustments, and consequences. It was alive and unpredictable, bound to music, but also free within it. Class and rehearsal were for learning the steps and knowing the limits, but in performance it was up to the dancer to take on the complexities of the music and dance. Some dancers made more interesting guides than others, which is why *who* was dancing mattered terribly—to us and to Balanchine. He made ballets for dancers to live in, and when everything worked, they ran free.

Free, especially, from him. Whatever stains his faults left on their lives, whatever his efforts to carve their bodies, on stage no one could touch them, and that was part of his point. The power of their liberation—and of him watching them free themselves from him with the tools he had given them—was part of the drama of his dances. Another part was cohesion. Every dancer is an island, a single isolated individual in an interlocking whole—remember, while she dances, she cannot *see* herself or the ballet she is in and must trust the pattern and her small part in it. Balanchine's ballets brought them all together in a synchronous musical world, a community governed by the strictures and freedoms of his art. How could real life ever compete?

"Ballet is woman." He said it over and over again, but what did it mean? It was the crux of his whole being, the great theme of his life, sunk into his soul with the distance of time and exile. *His* freedom was not what Americans seemed to take it to be. It had less to do with free will or economic gain or some woebegone idea of happiness than with the pursuit of an existence beyond earthly three-dimensional space. George believed in the Beautiful Lady and Divine Sophia of Blok and Soloviev; in Goethe's eternal feminine; in eternal Russia and in women (as the Russian philosopher Berdyaev put it) as "a craving for the beauty of a transfigured cosmos." The emotional vulnerability of individual women—Heidi, Holly, now Maria, soon to be Tanny, Diana, Allegra, and Suzanne, not to mention any number of other minor interests—didn't figure in his calculus. It has been said that the true monk takes nothing with him but his lyre, and this true artist could be cold, cold.[49]

The company, a seemingly contradictory mix of external hierarchy and internal anarchy—"Do what you do"—was their little chaotic collectivity.[50] Like all utopias, it was riven with pettiness, but it also had a strong communal sense and almost sacred ethic of work. With him, they were larger than themselves. They all believed in love more than virtue, and as Balanchine later put it, they were "a bit more than the third dimension—little above; we have something, we are talking about certain ideas that are more interesting than what to eat or how to travel, you see, a little bit higher than other people, you see . . . because our life is different and we are different animals you see."[51]

Should we say that they were less servants of God than vassals of his art? Should we say that the higher purpose they all spoke of was just a grandiose ego masquerading as art? We could, but they might respond—and do—that they weren't serving him, and he wasn't serving himself. He barely existed. It was Quixote, Faust, E.T.A. Hoffmann, Nietzsche, Christ, the book of Revelation. Music can be that too—its own world accountable to no one and nothing but itself.

Chapter 17

TANNY AND JERRY

Balanchine was dead set against it. *Firebird* had been Diaghilev's first "Russian" ballet in Paris in 1910, and as far as he was concerned, he and Lincoln hadn't gone through all they had in order to restage old Russian dances. But Morton Baum was pushing—hard.[1] Money was shorter than ever, and Russian ballets had a box-office appeal that George's new works could not match. The impresario Sol Hurok, a Ukrainian émigré George knew, owned old sets and costumes designed by Marc Chagall for a 1945 Ballet Theatre production and was offering them for a good price.[2] Hurok, knowing he would have to convince George, approached him one evening at the Russian Tea Room while he was dining with Maria and suggested, in his Yiddish-inflected Russian, that George choreograph a new version of *Firebird* for his Indian wife.[3] George, ever practical, finally said yes. Lincoln later said that George did the whole thing "with his tongue in his cheek, because everyone says we are so high brow. . . . We don't care about the PEUPLE. Alright, Buster, we give em *Fireboid*."[4]

Balanchine said quite frankly that it was an impossible ballet: "You can never make it convincing that the ballerina really is fire—she's just a dancer in a red tutu. The story is too complicated. . . . It's about eggs, pike, ducks, apples, and Katchei lives thousands of years, you can't make a ballet out of it." But he did, and he rallied his burgeoning company around its ur-Russian exoticism, chiding them, "Your mother Russian, your father Polish and still you don't understand—go to Met and see Russian icons!"[5] No one, however, was more exotically Russian-looking than Tallchief, and when *Firebird* premiered at City Center on November 27, 1949, with Barzin at the podium, and dramatic lighting by Jean Rosenthal, it was met with a "touchdown roar" (*Time* magazine) from audiences, who chanted: "Tall-chief! Tall-chief!"[6]

Balanchine remained ambivalent, especially about Chagall's spectacular sets, which threatened to upstage both Maria and the choreography, even if they were hopelessly old and musty—"rags," as he put it, pulled from years of deep storage. He didn't bother to contact Chagall, who was living in Paris, nor did he answer the artist's later admiring and finally annoyed letters regretting that they had not been able to work together on the production. Instead, Balanchine dimmed the lights on the decaying backdrop and threw Maria and her partner Francisco Moncion into a bright spot. When the company performed the ballet in Paris in 1952, he still didn't contact Chagall, who finally published an angry letter denouncing the broken-down state of his decor. Balanchine was furious at this intrusion and appeared backstage with scissors and began cutting through the moldy sets and costumes, infested with insects nesting in the cracked paint.[7]

Still, success was success, and they needed it. Just weeks before, London's Sadler's Wells Theatre Ballet, soon to be dubbed Britain's Royal Ballet, had presented *The Sleeping Beauty* featuring Margot Fonteyn at the Met to wild public acclaim—and far-reaching postwar symbolism. On the opening night, after some twenty curtain calls, an emotional Ninette de Valois, the company's director, told the cheering audience, "As long as there's an America, there'll always be an England." Thanks to Lincoln, the NYCB reciprocated the following year, affirming this Anglo-American cultural alliance with a tour to Britain, featuring—*Firebird*.

The company traveled on chartered transport planes, and the dancers found London cold and dank, with burned-out buildings and piled ruins from the Blitz. They fanned out across the depleted landscape in search of cheap hotels, often with no heat, and there were food shortages and ration tickets.

They were lucky to dine on horsemeat. Maria sprained her instep, and George quickly amended her roles to accommodate her injury. The company was popular with audiences, but the critics were savage and accused Balanchine of being cold, impersonal, and overly analytic—they didn't even like *Firebird*. Lincoln, already exhausted and operating at a high pitch, broke under the strain and had a nervous breakdown. "I was frightfully violent," he recounted to Mina, "and have become a sort of horror story here." Fortunately, he added, "Balanchine is a rock." A rock, but by the end of the tour, he had reached the end with Maria, Lincoln reported, "whether she realizes it or not."[8]

Their divorce—just four years after their wedding—was as matter-of-fact as their marriage. Maria fell in love with a pilot and tried to rouse George's jealousy, but he stoically waited for her to leave and avoided any confrontation. When she moved out and went to live with another dancer, George helped to redesign her new cramped fourth-floor walk-up apartment. He looked at this new stage set for her life and said that they needed mirrors to make the place appear more spacious, so he bought mirrors and hammered them onto the surfaces everywhere—even the kitchen cabinets. Several months later he and Maria signed a formal annulment, a commonplace provision preserving Maria's Catholic status as an unmarried woman.[9] Their marriage was erased, as if it had never happened. She said it was because she wanted to have children, but the real reason was that he was losing interest in her dancing—and falling in love with her close friend Tanaquil Le Clercq.

He had already cast Tanny in 1946 as the polio-stricken girl in *Resurgence* and as the fiery, unpredictable Choleric in *The Four Temperaments*. She was a seductive Ariadne in a bacchic love affair in *Ariadne and Bacchus* and the leader of the wild, sexualized Bacchants in *Orpheus*, and it was Tanny that George cast in the emotionally vulnerable adagio in *Symphony in C*. He even saw her barefoot with hair flowing in *Élégie*, a knotted and voluptuous pas de deux with her close friend Pat McBride in which they "just sort of twinned around," Tanny recalled; "they said it was a lesbian thing, two wild girls, upside down, leg in the crotch, very pretty.... But nobody liked it except maybe Mr. B."[10] Now, at twenty-one, she was a serene and spirited beauty with a fragile but fascinating technique, not strong, a bit wild, and interesting. Her relationship with "Mr. B" was moving fast but it was rarely entirely her own: the age gap was twenty-six years, and her mother, Edith, still accompanied her daughter everywhere. George found himself in an all too familiar ménage à trois.

He did what he had always done. He dressed her: clothing, costumes, perfume, jewels.[11] Her breathtaking appearance made her a natural in the fashion world, and Richard Avedon, Cecil Beaton, Irving Penn, and George Platt Lynes all photographed her for spreads in glossy magazines.[12] *Vogue* was run by the Russian émigré Alex Lieberman and his wife, Tatiana Yakovleva (Mayakovsky's last love—the "cloud in trousers" was never far behind), and Lieberman published a series of artistic portraits by Irving Penn (himself from an émigré Russian-Jewish family), including one of Tanny that captured her youthful eroticism, slouched and thin in a flung-back tutu, legs carelessly thrown open as if she were in a Balthus painting; or Balanchine, Corrado Cagli, and Vittorio Rieti (the Ariadne team) lounging fully suited on the floor, coats flung carelessly to the side and staring vacantly into space, with Tanny as Ariadne standing over them like an antique statue, half-nude in Grecian drapery. Penn became a friend and wrote notes to "my favorite dancer and ice-cream soda queen."[13] For George, Tanny was a kind of nymphet too, childlike in her freedoms but also a powerful womanly presence. As their romance developed, he wrote loving notes to his "boopsy woopsy," his "baby pussy," and his "darling baby love" and signed off with quick sketches of himself as MM (mousi-mouse) and drew her as a large and imposing PC (pussy cat), or he called her "My darling Pipistrella" (a bat-like figure) and signed off "I love you your topolino" ("little mouse" and also the Italian name for Micky Mouse).[14]

Tanny was herself an accomplished photographer, and her candid shots of George show him in jeans and a T-shirt, looking relaxed, with a rugged Brando sexiness that no other woman brought out in him; or joking around at Natasha Molostwoff's home on Fire Island childishly pretending to pee from a fountain.[15] In Florida on vacation, they jokingly staged shots of George pretentiously smoking and slumped in pseudo-thought "pretending to be E. Hemingway waiting for an idea," or in a drunken stupor, cradling a bottle of liquor—everything *he* didn't need to make dances. He and Tanny were both politically conservative, and Tanny fit in easily with George's virulent anti-Communism and Eisenhower Republicanism.[16]

Above all, they both loved words, puns, crossword puzzles, and acrostics, and George played with her name, "Le Clercq"—"Le Cleric," and eventually presented her with an erotic limerick that spelled LECLERCQ vertically in red ink. She kept the poem, labeling it simply, "GB's poem to me."

Luscious falsies
Evil thighs
Casting couchie
Lovely eyes
Elongation
Rape at glance
Combination:
Queen of Dance.[17]

What kind of love was this, really? It wasn't formal—they could lounge on the bed watching TV together, and they were both unpretentious and plainspoken—but it wasn't easy or familiar, either. It wasn't too aloof, like being with Prince Myshkin (as Tallchief had put it)—Tanny was up to it—up to the dancing and up to him. She had the background and above all the natural confidence of her own quick and spiky intellect. They got along because neither was bored and because there was some large part of her that didn't want to be close or share confidences or affection—which he never would or did. But it was still true that everything between them, the cooking and antics and gossip and gardening and carpentry, was all ultimately tied to caring and dancing, which was the core intimacy between them. The poem said it all: not a lover or a wife, but *Queen of Dance*. It was all in the dance, and as long as that was good, they were good. And yet, call it her American side, which could lay her heart flat on the page in some wickedly honest revelation, Tanny—that easy-gaited, all-in girl—really loved in her deepest self only one man and it was not George, but Jerry—Jerome Robbins, the dancer and choreographer George had recently appointed as dancer and associate artistic director of the NYCB.

Robbins was in love with her too—had been, he admitted, ever since he had seen her in the opening-night performance of *Symphony in C* in 1948.

The sight of her falling into the arms of her partner in Bizet moved him to tears and he never looked back, even though their relationship would be intermittent and rocky: Tanny's picture still sat on his bedside table when he died. After seeing her dance that night, he immediately wrote to Balanchine offering his services to him and the company—or was it to her, or did he even know? He was overwhelmed because in a single breath he had encountered the woman of his life and the choreographer he would revere. He would do anything he said: dance, make dances, help out, whatever was needed. George called him at once and said, "Come on."[18]

Robbins was the only living choreographer that Balanchine truly admired, with the exception of Frederick Ashton, and with only a brief interlude, Jerry would spend the rest of his life at the NYCB. For the moment, Tanny occupied a coveted if impossible place between them. Coveted because they both loved her and made dances for her to show it and because the choice between them was hers. Impossible because although she would marry George, the greatest love of her life would always be Jerry, a stubborn fact that would have consequences for them all.

It was not the first time George and Jerry had met. Jerry was fifteen years younger and had already danced for George on Broadway and at Ballet Theatre. Marked as one of the brightest choreographers of his generation, he had an impressive roster of original ballets and hit shows to his credit, including the ballet *Fancy Free*, which soon became the musical *On the Town* (1944), about three sailors on leave for twenty-four hours in New York, a collaboration with the equally young Leonard Bernstein. Jerry's work was youthful, jazzy, and colloquial—"ballet in dungarees," he called it—and he had no shortage of lucrative commercial offers.[19] But when he fell in love with Tanny that night, he also fell in love with George, who would become—his words—his God, his Christ, his father, mentor, and boss. Which did not mean that he was a disciple or imitator. To the contrary, George chose him in part because he was so different. Bringing Jerry on board, as Lincoln put it, was "a smart move," a way of de-Russianizing the company and giving it a strong American stamp.

But not too American. Robbins was born Jerome Wilson (after the president) Rabinowitz in New York City in 1918 to a family of Russian Jews. His roots lay in the "other" Russia—not George's imperial homeland, but the Pale of Settlement. It was a classic immigrant story. His father, Herschel (Harry) Rabinowitz, had left his native shtetl of Rozhanka, not far from Pinsk, as a teenager around 1905, to escape conscription in the Russian army—certain death for a poor Jew. Jerry's mother was Lena Ripps, daughter of a garment cutter from Minsk who settled in New Jersey. Harry and Lena had a kosher deli on East Ninety-seventh Street, but when Harry got a job managing the Comfort Corset company, they moved their young family and settled in Weehawken, New Jersey. Lena and Harry were both active in the Jewish community, and as a child Jerry studied the Torah and performed his bar mitzvah—although he later recalled his humiliation at being taunted by neighborhood boys and his burning desire to say "'That's it' to the whole business" of being Jewish.[20]

He studied music too and was something of a child prodigy, but it was dance that captured his imagination. In 1936, against his father's wishes, he politely turned down a place in the corset factory and moved to New York to dance. He took classes in everything: "art dance" à la Martha Graham and Mary Wigman, flamenco, oriental dance, acting, composition (at the politically radical New Dance Group). He studied ballet with Ella Daganova, a Russified American who had danced with Anna Pavlova, and swept her floors to pay for his lessons. Most important of all, however, was Gluck Sandor (also known as Senia Gluck-Sandor or Sammy Gluck), of Jewish, Polish, and Hungarian descent—who had worked with Fokine and performed on the vaudeville circuit and in Germany with Wigman. Sandor had a small studio and theater where he presented Russian ballets and his own "modern" dances on serious themes. He made a ballet about the Spanish Civil War, for example, and a dance about race to poems by Langston Hughes.[21]

Robbins was voracious and also performed in *The Brothers Ashkenazi*, adapted from the I. J. Singer novel at the Yiddish Art Theatre, choreographed by Sandor (Robbins sang "The Internationale" in a revolutionary crowd), and in the late 1930s he spent summers on staff at Camp Tamiment, another left-leaning and largely Jewish group, where he worked with Danny Kaye on a Yiddish version of Gilbert and Sullivan's *The Mikado* (they called it the *Richtige Mikado*). Back in New York, he danced on Broadway alongside Jimmy

Durante, Ray Bolger, Jackie Gleason—and George Balanchine. In 1939, with minimal ballet training but lots of theatrical experience, Robbins joined Lucia Chase's new Ballet Theatre, where he worked with Massine, Fokine, and above all the English choreographer Antony Tudor.

Robbins's early ballets were often dark, almost Tudor-like, in tone. Tudor was a major figure on the scene, invited by Lucia Chase in 1939 to represent "English Ballet" at Ballet Theatre. His dances were "Freudian" (critics said) psychological studies of repressed emotion. *Lilac Garden* (1936, with a 1940 American premiere) was a story of suppressed sexuality at an Edwardian garden party; *Undertow* (1945) took on sexual abuse, rape, and murder. None of this was melodramatic; Tudor wanted his dancers to perform his roiling dances "in cold blood," and their emotional power depended on the dancers' physical restraint. He drilled them, including Robbins, in Stanislavsky-like mental tasks and was known for "breaking" dancers with cutting personal attacks that pulled them into spirals of self-hatred until they felt empty and lost. He then set to work rebuilding the person—up from the ashes. Robbins took it all in, and in 1946 for Ballet Theatre he made *Facsimile* to music by Bernstein (again) with two of Tudor's most loyal dancers: Hugh Laing, who was Tudor's lover, and Nora Kaye. Kaye, née Koreff, was another child of Russian Jews, and a self-styled antiballerina—earthy and dramatic, with a knotted body and cropped hair. *Facsimile* had a rough, rebellious edge: "Scene: a lonely place." Action: kissing, seduction, rejection, a tangle of bodies pressing toward violence when Kaye shouts "STOP!" and they all abruptly leave the stage.

Robbins was also involved with the Stanislavsky-inspired Actors Studio, founded by Elia Kazan and Cheryl Crawford in 1947, where he worked with Marlon Brando and Montgomery Clift (his lover for a time). Robbins incorporated into his dancing the Actors Studio's focus on "inner action" and often did voluminous research. His instincts were theatrical and ethnographic, and he kept thick files of photos cut from newspapers. His annotations show him poring over the details of a striking face or gesture and analyzing movements drawn from sports, war, religion, and events around the world. His ballets *did* have stories, and he often asked his dancers to invent elaborate backstories to match. No one—even George—had a keener dramatic eye.

All of this was the opposite of Balanchine's approach, and in the studio,

Jerry was George's opposite too. He was not nice or even civil, and the work could be agonizing. Steps and phrases did not pour out of him "like water," as they seemed to from George, and the dancers knew they could be stuck in Jerry's mud for hours as he painfully eked out steps and his temper broke.[22] Anxious and moody, he often succumbed to the "black pall,"[23] as one dancer put it, and could without warning turn viciously on his dancers—who referred to him then as "the black Jerome." Like Tudor, Robbins traded openly in humiliation and fear, picking fights, hissing obscenities, and scapegoating.[24] He was using his dancers to break through his own mental blocks, assuaging his insecurities by preying on theirs, but he was also preparing them for a role. ("Do you hate me?" he once shouted at a dancer he had tormented. When the dancer meekly demurred, Robbins shot back: "Before you go onstage tonight, I want you to think of something to hate.")[25] He was known for pitting dancers sadistically against each other—switching them in and out of a role (who would he choose?) until they were emotionally wracked and drained of confidence.

Dancing his ballets was like performing a strictly regulated ritual and required an orthodox attention to detail—no step out of place. He often made multiple versions of a dance, each with hair-split variations in the steps, and the dancers dutifully memorized version A, B, C, D, et cetera. Robbins would rush on stage just before the curtain and shout, "Version B, change to version B!"—sending his dancers through a mind-spinning physical recalibration and setting their nerves on edge. He knew every move of his dances and patrolled them mercilessly. Afterward, any poor soul who deviated or made the tiniest mistake could expect to suffer Robbins's wrath. His dancers often hated him, truly hated him, but most of them also stuck it out or came back for more. For all the misery, Robbins pulled from people intense acting—and some of the best dancing on the American stage.

Driving it all was Jerry's embattled inner life. He was a Jew who didn't want to be a Jew, a homosexual who didn't want to be a homosexual and who also genuinely at moments loved women—Tanny—and a man who never found a way to feel at home in his own skin. His Jewishness lay at the heart of his anguish, and he was alternately repulsed and entranced by his family heritage: "I didn't like my father," he later reflected; "I didn't like his accent. . . . I didn't like that he seemed drenched in some murky, foul, unclean, unkempt, mysterious filth and dirt, which the whole of Judaism, as it was practiced, seemed to be. . . . It revolted me. And I laid my knife against it." And yet, recalling the experience of visiting Rozhanka as a child with his parents, he could wax rhapsodic: "They told me I spoke Yiddish there & that I played with the children of the *shtetl* all day long in the fields, in the yards. . . . I do not remember one unhappy moment there."[26] Tanny photographed Jerry through cracked glass or in a split mirror image, and she was right. He was a fractured soul, a man divided against himself.

His homosexuality haunted him. He was a romantic and fell passionately and hard—for men and for women, but it was men who occupied his deepest erotic fantasies. He had been born at the wrong time, long before homosexuality was open or legal. "Please save me from being 'gay' and dirty," he wrote helplessly in his diary in 1942, and he spent years in psychotherapy trying to expunge his illicit desires, knowing all along that he couldn't and wouldn't.[27] To make matters worse, he was knotted up inside with an intense ambition and overweening desire for social acceptance, compounded by fear. Fear, not unfounded, that in the America he was born into, who he was—Jewish and gay—would halt his rise to success and fame. In 1944, when his breakthrough came with *Fancy Free* and *On the Town,* he (and his parents) officially dispensed with Rabinowitz and changed the family name to something more suitable: Robbins.[28]

Ballet—and Balanchine—were both a problem and a solution. For himself, Robbins later reflected, ballet was Catholic, a way of "civilizationizing . . . my Jewishness. I affect a discipline over my body & take on another language . . . the language of court & christianity—church and state—a completely artificial convention of movement—one that deforms & reforms the body & imposes a set of artificial conventions of beauty."[29] But Balanchine's more abstracted, nonnarrative ballets were also a relief. They seemed to offer a kind of absolution, an escape from Jerry's own troubled identity and the gritty life stories that were the blood of his own dances. He had, in his way, a religious mind, and Balanchine's mysticism and spirituality both drew him and threw him back on his more Old Testament instincts. He yearned to be a part of Balanchine's world, but he also mightily resisted it.

George had inner conflicts about Jerry too, but they didn't gnaw at him. By inviting Jerry into the NYCB, he was inviting into his new home an entire wing of American theater and dance that he did not himself represent. He did it for one reason: it was good for the company. Not to mention that he and Lincoln were still vying with Ballet Theatre (George wrote to Tanny from Florence, "My presence here is very important now, as I using lots of poison against Lucia Chase"),[30] and soon after Robbins arrived, George and Lincoln also invited Tudor to "defect," which he did, bringing with him his closest dancers and relations: Hugh Laing, Diana Adams, and Nora Kaye.[31] It was a coup against Ballet Theatre, but for George it was primarily a way of getting Diana, to whom he was instantly drawn. Tudor wouldn't last. George didn't much like his psychological dances, and the choreographer would soon return to Ballet Theatre and eventually retreat into Buddhist isolation. Kaye, a dramatic dancer who interested him less (and Jerry more), would go her own way too. Diana stayed and was soon Tanny's best friend—and an object of Balanchine's desire.

These were the inclusive years when Lincoln was working to bring in a multiplicity of choreographic talent. Dances by Frederick Ashton, Merce Cunningham, and John Cranko were briefly added to the repertorial mix from the late 1940s into the early 1950s. (Lincoln also approached Agnes de Mille, but then backed out—and George drew the line at Ruth Page, who was just too awful, he said.)[32] Lincoln was pushing to establish the company on the widest possible basis, co-opting their rivals and playing Diaghilev again, but George didn't really like having any of them around; he preferred to give his own dancers a chance, including Todd Bolender, Lew Christensen, William Dollar, and Ruthanna Boris. Meanwhile, he obstructed Ashton (who, according to Lincoln, was already "in a blue funk having to work so close to Balanchine" and "frightened at how well our kids dance") by abruptly pulling dancers from Ashton's rehearsals, until Ashton finally scolded him for his shameful manners—"if you were a guest in my home"; Balanchine blanched and gave him what he needed, but by the late 1950s, Ashton and most other serious interlopers were gone.[33] Jerry was the only one who stayed—and stayed independent. "Please be friendly to Jerry," George cautioned Betty Cage, "he is still only one good choreographer."[34] Lincoln, who ran hot and cold on

Jerry, just said, "Jerry is a complex combination of vanity, guilt, fright, inadequacy, talent, viciousness, sweetness, ambition, greed and gifts—like most of us, only he has more gifts."[35]

George and Jerry's relationship worked because Jerry was both good and in awe of George from the start. He knew—they both knew—that Balanchine was in his own league. And when Jerry strayed to Broadway or threatened to surpass George in popular or critical success, which he would at times, George would take it and even cheer Jerry on. Good for the company. But he could be petty too, and what he took to be Jerry's defects frankly suited him. He made it clear to the dancers that *George Balanchine* didn't need all that rehearsal time, or all that abuse, to make a great dance, and everyone knew that "Mr. B" routinely surrendered prime rehearsal space, time, and dancers to the lesser and more anguished Robbins. Not least, "Jerry the fairy," as George disparagingly called him behind his back, was no competition with the women George loved.[36]

Except Tanny. At first, George seemed to encourage Jerry and Tanny's flirtations. He cast them together. It was Jerry and Tanny in the comic *Bourrée Fantasque*. It was Jerry and George and Tanny making *Jones Beach*, a silly dance paid for by the Jantzen bathing-suit company, with a limp, bikini-clad Tanny undergoing mouth-to-mouth resuscitation and "the kids," as Lincoln put it, looking "attractively naked."[37] It was Tanny in the lead of Jerry's *The Age of Anxiety*, with a score by Bernstein to a poem by Auden. And it was often Tanny, Jerry, and George at dinner with friends or playing charades into the night. Jerry sent Tanny notes with flowers before a show, "Dearest Pussy, nothing to say but know you will be just wonderful. Love and thanks, Jerry" or "Just take your body with you. Love and good luck. Jerry."[38] But when Jerry wanted Tanny for the lead role in *The Cage* (1951), a new ballet he was working on to music by Stravinsky, George said flatly no: Tanny was busy working with *him* on a new dance and was unavailable. They had hit a wall.

Jerry retreated and cast Nora Kaye in the role instead.[39] But *The Cage* was also a problem because it was an unexpected smash hit, "the greatest numero we ever numeroed," as Lincoln put it.[40] The subject was unlikely: it was a fifteen-minute dance about a "race or cult" (as the program put it) of female insects who savagely seduce, kill, and feed on the corpses of male "intruders" with explicit thigh-rubbing satisfaction. When the company went on tour, the Dutch government banned *The Cage*—too violent and taken to be pornographic, which naturally increased ticket sales and Robbins's fame. George just sniffed and noted that it was derivative of the Bacchants in *Orpheus*, which was true, but he let it go—good for the company. Still, at least one dancer noticed that George deliberately turned his back on anyone who raised the subject of *The Cage* and put it down if he had a chance.[41] He was jealous but also annoyed that the public would flock to dances that he didn't particularly admire.

The dance *he* was making for Tanny was entirely different. *La Valse*, to music by Ravel, comprised two pieces: *Valses Nobles et Sentimentales*, composed in 1911, and *La Valse*, which had originally been commissioned by Diaghilev in 1920 at a difficult moment in Ravel's life. Distraught by World War I and weakened from dysentery acquired during his military service, he was also suffering from the loss of his mother. The score, with its disturbing moodiness and undercurrents of violence, evoked the decadence of the collapsing Austro-Hungarian Empire. Ravel called it "a fatefully inescapable whirlpool" and wrote darkly in notes to himself, "We are dancing on the edge of a volcano."[42]

Tanny danced the role of a glamorous young woman at a ball, presided over by three Fates and a looming black figure of Death. Balanchine stopped Francisco Moncion on a stairwell in the theater: "How would you like to be Death in a new dance?"[43] The ballet began in the ballroom, beneath an ominously glittering black chandelier, with the Fates in tulle gowns and long white gloves performing elegant—too elegant—movements. Their cold beauty and the dark musical undercurrents hinted at events to come, but for the moment, all was glassy and smooth as couples entered and waltzed with apparent order and poise.

As the music shifted to the more tumultuous *La Valse*, the set changed from ballroom to wilderness, and the chandelier morphed into a burnt and blackened tree. Tanny was there in a resplendent white gown, and a man tried to dance with her, but she had eyes only for the black-clad figure of Death, who seduced her with gleaming black jewels. She clutched at them compulsively and beguiled herself with her own beauty, dangerously refracted through a broken mirror. Death tempted her with long black silk gloves, and in a moment of sheer extravagance, mesmerized and irresistibly drawn by her own beauty and his sexual magnetism, she plunged her arms into the gloves. He had won.

Wrapped in a black net overgown, she danced with Death. It was an impassioned and dismantled dance, full of broken, flinging movements and contractions, drawn from Weimar and plastique, Balanchine said. When Death finally left her, she collapsed to the floor, dead. The waltz churned on, as the other dancers, with the Fates triumphant, whirled around her corpse in a frenzied circle dance. Finally, in an image reminiscent of the sacrificial "chosen one" in Nijinsky's *Sacre du Printemps,* she was lifted overhead, lifeless and supine, above the dizzying fray, as the curtain fell.[44]

In Tanny and Ravel, George found one of his greatest themes: fatal loss and the trancelike power of erotic love. In his dance, Tanny found in herself a deeply romantic woman. The ballet was not "about" either of them, necessarily, but it emerged from their encounter and their inner lives, and although it would later be danced by others, it would always be Tanny's. She had no understudy, and of the dozens of roles she danced, *La Valse* was her personal favorite. For once, she was not witty and ironic, a girlishly long-limbed upstart, or the translucent angel falling into a lover's arms. She was a daring and tragic figure, tied in some inexplicable way to the implosion of a European world they had both come from.

Soon after *La Valse,* Jerry left the country. By late 1951 he had been targeted by the House Un-American Activities Committee (HUAC) and the FBI, who wanted him to testify and "name names," implicating colleagues and friends who had attended Communist Party meetings. At first he had refused, but when the TV personality Ed Sullivan abruptly canceled Robbins's scheduled appearance on his popular show, insinuating that the choreographer's success might have been engineered by the party, Robbins panicked. He was terrified that McCarthy would cut off his blossoming career—that his American success story would be derailed, sending him back to his Weehawken shtetl. Many of the entertainment industry's most famous and promising luminaries had been blacklisted, and the group calling itself Counterattack had recently published a long report—*Red Channels*—pointing to TV and radio personalities who might be "potential subversives" (spies): Leonard Bernstein and Aaron Copland made the list, and dozens of actors, directors, composers, and choreographers had been called to testify before Congress. Many who refused to cooperate lost their jobs, although Hollywood was much harder hit than Broadway. In 1953, in an act that ashamed him for the rest of his life, Robbins would name names, but for the moment he kept quiet and fled, hoping to stay away long enough to avoid a subpoena.

He wrote longingly to Tanny from Europe, asking if she had married George. No, she had not married George, she curtly responded, with no idea why he had left. Jerry made his case to her, even though he was already romantically involved with a man, because he still loved her and couldn't help competing for her favor:

> If my output is small, you mustn't judge by George, who is older, works differently and has other talents and approaches.... George is your ideal. Good. But don't be a little girl about it and expect everyone else to be like him. He is my ideal too. I adore him as a person and he is my God as an artist. He has helped me a lot and just his respect in me has felt like the blessing of Jesus. I want to help him too if I can, and I feel I can. You must feel very strangely. And your feelings around him must affect your feelings to me. More than anything I've always looked toward your letters and you in them this summer. And I have changed Tanny.[45]

She was annoyed: where was he? George was planning a new ballet just for him, she said. It was *Tyl Eulenspiegel*, to a tone poem by Richard Strauss, about the legendary trickster. And it was (perhaps not coincidentally) "all Spanish, inquisisionish [*sic*] dark and moody," as Lincoln wrote, begging Jerry to return for rehearsals of *Tyl*, which would be based on paintings by Bosch and would be "a great spectacle involving the liberation of the provinces of Belgium from Philip II... [with] wild inquisition scenes, ball-tortures... furiously cruel" and ending with an execution.[46] Jerry couldn't hear it and, too fearful to explain his HUAC dilemma in writing, he stalled, hoping that George would wait for him for *Tyl*, which he would.

Tanny didn't get it at all and wrote tetchily:

> Hy—just heard the news. I think you stink. . . . If you are sick why don't you come back? . . . If you can't dance you could at least come back and help. . . . You are a wonderful dancer, and you never dance—the best young choreographer and never choreograph. What the hell goes on? I'm sorry if this makes you so mad you won't write to me, I wish you would just explain—I'm understanding up to a point. Love, Tan.

Jerry, pressing the real point:

> I am not angry at you. I love you . . . but have some understanding and think deeper about me. I have been here sort of stranded in Paris, like between stations—not knowing what would happen next or if I'd ever be able to return. . . . Was it because of George that you were so angry with me . . . or was it you, because of you. And where do I stand anywhere, anyways with you.

She responded:

> You say you were "stranded in Paris." . . . Did you bump someone off? Is somebody having a baby? Are you married? In love? Is it your family? My goodness what is one to think? A little after in your letter you ask "doesn't anyone know what's happening to me?" Frankly I think not. . . . I knew we would get around to the who stands where? and with who. I just love you, to talk to, go around with, play games, laugh like hell etc. However I'm in love with George. Maybe it's a case of, he got her first. Maybe not. I don't know—anyway I'm staying with him. Can't we be friends? Like they say in the movies.[47]

In the end, Jerry and George did do *Tyl Eulenspiegel* (1951) together, and it was *them* at their best: two tricksters at work, playful, irreverent, with Jerry cracking up over the way George showed him how to wipe his nose or pull up his pants and George indulging to the hilt Jerry's rare comic knack.[48] Balanchine had slapstick, but his sense of comedy was otherwise painfully hamfisted and no match for Jerry's. It was a register he didn't have, as if humor had been ruined by irony, or Russian by English. He didn't laugh a lot, but with Jerry on a good day, he did.

By then George and Tanny were involved, and George was in full command of her talent. Jerry bristled with competitive angst and complained that George was downplaying *The Cage*, making excuses not to schedule it on tour. Worse, he wrote to a friend, Tanny was "acting like a queen bee (and not very well)," and the women in the company were upset because "George [was] favoring her more than he ever did anyone. . . . She just isn't ready yet for the role she's playing and so it all comes out like a childish bitch." The real problem: "I don't see much of her as George dictates everything."[49] Jerry and Tanny didn't end there; they would love each other, in a deflected kind of way, for the rest of their lives, and Jerry would long outlast George in Tanny's life. But in the studio: no. Jerry made only one other ballet that gave Tanny a role. That part was over.[50] George dictated everything.

On New Year's Eve 1952 in a small civil ceremony, Tanaquil Le Clercq and George Balanchine were married. That night, they celebrated at home. Jerry was not present; nor were many of Tanny's friends.[51] The couple posed stiffly for a snapshot, and Tanny—usually so vivacious and free-spirited—appeared oddly formal and ill at ease in her neat suit, holding a prim bouquet of flowers. George was in his usual bow tie, eyes glassy and remote, as if he were somewhere else. As the mostly Russian guests streamed in, Tanny turned to Lincoln, only half-joking: "Oh god, what have I got Myself IN FOR?" She was George's fifth wife, and Lincoln wondered if the "disembodied resentments" of Geva, Danilova, Zorina, Tallchief wouldn't also be "quite a load on Tanny's neck."[52] George proudly sent pictures of himself with Tanny ("She is a dancer") home to his brother, Andrei, in Tbilisi, with heartfelt love to "my dearest mommy."[53] Was it possible that finally, with this fifth and French American wife, he might find a home?

They tried. In addition to their small apartment in New York, he ordered a modest (this time yellow) prefab house for the land he had acquired in Weston, Connecticut. In the years to come, he and Tanny would work hard to make it theirs, and Tanny would photograph it all: George, bare-chested on the roof hammering planks or at a sawhorse sawing boards or lifting wood. George crouched in front of a large cupboard he had built by hand and painted in a colorful Russian style. George clearing the land with Eddie Bigelow and stopping to jokingly pose with him for the camera with axe and sickle triumphantly lifted and crossed, fists clenched, Soviet-style. Pictures of George planting, weeding, mowing, and cooking, always cooking: George making Tanny a steak; George spooning something soft and delicious, goglmogl-like, into her mouth; George scribbling to Tanny a "Me-n-you" ("Sardines, Vichyssoise, Ham, Muffins, Milk, Eggs, ets. Love,—") and signing with a sketched profile of himself.[54] Or sitting in the kitchen drinking vodka and eating caviar with a spoon or entertaining friends from the "Royal Family" of dancers they hung around with, which included Richard Rapp, Nicholas Magallanes, and Diana Adams—a constant presence and unspoken tension in their lives.[55] Connecticut was becoming his Finland, and he was doing what he loved to do the most: working with his hands. Making things for other people. Serving them. He was the chef, the gardener, the carpenter, the builder.

None of this was trivial. His marriage to Tanny was finally integrating his life. For the first time ever, it seemed, he had a house and a wife he was successfully building, tending, dressing, making. It is no accident that the domesticity he and Tanny shared became his primary metaphor for building the NYCB. He liked to say that he was a gardener, and the dancers were the plants he was cultivating; that he was a carpenter, assembling steps and dances; above all, that he was a chef, concocting delicious ballet menus. The split soul of the "cloud in trousers" was finally coming together. The bodily man in trousers was feeding, clothing, and building the wife and the dancers who would inhabit the fantasy "cloud" world of his ballets. Only the full-scale project of the NYCB could rivet George to himself, and Tanny was key—because of their life together, because of her European roots, because of the company, which turned out to be his real and only home. As usual, Lincoln saw the irony: "Balanchine and Tanny seem very happy; she is turning into a devoted domestic type, and has less personal relationship to him, I should say, than before she was Mrs. B."[56]

Home had political overtones too, and the hammer and sickle of Tanny's photograph was part of it. Balanchine was clear about the anti-Communist, anti-Soviet, pro-liberal American impulse behind everything he did, and as the Cold War accelerated, so did his involvement in winning it. The year he and Tanny were married, the company flew to Europe for a long tour that included performances in Paris at a festival organized by Nicky Nabokov and the anti-Communist Congress for Cultural Freedom. The Congress had been founded in 1950 (and briefly led by Arthur Koestler) to show the strength of culture in the free world. When Nicky took it over, he probably didn't know that it was being covertly funded in part by the CIA, nor is it clear that he—or Balanchine—would have cared. For them, it was all part of the Marshall Plan and restoring a European civilization that the wars and revolution had destroyed. Nicky called on his friends: Stravinsky, Rieti, Schoenberg, Copland, Ives, Thomson, and Stokowski; and from the literary world, Raymond Aron, Stephen Spender, André Malraux, Ignazio Silone, and Jean Guéhenno. Even his old friend Jacques Maritain, by then a leading figure in liberal Catholic circles, was involved. Balanchine and the NYCB took a prominent role and performed *The Four Temperaments*, *Prodigal Son*, *The Cage*, *Firebird*, and *Orpheus*.[57]

Later on the tour, George, Tanny, and Betty Cage, along with some of the dancers, traveled from Edinburgh to Berlin to perform at the Berliner Festival. They went by cargo plane, with no insulation, freezing cold, deafening noise, fumes, and condensed water dripping onto their backs. The rest of the company went by sealed train through East Germany ("behind enemy lines," Horgan reported excitedly to her parents).[58] They stayed in the British sector and were there, Lincoln noted, "to compete with the Russians who had sent their great troupes to East Berlin."[59] The city was still a bomb site, and the stunned dancers, many of whom knew little of Nazism or Communism or what was happening in their midst, were given a bus tour through the Russian sector—complete with an army escort "so George will be safe," Betty assured Lincoln.[60] The following year, they danced in Trieste "to bolster our prestige there," Lincoln said, and there were plans in the works with the State Department to send the company as an informal ambassador to Egypt, Greece, Turkey, and Israel (Lincoln demurred, but George went).[61] Lincoln paid attention to the politics: "If we lost two directors of the Board of the City Center because we went to [Franco's] Barcelona," he wrote to Betty Cage, "we would lose the rest if we went to the country of Peron, who destroyed *La Prensa*, and every newspaper in New York would be against us."[62]

That same year, George composed a letter to General Eisenhower. "My Dear General," he wrote, proudly noting the company's success in Berlin as a representative of the United States and enthusiastically endorsing Eisenhower's presidential candidacy, "you are the man to lead this country in its fight against communism." The ballet, he offered, could help. Everyone was worried about the "material" health of the people, he said, but artists were concerned with something even more essential: the "spiritual life of the nation," and he hoped Eisenhower would make this integral to his political platform.[63] He was hammering away at his most insistent theme: the spiritual revolution, not Lenin's—or capitalism's—material revolution, was the only true path forward, and Balanchine and the NYCB were ready to play their part. Eisenhower's office responded warmly, if vaguely, and the company toured Europe widely in these years, often with State Department support: 1952, 1953, 1955, 1956.

He saw this as a "progressive" position and wrote to Lincoln by hand in 1952:

> There is no progress in just inventing new small ballets every season just to exist. Until now, somehow we have created new ideas and we were progressive and now the company is established. . . . But that is not enough. We shouldn't do millions of little *hors d'oeuvres*. It is no longer progressive. And it is impossible to do new things so fast. It must be a process of evolution. . . . It would be better to think about my idea of free performances for children. Not only ballet, but drama . . . and opera . . . the new generation which would come to the performances will be the future citizens of the United States. . . . We have to do something for their souls and minds. . . . It is true that in the beginning there will be a loss. But we would have a loss anyway.

TV cartoons, widely popular at the time, were a poor substitute for fairy tales, he told Betty, reiterating his belief that the ballet could provide a whole new fantasy world for children.[64] Besides, it would be easier to raise money for the spiritual well-being of America's youth: no one is "interested in giving us money to pay Frank Moncion's salary. . . . Please, Lincoln, think about this. It's not as stupid as it sounds at first." He ended by reassuring Lincoln, whose mother had just died: "Don't worry about anything, Lincoln. Everything is all right. Love George. P.S. Time must decide everything. Think twenty-four times and do it once. Wait. Wait. And wait."[65]

But he did not wait. The early 1950s brought an outpouring of new dances, and the range from light to dark, from pleasure and beauty to pain, was impressive. Looking back, we can see that the NYCB repertory already had everything: founding texts like *Serenade, Apollo, Concerto Barocco, The Four Temperaments,* and *Symphony in C;* an ancient-seeming heritage in *Firebird* and *Swan Lake* and (soon) *The Nutcracker;* George's own lighter fare, like *Western Symphony* (1954), an exuberant and kitschy hoedown to music by Hersey Kay in which the dancers rollicked to "Red River Valley" and "Oh, Dem Golden Slippers"; and finally, new "progressive" ballets to the music that occupied George most: Hindemith, Stravinsky, and soon Schoenberg and Ives. George was gathering his dancers around his lifelong themes, starting as he often did at the end—and the end at the moment was Tanny, who stood at the epicenter of what can only be described as Balanchine's postwar return, with her and his company, to *Mitteleuropa.*

Metamorphoses (1952), to Hindemith's 1943 composition Symphonic Metamorphosis of Themes by Carl Maria von Weber, was George's own bug ballet, inspired in part by Kafka's story, along with the oriental themes Hindemith had elaborated from Weber; Jean Rosenthal's decor involved curved bamboo that dangled bedsprings sprayed with gold. The ballet is lost, but Todd Bolender was the cockroach, an "earthy, black, ageless kind of thing," ugly, small, with a "hump of shell" on his back that entrapped him in an insect body. He skittered around on hands and knees, scattering the terrified cast, who were dressed in "an orgy" (Lincoln) of satin; one dancer recalled that Balanchine originally wanted them to shed their clothing on stage and "transform" into something else while dancing. Tanny was the insect's love object, a beautiful dragonfly-like creature in a sequined Balinese-style bra with a fancy wired headdress and wings. Like the sister in Kafka's story, she was the only one who deigned to love the disgusting cockroach. In their pas de deux, the ugly beetle Bolender partnered Tanny literally on his knees, pitifully clutching her calves or ankles as she towered over him, until she finally folded herself awkwardly down into his bug-like arms.[66] The ballet ended, like Kafka's story, with an exuberant dance, except that this was no intimate family circling. Instead, Lincoln said, George staged an astonishing "wild night ride of angels in sweeping pinions. . . . Mercy." It was "mellow-acrid Balanchine," he noted, a dance that was "HUGE . . . VAST." Hindemith was there—and approved.[67]

By 1953 Balanchine was also hard at work directing the American premiere of Stravinsky's *The Rake's Progress* at the Metropolitan Opera. Inspired by William Hogarth's prints and with a libretto by Auden and his partner Chester Kallman, it was another Faustian tale about a man gone wrong, a wager with the Devil, and a pure woman who remains true to the bitter end. The opening in Venice in 1951 had been harshly criticized. Stravinsky, who was turning seventy, stood accused of a backward-looking neoclassicism and unrepentant rejection of serialism, Schoenberg, and everything deemed modern in music. He had lost his edge, critics said, marking him as "old-fashioned," "worn out," even "impotent." This critical failure plunged the strictly ordered Stravinsky into a rare emotional tumult. In 1952, over lunch in the Mojave Desert with Robert Craft—a young composer whose brilliant musical mind already wielded an occult-like power over the aging composer—Stravinsky wept openly and confessed his inner doubts. The critics were right, he said, he was creatively spent. In the months and years to come, Craft would push the elderly Stravinsky to reinvent himself, and serialism—and Balanchine—would be key resources.[68]

Balanchine threw himself into *The Rake's Progress* and defended Stravinsky. "I like Stravinsky's music," he told a reporter. "It is so strict, so solid. It never comes apart. You cannot improve upon it. It is built like mathematics."[69] Besides, *Rake* offered just the kind of comic and philosophical narrative that drew him, and he staged Stravinsky's opera as a danced ritual, including a full-scale religious procession circling the dead body of the protagonist. Lincoln thought it was marvelous and should go to Broadway, but it never did.[70]

Instead, the following year Balanchine made *Opus 34* (1954), set to

Schoenberg's twelve-tone Accompaniment to a Cinematographic Scene, op. 34. It was an old and minor score, composed in 1930 in Berlin with cinema in mind: "Threatening Fear—Danger—Catastrophe." It was brief—ten minutes—and the ballet George made repeated it twice. The first time (the "worm part," as the dancers called it) was for thirteen dancers in white with a black "thing," or tube, which slithered downstage, lit with pale green and lavender downlights designed by Rosenthal to look as if "coal had come alive."[71] We know about this long since lost dance from Edwin Denby, who tells us that the dancers began scattered on stage facing the audience: they "quiver a knee and stop; they lunge forward and stop; they dangle their hands; crouching, they throw a hand wide, slip it between the legs, grab a knee and stop." It felt, he wrote, "as if people were under an oppressive force, meeting it keenly and swiftly," and at the end, they wormed their way into a comforting larva-like clump.

The second part was shocking. A brother (Herbert Bliss) and sister (Tanny) stand alone on an empty and darkened stage, their backs to the audience. They are walking away into the darkness, but a witch appears and pulls them back. Suddenly, with the abrupt logic of a nightmare, they are lying on large operating tables surrounded by doctors and nurses in white coats under a bright surgical light. With outsized forceps and reams of bloodstained bandages, the doctors are flaying their bodies, like a Platonic whole cut in two. Tanny's half emerges as a gray skeletal cross section, with exposed nerves and innards printed on her front and a wig of floor-length silken hair. Bliss is the other half, crosscut to show muscles and arteries. Their faces are eerily flattened by tight nylon stockings pulled over their heads. These feeble creatures reach out but can't find each other and are intermittently swallowed up by Rosenthal's black "slithery heap of something viscous." At the end, Bliss mechanically straps his half body into a tubular bag and is lifted up into the light. Tanny, alone on the stage, wraps herself in a bloodied cloth he has left behind. Suddenly she turns her back to the audience and a battery of powerful klieg lights "hit her head-on, set fire to her, and, erect, she paces on into them." The audience is blinded too, and on the opening night, people screamed. "It was like flinging something foul in their faces, like a pail of cold filth," one dancer recalled.

Opus 34 reminded the dancers of *Nosferatu* or *The Cabinet of Dr. Caligari.* Denby called it a fairy tale, with "a few solid gobs of nightmare," and insisted that it was not Weimar or expressionistic at all. He described it instead as a stark classical world with movement that "was oppressive not because the dancer dances it oppressively, but because of its own visual and rhythmic nature." He marveled that balletically trained dancers could perform even the most grotesque movements with a kind of clarity and elevation, "Whatever it says is said nobly." It was a dance, he concluded, that affirmed "the company's stand as the most adventurous anywhere." For Tanny, it was a bit too close to life: three weeks later, she went to the hospital for an emergency appendectomy, and the ballet had to be canceled.[72]

That same year, Balanchine made *Ivesiana* to a score by Ives. It was musically complex and required two conductors in the pit, with Balanchine in the first wing signaling counts to the dancers. The most striking section of the dance was "Unanswered Question," and it was not for Tanny. Instead, it was for five men and Allegra Kent, who was emerging as a new figure in Balanchine's imagination. There was a conceit—a limit Balanchine imposed on himself and her: Allegra never touched the ground, a not inaccurate description of who she was. As it began, two of the men made a "chair" and lifted her to a standing position high on their shoulders; two others took her arms, and together they pulled her like a rope around and through their bodies, winding her between their legs, overhead, with her flexible limbs pulled into splits and pretzels. The men were her "spaceship," as she thought of it, and she was like an "elastic icon," impassive and unattainable, alone in her own stratosphere. Dressed in a simple white leotard and nothing else, she felt dangerously exposed. Todd Bolender stood in front of her "spaceship," beaconing, or lay flat on his back on the floor before her in abject submission. At the end, Balanchine asked her to stand tall on the men's shoulders and lean backward "very slowly" until she fell from her towering pose into the blackness behind—a terrifying act of blind trust, even with a team of capable men ready to catch her. The audience gasped.[73]

No wonder Baum was pressing for more classics. He meddled and suggested *Don Juan* to the score by Richard Strauss, and Lincoln foolishly took it upon himself to meet with Eugene Berman, who came up with some period sketches. Balanchine saw them and bluntly said no. He considered Pushkin's version of the story, "The Stone Guest," and wanted instead "a closet in which the exhausted libertine had come to die. . . . It should be shut; only a hint of sky; all walls and arcades, the center of a maze from which there was no issue." Maybe a "silver studded coffin; nails. Black and silver . . . for Juan's funeral." He wanted Hugh Laing as Don Juan, Maria as the first woman on his famous list of lovers, next Tanny as a "lemon and sugar bride-type." Diana Adams would be a nun; Melissa Hayden, a gypsy; and Jerome Robbins, the evil Leporello "who keeps Juan's horses sleek for their swift final ride to hell."[74] But actually he didn't really like the music, so the project stalled.

Then came *The Nutcracker*, which had been in the works at least since 1950.[75] It opened on February 2, 1954, just a month after the premiere of *Opus 34*. George had danced Petipa and Tchaikovsky's 1892 ballet in his youth, and the version he made was a portrait of childhood drawn from fragments of his own past, not least the spectacular tree that grows to fantastic heights (heaved up with a hand crank and ropes) lit with candles and bursting with chocolate and oranges and gold paper angels and stars "tangled up in silver 'rain' or tinsel," he said. Even the mice who fought the Nutcracker brought back his past, and he told the dancers about catching rats, killing them, and eating them in the starving revolutionary years. The second act, "Land of the Sweets," recalled Eliseyev's elegant art-deco St. Petersburg shop full of delectable treats that his mother had frequented. The act opened with a dance for angels (later children, but this time grown women) gliding across the floor in a Georgian folk-dance style, and the music for the Arabian Dance reminded him of a Georgian lullaby. Maria was the maternal Sugar Plum Fairy, and Tanny danced the free-spirited Dewdrop in the Waltz of the Flowers. His idea with *The Nutcracker*, he later explained, was to evoke the fun but also the mystery of Christmas. "It wasn't the way it is now, with everyone shouting, running around panting as if it's a fire instead of Christmas. Back in St. Petersburg there was a stillness, a waiting: who's being born? Christ is born!" Besides, he said, turning to a favorite theme, Hoffmann's story was written as a critique of strict German manners that squelched childhood imagination.[76]

Hoffmann was key. The old St. Petersburg *Nutcracker* had been drawn from Alexandre Dumas's sweetened version of Hoffmann's bizarre tale, but George clearly had the crueler original to mind. In life, Hoffmann knew Marie and Fritz: they belonged to his stuffily bourgeois childhood friend, whose overly regulated children had no capacity for fantasy and imagination. Hoffmann pointedly called the stiff parents of his story the Stahlbaums (Steeltrees); Dumas (and Petipa) softened this to "Silberhaus" (Silver-house). Balanchine's parents were strictly Stahlbaum. The main character in Hoffmann's story is Drosselmeier—a supreme-court justice (like Hoffman himself) who is strange, ugly, and periwigged, with a patched eye and a taste for the occult. He is obsessed with clocks, which he repairs, and with building tiny mechanical people. He is never more himself than when occupied with the "inner construction" and "creative gear work" that sets these automatons in motion. Hoffmann's Drosselmeier is no odd but kindly uncle, à la Petipa; he is a skilled and secretive sorcerer, master of time and dolls, who helps Marie find a wondrous and nightmarish imaginary universe. And although the courtship between Marie and Fritz is a sexual awakening, the primary relationship in the story, and the ballet, is between Marie and Drosselmeier, made and maker, girl-child become woman. In the filmed version of the ballet in 1958, Balanchine played the Drosselmeier role in which Hoffmann had imagined himself. This awkward old magician, hanging on the grandfather clock in the Stahlbaum living room like a puppet muttering nonsensical verses, Hoffmann wrote, makes "the most splendid and most wonderous things, if you only have the right eyes to see them."[77]

Lincoln told Baum that creating this nonreal real world would cost a cool $40,000, knowing full well it was likely to cost closer to $90,000, which it did. When Baum found out that the tree alone would come in at $25,000, he said "No!," but Balanchine insisted: the ballet "*is* the tree!"[78] The production taxed their already thinly spread resources, and when Jerry and George went to Karinska's just hours before the opening curtain to check on the costumes, they found a team of seamstresses bent over the still-unfinished garments. George immediately sat down, threaded a needle, and started sewing. Jerry followed his lead, marveling at George's calm. As a secret talisman for the dancers, Karinska sewed miniature medallion images of George and Lincoln inside some of the costumes. When the show finally went up, it was "a smasharoo," as Lincoln gleefully reported to his sister. "We will extend the engagement to 7 weeks and do it on television and make a mint, we hope." Denby called it "Balanchine's *Oklahoma!*"[79]

The fragilities that seemed to run like the river Styx under their lives were naturally unquelled by success. In the spring of 1955, Lincoln was found "howling" in the woods at his brother's home in upstate New York and was so erratic that finally Fidelma had him hospitalized. Lincoln resisted and put up a monstrous struggle as the nurse strapped him in a straitjacket. Electric shock therapy followed, punctuated by long visits with Father William Lynch, a Catholic priest and intellectual, whose writings on faith and art echoed Jacques Maritain's, and who had become a calming presence in Lincoln's restless life. After his release, he finally agreed to see a psychiatrist ("I feel about psychoanalysis very much like I feel about the weather. No one can hope for equilibrium of sunshine and lovely weather all the time. Unhappiness is part of the human condition and it's not a valid category. . . . The only thing of importance is consciousness").[80]

As for Tanny, for all her feistiness, she had always been fragile, ever since George had imagined her polio-stricken body in *Resurgence* for the March of Dimes back in 1946. Now he wanted her to do *Swan Lake,* which had been in the repertory since 1951. It was another nineteenth-century Russian "ham and eggs" staple made famous by countless Russian spin-off productions across Europe and America, and George, who had no interest in adding this old classic to his company repertory, had staged it in only one act, expanded the ensemble, and stripped out mime and narrative. "Who needs it?"; it was all too silly and outdated, he said: "A prince comes out with a feather in his hat, that's the plot."[81] Maria had danced a more conventional version for Ballet Theatre, but she quickly discovered that George had something else in mind. He talked incessantly about the eerie performance of the white Swan Queen by Olga Spessivtseva, a dancer he had loved in his youth, whose fragile physique and fractured inner life eventually led her to insanity. She ate real birds' nests for breakfast before performing the swan role, George said, and was so cut off from the world that she could barely speak, making her a broken and remote bird.[82] Maria, who was so robust and capable, was at a loss, and although she danced the role to acclaim, it soon became clear that it was not she whom George had imagined in it at all. It was Tanny.[83]

George wanted Tanny to dance the Swan Queen, but the role terrified her and almost broke their marriage. Technically it was beyond her capacities. She was not a strong classical dancer and gaining that kind of control over her raucous limbs was no easy task. She had never wanted to dance that kind of nineteenth-century Petipa-style role, and she hated *Swan Lake*, dreaded it, routinely vomited from nerves when she had to perform it. Tough, smart, sophisticated Tanny reduced to a trembling heap. George pushed, insisted, and cast her in spite of herself—wouldn't let it go. She was exactly the swan he wanted: fearful, timid, introverted, and musically sensitive. On the night of her debut, she threw up in the wings just before her entrance and managed to get through her variation, but her knees buckled beneath her at the end, making this traditional dance of love and redemption into a stark portrait of physical and psychological collapse. The *New York Times* critic John Martin wrote of her shy fragility and eggshell nerves; she was a swan and a woman, he said, that any man would want to protect and care for.[84]

It was another omen, if George needed one. By then their marriage was strained. Tanny was still so young and wanted to live, not just dance, and rumors were circulating that they were planning to separate. The company really was his only home, and there he was in charge, the calm at the center of every inevitable storm. In his dances, where their real life together had taken place, Tanny could be coquettish, sassy, and kitschy (*Western Symphony*) or wild (*Orpheus, Firebird*), but, above all, she was fated, tragic, erotic, walking into death, burning up, a person who could be physically broken, languid, disjointed, destroyed: *Resurgence, The Four Temperaments, La Valse, Metamorphoses, Opus 34, Swan Lake*. It was as romantic and violent a view of a woman as he would ever entertain, especially because—to his horror—it was about to come true.

Chapter 18

AGON

In preparation for a company tour in August 1956, the dancers were advised to take the new Salk immunization against polio. In the years since George's 1946 ballet for the March of Dimes, the disease had become a national emergency. With tens of thousands afflicted annually (some fifty-eight thousand in 1952, a peak year, including three thousand deaths), the announcement of a safe vaccination in 1955 had been broadcast live over radio, piped through loudspeakers in department stores, and celebrated with church bells, sirens, and singing in the streets. But by the summer of 1956, there was still confusion: short supplies and fears that the vaccine might infect and kill persisted (at least two hundred people had died that year from a competing faulty vaccine). When the dancers lined up to receive the shot from a kindly looking doctor in a white coat, a few stepped aside. Allegra Kent declined on Christian Science grounds. Tanny didn't want to feel sick on the plane and said she would take it another time.[1]

Zurich, Venice, Berlin, Munich, Frankfurt, Brussels, Paris, Antwerp, Cologne, Copenhagen. It was a long and exhausting tour that seemed to gather the winds of fate against George. In early October, Stravinsky was in Berlin conducting when his hands suddenly dropped to his sides, limp and inert. He stood stunned and momentarily lost and barely managed to finish the performance. Afterward, his speech was slurred and his right side numb: he had suffered a major stroke, and the prognosis was uncertain.[2] When George found out, Betty Cage found him crying outside her hotel room's door, gasping and unable to speak. He left immediately to visit the composer, who was hospitalized in Munich, and returned feeling anxious and unmoored. He had no way of knowing just how much of his own emotional and creative life would collapse if Stravinsky, the only father he now had, were to become incapacitated—or die. Adding to the tension, rumors were still circulating that his marriage was failing, which was true. And in a sign that made everyone who knew shudder, Betty Cage read Tanny's tarot cards and didn't have the heart to tell her that they forecast disaster.[3]

By the time the company reached Copenhagen, Tanny wasn't feeling well. She was scheduled to dance the dreaded *Swan Lake*, and Horgie gave her a Miltown tranquilizer to relax her aching muscles and help her sleep. This did little to allay the increasingly alarming symptoms and on the afternoon of October 31, George sought medical help. At 3 P.M. he and Edith (who had accompanied her twenty-seven-year-old daughter on the tour) checked Tanny into the Diakonissestiftelsen, a solid red-brick "motherhouse" of Catholic deaconesses, nurses who had devoted their lives to Christian service. By then she was dizzy and vomiting bile, and her limbs were weak and achy; the nurses noted that she seemed confused and "battered . . . in pain." They immediately consulted Dr. From-Hansen, a Danish polio expert, and the following day Tanny was transferred to the Blegdamshospitalet with a devastating diagnosis: acute poliomyelitis. It was not clear whether she would survive.[4]

George woke Vida Brown at the hotel: "It's Tanny, she has polio." He was white, bleary-eyed, cheeks sunken, and they clung to each other weeping; Milly joined them and they all wept. Vida ordered coffee, but George just stood in the hallway, leaning on the wall in a daze and unable to speak. Edith went to Betty. In a state of near hysteria, Betty called Barbara Horgan and Natasha Molostwoff. Eddie Bigelow, who had cared for his own polio-stricken mother, was morose but tried to make himself useful. Lincoln and Jerry were notified in New York, and Jerry wrote immediately to George sending prayers; he wrote to Tanny directly with more prayers. Edith took the reins of her daughter's life and eventually wrote back to Jerry telling him not to come since Tanny was too weak to see him; he sent orchids and a large stuffed animal in his stead.[5] George wrote to Diana Adams, Tanny's best friend and a woman he was already in love with, asking her to please write to Tanny every day. Her charming letters would be a comfort, he said.[6]

As word spread of Tanny's dire condition, the company was unhinged. They were scheduled to depart for Sweden for a last round of performances before heading home, and as they boarded the train to Stockholm, "headquarters" went into action. Betty, Eddie, and Barbara were all in shock but managed nonetheless to divide the dancers between them and inform them of the situation, doing their best to allay the collective fear and anxiety, not to mention the panic of contagion. The authorities stopped the train at the border for immediate vaccinations. After the performances, the beleaguered dancers flew back to New York disoriented and uncertain. Would Tanny live? What would become of them now? Would the company fold? Even Lincoln was at a loss.

In Copenhagen the physical facts were grim, and George and Edith were shuttling anxiously between their new headquarters at the stately, wood-paneled Ambassador Hotel and Tanny's modest hospital room at Blegdams. There was not much they could do as the disease ravaged her body. By day two, her hips, legs, and right shoulder were paralyzed. She couldn't lift her head, and her fever was still dangerously high. She was catheterized and given a blood transfusion, but her vital capacities were falling fast. She was having trouble breathing. By day three, her diaphragm was collapsing, and she was sealed into an iron lung, a terrifying experience that gave her nightmares of suffocating. At times she sent George out of the room; her mother was all she could bear, and she did not want him to see her crying.

George was in shock, devastated and haggard, but also calm and determined. After all, he was a man who understood the mutability of flesh and bone, who knew how to train bodies and "work on statues," who had somehow vanquished TB and survived wars and revolution, and who above all believed in God and miracles. He didn't for a moment abide the doctors' prognosis of permanent disability. What did they know? He was inwardly certain that he could heal her, that he had to heal her: in his troubled mind, Tanny's illness was his fault, God's punishment for his past profligate ways.[7] *Resurgence* had been a terrible prophecy bestowed on Tanny through him in a cruel twist of fate, which he pinned to sin, and he felt sure that the only way to heal Tanny was through hard work and the sheer force of religious faith. Whatever the state of their marriage before her disease, he was now wedded to her cause. It was not self-sacrificial but matter-of-fact. The company he had been building for so long slipped to the back of his mind, and he found himself consumed with a new project: fix Tanny.

As the danger to her life passed, she gradually began spending a few hours daily out of the respirator. Still, for weeks she was in pain and could only swallow liquids. George made Jell-O in his hotel room and delivered it to her bedside.[8] Her neck and abdominal muscles were gone, and when she tried to sit up, her head lolled alarmingly to the side. He helped her practice sitting in a special chair outfitted with what looked like jail bars to hold her skull in place—first an agonizing two minutes, then three, then ten. She could barely hold a pen, and her wavering childlike missives to Jerry using her stronger left hand—an unsteady line or two was all she could manage—were another harsh reminder of her heartbreaking dependence. Edith took dictation, and George stoically occupied himself with solitaire as the nurses routinely turned his wife's body, like a piece of meat, to prevent sores and sent him out of the room to expertly deal with the "large gooey" (Tanny's words) accidents that she could not control. Soon she would begin therapy underwater in a Hubbard tank; electrotherapy was next. The nights, after George left, were a terror. Afraid to sleep, Tanny deliberated over when to take her "atomic bomb" sleeping pill, administered if she was lucky with a whiskey chaser by the night nurses, who were their own dark comedy: Miss Bang, Miss Bull, and the cigar-smoking Madame Christiansens.[9] Finally, the doctor tore up the calendar they were using to mark her glacial progress. Frankly, he said, time does not exist in this disease, there is only the present moment.

George set out to make Tanny's hospital room a home. As she moved to solid food, he arranged to use the kitchen of his old Russian colleague, the teacher Vera Volkova, to cook Tanny's meals, and he lobbied the American embassy to get her favorite American foods (Velveeta!). He worked hands-on with her body and learned to roll her over in bed, to hoist her into a chair, to "exercise" her dead limbs manually—pulling them into circles, arcs, bends, in an effort to lessen the stiffness and atrophy. Eventually, he figured out how to "partner" her by draping her limp body over his own like a rag doll and using his legs to push her feet out in front of her to practice walking—a futile exercise that didn't fool either of them into thinking she ever would. Her progress was slow, but he delighted in even the smallest of gains: thanks to his cooking, she was getting "plumpy," he noted, unable to disguise his ambivalence, and the day she sat for a half-hour in her jail-bar chair by herself, his whole temper lightened. At least she wouldn't be "chained" to her bed, he said. Tanny, who never missed a beat, wrote darkly to Jerry: "I would *almost* say he enjoys me this way. To have someone totally dependent on one seems to agree with some people."[10]

Jerry was constantly on her mind, and reverting to an old pattern that had never really ceased, she wrote him passionate love letters full of kisses, jokes, and confidences. He would understand her terror, her "shitting" in bed, and all of that, and she talked her way through long, frightening nights by performing fanciful monologues to Jerry ("We are always on the beach or a beachy-type place," she reported as her handwriting steadied). In her blackest moments, she found comfort in obsessively reciting his phone number. When George set out to convince her that they should return to New York, where she could receive care at Lenox Hill Hospital, he held out a carrot: from Lenox Hill, he baited almost sneeringly, Tanny could "call *Jeree*." "How well he knows me," she reported to Robbins; "well it is a thought, if I can get past your secretary. Tired kisses. . . . My how we have slipped—I love you, love you, my kisses are dull, but never tired. Xxx Tan."[11]

Even the sleeping pills George took didn't give him more than a few hours of rest, and he was growing thin and drinking and smoking too much—Parliaments sent from New York by Betty at his urgent request. "George looks badly, thin and extremely nervous," Edith reported to Betty.[12] He passed long hours in Tanny's room, and when he wasn't helping, he played solitaire and glumly listened to Russian radio, sourly mocking Soviet propaganda about heroic workers and brick factory quotas.[13] Geographically, they weren't far from old St. Petersburg, and Copenhagen, with its cold northern streets and intersecting frozen canals, even felt a bit like his childhood home, except that it was small and squarely Protestant. He even took on a bit of work setting dances on the Royal Danish Ballet (the "Great Danes," he and Tanny ironically called them) as he had back in the 1930s, but he still didn't much like its too-correct dancers, with their overly cautious and mincing movements. "Very nice," George distractedly said ("and that's death," Tanny noted).[14] When he saw "some old ballerina" dancing his *Night Shadow* in a black wig, he just sighed: she "looks like a gorilla."[15] He donated the proceeds of his endeavors to the hospital for polio research.

There were events: the queen, dressed elegantly in navy, visited one afternoon, causing a rush of nurses to hide "all unsightly instruments of torture," and amid a paradise of potted palms, Edith and George joined Her Majesty for "sherry, cigs and cakes." Tanny lay in bed alone reporting it all to Jerry.[16] On another day Tanny's father, Jacques, visited half-drunk with his new girlfriend. Playing out their sad family drama, George did his best to minimize conflict—anything to avoid conflict—by hiding from Edith the fact that this new couple were staying in the same hotel room. When Jacques announced that Tanny looked to him "just fine," a comment that reminded her that she had never really had a father after all, George shot bluntly back: "Yes, she is fine, except she can't move."[17]

Lincoln and Betty wrote long letters and sent clippings about the NYCB: please send everything to the hotel, George requested, so as not to upset Tanny.[18] He didn't approve of many of the decisions being made in his absence. "Please no 'Sebastian,'" he wrote adamantly to Betty; "it is the most dreadful ballet, lousy music, stinking story—better nothing than that. I don't like Cranko idea either. Don't spend money on this junk. Let Todd [Bolender] do his Poulenc ballet." When Betty reported that Lincoln had finally punched their insufferable guest conductor, Carlo Menotti, George just said,

> [Menotti] is a nice chappie but I don't like his tail of disciples, extras, connoisseurs, snobs, parasites, idiots, megalomaniacs, carnivorous lizards, etc., etc. I hope that Lincoln had enough of it. There is no need to be panicky and collect this garbage, even if it's a success. . . . I hear you have two pretenders in "poor Swan Lake." I highly disapprove of these

two girls dancing it. Certainly I am not going to see them in Swan when I return. (Not everybody should dance everything, as president Lincoln said.) Be good Betty and give my love to your slave secretary Barbara. With my love to you. Your, G.[19]

Betty was pressing to bring them home and working to have the March of Dimes sponsor the trip. George and Edith were by then desperate to get back too, but Tanny had come to depend on her little hospital home and was frightened to leave. Like conspiring parents, Edith and George went so far as to stage a scene, half-real, half-contrived, in which George enacted one of his rare "I mads": in a spit of supposed temper, he rushed up to the nurses and snatched Tanny's medication and angrily insulted the doctors for not properly caring for her. She would be better off in New York, he loudly announced. When Tanny relayed this tantrum in a letter to a friend, Edith—who mailed her letters—tacked on a secret note admitting that it had all been a ploy to convince their child-Tanny to return to New York.[20]

On March 13, 1957, after four months that felt like a lifetime at Blegdams, the three of them finally went home. Tanny still couldn't walk (she never would) or use a bedpan or feed herself, and she was paralyzed from the waist down, so the arrangements were elaborate: there was a stretcher to carry her aboard the airplane; four "skybeds" for sleeping, with specially fitted bolsters for her legs; and an accompanying nurse to help. Betty and Lincoln had cleared the way for them to get through customs quickly at Idlewild, and an ambulance carried Tanny to her hospital room at Lenox Hill. (To calm her panic, she wrote childishly to Jerry: "So—are you getting excited? Are you coming to see me? Am I back yet? Did I call you? Do tell me. Please write. [heart] T.")[21] George asked Lincoln, who had rescued him so many times in the past, to please come with him to the hospital.[22] The cost for the trip was overwhelming, a whopping $2,379.90, but thanks to Betty, the March of Dimes paid for it all. Lincoln would pick up the tab at Lenox Hill.[23]

Six weeks later, they did it all again. Tanny boarded another plane, with another skybed, accompanied by George and Edith, to Warm Springs, Georgia, where she would live for nearly five months, at Roosevelt's famous retreat—courtesy, once again, of the March of Dimes.[24] The intake nurse noted that Edith was by then "bitter, dispirited and quite overwhelmed" by her daughter's condition, and especially resentful of this grim outcome after she had fought so hard to make her daughter a star. The nurse found George, by contrast, surprisingly resigned: Tanny's polio was "one of those things," he said, and maybe even a relief for his wife since she never really loved dancing and had lots of friends and other interests. As for Tanny, she seemed to the nurse oddly "well adjusted" to her situation.[25]

She wasn't, but George was not wrong about her strange sense of relief: at least there would be no more *Swan Lake*s or throwing up in the wings. It was a sign of just how oppressive George's love, so tightly knotted to the demands of dancing, could feel. There was some relief when after a few excruciating days at Warm Springs—more therapy, more lifting, more hospital food, lots of whiskey—George put down twenty dollars to cover his wife's expenses, tucked her into her bright blue room with a view of grass and trees (next to the busy and very smelly bedpan-emptying room), and left.[26]

He didn't abandon her, it wasn't that—even though Jerry, for one, angrily thought he had. George visited, wrote, and called, but he was also back at work and engrossed with the company and especially with a new ballet he was making with Stravinsky, who had recovered from his stroke, for the fall season. The terms of their marriage had changed, and the deepest parts of his mind and imagination were already cordoned off from her. He could never again love her in that vital, sensual, dancerly way, and he instinctively cut her out of this part of his life. He didn't even want her and her wheelchair around the theater or the school: no, you can't teach ballet, he told her a bit cruelly when the issue arose; if you can't do it, you can't teach it.[27] Bound by her illness, they were growing apart. She had other things on her mind too—not least Jerry, who swooped in (and out), spiriting her away, for instance, on a romantic picnic in the countryside that made her forget for a moment that she was permanently crippled.

George never forgot, nor had he given up on her body—or on his faith: "It takes time," he assured her, "my friend upstairs [is] helping."[28] He wanted her to pray over his icons (she wouldn't), and one day he called to tell her excitedly that he had consulted a priest or medium, who promised to give him St. Peter's or St. Paul's cloak, a magical healing force, for her to wear (she didn't).[29] In the months to come, he would consult doctors, order potions and injections from Europe, and hire a German physical therapist, trained by Laban, who specialized in biomechanics—Meyerhold's old system from his way-back Russia days. This miracle worker could discover, he brightly explained, "if there's just the faintest glimmering of life in a muscle that others have taken for granted was dead."[30] He had no patience with New York's famous Dr. Rusk, known as "Dr. Live-Again," a rehabilitation expert with experience treating wounded soldiers during World War II. All Rusk offered, George said dismissively, was ingenious gadgets to breathe or eat for you: "That's not what a dancer like Tanny wants—she wants her own body back, or any little bit of it that she can get."[31] Instead, he set her up with Joseph Pilates, a German physical trainer, formerly a circus performer and boxer, who had invented an exercise system for paralyzed or bedridden soldiers in British internment camps during World War I.[32] George was still working on Tanny's statue.

And on their marriage: around this time, he sent her a copy of Erich Fromm's *The Art of Loving*, a book he "swore by," she said.[33] Fromm was a psychoanalyst influenced by the Frankfurt School's critique of capitalism, by Buddhism and other Eastern religious practices, and by the work of anthropologists such as Margaret Mead and George's old flame Katherine Dunham (with whom Fromm had a long affair). Love, Fromm said, is like the practice of an art: less sex and romance, more caring, discipline, patience, humility, and faith—like an artist's uniting with his materials. It required each partner to engage in daily physical practice and cultivation of the "inner self." It also required, he said, echoing Ouspensky and Gurdjieff, an entire reordering of society away from an economy of well-fed "automatons" or "zombies" and toward a new utopia of love. Isn't that what George had with Tanny? She was his wife, his patient, his child, his work of art (his dog to walk, she wryly put it).[34] Is polio what it took for him to finally find himself at home with a wife?

All they needed now was a home, that panacea that seemed to slip through his fingers at every turn. If he couldn't build a ballet around Tanny, at least he could build her a home. They had been living on East Seventy-fifth Street, but around this time George chose an apartment (6A) in the Apthorp, a palatial stone building on Seventy-eighth Street and Broadway with a fancy iron-gated horse-and-carriage courtyard and a touch of Old World grandeur. It was not a pink house, but it was close: "I must make these four rooms like a fairy tale for her," he told Lucia Davidova.[35] He had the doorways shaved down for easy wheelchair access and positioned his cherished baby grand pianos in the corner of the living room to give Tanny plenty of space to comfortably wheel around. The large kitchen—food and feeding her—would be the center of their lives. He even considered, against Tanny's objections, hiring a Chinese cook to help. Ever preoccupied with fixing her body, he specially designed the cabinets a bit too high, forcing her to reach for everything so as to improve her range of motion. He left his own mark too: a life-size Audubon eagle suspended from the wall and ample timepieces, including a pendulum antique brass clock in the living room and another clock with an oversized face hung on the kitchen wall, keeping time in their lives.[36]

Weston, his own little Finland, was the real outpost of George's soul, and he went all-out to make their tacky prefab house into a fantasy dream home. He rushed there whenever he could and busily made for them a pastoral paradise with dogwood, lilacs, and roses. He drew pictures of trellises and sent sweet notes to Tanny asking: "What color roses do you want here? And what here?" Maybe a Vespa shed? (She preferred a guest room.) He shipped off letter upon letter with childlike sketches of a small industrious mouse (him) gardening, carrying rocks, hoeing, or milking a cow and sending pots of frothy milk to Georgia or pouring it into a large bowl for her, his large and towering "pussy cat." He told her how lonely he was without her, and reported, "I am a haus waus maus, building, washing, squishing poison on poison ivy, preparing housy wousy for pussy wussy," and he drew a large cat holding hands with a small mouse as the mouse diligently hammered the planks of their little abode. He kissed the flowers and plants for her and imagined her with him here and in New York: "In my mind you are [there] every minute, even at the rehearsals in the morning. When I have my coffee, I eat two sugar buns, the second is yours and I [sit] in your chair. My heart is breaking when I think of you. I love you my darling baby pussy cat. Your g." Finally, a month before her scheduled return, he triumphantly announced his accomplishments: "Now is August and September 15th we will be in our little housee-wousee," and he sketched this:[37]

There was of course a big problem with this carefully staged domestic bliss. The only home that could really sustain George Balanchine was dancers and dancing, and Tanny could not dance—which may be why he didn't really want her back so soon. On a visit to Warm Springs in July, he blurted to the nurses that September was "much too soon" for her to come home. "Please ask them to keep my wife as long as they can," he instructed ("It was very funny. HA," Tanny bitterly reported to Jerry).[38] He needed time: time to build their paradise, time to work with his dancers and get the NYCB season off the ground, time above all to make his new dance with Stravinsky. Work and using his hands—planting flowers, sculpting bodies, arranging ballets—were the only ways he knew to calm his heart, and as he worked and the experience of her illness melted into his mind, something unexpected happened. Instead of taking him down, this new trauma in his life—her life—seemed to clear a way. It was as if years of silt were sinking to the bottom of his mind, and in the coming weeks, a torrent of pure dance flowed out. That fall, all at once, over a ten-week period, Balanchine made no fewer than four new ballets. One of them was *Agon*.

. . .

Agon was a culmination and a breakthrough. It stood at the midpoint of the century and at the midpoint of his life. It was one of his greatest works, the meeting of many roads that all seemed to come together under the two North Stars in his sky at the time: Tanny and Stravinsky. After the black hole of her illness and his near-death, *Agon* was a burst of clear light. It came from them, but it was also its own engine. Balanchine and Stravinsky had been chewing, gnawing, and gestating the idea for *Agon* for over a decade. It had all started the day after the opening of *Orpheus*, when Lincoln wrote to Stravinsky proposing a new ballet that might form, "a great lyric-drama" in three parts: *Apollo*, *Orpheus*, and "*?—."[39]

In the months and years to come, they sifted through many ideas for "*?—"; most were discarded, and all were rooted in ancient Greek literature or mythology. What about the *Bacchae*? *Hero as Builder of Cites*? *Aesculapius, the Doctor*? *Amphion the Architect*? W. H. Auden (via Lincoln) came up with *Apollo Architectons: Builder of Shelters and Bridges*; T. S. Eliot (via Lincoln again) thought his *Sweeney Agonistes* might work. None of these ideas gained traction; Balanchine wanted to do *Pulcinella* instead, but by 1953 he was losing interest. He did not want to do a Stravinsky Festival, he told Betty Cage: "No one will come."[40] But Kirstein hadn't given up and was still writing to Stravinsky about the idea of a dance about Terpsichore, a kind of all-star parade of Greek gods with entrances by Zeus, Apollo, Terpsichore, Cupid, Pegasus, Orpheus, Venus, Mars, and Prometheus. Stravinsky thought not. He countered instead with the Nausicaa episode from *The Odyssey*. Kirstein responded that although Balanchine was amused by the idea of a dance of laundry baskets, he felt the ending would be dramatically difficult: "What becomes of her? Ulysses returns to Penelope and nothing at all becomes of Nausicaa," he wrote.

Instead, Balanchine (via Lincoln) proposed something startlingly grandiose, almost apocalyptic. In Lincoln's perhaps embellished letter to Stravinsky on August 31 that year, we can already feel Balanchine moving away from plot and mythology toward something more conceptual, even mystical.

> [Balanchine] would like a ballet which would seem to be the enormous finale of a ballet to end all ballets the world has ever seen, mad

> dancing, variations, pas d'action, pas de deux, etc., with a final terrific and devastating curtain when everyone would be exhausted. He suggested a competition before the gods; the audience are statues; the gods are tired and old; the dancers re-animate them by a series of historic dances, the correct tempi of which you can quite ignore, but they are called courante, bransle, passepied, rigaudon, menuet, etc., etc. It is as if time calls the tune, and the dances which began quite simply in the sixteenth century took fire in the twentieth and exploded. . . . Balanchine sees a marvelous theatricalized cosmic space in an architectural frame, more like Palladio than baroque; your music is the drama; his dances would attempt to stage dramatic tensions entirely in terms of dancing, but the characters would be dressed with some reference to historic styles. Does this appeal to you? You are the boss.

George and Lincoln's favorite themes: the audience as statues—dead, inert, asleep—waiting to be awakened; the "old and tired" gods no longer capable of ordering society; sixteenth-century dance forms and "time calling the tune" in a "cosmic space." All of this was a gesture to the ancient and Renaissance origins of music and dance that Stravinsky and Balanchine could "explode" in a ballet that would "wake-up" today's comatose, sleepwalking souls and offer a new way to order life aligned with the eternal principles of music.

Stravinsky would have none of it:

> Your objections to Nausicaa are quite right. On the other hand, the idea you and George have of doing "a ballet to end all ballet"—well, limits are precisely what I need and am looking for above all in everything I compose. The limits generate the form. I will compose a kind of "Concerto for the dance" for which George will create a matching choreographic construction.

That was that.[41] But not quite. Lincoln, ever eager, had sent a seventeenth-century dance manual by F. de Lauze to Stravinsky, who was studying it "poco a poco," carefully marking his copy as he went.[42] Importantly, the edition was a modern one, which appended scholarly notes as well as excerpts of text and music by Marin Mersenne, a priest, musician, and contemporary of Descartes, Pascal, and Galileo, whom Stravinsky admired. For Mersenne, steeped in Neoplatonist thought, music was a "beautiful part of mathematics," and dance was a human representation of the order and precision of the planets in orbit: both were governed by rational laws, in perfect accord with the natural laws of the universe. Musicians, he said, were "Christian Orpheuses" who could calm the passions and steer men to reason, virtue, and sacrifice to God.[43]

De Lauze was careful to point out that ballet was an ethical code: "the science of behavior towards others." This too was a religious idea. It was respect, manners, breeding, an aristocratic practice that would perfect bodies and elevate souls. The elegance and precision of dancing illustrated and confirmed one's proximity to king and God alike. Stravinsky seems also to have paid close attention to the book's modern scholarly speculation about the ritual and pagan origins of various baroque dances, such as ring dances with witches circling the Devil. In his score, Stravinsky would eventually combine these pagan and baroque concerns with his increasing interest in twelve-tone serial techniques, and *Agon* would include both seventeenth- and twentieth-century tonal and atonal dances.[44]

The following summer, while the company was in Los Angeles performing at the Greek Theatre, Stravinsky and Balanchine worked together at the composer's flower-filled home on Wetherly Drive. Balanchine arrived bearing Stravinsky's second $5,000 fee, and the two men sat at Stravinsky's muted, out-of-tune piano—the composer could hear better that way, he said—amid his collection of Russian icons and tchotchkes, drawings by Cocteau of Nijinsky and Diaghilev, pictures of composers he admired, and his prized collection of clocks, timepieces, and metronomes.[45] A crucifix was mounted on the wall, and the bookshelves sagged with volumes of devotional literature and religious philosophy. Stravinsky's neatly ordered desk was like a map of his mind: evenly stacked rows of red and blue pencils, rulers, scrapers, knives, pens, and other tools of his trade. As he scribbled notes from their conversation, his trusty electric pencil sharpener whirred like a lawn mower.[46] They worked hard and continued their talk over long dinners, fueled by plenty of wine and vodka, with Vera and Robert Craft. ("I make cheesecake for Balanchine," Vera recorded in her diary.)[47]

We don't know exactly what was said in these sessions, but Stravinsky's notes sketched on scraps of paper and index cards, with plenty of cross-outs and revisions, show his and Balanchine's fascination with time and precise durations—limits—as they calculated the exact number of seconds for each dance. These calculations were often accompanied by rough sketches of male and female stick figures in various configurations (Craft said Balanchine

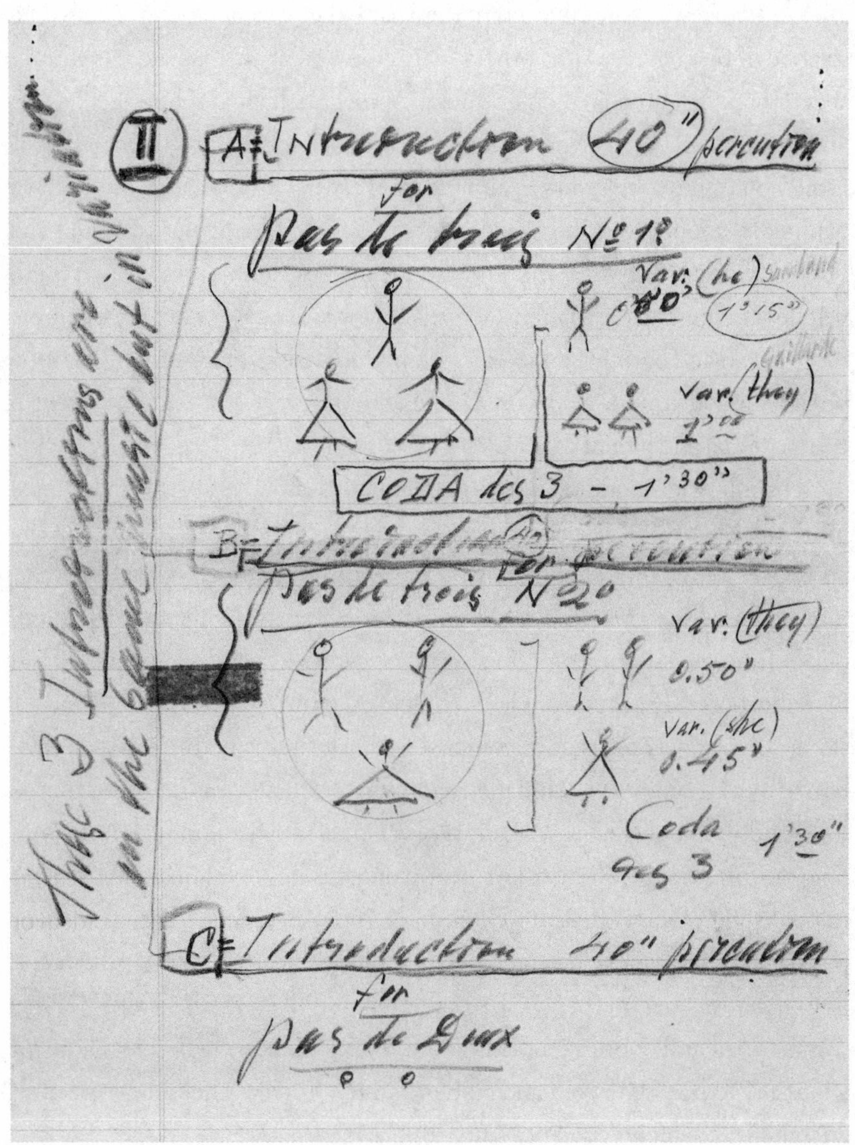

drew them)[48] with notes such as "dancer only turning her head" on this or that particular musical phrase.[49]

After Balanchine departed, Stravinsky confidently reported to Kirstein that they had successfully "established the whole structure of my new ballet. George will give you all details when he will see you back East." He added: "I have named it *Agon*—contest—Ballet for twelve dancers."[50] And across the title page, long before the score itself existed, Stravinsky neatly wrote by hand in large Greek letters: "AGON."

Agon is the Greek word for "contest" and describes the intensely competitive spirit of Greek social and political life. Stravinsky and Balanchine would have known of this idea from Nietzsche, a staple of their Russian minds and education. Nietzsche wrote admiringly of "agonist" culture and its concentration on perfecting the human body through discipline, physical training, and self-cultivation. This was not only a matter of personal vanity or gain: a competition was "won" for the city and seen as a public good. The idea was not egalitarian—it was instead to form an elite based on an aristocratic ideal of self. People don't "find" themselves, Nietzsche said, they *make* themselves by "sculpting," "pruning," "gardening" their minds and bodies. Without intense competition and a hierarchical "rank order," any society risked falling into an "abyss of a gruesome savagery."[51] It was an especially resonant idea to these Russian exiles, who had witnessed the collapse of the imperial order into the chaos of war and revolution. *Agon* would not be a literal enactment of a competition in an antique setting. It didn't have to be. Balanchine's company was an agon all by itself.[52]

They had a name, but still no finished score. Another push was needed, and they agreed that a new Stravinsky Festival, including the premiere of *Agon*, would take place in February 1956. That idea soon went by the wayside too: logistical complications and Stravinsky's weak health forced a delay, so they pushed the date out to the fall of 1957. Stravinsky, meanwhile, kept composing bits and pieces of *Agon* as he could. In June 1956 he finished the "Bransle Gai," and in August he worked on the "Bransle Double" in Venice on a pink grand piano in the darkly lit basement bar of the Bauer Grunwald Hotel. He was there waiting for the premiere of *Canticum Sacrum*, his first fully serial work. In this strange setting, he played with musical fragments from Mersenne, pushing them (with liberal use of blue and red pencils) through pitch rotations, inversion, and retrograde, and mixing tonal and atonal techniques.[53] Maybe the idea of baroque dance and musical forms "exploding" in the twentieth century was not so far off after all.

Stravinsky's stroke and Tanny's illness dealt a seemingly fatal blow to their elusive ballet. But Stravinsky eventually resumed, and in April 1957, soon after George had delivered Tanny to Warm Springs, Stravinsky finished the score. It was dense, a compressed twenty-four minutes: "I know that portions of *Agon* contain three times as much music for the same clock length as some other pieces of mine."[54] He immediately sent George a copy of the piano reduction, and when George "read" it, he was in awe. It was like the planets: "Not a single extra note, take one away and the whole thing crumbles," he told Jacques d'Amboise. That June, Balanchine and Stravinsky worked together again at Stravinsky's home in Los Angeles, and George attended the concert premiere of the music, which Stravinsky himself conducted, not accidentally, on his seventy-fifth birthday.[55] George left Los Angeles with an orchestral tape in hand, which meant he could *hear* as well as *see* the music (not yet commercially recorded).[56] That fall, with Tanny still at Warm Springs and a full roster of ballets in rehearsal at the theater, George called Diana Adams and Arthur Mitchell to the first rehearsal for *Agon*. Diana asked if

George could please start with someone else since she was busy that day. "No," he said flatly, "I must start with pas de deux."[57]

The pas de deux is by far the longest and most sustained dance in the ballet—Stravinsky clocked it at six minutes—and everything would flow into and out of its entangled forms. In the studio that day, however, it did not come easily. Balanchine tried out moves, threw things away, studied and restudied the score, and called additional rehearsals as he searched for movement that would suit their bodies and Stravinsky's tense sound. As they worked, he said very little, but he did tell Diana and Arthur, "The girl is like a doll, you're manipulating her, you must lead her. It's one long, long, long, long breath," and Mitchell has said that the key to the dance is for the woman to let the man move her, puppetlike, just as George had manipulated Tanny's inert limbs in all of those months of exercises. In an early film of the dance, Adams appears to move and contort her body almost without will. She watches Mitchell as he takes her foot, guides her leg, and holds her ankle, and she twists, turns, and supports herself on his body as if it were all happening to her. He doesn't embrace her but embraces her leg or her arabesque; she doesn't embrace him, but stands on pointe on one leg and places her other leg dangerously on his shoulder and waits.[58]

As a dancer, Diana was almost too perfect: ideally proportioned, flexible, long, elegant—strangely like Tanny but without her loose-limbed ironic wit or joie de vivre. Technically flawless but cold as ice, she moved the way she spoke: with precise schoolteacher diction and a formality that masked her anxious and frayed inner life. Arthur was her opposite: strong, outgoing, with "fire" in his movements, as Milly once put it, and it was the contrast between them that seemed to interest George. By then he had tried for years to pull his "alabaster princess," as he called her, out of herself, encouraging her to let go, do more, really dance. But she wouldn't, or couldn't. In *Agon* he finally found a way to use her maddening restraint: he made a dance *about* her remoteness and fragility. In the end it is Diana who moves us, not by conveying emotion but instead by withholding it.

In these rehearsals, George was deliberate too about the fact that Arthur was dark-black and Diana was pale-white—Southerners both, he from Harlem, she from Virginia, both via Georgia. They were working on the pas de deux during a particularly tense moment in the civil rights movement, soon after President Eisenhower had sent in the National Guard to enforce federally mandated desegregation of schools in Little Rock, Arkansas. Balanchine quietly emphasized Arthur's black on Diana's white skin: his bare arm crossed with hers, his black hand on her white body, his black body acrobatically twisted through her white limbs. Skin was like fabric—it was what they wore—and their costumes were otherwise minimal: simple black and white leotards and tights, not even a skirt for her—only a narrow waist belt. The fact of a black man and a white woman dancing together publicly, half naked and entwined, added to the tension of the dance. George said nothing; he just did it.

Another day he called Milly to rehearsal alone. There was no pianist, so George played himself and showed her how to count her counts—a five, two sevens, a five—against sixes in the music. As they began working, they quickly moved through her simple but rhythmically complicated steps, and she had to focus intensely to follow his physical math. In an hour, the dance was done.[59] We don't know exactly how it happened or what passed between George and the dancers in this and subsequent rehearsals with the rest of the cast. What we do know is that for the dancers, it was emotionally intense. They had been in Copenhagen; they had seen Balanchine disappear; they had feared for him, for Tanny, for the company, and for themselves. Now, after nearly a year on their own, he was back. No one said anything—they just got to work—but they all knew, and he knew they knew, that *Agon* was different from the other ballets they were busily producing that season. Balanchine was more focused, more intense, more excited than they had ever seen him.[60]

He didn't explain anything: the dancers didn't know why the dance was called *Agon*, had no idea of its genesis, and had never seen or heard the score; it was all a blank—they were all a blank, which is what George preferred. Often, he knew exactly what he wanted and showed them the steps, counting as he went; precision-trained, they accurately reproduced the movements immediately. Other times, he didn't exactly know: "Maybe we try . . . ," and the rest was timing, rhythm, imitation, touch, a quiet joke here or there, an occasional "BAM!" or "POW!" or "NOW!" for musical emphasis. When he flicked his index finger, gesturing delightedly, "That's right" or "You see," they knew they had it—whatever "it" was—and they scrambled to commit the steps to memory in their bodies. There was no other record. He depended on them to know it.[61] Some of them found the movement strange—"He's up there doing that weird stuff again," one dancer commented—but most were out there with him on the edge.[62]

They worked quickly, and by early November the ballet was almost complete. George nervously asked Stravinsky to come to rehearsals. He wasn't sure about his approach, he told Davidova, and wanted Stravinsky's eye. Having the composer there was for George like being in the presence of a god. He bowed, doted, and acquiesced, and photos of these extraordinary rehearsals show his bright and animated state. The toll of the past year was evident too, in his furrowed face and receding hairline—bald spot artfully covered at the back—and in his bony shoulders slumped over his barrel chest. If he hadn't been so lively, he might even have appeared disheveled in his casual knit shirt, loose-fitting trousers rolled up at the bottom, and feet indecorously stuffed into rumpled socks and scuffed dance shoes. Stravinsky, by contrast, was dapper in a woolen suit with vest and tie, sturdy loafers, and dark glasses pushed up over his forehead to better study the score.[63]

In these precious rehearsals, the two men were so engrossed in their work that they barely seemed to notice the observers sitting on the bench across the mirror at the front of the room: Davidova primly poised in Dior and her requisite string of pearls; Bernard Taper, a journalist writing a profile for *The New Yorker*; Martha Swope, a young photographer from Texas who had studied at SAB (Jerry had hired her for *West Side Story* and Lincoln called her to say "Be in the studio tomorrow morning," without mentioning what for);[64] Robert Craft; and Eddie, Lincoln, and a few others slipping in and out. The room was electric—intense but also lit with George's high spirits. Watching dancers can be like watching animal life, and George was everywhere, moving deftly from piano to bench to partnering, showing, stepping back to see, and threading his way into and through the dance. The dancers were everywhere too, dancing and trying out steps, but also sprawled on the floors, crouched under the piano, hanging on the barres, or hunched on the bench, intently watching. Lots was done, very little was said.

The concentration required of them all was mind-bending. One afternoon, faced with the unfamiliar exigencies of Stravinsky's new score, Kopeikine (hampered too by his vain refusal to wear eyeglasses) nervously admitted, "I'm terribly sorry. There are parts of this music I don't understand," to which Stravinsky responded, "It's perfectly all right. I don't understand them either!" George and Stravinsky plotted and gesticulated, bent over the score, and counted the music, with George snapping his fingers, hitting his leg, signaling the dancers, and lunging with outstretched arm, "Now!" The dancers strained to absorb the strange and irregular counts. In this new Stravinsky world, there were no standard waltzes or marches, and they found themselves instead in a forest of shifting fives, sevens, nines, and twelves; bewildered, some invented their own counts (Balanchine later cautioned: a five and a seven are not the same as a twelve).

Stravinsky had suggestions. Could the boys swing their arms more precisely so as not to appear lazy? Yes. Could Milly move faster in her solo? She did. Faster still? She did. Faster still? Barely, and they set the tempo there. Balanchine showed the composer what he had come up with to bridge the move in the score from tonality to atonality. He had the dancer Barbara Millberg perform sharp, angular arm gestures in silence—a "liminal zone," as she thought of it, before the music "corkscrewed into new machine-age techniques." Stravinsky didn't like it. As the dancers stood by, he and Balanchine argued passionately in Russian over this too-literal moment in the dance. In the end, George cut it entirely.[65] There were other things Stravinsky didn't like. He thought, for example, that there should be costumes because he found the idea of "dancing in practice kit" quaint and not very convincing.[66] On this, George held firm.

These were halcyon days, and we can only imagine how George felt when Stravinsky, mindful of his health and miffed that Lincoln could not afford his high conducting fee, decided to return to Los Angeles just two weeks before the opening of *Agon*.[67] Ruthless about money, Stravinsky could be coldly transactional and did not seem to realize (or perhaps he knew all too well) that George had made a ballet that would outshine him. *Agon* was more than a dance "to" Stravinsky's music. George's ballet was a musical composition unto itself—a composition that at times competed, agon-style, with Stravinsky's own score, which was stronger and more complete with the dances than it was alone. The son was about to join if not surpass the father, and Stravinsky, who never liked to be upstaged, stayed home and instinctively sent a telegram instead.[68]

Events crowded in. On November 21, the company premiered *Square Dance,* to music by Vivaldi and Corelli, in which Balanchine "exploded" these seventeenth- and eighteenth-century musical forms too—this time with live fiddlers and a veteran square-dance caller from North Carolina presiding on stage ("You just do like you do," Balanchine told the nervous caller). It was fun and technically demanding, featuring the company's ace, Pat Wilde, in a bravura display: "Now make your feet go wickety whack! / Hurry up, girls, 'cause here comes Pat!"[69] Two days later, on November 23, Tanny came home, accompanied by Edith, and George raced back and forth from the theater to help care for her. She still could not dress herself, manage doors, get into or out of chairs or cars, and she arrived with an array of Rusk-style apparatuses: wheelchair, corset, crutches, hand splints, feeders, lapboard, sliding board, toilet blocks.[70] She was there just in time. The November 27 gala premiere of *Agon* was for her, although it is not clear that she came: it was a benefit performance for the March of Dimes.[71] The official opening followed on December 1.

That night everyone was nervous and on edge. The dancers had barely heard the music with a full orchestra. Everything sounded different than it had in the piano rehearsals, and one dancer recalled her panic: "Oh my God, where are my counts?" They had to concentrate and listen very, very hard. Their eyes were trained on Barzin, who conducted and was their only lifeline. Meanwhile, the musicians were concentrating and listening hard too: Barzin was not a Stravinsky expert, and the orchestra had their own troubles with the irregular tempos and complicated demands of the new score.[72] Add to this the blindingly bright lights hitting the dancers at eye level from the wings, as they hissed competing versions of the counts (Diana and Milly led two opposing factions) and tried to keep up and stay together, and it is no wonder many recall feeling unnervingly exposed and alone on the empty stage that night with no plot, no costumes, only those elusive counts to hold on to. One dancer later said it was like being on the high peak of a mountain or balancing on a platform suspended in light.[73]

The curtain rose in silence. The stage was empty except for four men with their backs to the audience standing across the rear. They were dressed in simple white T-shirts, black tights, and white ballet shoes, and they were doing nothing. Just standing. There was no set, no decor, no theatrical dressing of any kind—only space, light, and a blue cyclorama stretched behind them like the sky. Nameless, faceless, nothing but four men's blank backs and silence—a shocking start.

Then they swiveled in unison to face the audience. Now it was not silent anymore: this first move came on a musical rest, and although no one heard it, the beat was there, like the first beat of the universe. The men caught it, took life, and began to move. They bent their knees, walking, walking, counting paces, in diagonals, marking time, little catch steps, walking, walking, in twos and fours, until walking became dancing and they were off. From this moment until the ballet's end—precisely twenty-four minutes later—there was no respite: the pulse that had begun in silence seemed unrelenting, and the four men were joined by eight women in black leotards, flesh tights and toe shoes, hair pulled tightly back, almost nude.

Agon was everything Balanchine and Stravinsky had planned: twelve bodies in propulsive motion to a suite of dances patterned on seventeenth-century dance and musical forms, "exploded" in the twentieth century with twelve-tone musical techniques. It was elegant, refined, gay; dissonant, broken, and jarring. It was about math: there were four parts, twelve sections, and dances for two, three, four, eight, twelve dancers that accumulated with astonishing precision as dancers tore across the stage, bending, contorting, toe shoes digging, pulling, striking their way through intricate footwork, legs flying, switchbacks, acrobatic extensions, gracious bows, physical and musical wit, and always on time, in time—the pulse, the pulse.[74]

The dancers moved like the decor—plain, direct, exposed, calm-faced, no acting. They looked front, bodies front, eyes front—even positions in contrapposto or with a lilting épaulement did not seem lilting but appeared direct and straightforward. It was the position of an icon, and the conventions of a proscenium stage as a real—or surreal—space grounding a human subject in the material stuff of living had been jettisoned in favor of the only approximation of infinity we know: light.

The original lighting was by Nananne Porcher, closely supervised by Balanchine, and built around Jean Rosenthal's ideas of "light all around": cold blue light pouring in from all directions—no follow spots, take out the gels, burn the brights—and not just from the footlights but from the side wings too. The dancers flinched at the "shin-busters"—blaring lights placed in the middle of a wing (where the dancers rammed into them with their shins while exiting the stage).[75] Under this kind of light, they appeared translucent, nothing hidden. The idea—far more radical than any set design—was of a stage without shadows or dim corners so that every curve, line, bone, ligament of the body would be X-ray visible.[76] It was a paradoxical combination of unreal and hyperreal, a kind of ghostly or angelic muscularity, accentuating their highly trained and not-quite-human bodies. The dancers' simple leotards and tights similarly recalled at once an idealized classical nude and a concrete contemporary reference: work clothes, a uniform—black and white, impersonal and anonymous. Wearing them made the dancers feel that way too: efficient, straightforward, not "playing" a character, just dancing.

The movement vocabulary of *Agon* was basic, almost pedestrian at times: walking, small steps, the legs—turn in and turn out—showing the human body from every angle, and building to a complicated series of intricate movements recalling baroque steps but rarely strictly classical in form. The dances were elemental, more about the mechanics of the body than about steps, beauty, or line. There was visible effort, and the dancers in early films of the ballet could often barely do what was asked of them, which meant audiences were with them in the raw moment of physical exertion, as they calculated and improvised their way into and out of a step as if for the first time—itself a kind of intimacy. They were in nearly every possible way exposed.

Who are these twelve dancers? Like the twelve tones in the music, they are an ensemble of equals, and the traditional hierarchies of ballet no longer exist. Soon after the ballet begins, there is a kind of family portrait: they are all there, posed as in a family or clan gathering or a painting of the twelve disciples. This is our group, and their dances break out from here and pile up, like episodes stacked one on top of another. Even Arthur and Diana are not "stars" but part of the ensemble and the clock-ticking order of the ballet. Moreover, the three interludes, as Stravinsky noted, repeat the same music "but in variation," which keeps the dancers oriented but also pulls them into a ritual repetition, like an event compulsively replayed with new people; with a bow or final gesture, a dance seems over and gone—but in fact we are not done with it yet.

Agon is a woman's world. The four men open and close the performance and have the first and last breath, but the eight women dominate: they are confident, even aggressive, and with the notable exception of the pas de deux, barely in need of male support. Their music is often rivetingly chromatic, recalling *Le Sacre du Printemps*, and they are the source of the ballet's primal energy and self-assurance and of its humble grace. They are on pointe, but their toe shoes are not used to emphasize the ethereal and are instead made to dart into the floor, propel the body, mark time, extend the leg not up but down into the ground, weight slung low, or precariously suspended. They are instruments of mathematical precision, of logic and calculation, not of emotion or feeling.

The shoes, like the costumes and light, add to the abstract, intellectual atmosphere of this dance "controlled by an electronic brain," as Balanchine liked to put it.[77] Even when the woman in the pas de deux, for example, finds herself on one leg in arabesque on pointe, she is not gracefully posed but fighting to stay up, gripping her partner's hand, arm quivering with effort as he flips onto his back on the floor, barely within her reach. The dime-sized tip of her pointe shoe, the only part of her body touching the ground, is not raising her to the heavens but daring her to balance here on earth.

Events unfold. There is no "story" or traditional narrative flow. Instead, everything feels compressed and discrete, brick on brick, mass on mass, like a kind of ballet montage. The only story is the pulse—time—that pushes irretrievably on and keeps the dancers—and us—in its grip. We hang on every beat, and the experience is intense, engrossing, but also joyful and fun, because it is fun to be on time and in time—to divide, count, multiply, keep up. When on opening night Melissa Hayden coolly resolved the competing rhythms in her riveting dance, the audience, Denby reported, "caught the acute edge of risk" and broke into a spontaneous "roar" of applause.[78] The bravura was never the show-off kind, and in a nod to the seventeenth century, the dancers were impeccably behaved: they bowed and gestured gracefully even as they sped through the intricate traffic patterns and involved physicality of the dances.

Nowhere in *Agon* is Balanchine's strange and unhinged classicism more fully explored than in the pas de deux for Diana and Arthur, which turned traditional balletic conventions inside out. There was no woman on a pedestal, no romance or courtship, no sentimental display; this dance was a black and white abstraction, but also intimate, internal, between them. The audience was almost spying, like George in his hidden first-wing post. The dance began in silence as Diana and Arthur entered and stood at the far back corner of the stage facing the audience. When the music sounded, they raced out across the space on a diagonal. This was no polite encounter. It was a chase: her first, him close behind, sweeping legs, double turn (her), double turn (him) in hot pursuit until she dove forward and whipped her leg backward, catching him around his head and they stopped. In this striking and unstable position, time seemed for a moment to suspend.

They gathered themselves with small classical steps and a return to manners, holding hands, in unison. Then they faced each other close—too close—body to body, face to face, but quickly flipped back-to-back, and she leaned, spiderlike, almost crawling on his spine. And so they continued: back-to-back, never really looking at each other, limbs and bodies interlacing with effort—leaning, pressing, and sustaining their mutual dependence in uneasy and precariously counterbalanced partnering. The music was strictly measured but irregular, with atonal gestures, and as Arthur and Diana moved through it, in "one long, long, long breath," they seemed to exist out of time—unhinged from Stravinsky's already irregular beat.[79] It is the only dance in the ballet that was not counted. There was always the fact of sex in the movements, which were nonetheless performed matter-of-factly—his hand through her crotch, his head diving between her legs, her legs in the air split wide. By the end he was on his knee to her, gazing up—a courtly pose, almost, but instead of his taking her hand, they circled their arms, each in their own orbit, without finding their way to any possible embrace. On the last beat—or the beat George designated the last beat, which was not Stravinsky's last beat at all—her arm fell heavily on his head as they both slumped, her over him. Defeated.

As they all reached the end of the ballet, which returned to the opening music, the stage cleared except for the four men who had started the festivities. These men made their way upstage with sweeping arm gestures and took their places at the back across the blue light, facing the audience, recalling the opening. Suddenly, they abruptly turned from the audience and froze in profile. The music stopped. But there is a final rest in the score—and in its silence, they swiveled to their original pose, backs to the audience.[80] Their faces disappeared. The pulse stopped. They stopped. It was over, and the curtain fell.

The exhausted dancers listened from behind the fallen curtain, unsure of how this difficult new work would be received. They were shocked when the audience rose to a spontaneous ovation, with shouting, whistling, and curtain calls, until finally Balanchine walked from his first-wing post to center stage and bowed humbly before slipping away again. Stravinsky received an avalanche of excited cables from friends, and his son Soulima reported the success: "Have no words telling my enthusiasm. . . . Your music phenomenal Balanchine dances superb enormous success."[81] Lincoln wrote to the composer saying it had been "the most thrilling evening of my life."[82] Marcel Duchamp said it felt like the opening night of *Le Sacre du Printemps* in 1913, almost half a century before, and the poet Frank O'Hara, a regular at the ballet, said *Agon* was as life changing as Picasso's *Guernica*.[83]

Agon was a dance about dancing, and nothing else. "On the surface it is quite insane," the critic John Martin wrote the next morning, "but it has an irrefutable logic of its own, and it is done with a supreme dignity that is not to be denied."[84] Martin had been slow to recognize Balanchine's talent (George and Betty called him Frankenstein),[85] but this time he was overcome. He noted too that *Apollo*, performed in the same program, had been similarly stripped: no sets, no costumes, just dancers in practice clothes. "Such a program makes us realize that an entirely new era of the ballet has been evolved before our eyes. . . . And that must come, even to the most inveterate of us, as something of a revelation."[86] Other critics had the same deer-in-the-headlights feeling, but if no one quite knew what to make of this "brainy" new dance bristling with "atomic" energy, they at least agreed on the momentousness of the occasion. Here, finally, was a dance that, like a rose, had no "why." It simply existed. "We're like flowers," Balanchine said, "a flower doesn't tell you a story. It's in itself a beautiful thing."[87] *Agon,* far from being difficult and inaccessible, was a surprise box-office hit, and Lincoln scrambled to add performances. Stravinsky gave George the greatest compliment he knew how to give: exclusive rights to perform and stage his ballet.[88]

Agon, George said with a hint of pride, was the product of poverty. Poverty was its own artistic limit, and being too poor to afford fancy sets and costumes had forced him to find ways to make his dances stand alone. He had staged *Barocco* in practice clothes when Eugene Berman moodily pulled his sets and costumes in 1945, and by 1951 no one (except maybe Lincoln) wanted them back. George had taken large scissors to the clunky clothing for *The Four Temperaments* in 1946, and by 1951 that ballet too was officially restaged in black and white uniform. *Ivesiana* in 1954 was also danced in practice clothes, and that same year the company was so poor that *Western Symphony,* later extravagantly attired, premiered with no sets and the dancers clothed in makeshift shirts, frontier pants, and cowboy string ties for the men, with practice wear for the women. As early as 1954, Balanchine had imagined that *Apollo* "done with stark simplicity for Jacques d'Amboise . . . will be a revelation,"[89] and in 1957 d'Amboise danced the role bare-chested in simple black practice clothes—with no golden Louis XIV curls. He wanted to look *his* way, like a kid from New York, black hair slicked back Elvis-style, and Balanchine approved. Even *Square Dance* (1957) had plain dress.

In the program notes, Balanchine talked about *Agon* in all his usual ways.[90] He was a cook, he said, inventing new dishes using Stravinsky's "tasty, eatable, digestible and memorable" music. Or a carpenter building cabinets—in the case of *Agon,* he admitted, a complicated cabinet more like "an IBM electronic computer . . . a machine, but a machine that thinks"—a reference to the recently announced invention of one of the most impressive early computers, the IBM 305 RAMAC "electronic brain."[91] But, sounding a familiar theme, he added: "The mind is also involved. Also morality, the manners and behavior of people, of dancers, of the audience," which was a way of saying that everything was involved. With this sly comment, he was back at de Lauze and "the science of behavior towards others" and also at Nietzsche and the pruning and sculpting of bodies and the ways that Greek festivals and the Orphic power of music and dance might make a new and better kind of person and society. George wasn't worried about Nietzsche's death of God; for him, the problem was the murder of God by the Communist state and the lost path of the spirit.[92] Even America, besotted in its own way with material things, he found spiritually lacking; a favorite film was the 1956 Cold War sci-fi *Invasion of the Body Snatchers*, about a small population duplicated by aliens with no emotion. His job (as he had put it to President Eisenhower) was to feed the languishing spiritual soul of the nation. Love as a work of art was one thing; *Agon* was life as a work of art—and ballet as service to God. Christ too was a carpenter.

"Sure," George said casually to an interviewer, "you could say [*Agon*] is a competition, or a circus, you buy your tickets and come to see something lively and gay—it is gay."[93] And it was gay—gay in the spirit of *The Gay Science*, Nietzsche's book written after his own health crisis and retreat to his secluded and beloved "rescue-place" at Sils Maria in the Alps. He was reading Spinoza and the American mystic Ralph Waldo Emerson. What "we convalescents" need, Nietzsche later wrote, is not "the theatrical scream of passion . . . the whole romantic uproar and tumult"; what we need instead is "a mocking, light, fleeting, divinely untroubled, divinely artificial art that, like a bright flame, blazes into an unclouded sky." What we need is the minstrel and the knight, "free spirits" unconstrained by a conformist "herd" mentality; what we need, he said, drawing on a Provençal idea, is a "gay science."[94]

The science of *Agon* came from technique and math, but it also came from secrets: magical numbers, letters, and names tucked like talismans into the fabric of the dance like Karinska's medallions sewn into the hems of costumes. The critic Arlene Croce saw the trick of twelve recurring like an incantation, a sign of the mathematical beauty of music and dance: the twelve dancers and twelve notes of the atonal scale; the twelve Milly counted and scribbled in her notes composed of five, seven, seven, five against phrases of six—all twelves, which finally resolved on . . . the twelfth measure.[95] Taken further, there was the twelve of the five and seven of 1957, the twelve of Stravinsky's seventy-fifth birthday and the music's orchestral premiere, the twelve hours of day and night, the twelve gods of Olympus, the twelve hours of Adam's first day, the twelve apostles, and *The Twelve* of Blok's poem about the apostles that stood at the beginning of Balanchine's career.[96] *Agon* "starts with twelve dancers," Balanchine reiterated, "and then all the ways it can be divided, one and two, four and four, and so forth. . . . I think we found every possible division of twelve."[97] Twelve was a binary too: like the new computer science of the "machine that thinks" and like the binaries of black/white, male/female, and tonal/atonal that structured the dance. It was also a sign of God's universe, given in measure and number and weight.

The Greek letters *AGON* that Stravinsky inscribed so carefully across his score mattered too. Greek was the language of the Orthodox Bible, and although the word had a pagan context, it also contained the alpha and omega, the first and last letters of the Greek alphabet, which John spoke of in the book of Revelation, "Saying, I am Alpha and Omega, the first and the last: and, What thou seest, write in a book, and send it unto the seven churches which are in Asia."[98] You could find the alpha and omega inscribed in Catholic painting, and the alpha was prized too among mystical thinkers drawing on the Kabbalah who saw in it, like the Hebrew aleph, the source of all sound, holding within its open-throated vault all other letters and sounds and the whole of human discourse.[99] *Agon*'s steps were similarly elemental. Stand, swivel, walk presented a whole new (and very old) alphabet of dance that held within it the whole of the body's physical discourse. These were the basic steps—the elements—that George had been working on in classes with his dancers for all those years.

In George's playful and esoteric mind, even names were a clue: Diana, the Roman goddess of the hunt and of chastity, was the voluptuous divinity who had stunned the mortal Actaeon when he chanced upon her bathing; and Diana herself could be found marveling at the godlike beauty of Endymion. To the Greeks, Diana was Artemis—Apollo's twin sister, who fell with him from the womb of Leto. In his own dance of *Apollo*, George had left Artemis out, but now, in *Agon*, he had found her: no one was more coolly Apollonian than Diana Adams. Entangling names further still, George loved it that Diana was from her (not his) Georgia, and continuing the game, Diana would later name her only daughter—rumored (incorrectly) to be George's—Georgiana. As for her last name: "Adams" made Diana like Adam's Eve, and she and Arthur Mitchell—black and white—were at once an American spectacle and a kind of primal couple, undressed, presocial, existing in the liminal light before sin and civilization.

In this sense, *Agon* was less a stripping away than a derobing. Balanchine had removed the garments of narrative to expose the secret underneath: the nut inside the shell, the orange peeled, the body under the cloak. It was a ballet with no worldly context, only light, the measure of Stravinsky's time, and the beautiful bodies of Balanchine's dancers. These bodies were by then so highly trained and sculpted as to appear not-quite-human. The women in particular, with their pinhead look, hair fastened tightly back and severe black and white uniforms and flat movements, were time people, icons or instruments of the music that enlivened their spirits. Tanny had been the first such creature, and these dancers, whatever their individual shapes, had been trained to her long and flexible likeness. *Agon* was not a tribute to her, but it was in her image. The ballet was a testimony too, and the dancers could be seen as black and white signs of themselves on the stage, like ink on a page. They encompassed the beginning and the end of time, the first beat and the last swivel, the face of man into the world and away from it. Only the women were eternal.

Finally, if we think about *Apollo*, *Orpheus*, and *Agon* as a trilogy, as George and Lincoln certainly did, we are faced with a revealing artistic arc. *Apollo* was clarity and order. For Stravinsky and Balanchine, each for their own reasons, it had been part of a turn away from Russia, and the Scythian and peasant worlds of *Le Sacre du Printemps* and *Les Noces*, and toward Malevich, or a blank slate, and a more neoclassical tonality and calm. *Orpheus*, with its wild furies and tragic love story, was more Dionysian—even though Orpheus was himself an Apollonian character who used the lyre to tame passions. *Agon* was both. It had the Dionysian pulse, the dissonance, the static but driving ritual force, the physical brinksmanship, the gymnastic extremes, the sex, the aggression, and blocks of bodies. But musically and visually all of this was delivered with restraint and cold assurance, wit, irony, and lots of charm. So the trilogy was less a triptych than a circling back to a Russia that didn't exist—probably never had. *Agon* returned to the propulsive energy and "risk" of

Sacre, but with none of the excess. It was spare, disciplined, "lean," as Balanchine liked to say, and "without fat."[100]

On a more personal level, *Agon* revealed Balanchine's innermost ambition. It came from the thing he had come to care about most: service. Service to music, to women, to dancers, to Tanny, and to God—wasn't it all the same thing? Every dance has many authors, and George never stopped saying that without his dancers he would have no dances. It was they who absorbed his pulse and timing, his gestures and images, his dance. He moved *through* them. In these moments, he had no individuality, no "man-ness," no self: all cloud, no trousers. And those months and years of near-impossible ballet classes had broken his dancers of excess—they were trained to execute steps as accurately and precisely as possible, nothing more. Who had time to do anything in *Agon* but count to stay alive? Which does not mean their individuality was erased. To the contrary, George built the dances around who they were. He just didn't want them to *add* anything extra to who they were, no sauce, no affectation, no drama, no acting, no interpretation. On stage that night, he resolved the paradox. They were at once themselves and a company of selfless dancers in service to *Agon*. Even a ballet could be an emanation of God. It was a moment: Balanchine had become Balanchine.

Which is why it was so shocking that as the curtain fell, even before it fell, George was filled with an urgent desire to rid himself of them all and start over again. It was an old and cruel reflex: when had he not started over, without them or anyone? Being settled—even being himself—was anathema, and faced with success, the company he had made suddenly felt like a threat. Sleepwalking, zombies, home, deadening bourgeois life—byt—don't settle, keep moving, run, run, run. Having finally arrived at *Agon*, he returned instinctively, with a touch of violence even, to the task of gardening—this time to the ruthless job of weeding them out. In the months to come, he would gradually ignore, sideline, discourage, and neglect the dancers who no longer interested him or could be replaced with a whole new generation—younger, stronger, and more beautiful. The old guard would go—of their own accord, discouraged and unloved, or with a quiet word from Betty, "Mr. Balanchine does not wish to encourage you," or with a little pink slip cruelly wedged into their weekly envelope of cash pay, no comment necessary.[101] Lincoln called it Balanchine's "purge."[102]

The question of *Agon* was the question of ballet itself. What is this thing that banishes fear and pain and yet is itself based on fear and pain; that admits no bestiality and yet is itself bestial or at least animalistic; that hangs its harmonious bodies like angels in blue light but screams flesh and blood; that coldly strips the body of ornament and display, fabric and costumes, removing it once and for all from the clothed civility of society? That insists that the deed—the dance—is greater than the word and that a dance has no past, only a fleeting present.[103] You will not glimpse these creatures in all the history of art. Who are these strangely voluptuous and depleted figures, seemingly bent on weight and their own physical and erotic presence but also on disappearance into the nothingness of spirit and air? *Agon* was one answer.

Chapter 19

COLD WAR

By 1962 the State Department wanted Balanchine to take his American company and his American dances, even the antinomian *Agon*, on a Cold War tour in service of his adoptive country. This time the destination would not be Western Europe. They were asking him to cross the Iron Curtain to perform in the place he hated and dreaded most, the USSR. He didn't want to go, and the fact that Stalin had died in 1953 and Khrushchev's "thaw" was by then well under way had done nothing to allay his feelings of anger and fear toward his ruined homeland. He had already turned down invitations in 1956 and 1957; in 1960 he inched closer by securing a visa, but still didn't go. This time he finally gave way, but the dread did not. Even the thought of setting foot on Soviet soil made him feel sick. What if they wouldn't let him leave?[1]

Cultural exchange had by then become an arm of foreign policy, and as contact between the superpowers increased, so did competitive tensions. There were plenty of chits on both sides. The announcement in 1956 of the IBM 305 RAMAC computer, which Balanchine had referenced with *Agon*, was part of the race to prove the industrial, military, and cultural superiority of capitalism over its Communist rivals. In 1957 the Soviets successfully launched Sputnik, taking a firm lead in space. The U.S. government created NASA. And in 1959 American industry was set on display for some three million Russians at the American National Exhibition in Moscow. In a magnificent fifty-thousand-square-foot pavilion, Soviet citizens surveyed American food, clothing, toys, newspapers, hi-fi systems, color TVs, not to mention the famous IBM computer (which charmingly obliged by answering questions in Russian). A model kitchen outfitted with the latest American gadgets spurred the famous "Kitchen Debate" between Nixon and Khrushchev, as a barbed exchange over refrigerators quickly escalated into a tense debate over America's presence in Berlin.

Music and dance were a vital competitive arena, and by the time Balanchine entered it, the way had been paved. As early as 1955, after years of jammed airways, Voice of America had successfully launched *Music USA* to broadcast jazz and popular music to Soviet youth. An industry grew up around the discovery that medical X-ray film could conduct sound, and "recordings on bones" or "X-ray editions" of popular albums circulated widely among *statniki*, or States-lovers, besotted with Western fashion, music, and dance. In this environment, dances such as the twist became coveted signs of growing political and sexual freedoms, and in the late 1950s, Benny Goodman, Woody Herman, and Duke Ellington played the USSR. American classical music was represented with tours of *Porgy and Bess* in 1956, followed by symphony orchestras from Boston, San Francisco, and New York, including appearances by Isaac Stern and Leonard Bernstein. The Russians sent David Oistrakh and Mstislav Rostropovich in return, and in 1958 the Texan Van Cliburn even won the International Tchaikovsky Competition in Moscow.

When Moscow's Bolshoi Ballet arrived in New York for the first time ever in 1959, following a momentous 1956 visit to London, performances sold out in advance and the queue for standing room started thirty-nine hours before the opening night at the old Metropolitan Opera House. That evening the theater was packed, with more than two hundred people crowded around the sides and American and Soviet flags draped like banners from the boxes. The orchestra performed the national anthems of both countries before the ballet began, and although reviews were mixed, Khrushchev, who was in America that year for the first time too, was delighted with the audience enthusiasm and cooed to the press: "Which country has the best ballet? Yours? You do not even have a permanent opera and ballet theater. Your theater thrives on what is given them by rich people. In our country it is the state that gives it money. And the best ballet is in the Soviet Union."[2]

Balanchine had worked with Leonid Lavrovsky, the Bolshoi's artistic director, back in Petrograd in the early 1920s, but since then Lavrovsky had become part of the "retardative and uncreative" side of dance in the USSR, what Balanchine later called "Soviet garbage."[3] When the two former friends were reunited at a reception at City Center, they exchanged veiled insults in Russian while feigning niceties before a throng of journalists and flashing cameras.[4] The Bolshoi dancers were not much interested in Balanchine either—they flocked instead to Robbins's *West Side Story*, which had just opened on Broadway. Watching the Russians perform nonetheless had its effect, and the NYCB dancers noticed that class with Balanchine got longer and harder, with a new emphasis on the upper body and the details of hands and fingers, a Russian specialty. Still, when Khrushchev made a scene at the United Nations and banged his shoe on the table, Balanchine angrily railed to the company about the coarse language and vulgarity. Anything Communist was hard for him to stomach, so in 1960 Ballet Theatre became the first U.S. ballet company to tour the USSR.[5]

In May of that year, relations between the superpowers deteriorated dramatically. The American pilot Gary Powers's U-2 spy plane was shot down over Soviet airspace, and the infuriated Soviets walked out of the Paris summit. In November, John F. Kennedy won the presidential election on a strong anti-Communist platform. Fidel Castro's regime in Cuba was an immediate concern, and in April 1961, Kennedy launched the disastrous and humiliating Bay of Pigs invasion. That same month the Soviet astronaut Yuri Gagarin became the first man in space, and escalating tensions further, in June, the Kirov Ballet—Balanchine's old Mariinsky alma mater, renamed by Stalin after his murdered colleague Sergei Kirov—toured the West and Rudolf Nureyev, the company's greatest star, defected at Le Bourget Airport in Paris. His dramatic struggle with KGB operatives as he threw himself into the arms of the French authorities and begged for asylum made banner headlines across Europe and America and was a serious blow to Soviet prestige. In June the Vienna summit between Khrushchev and Kennedy ended in a tense deadlock, and in August the Soviets began building the Berlin Wall, cautiously starting with barbed wire but quickly moving to concrete.

In this worsening political environment, cultural exchange became all the more important, and close relations between the Kennedys and the NYCB made the company a natural ally. Kirstein attended Jack's inauguration, and Balanchine was among the first guests invited to the White House to visit with Jackie. They had tea (he asked for scotch instead), and Jackie became an enthusiastic supporter, lending Kennedy glamour and sheen to the NYCB. Balanchine pressed his case in a follow-up letter, imploring her to be a guardian of art: "I mean to distinguish between material things and things of the spirit—art, beauty. . . . Man takes care of the material things and woman takes care of the soul. Woman is the world and man lives in it." He hoped she would be not only "the First Lady" but "the First Woman," and would unite "the soul of the United States." He reiterated the point in a luncheon address at the Woman's National Democratic Club in Washington, D.C., titled "If I Were President," in which he said that he hoped Mrs. Kennedy could reach children and bring out their "inner nobility" and "safeguard them from the cynicism of utilitarianism." He later gave a TV interview with a wifelike Diana Adams by his side, hair pinned neatly under a pillbox hat, in which he told a bewildered journalist that he hoped the First Lady would be "America's Faerie Queene," referring to Edmund Spenser's sixteenth-century courtly poem.[6]

As a sign of his ongoing enthusiasm, Balanchine accepted the president's invitation to serve on the advisory committee for a new National Cultural Center to compete with the Soviets in the cultural Cold War (renamed the Kennedy Center after Kennedy's assassination).[7] Meanwhile, Kirstein, with Baum, was involved with a group of prominent New York leaders—including his old friend Nelson Rockefeller, Nelson's brother John D. Rockefeller III, and the city's "master builder" Robert Moses—in planning a new arts center in midtown Manhattan. Slated to be the largest in the world, Lincoln Center for the Performing Arts was another Cold War project, modeled on the great opera houses of Europe and Russia, and the NYCB would become a constituent member. Balanchine and Kirstein were working too with "Nelson

Rocks," as Lincoln sometimes called him, and another Lincoln Center colleague, Dick Leach, to plan a new performing arts center in Saratoga Springs, New York.[8] They envisioned it as a European arts festival—theater, music, dance, film—and a summer home for the NYCB. Balanchine hoped it would be New York's Salzburg Festival, like the one cofounded in 1920 by his old colleague Max Reinhardt.

Adding to the momentum, that same year the Ford Foundation awarded Balanchine and his colleagues the first of several transformative grants, with an eye to establishing a national training system in dance. They sent George on the road to survey the state of ballet in America. W. McNeil "Mac" Lowry, Ford's director of programming in the humanities and the arts, was a Balanchine convert. Kansas-born, Mac Lowry had served in the navy during World War II and worked as a journalist before he arrived in New York and got a job at Ford in 1953. He became a regular at City Center, knew Lincoln, and immediately targeted Balanchine as a great artist who could help Ford foster dance in America. For Lincoln and George, it was another Cold War project, and a chance to finally fulfill their original goal of a national ballet company. Lincoln put it this way in a note on the 1959 grant proposal:

> In Russia . . . 22 national ballet and opera companies feed into the two great companies of Leningrad and Moscow. There the status of dancer, from pupil to performer, is assured; money is no problem. . . . The national necessity for the performing artist is equated with the need for scientists, soldiers and farmers. Without this necessity acknowledged there can be no national policy or program worthy of the name.[9]

In the coming months, Balanchine personally traveled to ballet schools across the country—he visited eleven schools in Buffalo, New York, alone—and sent teams of dancers, along with Eugenie Ouroussow and Betty Cage, to scout talent and set up scholarships and teacher training that would feed back into SAB and the NYCB. He lectured and taught widely, and in 1961 he personally led a series of free two-week summer seminars at SAB on ballet technique for teachers from dance schools across the country. Spreading his reach even further, he offered his ballets *gratuit* to regional companies—"The earth gives free what plants need to grow"—and the company gave free performances for children in New York.[10]

It was all part of an ambitious plan for the future, eventually set forth in a white paper to Ford in hope of further funding. This extraordinary document, assembled by a Ballet Society committee that included Balanchine, Kirstein, Ouroussow, and Cage, began with a frank assessment of the culturally impoverished American landscape. Many communities across the country, the committee observed, had plenty of ballet, but most of it was depressingly amateur. These communities "play at ballet" just the way children "play house," and what they are doing is "not ballet at all" but instead a "clumsy and ignorant parody." It would take a nationwide professional program, they argued, administered by Ballet Society and led by Balanchine, to develop a national academy and a national company. The document ended with a plea for the "Utopia" they envisioned:

> A program of assistance must provide an atmosphere in which we can breathe. Ballet is not an industry in which you can measure so many pounds of raw material and count on obtaining so many ounces of finished product. It is more comparable to friendship, religion, or the trust an animal has for the person who feeds him. We must be friends and we must help those who want us to help them. We must not try to pump artificially a soul into an inert mass which does not want a soul.
>
> We are honest and responsible and we do not think of personal gain. We are poor. We use what we have for our art. If no one helps us, we will still do what we can. If we are helped we can accelerate the process. We are working toward the pure tradition of classic ballet as it has been handed down to us. It is exquisite—pure and crystal like a precious stone. We must respect art and music and we must put all our human energy, heart, and soul into it.
>
> Europe is dead. They look to us for inspiration, for new ballets. Only in America is there still the willingness to sacrifice everything to our art.
>
> We have a vision of Utopia. If our vision as vision is to be trusted, we must be trusted to make it happen.[11]

Finally, in the spring of 1962, Balanchine agreed to take the NYCB to the USSR. The troupe would go that fall, but only if he had a personal marine corps guard and a diplomatic passport, and only if the State Department would also pay for an adjoining five-week tour for the company in Western Europe, guaranteeing more work for his dancers. "Soviet trip impossible without it," Kirstein wrote to his State Department contact, suggesting that he speak directly to Balanchine if he didn't believe it.[12] The details were finally hammered out (and the marine guard dropped). It would be an exchange: while the NYCB performed in the USSR, the Bolshoi Ballet would tour the United States.[13] "We will have the biggest failure since the 4th 5-year plan," George gloomily joked to Lincoln.[14]

Balanchine fought with the Soviets over repertory. They didn't want *Prodigal Son* (too religious), or *Agon* (too abstract). They liked *Western Symphony*, which seemed to them folkish, and they wanted *Swan Lake* and *Firebird* (which they considered their turf), but Balanchine refused. Lincoln put it this way to a friend: "No *Cage*, no *Agon*, no *Faun*, since these are straigfnyghly erotishky [*sic*]. . . . No *Orpheus*, no *Gesualdo*, but *Firebird*, da. Balanchine: *Firebird*, NYET."[15] "We want people to think of you as second Fokine," a Russian negotiator told Balanchine, who responded simply, "I want to be first Balanchine."[16] This meant *Agon*, along with *Episodes* (a new ballet to an atonal score by Webern), were nonnegotiable. The Russians finally relented, and they settled on a list that also included *Symphony in C*, *Serenade*, *Allegro Brillante*, *Concerto Barocco*, *La Valse*, *Tchaikovsky Pas de Deux*, and *Donizetti Variations*.[17]

Looking back on the work he made in the years between *Agon* and his departure for the USSR, we are faced with the sense that he was preparing himself, consciously or otherwise, for this momentous return to his homeland. We find him walking his way backward, retracing his steps to 1924, when he boarded the steamer to Germany, and back even further into his Russian childhood. He was girding himself with his own past, as if it would armor him for a trip that frankly terrified him. Not accidentally, he also made at this time some of the most political dances he had ever created, laying out his allegiances as the Cold War escalated. It was a dangerous internal bifurcation: he was doing, talking, performing, and externalizing himself more than he ever had, and he was on full media display—*Time, Newsweek*, TV, interviews—as he and Lincoln worked to finally solidify and stabilize the company they had founded. But his body and soul were as preoccupied as ever with music, dances, and the people who would perform them. As he moved from success to success in the public sphere, his dances were revealing a darker and more anxious story, another backdrop to his trip back home.

In January 1958, a month after the premiere of *Agon*, he made *Stars and Stripes*, to music by John Philip Sousa (orchestrated by Hershy Kay). It was an all-out, almost embarrassingly campy celebration of the red, white, and blue, featuring five "regiments" of neatly uniformed men and baton-wielding women who pranced like cheerleaders to Sousa's martial tunes. Jacques and Milly, who danced the pas de deux, were like "Ike and Mami,"[18] George liked to say, and the grand finale was a full-cast march to "The Stars and Stripes Forever" ("Hurrah for the flag of the free!") performed against a huge American flag unfurled across the backdrop and a full-company salute. "Calculated vulgarity is a useful ingredient," he said, defending his "big casserole my critics refer to as an applause machine." The critic John Martin was flummoxed: "Is it as innocent as it seems? Or is it a colossal piece of cynicism?"[19] It was both: pure kitsch and deadly serious. Balanchine had by then awarded himself three badges of Americana: *Western Symphony, Square Dance*, and *Stars and Stripes*.[20] Who could doubt his patriotism now?

At the same time, he was pushing further into nonnarrative forms. The Cold War was being fought in part on the battlefield of abstraction, and Balanchine saw himself strictly in the vanguard. Stalin's officially decreed Socialist Realism had long since prohibited "abstract" dance in favor of lavish narrative "dramballets," often with Socialist themes and workers wielding hammers and sickles building an earthly paradise, but also drawn from Shakespeare and other approved literary classics. Abstraction was deemed a political threat—a slippery artistic form dangerously free of words and story that could be censored. (Who could exactly say what *Agon* was about?)[21] *Agon* was all that it was, but it was also a weapon in the Cold War.

Episodes, made in 1959, was another. It would go to Russia too, and as he was making it, George received a telegram from Andrei announcing (in Russian) their mother's death: "Mother died 28 February. Let me know your new address." There is no record of George's reaction, but he was by then so cut off from his family that Andrei didn't know where to send the cable, and it was routed to the theater by Western Union.[22] *Episodes,* meanwhile, was pieced together from several scores by Webern that Balanchine had been studying for some time, composed mostly in Webern's Weimar years, and it was in the realm of *Agon* but even more disjointed and fragmented. Lincoln wanted to bring in Martha Graham to work on the ballet with George. Good politics, he said, and George just nodded, noting wryly that the company motto seemed to be "chock full o' nuts" (referring to the coffee jingle).[23] So the first half of the ballet was Graham, who made an elaborate full-dress drama about Mary, Queen of Scots (with herself as Mary). The second half was Balanchine, who did the opposite: five plotless dances in practice clothes with a minimal set made of four poles arranged on the stage: "Do what you do" was George's only instruction to the designer David Hays, another Lincoln recruit from Harvard days.[24] Graham's half of the ballet was later summarily dropped, and *Episodes* quickly became Balanchine's half only. They worked separately, with little contact, and he was focused on the music, which he carefully transcribed (in the case of opus 21, twice), working quietly at a table in pencil.[25]

The pas de deux was for Diana again, this time with Jacques, to Webern's Six Pieces for Orchestra, op. 6. Balanchine wanted them naked and afraid, like Adam and Eve just after they ate the apple, he told them. As they worked, according to d'Amboise, what came out was a nightmarish dance built on the idea of a bat-like witch, hitched to a turtle or toad, with forty feet of hair that wound them into a ball and flung them out, naked again, onto a stage strewn with clothing. Then a dance of Adam and Eve clothing themselves. As they were finishing this dance, Graham walked into the studio and said she needed more music. Balanchine simply handed her his score for Webern's Six Pieces and said, here, use this. He threw out the dance they had just made—maybe another time, he told the bewildered dancers—and walked out.

At the next rehearsal, he made a completely different dance, this time to Webern's Five Pieces for Orchestra, op. 10. Now Diana and Jacques were in total darkness, each under a separate spotlight. She was dressed in luminous white; he was nearly invisible in black. Their steps were hieratic, angular, with splayed, trapped movements and tangled deadweight arms, and they were engrossed with each other but disconnected, with a musical but no narrative arc. At one point Jacques lifted Diana upside down on his back with her legs split like antler's horns around his head, which now seemed to emerge from her crotch. This abstract but sexualized image, a close copy of a move he probably saw in Petrograd in a production by Foregger around 1923, made the audience laugh uncomfortably—which made George furious. "Idiots," he said; "just because they see new kinds of movement—what's funny about that?"[26]

There was a solo too for Paul Taylor, a dancer in Graham's company. Lincoln called him up: "Geek" (his name for Taylor), "you're being drafted, George says he wants you in a new ballet of his." Taylor was a large, soft man with a malleable, wide face and a flexible, muscular, but puttylike body, which made his powerful, full-bodied dancing all the more astonishing. The movements Balanchine gave him made him feel as if his limbs "were being sharply jerked around by a succession of invisible strings. I'm being reined in . . . pent up. It's disagreeable. Hurts. Besides, keeping to the music is too tricky, and this whole business is totally foreign to my usual way of moving." Balanchine nodded, "Is like fly in glass of milk, yes?" And Taylor imagined the fly drowning, subhuman, ugly, caught in a "deadly vortex of its own making . . . an epigram about self-ordained patterns and death." Very German expressionist, he later reflected.[27]

The last section of the ballet veered in another directly entirely. After the "fly in glass of milk" solo came Webern's tribute to Bach's ricercars (from *The Musical Offering*)—calm, harmonious, "like being in church," one dancer recalled. The movements and music took Balanchine home with slight references, via Webern, to his own *Concerto Barocco* from 1941, stripped now to flat, semaphore gestures and ending with all bodies facing front, turned in, arms down, heads bowed. It was another conversation between the seventeenth and twentieth centuries, between Bach, Webern, and Balanchine. Overall, this fractured ballet brought to the minds of critics such words and phrases as "shocking," "transmutation into monsters," and "a coordinated assemblage of bones, muscles and nerves . . . without the impulsion of human motive." Denby called it a "counter-classic classicism," with a "lucid abnormality" and "a wit like Beckett."[28]

Next, he tried out jazz-inspired and experimental music, some of it new, much of it old, all of it with Diana Adams. It was the kind of music—and dance—the Soviets would outlaw, which was not the reason to make it, but it was a sign of his taste at the time. *Ragtime* (1918, Stravinsky), *Modern Jazz Quartet* (1961, Gunther Schuller conducting his quartet), and, above all, *Electronics* (1961), a wild sci-fi dance to an electronic tape by the composer Remi Gassmann, with a set made of plastic columns and cellophane and the dancers as creatures dressed in plastic (that aggravatingly glued itself to their noses and mouths). The dance featured a sinuous, acrobatic, and coldly sexual pas de deux with Diana and Jacques rolling around on the floor clutching each other in embrace. The dancers, who didn't much like it, called it "Electronic—ca-ca," and when one asked George where he got such a dehumanizing idea, he said simply, "This is what life will be in the future, you see."[29] The critic John Martin called it "synthetic," part of Balanchine's seeming interest in "choreographic outer space." Edwin Denby, who was among Balanchine's most insightful critical interlocutors, was unconvinced. He thought *Electronics* was "a fake," a "middlebrow Radio City corn" masquerading as a "highbrow act."[30] Jerome Robbins disagreed:

> The ballet takes place in the heart of the sexual act . . . and don't let anyone tell you otherwise. Things happen on that stage that could not and would not be allowed to happen anywhere else ever on any stage. If it weren't for the camouflage of decor and costume and the occasional strangeness of the music, the joint would be raided. . . . A woman enters. She is led into the act. At first against her open wish, but then with her surrender and acceptance and fulfillment, with marvelous feminine yielding. Knowledge is released, and others eat of the forbidden apple. The world becomes one of female genitals [he wrote "cunt," but crossed it out]. Literally all over the stage girls are on their backs with legs spread apart, or making backbends to the floor with crotches front. . . . King and chosen mate return. Slowly, oh so slowly, they involve themselves with each other . . . and in a fantastic copulative meshing on the floor cover each other as they roll in slow motion hypnotically on the floor—lights fade out. Curtain.[31]

The ballet quickly fell out of the repertory and was lost, but photographs of Jacques and Diana in the pas de deux suggest Robbins was not making it up. *Electronics* would not go to the USSR, and even if Balanchine had wanted it to, a ballet with that much sex was unlikely to get past the Soviet censors—sex was the one thing they could spot every time.

That same year Balanchine reached back to Weimar Germany, again, this time to Les Ballets 1933 and *The Seven Deadly Sins*. He restaged Weill and Brecht's old anti-Fascist, anticapitalist show for the nubile Allegra Kent—his Brigitte Bardot, he liked to say. Lotte Lenya, his original Anna 1, returned as Kent's double: Anna 1 and Anna 2, a pitiful pair, mother and daughter, talking singer and mute dancer, Weimar and now. The opening image saw them clinging to each other and wrapped in a single black cape—a prison, Allegra said, in the void of a pitch-black stage. Rouben Ter-Arutunian, a Georgian-born émigré artist of Armenian parents who fled Tbilisi for Paris and Berlin after the revolution, redid the sets as a "*Salade Niçoise* of German Expressionism," drawing especially on harrowing interwar images from George Grosz. Karinska, who made the costumes, had discovered a new synthetic fabric that smoothed flush to the dancers' bodies. So the women wore these new flesh-colored nylon unitards with cabaret-style G-strings, bras with rubies on the nipples, high leather boots, and wigs. Masks, they needed masks, George said, and he sent Rouben to Forty-second Street to get them. A few dancers prissily refused to be seen in such revealing gear and were given the more modest (and sweaty) option of a skintight rubber covering over their nude unitards.

Still, it was a Weimar world that many of them knew from their émigré parents or from the movies—*Lilli Marlene*, *The Blue Angel*, and *The Threepenny Opera* were all there in Lenya's husky voice ("Right, Annie? Right, Annie?")—and George knew that Allegra knew these references and had her own: in real life, she was trapped by her controlling mother and had a new and troubling fashion-photographer boyfriend, soon to be a failed husband. The strictures of dancing and Christian Science had kept Allegra, though twenty-one, childlike and mute, but ballet also fed her naturally sensual, needy, uninhibited, and at times almost exhibitionist character. She was a creature of the stage and easier to unlock than Diana, and Allegra felt, probably rightly, that

George was in love with her then. When she was paraded across the stage sitting high on a giant cellophane-wrapped platter as a delectable appetizer (wearing a glittering bra and skimpy panties) with nightmarishly giant knives and forks poised for attack, Balanchine threw the task of the choreography to her: invent something, he said. She improvised, capturing perfectly the lost Weimar spirit on the eve of Hitler's rule and the lurid sins of capitalism. By the end of the ballet, even sin was insufficient for survival, and Anna 2 rebelled. She "takes over for herself," as Kent later put it, and commits suicide. "I knew how to go back to the moon over Louisiana," she said, and smiled faintly as she quoted the libretto decades later and described her headfirst dive in black bra and panties through a silver aluminum-foil vortex at the back of the stage. As she broke the silver and disappeared into the abyss, bright lights blinded the audience. A final image before the curtain fell: the two Annas walking forward, huddled together under the black prison cape.[32]

In 1960 came more revivals, and at this point we begin to fully realize just how much Balanchine's taste was gathering around themes and styles that would have positioned him against the USSR. It was not deliberate, necessarily, and what he chose to revive and when often had to do with more practical matters—what they could afford, what music he had, what the dancers remembered, whether there were costumes that could be repurposed, et cetera. But still, he chose *this* and not *that*, and in retrospect, we can see him tied back more and more, in various ways, to the "realer than real" world of spirit.

He found a new lead for *Prodigal Son*, and offered it to the anti-God Soviets knowing they would refuse it, which they did ("too religious"). In New York he cast this "too religious" dance with Diana as the Siren and Edward Villella, a machismo former boxer from Bayside, Queens, as the son. Villella came from a working-class Italian émigré family; his father was a truck driver, and his mother worked at Loft's candy factory. Even as a child, Villella was looking for a way out and found it in boxing, baseball, and *ballet*, which he stumbled into at age ten, tagging along after his sister. He quit—under pressure from his father—to attend Maritime College, but he kept training himself secretly and joined the NYCB five years later, in the fall of 1957. The company reminded him of his "godfather" family and patriarchal grandfather—"the pourer of the wine"—who seemed to have the information one needed to live, and Balanchine had it too. "I could jump but needed to know the rest, and he opened the world to me," Villella later reflected. He was dark and sexy, with a muscularly compressed body and all-out machismo style. He begged to do *Prodigal Son*, and Balanchine finally gave it to him, like "an old coat" he didn't much like, and let it serve as a vehicle for Villella's immense talent.[33]

In another key, that same year, he brought back *La Sonnambula* for Allegra Kent. He had made this dance, originally titled *Night Shadow*, in 1946 for Danilova (who was herself a sleepwalker). It was an otherworldly story about a haunted sleepwalker and a poet who loves her but cannot not wake her. When he is murdered by a jealous husband, she lifts his dead body in her arms but then leaves him to continue her eternal trancelike walk up the walls and over the roof. Balanchine wrote to John Taras when Taras was staging the ballet a few years earlier:

> The main point is that [after the death of the poet] the Sleepwalker should not go through the rooms, inside the house. . . . She is supposed to walk on the roof of the house and go down the side gutter. When she takes him away she likewise goes up by a wall and by the roof and the spotlight that [is] the illusion of her . . . goes to opposite side of the stage by going across backdrop, high up, and disappears. . . . The illusion is that she is going away into another world and is not going to stay with him in the room.[34]

In another spiritual mode, he made a new and magnificent, nostalgia-tinged waltz ballet, *Liebeslieder Walzer*, to music by Brahms for four couples (including Diana). The first half was romantic waltzes in period dress in a ballroom setting designed by David Hayes. In the second half, they revealed their souls: the walls fell away, the chandelier became stars, and the women changed into pointe shoes and tulle, which threw their polite society dance into close and intimate embrace.[35]

In perhaps the most unlikely otherworldly dance of all, Balanchine staged his own full-length narrative ballet, *A Midsummer Night's Dream*. He had been thinking about it for a long time, weaving together a score out of seven distinct pieces by Mendelssohn—a kind of composition all its own.[36] He told the dancers that he knew Shakespeare's text "better in Russian than a lot of people know it in English," and as they worked, he freely quoted long passages from memory.[37] It was a kind of homecoming: as a child, he had played a *Dream* elf on the Mariinsky stage. This new production was also supposed to go to the USSR, but when Balanchine requested that the child roles be locally cast, the Soviets objected that they did not want Russian children working with American dancers.

He began the ballet with a small spirit-like child in the upstage corner, poised to dance, bringing to mind George's own memory of himself as an elf. The child runs; the stage fills with bugs, butterflies, and sprites; and we soon meet Puck, along with the fairy queen and king, Titania and Oberon. Already this is a departure from Shakespeare's play, which opens decorously at court with a show of pomp and circumstance as Theseus and Hippolyta confront the lovers and impose law and reason over unruly youthful passion; the forest and the fairies come later. For Balanchine, by contrast, the forest is everything. He compresses Shakespeare's five acts into two and brings everyone—everyone—into the forest and keeps them there, playing out all their various dramas under the enchanted night sky and only bringing them to court for the wedding divertissements at the end. This reversal of Shakespeare—but also of traditional ballet form, in which the court (the real world) comes first and anchors supernatural flight—was Balanchine's way of showing where *he* located the real "real" world.

Balanchine's forest, moreover, is no ordinary forest. We feel the trees all around, but the stage itself is empty. There will be no lovers bushwhacking through branches and dew-covered trees: in this open and unencumbered space, the entire design of the ballet unfolds with astonishing clarity, and a central fact of the play comes immediately to the fore. We see that the lovers are not characters with complex psychological inner lives; they are anonymous figures, actors who switch and change at first sight for no apparent reason but their own fickle imaginations, addled by a bit of magic. The story lies in their movements, not in their minds, and Balanchine shows them racing across the stage with great purpose, pursuing, following, chasing, yearning, falling in love, and asleep; awaking and running off to do it all again in a different order, with Puck pushing, pulling, and orchestrating the whole game in gleeful delight. The mortals don't even know they are part of a larger design ("Shall we their fond pageant see? / Lord, what fools these mortals be!"). It was narrative ballet, Balanchine style.

Even Balanchine's second-act court looks strangely like his forest. The dark woodland trees are still there, shimmering in the distance over the regal balustrade, and in a later staging, he made a point of asking the designer to make sure that there were trees growing inside the royal tent too—and would he please also create a garden with cypress trees like those from *The Lady and the Unicorn* tapestries in Paris, styled to make the forest and the court appear more alike? When the scene melts from the court back into the forest at the end of the ballet and Puck flies away into the night, the transformation is so smooth that you can miss it in the glow of fireflies flitting across the stage. Did we ever leave the forest, really?

Balanchine cast Diana Adams, with whom he was still deeply in love, as Titania. He was married to Tanny, of course, and by then (*Dream*-like) Adams was married to Ronnie Bates, and they were all trying to find love's spot. Shakespeare had drawn his Titania in part from Ovid. Titania was Ovid's other name for Diana in his retelling of the Diana and Actaeon story, and Ovid calls her "Titania" at the precise moment when the hunter Actaeon enters her grove and sees her bathing—an erotic trespass and revelation for which he is punished by being turned into a stag (Shakespeare's ass) and then ripped apart by his own dogs. Diana, moreover, is the goddess of the moon, shining over the midsummer night, and of hunting and chastity. Balanchine framed *his* Diana in what he called her "Primavera" throne, referring to Botticelli's painting and to the seashell cove in the painter's *Birth of Venus*, which was replicated in the ballet.

Oberon was Eddie Villella, which initially seemed a surprising choice to many of the dancers, including Villella himself. This short and muscly dancer seemed an unlikely match for a kingly role—or for the regal (and much taller) Adams. But Balanchine wanted a shorter Oberon in keeping with literary traditions—cursed with stunted growth, Oberon was known as the "little king"—another "Maloross." The scherzo that Villella danced so brilliantly demanded nobility, power, and (as he put it) "super-human" technical accomplishment, making him the perfect otherworldly patriarch.

Puck was traditionally a hobgoblin or demon, or a house spirit sweeping the stage with a broom, who helped women with their chores and their romantic quandaries. Balanchine cast Arthur Mitchell in this role, telling him his dark skin would make him seem to disappear into the trees and the forest night. They fussed over his costume, couldn't get it right, until finally Mitchell went home one night and traced his muscles with Abolene and sprinkled his gleaming bare body (minimally clothed) with glitter—like dew—which delighted Balanchine.

If Balanchine imagined himself in a role, it was Bottom, Shakespeare's simple weaver and amateur actor turned ass. The pas de deux between Titania and Bottom is among the most poignant moments in the ballet—a dance of loving domesticity, in which Titania (a goddess) feeds, caresses, and adores her awkward and very mortal ass, and a fantasy of a younger beauty doting on an aging man. (Bottom: "I am a man as other men are"; Titania: "I will purge thy mortal grossness so / That thou shalt like an airy spirit go.") Sensing Diana's growing lack of inner commitment, to him and to the role (she would bow out, pregnant once again, and "Mighty Milly" would step in), Balanchine also asked a younger dancer, aged sixteen, who had recently joined the company to learn the part. She was Suzanne Farrell, who would soon take Diana's place, in this dance and in Balanchine's heart.

As to the meaning of it all, he loved to quote Bottom, noting with pleasure Shakespeare's clever play on St. Paul's First Epistle to the Corinthians:

> The eye of man hath not heard, the ear of man hath not seen,
> man's hand is not able to taste, his tongue to conceive,
> nor his heart to report, what my dream was.

"At that moment," Balanchine later explained, freely mixing traditions, "Shakespeare was Sufi," in the sense that "like Sufism always double, triple meaning." He went on, "What Bottom says sounds as if the parts of the body were quarreling with each other, but it's really as if he were somewhere in the *Real World*. He loses his man's head and brain and experiences a revelation." A "revelation," that is, without words. Which is what Balanchine believed dance might also achieve, and why words were useless to describe it. Not quite satisfied with his ending, Balanchine admitted he had wanted to follow the more conventional court entertainments with something more like "Bottom's Dream," the "ballet" Bottom promises to "sing" at the end of their play within a play. He had thought to use Mendelssohn's St. Paul Oratorio for this scene: "A big vision of Mary standing on the sun, wrapped in the moon, with a crown of twelve stars on her head and a red dragon with seven heads and ten horns . . . the Revelation of St. John!" He didn't do it because "nobody would understand it. . . . People would think I was an idiot."[38]

Maybe, but he also left something out. In the book of Revelation, the red dragon with seven heads and ten horns, after all, wreaks havoc in heaven, and the woman "clothed in the sun and wrapped in the moon" is not just a woman, she is pregnant—and the dragon is a horrible beast waiting to devour her child as soon as it is born. Then war breaks out in heaven, and the evil dragon is finally thrown down to earth, where he terrorizes communities until the whole earth succumbs and worships him and the ugly beasts he has wrought.[39] It was a grim vision from a war-torn era, with a clear analogue in modern fears that the USSR would take over the world. The fact that he prettified the story from Revelation—left the dark parts out—reads less as a solution than as a kind of anxious postscript to an otherwise delightful if flawed ballet. Any forest or dream, after all, could come to an end. In his next ballet, his last before leaving for the USSR, it did: *Noah and the Flood*.

Noah and the Flood was a bizarre made-for-TV "choreographic allegory" devised by Balanchine and Stravinsky for the CBS network on the occasion of the composer's eightieth birthday. It was not a joyous occasion. Instead, the production was meant as an allegory, as Stravinsky put it, for "the atomic destruction of the world with the new life of the new beginning." The production would be designed by Ter-Arutunian, whose Orthodox background and artistic fascination with light and luminosity, the "alabaster appearance of a layer of nothingness" that suggests something beyond, made him a natural collaborator.[40] The libretto would be drawn from miracle plays and the book of Genesis, and Balanchine and Stravinsky saw Noah as a second Adam or Christ figure. The subject of the story, they agreed, was "SIN" in a nuclear age—a direct reference to the U.S.-Soviet arms race.

They met in Los Angeles in the early summer of 1962 to hammer out details, and Robert Craft (who had a hand in the libretto) took notes. The program would begin and end, they agreed, with an iconostasis of seraphim: "Russian style" angels framed by a Byzantine altar and topped "with the Chiasma or X symbol," a cross, but also a rhetorical structuring device they both apparently recognized in the Noah story. God, it was decided, would be a spoken voice and visually represented by a sunburst of crystalline light and divine rays; Balanchine thought this might be achieved with lights shown through plastic tubing, and he also suggested a shower of gold dust on the screen every time God sang—or two ellipses that might parallel two sung voices, since half ellipses formed a divine ideogram. For the building of the Ark, he reached for the divine clockmaker, envisioning the construction "as mechanical as a watch, and the builders' arms should work like semaphores." The animals would be depicted with children's toys set on a factory conveyor belt and "thrown" into the laps of audiences in their living rooms. For the flood itself, he fell back on the old trick of a black plastic sheet or silk curtain with men underneath making waves and "swallowing" the women "in the folds of their black substance." Audiences would feel, he hoped, that they were drowning too.

The show, which aired on June 14, began with an opening monologue delivered by the British movie star Laurence Harvey, who ponderously narrated the drama. After a long discourse on versions of the Noah story around the world, Harvey turned to face the camera: "As we watch Noah's story, danced for us now, we may well wonder, with Atoms at our command, if there are lovers among us worth the grace given to Deucalion and Pyrrha, or one man who could build a seaworthy ark." With this, the story began, "And God said . . . ," and the screen showed rays of sun, watery drops, and amoeba-like shapes; "And God said . . . ," as an amoeba became Adam, who reached for Eve, and their index fingers met in the image of Michelangelo's Sistine Chapel painting of the Creation of Adam (which George had used in *Apollo*).

Jacques d'Amboise performed Adam to Diana Adams's Eve, and he later recalled Balanchine's pleasure in showing him just how to partner Diana as they embraced in the act of original sin, and then running back to see what they would look like through a camera lens. Finally, they would have their Adam and Eve dance—except that, true to form, Diana was indisposed at the last moment and had to be replaced. Jacques also danced Lucifer, bejeweled, sequined, in gold—"queer," as Lincoln saw it, but Jacques saw himself as a "giant, glittering, winged Azazel," after the demon-like figure of Jewish lore, and in the Bible a goat, carrying man's sins into the wilderness and pitching them over the precipice. Balanchine had Jacques suspended at eighteen feet on a hidden ladder and shot from below. As he fell, the screen switched to a body spinning through darkness into fire, and the narrator warned: "In a world like this, will *he* win?"

So it went, through the Building of the Ark, the Flood, and the Covenant of the Rainbow. The dancers, all women, were angelic: clad in skin-colored leotards and tights and covered with white makeup, hair pulled tightly back or under smooth bathing cap–like hats, and performing abstract, *Agon*-style steps. Noah and his wife were masked and of this world, trapped in a (frankly silly) pantomime. The program ended with Stravinsky's "Sanctus," sung to the somber (and today almost comical) image of the seraphim dolls, rolled in on carts, each wrapped in six feathered wings, heads bobbing.[41]

Balanchine had naïvely hoped that *Noah and the Flood* would run without advertising breaks. He was wrong—and very angry. The show was "brought to you" by the Breck Golden Showcase, and the vaulting biblical narrative was routinely interrupted by sleek models showing off their hairdos: "Beautiful hair . . . Breck mist in two types . . . for softness, manageability, and luster." Enraged at this commercialization of a sacred text, George gave an interview in which he painted a Gogol-esque portrait of the dystopian "panic" that controlled the TV industry.

> It's a pyramid. Everybody's afraid of somebody else on top. Comes to the point when you ask who is the boss and the boss is nobody because the boss is—the sponsor. A sponsor is not a man, a sponsor is a thing, a toothpaste. And toothpaste is sponsored by millions of shareholders. . . . So a kind of fear is squeezed through the plastic tube and a devil operates the top and laughs at everybody. Everybody thinks the other guy is important but the important guy is scared to death, of somebody who doesn't exist.

The result was that televised dance was "as far from the real thing as a newspaper report of a murder is from the actual terrifying murder itself." Balanchine sarcastically noted that he was considering a consumer protection label to warn viewers that they were not getting the product as advertised. But in truth it was not only Breck shampoo that spoiled the show. As Lincoln put it, "*Noah and the Flood* was ghastly."[42]

With this failed but dire biblical allegory of the apocalyptic danger posed by U.S.-Soviet tensions and the nuclear-arms race, Balanchine and the NYCB prepared to depart for the USSR.

Chapter 20

USSR

On October 6, 1962, the NYCB boarded a plane in Vienna, bound for Moscow. They numbered almost ninety, including the dancers; the conductor, Robert Irving; two mothers (escorting underaged dancers); several translators; and the company doctor. John Martin, chief dance critic for *The New York Times*, also joined the tour to document Balanchine's homecoming. The dancers had stocked up on peanut butter, candy, toilet paper, cereal, tuna, chewing gum, pens, lipstick, stockings, Spam, potato chips, instant coffee, and other necessities. Balanchine had also asked that they please dress well, since he wanted his company to present an elegant image. He was also concerned about the many dancers with Russian backgrounds and had personally arranged a publicity poster with the full name of every company member in large type, so that family members in the USSR would be able to identify and find them.[1]

When they landed at Sheremetyevo, Balanchine was the last one off the plane. He emerged onto the jetway in a suit and bow tie, trench coat draped casually over his arm. Diana Adams took her place by his side, and he proudly introduced his star ballerina all around. A full-court reception awaited him: klieg lights, flashing cameras, Soviet officials, American diplomats, and a press corps eager to record his return. The sparring began immediately: "Welcome to Russia, home of classical ballet," one of his hosts began, shaking George's hand, to which George proudly responded, "No, Russia is home of Romantic ballet, America is the home of classical ballet," and he flashed his American passport in case they didn't get the message. But his attention was not fully there. He had seen his brother, Andrei, who was standing patiently to one side, waiting.[2]

"Andruska! It's you," he said, as they embraced and his expression softened with emotion. He was surprised that Andrei was so small, "a very short brother," and it was true that George, who thought of himself as Maloross, seemed to tower over him. At fifty-seven Andrei was prematurely gray, and next to his dapper sibling, he appeared aged and shy, with frayed white locks of unkempt hair, a sweet, toothless-like smile, and a rumpled suit with drooping, oversized pockets (stuffed with tobacco, sugar, and papers for rolling cigarettes). Unlike George, he spoke Russian with a Georgian accent. Lincoln called him "a nice puddle duck from the country," but it was sadder than that.[3] Andrei was younger than George by a year but more spent by a decade. By then a well-known Georgian composer, like their father, his life had nonetheless been constrained by the harsh realities of Soviet existence—and by his brother's American success. They had not seen each other for some forty years, since they were children, before the revolution had torn their family apart. George had received only one letter from Andrei, and it had been delivered to him by a man he suspected of being an agent of the secret police. In it Andrei had implored George to return to the USSR, but George correctly sensed that his brother had written under duress and ignored it. Andrei had also sent those terse cables, notifying him of their father's death and, more recently, of their mother's passing. That had been the extent of their communication.[4]

The brothers went to dinner together at a nearby Georgian restaurant. George eagerly selected favorite dishes from the menu, only to be told one after another that none were available, so they finally settled on coriander chicken—the only thing on offer that evening. The Hotel Ukraina, where he was staying with the company, had a similar empty grandeur. It was massive, monumental, a fortresslike complex in yellow stone with eight flagged turrets and a central tower with a high spire topped with a Soviet star. One of the "Seven Sisters" commissioned by Stalin to compete with American skyscrapers (and modeled in part on the Manhattan Municipal Building), the Hotel Ukraina was built in "a Stalinoid Gothic" style, as Lincoln put it, devoid of human scale.[5] Completed in 1957 and named by Khrushchev (who was born in Ukraine of Russian parents) in honor of the three hundredth anniversary of the unification of Russia and Ukraine, it already felt old and run-down.

The enormous gray marble lobby resembled a train station, with a post office, banks, shops, a telephone station, and a large restaurant emitting a pervasive Soviet smell of onions and cabbage. The thirty-four floors and more than one thousand rooms were served by only four very slow elevators, manned by stolid, suited ladies, and the wait could be over half an hour to travel a few floors. Stairs were strictly prohibited. The thirteenth floor was said to house the bugging apparatus for the whole building, and each floor was armed with a uniformed matron who sat stoically (with a cot for sleeping), controlling keys and entry at all times. Once a guest passed her muster, the walk to a room could seem miles long, down dreary carpeted corridors, and the rooms themselves were decorated in a worn Biedermeier style with oriental throws and unvarnished parquet floors prone to splinters. They all knew that the ceilings were lined with bugging devices, and the dancers made sport of discovering them.

They ate at the restaurant in the lobby: piroshki, dark bread, cucumbers, pickles, borscht, chicken Kiev ("mystery meat"), bottled sweet sodas, Russian ice cream. Balanchine asked for Borzhomi, a sulfurous mineral water he remembered from childhood that to the dancers reeked of rotten eggs, but he guzzled it down. A pall of surveillance hung over everything. Their movements outside the hotel were tightly controlled, and three large buses carried them to rehearsals every morning, as well-wishers shouted, "No politic, no politic!" A few of the dancers ignored the restrictions and walked through the wide streets and crowded markets anyway. The requisite "interpreters" (undercover secret police) were their constant companions and occasional adversaries in chess matches, played with ice hockey blaring on TV in the background. Contact with family back home was difficult. Mail arrived erratically via diplomatic pouch, often already opened, and making an international phone call could take hours. If the caller was lucky enough to get a connection, it was often only one-way—the person in Moscow could hear but not be heard, as operators controlled the flow of information leaving the USSR.[6]

On October 9, after three days of rehearsals, the NYCB opened at the Bolshoi Theater—elegant, Old World, plush red and gold, with crystal chandeliers—to a house packed with Soviet brass, including Yekaterina Furtseva, the minister of culture, a tough and cultivated woman neatly dressed à la Ninotchka, whom Balanchine grew to like, perhaps in part because she had fallen out of favor with the regime the year before. Khrushchev himself was notably missing from his bulletproof private box. As the evening began, the audience solemnly stood for the Russian national anthem, followed by "The Star-Spangled Banner," with Robert Irving at the podium conducting an orchestra of Soviet musicians. Balanchine had chosen a program of four ballets, all but one plotless: *Serenade*, *Interplay* (Robbins), *Agon*, and the full-dress *Western Symphony*. For this momentous opening night, he wore his Sunday best: Mississippi riverboat gambler's pegged pants with a rodeo rider's silver-embroidered shirt and string tie.

The audience response to the performance was polite but restrained, and George found himself devastated, confused, and angry that he was angry or cared at all. Once the official contingent finally cleared, however, a group of students from the upper balconies rushed enthusiastically to the front and clapped in unison for the dancers. A fancy reception followed, hosted by the American ambassador, Foy Kohler, at Spaso House, his elegant residence in an old sugar-merchant's palace. The gracious nineteenth-century-style imperial rooms were crowded with dancers and the Soviet artistic and political elite—including, it was noted, Khrushchev's son-in-law, whom Balanchine studiously avoided to minimize any political complications.[7]

The next day, the company moved to the gigantic four-thousand-seat Palace of Congresses, which had been sold out for weeks. It was an impressive, if cold, new theater—a monumental stone and glass structure originally built to host the Twenty-second Congress of the Communist Party in 1961. The dancers were amazed to find TVs in their dressing rooms, a fully stocked restaurant, and marble bathrooms with plenty of toilet paper. They were apparently unaware that the inaugural party meeting just a year before had been a spectacle of anti-Stalinist vitriol (or that Stalin's body, which then still lay in Lenin's nearby mausoleum, was dug up, thrown in a pit, and covered in concrete). Seeing the cavernous stage, Balanchine immediately pulled the "short" cast of *Serenade* and replaced them with the "tall" cast, since the dancers could barely be seen in the vast auditorium.[8] The audience response that evening, and for the rest of the run, was overwhelming. Night after night, the Soviet people stood and cheered for the company, urging on their favorite artists by chanting their names ("Meetch-ell! Meetch-ell!" for Arthur Mitchell) and, at the end, calling for George to take a bow—"Bal-an-chine! Bal-an-chine! Spa-si-bo! Spa-si-bo!"—until he appeared shyly from the wings and bowed modestly. As the Russian crew began to extinguish the lights, he gently urged the audience to go home; the dancers needed to rest.[9]

He had to admit his immense satisfaction that audiences especially loved *Episodes* and *Agon*. Allegra Kent—who took over for the again-injured Diana—was even dubbed "the American Ulanova." Critics were more ideologically constrained and dutifully complained that these dances were cold and lacked the warmth of theatrical dress and a human story. George patiently endured interview after interview, tirelessly explaining his approach to beauty and the human figure. His un-Sovietized Russian flowed, and at times his facial tic even melted away as he meticulously answered in his native tongue those who called his work mechanical or grotesque and "repulsive," but when a prominent critic told him he had no soul, he sharply retorted that since Soviet critics didn't believe in God, they couldn't know about the soul.[10] And when a delegation from the Ministry of Culture asked him, please, to cancel *Episodes* because "the people" couldn't understand it, he responded succinctly with a Russian equivalent of "Fuck you" and walked out.[11]

It all wore on him. The daily petty humiliation of waiting in the freezing cold while some "idiot" guard, who by then knew exactly who Balanchine was, double- and triple-checked his papers before allowing him into the Kremlin or the theater. One day he forgot his official pass, and the guard turned him away, leaving a gaggle of frustrated journalists shouting from the other side of the barrier, a scene that delighted him for exposing the comedy of Soviet officialdom. Everything seemed grim and gray, he said, the food, the people, the ways they warily checked their every bodily movement, even while walking down the street. His stomach clenched when an old friend invited him to his home, two cramped and dingy rooms, and proudly showed him that he had his own toilet. Lincoln went to see Eisenstein's widow and learned of the filmmaker's sad fate and of Meyerhold's gruesome murder by the secret police.[12] As the days went by, George complained that the phone in his hotel room rang mysteriously in the middle of the night and that the radio suddenly turned on. He was haunted by nightmares about losing his passport or being thrown into prison or suffocating. "A little green devil is following me," he said, and he was not joking. In a moment of black humor, he wrote to Tanny: "Impossible to describe. . . . Remember? Invas. of the body snach!"—his go-to allegory for Communist takeover. He was losing weight fast and looked noticeably gaunt and thin. Making matters worse, the bursitis in his shoulder was inflamed and painful.[13]

His temper flared. One night, after a bravura technical performance of *Donizetti Variations*, the cheering audience called Eddie Villella back for bow after bow, until finally Villella signaled Irving for an impromptu encore. Balanchine was beside himself with rage and gave Eddie hell as a group of hushed dancers stood by: "What you do? How dare you—there is no repeat in music, this not circus." It was everything he had fought against, and he was angrier than they had ever seen him at this breach of musical taste and trust. They were on edge too: one dancer, already a difficult person, got so drunk at a reception that he started smashing glasses and bad-mouthing "America of purple mountains majesties," until he was promptly escorted out and put on a plane back to the United States. Allegra went wild at a party one night too—literally climbing the walls and performing a too-sexy "improvised beatnik twist" for a gathering crowd of astonished Russians—and had to be forcibly dragged away by friends. Betty, who was suffering her own debilitating depression, just sighed, "We need her more than we needed him, so we cope and try to get her to settle down." There were incidents and whispers, some true, of dancers having affairs with their KGB handlers and falling in love with Soviet musicians, for instance, or of the dancer Shaun O'Brien being arrested for taking pictures of pigeon tracks in the snow and held in custody for hours, where he was questioned at length about Little Rock, Marilyn Monroe—and Cuba.

Cuba. On October 22, in the middle of the company's Moscow run, Kennedy went on national TV to inform the American people that the USSR had installed offensive nuclear missiles in Castro's Cuba that were capable of reaching cities across the United States. He coolly announced a strict blockade of the island and the willingness of the United States to retaliate on Soviet soil in the event of a nuclear strike. When the news of this terrifying standoff reached the embassy in Moscow, Kirstein, Balanchine, Betty Cage, and Natasha Molostwoff were informed of the situation. Lincoln and Betty quickly came up with a disaster plan, in the event of hostilities. Plan A was to charter a plane, and if the word came from the embassy, the dancers could board waiting buses to the airport and take off immediately. If they couldn't get to the airport, plan B was to get everyone inside the embassy. Plan C was to then arrange a "prisoner swap" with the Bolshoi dancers in New York. When Lincoln shared these wildly unrealistic scenarios with the embassy, the response was swift: "The first thing we will know at the Embassy is that the phone will be cut off."

For the moment, he was told, there were no plans for evacuation, and the ambassador would attend rehearsals to allay any panic. As a comfort, the embassy kitchen was made available to the dancers, who occupied themselves making hamburgers and steaks, and in a touching sign of solidarity, the staff at the Ukraina placed huge vats of flowers on the tables for the company. On October 25, in an effort to signal calm (while still snubbing Balanchine), Khrushchev and the presidium attended a performance at the Bolshoi Theater, while the NYCB performed at the Palace of Congresses (Lincoln nervously scuttled back and forth).

On October 27, "Black Saturday," an American U-2 plane was shot down over Cuba and the pilot killed. Information was not widely available, and secret negotiations were under way, but the surprise downing of the U-2 (by a local commander) further frayed nerves in Washington, Moscow, and Havana. By then, the United States was already at DEFCON 2, one level below war, U.S. long-range missiles and bombers were on alert, and planes with atomic bombs were taking off around the clock, ready to move on targets in the USSR. In Cuba, armed surface-to-surface missiles with nuclear warheads were ready in the event of war, accidental or otherwise.[14]

In Moscow that afternoon, in a separate incident, Soviet troops moved into place around the American embassy to protect protesters who were throwing ink and rocks in a large demonstration against the imperial capitalist United States (staged, it later transpired, by Soviet authorities, who bused in confused workers for the event and supplied them with large posters, along with ink and eggs to throw). The American ambassador told the dancers to stay away and informed Lincoln that in the event of war, he would be powerless to help them, and they would all have to use their wits to survive. He warned that the audience that night might rush the stage and advised that the company be prepared to immediately bring down the heavy safety curtain in the event of a riot.

That evening, the dancers, aware of some vague but imminent danger, nervously gathered at the theater. Balanchine was strangely calm and commented dryly that he hadn't yet seen Siberia. He never believed there would be a war, he later explained, because neither Khrushchev nor Kennedy wanted one, but there was more to his detachment than that. Russia had held a gun to his head once before with the revolution, and this time he had been training himself for years to expect death and to live only in the present moment. That for him was one of the greatest skills of ballet. As the curtain rose on *Symphony in C*, the dancers, who were trained too, stood for a moment in disciplined anticipation staring into the blackened house of the theater. Irving stood poised at the podium, baton raised for the downbeat, and at that moment, the audience suddenly grew larger than itself and rose in spontaneous applause. As Irving signaled the first note, an adrenaline rush of pent-up fear and relief flowed through the dancers' bodies, and they danced with the energy of life-giving release. When they reached the end of *Symphony in C*, with its tragic pathos and patterned beauty, and Bizet and Balanchine's exuberant and decisive close, the Russians began their rhythmic chanting until finally Balanchine, looking small and thin, stood center stage and spoke quietly into the hushed auditorium. He thanked them all and then asked them to please go home; the dancers were tired and would be back tomorrow.

When tomorrow came, Armageddon had been averted. Kennedy and Khrushchev had reached an agreement, and late that afternoon, the news was broadcast in Russia and around the world. As it happened, that night was the NYCB's last performance in Moscow, and after the cheering and chanting at the end of the show, Balanchine took the stage again. This time he graciously invited the audience to follow the company to their next destination, which would be Petrograd, he said, deliberately using the old World War I name for his native St. Petersburg. He despised Lenin and refused to call his beloved city Leningrad.[15]

The moment they arrived and checked into the Astoria Hotel, Balanchine grabbed Natasha, Betty, and Jacques: "Let's go to my old house." Not the fancy apartment of the lottery years, but his aunt's old rooms at 1-3 Bolshaya Moskovskaya, across from the old Vladimir Cathedral, which he had escaped to from the Imperial Theater School. They followed him at a clip as his legs carried him down the still familiar streets from the hotel, across the canals, until they reached the spot. The apartment building was still there, and he could see the window where they had lived, but his heart fell when he saw that the once beautiful house of worship across the street was now a factory. Worse, the mighty Kazan Cathedral, which they had passed on the way, had been converted into an anti-God museum. Still, he raced, his small entourage trotting behind to keep up, to the Theater School on Rossi Street—but to their surprise, he stopped short at the entrance. His mind locked, and he couldn't go inside. How would he manage the memories that were so tightly packed inside this old building that had served as his erstwhile home for so many difficult and momentous years? He found a small church that was still open and lit a candle inside instead.[16]

The people he had known were still alive; he just didn't recognize them—didn't want to recognize them, perhaps, such as Elizaveta Gerdt, his once beautiful young teacher, who was now an old woman, he sadly noted. He had wanted to see Goleizovsky, scion of his youth, but when he saw the choreographer's *Scriabiniana* performed by the Bolshoi, he was so embarrassed that he canceled the visit. He didn't want to meet a feeble and wrinkled old man and preferred his memories of this crucial iconoclast.[17] In Leningrad a few members of his early 1920s Young Ballet appeared, but now they just seemed to him "old and brown and bent . . . like mushrooms. How can you feel affectionate and sentimental about a mushroom?"[18] He did want to see Fedor Lopokov, whose *Dance Symphony* had been such a formative influence, but the old choreographer declined a visit.[19] George's obsession with age and aging was irrational, of course, and he was older too, but he couldn't stand that his colleagues, who had been so beautiful and vibrant, had grown old and "dumpy," as if the ruin of their bodies was part of the ruin of Russia itself.

The more he was fêted, applauded, and celebrated, the more depressed, stoic, controlled, and in charge he became. When he learned that students and artists couldn't get tickets for the company's performances, he arranged a free performance for them all at the Palace of Culture: *Apollo*, *Agon*, and *Episodes*. He met with Soviet choreographers at the Leningrad State Choreographic Institute to discuss the principles of his art, and when the youngest among them asked for more, he met them again informally at the theater. When Konstantin Sergeyev, artistic director of the Kirov Ballet and a professional apparatchik, obsequiously presented him with a silver samovar on stage one evening, George just looked at the floor and thanked him politely in his best imperial Russian, and when Sergeyev presented flowers too, adding that Leningrad was George's native city, George pointedly accepted on behalf of New York and America.[20] It all reminded Lincoln of the coronation scene in Eisenstein's *Ivan the Terrible*: "Do you remember that scene? Ivan is on his throne. The nobles bow down before him; they heap gold upon him. And he sits there, implacable—he is absolutely implacable."[21]

George was also tense, moody, competitive, and despondent. When he taught class at the theater, he seemed to the dancers distracted, and they watched quietly as he peered out the window in a daze, vacantly recalling how he had watched the czar's uniformed parades out of these very windows as a child.[22] Ironically, the company happened to be there for the anniversary of the Bolshevik Revolution, which brought out the Russian fleet, flags, tanks, banners, huge photographs of Lenin, parades, loud slogans, and carousing crowds. What *he* remembered was bitter cold and starvation, eating dead horses and rats. At the theater the celebrations were marked by the cancellation of *Episodes* because the musicians were too drunk. It was hard for George not to see everything through 1917, or through the rose-tinted glass of the czar's kingdom, and he angrily complained that the theater was full of dowdy working-class people who ate and drank noisily during the performance and didn't care a whit for what they were seeing—which was manifestly untrue.[23] One night he stood immobilized in the wings as the crowds chanted, and when one of the dancers urged him to go on stage, he refused to move, saying "What if I were dead?" Betty worried. She wasn't sleeping, in spite of pills and brandy, and she found herself chanting the Volga Boatman (ai da, ai da, ai da, ai da . . .) and reading Dostoyevsky into the night. She thought Balanchine was on the verge of collapse and had already arranged for him to skip Kyiv, the company's next stop, and return to New York for a week before rejoining the company for their final performances in Tbilisi and Baku. He needed a break. This time it was George who was going crazy, Lincoln said. Being in Russia was for him "a kind of crucifixion."[24]

On November 8, George flew to Helsinki, spent the night, and left the next morning for New York. Eugenie Ouroussow and Edith Le Clercq met him at Idlewild. Ouroussow reported in a letter to her son the two "main points" he had pressed on them on the car ride home: that the company had produced an artistic revolution in Russia and that Russia had "crushed" Balanchine. This was Russia in the cruel days before Peter the Great, George told her, and he described a horrible weight pressing down on everyone. That week he and Tanny entertained guests constantly, as if cooking and food could repair his battered mind and solder their still close but corroding relationship, made ever more difficult by George's long and evident infatuation with the elusive Diana. It was a haggard visit, a reminder once again that he was the wrong generation, the wrong person, really, to ever feel at home. Even Stravinsky, who was just back from Russia too, had fallen in love all over again, greedily drinking in the official acclaim and fawning on Khrushchev, an important and good man, he said. It was another disorienting loss: an idol who mistook a tyrant for a father and himself for the Prodigal Son.[25] Russia made Balanchine feel more American and less at home.

Barely a week later, he departed again for the USSR, bags stuffed with extra pointe shoes for the dancers. He rejoined the company in Kyiv just in time to board the plane for Tbilisi. When he stepped onto the tarmac in his father's native Georgia, Andrei was waiting with family and flowers. It was a looking-glass moment, the life he might have had. Suddenly, he was Georgik, Georgi, a little boy-man to Andrei's short-man brother, and he met the relatives he did not know: Andrei's glamorous wife and their darkly handsome son, Jorge (named after him), and daughter, Tsiskari, a dancer who hoped her uncle would invite her to dance with the NYCB, but he never did. Apollon Balanchivadze, George's half-brother from his father's first marriage, whom he had known briefly as a child, was present too. Talking freely was difficult. They were shadowed, and at Andrei's apartment George nervously pointed to the ceiling, indicating that everything was bugged and they couldn't talk. Still, in snatches and pieces, he learned the story of his family's sad fate.

Tamara. His voice later turned ashen when he spoke of her, in the only recording we have of his account of her tragic death, which Andrei now told him. He had last seen her as a child, and in the years after he left Russia, Tamara had grown tall and angular, with intense, skeptical eyes and none of her mother's snowy beauty. She had become a set designer after all, and like their mother's mother, she had married a German who deserted her to return to Germany, adding a second absent German husband to the family. She moved to Leningrad alone, where she worked with the acclaimed Obraztov Puppet Theater. She wrote gaily of visits to the Almedingens, but the last anyone heard from her was just days before the German siege of the city, when she sent Andrei a birthday note: "Andriushen/ka!" She may have been killed during the siege or died of illness or starvation or perhaps on a train in the war zone trying to get back to Georgia. No one quite knows. She simply disappeared.[26]

Andrei was a survivor. Like Meliton, he was lively, outgoing, and long-winded, prone to excessive toasts and speeches, and had a wonderful singing voice. He won medals and honors for his Georgian-style music—the Order of Lenin, Stalin Prize, Order of Red Banner of Labor, People's Artist of the Georgian State Socialist Republic, et cetera—and liked to array them on his jacket like a general's insignia. At the right moment, he would strip them off, grinning, make some loud anti-Soviet declaration, and then restore them all again. He knew Dmitry Shostakovich and had publicly supported the composer in 1936, when Stalin banned his opera *Lady Macbeth of Mtsensk District*, and he had also later proudly refused to sign a letter condemning

Pasternak after the publication in the West, in 1957, of *Doctor Zhivago*. Andrei played at the margins, calculating in part that the cost to the authorities of arresting the brother of the famous George Balanchine would be too high. But in fact he also did everything he was supposed to do: led the composers' union, taught at the academy, composed music in the correct style, and won the requisite awards. So they let him play the jester—within limits. Over the years he was pressured to denounce his brother as an "enemy of the people," which he did—and didn't—depending on the "limits" of the situation. His career was celebrated, but he was also constrained and rarely permitted to travel to the West. He must not defect, and he never tried.

Apollon was older and less fortunate. Arrested and indicted in 1924 for fighting in a special gendarmes unit of the White Army, he had spent years in isolation, and although he was eventually released, he was arrested again in 1942 and this time sent into ten years of hard labor in Kazakhstan.[27] Upon his release he took on the family mantle as a quietly practicing priest in Kutaisi. He organized a vespers service at a local church specially for George.

George knew his mother had died three years earlier, but he knew little of her sad life. After she left him in Petrograd, she had joined Meliton in Tiflis where, thanks to his position and rank, she eventually lived modestly on a small street—Perovskaya, No. 2—in an old church converted by the Bolsheviks into apartments. The frescoes were still on the walls, and some of the nuns who had once made fresh Communion bread in the front rooms resided there too. Maria lived upstairs in the company of a heavy solid-wood bed and cupboard, and an icon of the Virgin Mary lodged in the ceiling corner near the door. Often alone, she wore a brooch with pictures of Tamara, Georgi, and Andrei, and in the early years would sit anxiously by the radio listening for word of her Georgi—would they ever let him come home? She watched the mail closely and couldn't understand why he wrote to say how much he hoped to receive letters from her but didn't send a return address. She worried in sad disbelief that they had lost the "thread of connection to Georgi. Where is he?!"[28]

Meanwhile, aside from daily excursions up the road to the modest onion-domed Russian church, one of the few left open, Maria had occupied herself with family and carefully tracking her expenses with the large beads on a wooden counting block.[29] Andrei visited with his family when he could, and his children fondly called her the "white grandmother" for her almost ghostly pale appearance, as opposed to Meliton's first wife, who was the "black grandmother." Maria faded away as quietly as she had lived. No one thought she would care to be buried near Meliton, so instead Andrei arranged a small plot in a large and prestigious cemetery in Tbilisi, home to the dead of well-to-do Communist families and a fitting tribute to his stature as a famous Georgian composer.[30]

Balanchine wanted to visit his father's grave. Not his mother's—she had always been a kind of spirit figure in his mind, and he didn't need her earth or bones; he had her snowy ethereality instead. Was it enough? She had loved him, she had given him their Finland home, but she had also left him—twice. First at the school "like a dog," and it didn't matter to him why or what her intentions had been, he always remembered and never forgave, he didn't have that kind of empathy. He responded instead with detachment and yearning. During the revolutionary years, when the whole family had gone to Georgia, she had left again, and he was alone—again. Just as he was alone with TB on the mountaintop, when he plaintively, anxiously wrote to her and got a void in return. He wanted her approval and proudly told her about Brigitta and then Tanny—see, see—but all he got was the void of terror and war again. So why was the image of his father propped on his bedside table all those years, instead of his mother's? Meliton left early, barely wrote, and then he died. And he had chosen Andrei, not George, as his musical son and successor. The image of his father, next to his icons, wasn't really there for comfort, like a family album. It was there to *show him.* See me. Watch me. I am a musician too. He wanted to *see* his father's grave because any eulogy to his mother naturally ended in his father. Not because he loved him—seeing is not the same as loving—but because his father was music and what he had become, and his mother was the soft inner sanctum that was destroyed, or left behind, that he could only get to through music and women, if it even existed.

Besides, his father was his roots, his soil, and he wanted to see and smell the Georgian heritage he had claimed for so long as his own. Meliton was buried in Kutaisi, near the Balanchivadze family enclave of Banoja, some few hours west of Tbilisi, and George went with Andrei, Apollon, Jorge, and Natasha Molostwoff, accompanied by the inevitable KGB posse. They departed by train at 7 A.M. As luck would have it, Natasha later recalled, their car was full of "wild Georgians," who flocked around Balanchine, taking pictures, talking, touching, celebrating their lucky encounter with this famous artist. When they finally arrived in Kutaisi, exhausted, Balanchine insisted that he and his brothers go alone to Meliton's grave. Their escorts waited at the tall iron gates to the cemetery.[31]

The story of Meliton's death that November 1937, it turned out, was not simple. Andrei told George that Meliton had died of a gangrenous leg he'd refused to have amputated, and that he had found their father lying in bed at home saying that death was a beautiful girl who was coming to take him in her arms, and that he was looking forward to it. But it was later whispered among grave keepers that this kindly man had been taken away in the night and shot before being ceremoniously buried—not here, but in the "Pantheon" of famous Georgians under a large pine tree at the foot of the Bagrat Cathedral, a magnificent church turned into a historical museum by the Bolsheviks. The rumors weren't true: Meliton more likely died of gangrene, as Andrei had said, but they were a sign of the violence engulfing Georgian life at the time, and they cast a double pall over Meliton's passing. It was the height of Stalin's Great Terror, led in Georgia by Beria, a fellow Georgian and one of Stalin's cruelest henchmen. In the year before Meliton's death, Beria had begun purging the local party and intelligentsia at a harrowing rate, killing or expelling to the Gulag thousands weekly, including family and friends close to Meliton and Andrei. It was at dinner before a performance in 1936 of Andrei's "first" Georgian ballet, *Heart of the Mountains*, that Beria secretly poisoned the stalwart Yagoda (fallen from Stalin's favor) and then escorted him to the elegant Moorish and art deco–style opera house, where the Tbilisi elite witnessed the spectacle of his agonizing convulsions as the ballet played on; he died the following morning.[32]

Friends of Meliton, whom Georgi and Andrei had met in their home as children, had been victims too. Mamia Orakhelashvili, by then dangerously highly placed in the party, was arrested on June 26, 1937, and tortured in front of his wife, Maria, who watched as Beria personally gouged out her husband's eyes and perforated his eardrums before he was shot. She and her daughter were then arrested and sent to the Gulag, and her daughter's husband, the famous conductor Evgeni Mikeladze—who had taken little Andrei over the mountains in a cart from Petrograd to Tiflis during the revolution—was blindfolded, tortured, and eventually executed.[33] There were show trials broadcast by radio, and Beria's agents had quotas and routinely slaughtered hundreds of "enemies" in a single night. No one was safe. Even the celebrated director of the Rustaveli Theater, who had recently staged a celebration of Georgian culture in Moscow for Stalin himself—including Meliton's Georgian opera—was arrested, tortured to the point of paralysis, and executed on June 27, 1937.[34] Circling closer to home, Meliton's nephew Irakli Balanchivadze was arrested later that year for "Trotskyism" and shot.

But not Meliton, who was probably too old and too studiously apolitical to matter. Official reports did not mention his gangrene and merely noted that his dead body lay in state in the main hall of the music school he had founded in Kutaisi and that a small service was performed by a local folk choir before he was interred under the pine tree at Bagrat. This was not to be his final resting place. In a macabre finale to his already bizarre death, in 1957 Meliton's bones were dug up and reinterred in a new official Pantheon at the Green Flower Monastery (Mtsvane Kvavila), where he now lay near a small church used by the Bolsheviks, it was said, to store cement.[35] His grave, unlike the others around it, was left unmarked except for a large rock and a miniature carving of piano keys. The KGB didn't give George or Andrei much time with their father, but before they left, the brothers poured some wine and spilled the first glass over the grave in the Georgian way.[36]

They visited too the medieval Orthodox Gelati Monastery, high on a misty mountain above Kutaisi. Founded in 1106, it had been closed by the Communists in 1922 but preserved as a historical monument since kings were buried there, including the legendary "Golden Age" Georgian King David. David was "the builder," who built Gelati, among other monuments, envisioning it as a "second Jerusalem" and a center of Christian culture and especially of Neoplatonism. Its misty grounds, practically in the clouds on a wooded hillside, include the Church of St. George, the Church of St. Nicholas, and the astonishing Cathedral of the Virgin. It was everything Balanchine came from and believed in—these were his saints—and although formal worship was not permitted and the monks long since dispersed, he and his entourage were allowed inside the vaulted cathedral. There they found themselves under a massive arch reaching as high as heaven itself, with light flooding in through the small windows onto the faded but still colorful ancient frescoes. An intricate mosaic of the Virgin and Child with the archangels Michael and Gabriel appeared high in the apse, and a photo shows George in his trench coat standing stoically before them.[37]

Balanchivadzes, meanwhile, seemed to be everywhere. George didn't make it to his father's nearby peasant enclave of Banoja, thick with descendants, but one Bidzina Balanchivadze, a musician and relative of Meliton's brother Ivan, hosted a traditional *supra* in George's honor at his home in Kutaisi, with ample Georgian wine and endless toasts to the living and the dead delivered mostly in Georgian—which George didn't speak and couldn't understand.[38] By the time they left Kutaisi on the night train back to Tbilisi, they were exhausted, and it was pouring rain, but George had seen what he had come for: his father's Georgia was now his own. It felt to him primal, a biblical land, and he even enthused to some of the dancers that after Noah's Flood, there had been a flight to the Caucasus. Ancient Greece, he said, was settled by Georgian tribes, and these were his tribes, his people. Being Georgian was another way too of setting himself against Russia. No wonder some of the dancers were sure he had been born there. He had told them so. At moments, he may even have believed it.[39]

None of this helped with Andrei, who enthusiastically proposed that they make a ballet together, as they had as children. After dinner one evening at his home, he hopefully played recordings of his music for George and even sat at the piano and regaled his brother with his prize-winning compositions. Balanchine sat bent with his head buried in his hands and said nothing. Finally, in frustration and despair, Andrei stopped and waited in painful silence, until someone awkwardly changed the subject. Natasha Molostwoff, who was there, was appalled: couldn't George just say something nice, anything at all? He couldn't.[40]

There were more feasts and more toasts, this time high on a hill above Tbilisi for the full company, complete with a performance by a traditional Georgian folk-dance troupe in full regalia. Balanchine's dancers, who were by then stone drunk on the strong Georgian wine, joined the folk dancers, squatting and kicking until they all resorted to newly common ground: the twist. These were the artists George loved. Skip the State Ballet of Georgia: he had no patience for its extravagant dramballets or for its "star" choreographer and dancer, Vakhtang Chaboukiani, who had worked with Andrei on *Heart of the Mountains* back in 1936, and whose schmaltzy, charismatic stage presence and lavish bows enchanted Jacques d'Amboise and others. "You see poster, Chaboukiani, Chaboukiani, you see only Chaboukiani. You see our poster? Where is my name?"[41] Ballets were God-given, and anything else was hubris.

The NYCB performances were sold out and on opening night, the streets around the opera house were thick with crowds, as a sea of people reached out and parted for George as he made his way into the theater, as if he were some kind of Christ figure—or movie star.[42] The police had been summoned, anticipating a crush of people pushing their way in, but the crowds were orderly and civil as, night after night, they pressed into the packed house. On the last night, after the final curtain fell, George stepped onto the apron of the stage to thank them all. Before they all boarded the train to Baku, the dancers piled their extra tights, leotards, leg warmers, and pointe shoes into a bin and left them for Chaboukiani's dancers, who had none.

"Baku or bust": for the dancers, Baku was a countdown. They marched through four days of performances, and on the final night, a group of them stayed up until dawn dancing and playing strip poker with no heat and the hot-water faucets running full blast until the walls sweated. Sleepless but wide awake, they all packed into buses and departed on a rickety plane for Moscow. It was snowing hard as they changed for a flight to Copenhagen, destination New York, and by this time, the dancers were all chanting in their own unison: "Go, go, go, go!" As the jet lifted off the icy tarmac at Sheremetyevo, the exhausted company broke into cheers, relieved to "get the hell out of the USSR" as d'Amboise put it.[43] No one was more relieved than the gaunt George. "That's not Russia," he said; "that's a completely different country, which happens to speak Russian."[44]

Soon after landing at Idlewild, Balanchine made the trip to Washington for a debriefing at the State Department. By all accounts the tour had been a personal and political victory beyond imagining, but Balanchine was stoic and unmoved. To him, their success meant nothing. Instead, this was the moment when the mirror broke in his mind. He could no longer hold a nostalgic reflection of himself and an imagined czarist past. That image, which had sustained him even as he also stood against it, had crumbled—didn't exist—and for all his proclamations of Americanness, he was left feeling even more homeless and unmoored than he had felt before he set out. Russia really had disappeared. There was no more place to be exiled from; exile was no longer a state of being; it was a flight—a flight into the pure glass and mirrored realm of the imagination, its own kind of home. He had seen it coming: a few days after his return, he commissioned a score from Nicky Nabokov for a full-length ballet based on Cervantes's chivalric tale of perhaps the most mirrored and spiritual life ever lived: *Don Quixote*, with himself in the role of the Don.[45]

The show would not go up until the late spring of 1965, but there was much to be done before then, and it could be said that the intermittent three years were all a preparation for this epic production. In the spirit of the novel and its knight errant, he set out to build a new theater, a bigger company, a whole new landscape for his character to live in. He was both author and player, and like Quixote, he couldn't fully control all the parts, least of all his own.

Chapter 21

MASTER BUILDER

It all began a few days after his return, when he dove headlong into a series of meetings with Lincoln's old friend Mac Lowry of the Ford Foundation. These "martini sessions," as he later called them, generally took place in the afternoon, lasted into the evening, and included Eugenie Ouroussow and Betty Cage.[1] When Lowry left, the others continued at a local bar over more drinks. There was something giddy about this unlikely meeting of minds. Lowry, after all, was an avowed Socialist. He and George had already worked together closely, but George had also angrily walked out of more than one dinner at Lowry's home, unable to tolerate the left-wing intellectuals and Communist sympathizers at the table.[2] No matter: Lowry wanted a national arts policy for dance as comprehensive as the state-supported systems of Europe and the USSR, and he was in a position to fund it. Balanchine wanted that too, although for him it was the czar's theaters combined with a spiritual order of the "progressive" avant-garde. Ouroussow was moving back and forth between their discussions and her own scholarly writings on Pasternak, Soloviev, Blok, and Russian mysticism, a pursuit that tied her ever more deeply to George. ("Pasternak would have been mildly annoyed I imagine if he knew that working on his Zhivago had prepared me for writing a report on ballet dancing in America.")[3] Cage was still a practicing witch with her own mix of magic realism and brass-tacks practicality. Kirstein worked with Lowry behind the scenes but otherwise lay low: he knew he couldn't pay for it all.

The company's money problems were vexing as ever. Balanchine (and Kirstein) were still not salaried, and to make ends meet, Balanchine took commercial work that didn't interest him. He had been looking for a solution for some time and, in 1952, had even considered opening a Vespa store in New York with one of his dancers and a couple of mechanics he had met in England. "You see," he wrote to his agent, "I must find a way to make some money, because, as you know, what I get from the ballet company does not even cover my expenses, and I don't want to have to do Broadway shows in order to live."[4] It didn't work out, of course, and the problem was ongoing. The company's short New York seasons, moreover, made extensive touring necessary to keep everyone employed and their organization alive. The dancers, who were unionized, were by then making a meager $3,500 to $7,000 annually, depending on rank, and top teachers at the school were earning $5,000 or less. With more than four hundred students, faculty, and staff, the school was being run by a small coterie of underpaid women, led by the "Three Graces": Ouroussow, Molostwoff, and Gleboff. The NYCB, they told Lowry, was still "wholly dependent on Lincoln Kirstein's energies, money and the contributions of three regular patrons," amounting to about $50,000 a year above box-office receipts—too little to cover operating costs and new productions, especially since City Center was trying valiantly to "keep prices LOW. Result: deficits."[5]

The NYCB was also subject to the instability of City Center, which, in addition to the ballet, housed opera and theater companies. Baum waged constant battles with the city, arguing at one point that as a people's theater serving the city's working classes, students, and artists, City Center deserved the same $1-a-year rent afforded to the Brooklyn Academy of Music. Lincoln spent most of his time raising money and positioning the company with the city's notables, including the building czar Robert Moses (who remembered Lincoln's father well) and the inevitable Rockefellers. Even so, things remained difficult, and the company was constantly on the brink. When Lincoln wangled a three-year grant for new works from the Rockefellers in 1953, for example, the company was still hamstrung by a fiscal crisis engulfing the theater—what good was new work, if City Center itself was insolvent? The bottom line was ticket sales. The invented tradition of *The Nutcracker* was a help, but not enough. George took these endless crises with his usual preternatural calm, with occasional outbursts of impatience to Betty.

To boot, he was at the time already furious with Baum and feeling unusually touchy about money. Baum and his colleagues had picked at George over *A Midsummer Night's Dream,* which he was already worried about. Why Mendelssohn? Do you really think he is such a great composer? Why not Richard Strauss? And isn't it too long—can't you cut it to a single act? Finally, in a fit of pique, George lost his temper and screamed at them, "You go to Hell!" and walked out. He then asked Betty to ask Baum (instinctively avoiding further confrontation) to give him a salary, and Baum came back with a stingy offer: a small salary, on condition that his royalties—all he was paid at the time—revert to City Center. Tanny was furious: "I think this hurt George just terribly—he and Baum have been together for about 25 years—I could just cry—No, I could just kill them."[6] Balanchine absorbed it, but it was a breach—another confirmation that he could trust no one.

Then, on December 16, 1963, a windfall. The Ford Foundation announced a major grant of $7,756,000 to "strengthen classical ballet in the United States."[7] It was an unprecedented sum—a bit like his parents' winning the lottery—and the lion's share went to Balanchine. SAB received a whopping $2,400,000 over ten years, and an additional $1,500,000 to dole out at its discretion to teachers and schools across the country. (The thrifty Ouroussow made the most of the money by squirreling it away in small interest-earning accounts in banks all over the city.) In addition, Lowry helped negotiate a plan for SAB to eventually move into the Juilliard School building at the new Lincoln Center.[8] As for the NYCB, they received $2,500,000. "We had hoped," Balanchine's official announcement read, "that someday a miracle would happen—and here it is. . . . We can breathe."[9] Six smaller companies around the country received (lesser) funding too—four of them run by Balanchine acolytes. Lucia Chase's American Ballet Theatre received nothing, and modern dance was entirely ignored.[10] Lowry had almost single-handedly made SAB and the NYCB the country's de facto national ballet.

The retribution for this sudden amassing of power and resources was swift and harsh. Martha Graham phoned Lincoln and angrily shouted "Thief!"; he cursed at her and hung up. He was approached by disapproving strangers on the street and in restaurants: "How does it feel to take bread out of other people's mouths?"[11] Prominent modern dancers fired off furious, disappointed letters to Lowry, complaining that Ford seemed entirely blind to the only truly American tradition the country possessed: them. *Time* magazine even reported the backlash and the fear that Balanchine was out to impose his "American style" on "the entire US dance world." He had achieved, the magazine noted, a kind of cult status, and his young dancers spoke of him "as if he were Yahweh." But none of these "howls of rage," as Lincoln put it to Jerry, seemed to bother George, for the practical reason, he said, that "the money is granted."[12] But inside he was hurt, and as he strengthened his armor against the outside world, he noted resentfully that no one seemed to notice that he was using "Ford's millions" to help raise the standards of dance for them all and also giving the gift of his own ballets, *free*.[13]

If Ford was not enough, the new Lincoln Center for the Performing Arts, which had been in planning stages since the late 1950s, was finally under construction. Its central square, inspired by the Piazza San Marco in Venice, would be composed of three large white travertine buildings set off like jewels on an elevated clearing, rising up near Central Park. From a distance you could already see the outline of this new "Athens on the Subway," as it was dubbed by the press: the Metropolitan Opera (still a shell), the newly completed Philharmonic Hall, and the New York State Theater.[14] The $185 million campus would also eventually include the Lincoln Center Performing Arts Library and Museum, the Vivian Beaumont Theater, the Juilliard School, Damrosch Park, and the Guggenheim Bandshell. Surrounding this theatrical core, a small society was laid out: an outpost of Fordham University, two public schools, a shopping center, parking garages, a hotel, an office building, and more than four thousand new luxury and middle-income apartments.[15] That April, when much of the complex was still a hole in the ground, the NYCB moved into its spanking new home at the New York State Theater, one of the first of the buildings to be completed. Slated to be the largest performing arts complex in the world—to rival anything in the USSR—

Lincoln Center was a planned utopia of art, and no one closely involved seemed to terribly mind the great irony that this utopia would be built up from an immigrant community razed for the purpose.

The festivities in April 1964 for the opening of the New York State Theater were beamed live into living rooms across the country on CBS TV, with George, Lincoln, and an invited audience studded with New York's political and artistic elite in attendance. There was a tour of the auditorium and a flowery speech by Lincoln's old friend Nelson Rockefeller, now the governor of New York, extolling this "first theater ever created by a legislature," by and for the people, and another by Nelson's brother John D. Rockefeller III, among other dignitaries. Lincoln and George, looking like the odd couple, one huge and hulking, the other small and spritely, were interviewed in the lobby, and the performance featured selections from *Carousel* and the NYCB at its most patriotic with *Stars and Stripes*.[16]

The New York State Theater was Lincoln's baby. It had taken a decade to accomplish, and the negotiations had brought him, along with Morton Baum and Betty Cage, up against the powerful Robert Moses and an array of wealthy interests hoping to capitalize on the venture. Lincoln's personal relationship with the Rockefellers was key. Moses had realized he could use a modest plan to relocate the Metropolitan Opera, which he didn't care about, to help fund something he did care about: the largest urban-renewal project in the nation. With funding for slum clearance under Title 1 of the Federal Housing Act, along with bits of other city, state, and private funding, plans were thus set in motion to redevelop the area of Lincoln Square—or San Juan Hill, as residents called it. This meant bulldozing fourteen city blocks, between Sixty-second and Seventieth Streets, between Broadway and Amsterdam Avenues, and displacing some seven thousand low-income families ("You cannot make an omelet without breaking some eggs," Moses chimed), an ugly social fact, which led to a public outcry that Lincoln both agreed with and helped Nelson to allay. Jerry Robbins, seizing the moment and documenting the crime, shot the opening scenes of the film of *West Side Story* on the leveled ruins that would become Lincoln Center and the house of Balanchine.[17]

By that time, Nelson had arranged for New York State to help fund the so-named State Theater by linking it to the 1964 World's Fair. Rockefeller put in $15,000,000 in New York State funds and the city and private donors each put in $2,150,000 to help meet the total projected cost of $19,300,000. Meanwhile, Lincoln was busy winnowing the competition. It was Ford all over again: Martha Graham and Lucia Chase wanted in, but he campaigned effectively against them, using his contacts and friendship with the Rockefellers to make the case that the future lay with Balanchine. He had been making this case for most of his life, and it was finally taking hold in the inner sanctums of boardroom power. Next, he threw his weight behind the design of the building and pressed for Phil Johnson, his old and now famous friend, to design the theater in close consultation with Balanchine.[18]

After more than forty years of roaming, George was on the brink of having his own theater, and he plunged into the designs. He wanted a festive civic space, good sight lines, and none of the pomp and hierarchy of European houses. He referred to the theater as "our church," and Johnson, who agreed for his own reasons, described his State Theater as a modern *Volkstheater*, a "non aristocratic, large house with elegance" in a light, neoclassical style. Critics generally approved, although adherents of brutalism, with its Socialist undertow, pejoratively referred to it as Johnson's "ballet class style," and it was true that the building was a kind of pure artifice that, like ballet, hid its inner strength and tucked steel trusses and support structures, for example, behind a jeweled ceiling.

But it also had a deliberately democratic feel. The lobby was large and airy with clean lines flanked by wide banks of stairs that carried audiences to a spacious second-floor promenade. This "great hall," as it was called, was fifty feet long, sixty feet wide, and two hundred feet high and felt like a grand indoor plaza or agora, joined at every level by Italianate balcony walkways where people could congregate around its elegant central space—Balanchine liked it because it was modern but still made him feel like he was in Venice. The huge wall facing the outdoor plaza was transparent—a stunning seven thousand square feet of glass—hung with eight million gold-anodized aluminum beads, one for each citizen of New York City. Further emphasizing its nonhierarchical identity, the house had Continental seating—no center aisles—to bring its audience into a single community, and the five rings rose steeply so that most of the 2,729 seats were within one hundred feet of the stage. Johnson called this "papering the walls with people," and there were no boxes for the wealthy, and the ceiling chandelier, which Balanchine had imagined as a "marvel of cut-crystal," was instead made of everyday plastic and mirrors shaped into a gaudy jewel-like fixture. Tanny and Jerry thought it looked like headlights, or cheap rhinestones, which it did.[19]

The backstage areas, which interested Johnson less and Balanchine more, were a problem. The windowless rehearsal rooms were lit with harsh fluorescent lights and cooled with air-conditioning that left the dancers dry and gasping, and the floors were dangerously sticky. Balanchine let it go, but he drew the line at the stage, which was a disaster. It was large enough, but the floor was concrete covered in a mauve linoleum that reflected eerily onto the dancers' costumes.[20] "If you had a race horse, would you run it on concrete?" he asked, as he firmly insisted on the installation of a costly woven-wood floor, sprung to ease the impact on human joints of landing from high jumps, and covered in a durable nonslip battleship-gray linoleum used by the navy.

Next came the orchestra pit, which he had specifically designated for a full symphony orchestra. He was in Russia, in 1962, when he learned that it had been shrunk to a Broadway-style pit, and when he returned, he said it would simply have to be dynamited and properly rebuilt, nonnegotiable. No one was happy with this extra work, and when the ceiling in one of the studios fell in and missed killing George by inches, it was said that the disgruntled workers had done it on purpose.[21] (Balanchine just stepped calmly aside and said, "Rebecca Harkness," referring to the competitive heiress who was building her own rehearsal studios with chandeliers.)[22] Lincoln, for his part, moved to anchor the airy promenade with two large and sensual Nadelman women placed at either end of the hall like giant folk goddesses presiding over their new realm. To get these nineteen-foot, twelve-ton sculptures into the theater, crews were forced to blast a large hole in one of the already constructed walls.[23] More grumbling, but they did it.

No sooner was the theater completed than the deal collapsed. The breaking point was ticket prices and control of the theater's schedule. Lincoln, Betty, and Baum were fighting hard to keep prices low and to secure a dependable season for the company, but Lincoln Center wanted board control so they could rent the theater to the highest bidder and set ticket prices to cover costs—the NYCB would get whatever time was left over. Lincoln was furious. "We are being thrown out of the State Theater, having built it; it is all too ghastly, but inevitable and I long foresaw it. . . . They want to raise the prices, steal the house, and get in a ballet company which they say will be more 'eclectic' than Balanchine."[24] Lincoln was fighting his oldest fight: against the blue-blood wealth of New York and the (openly anti-Semitic) Metropolitan Opera board, in the interests of the scrappier, more creative émigrés at Baum's City Center. "Your associates are not inimical to art," he wrote to Nelson, finally laying it on the level in a burst of temper; "to them it is not real. Their habit is compulsive charity to maintain dynastic prestige." He blasted the Lincoln Center leadership in print, explaining sourly to a friend, "I doubt if we will remain long in Lincoln Center; they really hate us, and musical-comedy, after all, is the great American art-form. Or something."[25] Finally, the men of Lincoln Center gave in, and in 1965 the City Center of Music and Drama leased the New York State Theater for twenty-five years, renewable, and the NYCB became a constituent member of Lincoln Center—with full control of ticket prices. They had won.[26]

Balanchine had his Mariinsky.[27] To fill this enormous new house, he would need bigger dances—*Don Quixote* would be one—and better dancers. Thanks to the Ford Foundation scholarships and to Balanchine's "purge" and renewal of the company after *Agon*, a whole new generation of young and more highly trained dancers was flowing in. This "new breed," as they were dubbed by *Newsweek*, came from all over the United States. Some started at SAB, which, like the old Theater School in St. Petersburg, had become a pipeline to the company. Balanchine wanted them young—eight or nine, as young as he had been in Russia. The idea was that they would grow up dancing child roles in ballets such as *The Nutcracker* before moving seamlessly into the company—no audition, just a casual comment from Ouroussow or Cage: "You have rehearsal today at the theater," and that was that. In the meantime, thanks to Ford, the school was also bringing in dancers trained at satellite schools across the nation. It was the achievement Balanchine had long ago envisioned, but it came with consequences. The company was no longer an intimate family of dancers, and the dancers were no longer Balanchine's peers. At sixty he was old enough to be their father—grandfather even—and George and Lincoln's "progressive" troupe was quickly becoming a large and established institution.

Still, many of Balanchine's new daughters and sons were from the usual old stock: European and Russian backgrounds, émigré families, women without fathers, men who were gay or had fallen into ballet somehow, by luck or by chance. George, who personally selected each and every dancer, "papered" his theater with people he intuitively knew. Kay Mazzo, from Chicago, came from an Italian and Yugoslavian family and was at the school from age eleven. Carol Sumner's parents were Lithuanian. Bettijane Sills's father was Polish and Jewish. Victoria Simon's parents were Russian and Austro-Hungarian. Mimi Paul's mother was French Catholic, and her father was an Odessan Jew. Lynne Stetson, from Dallas, had English Mennonite and Swiss German parents. Patricia McBride was raised in Teaneck, New Jersey, by her Swiss mother after her father disappeared; and Violette Verdy (née Nelly Amande Guillerm) was French and also fatherless. She survived World War II with her mother, who was Catholic and a devotee of Eastern mysticism. Patricia Neary lost her father at nineteen—her sister Colleen was nine—and their mother kept a rooming house for dancers and manned the canteen (and the gossip mill) at the theater. Karin von Aroldingen was East German, raised by her mother and aunt after her father was killed during World War II. Among the men, John Prinz was from Chicago, of Austro-Hungarian and Slavic origin. Conrad Ludlow was a shy dyslexic kid from Montana who found a world studying Yugoslavian folk dance before joining Balanchine. Kent Stowell was from a polygamist Mormon family in Utah (he had twenty-five brothers and sisters), and ballet was a way out. Suki Schorer, petite with a quick, analytic mind and a body recovered from childhood polio, came from a literary family, and her father, Mark Schorer, tried to write a biography of Balanchine, who finally said no and declined to cooperate.[28] The list goes on.

Gordon Boelzner was another new arrival in 1959. A piano prodigy of sorts, he had impeccable training—the Eastman and Manhattan schools of music—and might have had a concert career but ended up with Balanchine instead. Boyish and anxious, Gordon was gay, moody, and a loner with a dark side and a mischievous sense of humor. He had a counterculture sensibility, read philosophy, studied with John Cage, hung around with Christopher Isherwood and later with Andy Warhol at the Factory. (Gordon's apartment had a bleeding finger on the sink, an arm on the kitchen wall, and a huge fish in the bathtub, and the only chair was a dentist's chair.) He could sight-read a difficult orchestral score on the spot, transposing as he went—a rare skill—and Balanchine quickly came to depend on his musical knowledge and instincts. "Where's Gordon?" he would say as he arrived at the theater with his own piano transcription of a score tucked under his arm, and Gordon, dressed informally except for some wild pair of shoes or a single shocking sock, would stuff the score into his old leather schoolboy satchel, and later pull it out for George—"Not bad, EXCEPT . . ."—and they would dive into the music together. Gordon was at the theater day and night, and for morning class, he would lighten the mood with improvised versions of Motown, the Beatles, Gershwin, show tunes ("Bali Ha'i"), or old World War I ditties, such as "The Whistler and His Dog" or "The Glow Worm." Emotionally mercurial, Gordon had a rocky private life, and Balanchine became his anchor, his father, his mentor. Balanchine, who depended on no one, depended on Gordon.[29]

Gordon also served as a foil to the company's new conductor, Robert Irving, "the Duke," who arrived in 1963 (when Barzin left) and conducted the orchestra until after Balanchine's death. Tall and fattish with a flushed, moon-shaped face and saucer mouth, as Tanny noted, Irving was terribly British—Winchester, Royal Air Force, Oxford—and had narrowly lost out as the principal conductor of the London Philharmonic Orchestra. He had come from Ashton and London's Sadler's Wells Ballet, perhaps drawn to NYCB by its more adventurous musical repertory.[30] Spiky and gay, with a taste for wealthy friends, racehorses, and drink (he routinely slipped out to O'Neil's during intermission and downed a whiskey waiting for him on the bar), he settled for Balanchine, who respected him enormously and fought with him constantly over tempos and interpretation. Gordon knew how to tease this stuffy Englishman and relax a tense situation with Balanchine by sardonically delivering silly jokes—"Blah-nheim not Blenheim, isn't it?" he would tease the red-faced Irving, and on they went. Jerry Zimmerman, a fine Juilliard-trained pianist—who was also gay, funny, soulful, and might have had a concert career—joined them in 1969 and stayed until after Balanchine's death. It was a world-class team of artists with the talent but not the temperament for major musical careers.

As for dances, to fill his new Mariinsky, Balanchine took the seams out of his existing ballets. Some, like *Symphony in C*, got larger casts, but mostly the dancers expanded the ballets from within as they learned to move farther, faster, bigger—"More!" he shouted, as they took running starts, pushing off from the back walls of the wings to fly to center stage. For repertory, he instinctively turned back to Russia and the imperial past: Tchaikovsky, Glinka, Petipa, early Stravinsky, and the full-length narrative ballets of his childhood at the Imperial Theater. It was a conservative turn, not nostalgia so much as a way of giving his young dancers the education he had received. Nothing would make them stronger than the strict exigencies of Petipa's classical form, and in the course of the 1960s and 1970s, he filled his theater with new and old dances inspired by the imperial past: *Ballet Imperial, Harlequinade, Tarantella, Glinkiana, Valse Fantaisie, Firebird.* But the point was also emotional. Petipa, then and later, was a touchstone for Balanchine—a tradition, place, person he could trust and draw upon. It was his garden—an ordered and artful style, like the court to which it belonged, nothing wild or dismembered. It was whole in its way, complete, and it could be trusted and expanded upon; he could make it plotless and his own, in speed, timing, and gesture, without losing Petipa, as he did in many pure dance ballets of immense beauty, pattern, and musical design, including *Allegro Brillante, Divertimento No.15, Theme and Variations, Brahms-Schoenberg Quartet,* and *Tchaikovsky Piano Concerto No. 2.* To dress these works, many of them tutu ballets, in the lavish style they required, Balanchine and Karinska established a fully equipped costume shop, another piece of Russia permanently annexed to his Lincoln Center realm.

His rule was personal, and even as the company grew, he knew everyone who worked for him, from the principal dancers to the musicians, dressers, costume designers, stage managers, and lighting techs down to the lowliest stagehands. He knew how to talk to them all, he took the time, and he knew in a split second—and they knew he knew—if someone was faking it. He studied their flaws and eccentricities and had a feel for their lives, loved gossip, found out where they were from, what they read, who they slept with, where they liked to eat and drink, which TV shows they watched. His quiet good manners were genuine and gracious, and Mr. B, they all said, was "everywhere" in the theater, even when he was spending months of the year abroad. All he had to do was put his head into a rehearsal room or silently cross the stage and everyone sat up straighter and stepped up a notch. He had a kind of omniscience—calm, selfless, certain of them and the enterprise they were all serving—and something in his manner and aura made them seek his approval.

Lincoln Center was only a start. On June 30, 1964, Nelson Rockefeller, with Lincoln at his side, broke ground upstate for the NYCB's summer home, the Saratoga Performing Arts Center (SPAC). It was another spanking-new arts center, this time for the entire state of New York, that would include ballet, music, theater (directed by Lincoln's old friend John Houseman), film, and popular entertainments, along with a summer dance and music school. Saratoga had been a summer destination for high society (the Whitneys, Vanderbilts, Paysons, Wideners) ever since the nineteenth century. It was a prime location that already boasted baths, casinos, a racetrack, and now a 5,100-seat open amphitheater, situated in a 1,500-acre park, with room for an additional seven thousand people on the lawn stretching out from the stage. Once again, Balanchine had a hand in the planning: acoustics, lighting, stage design, rehearsal spaces, auditorium, even the shifting of a waterfall and removal of crickets threatening to disrupt the orchestral sound. Like Lincoln Center, SPAC included provisions for the surrounding society—in this case, a new eighteen-hole golf course, pools, tennis courts, a picnic area, and a facelift for the once elegant Gideon Putnam Hotel.[31]

The opening was slated for the summer of 1966, and Nelson hired Dick Leach to run it. Leach was Sorbonne-educated and a former navy lieutenant who had founded the Aspen Music Festival and worked closely with John D. Rockefeller III at Lincoln Center. Leach wanted Saratoga to be like a European festival too, and for the next two decades, the NYCB would spend summers at SPAC, and Balanchine would live at River Run, the Leach family estate, where he rented a modest guest cottage next to the richly appointed main house.

As if this were not a wide enough wingspan, Balanchine set out that same year to help establish a new company in Los Angeles. He would give his name and ballets, along with support from NYCB rehearsal masters. They were well into the planning when the director, James Doolittle, went rogue and asked the recently defected Kirov star Rudolf Nureyev and his British ballerina, Margot Fonteyn, to dance a gala benefit. George angrily pulled out. The company, he wrote in a long and devastating letter to Doolittle, "has become something that I didn't want." It should be "an independent . . . company for the city with civic support," not a commercially produced Doolittle enterprise dependent on celebrity superstars. There were no Nureyevs in *his* company, he later explained. "We are all Americans. We don't have these great names but we have dancers who can dance everything."[32] If Doolittle didn't want that, Balanchine didn't want Doolittle.

Requests for advice, support, and ballets flooded in from across the country—the Western Ballet, the Louisville Ballet, the Lyric Opera of Chicago, and a company in New Orleans, among many others—along with stacks of gold-embossed invitations (most politely refused) to embassies, parties, events, and inaugurations. To field these burgeoning requests, Balanchine needed a gatekeeper, and in 1963 he used his new salary at the school to hire Barbara Horgan, who had briefly left the company, as his personal assistant. For the next twenty years, she would be his closest companion, the woman who organized and ran his life. She called him at seven every morning, and he would often answer from the bathtub, and they would discuss the day's schedule while he soaked. She handled his growing correspondence ("Mr. Balanchine doesn't feel he can") and managed his schedule, money (he didn't know or care how much he had), insurance, doctors, foreign travel, hotels, and anything else going on at "headquarters" that Betty shunted her way.[33]

His career in Europe was exploding too, and he was staging operas and mounting his ballets in Berlin, Cologne, Hamburg, Paris, London, Vienna, Geneva, Zurich, Copenhagen, and Milan. He did it because the projects were interesting and because he liked being in Europe. In 1959 Balanchine had proposed that his dances be distributed through a "lend-lease" style program overseen by the State Department's Bureau of International Cultural Relations, and for a moment they were.[34] To the frustration of his European agent, the Russian impresario Leonide Leonidoff, Balanchine still didn't care about money and constantly refused fees: give my fee to Allegra to pay for her mother to come; or to Una Kai or Francia Russell, who were staging the ballets. "I will help," he said to the director in Berlin (via Barbara), but please, expenses only: no title, no terms, no fee, no contract. He still hated contracts, and Leonidoff pressed the point: Why should you subsidize state administrations? And besides, by taking less you undercut my ability to get more. "Why shouldn't you be paid? It's not personal!"[35] Barbara pressed too, noting that Balanchine could ill afford his own generosity, but he didn't care. He didn't want to be tied down by anyone or anything and wouldn't change. Besides, eschewing money was a deliberate stance, part of his war against mundane material desires and bourgeois culture (except good wine, first-class travel and hotels). The byt that came with success was fast encroaching on his life.[36]

Artistically, the Hamburg State Opera held a special place. It was directed by Rolf Liebermann, a Swiss Jew and a composer and conductor with adventurous taste and a strong interest in contemporary music. Appointed in 1957, he made the Hamburg opera one of the leading houses in postwar Europe. He and George had met in 1959 through Nicky Nabokov, and Liebermann often invited George to stage both operas and ballets. George liked Liebermann, and he liked Hamburg. George's German was good enough, and he appreciated the ordered and gemütlich feel of the city and the restrained Old World grandeur of the Hotel Vier Jahreszeiten, where he stayed. The opera house, bombed to a shell during the war, had been rebuilt as an appealingly functional civic opera house, glass with a simple brown wood.

He didn't care about money, but he did care about his dances and tightly controlled their dissemination and performance. "No, you may not stage *Episodes*," Barbara wrote to Liebermann in a rare refusal; "it is a very difficult work and requires a very well-trained company. Mr. Balanchine feels it could not be danced by any company other than his own."[37] No to *Agon, Movements, Monumentum* too, only his company could do them, he said. Liebermann pressed: what about *Liebeslieder Walzer*? Impossible, George responded (through Barbara), only the eight original dancers know the ballet, and even he could not mount it. To help stage the ballets he did approve, he developed a front line of trusted stagers from among his former dancers, including Una Kai and Francia Russell, who fanned out across Europe mounting his dances.[38]

He even thought, vaguely, about succession—about sons he didn't have or could train. It had to be a son—a woman couldn't make dances for women; only a man who loves women could do that, he believed. So he continued to encourage a few, such as Jacques d'Amboise, John Taras, Francisco Moncion (briefly), and Eddie Villella (more briefly). And soon Paul Mejia, John Clifford, and finally (in the 1970s) Peter Martins. Balanchine helped with music (Ralph Vaughan Williams's *Fantasia* is too "mooshy," he counseled and then relented, but no Wagner, please, too heavy), watched their progress, solved problems, and suggested changes.[39] He even at one point invited Massine's son, Lorca Massine, but that was more of a barb at the father—see who's king now—than a vote for his mediocre progeny. With Robbins absent and working mostly on Broadway, it was a way of taking some of the weight off himself, but artistically it was always a bit halfhearted. Who could measure up to him or to Jerry? None did.

Balanchine's schedule could still be punishing. In 1964 alone he traveled for Ford to Cincinnati, Dayton, Cleveland, Buffalo, Nashville, then back to New York for the premiere of a new ballet; then briefly to London and Vienna before rejoining the company in Washington and New York; and then out again to Montreal and back to New York for the Ford-sponsored choreographers and teachers seminars that he personally ran at SAB, followed by tours with the company to Chicago and Los Angeles.[40] Not to mention producing a steady stream of new ballets. Ouroussow was not the only one to note the mounting strain: "With Balanchine it has become quite difficult in recent times," she confided to her son; "he is overtired and wants to do everything himself. . . . The more millions one gets, the worse one sleeps."[41]

It is worth pausing for a moment over his achievement. He knew what he was aiming for—he had grown up with it in St. Petersburg—but he was building from thin air what had taken centuries for kings and czars and commissars to establish across Russia and Europe. He had many helpers, Lincoln for one, and the wind of the Cold War behind him, but it is nonetheless astonishing that he was able to build from the ground up not only the ballets but the institutions of a new American art. He was a magnet—people were drawn to him, and they didn't often leave. And although he could be autocratic, he also trusted; they stayed because he left them alone to invent their roles. At moments his ego was as huge and petty as anyone's, full of the vanities and virtues of his nature, but his company, like his dances, was something apart—or above. He was a great builder for the same reason that he was a great artist: he gave them all a purpose greater than himself. Greater than themselves.

The artistic and personal cost of building an empire was nonetheless high, and as he rose his inner life fell to ruin. The 1960s were an apex, but they were also the years his health broke. His marriage broke. His art broke. He became moody and irritable, even when he was in his element—charming the press, training dancers, putting up shows, and presiding over the expanding court of Balanchine. Some part of him knew that success and establishment standing were a poisoned chalice, and his instinct to run was almost as strong as his instinct to rule. He kept running in reserve; even at the sumptuous celebrations for the opening of Lincoln Center, he had nervously assured one astonished dancer that he could always flee and start another company somewhere else.[42] He knew he was in danger, even as he reached for the prize.

The danger started with Tanny, if it started anywhere. She had grown softer and fuller, the glamorously chiseled edges of her youth sunk into her broadening face and whitening wispy hair, her lower body ever-inert. Their life had grown softer and fuller too, a comfortable but routine domestic affair, full of cooking (she wrote a book of dancers' recipes) and cats (another on how their cat Mourka could be trained to leap like a dancer). Her ecstasies over food, recorded in countless letters with detailed descriptions of meals, were the most lasting thing between them: "First we had Vodka with dill in it (I didn't) then we had Westphalian ham with a deliciously ripe melon. Then we had 2½ inch thick charcoal broiled steak. Yummy we ate inside but cooked the steak outside—with the steak we had potatoes home fried, and cauliflower with a creamy parmesan gravy—then we had endive with herbs from the garden basil and thyme then coffee fudge ice cream." There were plans for gardening in Weston ("George put a picket fence with an arbor thing around the tool house," she reported excitedly to a friend).[43] Home improvements, visitors, and dinner parties filled their lives as he relinquished any hope of ever restoring her crippled form. But these domesticities couldn't make up for what they—or he—had lost in the studio, and it didn't help that their intimate life since her illness had apparently not gone well. Snapshots of them together in their beloved Weston show George dimmed and preoccupied. Living with her broken body was too hard, he later said. It was destroying him.[44]

Even the love triangles were familiar: George, Tanny, and the annoyingly intrusive Edith: "Do you know she goes up every Friday to the country? Rearranges all the furniture? Brings her dishes and glassware from NY. . . . Don't tell me to be nice to my mother. She is overpowering, and quite selfish at times. . . . And she doesn't work or do anything for anyone (George says) except herself."[45] Or even more awkwardly: George, Diana, and Tanny. Diana was still Tanny's best friend and a love object for George, and she was still at their home a lot in a tense and unspoken ménage à trois that revolved around cooking and food, with Balanchine's frustrated desires in Diana's hands. She controlled the two things that mattered to him most, whether she danced and whether she loved. Or even George, Tanny, and Jerry: "Jerry came over last night, and was most charming—he came late, and gave George a Soviet lacquer box, with a dancing peasant on it, which he, (George) disliked natch."[46] Another time they played word games at Jerry's, and George couldn't keep up with Tanny and Jerry's quick-witted banter and went home feeling angry and slighted. Tanny and Jerry ran hot and cold, but their correspondence (he called her Lucy, she called him Charlie Brown) shows a deep and ongoing intimacy. Meanwhile, with George often away or occupied at the theater, Tanny was retreating into her own society of helpers and friends, and a glass menagerie of homespun theatrics, such as the miniature stage she designed with photos of their cat Mourka variously dressed as pope, cardinal, and king or set as the Three Musketeers in period style with red velvet curtains thrown over a table, hand sewn with fringe and tassels.

A word about cats. Balanchine loved them, and Tanny did too. Mourka was something to care for, the child they never had, but there was more to it than that. Cats are loyal, detached, and self-sufficient—loners. Mourka was domesticated, but only in the sense that she was kept indoors. Cats don't lose the wild, but they adapt and accept the world they are given. They aren't emotionally dependent and don't try to win love, as dogs do. They just exist, like flowers and ballets. Balanchine adored cats, which, in many ways, were easier to love than women. He even trained Mourka to jump, and he and Tanny had her perform at their annual Christmas party for Stravinsky. The family picture on Balanchine's wall at the theater was—Mourka.[47]

Diana was by then a serious problem. Balanchine's marriage, in spite of its domestic reassurances, was failing, and he couldn't get Diana out of his mind. "She's holding my head under water," he despaired to Lucia Davidova, who worried at one point that his despair was suicidal. There had even been a child, his child, he told Lucia (and later Jacques), and Diana had promised she would go to Canada to have it, but she miscarried.[48] Whatever the truth of this story—and Lucia had her own complicated attachment to Balanchine—George froze when he heard the news. "I am weak," he confided to Jacques one afternoon in 1963 when they met on a street corner; "it is only monks who deny their bodies who succeed," he said, but to make a dance, he had to think of "how beautiful the girl is" and how much he would like to touch her and kiss her.[49]

Loneliness stood like an axe over his gift. To make dances, he needed to be physically attracted to a dancer, and she had to be a great dancer—or to have that potential, some ember or light inside her. He was like an animal sniffing out this light. "The conception of the sacred—not church—but an even more distilled form of perfection, that's what Balanchine was after, an atmosphere, a scent, *cette personne a quelque chose*," as Violette Verdy put it.[50] Pursuing a woman, winning her, and nurturing and lavishing everything he knew upon her—that was the primary object of his life and art. Without love and eroticism, he would shrivel up inside and run dry. That's what the NYCB was—a whole company of women who might, just might, become great dancers—and their striving and womanly beauty, if he could help them find it, was the material of his dances. Love of a woman was his breath, his inspiration, "the one thing that you want to do . . . You are inspired to get up and do things, and you shout in the night."[51] It was his old Pygmalion conundrum, except that his statues were already alive—and not always cooperative. As Tanny receded and Diana refused, and as he grew older and more preoccupied with the business of running a large institution, he found himself dangerously stranded and alone.

So he availed himself of his "new breed" of young dancers. "The history of man over forty is *Lolita*," he later ruefully noted.[52] Except that now he was sixty with an ever-receding hairline, wrinkling skin, and a noticeable paunch—a fact that only intensified the urgency of his desires. He was who he was: a genius, elegant, restrained, a true gentleman in an old courtly-love style—but also at times vulgar and lewd, a dirty old man (they said, brushing it off) or an adolescent boy, making a fucking motion with his hands and trading sexual exploits in backstage locker-room talk with stagehands, or with Ronnie, Eddie, or Ducky, the wry and very gay English dresser down the hall from his office on the fourth floor, who also joined the company around this time. Balanchine consorted more and more with gay men—no competition—and awkwardly "played sugar daddy," as Jacques put it, annoyed for his own reasons, to his young dancers.[53]

There was perfume for a dancer he admired, even if he didn't sleep with her, and he liked it that he could smell his favorites in the theater (you worried if you *didn't* get perfume, one said). He wore perfume too—a light scent of Coty's Emeraude wafting from a silk foulard.[54] Made from the oils or "souls" of dead flowers, perfume was part of the theatrical atmosphere backstage, which was its own zone of seduction and artifice. Perfume masked a woman's natural smell, and signaled her femininity, her presence, and, above all, his possession. (Even perfume had Cold War resonance in the USSR. Like lipstick, it was considered a bourgeois opiate and made unavailable. He sent large bottles of it to his family.) Another favorite gift was wine—by the case—delivered to a dancer's door from Sherry-Lehmann on Madison Avenue. A dancer who cooked for him at her apartment received, more practically, a Farberware rotisserie and a stainless-steel carving knife. He even bought her a refrigerator. He dressed the women in his life the way he dressed his wives—the way he dressed up in his mother's finest as a child, the way he admired the fine clothing of gay men, or bent over costume fittings, engrossed in the details of a skirt or bodice. He shopped with them, or for them, in Paris, Rome, Berlin: a coveted pair of shoes, a Dior dress, an expensive handbag or hat. In airports he liked to stock up on silk scarves, duty-free.

He was discreet, sort of, perhaps for Tanny's sake. Una Kai was setting his ballets across Europe and became a lover, or so she claimed, in the early 1960s, when he joined her to help. She was shy and had been scared of him since her dancing days and long-since-ended marriage to Eddie Bigelow, and one afternoon in his office, he had taken her face impulsively in his hands and kissed her hard on the lips. Gifts followed: a smooth, almond-colored leather handbag in Hamburg, dinners in Paris, hotels with connecting rooms, a kitschy poolside seduction at Rouben Ter-Arutunian's home in Los Angeles—she in a white bikini and he in tight swimming shorts looking like a red lobster. Finally she got pregnant (Is it mine?—No, not yours), and their liaison faded. It reads like a girlish romance novel; she wished she had kissed him back, shown her feelings; he was a wonderful lover and said the things that make any woman feel beautiful—but had any of it really happened? She told no one until she was close to death, and even Barbara, who knew most everything, didn't know, or didn't want to know, or pretended not to know. Reticent, pushy Una—all that life since lived, and Balanchine was the sticking place.[55]

For Balanchine, she was part of the landscape, and there were other encounters with dancers in lonely hotel rooms as they traveled on Ford Foundation excursions, as well as ongoing sporadic relations with women in the company, which in at least one case went on intermittently for years. There were women who told all, women who denied it ("I want to be classy, like the wives"), women who said it was so when it wasn't, and everything in between. Even his relationship with Barbara Horgan (who later lived with a woman) slid occasionally into sex, and it was Barbara, young and giddy with a fancy new dress, who had accompanied George to the Lincoln Center opening, while Tanny stayed at home.

As the list grows, it starts to look like Don Juan's catalogue. But it wasn't, really. He didn't lie, he didn't propose marriage as a ruse, he wasn't smooth or by then particularly physically seductive even, although some found him sexy, and he didn't collect lovers like prizes. Conquest was part of it, but as the years went on, there was something impersonal about these encounters, which seemed to carry little weight and minimal sex. Listening to the women who had them calls to mind a voyeur or perennial watcher, a first-wing vantage point even in his own affairs. His pursuits—even if he loved the chase—could sound lonely, such as his postperformance visits for "drinks" with a dancer who bore an uncanny resemblance to Tanny, or the way he would invite a dancer or two or three to dine with him after a show, often impromptu, and they would leave the theater, arms gaily linked, for the Russian Tea Room or another local spot where he was a regular and kept a tab. Women fortified him. He could be charming and held forth, nose in the air, index finger raised, about wine and pairings, food and fine desserts, and he bubbled on about Plato and Nietzsche, the Bible and Sufism, Communism and politics, sports, current events, the dances they were performing. Being in his presence and the object of his attention was interesting and made them feel beautiful and special; being in their presence enlivened him. The walk home, when there was one, was like a B-grade movie: the kiss at the door, the hopeful gentleman, the invitation upstairs or the quiet rebuff. Some did; others didn't. He was always polite and never pushed.

Sex: did he, didn't he, could he, couldn't he, with whom, when, how many times? Rumors flew and every inch of his body and behavior was a subject of obsessive scrutiny by his dancers, a fact he knew and also had to incorporate. He was small, they whispered, and by then he was having trouble getting an erection and seeking out the virility potions that would preoccupy him for the rest of his life. He liked finger sex or oral sex, they said, or just wanted to touch, a brief intimacy; call me Georgi, he begged, but none of them would. He didn't stay and slept alone. He was not impotent, let's establish that, and there were pregnancies and abortions, though surprisingly few, at least that we know about, probably because he withdrew or refrained from intercourse. He loved most the dancer in the woman, less the woman herself. They knew about the wives, knew he fell in love with his dancers, married them, lavished them with the ballets they were all so desperate to dance. Who would be next—could it be me? Am I beautiful enough, good enough, strong enough? What *does* he want? Some who flirted or made love to him, if that's what it was, gained a role or two they might not otherwise have had, but others got nothing, and proof of performance was always the final arbiter. "Why am I not cast for a second performance of *Barocco*?" one asked. "Well, dear," he sniffed, "knees don't straighten and feet don't point." Sex was profane, work was sacred, and although they reflected back on each other, he knew the difference.[56]

We could list them; they could list themselves, but they won't. Family business, dirty laundry, the secret circle, and undying loyalty—to him and dancing, but also to themselves. Does it really matter, they ask, these were private encounters and they made themselves available, or didn't, even in the cycles of pride, pain, and self-recrimination his attentions could unleash inside. And there were cycles of pain. They were young, so young, and the secrecy was a dark sign of the shame and confusion that could burden their minds as they strove to make themselves into the objects and instruments of his art. It was not only sex and their bodies; it was their whole beings that were at stake; their very selves were the clay of his ballets, and it was not surprising that love and sex were so intimately and at times confusingly conjoined in their art. He had an X-ray vision and a love of each and every woman, and his dances were a kind of intimate gift—he really did know them better than they knew themselves. But he could also be "coldly instrumental." When he promoted one who had refused his advances, she said, "How kind"; he said, "Not kind at all, I run a theater, and I promoted you to see if you can make something of yourself."

We could say sex is power, but that would only be an inch of the truth. The mile would be that the whole premise of the NYCB was that Balanchine's love of women, of *them*, including the ones he didn't love or court, promised to give to them their best possible selves in dancing, a seduction few refused. This didn't mean their most moral selves, or their most pure selves, it meant their deepest "Yes, that's me" selves. The real allure lay in the work, their bodies daily before him, his soul nightly before them in his dances. These were women willing to give everything *for that*. There were no boundaries, and he sensed it, instinctively chose (and was chosen by) women partly for it—and that unboundedness, and their fight against it, was part of what made them so magnetic on stage. They were a family without sexual or incest taboos, but the fact, which was also a fuel, was that they all cared more about ballet and music than anything—and he cared about it most of all. They were all married to *that*—not to him but to dance. His dancers, he said, were simply "what I like," and the erotic impulse, the life force that he tapped, unleashed, manipulated, inspired, instilled, distorted, and needed was part of the energy behind the art and institutions he was building. They didn't expect to like him;

that's not why they were there. They loved him, and he loved them, for his dances and their dancing. As for the rest, well, that was life and it flowed through him, at least, like water and air.

It's not that it was easy to be the way he was, but he didn't think too much about it either. He wasn't psychological and had an inner humility that was both nihilistic (who cares) and liberating (anything goes). He seemed different, airy, apart, and some of the young women he approached were shocked to hear this godlike figure in their lives confess, "I am man too, you know dear." He never found a way to integrate his two bodies, and as he aged, the gap grew. Violette Verdy's mystic mother once read his tarot cards: "You are someone who does not want to be idolized; you want to be a normal man, to find that kind of life,"[57] and he said, yes, that's right, but he also knew it wasn't right, or at least it wasn't possible. He couldn't live that way, and he was asking his dancers not to live that way either. He wanted to be "normal" and wasn't, wanted a wife and couldn't bear the life, desired a woman and got a dancer, wished to be a saint and found himself a man. Governed by dance, he wasn't ashamed of his desires, or theirs, didn't ruminate on whether he was right or good or useful; that wasn't his business.

He also delighted in taking care of them. Sometime in the 1960s, for example, he invited one of his dancers to dinner with her French boyfriend. When the boyfriend failed to show up, Balanchine serenaded her over a meal and a bottle of wine with advice about unrequited love and walked her through the steps of what to say to the errant boyfriend when he called. They left the restaurant around midnight, and she went home to bed. In the middle of the night, the phone rang. It was Mr. B pretending to be her French boyfriend, complete with fake Parisian accent. He ran through a catalogue of excuses and apologies for his behavior, and she went along with the game and played her role as he had coached her, until he finally broke into his own voice and said, "Not bad dear," then hung up. When he passed her the next morning at the barre, he just nodded, and they never spoke of it again.[58] On another evening, he walked a dancer back to her hotel, but before dropping her off, he stopped at Betty Cage's brownstone to show her a print by Picasso of a cat eating a bird, just to see her reaction.[59]

In 1963 he made three new dances about the women who were most on his mind. *Bugaku* had begun several years back in the late 1950s, with Lincoln's fascination with Japanese Gagaku and Bugaku, ancient feudal musical and dance forms derived primarily from China, Korea, and India and developed in the seventh and eighth centuries at the Japanese court. Masked and lavishly costumed, Bugaku dances were slow and ritualized, often with militaristic themes. As usual Kirstein read everything—and deposited a stack of books on Balanchine's desk with no comment. In 1959 he worked with his friend Dag Hammarskjöld, United Nations secretary general, to bring the Japanese Imperial Court orchestra and dancers to City Center and to the United Nations for a series of performances and arranged for the publication of an accompanying book on the subject. Hammarskjöld, it turned out, was a great admirer of Balanchine. A serious student of mystical thought and close to Saint-John Perse and W. H. Auden (who translated Perse), he saw his mission at the United Nations in Christian terms and, echoing Balanchine, spoke openly of his desire to surpass material reality and "to influence the development of the world from within as a spiritual thing."[60]

Balanchine was interested and commissioned a Bugaku-inspired score from Toshiro Mayuzumi, a composer versed in traditional Japanese musical traditions and the Western avant-garde, for a ceremonial dance of courtship and marriage. He made this dance for Allegra, who was as erratic and elusive as ever. She warmed up before class or performances alone in her own corner off to the side at the theater, erupting into strange, sinuous movements, her flexible limbs twisted like pretzels, and sometimes she literally climbed the walls (an acquaintance recalled her sitting in a taxi with her big toe fixed to the ceiling).[61] As he began work on the central pas de deux with her and Eddie Villella (no understudies), he asked Allegra to extend one leg very high to the front while holding her foot in her hands as it extended over her head—something the pliable Kent could easily achieve. "Next Mr. B instructed Eddie to press me very close" to his own body. "Eddie and I were both a little shocked when Mr. B asked us to do movements that seemed to consummate a sexual encounter. When [he] asked me to spread my legs to the audience, I gave him the shocked look of a Salvation Army major—which he disregarded—so I did what he requested."[62]

Karinska dressed Allegra in a delicate white bikini and flowers. "I have never felt so . . . exposed," she later said, and her compressed and tensile movements, weighted by "invisible pressures on the body," worked against Eddie's macho warrior-like figure in an involuted and eroticized dance.[63] To prepare herself, Kent watched Kurosawa's *Throne of Blood* and *Rashomon*. A "sukiyaki," Balanchine lightly called it, but he guarded the ballet tightly, refusing at the time to allow it to be staged or danced by anyone else.[64] A few weeks later, Allegra appeared in class announcing that she was pregnant again. As her family grew and her marriage imploded, she moved to Scarsdale (and wrote to Balanchine: "I hope the company can wait for me. Otherwise I think I'll be the only person in Scarsdale on welfare"), moved back, had a third child, veered in and out of shape, and never fully recovered her dancing life. She sent pleading and self-excoriating notes written on scraps of paper with colored childlike circles or scrawled on the back of an envelope, asking for time, a leave of absence, and expressing her fear of being fired and dismay at her own inability to dance: "Instead of increasing my efforts, I just stopped. What am I thinking about?" Her talent was huge, and he kept her on full salary until he died, even though she was barely there, just in case she decided to come back and "make something of herself." Privately he was bitterly disappointed, but he never gave up. "Wait, wait, and wait."[65]

He turned to Diana again, this time for a pas de deux with Jacques to Stravinsky's Movements for Piano and Orchestra. It was a once-and-for-all effort to engage her, but she was only half there. "Can't take Di she really just doesn't want to dance and is fooling herself acting interested," Jacques noted in his diary. Balanchine was in a foul temper: "Like some nut—yelling at everyone very tired and impatient . . . Heading for a nervous breakdown again if he keeps this up."[66] Soon after the ballet was done, Diana announced that she was pregnant, again, and could not dance. It wasn't easy to raise Balanchine's ire, but this time he was enraged: "She stabbed me in the back," he ranted to Jacques; "she could have told me, she could have waited, there are ways, she did it on purpose."[67] He had been waiting for her all these years, he said; everything else was just work, but she inspired him, and now, "I don't know what to do." He went home, shut the door, and refused to answer the phone.

He was in a state, and the whole knotted problem of woman and statue, free will, love, and art was before them in a monolithic fight over her body. The days of *Agon* and *Episodes*, a struggle, but a struggle that worked, were over, and the intense and buried inner yearnings in play between them had been going on for too long—nearly a decade. She *really* didn't want to dance, and *that* could only take Balanchine so far. He kept pushing—why? He loved her, that's all, and she instinctively knew that her withholding was part of her power—a power that he insisted on and she didn't even exactly want but didn't relinquish either. She wanted a child, but *that* eluded her, and so they chased around what they couldn't have of each other, locked in a pattern with no resolution. And there they were again, she wouldn't, and he couldn't—Diana had no understudy. But Jacques thought that the young Suzanne Farrell, age seventeen, might be able to take on the role.

Farrell was Roberta Sue Ficker, a Midwestern girl born in Mt. Healthy, near Cincinnati, of all places, and her girlish fantasies were already wrapped up with Diana—and with Jacques. As a child she had named an armchair in her living room "Jacques d'Amboise" and danced with it, and when "Miss Adams" came to her local ballet school in search of talent and invited her to study in New York for the summer, she christened her diary "Diana." Her divorced mother—she barely knew her father, who worked in the meatpacking industry—took the chance and loaded Roberta Sue and her sisters into her 1952 Ford and drove to New York. A stolid, jaw-set woman, Catholic, from a line of independent women, she worked the night shift as a nurse's aide to make ends meet. That summer, Balanchine personally auditioned Roberta Sue—who danced and sang her dinky recital numbers—and offered her a Ford Foundation scholarship to stay, so she and her mother and sisters moved into a small flat together. The following year, Balanchine slipped in to watch class one afternoon at the school, and Barbara Horgan pulled Suzanne aside afterward to tell her that Mr. B had chosen her and one other student to join the company. She opened the phone book in search of a name more suited to the sophisticated life she now imagined for herself. Her finger landed on Farrell, Suzanne Farrell.

She became Diana's double and Balanchine's second "alabaster princess." That's when he asked her to learn Diana's role as Titania in *A Midsummer Night's Dream*, a highly unusual request (that unleashed a wave of jealous whispers) since Diana had no understudy and Suzanne was a mere newcomer. He spoke to her warmly, even romantically, in ways that filled her with emotion, and in Russia (still under eighteen, she went accompanied by her mother) he gave her flowers and took a personal interest in her knee injury, encouraging her to rest. "I want you more than you want me," he told her, and she confided these overwhelming words to her "Diana" diary. And now Jacques d'Amboise, her childhood crush, was asking her to step into Diana's role in *Movements* with him. But this was Stravinsky, and Balanchine was skeptical and didn't want anything to do with a novice substitution. Jacques persisted and convinced "Di" to teach the role to "Suzi" from her living room couch, an almost impossible task since Suzanne had never heard the music and had to quickly memorize the off-kilter, angular movements in her street clothes to Diana's humming and hand gestures, without any sense of time or space.

When Balanchine finally sullenly agreed to look, he was immediately up and "lifting her leg, molding her gestures," and demonstrating to Jacques how he should hold Suzanne. In that moment, Jacques later reflected, "Suzanne became an extension of Diana," and Diana "passed Balanchine to Suzanne." Two weeks later, Farrell rushed in late to rehearsal, delayed at school by an algebra test, to find Stravinsky, Craft, Ter-Arutunian, Kirstein, and the conductor Irving waiting. She threw on her pointe shoes and plunged into *Movements.* Stravinsky leaned over and asked George who in the world she was, and he responded simply: "Suzanne Farrell, just born." Finalizing this mythic succession, Diana passed to Suzanne an old Russian medal of the Madonna that George had once given to her.[68]

The third ballet in the row was a new pas de deux, this time for Suzanne and Jacques to Tchaikovsky's Meditation, op. 42, no. 1. Now *she* had no understudy. Before the opening night, Balanchine sent her a note from Hamburg, where he was staging Gluck's *Orpheus and Eurydice,* quoting a favorite Pushkin poem, "I Remember a Wondrous Moment":

> Dear Suzanne,
>
> Here is the poem I promise to you before I went to Hamburg. That is how Jacques should feel when he is dancing pas de deux with you.

Show to him and to Diana. She is your guarDIANAangel! But not to anyone else.

[*in red ink*]

I can't forget this blessed vision,
In front of me you stood my love,
Like instant moment of decision,
Like spirit beauteous from above.

Through languor, through despair and sorrow,
Through clamor and through restless space,
I heard your voice from night to morrow
And dreamt and dreamt of darling face

The years of storm compel surrender,
Dispel and scattered dream of mine,
And I have lost your voice so tender
And face so heavenly divine.

[*in blue ink*]:

p.s. I hope by now you are thin and beautiful and light to lift. See you soon, your GB.[69]

The ballet premiered on December 10, 1963, without George—he was in Paris on business. As a dance, it was a trifle ("more than usual corn," Lincoln noted), and Balanchine admitted a bit defensively to an interviewer, "Yes, it is emotions. . . . I hope it looks like what it is. It is the life of two people . . . a couple . . . that *almost* get together, two people *almost*—If this or if that, if it is the age, or if it is the time, but it didn't happen."[70] It was a final goodbye to Diana, announced through Suzanne, but it was also a sign of the paralyzing effect a woman could have on his imagination. It had happened with Zorina—immense passion, second-rate dances—and now, after the glories of *Agon* and *Episodes,* he had reduced Diana, through Suzanne, to a melodramatic episode. The hostility of the act should not go unnoticed, nor should the lingering power of Diana's presence in his mind, even as Suzanne took her place.

Tanny, no doubt sensing a drama, made her own barbed gesture to their failing marriage. For George's birthday in January 1964, she gave him a joke *Playboy* magazine, with a cover featuring George cuddling their cat Mourka surrounded by Playboy Bunnies in various states of undress. She accompanied it with a rendition of *Time* magazine, this time with Mourka in George's place as "Man of the Year."[71]

Several months later, Diana, by then six months pregnant, had her fourth miscarriage. Tanny and George were among the first to hear the news, and three days later, George distractedly sliced off his left index forefinger while mowing the lawn in Weston with a "little Jerry" mower. "He has an open wound.... Looks like meat," Tanny reported to a friend. In the merry-go-round of their lives, Ronnie Bates happened to be there and rushed Balanchine to a local Norwalk hospital, where a surgeon amputated his finger at the knuckle joint, leaving a painful stub. It was a devastating blow: he could no longer play the piano and was consigned to pecking out tunes, and the stub made him feel old and vulnerable. A month later the left side of his face mysteriously melted in a terrifying and inexplicable paralysis. It was eventually diagnosed as Bell's palsy, a temporary condition that would eventually subside, but for the moment there was nothing he could do but endure it. Adding insult to injury, he was also being treated for glaucoma and undergoing major dental work.[72]

His body was failing him, again. As he turned to the ambitious evening-length production of *Don Quixote* that he and Nicky had been working on, he was feeling more and more like the old Don himself, aging and a bit weathered—so alike that it would have been easy to mistake one for the other, and in a way, he did. And if the recalcitrant Diana had refused to accompany him into the mirrored "realer than real" world of fantasy and the spirit that was now his overwhelming purpose, he had already found someone more suited to the role. That spring he asked Suzanne Farrell to dance Dulcinea to his Quixote.[73]

Chapter 22

DON QUIXOTE

If you were painting her, you'd have to start with an outline of her body. The face would be hard to fill in. Her wide eyes and narrow lips, cheeks rounded slightly with baby fat, seemed to disappear behind a sweetly ironic smile, so that all you noticed was her body, which was long but not lanky, womanly but with none of Tanny's or Diana's pure sculptural beauty. There was nothing open about her composure, only a whiff, perhaps, of Balanchine's mother, Maria, in the wispy pallor. Even her girlish voice was naturally reedlike and restrained, a bit aloof or distant, as if everything she thought and felt lay sequestered in body and bone. You wouldn't notice her if she was standing still, but the moment she moved, she was unavoidable. It was a body whose parts seemed to fit or blend naturally, but the mechanics of her technique were baffling. The turnout of her legs, so fundamental to classical form, seemed to come from the feet rather than the hips, which left her knees facing forward as her feet folded into an uncanny perfect fifth position, like a closed envelope, tightly sealed. Her hips were a blank, her whole midtorso was a blank, actually, not muscularly sculpted or defined at all, or not to plain sight. It is not that she moved effortlessly—her endless tapered legs took power to hoist—but her dancing still seemed to bypass muscle. It was never clear where it came from or how she did what she did, but movement—not steps—flowed from her in unexpected and unmediated ways. He called her a dolphin for her mind, a cheetah for her speed.

Suzanne was no mere infatuation, she was a grand obsession, an all-consuming love that fell upon him with a force and urgency that astounded everyone around him. He wanted to see her in everything and immediately cast her in most of Diana's roles, and many others besides, but Dulcinea was the role he envisioned for her most. *Don Quixote* was slated to open in the spring of 1965, and he was anxiously clearing his schedule as he prepared to mount this epic production. Farrell rushed to buy the book, but four hundred pages in, she still couldn't find the entrance of her Dulcinea. "Don't worry," he said, "you don't need to read the book."[1]

Balanchine, however, had been circling *Don Quixote* for most of his life. Cervantes's novel was a Russian obsession, and he had danced as a child in Petipa's silly imperial ballet on the subject—"Not a serious work," he later noted dismissively.[2] In years to come, he had read and reread it in French and English, and he and Nicky, who shared his passion, had been planning their own ballet based closely on the text since the 1930s, but other projects had intervened. Finally, a few days after his return from the USSR, he had commissioned the score.[3] For the next three years, while he was busy building institutions, he was also working closely with his old friend, usually long-distance since Nicky was at the time living in Berlin. ("Dear Reverend" and "Father," they jokingly wrote, and George assured him, "Don't worry, we will get everything done . . . but no more girls until you finish the whole thing!")[4]

He finally began working on the dances with Farrell one afternoon during a company layoff just before rehearsals were scheduled to begin. She was at the empty theater practicing alone when Balanchine looked in: "Do you want to work?" He began at the end of the ballet, with her third-act variation, which took place in a dream. Gordon Boelzner showed up too, and they worked long hours, completely engrossed in the dance. "The beginning was difficult," she later recalled, "full of a repeated rhythm that I had to absorb into my body without the aid of any conventional ballet steps. "I want pulsing, pulsing," Balanchine said; "how about we try . . . ?" As she tore into musical phrases and veered dangerously off balance, he encouraged her: "Perfection is boring."

They were no longer working, she later explained, in "the conventional space . . . of up and down, left and right," but had moved instead into "a tilted, revolving circle" and "an unorthodox relation to gravity." Gordon broke the intensity—he was irreverent and fun, always checking Balanchine against the score: "You don't have a repeat there, Mr. B, you made it up and it doesn't exist." Farrell's Midwestern simplicity and Catholic piety were cut with sharp wit, and she was always ready with a softly uttered quip to take the edge off a silence. After these sessions, Farrell continued their work alone, often late at night in a studio by herself, committing the material they had come up with to her body as she hummed the music. She forced herself to run the whole variation start to finish over and again as a way of uncovering its emotional range and structure. The point was never to nail it down, and she taught herself, as she later put it, to rehearse options not opinions, knowing that it was impossible to predict what she would do on stage until she was there.[5]

When the full company returned, Farrell attended all the rehearsals for *Quixote*. Balanchine was everywhere during these long days in the studio, and pictures show him animatedly playing every part, joking, laughing, and demonstrating—up on Henry the horse, "Cue Henry's music, please"[6]—or bent and grimacing, yearning, angry, or enraptured, as he energetically acted out the whole ballet, drawing on everything he knew about commedia dell'arte and pantomime. He had cast himself as Quixote, but he couldn't possibly perform the full two-week run, much less all the rehearsals, so he also put the dancer Richard Rapp, along with Jacques, his trusted double, into the role too. Nabokov's score, as it turned out, was a problem, and Balanchine struggled to fit his friend's music to the fantastical world he was imagining. In his enthusiasm to make it work, he promised things he didn't have: Nabokov originally scored the ballet for two trumpets and two trombones, but when Balanchine heard the music, he wanted the final funeral scene to have three trumpets, three trombones, and church bells—and he assured Nicky that his orchestra could "absolutely" provide them. Irving flinched: not so, and they had to hire extra players.[7] It was a problem too because the musicians found the score facile, and George had to enforce rank: he angrily walked out of rehearsal one afternoon when Irving was making fun of the music.[8] To get this production off the ground, they all had to believe in it, and he brooked no dissent.

As he worked, his intimacy with Farrell grew and spilled over from the studio into the street as they left the theater together, often after midnight, and stopped for a bite to eat at the Tip Toe Inn, a local spot, for an omelet and iced coffee (her) and cold potatoes with herring and onion and a beer chaser or shot of vodka (him). Eddie Bigelow often came too—the usual threesome—and they would escort Suzanne to her apartment on Seventy-sixth Street, where George would "deposit her," he liked to say, safely with her mother, before making his way to the Apthorp and Tanny on Seventy-ninth Street. When he was away or unavailable, Eddie would take Suzi for a bite and escort her home. This time, Balanchine wasn't taking any chances.[9]

He couldn't. Quixote was him. Not metaphorically, but really, starting with Cervantes's famous opening passage about a gentleman, not yet Quixote, who lived "somewhere in La Mancha." Like him, George was known for his composure and civility, lived modestly, and rarely lost his temper. He liked hearty good food (a treat of paskha and *kulich* on Easter Sunday), dressed neatly, and had no family to speak of. His marriages had all failed—or were failing. He depended instead on his devoted staff, and he too had a trusted man-of-all-work in the Sancho-like Eddie Bigelow. He was even middle-aged and a bit weathered: watching Balanchine perform, Jacques noted that he seemed "a little pudgy, and, with his one healthy lung, huffed and wheezed his way through the difficult passages of choreography."[10]

In the novel, of course, this gentleman reads so much chivalric literature that he loses his mind and goes mad, or sane, and decides to become, at his advanced age, a knight errant. It is a midlife crisis of sorts, and we see him starting out anew in his fifties: he takes a new name, Don Quixote, and a new costume (an old helmet and rusty armor), grandly christens his ancient dray horse Rosinante ("formerly, old nag"), and leaves his home and his village to set out across the countryside to reimagine his life. He invents his lady, Dulcinea—an idealized vision of a simple village girl he once loved, although we never see her, and he later admits he doesn't even know if she exists. As he does all of this, Cervantes looks back at a dying feudal order, evoking in his mind its purest chivalric ideals even as he mercilessly mocks them and moves on.

In Balanchine's mind, ballet was like chivalry, both in its aristocratic origins and in its ethic of devotion and self-denial in pursuit of a noble ideal. He admired the equestrian arts—loved Lipizzan shows, the circus, the racetrack—and thought of his dancers as highly trained stallions. And chivalry, like ballet, involved the adoration of women. "Everything a man does," he explained as he was making his *Quixote*, "he does for his ideal woman. You live only one life and you believe in something and I believe in a little thing like that."[11] In order to work, he had to be in love, and this "little thing" ordered his mind and their lives; it was the whole premise of ballet, his ballet, and Farrell and the dancers believed in it too. And Balanchine had a dying Old World order somewhere in the back of his mind too: the imperial Russia of his childhood, with its dizzying array of ancient Petipa ballets—also predicated on women—texts he had immersed himself in like Quixote's maddening chivalric novels. As he worked, it became clear that the dimensions of Farrell's dancing were also the dimensions of the ballet, which took classical forms and spun them into the "tilted, revolving circle" of Cervantes's novel and his own mind.

The ballet followed the plot of the book's two parts, written sequentially, that famously play off each other, so that many of the characters in the second part have already read the first part. They know its players and its plot, and the author of the book shifts and changes as we are led deeper and deeper into a complicated theatrical world. The events of Quixote's "life" are now staged by the duplicitous Duke and Duchess and various enchanters, imposters, and doubles, but also by Quixote's friends back home who join the fray, and of course by Quixote and Sancho themselves. Everyone is acting, everyone is enchanted, and whatever "real world" may have existed disappears into a fractured multiplicity of worlds within worlds. In this sense the ballet was its own enchantment, and like Quixote's impersonator Carrasco, or the Knight of the Silver Moon, or the Knight of the Mirrors, Balanchine himself may or may not have been the Don.

The sets were designed by the Spanish artist Esteban Francés, who had already worked with Balanchine for nearly two decades—*Prodigal Son* (after Rouault), *Tyl Eulenspiegel*, *Night Shadow*, *Figure in the Carpet*—and had a deep interest in surrealism, magic, and the occult.[12] (As Francés was designing *Quixote*, he also painted a puppet theater for Robert Graves, a mutual friend and the author of *The White Goddess* [1948], about pre-Christian ritual worship of women.) Francés worked to build a fantastical world on stage, and George also enlisted Kermit Love to create the giant puppet knight that grew to a terrifying twenty-foot height and loomed over Quixote. Kermit was a kindred spirit—they talked "fairy talk" together, Horgan said—and Kermit later noted with delight that Balanchine "believed in Big Bird, he accepted it totally—there was nobody inside it, it was Big Bird."[13] Karinska worked with Francés to make more than one hundred lavish costumes. Makeup—Quixote's in particular—was by George's old friend, the émigré dancer and makeup artist Misha Arshansky, and it is hard not to see in the image they created a reflection of Feodor Chaliapin, the Russian bass whom Balanchine knew from Diaghilev days, famed for his portrayal of Quixote in opera and film.[14]

It was a monster of a production, with three acts, seven scene changes, and a full-company cast of more than 150 dancers and musicians, plus children, live animals—a donkey for Sancho and a white horse (Henry) for Quixote, along with a corps de ballet of pigs—a sturdy wooden-peg horse complete with explosives, and Kermit's giant puppet, along with three stately thirty-foot windmills with arms that turned (with a huge crank). On stage it was big, messy, loud, and smelly (the animals relieved themselves at will) with dry-ice fog, plenty of sweat, and burning incense for the death scene. There were complicated set and costume changes, and crowds of people backstage as dancers clamored to their positions in elaborate dress and milled about warming up, ready to set forth, only to be vanquished by Quixote and sent tumbling back into the wings. Kermit's giant puppet had a big club and had to hit the Don, and when Balanchine danced the role, he wanted Eddie Parks—who operated the monster—to *really* hit him, so he did. He knocked him over every night, and Balanchine gave Parks a bottle of his favorite rye whiskey in thanks.[15] There were even elaborate program notes—probably Lincoln's contribution—with lengthy excerpts from the novel and from Auden's essay on Quixote and Sancho as the "spirit-nature pair," along with illustrations by Gustave Doré of scenes from the novel, faithfully reproduced by Balanchine in many of the tableaus on stage.[16]

On the gala night of the ballet's world premiere, the theater was packed with notables and celebrities, including many of the lead characters in Balanchine's life: Nicky Nabokov, Jerome Robbins, Philip Johnson, and John D. Rockefeller III were all there.[17] Tanny was there too, seated on a side aisle for easy wheelchair access, and Suzanne's mother and sister naturally attended in their finest. In another turn of the fictional key, and echoing the moment at the end of the novel's first part when the parchment papers continuing the story are recovered in an old leaden box, Allegra's husband, the photographer Bert Stern, secretly set up a camera at the back of the theater and filmed the entire performance, capturing Balanchine's rare appearance and adding yet another character—and author—to the production.[18]

In this charged environment, and with much anticipation of this major new work and of Balanchine's performance, George sat in his dressing room backstage as Arshansky applied a final layer of glue to his mustache and beard, blackened his eyebrows, and furrowed his brow. It was the first time Balanchine had ever taken a principal role in one of his own works, and when he appeared in the wings fully costumed, Farrell, who was herself near tears, could feel his emotion. As the curtain rose, he was sitting alone in his dusty study slumped in a chair and surrounded by a cacophony of outsized books, à la Doré. He had been so busy supervising the whole production that he barely knew his part, and the dancers too were still finding their way through the complicated labyrinth they had all made. As Balanchine wound himself into a knightly fury to save a young damsel, he began attacking his phantom toy adversaries, played by students from the school, wielding his makeshift lance like a madman and sending the terrified children flying as he tore at them unpredictably and they ran for their lives.[19]

For the next three hours, the ballet piled life and dancers on stage and piled the teeming episodes of the book together, one after another, in a grand pantomimed narrative. Audiences watched Quixote go mad, declare his devotion to Dulcinea and knight errantry, encounter the galley slaves and the boy who was lashed; saw Sancho bounced at the inn; and attended the puppet show, which Quixote naturally attacked, leaving the stage strewn with rubble as the act came to a close. But the heart of the ballet lay in the Inquisition-suffused act 2 court of the Duke and Duchess, where Quixote found himself cruelly tricked by enchanters working to undermine him. He was awkward and out of place, blindfolded, pinched, tripped, and sent flying in a ballroom dance, and as he finally glimpsed a vision of Dulcinea, his face was meanly soaped with a shaving-cream pie; he and Sancho valiantly rode the wooden-peg horse, which exploded—more ruins and rubble—leaving Quixote defeated and indecorously passed out on his own horse. Act 3 was devoted to a dream ballet in which Quixote slept and saw beautiful dances—Mimi Paul, Marnee Morris, Suki Schorer—but woke to further humiliations, plotted by his enemy enchanters: windmills and the giant knight; stampeding half-human pigs; and, finally, caged like an injured wild beast, our poor old gentleman knight was carted home by Sancho Panza in a fevered state to attend to the final spectacle of his life—his own funeral march.[20]

Underneath the story of this knight vexed and crossed by the menacing world around him lay the counternarrative of Quixote's heart. In the ballet, Dulcinea appears right away: Farrell is there as the barefoot country girl who opens the curtains and washes his feet in the opening scene and kneels to dry them, Magdalene-like, with her hair; she is the vision of the Virgin Mary, with her own musical theme drawn from an old Russian folk song Balanchine knew, who appears icon-like and elevated, haloed, and bathed in a shaft of light—"Suzi's light," he called it. Farrell, a devout Catholic, was overwhelmed to find herself in the Virgin's crown and veil, tottering on a pedestal above her knight errant as he fell to his knees before her, head bowed in reverence. She may not have realized that as the Virgin, she also evoked in the Russian mind the holy Mother Russia, and Balanchine was bowing to that too. It seemed all too real, even in rehearsals, but "Balanchine was not a man embarrassed by his faith, or others' fear of it," she later reflected, "and in *Don Quixote* his blatant belief shocked his audience."[21]

She was Marcela, the woman who killed a man by breaking his heart ("I was born free"). And when he found himself seated on a throne, clothed, Christlike, in a red cloak and a misshapen crown, she removed the cloak and crown from this pitiful ramshackle man, and they danced a fragile pas de deux, full of gentle leading and following. He led her, she led him, he lost his way in the choreography and whispered to her, "What's next?," and, improvising, she wrapped an arm around his shoulder from behind and pointed him in the direction he should take her. Or like the Dark Angel of fate in *Serenade*, she draped herself over his back and pointed the way, and he pointed his own finger too. He fell to his knees and crawled after her, like the helpless donkey in *A Midsummer Night's Dream*, happily eating from her hand. She cradled him like a child.

But it was Farrell's wild solo in the dream sequence of act 3 that broke all barriers. No one had moved like that before, and even the scratchy film of her performance on that gala night is astonishing today. She had found a way to track the "pulsing, pulsing" in a kind of inner beat through her chest and back as she reached, pulled back, thrust out again, off-balance in ways that made her seem completely in control and utterly lost at the same time. At one point, her arabesque was so lush and deep that her neck broke extravagantly back. Her focus was to the diagonal corner, where Quixote was lying captured under a net asleep—dreaming her—except that on that opening night, he slipped imperceptibly out of the netting to watch her from the first wing, his other role in her dance. As she approached him, and the conjuror Merlin continued his torments, she despaired and flew through a range of feelings with such speed that no one could catch them until she seemed about to end in a traditional way, kneeling or posed at his feet, when suddenly she reversed and backed up as if thrown by a wave and fell hard to her knee, head in her hands in anguish before him. It was raw and exposed, and watching from the wings, Jacques was aghast: "What's happened to Suzi? . . . Who's in there transforming her? . . . Suzanne danced possessed."[22]

As for Balanchine, his Quixote was equally possessed—he was driven, worn, drawn, and above all living in his own mind as he wandered through the ballet, and Farrell and the dancers often had to take his hand to lead him through its episodes. His visions were his only real company, and the heaps of life swirling around him on the stage had strangely little to do with him, even when he was engaged in fierce battle against them. Even his dances with Farrell had the far-off look of a man who doesn't quite live in his body. Which may explain why Sancho Panza is so diminished in the ballet. He is there with Quixote, of course, and Balanchine gestured now and then to Auden's "spirit-nature pair." When Sancho is so rudely bounced in the blanket, for instance, Quixote helps him to a meal: the flesh-and-blood Sancho must eat and gobbles his food, while Quixote—all spirit—stands by. But this Sancho never joins with his great friend in the absorbing ways that he does in the novel, and without him, Balanchine's Quixote takes on an increasingly far-off aspect—all spirit, no nature. As Balanchine saw it, "Sancho Panza is the 'people', he's the 'crowd' . . . that doesn't see anything beyond the stomach. . . . And [he] trie[s] desperately to drag the white horse, and the knight on the white horse, down to his level. . . . It's the same with every one of us. It's difficult for us to follow Quixote into those realms of light and truth that are beyond our stomach. . . . Don Quixote is almost like the Second Coming of Christ."[23]

It was a very Russian reading—Quixote as the knowing and suffering Christ, with echoes of Dostoyevsky. It was true that at times Balanchine spoke of himself as a Christ figure, showing the way and misunderstood when his dancers refused to follow or when he was undermined by critics, or "idiots," and other "stupid" people. But on stage, Balanchine's Quixote was too frail and ramshackle to be Christlike, too devoted to his ideal woman. "Although he gives his whole life for her, he never really sees her. He is, if you like," Balanchine later said, "a kind of secular saint whom no one believes in. Finally, his death brings him face-to-face with himself, seemingly defeated, but having lived as he believed."[24] Balanchine took pains to expose the loneliness of the quest. At the peak of Quixote's humiliations and with Sancho gone to govern his island nation, we find the gaunt knight alone on an emptied stage, collapsed and bent in defeat, battered, beaten, and isolated. There is only darkness and doubt—and Dulcinea, who appears for a moment as a vision, before the humiliations resume. His extreme loneliness marks a divergence from the novel, in which Quixote is a loner but rarely alone: even in this darkest hour, his story is deeply social. Not Balanchine, whose Don had the haggard look of a monk or mystic living in a kind of inner exile. He is void, a man without country or companionship, alone on stage by himself in the dark.

By the time we reach his death, we have left the novel for good. Cervantes's Quixote comes home and has a revelation: the scales fall from his eyes, and he renounces chivalry, calls for a priest, and prepares to die. "I was mad, and now I am sane." We know of course that this "sanity" may well be another kind of madness; the enchanters, after all, are still at work everywhere, and he is among them. But death is the one trick that only reality can play, and we are told that Quixote "gives up the ghost"—the ghost of chivalry and the ghost of his life—"that is to say, he dies."[25] "He dies" in plain, undecorated prose, surrounded by Sancho and the few loyal friends and little family he has always had.

Balanchine's Quixote has a different kind of death. He envisions an elaborate and formal ceremony recalling an Orthodox service, with a pageant of cardinals and priests swinging incense, monks in dark hooded cloaks bearing crosses, knights, earls, and dukes—like *The Burial of the Count of Orgaz* by El Greco, the scenario instructs—along with the entire cast of dancers, who shuffle past to echoes of "Gloria in excelsis Deo." As the procession ends, we find Quixote, a wan spirit in his white nightshirt, standing awkwardly in his bed, as he is lifted (by a noisy mechanical hoist) into the air and elongated like an El Greco figure, ghost-gown trailing, all spirit. In the distant light, he sees a floating vision of the Madonna—the gold-wreathed Farrell—blessing him as he rises and reaches for her, before collapsing abruptly back to the bed.

In the final scene, Farrell enters barefoot once more as the country servant girl and stands by his bed; his close companions are there too, in the shadows. He and Farrell embrace. She goes to close the window curtains. The orchestra stops and silence shrouds the theater as she walks slowly back to him across the stage—"Don't rush it, take all the time," Balanchine told her. She picks up two sticks, fits them together as a cross and walks—slowly—back to the dying Quixote. Still in silence, she places the cross on his chest and falls on him in grief as the music resumes; he reaches up once more in his delirium and falls back dead. Farrell, still collapsed on his body, sinks to her knees as the curtain falls. On that first night, as her arm slid over his body, the dead Balanchine, in a gesture to her but also to the playful reality at the heart of the ballet, surreptitiously reached out and took her hand.[26]

When the curtain rose again, they bowed many times, before Balanchine finally nodded and slipped back into the wings, leaving Farrell alone on the flower-strewn stage holding a bouquet of red roses. When it was all over, he exchanged his armor for a tuxedo and bow tie and escorted her to the gala champagne party in the theater's great hall. She wore a white gown and long white gloves (washable, a gift from Davidova) with a pearl pendant from

George and her hair swept into a youthful 1960s ponytail. They were fêted and applauded and danced together on the promenade before disappearing once again backstage. Suzanne changed into street clothes, and they left the theater. Following their usual path, they walked up Broadway, arm in arm, and stopped at the twenty-four-hour Dunkin' Donuts on Seventy-fourth Street for cream donuts and coffee.[27]

The press, which he did read but couldn't abide, was ambivalent. Farrell, it was agreed, was a marvel, but the ballet was deemed everything from magnificent to a tasteless Christian allegory and a sign that Balanchine had been "paralyzed by success, money and a big house to be filled." The score was thought at best undistinguished, at worst a dull "horror." Balanchine didn't care: when Farrell read him a review that began by saying that he was one of three great contemporary choreographers, he just looked up: "And Suzi, who are the other two?"[28]

But in his own mind, his ballet did not entirely succeed. Like Quixote, he had tried to reinvent the story-ballet and Petipa's old and outmoded chivalric form. He had made a sprawling ballet about failures and ruins, about leaving home, a journey, and the comedy and futility of it all. It was a serious work, perhaps too serious, since it was still beholden in the end to a more limited Petipa-style genre of pantomime and divertissement, even if it also burst these old seams by sheer force of epic reach. In this sense it was a reckoning, and to the extent it failed, it was one of his most absorbing failures, a production that would continue to occupy him for the rest of his life. He immediately began changing it, adding, subtracting, and fussing over the details to try to get it right. It later fell out of repertory, but before his death, he had in mind a new, shorter, two-act version. As for the title role, that would continue to absorb him too: he would step in several times, well into the 1970s. His audiences, critics, and a later generation of dancers tried to like the ballet over the years, but most found it frankly baffling.

But *Quixote* was not for them. Balanchine had thrown open the doors to a wider public and his current generation of dancers, and *Don Quixote* was a way of sweeping them all into his fold. It was not a perfect machine, but more of a rickety house lived in by the company that had made it. They were its hallways and back rooms, its eaves and shutters, the stones and dirt of its very foundation. He needed them, every single one of them, down to the last stagehand and the youngest child. He needed their full attention, and he needed them to believe. He was a player in this growing house, and *Don Quixote* was a way of saying something to them, and to the air above, about a kind of total belief that can overwhelm everything—belief in God, in a woman, or in ballet as a chivalric ideal. It was a kind of consuming belief that could carry villages, countrysides, and whole towns with it, pulling in actors and assigning parts, rushing past any obstruction, fooling everyone, laughing, donning masks, playing roles, even committing cruelties in its name (Tanny was one). This is what Dulcineas can inspire. This is what the NYCB was made for.[29] Like the novel, the ballet was a kind of enchantment, and like Quixote, Balanchine was one of the greatest enchanters of them all. As for Dulcinea, everyone knows she doesn't exist.

He had done it. He had his company, he had his empire, and he had his lady. He had declared his love and established his kingdom. What came next had the inevitable logic of fate, or a script that had already been written. After the premiere of *Don Quixote,* he and Farrell set out on a path that would leave his kingdom, and his life, in ruins.

Chapter 23

THE ALABASTER PRINCESS

By then Suzanne belonged to Balanchine. At least that's how Balanchine seemed to see it. After the premiere of *Don Quixote*, the company departed on tour for Europe and the Middle East, and Suzanne—still accompanied by her mother—was by his side at every moment. In Paris they dined together, alone, at Maxim's, Fouquet's, and Brasserie Lorraine. They walked down the Seine in the moonlight, arm in arm. He took her to see *The Lady and the Unicorn* tapestries at the Musée de Cluny, romancing her with a ballet he was planning for her about the story of the unicorn with a new score by Nicky; it was a role, he said, that could be danced only by a virgin girl. He took her to see Botticelli at the Louvre, telling her that she looked like Venus in *The Birth of Venus*. Rome, Venice (he was away but told her to take a gondola and eat gelato on the Piazza San Marco), Dubrovnik with fine dining and a belly-dancing show, Athens, Salzburg, and London. When they got to Jerusalem, he left his astonished company to rehearse alone while he took Suzanne sightseeing. He even endowed his beloved with supernatural powers. When the flight home landed safely in a pea-soup fog, he insisted that it was thanks to the "miracle" of Suzanne's prayers, and Jacques noted irritably that "she acquiesces to that bullshit."[1]

The company watched in dismay as Balanchine disappeared into Suzanne. He saw only her, cast her in everything, hovered over her every move, fussed with schedules to make sure his precious "alabaster princess" didn't exhaust herself. He routinely left the theater when she finished dancing to walk her home or take her to dinner, leaving the rest of the company to carry on in his absence. In class he catered to her every whim. If Suzanne had a bad knee—"Was it very bad?" he would ask attentively; "Well, yes," she would say quietly; and they would skip grand pliés, lest these deep knee bends aggravate her condition. The men who partnered her walked on eggshells: when she fell in a performance with Jacques, Balanchine flew backstage and wildly berated him for "throwing her to the floor." Jacques shouted back—"I would never do that. . . . If you don't like it, get someone else to dance"—and Eddie had to stop them from coming to blows as Suzanne stood nervously watching.[2] By then she was taking her rehearsal breaks in Balanchine's private office and could be seen lounging on the couch in her robe, conferring with him on casting or bent over a crossword puzzle as he caressed her leg. Her wish was his command: one afternoon at the casting board surrounded by other dancers, she said that *she'd* like to dance *Barocco* after all, and Balanchine immediately crossed off "Mimi Paul" and wrote "Farrell" in her place. "Who would ever have believed that we could lose respect for Balanchine," another dancer sighed. "But we did."[3]

He didn't care. Balanchine and Farrell traveled together, alone, on company breaks—Paris, London, Brussels, Rome. In New York, she took him to his first baseball game (he was bored), and they met for breakfast and often went for lunch and dinner at their favorite local restaurants and could be seen walking arm in arm engrossed like lovers in intimate conversation. At night he filled her dressing room with large bouquets of flowers, and when they were apart, he wrote lovingly to his "Dulcinea":

> Dearest dul, This is just to tell you that there is no news since I wrote to you last. My days are the same routine; morning in the theater, pouring water into the sieve. This afternoon I talked to about twenty reporters, some of them trying to spank me for being mechanical and soulless

> monster. Thank God, soon I'll be nearer to you! Love you, miss you, Pest you—George [*and he drew a small black bug*][4]

Farrell says they were never lovers, and although there were plenty of rumors (unsubstantiated) that she slept with him, and even got pregnant, we have no reason not to believe her—after all, *à quoi ça sert*? She was exactly where she wanted to be—or on the only ledge she could find. Eventually she would have to jump one way or the other, but for the moment, they were living in a precarious erotic balance, pursuer and pursued. "Pest you," the great Balanchine as a Kafkaesque black bug—not even a mouse to Tanny's looming cat—only an insect with little legs racing after his glorious golden-wreathed girl.

She *was* a girl. At home her mother and sister still called her "bean," for her childish figure, and on their fridge, she posted a list of the season's ballets, and every night she would grade her own performance, writing G (good), VG (very good), E (excellent), or N (no good) next to the ballets she had danced. She had a cat named "Girl" too, the same cat she also called "Bottom" since she had gotten her at Balanchine's suggestion while working with him on the pas de deux between Titania and the ass in *A Midsummer Night's Dream* ("Don't you have an animal at home that you play with or talk to? . . . You should have one").[5] Yet she was also not a girl at all, and thanks in part to Balanchine's attentions, she instinctively knew the power of her own sexual allure and even (especially) of withholding. The age gap—forty-one years—was huge, and she had seen him with his shirt off and told a friend her skin crawled at his sagging flesh. She wanted Mr. B the choreographer (wasn't their physicality in the studio a kind of love?), and she even wanted the courtship, the intimacy, and his desire, but she did not want the man George Balanchine. *He* was old and married, and *she* had no intention of becoming, as she later put it, his Mrs. Sixth Wife. In fact, she was a first: the first of his chosen women to say no and hold him to his own antimarriage mantra. He didn't want his dancers to marry? Well, she wouldn't either—or she might, but not him.

Instead, to his astonishment, she acquired a boyfriend. Roger was tall, slender, Jewish, a doctor, and a fan who left anonymous notes and romantic outpourings at the stage door, signed "the poet." He avidly followed her performances, stood silently in the shadows, and sent perfume—Réplique, a scent that George unknowingly approved. When Roger finally introduced himself to Suzanne sometime in 1966, they began discreetly dating. It was a secret from George, and a secret from her mother, who had by then decided that her daughter should marry Balanchine. "It wouldn't be so bad to be Mrs. George Balanchine," she insisted. After all, he was famous, financially secure, and charming, and George had taken care to woo the mother too, inviting her to her daughter's performances and on tour, and when he "deposited" Suzanne at home, he stayed to talk warmly with her mother about cooking and cats.[6]

"Bal going on the rocks," Jacques noted in his diary; "he knows Su F is interested in another man and fears what will happen."[7] Depressed and moody, Balanchine chased faster and more ardently, wooing Suzanne in any way he could think of. He took her to Princeton, for instance, for dinner with Nicky and his very young French wife, Dominique (Nicky could have a young wife, why couldn't George?), and the Russian émigré philosopher Isaiah Berlin. He called ahead to make sure everything would be just right, but when they got there, his Suzi just seemed bored and out of place.[8] He wooed her above all with the thing they both cared about most: his dances. That year, she turned twenty-one, and he formally bestowed upon her the rights to *Meditation*—it was her dance now. He cast her in Diana's role in the movie version of *Midsummer Night's Dream*, which they filmed that spring, and asked her to wear the pearl necklace he had given to her—a sign of his possession. Every new ballet he made that year was for her, with a few bones thrown to other dancers, and she teased that she was his truck driver, nightly hauling the great load of his dances. The more she withheld sexually, the more obsessed he became, and he told her so in at least one cringeworthy erotic poem playfully dedicated to her "in recognition of your service to me as a truck driver" and signed, "Lord George B."

> Oh you suzi, my la-zy Suzi Com[e] on turn your dish for me, don't be choosy you lazy Suzi twist and turn for all to see. Roll you[r] stuff-in, show your muf-fin, put out light and give me bite! What a pleasure to be at leisure when she stirs my a-ppe-tite.[9]

On her birthday, he was in Paris and visited her favorite church. He lovingly wrote that he had stumbled into a small chapel of St. Suzanne—"How strange!"—and lit two candles, one for each of her vulnerable knees. "Let your knees and feet be quiet for awhile," he wrote. "Let your brain work—read *War and Peace*. God bless you. Love, George."[10]

But Roger was moving fast too, and he soon presented Suzanne with a ring: two pearls, one black, one white, set in a circle of diamonds. She was careful, but not too careful, to hide it from George, and when he finally saw it on her ring finger, he exploded in anger: "I don't like it, take it off." She did and eventually returned the ring to Roger, who got the message and faded from the scene. A week later, Barbara Horgan informed Balanchine that the ring *he* had ordered was ready to be picked up from the jeweler. It was a pearl too, set in a circle of diamonds, but (naturally) larger than Roger's. According to Farrell, he presented it to her in her hotel room one morning when the company was performing in Philadelphia. She took one look and told him she couldn't accept it. He threw the ring angrily across the room, and she retrieved it on hands and knees from under the bed, pushed it roughly onto her finger, and stormed out.

Trapped between George, her mother, and her own confused desires, Farrell sought help. She went to Betty Cage. She visited two Marist brothers, Paul and Damian, friends of Jacques d'Amboise, in a Catholic community in Manhasset, Long Island. She talked to a priest. Nothing helped. The impossible knot of creativity, love, desire, fragility, need, and pursuit between them was impossible to unravel, perhaps even for them. Yes, she was by then spoiled and manipulative, "La Farrell," "the princess," as some dancers thought of her, a child-woman accustomed to getting her way, but she was also anxious, not sleeping, feeling pressured and suffocated by his love and her situation. It was some version of what Diana, Tanny, Maria, Brigitta, and Tamara had all felt before her. They had all reigned, and they had all run from Balanchine's overbearing love. Yet Suzanne was even younger, and he was even older, and she had a soaring talent and desire to dance that none of them ever fully possessed. She was the only one, he later said, who truly *submitted*—not to him, crucially, but to dancing. She was also the only one with such a fierce independence and rebellious streak. Between them, there was no clear right or wrong, no should or shouldn't—they were past all that, mired in the barely conscious drama of who they were and what they did.

The following year he presented her with another gift: *Diamonds,* the final act of a new and plotless evening-length ballet that would eventually be titled *Jewels.* The idea for the ballet grew out of a meeting with Claude Arpels of the Parisian jewelry firm Van Cleef & Arpels. Over dinner at the home of Nathan Milstein, they came up with the idea of a ballet loosely based on the mining and crafting of stones (like dancers) into beautiful objets d'art. Arpels was looking to popularize his family company's luxury brand, and Balanchine similarly needed a new "hit" to fill his large Lincoln Center house. The ballet, as Lincoln put it, "sounded expensive before any step was taken," and in the lead-up to the premiere, Balanchine took Farrell to the Arpels showroom for a publicity shoot. Fully costumed in an elegant white tutu, she played dress-up with necklaces and tiaras once belonging to the Empress Josephine and a Russian czarina.[11]

Jewels had three acts to music by three different composers: *Emeralds* to a score Balanchine stitched together from Fauré's Suite from *Pelléas et Mélisande* and *Shylock, Rubies* to Stravinsky's jazz-age Capriccio for Piano and Orchestra, and *Diamonds* to the last three movements of Tchaikovsky's Symphony no. 3 in D Major. It is known as the first full-evening plotless ballet organized around a single concept: Van Cleef's jewels (and presumed sponsorship). More personally, *Jewels* was a walk through the musical geography of Balanchine's life, beginning in France, moving to Stravinsky's America, and culminating in a nostalgic rendition of a Russian imperial ball.[12]

It was also, and perhaps above all, a gift to his dancers. *Emeralds* was for the French Violette Verdy (he called her Mistinguett)—open-necked, soft arms, full but reluctant embraces—and for Mimi Paul, who was of French Swiss and Russian parentage. "Show me your Russian soul," he once said to her, and her melancholy pas de deux with Francisco Moncion was a long and pensive walk on pointe: "You are going forever on that walk," she said. *Rubies* was jazzy, weighted, angular, syncopated, full of prances, running, *Agon*-like thrusts, and cabaret moves. It played to the street smarts of Patti McBride and Eddie Villella, kids from New Jersey and Queens. McBride was the kind of performer who arrived at the theater just before curtain, Coca-Cola in hand, threw on her costume, and barely had to warm up before charging onto stage. She never danced what she rehearsed—nothing canned, everything spontaneous. Balanchine loved her but didn't *love* her (she later married), and it was for Patti that he made some of his loveliest work in these years. She was a relief, no drama—"I just accepted it," she said, whatever "it" was, and danced her heart out. *Rubies* was also Pat Neary—tough, aggressive, sexy in a brawny way—"the Irish policeman," some called her for her bossy personality. In *Rubies*, Balanchine gave her an angular dance with four men manipulating her limbs, like *Agon* gone red satin sheen.[13]

Diamonds, the stone of marriages and coronations, was for Farrell. It was all in white, grand, ceremonial, and her pas de deux with d'Amboise to Tchaikovsky's lush score had the high drama of a great romance. The sets, designed by Peter Harvey, were a key to the dance: Balanchine wanted a Versailles-like hall of mirrors, except asymmetrical, with mirrors on one side and windows on the other, under a starry night sky. Jewels were like stars, he said, and he insisted on a set hung with shimmering reflective rhinestones. Harvey tried lighting them from the inside, but Balanchine said no. *Jewels* were all surfaces—a play of windows and mirrors, real and reflected, appearances and light.[14]

When he met with Suzanne and Jacques to make their dance, Balanchine didn't know how to start and began instead in the middle; he choreographed the famous beginning last, after the whole dance was completed. Farrell and d'Amboise entered from opposite diagonals of the stage, walking formally and slowly toward each other to a lonely French horn: three steps and a pause to graciously open an arm to each other, until they finally met and began their stately but impassioned dance. Balanchine then surrounded them with a full-scale polonaise straight out of *War and Peace*, with thirty-four dancers in white and gold tutus, and at the end, d'Amboise fell to his knee and kissed Farrell's hand—not at her feet, like a prince, but instead softly beside her, as she turned her head to look. The dance was grand and simple, formal and intimate, full of a kind of melodrama only Farrell could cut through and dignify.

Rumors were flying: Mr. B was engaged to Suzanne; Mr. B had married Suzanne; Mr. B was divorcing Tanny. Finally, four days after the opening of

Jewels, things came to a breaking point. George was to attend the opening-night festivities at Lincoln Center for his new, recently completed film of *A Midsummer Night's Dream* starring, naturally, Suzanne. That night he informed Tanny that he would not be attending this splashy event with her; instead, he would be taking Suzanne—who wore for the occasion a gown specially designed by Karinska, black, form-fitting, and strapless, with blue silk lining and bust pads. For Tanny, it was one humiliation too far, the *Don Quixote* gala all over again, and this time she couldn't bear it. That night, with Eddie Bigelow and Martha Swope's help, she angrily threw a pile of George's things out of their apartment and into the hallway and checked into the Mayflower Hotel. George, sensing the end, called Barbara to say that *he* had checked into the Empire Hotel and would not be going home.[15]

A week later, Balanchine signed a lease for a studio apartment at the Lincoln Square Apartments on West End Avenue and moved out of the Apthorp. Eddie, who managed to walk the thin line between George and Tanny, brought over whatever possessions Tanny was willing to relinquish: several cartons of books, a rickety bed, and (a Tanny barb) the table and chairs designed by Alvar Aalto that Lincoln had given to George when Brigitta left him. Tanny kept everything else, including *Les Intermittences du Coeur*, a valuable painting by René Magritte (guilt money), two paintings by Tchelitchew, and works by Esteban Francés, Dalí, and Benois.[16] To ensure her stability (more guilt money), George took out a life insurance policy payable to her.[17] Someone, maybe him, maybe Tanny—the records are unclear—inquired about selling the Weston property, but it didn't happen. He wasn't divorced yet, but now Suzanne could come for breakfast at his bachelor flat, which she did.

By then Suzanne's isolation in the company was near complete. Even Jacques, who had championed her and still served as her primary partner, had no patience for what he took to be her cunning and manipulative pouts and scenes. The "princess" had only one friend, the petite, dark-haired, and sweet-faced Gail Crisa, known to the dancers as "the maid." Suzanne liked to have Gail along to cut the intensity with George, and Gail was just young and insecure enough to play this role. An anxious and ferreted creature afraid to eat or even exist in front of Balanchine but desperate to be "in his presence," she obediently trailed after the glamorous Farrell. The princess and the maid were joined by the "prince," also known as the "butler," depending on how you saw things. That was Paul Mejia, and in a fateful turn of events, he was in love with Suzanne too.

Mejia was born Pablo Roman Mejia Kryzanowsky. He had arrived at the school as a boy of eleven in 1958, and he looked uncannily like the boy-Balanchine: the same dark pallor and wide face with a high forehead and slightly retreated, cinched eyes; the same shortish height; and the same strong legs, quick muscles, and easy physicality, not elegant but agile, the kind of body that seemed to drive itself. Balanchine immediately fixed on Paul with such paternal attentiveness that even people close to him thought that Paul must be his biological son. There was no proof—only talk of a possible affair with Paul's mother, the dancer Romana Kryzanowska.[18] But talk was enough, part of a blur of fact and emotion that grew into feelings so strong they played a role in real life.

The roads wound back to where they always did. Romana was the daughter of Roman Kryzanowsky, a White Russian from a wealthy Polish Catholic landowning family in southwest Ukraine. It was a family scarred by an ill-starred romance with dance. Roman's father, a bit like Balanchine's Meliton, had an artistic bent and a passion for traveling to villages to study local peasant dances, and family lore had it that Roman had broken his marriage and fled to America in a passionate affair with a ballerina, leaving his family in ruins. The mother, strong-willed, wealthy, humiliated, moved to St. Petersburg; Roman studied art and even spent time working in Paris, and eventually became a successful painter. The family fled to Poland during the revolution, but by then Roman had already left and found his way to America—Detroit—where he finagled U.S. citizenship and married, of all things, a Kentucky-born Quaker, Sari Pickett. He painted landscapes, portraits, and icons (many of his paintings still hang on Mejia's walls), but he died suddenly in 1929, leaving Sari alone with their five-year-old daughter, Romana. As it turned out, Sari was not only beautiful but restless and bohemian, and she traveled, remarried (several times), and finally settled in New York, where in 1942 she enrolled Romana at the School of American Ballet.

There are pictures of this young Romana, a full-figured girl, large boned, with a tight but joyous smile, in the ballet studio with Tanny and George in the 1940s. But instead of dancing for Balanchine, she married a wealthy Peruvian businessman, Pablo Mejia, and moved to Lima, where Paul was born in 1947. Her husband prohibited her career, which he found unsuited to her newly elevated station, and when she danced anyway, he stormed out of the opera house one night in a rage, dragging little Paul behind him. When he refused to build her dream house—*Swan Lake*, she called it—she finally took the children and moved back to New York near her mother Sari and enrolled Paul and his sister at the School of American Ballet.[19]

So there was little Paul, with a family history of exile and strong women, fatherless children, and the mythic power of dancing. Dance had broken his family—twice—and the weight of his Russo-Peruvian past and his mother's own frustrated artistic dreams now lay squarely on his boyish shoulders. He had more than a touch of Latin machismo and found himself the only "man" in a family of powerful women—his grandmother Sari; his mother, Romana; and his sister (also Sari). When the divorce papers arrived from Peru, Paul threw the delivery man down the stairs in a fit of temper and proudly refused for years to reconcile with his father. Who was head of the house and his mother's protector now?

The short answer was Balanchine. When he visited the house, Romana made George's favorite piroshki, which he greedily stuffed into his mouth two or three at a time. She took up work with Joseph Pilates, George and Tanny's trusted German trainer, and made herself a fixture in the lives of injured dancers, many of them Balanchine's. Most of all, Balanchine took on Paul as protégé and son: he arranged for Paul to study piano with Kyriena Siloti, daughter of the famed Russian composer Alexander Siloti, who had studied with Glazunov at the imperial conservatory in St. Petersburg, where Balanchine himself had studied as a child. Kyriena was an eccentric woman, tall and square-faced, who lived alone with dozens of pet birds that flew madly around her apartment for their daily exercise (visitors received a newspaper to shield their heads from the droppings). "Teach him what good music is," Balanchine told her, and she taught him piano and took him to concerts, laying her large hands on his to emphasize a musical point.[20]

In 1959—at age twelve—Paul choreographed a ballet for some of his fellow dancers at the school, called *The Cockfight,* with a scenario by Romana and music by a close family friend, "Uncle George" Wehner.[21] Wehner was a composer, psychic, and Theosophist from the world of Gurdjieff and Ouspensky who claimed to speak through Madame Blavatsky, another connection to George's (and Lincoln's) past and life; Sari painted Wehner's portrait, along with a study of Madame Blavatsky herself, and Wehner took Paul and the family to dinners at a local restaurant, Coq au Vin.[22] Balanchine was unimpressed with the score, but he liked Paul's choreography and arranged for the young dancer to participate in his Ford Foundation choreographic workshops, along with Jacques, Eddie, and a few others aspiring to choreograph. He gave them each several dancers and ten minutes in a studio to make a short dance and then tore apart and rebuilt what they had done, sitting at the piano modulating between major and minor chords and jumping up to show them how to modulate visually with dancers. Soon after, Ouroussow informed Paul that Mr. B wanted him to take Madame Doubrovska's advanced "special" technique class for women. He would be the only boy in the class, she explained, but Balanchine wanted him to learn more about the mechanics of women's bodies and how they move. He also wanted Paul—still a youngster in the school—to learn Oberon, Villella's lead role in *A Midsummer Night's Dream.* Eyebrows were raised, and Villella pointedly refused to show up to rehearsal to teach this novice his part. But Paul was perfect for Oberon, who—like Villella and Balanchine himself—was also short, and a king.

George was protective of his young charge: when he noticed that Nicky Magallanes was falling in love with this dark and handsome youth, he called Romana: "Are there any men living in the house, any father figure?" When Paul heard of this intrusion, he was enraged; he didn't want or need a father and resented Balanchine's paternalism, even as he was falling under the master's sway. In 1964 Balanchine invited Paul to join NYCB, and eyebrows were raised again as he quickly entrusted Paul with coveted roles. He even added a new dance to *Don Quixote* especially for Paul. It was a classic situation:

fiercely ambitious and filled with Balanchine's confidence in his own promise, Paul began to build an image of himself as a young Balanchine, a disciple and son even, maybe, destined to inherit the kingdom. Everything in his life was pressing him to succeed in this coveted realm, so it is perhaps not as surprising as it might seem that when Suzanne Farrell danced Allegra's erotic role in *Bugaku*, Paul did an astonishing thing: he sent a large bouquet of flowers to her dressing room and invited her to take a partnering class with him—a bit like inviting the boss's girl to the prom. And so the son began courting the father's greatest love and would-be wife. It was Oedipal, except that Suzanne was young enough to be Balanchine's daughter—or Paul's wife.[23]

Oblivious to Paul's growing feelings for Suzanne, Balanchine continued to shower this promising young prince with opportunities—partly at Suzanne's request. Paul danced Oberon to her Titania, for instance, and in 1967, in Edinburgh, Balanchine gave him a plum role in *Agon* (and meanly removed the previous dancer, saying that he was a "fairy interior decorator" ruining the choreography).[24] That Christmas, in a *Godfather*-like scene, Balanchine took Suzanne to Romana's annual Russian dinner party, and Paul and Balanchine sat together, like father and son, at the piano playing for the guests while Paul gazed longingly at Suzanne. "She's Balanchine's girl," his toughened grandmother Sari warned, but he was already in love. After all, he told himself, his relationship with Suzi was based on their mutual worship of Balanchine. That's all they talked about, and Suzanne saw Paul the same way Paul saw Paul—as a young George.

Secretly—secretly—he began inviting Suzanne to dinner and the movies, wearing his best pinstripe suit and becoming her confidant in her struggle with her mother and George. He would come to her apartment late at night (while her mother was at work) and stay until two or three in the morning, or they would meet at Éclair on Seventy-second Street for breakfast. The usually astute George, attuned to every hint of gossip, missed it all. It simply didn't occur to him that the boyish Paul would be any competition for the great George Balanchine. It was another triangle—Tanny, Jerry, George, but now in a darker key—and George soon asked the trusted son Paul to take his place with Suzanne while he was traveling. Paul could be her escort and protector, another Eddie Bigelow, he said, facing straight into the headlights.[25]

His company, meanwhile, was in a state of mutiny. The jealousy, envy, and finally rage among his youngest and most talented dancers at his seeming disregard of *them* was reaching a boiling point. The women, but also the men, felt deserted, as if by a lover, they said, and they let out a collective cry: what about *me*? Fed up with the rule of Farrell, several angrily quit, including Pat Neary, Mimi Paul, Gloria Govrin, and John Prinz. Paul and Prinz later changed their minds and tried to come back, but Balanchine ("the rat," said Jacques angrily) refused to let these traitors return. Govrin wanted to come back too, and this time Balanchine allowed it; unlike the proud Mimi, Gloria begged and wept and promised to work hard and stay thin. Fearful that the company would collapse, senior dancers such as Melissa Hayden and Arthur Mitchell pulled Suzanne aside: "Things are falling apart, why don't you just sleep with him?"[26] Balanchine was losing weight, and "headquarters" was worried too: couldn't Suzanne do something? She refused—"It was not my religion, not my faith, not who I was." They were all living in this strangely public sexual and romantic stalemate, which was getting in the way of work and seemed to be destroying everything else in its wake. It was fair to wonder: did Balanchine even want the company to survive?

Adding to the crisis, at this very moment Lincoln disappeared into one of his worst bipolar episodes yet. It happened in August 1967, while he was away at Harvard directing a play he had written about Abraham Lincoln, with the young John Lithgow in the leading role. Lithgow watched in amazement as Lincoln, a "turbulent, fast-moving human storm system," arrived on set drinking and haggard and, in the course of rehearsals, came to believe that *he* was Abraham Lincoln, and *they* were all characters in *his* Lincoln's life. Finally, he banished the actors to the audience and enacted the entire play himself in a "frenzied pantomime" performance before racing out of the theater with a pineapple in one hand and a knife in the other. Wielding this puny sword like an indecorous Quixote, he stormed into his hotel, walked into the wrong room, and peed on a woman asleep in bed before he was finally constrained and eventually committed to Baldpate Hospital outside Boston. Sidelined at home for nearly a year, he began compulsively planning his own succession, writing to Morton Baum that perhaps it was time Jacques took his place. In another blow, a few months later, Baum himself died suddenly of a heart attack. The pillars supporting the NYCB seemed to be collapsing under their own weight.[27]

The problem was bigger than any of them thought. It was not only Suzanne, and in some ways she was as much symptom as cause, more a woman of the 1960s than she or anyone else recognized. The fact was: the era of hippies and miniskirts, rock and roll and flower power, Vietnam and Martin Luther King Jr., was seeping into the NYCB and disturbing its well-worn hierarchies and obedient peace. For the first time ever, the company was producing significant dissenting voices, and a divisive generation gap opened between Balanchine and his dancers. His "new breed," after all, were children of the 1960s, and as the decade wore on, an angry anti-Balanchine chorus emerged. They were not against his art—his genius was indisputable—but they were opposed to "the cult," as some of them now called it, that had grown up around him.

As usual, the battle was waged over their bodies. It started, you might say, with hair: *Hair* was the 1967 rock musical, hair was the "summer of love," hair was a political statement, and Balanchine would have none of it. He mandated short hair for the men, please, no beards, no mustaches, no sideburns. The theater is a church, he said; "don't bring garbage and dirt from the street Hippies." The result was predictable: Tony Blum came to the theater with hair teased to the heights, while others resentfully shaved or got haircuts. The women, more submissive and desperate for Balanchine's attention in a Farrell-blind world, began adorning themselves in perfect makeup and low-cut leotards with perfume and matching flowers neatly tucked into a French twist—a kind of anti-"flower child" statement of cultish loyalty, although one dancer did shear her gorgeous locks and walk out.[28]

Weight was an ongoing and ever-crueler conflict, and Balanchine even suspended or fired dancers for a few extra pounds. If they got too thin, he fired them for that too. Not in person—he still hated confrontation and sent Betty or Barbara (or pink slips) instead. Their bodies were his instruments, and as they became younger and wilder, he tightened the screws. He reminded them that they were dispensable. The school, after all, was churning out dancers—"You see, we have a meat grinder," he said deviously to one journalist; "we supply more and more." The dancers protested in the only childish and self-punishing ways they knew: by gaining weight (so there!), which they then hated themselves for, or by doing helpless things like posting signs in their dressing rooms: "CURSE NOT THINE FAT."[29] But the ethic—and it was an ethic—of sleek bodies that revealed their form ("You can't *see* a fat body") was so strong that even Gordon, sweet Gordon, who seemed to absorb all the company's woes while sitting silently playing the piano watching the dancers day and night, began losing weight too as if in sympathy. They were all alarmed to see his cheekbones emerging sharply from his craterous face, but Balanchine said nothing. Not his business.[30]

Marriage was a trickier battleground. Feminism was all but putting an end to the idea of pedestals and the eternal feminine, and as tense national debates about a woman's place trickled into their lives, the dancers seemed ironically to rebel in the opposite direction: Balanchine didn't want boyfriends or marriages? Well, they would marry. As he ranted about them becoming "Mrs. Him" and losing their independence, they defied him in matrimony. Patti McBride, Mimi Paul, Linda Homek, Lynne Stetson, Suki Schorer, and Karin von Aroldingen, among others, all married in these years—and kept dancing. He didn't like it, but his tirades started to sound like a broken record. The day Karin wed and was absent from an afternoon rehearsal, one dancer noted laconically in her diary: "Mr. B gave a lecture on how dancers shouldn't get married except to other dancers. He said, 'I know what happens. . . . They start having babies.' He was in a pretty foul mood."[31]

He drew the line at drugs. Marijuana, LSD, and acid were grounds for dismissal, and in 1968, in a dramatic purge, he fired several dancers at once. Ricky Weiss, who had joined the company in 1966, was among them, but he was too good to lose, and Balanchine hired him back. Still, the message was clear.[32]

The union was another site of contention. Weiss was a union representative, and he would intervene, to Balanchine's immense annoyance, if a rehearsal ran through a union-required break, and Weiss and others also fought for increased overtime wages. Balanchine's approach to the union was simple: he didn't want it; he didn't need it. *L'état c'est moi*: "Not they, somebody, office—but ME—I am the New York City Ballet."[33] At meetings challenging his authority or threatening a strike, he didn't hesitate to calmly play his trump card: Fine, he would say, I will take the dancers who want to come, and we'll go to Brooklyn (or Monte Carlo or Milan or wherever) and start a new company. I have done it before and will do it again. At which point, all but a few would line up and close ranks around him.[34]

At least they could boycott his class, a slap in the face that enraged him. It was a way of taking back their bodies, even if they still wanted to dance his way—and it is no accident that it was the male dancers, who were still scarce and less dispensable, who led this revolt. Dancing Balanchine's ballets was physically demanding, and the larger stage and longer season—signs of success—intensified the strain and threat of injury. Villella rose daily in pain and would make his way to a hot bath by inching his body along the walls, part of an agonizing daily process of bringing his cramped and aching limbs to peak condition for the evening performance. For him and others, Balanchine's class was too fast, too demanding, and too weighted with quaint homilies and philosophical diversions. Their bodies grew cold and stiff as they stood resentfully listening to his ramblings: "You don't participate in putting your foot down, you don't even know you are putting it down! With Newton . . . You don't have to do anything! What we do is reverse, we fight, we don't let it, we put down against the force. . . . Could you show me, from there to there. NO, I didn't see it!! Force it down, and I want to see it"—followed by a long story about preparing lamb chops.[35] Unwilling disciples, they abandoned his class and went instead to the school to study with Stanley Williams, who was attracting his own kind of cult following.

Williams had come from the Royal Danish Ballet, where he and Balanchine had met in 1956 during Tanny's hospitalization. In 1960 Balanchine invited him to New York to teach at the school, and he never left. Williams's acolytes claimed he taught them what "Balanchine wanted" better than Balanchine could, and although Balanchine irritably dismissed him as a guru, he never fired him. Williams's classes were quiet and analytic, and the dancers who studied with him developed a sophisticated physical intelligence and ultrarefined technique. What's more, Williams's classes, and his men's class in particular, had an alluring celebrity quotient, another annoying sign of the "me generation" 1960s, as Balanchine saw it: Villella, Nureyev, and eventually Mikhail Baryshnikov, Peter Martins, and Fernando Bujones were "Stanley people," and the physical and star power in the room was palpable.

Martins was a special case. His history with Balanchine began before he was born. His maternal uncle was Leif Ørnberg, a dancer with the Royal Danish Ballet who had worked with Balanchine in the early 1930s. Ørnberg was Balanchine's first Danish Apollo, a role that Martins himself would later occupy with distinction, and Martins was Ørnberg's spitting image: blond, square-jawed, and strikingly handsome, with a soft, pliable musculature. But Ørnberg was a heavy legacy to carry in other ways too. In 1936 he had joined the Fascist DNSAP (National Socialist Workers' Party of Denmark), and during the Nazi occupation, he was part of the (SS-inspired) Landstormen and produced Nazi propaganda and SS radio broadcasts. He and his wife (also a collaborator) terrorized members of the theater who were sympathetic with the resistance, even threatening them with death. He personally shadowed Balanchine's close colleague and friend Kjeld Abell and was known to show up at the theater armed and in uniform, in an armored car with bodyguards. When the occupation ended, he was immediately arrested, sentenced, and imprisoned, and he later fled into exile in Spain.[36]

Martins was born in 1946, just as the war was ending, and when he enrolled at the Theater School as a child, he bore the brunt of his uncle's past with teachers who despised his family. Making matters worse, his father disappeared when Martins was two, leaving his mother, a pianist, to cope with her three children alone—another fatherless child. At the Royal Danish Ballet School, the child Martins was both a great talent and a terror. He picked fights, shot up a studio with a pellet rifle, locked classmates in their lockers, bashed the coat hooks off the walls by wildly swinging a baseball bat, and went AWOL from classes. Finally, when he was twelve, the school tried to throw him out, but Stanley Williams, who was on the faculty at the time, saved him—if we can't deal with a rebellious twelve-year-old, who are we? So Martins stayed and worked with Williams until Balanchine brought them both, separately but around the same time, to the NYCB. Martins joined in 1970 as a principal dancer. Balanchine would mock him for years for his stiff classicism, and Martins would childishly fight back, slinking lazily to the fringes of the room, sitting glumly under the piano in rehearsals—and skipping Balanchine's class altogether to flee to Stanley.[37]

Women also flocked to Stanley: Melissa Hayden, Allegra Kent, Mimi Paul, Merrill Ashley—all took sanctuary for a time. Worse, as Balanchine saw it, was the teacher Maggie Black, who in many ways opposed Balanchine's teachings and who also had a cult following in New York in these years. Balanchine called her "black magic," and she attracted an even harder-core opposition, such as Gelsey Kirkland, who joined the company in 1968 at age fifteen and soon angrily quit. She was a wunderkind, and in spite of or because of Balanchine's immediate interest in her extraordinary dancing, she rubbed Maggie's apostasies in his face, not-so-secretly seeking her teacher's private coaching and even sneaking Maggie into the theater. Testing the limits, Gelsey liked to stand in the wings wearing headphones and performing Maggie's tape-recorded barre while Balanchine taught his own class on stage. Balanchine feigned indifference, but it got to him. One morning he counted only thirty-four dancers in company class. "You know," he said bitterly, "there are 80 people in the company, the rest of them must be in church."[38]

Farrell was a lightning rod, not only for her position but for her dancing. She was everything that Stanley Williams was not: impulsive, daring, physically outrageous, an exemplar of Balanchine's most radical departures from classical form. The irony was not lost either on her or on the women—there would be many—who took her as an idol and inspiration. Like her or not, there was no denying the astonishing power of Farrell's dancing. She was the new pure Balanchine, a believer in the cult if ever there was one, but it was she, not the rebels, who was destroying, with Balanchine, his own orthodoxies. *She* was always in class; it was their laboratory. Many of the older generation sneered at her innovations: Pat Wilde disparaged the way Farrell "whacked" her legs high, broke her wrists, distorted her line, and ran roughshod over the niceties of form in the interests of some newfangled freedom or no-holds-barred sexuality.[39] On stage, Farrell seemed, as the critic Arlene Croce (who at first counted herself among the skeptics) later put it, like "the freest woman alive."[40] She had plenty of technique, but never allowed herself to be ruled by it, and it was Farrell—not Stanley or any other rebel cause—who was changing the art. As usual, Balanchine was in the avant-garde, and as usual a woman was taking him there.

Metastaseis and Pithoprakta, to music by Iannis Xenakis, was proof. Balanchine first met Xenakis in Berlin in 1964 and was interested in his music; after a correspondence, they settled in 1967 on two scores for a new ballet, *Metastaseis* (1953–54) and *Pithoprakta* (1955–56). Meanwhile, the State Department invited the NYCB to perform at Expo 67, an international exposition in Montreal, where Xenakis was building, with Le Corbusier, a multimedia installation that turned the French pavilion into an architectural realization of *Metastaseis*—and a setting for a performance of Edgard Varèse's *Poème Électronique* along with a film by Le Corbusier, a "ballet" of mechanical images, eyes, animals, and human faces. For this immersive event, Balanchine walked with hundreds of people through a massive, spiky, futuristic tent on many levels, with swiveling paraboloids suspended from steel cables and rapid beams of light flashing in mathematically and spatially determined patterns. Every eight minutes (the length of the musical score), the pattern would resolve—and repeat.[41]

Xenakis was another Balanchine person. A Romanian-born Greek, he had fought in the resistance during the war, an experience that had left him blind in one eye, stateless, and sentenced to death. He took refuge in Paris, where he found work with Le Corbusier and became an architect. But Xenakis wanted to be a composer, so he also studied music, physics, and mathematics and invented a new style of musical composition based on "the calculus of chance, the determination of probabilities—the calculation of accident." He used game theory, set theory, the law of large numbers, and an IBM computer among his compositional tools, along with architectural ideas about space, load, and building structure. It was an effort to push composition beyond serialism, and even his notation—thick forests of dots and lines ordered on an *x* and a *y* axis—departed from established musical convention. *Metastaseis*, which premiered in Germany in 1955, was his breakthrough composition—even the European musical avant-garde didn't know what to do with this "atomic music."

It was just the kind of mélange of cosmic scientific and mathematical concepts that appealed to Balanchine. "Metastaseis" meant "beyond immobility," and Xenakis said it also referred to "clouds" and "galaxies" of sound governed by mathematical probabilities—some of its pitch manipulations were calibrated, for example, to the ancient Fibonacci sequence, thought to reflect the natural order. In another tie, Xenakis said that his head at the time was filled with the sounds of his past: the Romany music and Orthodox liturgies of his native Romania; the calming seas of Greece; the harsh dissonance of Nazi chanting, tanks, and machine-gun fire; and even the agonizing suspense of house-to-house skirmishes.[42]

Metastaseis was scored for sixty-one parts, forty-nine of them strings. It began with the strings: all of them, each playing a different note to produce a loud and dissonant wall of sound, no rhythm, just a sonic blast that diminished as each player faded out, like voices silenced in a crowd. To this disorienting cry, Balanchine set a "great mass of figures"—twenty-two women in white—lying in a wheel-shaped mound on the stage. The ballet has long since been forgotten, but observers described how this pale mass heaved and undulated, until the dancers rose and formed new clumps—like "lost cities," one observer said—or spilled out, "as mercury breaks from its phial to . . . roll in little globules." Beams of light rhythmically crisscrossed their bodies. They seemed to observers like a "lump of clay" or like "lava being flung out of the mouth of a volcano"—more "matter" than man—and at the end, they folded back into a dirt-like mound.[43]

Pithoprakta, Farrell's dance with Arthur Mitchell and a corps of twelve dancers, meant "actions by probabilities"—not a bad description of her dancing. But even Farrell, who was used to "swimming around," as Balanchine put it, in his dances, was lost. "Crazy sounds, no counts, very vague choreography, crazy costume," she said, and the lighting—bright spotlights on a black stage—was jarring to them all. There were plans for scenery hanging in the auditorium and lighting that would "bomb the audience by computer," Lincoln said.[44] The costumes had a mod sartorial sheen: Farrell in a white bikini with gold fringe, hair loose, and Mitchell bare-chested in sleek, sparkling pants.

The choreography was so strange that they videotaped the pas de deux when it was done so that they could remember it, except that Mitchell missed the taping, so Farrell did their dance alone. When Balanchine saw the footage, he liked the look of Mitchell's absence and asked him to perform the dance as if he wasn't there. So Mitchell and Farrell barely touched and improvised their way around discernable musical landmarks. The corps de ballet had similar rein. "We liked it, went crazy, percussion, jerky, clangy . . . then a bang and we froze," one recalled.[45] Critics described Farrell as puppetlike, part mannequin and part insect, "spasmodic," or a human machine performing at its most extreme limits while "black creatures rolled past her feet like so much dust."[46] The dance ended with a startlingly poignant and enigmatic image: Farrell alone on her knees, arms wrapped around her own head, and one wide-open hand covering her face like a mask.

It was a dance in the radical lineage of *The Four Temperaments*, *Agon*, and *Episodes*, except where they built, this seemed to destruct. The reviews were strong, very strong, but Balanchine never brought it back, and Lincoln was less sure: "As far as I can judge," he wrote to a friend, "it's about marijuana, heroin and the effects of LSD on the human body."[47] But if the ballet had a psychedelic feel, it was not as loose or undone as it appeared, nor was it as original in its methods. John Cage and his collaborator and partner Merce Cunningham had long since been experimenting with chance and probability, using throws of dice and readings of the I Ching, for example, as compositional tools. Their idea was to inject an element of randomness into the making of art, as a way of disrupting convention and their own thought patterns, even if the dances themselves were then strictly choreographed. Cunningham had recently staged *Summerspace* at the NYCB with music by Morton Feldman, another composer in Cage's circle. Feldman used his own graphic notation and prescribed rhythmic and tonal limits but otherwise allowed his instrumentalists to play whatever notes they chose.

Whatever the influence, Xenakis's methods and goals were opposed. "Chance needs to be calculated," Xenakis said. "I have tried to inject determinism in what we call chance." He had this in common with Balanchine. They had both witnessed the violent unraveling of a society, one reason not to be interested in randomness or disengagement of human will, and they both wanted to impose control over chaos. "That is my definition of an artist and of a man: to control," Xenakis explained.[48] But of course control in a structure inhabited by free-willed dancers was a paradox, or at least a kind of controlled anarchy. Balanchine never entirely set his dances—they were musically formal but also unstable, freely dependent on the dancers.

Control was harder and harder to achieve as the political storms of the 1960s gathered force, and by 1968 even the thick monastic walls of the theater could not keep the turmoil of the outside world at bay: Vietnam (the Tet offensive, the My Lai massacre), violent student protests, police brutality, the Chicago Democratic Convention, the assassinations of Martin Luther King Jr. and Bobby Kennedy. "Leave that outside," Balanchine said to the dancers he found lying on the plaza protesting the Vietnam War or wearing black armbands to the theater; "this is our church." But they knew he was not on their side. Anti-Communist to the core, he supported the war in Vietnam (including the bombing of Cambodia), admired Nixon, and doted on Kissinger when they met the following year (Kissinger would even later serve as chairman of a fundraising committee for the company).[49]

But when King was shot in April, Balanchine opened the doors of his church. Kirstein had marched at Selma, and he and Balanchine talked at length with Arthur Mitchell about what to do. A month later, Balanchine produced a memorial dance to Stravinsky's *Requiem Canticles*, with Arthur Mitchell and Suzanne Farrell in the lead roles. Stravinsky had written the score in 1965–66—he was eighty-four years old and in poor health—to be performed after his own death, and his notes for it included obituaries of friends who had died while he was composing it (Edgard Varèse, Alberto Giacometti, Evelyn Waugh) along with pictures of crucifixes and other "practical commentary."[50]

Requiem Canticles was a fifteen-minute lament, twelve-tone but also drawing on traditions of Christian chorale and dirge and the octatonic chromaticism characteristic of Stravinsky's most Russian and ritualized works. The text consisted of Latin fragments from the Catholic requiem mass, and the "chords of death" at the end rang with funeral bells, chimes, xylophones, and celesta. The chorus sang but also chanted, in a sound as close to *Les Noces* or *Sacre* as anything Balanchine had choreographed. As for the dance, which was performed only once and then lost, Kirstein called it "a combination of Dalcroze, Eurythmics, *Sacre* (by Nijinsky), *Agon* and the Montgomery and Washington Marches. It will be a stupendous historic occasion, the first time a major American-Russian artist has directly involved himself in a piece of political action. . . . The public won't know whether to shit or go blind."[51]

According to photographs and contemporary accounts, this "piece of political action" was a religious rite performed by fifty dancers in long white robes carrying large candelabras, each crowned with a trinity of light. The candles were real, and the dancers moved into formations—a cross, an altar.[52] At times the stage went dark and only the candlelight showed and moved, as Suzanne threaded through the night searching for someone who no longer existed. Mitchell was King, dressed in silver and purple vestments, and he stood with arms outstretched or kneeled at the human altar, a black man with the translucent Farrell, hair down, positioned above him like an angel in a painting. Finally, Mitchell's body rose high above the mourning crowd. This was not Balanchine's first (or last) elegy, but few present at the time knew just how far back his dances of grief went, beginning with *The Twelve* and his early Russian pageants for the dead, and moving through to *Serenade*, Bach's St. Matthew Passion (for the children of World War II), and his own death march in *Quixote*. After the curtain fell, the hushed audience filed silently out of the theater. A month later, Bobby Kennedy was shot.

There were complaints that this ceremonial act one whole month after King's murder was too little too late, but Kirstein and Balanchine were understandably defensive. Kirstein, referring to a poem he had written after Selma, noted, "We do not have instant grief," and we do not get on the bandwagon "over King's bones." By then Balanchine was already working to help Arthur Mitchell to found, with Karel Shook, the Dance Theatre of Harlem (DTH). Balanchine gave his ballets and his blessing and accepted the position of chairman of the board, and he and Lincoln tried to help raise money. Tanny eventually taught there, and Balanchine provided sets and costumes *gratuit* whenever he could.

By then, as part of a scholarship program funded by the Ford Foundation, Balanchine and his colleagues at the school had been trying for years, without great success, to recruit young black dancers from the Jones-Haywood Dance School in Washington, D.C., and from Constance Harding's school in Bristol. Doris Jones, who had taught herself ballet after being turned away by white schools, had founded a school in D.C., in 1940, with Claire Haywood, a former student with a doctorate from Catholic University. Together, they also started the racially integrated Capitol Ballet Company in 1961, and although they were happy to have Balanchine's help, they were frustrated at not receiving Ford money of their own—why should they lose their best dancers to Balanchine? By 1963 it was true that young black girls were appearing at SAB auditions, and Lincoln told Eugenie Ouroussow that "the influence of Italians and Jews on American art is on the wane and that we must now enter an era of Negro and Puerto Rican influence." Two years later, Eugenie reported optimistically, and with assumptions all too common at the time, on her visit to an all-black dance school: "Ballet is turning out to be a very sharp instrument of integration. They had boys who seemed to be almost picked off the street and girls who held themselves regally like Queens. . . . The Negroes are not quite built for the ballet but they take it and its atmosphere as a magic of the highest order and do their exercise with pride and concentration."[53]

None of this had led to an increase in black dancers in the NYCB, which remained lily-white, with few exceptions. "They never stay long enough to become dancers," Balanchine complained, but the problem was of course deeper, and King's assassination and Mitchell's desire to form his own troupe brought it to the fore. Balanchine had his views, and he stuck to them. "Why integrate? Why? Why? . . . We have to change its like evolution, it will take Arthur 20 years," just as it had taken him years to change minds and establish a lasting company. When Balanchine invited DTH dancers to perform with the NYCB two years later at a gala to raise money for Mitchell's efforts, he came under heavy criticism for setting the black dancers apart, as if they were some lesser "ethnicity." He was infuriated, and lashed out at the public and the press: Mitchell's dancers were not unionized and could not perform with the NYCB, he schooled a reporter, and besides, what were all his critics doing for Mitchell and his dancers? "Let them sponsor. . . . I wish they would give a million dollars to Arthur and buy him a theater, but they won't do that, they only talk, but I don't talk, I help."

As for the NYCB, he said, temper rising, "Emperor Jones is Emperor Jones. You don't want *me*—a Caucasian Georgian from the Caucasus—as Emperor Jones do you?" He went on, "I absolutely know I don't want to see two Japanese girls in my *Swan Lake*. I just don't want to see. . . . It's not done for them. Same thing like . . . American blond [as] Geisha. Why? This is something else. . . . Not even tradition, it belongs to a special thing . . . looking that way. Chinese art is different, it's not Japanese."[54] He believed in cultural difference, and in appearances in casting, although it was hard not to notice that he had readily outfitted Allegra in a black wig to play a geisha-like woman in *Bugaku*.[55] He wanted a doctor to look like a doctor, a lawyer to look like a lawyer, a geisha to look like a geisha, a sylph to look like a sylph—except of course, there is no such thing as a sylph. Besides, the dancers of color in his company were mostly men, and he cast them according to whatever stereotypes he possessed, and he had many of the prejudices of his time—Mitchell did too. And so he cast Mitchell in exoticized roles, fewer clothes, please, oil and glitter, bare-chested with shiny trousers; black is beautiful, *Ebony* magazine or Carl Van Vechten's homoerotic photographs, which Mitchell fondly collected. In Balanchine's mind, dark people played dark roles: the Puerto Rican Moncion was Death in *La Valse*, but not suited to *Liebeslieder*: "You see you are Islander, dear," he explained.[56] Mel Tomlinson, very black, would arrive in 1981 and was perfect for Pluto (when Tomlinson cut his regal Afro the day before the opening, Balanchine was upset: "What have you done!").

Did ballet—or Balanchine's ballet—bleach blackness? Tomlinson thought it did, but he was the next generation up from Mitchell and saw differently and more. Mitchell was honored to cope. When he went on stage for *Divertimento No. 15*, he told Milly that he just thought "elegant and white. What else was I supposed to do with all of these white kids all around me?"[57] Tomlinson wondered why he was there. "Am I here to sell tickets, am I 'the onlyist,' the token black?" Balanchine said no; the company is like a garden and there are many kinds of flowers. "You are my dark prince"—which didn't particularly please Tomlinson, but he stayed anyway. "He taught me to command the stage without doing anything, let audience come to you, don't go to them," and he later commented sardonically that if the black had been bleached out of him, the white had been bleached out of them too.[58] They were *all* creatures.

It had nothing to do with politics, Balanchine insisted; it was pure aesthetics:

> It is what I like—if I don't like it, I don't take, white or black or any other thing. . . . They say he is a dictator; Yes, he is, I am, because I don't like or I like. I don't like this councilism, ten people decide to give scholarship but nothing happens because they don't understand anything. Even at my own school and company, good teacher don't really see the important things that are wrong or right, but I see, you see that's what I am I was born that way. I am like a dog, you know like a German Shepherd, I can see, I can smell, I am stupid, I cannot write or read, you see, I am not intellectual, but I can see, smell and hear.[59]

And what he liked was talented, mostly white dancers, even if he dressed and trained them to move with rhythms and timing he had absorbed in part from black dancers. Skin was costume—he didn't even want his alabaster dancers sitting in the sun before *Swan Lake*. He was interested in black dancers—another human color and variety in his palette, another beautiful flower. But integration, segregation, separatism, civil rights, black power, social justice—not his responsibilities. It was another way that the 1960s were passing him by.

Meanwhile, the agonizing drama with Suzanne wore on. Finally, one morning Balanchine was on the 104 bus on his way to the theater when Suzanne and Paul got on after breakfast at Éclair. They were all going to the theater and made small talk, but everyone knew what had happened. Then Balanchine was sitting in a pew in Suzanne's favorite church when Paul and Suzanne walked in. One of the dancers even saw an uncharacteristically rumpled Balanchine standing hunched behind a marquee on Broadway spying on Suzanne and Paul as they stood talking.[60] His reaction to the rivalry of Paul, now that he finally saw it, bordered on panic. He was still married to Tanny, but in a last-ditch effort, he abruptly proposed marriage to Suzanne. They could have a child, he said. She thought he was desperate, but he still couldn't imagine how she could refuse *him,* who would give her everything, for the nothing Paul. But she did. Her mother was enraged and called Betty, who defended Suzanne and Paul, so she called George himself to say that Betty was fomenting Suzanne's betrayal of them both. Suzanne moved out.[61]

Balanchine had only one weapon, and he began wielding it with scathing precision. Dismantling Paul's career was not hard—he had made it; he could break it. "You have never begged in your life," he chided Paul, his once-protégé, angrily in a rehearsal for the solo he had choreographed for him in *Quixote*, and he made Paul grovel humiliatingly lower and lower, while his colleagues stood silently watching. Then he cut the solo entirely. Other favored roles were retracted or reassigned, leaving Paul sitting despondently night after night in the wings, watching. But Farrell, no. Balanchine did not punish her and was still prepared to go to the wall to win her, although he was planning at the time a ballet based on Lermontov's poem about Thamar, the beautiful and cruel Georgian queen who seduced men for a night of love and then in the morning, with a sorrowful sigh, threw them off a cliff to a rocky death.[62]

On January 31, 1969, seventeen years after he and Tanny had wed, Balanchine traveled alone to El Paso, Texas, and crossed the border to get a Mexican divorce. He called Tanny in tears of pain and guilt to tell her. Echoing the range of her cynicism and despair, she just said, "nice"—and hung up the phone and called Jerry.[63] Now his marriage was out of the way, and he was free to marry Suzanne. What he didn't yet know was that Suzanne was already secretly planning her own wedding with Paul. Like naughty or frightened children, they planned to do it when Balanchine was away in Hamburg staging Glinka's Pushkin-inspired *Ruslan and Ludmilla*. The day before he departed, in an act of melancholy whimsy, as if he knew he was losing control, Balanchine gathered a group of musicians and dancers in a small studio at the theater to record a sentimental song he had composed. He sat at the piano and crooned "Love Is a Simple Thing," a thinly disguised ballad to Farrell: "I am 23 . . . I'm taking ballet dance, I keep my diary neat and take no chance . . . Love is a simple thing, One look, one kiss, one ring."[64] When he arrived at the airport, his anxiety spiraled until he finally called Lucia Davidova for solace—and missed his plane. Barbara got the next call and tried to talk him down from his panicked state. She arranged another flight, but on the plane he was restless, couldn't sleep, and suffered from diarrhea, and he arrived in Hamburg exhausted and undone.

Five days later, in New York, Suzanne and Paul were married. It was a small wedding, almost hidden, in a side chapel of the Church of St. Paul the Apostle on West Sixtieth Street. Ricky Weiss was best man ("Are you sure you want to do this?" he cautioned Paul), and Gail Crisa was maid of honor. Suzanne wore a simple white lace dress made specially by Karinska, who was there along with Barbara, Betty, Eddie, and a few dancers—not many—and others from the school. Suzanne's mother sat slumped at the back of the chapel and howled her disapproval like a chorus of one, loudly wailing and weeping for the entirety of the service. Romana hosted a reception at her apartment on Sixty-fifth Street, and Paul and Suzanne then left for their honeymoon in Hawaii. No one said a word to Balanchine.

When news reached him at his hotel in Hamburg, he immediately called Barbara, enraged that she too had betrayed him and unleashing a torrent of anguish, hurt, and fury. He insisted she come to Hamburg immediately; he had already booked her a flight. When she arrived at the elegant Hotel Vier Jahreszeiten, she sat with him for hours at a corner table in the hotel's wood-paneled dining room as he drank—double Steinhägers with beer chasers—and burrowed into an obsessive hole about Farrell: how could she, why, why, why—over and over again in a thousand iterations. He wept and couldn't seem to escape his own despairing thoughts, until Barbara, finally exasperated, lost patience: "You're better than this. . . . Enough!" When she left, Eddie Bigelow replaced her. Nicky Nabokov came with his Dominique (small consolation), and Lincoln too arrived with Ronnie Bates. As usual, Lincoln said little, but they all went to the opera together and Ronnie stayed up into the night drinking with George.[65]

Through it all, Balanchine never stopped working, his salvation. He plunged into *Ruslan and Ludmilla*, traveled to Berlin to help the West Berlin Ballet Ensemble, and went to see Maurice Béjart's Ballet of the Twentieth Century, another reminder of just how out of sync he was with the 1960s. Béjart's blend of Eastern mysticism, revolution, philosophy, and sex (often openly homoerotic) was playing to huge crowds in stadiums and outdoor venues (fans wore buttons: "Béjart is sexier"). Not Balanchine's thing. Still, he threatened to stay in Europe—it had always been more his world, and he could always start a new company.

Another song, this one scribbled on Swiss Air stationery during his flight back to New York.

SILVER NIGHT.

Silver night moon is bright
And yet no sight can quench
My sorrow
You are my star above to far to reach
To love
In the sky angels flight to heaven
Where your treasures lie. They sing
A silent song the song of you
And I
With you around all stars are
Gleamming
With you away ther is no sky
Oh! Tell me why alone I'm left to cry
Where are you what am I to do?
To be alive alone for ever
It was my dream alas
My one and only dream.[66]

When Balanchine got back to the theater, he unleashed his fury at Paul. He wanted to fire him outright, but Lincoln said, No, you can't do that contractually; so instead Paul received a call saying he would be paid but should not come to the theater. When Paul threatened to go to the press, that was retracted too, which meant that although Paul was persona non grata at the theater, he was still around—impudently throwing kisses to Suzanne across the barre in class and cuddling with her in the canteen. As for Suzanne, Balanchine avoided her at all costs and turned his back and walked in the other direction if they met in the hallway. "She's a witch," he said, and knew that he had to exorcise her from his being. He assigned understudies to her roles and scheduled her to teach her parts to her former competitors. But nothing could blunt his pain. He was on medication to stave off a nervous breakdown, and he was acting strangely: "I am Zeus," he announced to a few dancers, who glanced nervously at one another or rolled their eyes. Many of his dancers were relieved to see the princess and the "Inca Finka," as they called Paul, demoted, but it wasn't clear that Balanchine would recover. When Suzanne took her place on stage during a rehearsal for *Don Quixote*, hair down and bathed in "Suzi's light," Balanchine noticeably flinched as a rush of emotion overtook him. He was like Don Juan after all, he said bitterly to Jacques, bringing beauty and doing his best for women, and they just left him and married "garbage" instead of being happy with a great man.[67]

Artistically, he was at a standstill—emptied out, barren. He went silent. Jerry Robbins, who had just returned to the company after years on Broadway, stepped into the void. He was flush and coming off two years of replenishing himself with experimental work at the American Theatre Lab, which he had founded for the purpose. With a group of leading actors, dancers, musicians, and writers—including Anna Sokolow, Marion Rich, Jay Harnick, Mary Hunger, Joseph Papp, Leonard Bernstein, and Robert Graves (they did hallucinogenic mushrooms together)—Robbins studied Japanese Noh, ancient Greek theater, Brecht, and Shakespeare. They worked on *Hamlet* and *The Bacchae* (Noh style). They reenacted John F. Kennedy's assassination, improvising being shot, body parts blown to bits, and incorporating sections of Lee Harvey Oswald's diaries and the Warren Commission's report. They experimented with the use of a chorus, repetition, role switching, double characters, and chanting. None of the Theatre Lab experiments were performed publicly—it was all grist for Robbins's mill, and when he dissolved the Lab and arrived back at the NYCB in 1968, he was teeming with energy and ideas.

Dances at a Gathering was for five couples to piano music by Chopin. To some of the dancers involved, it was thrilling: a ballet, finally, about them and *their* generation. Robbins was closer to the dancers in age than Balanchine was, and *Dances* had a "hippyish" feel, he said, and he loved it that a few of the men, who had just returned from a layoff, had long hair and beards. "We felt like flower children because we *were* flower children," one dancer explained; "I was part of that whole hippy thing and this ballet epitomized us." The movement was internal and intimate, classical but casual and simply dressed, and Robbins told the dancers to perform as if the audience was not there—no virtuosic displays, no pageantry, just friends dancing for each other, "easy baby, easy." *Dances* was also both a refutation and an embrace of the downtown New York avant-garde dance scene, with its earnest fragmentation and emphasis on pedestrian movements (walking, running, skipping). Robbins, who attended downtown "happenings" and Judson Church events, finally threw up his hands: "Why—I asked myself—does everything have to be so separated and alienated; so that there is this almost constant push to disconnect? The strange thing is that the young people—what you might call and I use it in quotes, the 'hippy' world—is for love. Is that bad?" Even Balanchine thought Robbins's new dance was wonderful.[68]

Dances at a Gathering premiered at a gala celebration on May 8, 1969, with Gordon Boelzner at the piano. That night, preoccupied with his ongoing vendetta, and apparently facing a casting dilemma, Balanchine abruptly took Paul Mejia out of his customary role in the third movement of *Symphony in C*, which was also on the program. Suzanne and Paul were furious. In a fit of outrage, Suzanne marched up to Betty's office and said it was impossible and Balanchine simply couldn't do this. A tizzy of conferences and calculations ensued, and when Balanchine refused to see Suzanne or Paul, they finally sent an ultimatum through Eddie Bigelow, who warned them not to: if Paul doesn't dance, I don't dance either, Farrell grandly proclaimed, and they both threatened to resign.

The response was swift and final. Balanchine canceled *Symphony in C* and replaced it with *Stars and Stripes*. Madame Pourmel, the little Russian wardrobe lady who delivered costumes to the dancers, appeared nervously in Suzanne's dressing room and removed her Bizet tutu. "I'm sorry, Suzanne, you are not dancing tonight," she said tearfully, and they both knew it was not just that night. Farrell was stunned. How could he do this? He had never not listened to *her*—and wasn't she—or at least her dancing—sacrosanct? It was not. Later that night, she numbly returned to the darkened theater to collect her things and walked out of the NYCB. As for Paul, "He's a lousy little bastard," Balanchine said bitterly. "How dare he even . . . think I will be scared to death and say okay. No, he is not going to dance. I have other people to dance." Besides, "he is like a scorpion that stings itself in its own head." The same, of course, could have been said of Balanchine.[69]

Meanwhile, *Dances at a Gathering* tore down the house. The applause that night was like a rock concert, and after its official premiere, critics rapturously embraced the ballet as "one of the most significant evenings in the American theater since O'Neill."[70] There was talk—lots of it—of succession: wasn't Balanchine old and creatively spent, and wasn't Robbins on a new creative high and ready to lead the way? With *Dances at a Gathering,* he had made a ballet for Americans, for the 1960s, and he had tapped something in his young dancers that Balanchine was probably too gray, and too Russian, to grasp. Even Lincoln reached for Jerry, writing obsequiously to offer him a blank check with the company. Balanchine "increasingly will be away; he says he cannot be milked like a cow any more" and has plans to work more in Milan, Hamburg, Geneva, Moscow, Teheran. "You can have our company," Lincoln told Jerry. "That is, if you want to cast your lot with us again, you can and no problems for you."[71]

It had been a fateful night. Paul and Suzanne gone: the exile of a son and daughter. Jerry returned, like the Prodigal Son he had once danced. And George, the father and king, knocked by them all from his throne. As Balanchine went home alone that night to his small and poorly furnished apartment, one thing was clear: he had been usurped—twice—once by each of his only two imagined sons. As for Suzanne, the experience had destroyed him.

When it was all over, it was easier to see what had happened. Suzanne had that mellifluous voice that glides past difficulties, and even in the inevitable interviews with a scandal-hungry press, you could hear eruptions of spirit—not quite anger, more incredulity and the indignant righteousness of a child who hadn't been allowed to explain *her* side. ("Balanchine doesn't even *know* what happened; he never talked to us.") Injured, sultry, a bit pious, she spoke with that little-girl voice, such a little-girl voice that it seemed at least partly a manipulation, but it worked on herself more than anyone else. That's how inside it all she was. She and Paul were in love, and Balanchine had cut them off in a single stroke, taken away their voices just like that. Suzanne, whose voice had rung so silent and clear through the theater during her reign, found this especially vexing, and she clearly had not expected it. She even showed up at the theater here and there in the weeks to come, just appeared in class or stopped Balanchine in the hallway wanting to talk. Make an appointment with Barbara, he said blankly. And when she told Barbara, "we" have decided to come back, Balanchine just said, "Who is this we?"[72] In interviews, she sounds young, never innocent, caressing, laughing, but injured too and smoothing the pain with her voice, like a woman smoothing the creases in a dress.

What, finally, did Balanchine see in this Midwestern *fille*? She was remote and could seem aloof—another alabaster princess—but she also had a sharp wit, loved puzzles and puns, carried her Catholicism proudly, and she worshipped him. Other women may have had that, but they did not dance the way she did, did not work the way she did, and did not make him laugh with the same easy irony. One can see them together—sitting there, existing together, like two rare single-stem flowers, poking toward the sky. They were airy people, tempered by humor and a physical alignment, wrapped in poses and a playful but detached sexuality, Suzi lounging in her robe in the office (there was that), Balanchine meek and mousy, but fully in his element in the studio as he made her—they made her—into herself, and he felt himself too, fully self-possessed and physically engaged in a way he wasn't anywhere else.

Being in love with her was loving her truly extraordinary talent, and he needed to get inside it, touch it, conquer it even, in order to set it free. We might ask: but why did he need to make love to her—couldn't he just *work* with her? He couldn't. His desire was cinched to her dancing—and truth be told, her dancing was cinched to his love. It was one of her great qualities that on stage, performing his dances, this girl-woman was more womanly, more fully feminine in a profound way, than any other dancer he had. The stalemate between them was a stalemate of sex, but more consequently for Balanchine and the world around him, it was a stalemate of art. If she couldn't submit, he couldn't keep going; if he couldn't relent, she couldn't submit. It was a steel trap with no way out but out. That path—the Suzanne path—was bouldered over.

It was the paradox of his life. He needed submission—her to him, but also him to her. Remember the man crawling like the bug at the woman's feet in *Metamorphoses*; the small mouse to Tanny's huge cat; Quixote prostrate before Dulcinea. His deepest impulse was to submit to Suzanne, or at least to the goddess of their making, and to set *her* free on stage. That happened. That they achieved—on stage she really was the freest woman in the world. But in life his love was suffocating, and she was no goddess but a very young woman with her own faults and frailties. He was morally blind to her age, her suffering, her desires, and even (especially) to her confusion and wily manipulations. He was trying to bleed art into life, which is why the suggestion of marriage came as such a shock. In the studio they had already given themselves to each other, but to propose a sacrament in life too was jarring. It sounded wrong. It couldn't work, and she fled.

The final irony: Suzanne and Paul went to Maurice Béjart's Ballet of the Twentieth Century, a company of men for Balanchine's most "ballet is woman" dancer. There, she was just another star, proof that without Balanchine she was not going to travel the same radical route, and by her own account of it, she spent most of her time with Béjart obsessively practicing and representing Balanchine. As for Paul, it depends on who you ask. He claimed, incredibly, that he didn't know she was Balanchine's girl, but she was *her,* after all, and this boyish innocence was not so innocent for a man who aspired—and was being groomed—to become the next Balanchine. As it was, he lost the most of them all, and his bright future disappeared into a mere shadow as he joined the ranks of good-enough dancers and directors populating the dance world.[73]

After Farrell's departure, Balanchine fell into an even deeper depression. He looked awful, his face gray and lumpy, as if he had aged a decade in a day.[74] He spent the week in Weston, "mowing Tanny's lawn, painting her house, and resting from the inevitable let down after the euphoria launched by Suzanne's exit," Lincoln reported to Jerry. "Everyone hopes that Balanchine will now go back to Tanny but the truth is she knows it would only be until Gelsey, or X. Y. or Z. are mature enough to move him. Oh dear."[75] The little cottage he rented on the Leaches' pastoral River Run estate in Saratoga was a respite. He took in an abandoned mutt he called Moka, who dug a hole under the window to sleep near him. He named the other dogs Serge and Igor (Samoyeds) and Sam (barbet); the cats were Dido and Aeneas. He helped with the goats and horses and cooked Georgian food for everyone. Kay Leach, it turns out, was an accomplished pianist (trained by Stokowski's Russian wife), and George played her grand piano, even with his missing finger, and they listened together to the classical-music station WMHT. That summer, he sat glued to the TV during the moon landing, an affirmation of progress, technology, and cosmic realms, and he read the morning newspaper on the lawn in his blue silk bathrobe with coffee and croissants from Mrs. London's bakery. He staged ballets and tended the theater; he ironed shirts, played solitaire, and went on a binge washing everyone's cars.[76]

His divorce from Tanny proceeded. There were lawyers, and Betty took Tanny's side in a nasty rupture with Balanchine that would never really heal. George was loyal to Tanny, though, and would send gifts and pay alimony and a percentage of his earnings for the rest of his life. And when Mourka, the cat that seemed to stand for the marriage they did and didn't have, ran away and Tanny called distraught, Balanchine dropped everything and drove from Saratoga to find her. He must have known that Tanny had been his only ever real wife.

He moved house, again, this time to a spacious apartment at 27 West Sixty-seventh Street, an elegant building off Central Park, not far from the theater. With Barbara's help, he furnished it simply with basic white plates and the like from Bloomingdale's and Macy's and the five-and-dime.[77] The apartment was to be done in "white . . . not style, nothing at all, no style," he said, and include only a few belongings: white sofa, green loveseats, a dining table, a small wine closet, and the requisite ironing board—no piano even. The second bedroom, a bit dark and dusty, was largely occupied by icons. In his bedroom, St. George stood on the bedside table, along with the photograph of Meliton. Balanchine's trajectory was comfortingly routine—home, theater, restaurants, home. Sometimes he appeared at the Milsteins', let himself into the kitchen, and started cooking; once he made *kissel* and ate the whole thing himself.[78]

At the theater, he seemed lifeless and disinterested, fragile even. Jerry, who was on a creative roll, was a source of anxiety. In a rehearsal around this time, Balanchine went on a rant against him and the dancers loyal to him and finally blurted out, "Do you know Dostoyevsky's inquisitor? I am the inquisitor," and when the dancer Francis Sackett said he knew the novel and saw the point, Balanchine turned to Gordon at the piano, "See, *he* likes me!"[79] Even the hallways seemed haunted. "Don't wear that perfume, she wore it," he said listlessly to one dancer. Some days he didn't show up at all. He glumly tolerated the dreary business of his ballerinas vying for Suzanne's roles. Karin von Aroldingen and Kay Mazzo, the "two Kakas," as the gossip mill cattishly called them, took over most of Farrell's territory. Kay was petite, refined—and wary. She knew she didn't want to be the next ex-Farrell, but Karin, who was married and had a child, immediately made herself into a Suzanne look-alike: she stood at Suzanne's place at the barre and wore the same rubber fisherman's pants Suzanne wore, the same scarf around the middle, the same ponytail. She even seemed to develop the same Farrell overbite.[80]

Ramparts down, Balanchine began dating Karin. (Barbara called her "the German bombshell" and wasn't the only one to observe that Karin "threw herself" at Balanchine.) At least she was European—German. Karin's husband, Morty—charming, insecure, in real estate—was apparently flattered by the association with the famous George Balanchine and also knew he would lose Karin if he didn't accept him. It was another awkward trio; Balanchine was even godfather to their daughter. It was a solution, of sorts, but it was also a capitulation. He wanted a woman, but he was done forever with muses and marriage and romantic love. As a dancer, Karin couldn't hold a candle to Suzanne. When she got a small apartment of her own and offered to leave her husband for him, he said no, please don't, really, he wanted to be alone.[81]

The final blow that seemed to end an era in his life came on April 6, 1971, when Igor Stravinsky died in New York. That night, Balanchine made his way through the sleeting rain to a prayer service at the Frank E. Campbell Funeral Chapel on Madison Avenue. Several days later, he attended the Orthodox funeral. "It was very touching to see Balanchine on his knees," Lincoln noted, "after all he is a very God-fearing man." Stravinsky's body was sent to Venice for burial in a plot next to Diaghilev, but Balanchine stayed home. He hated Venice—too wet and too cold—but also, perhaps, too past. "Stravinsky was only one who knew I [was once a] young man," he told a colleague. It was enough that Balanchine had lost a father, a friend, and a mentor—the musical "ground" that had anchored his life and art.[82]

What came next was *PAMTGG*, maybe the worst ballet he ever made. It was based on an airline jingle, "Pan Am Makes the Going Great." He liked TV commercials and had hoped that Pan Am might sponsor the company's air travel (they didn't). He was moody during rehearsals, as low as anyone had ever seen him, and he walked out several times. He knew the ballet was bad, and it was. It took place on an airport runway, with stewardesses, signalers, piles of Lucite luggage, and a cast of jet-setters, young lovers, and hippies. He got creamed in the press ("Balanchine—Has He Become Trivial?"; "take Robbins away and you find a mixture of tinsel and trash"; "not worth reviewing").[83] For the last performance, Balanchine scrapped the set and told the dancers to do whatever they wanted. They opened their closets and had a party: psychedelic halter tops and miniskirts, leather and fringe, motorcyclists in blue star-studded bell-bottomed pants with dark glasses, a Superman. It was the final revenge of the 1960s, a defeat all the more bitter since it came with another Robbins triumph, *The Goldberg Variations*, to Balanchine's beloved Bach. Even Barbara Horgan was stunned and wrote to Francia Russell, "Jerry's ballet [*Goldberg*] is a big hit. I am listening to it now on the intercom. Rave reviews, and nervous breakdowns for all of us. It is quite something. I like it very much, all one and one half hours of it. The company look superb in it. . . . Balanchine, on the other hand, has finished another piece of junk called PAMGG. . . . It is twenty minutes long, and Eddie and I figured that it will cost about $5,000 a minute. GB has been in a terrible mood, the worst I've seen in years . . . walking out of rehearsals mind you. . . . When do you remember that?"[84]

It was as if the whole weight of the 1960s had come crashing down on his head. It was not only Farrell and Mejia, it was sex, drugs, and rock and roll; feminism and the antiwar movement; hippies and "let it all hang out." But it was also success, empire, money, and the crippling demands of running a major arts organization. Suddenly, he was on the wrong side of everything. He had stood against the Mariinsky, against the Paris Opera, against the Metropolitan Opera, against the bad and boring people of boards, against money, critics, and convention. He had always been "progressive," as he put it, and now he found himself in the director's seat against the youth that had always been his primary inspiration. No wonder he flirted with abandoning it all and starting over again. And yet it wasn't so easy to make, feed, and house a family of dancers, and after thirty years in the wilderness, he had finally built them all a home. The paradox was excruciating: had he made a machine to feed his art only to watch the machine take over his life? As he saw it, Farrell was that too: had he given her everything only to have her break him? And all because he was older and aging. All because the dancers who had once been his peers were now daughters and sons staring at him over an impassable generational divide.

By this time, Balanchine was giving up on himself as a man. He was cut off, and, Quixote-like, he began moving once and for all into a world of his own making. From now on, the man-in-trousers Balanchine would play out his worldly life and fame—with plenty of appetite for food, drink, and sex—but the cloud Balanchine would retreat into the spirit realm of pure dancing. It was a false distinction, of course, since these two bodies were wrapped into a single man, but that's the way he experienced it inside. "Because you see, I am not a *male*, I am whatever it is, Aquarius and Aquarius [is] not supposed to be male at all, I am water and air and I am servant and whatever it is" (or, as Karin put it, "He's not a man, he's not a woman, he's a creature"). He added, "Ninety-nine percent of the world is your world, leave me my world, I like the way it is."[85]

It's all in the dances, he had once said, and now finally he was right.

Balanchine relaxing, Brando-like, with Tanny on Fire Island in the early 1950s.

George and Eddie Bigelow, a devoted friend and man of all
k, clearing the property George
hased in Weston, Connecticut,
d joking with hammer and sickle
bout being workers in a Socialist
paradise. Balanchine was always
hting the Cold War, and Tanny,
who was also a photographer, recorded the joke.

George in Florida on vacation with Tanny, who took this photo of him pretending to be Ernest Hemingway—drunk and in need of "inspiration" to write, which the craftsman George scoffed at.

Balanchine photographed in the 1950s by Tanny, the woman who knew him perhaps better than any other. Note the setting—a meal with wine—and the imagery of seeing through glass.

Balanchine on his Vespa, purchased during a company tour to Italy in the 1950s. He even considered opening a Vespa shop in the United States as a source of income to free him from commercial work so he could devote himself to the NYCB, from which he took no salary at the time.

Cats were a passion, as well as a connection between George and Tanny. Here are Mourka and Balanchine, dirty after planting flowers—another passion—at their home in Weston.

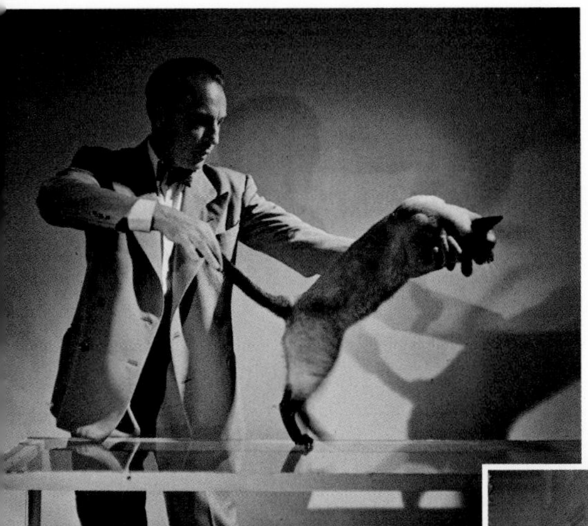

Balanchine teaching a cat to dance. He also often used cat metaphors with his dancers.

Tanny and George at home after she was crippled by polio. Cooking, along with cats and gardening, lay at the heart of their marriage—and of his self-description as a choreographer: I am chef, gardener, carpenter.

Diana Adams, Tanny's best friend, also lay at the heart of their marriage. Plain-faced but physically beautiful with what seemed to be golden-mean proportions, Adams was internal and troubled. Balanchine was in love with her as a dancer and as a woman, even after she married his lighting designer Ronnie Bates.

Arthur Mitchell joined the NYCB in 1956 and was soon a principal dancer. Mitchell's family had suffered after his father's incarceration, and Balanchine and Kirstein became father figures, Mitchell said. He is shown here holding Christmas angels.

In 1957, Balanchine made *Agon* in collaboration with Igor Stravinsky, who also attended rehearsals. Here, Stravinsky (lef Balanchine discuss the score in rehearsal with the pianist Nich Kopeikine (another Russian émigré). "I'm terribly sorry. There parts of this music I don't understand," Kopeikine admitted, to which Stravinsky responded, "It's perfectly all right. I don't understand them either!"

Agon was made for Adams and Mitchell in the leading roles. One of Balanchine's greatest works, it was plotless, was performed in practice clothes, and depended in part on the visual (and political) image of black skin on white.

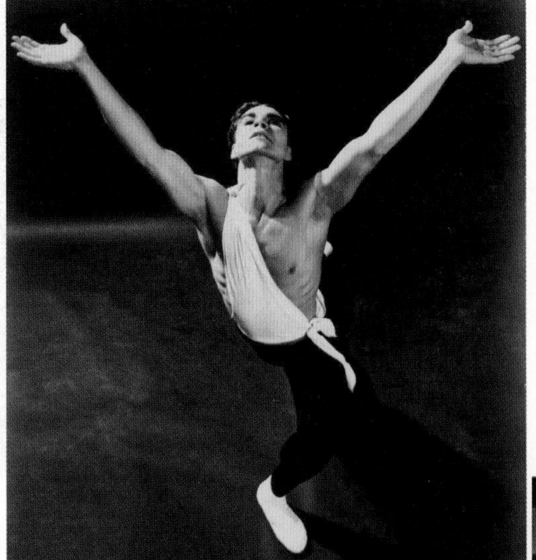

In the 1950s, Balanchine also stripped *Apollo* of its classical and eighteenth-century sets and costumes. Jacques d'Amboise performed the title role bare-chested, in simple black-and-white practice clothes. He wanted to look like who he was: a kid from New York, hair slicked back Elvis-style, and Balanchine approved.

ıcques d'Amboise in *Stars and ɒes* (1958), Balanchine's most ıy patriotic dance, to music by Philip Sousa and Hershy Kay. ɛ finale, performed against the ırling of a huge American flag, was a Cold War pledge of allegiance to America.

Allegra Kent, a bold new talent, in the 1958 revival of *The Seven Deadly Sins*. Balanchine remade this Brecht-Weill show, which he had originally choreographed in 1933, in a decadent Weimar style, for Kent and Lotte Lenya. Kent is seen here served on a platter to gluttonous men.

In 1959 Balanchine made *Episodes* to a score by Anton Webern, for Jacques d'Amboise and Diana Adam
the leading roles. Balanchine was enraged when the audience laughed at this move (left), which he may h
drawn, knowingly or otherwise, from *Pastoral* (1923) (right), by Nikolai Foregger and MASTFOR, a grou
Balanchine had worked with in Russia in the early 1920s.

Balanchine with Gordon Boelzner, an accomplished pianist, who joined the NYCB in 1959 and stayed until after Balanchine's death. Gordon was among Balanchine's closest musical colleagues, and they could often be seen bent together over a score.

Balanchine in rehearsal in the 1960s. Note his dynamism—"Pow!," "Bang!," and "Move!" were common imperatives.

Arthur Mitchell as Puck in *A Midsummer Night's Dream* (1962). When Balanchine had trouble imagining a costume, Mitchell went home and traced his muscles with Albolene and sprinkled his gleaming bare body (minimally clothed) with glitter—like dew—which delighted them both.

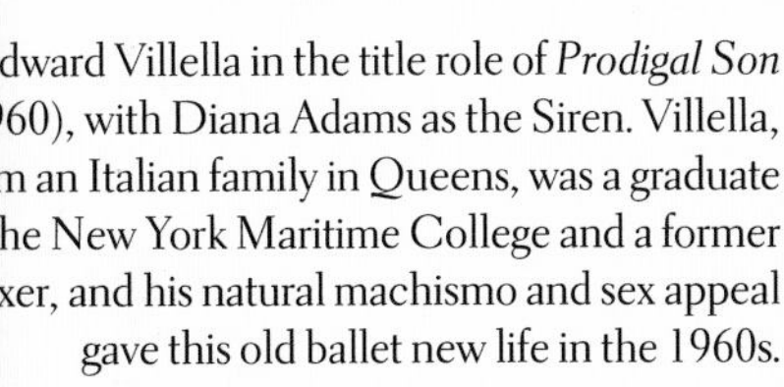

dward Villella in the title role of *Prodigal Son* 60), with Diana Adams as the Siren. Villella, m an Italian family in Queens, was a graduate he New York Maritime College and a former xer, and his natural machismo and sex appeal gave this old ballet new life in the 1960s.

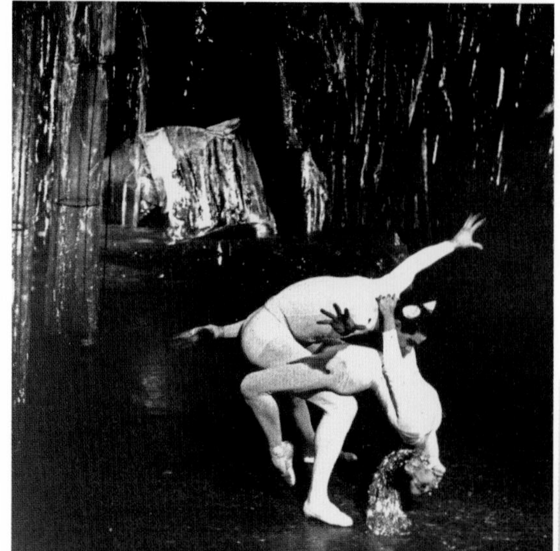

Jacques d'Amboise and Diana Adams in *Electronics* (1961), to a score by Remi Gassr in collaboration with Oskar Sala. The sets w sci-fi cellophane, and the subject, according Jerome Robbins, was sex—part of Balanchin efforts to keep up with the 1960s.

Balanchine with Jacqueline Kennedy at the ballet in 1962. He tried to convince her that she was not only the First Lady but "the First Woman" and could unite "the soul of the United States." He hoped that she would be "America's Faerie Queene," referring to Edmund Spenser's sixteenth-century courtly poem and invoking a long tradition of assigning to women moral and spiritual authority.

The NYCB tour to the USSR in 1962: Balanchine looking annoyed by Konstantin Sergeyev (far right), artistic director of the Kirov Ballet, whom he considered a mere apparatchik. Also present are choreographer Leonid Yakobson and ballerina Natalia Dudinskaya. When Sergeyev presented flowers to Balanchine on stage after a performance in the name of Balanchine's native Leningrad, Balanchine pointedly accepted on behalf of New York and America.

chine surrounded by his Georgian family upon landing in Tbilisi. The man in front with ite shocks of hair is his younger brother, Andrei. Balanchine is speaking to Apollon, his older half-brother from his father's first marriage. Balanchine considered Georgia his land even though this was his first time on Georgian soil.

The medieval Gelati Monastery, high on a misty mountain above Balanchine's father's home in Kutaisi, had once been a renowned center of Orthodox Christian worship and learning. The Communists left it open as a historical monument, and Balanchine (in the company of KGB agents) visited the Churches of St. George and St. Nicholas and the astonishing Cathedral of the Virgin, where we see him gazing at the ancient frescoes.

Crowds in Tbilisi part as Balanchine enters the theater for a performance. In Georgia, he was greeted like a hero or a saint.

Suzanne Farrell, an immense talent, joined the NYCB in 1961 at age seventeen. Balanchine soon fell passionately in love with her as a dancer and as a woman.

Balanchine in the title role of *Don Q*
(1965), a major full-company produc
based on Cervantes's novel, with mu
Nicolas Nabokov. For the opening ga
performance, Balanchine danced Q
to Suzanne Farrell's Dulcinea. We se
here on Henry the horse, who playe
the role of Rocinante.

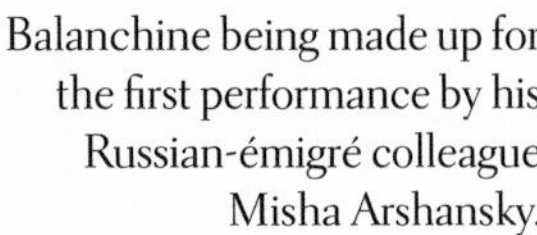

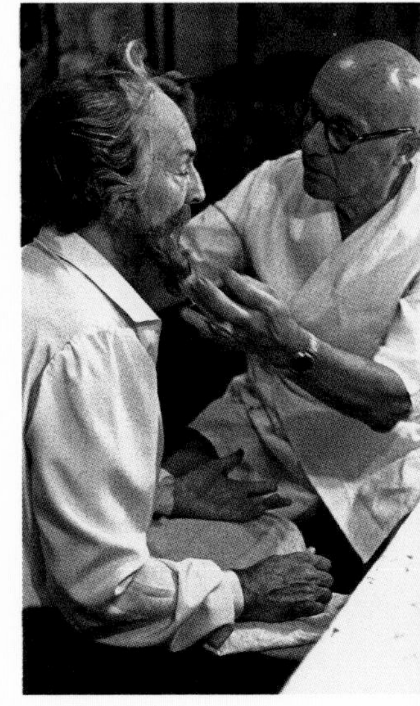

Balanchine being made up for the first performance by his Russian-émigré colleague Misha Arshansky.

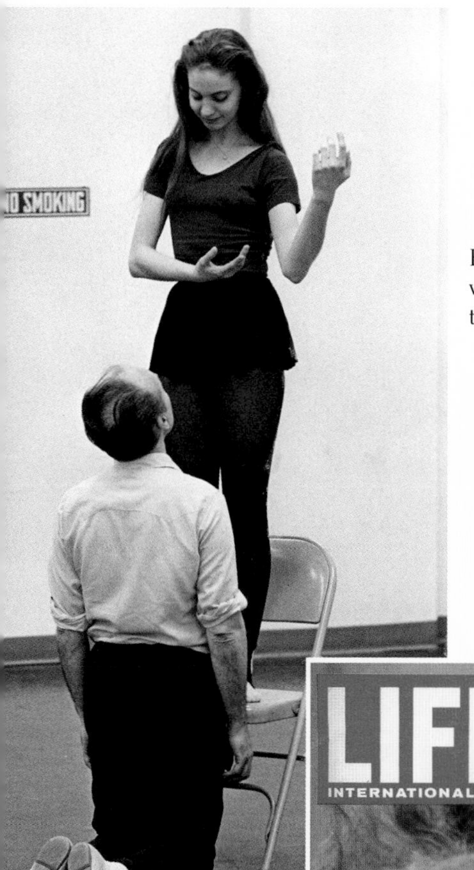

Balanchine rehearsing with Farrell, who in this scene was dressed like the Virgin Mary and haloed.

LIFE
INTERNATIONAL
KENNEDY: PART II—'His Biggest Mistake'
by ARTHUR M. SCHLESINGER JR.
Fantastic New Drug Which Causes Quints
George Balanchine
and Suzanne Farrell
in 'Don Quixote'
AUGUST 23, 1965

Balanchine and Farrell in *Quixote*, which made the cover of *Life* magazine.

Balanchine shows Edward Villella how to partner Patricia McBride in a 1967 rehearsal of *Glinkiana*. McBride was a spontaneous and carefree performer, a respite for Balanchine from the high drama of Farrell.

Soon after Farrell married Balanchine's protégé Paul Mejia, things finally exploded and they left the company together in 1969. Balanchine found himself at an all-time low. To make matters worse, Igor Stravinsky died in 1971. That year, Irving Penn took this series of photos.

After Farrell's departure, Karin von Aroldingen became Balanchine's partner and lov spite of the fact that she was married and had a young daughter. Karin was East Gern and had a wide back, long torso, muscular legs, and a dramatic spirit. She is seen here tearing across the stage in *Serenade*.

ıchine and Robbins in 1970, steadily working even as critics
·d that perhaps Balanchine's time was coming to a close
he more youthful Robbins, who'd seemed to have his finger
e pulse of the 1960s, would take over.

By 1972, Balanchine was back. The Stravinsky Festival was a tour de force week of thirty-one ballets—twenty-one of them new—including ten original and restaged dances by Balanchine. Here we see Lincoln and George in a vodka toast to Stravinsky on the opening night.

Kay Mazzo and Peter Martins in *Violin Concerto,* which premiered at the Stravinsky Festival. This moment falls at the end of their pas de deux. Is there a more vulnerable moment in all of ballet than this back-bent woman, head dangling behind her on the frail thread of a neck, eyes covered in darkness?

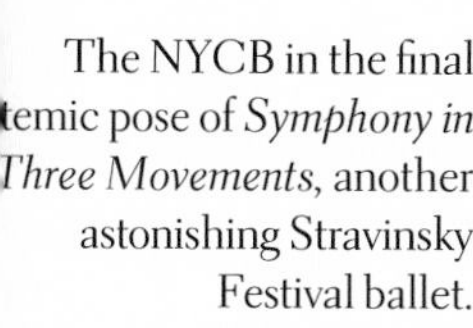

The NYCB in the final
temic pose of *Symphony in*
Three Movements, another
astonishing Stravinsky
Festival ballet.

In 1975, Suzanne Farrell returned to the company and Balanchine began making dances on her again. This photo of them in a rehearsal of her role in *Vienna Waltzes* in 1977 captures something of their relationship and the theme of yearning and unrequited love that marked so much of Balanchine's life and work.

Mikhail Baryshnikov defected from th
USSR in 1974 and joined the NYCB
briefly in 1978. Balanchine was sevent
four and his health was failing, but he
worked closely with Misha (as he fond
called Baryshnikov), who is seen here,
Christlike, in *Prodigal Son*.

As Balanchine grew old, the school continued to train talen
young dancers who fed into the company. Heather Watts w
from California, and Mel Tomlinson was from North Caro
and came to the NYCB from Arthur Mitchell's Dance The
of Harlem. They are seen here in *Agon* in the early 1980s.

Merrill Ashley took ballet technique to another level and Balanchine made for her *Ballo della Regina* (1978), perhaps his most technically demanding dance ever.

Alexandra Danilova rehearsing *Coppélia* with Balanchine in 1974. It was a ballet they had danced together as children in St. Petersburg. By then Danilova was also teaching at the school. See how he still loves and admires her.

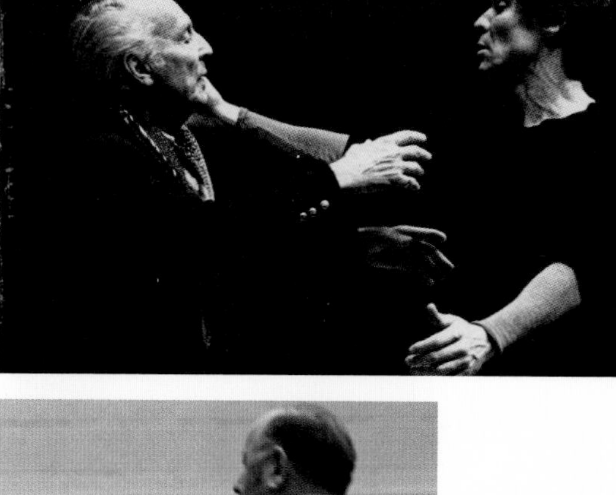

ﾠs Balanchine aged, so did Jacques mboise. Jacques was Balanchine's losest male dancer: it could be said that he doubled for Balanchine in many ballets, especially in dancing with Tanny, Diana, and Suzanne. This poetic gesture conveys their deep connection.

Balanchine playing around with the conductor Hugo Fiorato—"ego furioso," Balanchine called him. Fiorato had been with the company since 1948.

hine and Kirstein remained together like two trees in the ge wing, seen here in 1982. ad been standing together in n pursuit for half a century.

Karin von Aroldingen as Clara in *Robert Schumann's "Davidsbündlertänze"* (1980), a ballet about love, madness, and death. "You know how to mourn," Balanchine told her.

Even as his health declined, Balanchine continued to personally prepare his annual Easter dinner, a ritual he had performed most of his life. The dancers knew he would disappear intermittently from rehearsal the week before Easter to tend to a special dough or other details of this celebratory meal, shared with close friends.

Balanchine's funeral in 1983, with the flower-l casket under the chandelier of the former ballr a mansion that had been converted to an Orth church on Ninety-third Street.

By then, Balanchine had already staged his own death in *Adagio Lamentoso* (1981), to the final moveme Tchaikovsky's Sixth Symphony, with mourners, monks, a breathing human crucifix, and seraphim angels end, a small boy in white carrying a lit candle stood alone on a darkened stage. In a last breath, as the mu out, the boy blew out the candle. The theater plunged to black.

Chapter 24

A LEGION OF ANGELS

Call it survival. Call it relief. Call it genius or the grief from Stravinsky's passing or the lightness of this father finally departed. Or call it an invocation. It was all of these things, rushing in like antibodies to protect and revive a mind in crisis. He wasn't the kind of man to grieve openly, but it was always on the threshold of terror and loss, perfectly alone, that his heart gathered itself. His advantage was that in the Russian mind, the dead don't die, and so in June 1972, Balanchine invited Stravinsky into his theater to celebrate the composer's ninetieth birthday. He called it a party, a festival of music and dance to toast his dead friend and paterfamilias. "In Russia we don't cry when a person dies. We are very happy. We throw rice with nice sweet things in it—vanilla and natural things—into the grave. Then we go home and have an enormous table of food and drink and we drink to the health of the guy who dies. The body is gone—we don't need—but we drink to his spirit."[1] He was still in touch with Stravinsky, he said, and they talked often: "He called me on the phone and said 'George, it's all yours. Do what you want.' . . . His body is gone but he is here, what could he leave. . . . His nose?. . . . It's the music, that's what he left and he's here when they play the music."[2]

It was the least Balanchine could do. It was Stravinsky, after all, who had restored him to life with *Agon* after his half-dead days at the hospital caring for Tanny and her polio. It was Stravinsky who had lifted him up from TB and chronic illness in the early days with Lincoln and the first Stravinsky Festival in 1937. It was Stravinsky who had given him his start, even further back in the Diaghilev days, with *Apollon Musagète*. And it was Stravinsky who had been prohibited to him by the Soviet authorities in his youth when he had tried to make a dance to *Pulcinella*. Stravinsky had been the North Star of his life, his music the "floor" Balanchine stood upon, the earth beneath his feet. "Why do you love somebody?" he explained to a journalist: "I'll ask you. Are you married? Do you like your husband? Could I say why I love Stravinsky as a man, as a person, as a music? I love it. It's wonderful, delectable, delirious, and lots of Russian and lots of Latin, Catholic, pure Catholic."[3]

The Stravinsky Festival celebrated Stravinsky's music in one dense week of performances—seven nights in a row, like the seven days of creation. It was an astonishingly ambitious undertaking on a scale never before seen in the dance world: thirty-one ballets, twenty-one of them new, including ten original and restaged dances by Balanchine. All in all, thirty-five Stravinsky scores would be played, and alongside Balanchine, six other choreographers would make dances: Jerome Robbins, Richard Tanner, John Taras, John Clifford, Todd Bolender, and Lorca Massine. Frederick Ashton and Antony Tudor were invited but declined; Balanchine also went to see Alvin Ailey's *Myth* (1971) to music by Stravinsky but did not invite Ailey to join the festival.[4] Eliot Feld wanted to join, but schedules didn't align, so in the end, it would be a strictly NYCB affair. Balanchine knew very well that the festival would yield some "lousy" ballets, but that didn't matter. The point was to produce an event, a happening, that would bring together and celebrate the dancers, the company, the city, and, above all, his beloved Stravinsky.

It was also to heal himself. Farrell's departure, the *PAMTGG* debacle, and Stravinsky's death had left him empty and he spent the summer of 1971 with a pile of Stravinsky's recordings and scores in Saratoga, ensconced in his little cabin at River Run, where he immersed himself in his dear old friend, a comforting companion after the humiliations and depression that had engulfed him. Stravinsky was still "the only comfort I ever had," and the intimacy of sitting quietly in the morning hours over a piano reduction of, for example, the Symphony in E-Flat and carefully transcribing Stravinsky's notes in his own neat hand, stilled his mind. He spoke to Robbins: is there something you would like to choreograph? Robbins immediately seized on *Requiem Canticles*, which Balanchine himself had done in memoriam of Martin Luther King Jr. Fine, that's fine. That fall, he had lunch with Vera Stravinsky and Robert Craft, who loved the idea of a festival, and he and Craft worked on a list of possible scores. He even tried to excavate from the USSR a recently uncovered lost sonata from 1902. He failed, but his Parisian friend Madeleine Malraux memorized the scherzo section from an unpublished facsimile and delivered it to Balanchine that way instead. Calling in his closest collaborators, he and Barbara traveled to Europe, where he consulted with Nicky Nabokov and Rolf Liebermann, and he sought out Eugene Berman, to see if he would design a new *Pulcinella* (Diaghilev had done it with Massine and Picasso), this time after Tiepolo's great paintings.[5]

It all had to be paid for, so Lincoln enlisted Richard Clurman, chairman of the recently formed NYCB board of directors, whom George vaguely referred to as "Clurman or something." Lincoln told Clurman before his meeting with Balanchine that, above all, they needed to get George back to making dances. Clurman saw Balanchine the way Lincoln did, as the head of "a religious order," and promised George that he would raise the quarter of a million dollars the festival would cost, but that he could do it only if Balanchine would contribute new work. Balanchine calmly evaded these artistic intrusions and quietly made Clurman feel that he too was in service to their bold new artistic venture. Clurman went out and raised more than the necessary amount.

The festival was a retrospective. "We will show Stravinsky's life through sound and then you will see the whole thing in front of you," Balanchine told the press.[6] It was a special point of pride that he was giving this twentieth-century giant a hearing to rival any symphony orchestra's—almost a third of his oeuvre would be performed. If the dances are "lousy," he said, audiences could close their eyes and listen. What they were getting, however, was a partial hearing: this was Balanchine's Stravinsky, without the more "Scythian" works like *Sacre* and *Les Noces*, or even *Petrouchka*. They were overperformed, he said, but they also came from the period of World War I and the revolution, a time he didn't particularly wish to eulogize. "I danced [*Sacre*]," he explained, "but you can't do it, you can't dance to it, it's so powerful—why should you, you don't have to do anything to it, it's so great. Not supposed to be done. Music is enough. You need probably five hundred Russian dancers, gongs, I don't know, but you don't want to see because it is already there." As for *Les Noces*, which he had also danced in the 1920s with Nijinska's choreography, it was "impossible" too, he said (ignoring Nijinska's great dance). It is a great tragedy, he told one journalist, a cantata, and he sang from it, explaining that "the groom is saying 'we will live happily,' but they have never met, and the marriage will be a disaster, and the music is heavy—it is death, and it is a great tragedy. Not sexual, virginal really." He said he could never choreograph it.[7]

His Stravinsky was the Stravinsky of Apollonian renunciation; the Stravinsky who recovered his faith and returned to the Orthodox Church; the "Bach-y" (as a friend put it) and Tchaikovsky-loving Stravinsky, ringing the bells of imperial Russia and a Nietzschean aristocratic order. Skipping from the early Russian years, over the war and revolution, Balanchine moved straight into the composer's neoclassical 1920s and through to later serial works that gave his Russianness new forms, such as *Agon* (1957) and *Requiem Canticles* (1966). Now that Stravinsky was gone, he was even freer with his friend's scores, cutting, mixing, and molding the music to his own theatrical purposes.[8] He noted that his dances were never to music alone—he also had to take into account the personality of the composer, and Stravinsky was "a Turk, an acrobat, his music is at once oriental and very Russian . . . in the Scythian sense." And so the festival ended by doubling back to 1930 with the Symphony of Psalms, based on biblical stories and composed soon after Stravinsky's return to the Church.[9]

As early as the fall of 1971—some nine months before the festival—Balanchine was quietly turning his ship of state toward Stravinsky. He gave the other choreographers first choice of scores and dancers. He would cook with whatever was left, and in the days and weeks to come, the casting board was full as dancers were called to rehearsals for new ballets. The pace was fearsome, and the dancers—including children from the school—found themselves in the theater from morning to midnight, racing from studio to studio rehearsing dozens of new dances, not to mention their regular repertory—the season was in full swing, with performances nightly. They would sometimes even return to the studios after an evening show (racking up overtime hours) before dragging themselves home and falling into bed for a few hours before doing it all over again. They loved it: Balanchine was back, and they were relieved to find him everywhere in the theater again, in high spirits, focused, fun, and the calm at the center of the theatrical storm he was brewing around his great friend.

The logistics alone were mind boggling. Overwhelmed by the enormity of the undertaking, the administrative, artistic, and production staff met one afternoon to plan. Balanchine stuck his head in and said, "You discuss, I'll do," and left. There were only three studios and the stage, and these four spaces had to be shared among dancers, choreographers, conductors, musicians, designers, builders, and lighting and stage crews. At times there were several rehearsals going on in the same studio, and dancers practiced in every corner and hallway—even in the elevators—repeating unfamiliar steps, comparing notes, coaching one another on the intricacies of the vast new repertory they were committing to their bodies in record time. Rehearsal pianists were daily handed difficult scores to sight-read for the first time, demanding a level of concentration and commitment few had ever experienced. Irving, Fiorato, and the full orchestra worked at peak as they faced the challenges of performing dozens of difficult Stravinsky scores with scant rehearsal.[10]

By March 1972—three months and counting before the June 18 opening—the theater was in a state of high alert. They were nowhere near ready, and nine of the new ballets hadn't even been started yet. Balanchine pulled the company still closer around him. He called them back early from a scheduled layoff and cut the upcoming spring season short a week to give them all seven "dark" days in the theater to get the dances on stage before the festival's June 18 opening. Even then, it would be a close call. Ronnie Bates designed the lighting for the entire festival in one hectic week, often without the sets since most were completed only hours before the opening. His crew worked from 8 A.M. to midnight daily, and he scrambled to make ends meet by pulling old sets for new works. How about the backdrop from *Midsummer* with a scrim pulled over it for *Scenes de Ballet*? Could someone please buy some tennis rackets and net? He could use them with plastic plants borrowed from *Divertimento No. 15* to make a set for *Dumbarton Oaks*. Noguchi arrived to refit *Orpheus* to the larger State Theater, and Eddie Bigelow meanwhile managed to locate an old Ballet Russe de Monte Carlo set at Butler University—which he promptly purchased and installed. He also scavenged the theater attic for old costumes (rancid with sweat) that could be repurposed, and Karinska's shop worked madly to the final hour, often delivering costumes just before the curtain rose. For the "leotard" ballets, Balanchine asked the dancers to raid their personal drawers for practice clothes Karinska could copy. Lincoln was in his element and happily occupied himself with a thousand details, including the theater's lobby decor: new sculptures by Yasuhide Kobashi, and a beautiful banner designed by a favorite calligrapher.

In the studio, Balanchine's focus was intense, and he didn't waste a moment. When Kay Mazzo was home sick for several days and completely forgot the choreography he had made for *Violin Concerto*, for example, he just said: "So we try this instead" and started over. The dances seemed to flow out of him—"fast—we had to keep up and you had to stay at the highest level of concentration," she said. It was like doing complicated mathematics with your body all day long, and he worked with a metronome, or snapping fingers, and taught the music and the counts very precisely. "I talked to Stravinsky last night," he would say, and gaily explain the moves as they emerged: this one was "like Russian Tea Room waiters"; that one was "thumbs up for a toast to Stravinsky."[11]

Symphony in Three Movements was the only dance that didn't easily yield. He bent over the score and revised the movement constantly to find the look he wanted, which only rallied the dancers behind him more. The finale alone was a tour de force of complicated patterns performed by a large cast as they executed regimented, semaphore-like arm gestures. He set it on stage by taking each dancer personally by the hand to show the way, talking softly—"Maybe you go here"—as he patiently arranged the dancers like chess pieces, fixing collisions as he went. He didn't stand far off in the theater to check the pattern, nor did he boom his voice at them over the "God mic." He had it all in his head, like a battle plan, and as the pattern came into focus, one dancer was so overcome with the brilliance of the result that she whispered, "He isn't human."[12] He could see the workings of the clock; he knew the inside of the orange without breaking the skin, and he brought it all to life with consummate calm and civility. In this atmosphere, company tensions and petty disputes, so rampant in the months before, seemed to melt away; there was simply no time to complain, and they all felt the momentousness of the project at hand.

Robbins wrote giddily to friends:

> Frantic time! It's like being on an express train whizzing thru stations at breakneck speeds and as the stations flash by you almost can read the names "Pulcinella"—gone—"Violin Concerto"—gone—"Requiem"—GONE—and those flashes were the entire experience of visiting those places after having read about them, studied the maps, selected the sites and restaurants you wanted to see, found out about the weather, hotels, currency, visas, inoculations, etc. packed and voila—passed! It's going at a sickening speed now. George's *Violin Concerto* is George at his best—and its his top best. . . . G and I have become closer—sharing the same dressing room, ballet, and identical knee injury. I've loved helping him and know him better than ever. He seems very happy—excited and at the same time calm and patient. . . . Well, back to the express![13]

He was frankly in awe of George's approach. It is Tuesday, he told a reporter excitedly, and *Pulcinella* opens Friday, and the scenery and costumes are still in the shop, and nothing has been rehearsed on stage, much less with the orchestra. "In all my experience working on Broadway shows I have never seen anything comparable, nothing, nothing. . . . Never . . . it should be known that [at the NYCB] there is never a time when we have the completed work, lighting, costumes, orchestra. The first time all of that comes together is opening night. . . . These ballets are just going up." The reason it works, he said, irritably dismissing the reporter's petty questions about money,

> is *that man* and his leadership and the unassuming way he has led us, he is not what you would call a man of great oration and there's no such thing as pep talks and "we all got to get in there together," he's a man

who by his own personality and his own dedication and his own humanity has shown us how to follow his lead. It matters beyond all of us.

He wrote to a friend, "The short order cooks at the Stravinsky Restaurant are turning out their dishes, the most wonderful news is George is back on track again." Lincoln likened the festival to a miniature Normandy landing.[14]

At times, Balanchine faltered under the pressure. He and Irving fought like vipers over tempos, and more than once he abruptly left rehearsal spitting and raging at the conductor—one of the only people in the world who could raise his ire. The union was another, and when Jerry was late one day and the dancers packed up their things and left after fifteen minutes, per union rules, Balanchine was enraged. He furiously attacked the male dancers for leading an insurrection. It wasn't the women, he said; it was those men ("What a mad dictator," Jacques sighed). The next morning, Balanchine came to class armed with a paranoid speech. There were a few subversives, he said, his face agitated and twitching, that were trying to destroy him and the company. He knew it and could see it, he warned, but he and Stravinsky had a "legion of angels" behind them and would never lose. Besides, he threatened, index finger raised, nose defiantly to the sky, he could always leave and start a new company with a few people that "have respect."[15] But mostly, he floated above it all. When the renowned conductor Walter Hendl (father of one of the dancers) showed up stone drunk for a precious stage rehearsal just two days before the opening, George coaxed him out of the pit as Hendl shouted "Georgi!!!" and railed incoherently at the musicians. The next day, Balanchine quietly fired him.[16]

It was *Quixote* all over again. The up-to-the-minute rehearsals, the improvisational high jinks, the "all in" against impossible odds, and the around-the-clock schedule were ways of destabilizing their too-established company and "waking it up" from deadening and routinized regimes. By throwing the Stravinskyan kitchen sink and the full powers of his imagination at them with no time to think about tomorrow or yesterday, he pulled them all into *his* other world, and they found themselves happily battling windmills and playing the roles he assigned them.

On opening night it was pouring rain, and as the damp audience arrived at the warm and brightly decorated theater, Lincoln and George were there to greet them. The ceremonies began in front of the curtain with Lincoln "looking like a lost rhino," Tanny giggled, and George "woodchuckish, a little plump, dapper as hell." This very odd couple blundered winningly into an inadvertent comic act over the mic—too low for the towering Lincoln, too high for George craning on tippy-toe. The audience shouted, "Can't hear!," as Balanchine wandered to gesture to the orchestra, until finally they arrived at the appetizers: the lost smuggled scherzo played by heart by Madame Malraux for two dancers, a kind of aperitif whipped up among friends, followed by Stravinsky's orchestration of *Happy Birthday,* and ending with the *Fanfare* that had announced the opening of the State Theater nearly a decade before. Then, in one gulp, came two new Balanchine masterpieces: *Symphony in Three Movements* and, above all, *Violin Concerto.*

The reception that night was ecstatic. Jacques wrote in his diary: "BUT! *Violin Concerto* oh oh oh fab fab. . . . What a ballet on the order of *Apollo, Agon*—oh! Oh! I am inspired—so happy—thrilled—what a genius Bal is. . . . What an eve." Even Tanny, her customary irony disarmed, confided to a friend: "I mean you felt privileged to be there, glad to be alive now to see it. . . . *Symphony in 3 Movements, Violin Concerto*—a KNOCKOUT." The next morning, the critics raved and fawned as they rushed to restore Balanchine to his throne. He dryly told the dancers, "We don't listen to them."[17]

Even Balanchine thought *Violin Concerto* was his best ballet: "Like a Russian icon, constructed like good architecture, solid, pure, it is good."[18] The music had been with him for a long time, ever since 1940, when he had worked with Stravinsky and the violinist Samuel Dushkin (who inspired the original) on *Balustrade* (1941) to the same score, with larva-like tangles of people and surrealist sets by Tchelitchew showing two blood-red skeletal trees, veined like nerve ganglia. His new *Violin Concerto* ("Stravinsky never wrote *Balustrade;* he wrote *Violin Concerto*")[19] was in the lineage of *Agon*—black-and-white practice clothes, cyclone-blue backdrop, and a small corps of women and men dancing each musical section in various combinations. It even began like *Agon:* four men, this time facing front, feet front, with Kay Mazzo added in the center spot.

Balanchine was in full control of the style he had invented. *Violin Con-*

certo was walking, running, acrobatics, ballet, jazz, Georgian folk dance, and a whole life of movement fused into one. It was flat—head on, full light, no shadows, and this icon-like frontness took away depth and inverted the space: the horizon is not behind the dancers but flipped front, so that *we* are the horizon, and the dancers are in close and intimate conversation with each and every one of us. Partly this has to do with the bodies, or creatures or animals or transfigured beings—it is hard to describe how unhumanly human his dancers had finally become, and they were both intimate and detached—like the mysteriously yielding surface of a varnished icon.[20]

The first pas de deux, for example, was all Karin and Karinness: big-boned, wide back, ample hands that splayed, and a body imbued with a Central European ethos—not a classical bone in her being. With her, Balanchine put Jean-Pierre Bonnefoux, panther-like, weight down, a morphable body that could take any shape. Their dance was a study in avoidance and alienation—which somehow "looked" the way the music sounded, two bodies in the same orbit, but not the same life, as they circled and slunk around each other; at one point she went into a backbend bridge and pivoted upside down on all fours, as he laced through her. The ending encapsulated the whole, as she slid through his hands into a sinuous acrobatic back walkover and landed on her feet, arching back away from him into a deep back bend, neck broken and head hanging down her spine. On the last stroke of the music, he flipped like a fish onto his back, fully prostrate before her. In this final moment, they could not see or touch each other, but they were both fully exposed, belly-up and blind.

The second pas de deux was Kay and Kayness: delicate, long thin wrists, with a fragile strength, tenderly supported—or saved—at every perilous physical and musical juncture by the enigmatic Peter Martins, with his Apollonian beauty and don't-give-a-damn posture—except that really he knew just how to partner this breakable girl. Their dance begins with her dangling by a thin wrist from his large hand, on one leg, on pointe, off-kilter, righted by him as she runs away and takes a bold stance, two feet spread wide on pointe, arms and legs stretched to four diagonal points, as big and tall as her pin-like body could be, and then her knees abruptly collapse dangerously inward, a kind of crippling or falling, as he rushes to hold them—not her, the knees. He stops the collapse—but also traps her in a perilous and untenable balance, which they both instantly recognize, and she pushes herself up again, turning her back on him this time—though she is still precariously on pointe, balanced again by his large hand.

The ensuing lyrical and involuted dance ends with him standing flush behind her, two bodies as one. He reaches his long arm over her shoulder (an elephant's trunk, Balanchine said) and wraps it around her in embrace, her head nestled in his arm, which then opens out again like a searchlight scanning the horizon. Her head and eyes follow his arm, which takes them both into a low bow (begging, Balanchine said). From this humble point, his beacon-like arm raises them both up and gently pulls her head backward into a neckbreaking arch as he kneels behind her and slides his hand gently over her eyes. Her eyes are now in the palm of his hand—he is caring for and obliterating her at the same time. Is there a more vulnerable moment in all of ballet than this back-bent woman, head dangling behind her on the frail thread of a neck, eyes covered in darkness?

By the time the finale arrives, pulsing with rhythmic life, everything has dissolved into a joyous, pure (and purely invented) abstraction of a Russo-Georgian folk dance. We are back in the polyphonic world of Balanchine's father and his Georgian singers and dancers, drawn into a celebratory rite—not of spring or marriage, but of these strange and interesting human creatures who are all living in Stravinsky and Balanchine's musical time, coping with stasis and discontinuity, static moments and vertical chords; harmonies that seem to chase an elusive center, lose it, and build another one, like fragile villages made of sand. The dancers seem to track these multiple rhythms and dissolving centers in their bodies, weight down, fast and precise, as if the speed and skill of the dance could keep the score on track. They fly and whoosh here and then there and into an underarm turn, running themselves out to the end of the clock, barely holding the pace, until finally they stand facing us, feet forward, breathless—and we are breathless too—and not an instant is lost, tiny bow of the head, as the music stops and the curtain falls. The thrill and fullness the audience felt, as if Balanchine had gathered all of life into those intense twenty minutes, was not misplaced. His Russia—the one he and Stravinsky had invented—was finally fully there, on the stage and in the bodies of his American company.

Symphony in Three Movements (1946) was that too, but this time heavily laden with the moment of its composition. Stravinsky had completed the score three days after the atomic bombing of Hiroshima, and it was linked in his mind "with a concrete impression, very often cinematographic in origin, of the war."[21] Its martial and at times bombastic sound struck the dancers as harsh, and the ballet Balanchine made was abstract but ritualistic: flat and rhythmically driving—Scythian almost—with phalanxes of dancers in black and white practice clothes and a bacchic-like chorus of ponytailed women in white on a long diagonal kick line performing arm-swinging hieroglyphic gestures—"We were one animal."

Choreographically, it was like an anxious cross between Busby Berkeley and Leni Riefenstahl, tense, off-center, with flanks of split-bodied women stuck half in the wing and half out, slinging their arms in semaphore patterns or careening across the stage. "I felt like I was on Freeway 105 in LA," one dancer said.[22] The finale was all arms and legs signaling code against a blaze of syncopated sound until the engine of the music and Balanchine's patterning sent them to their final places: women standing across the stage like Stonehenge rocks, bodies facing front, feet front, arms extended like planks straight side or high overhead, and the men crouched in formation at the edge of the stage, cougars before the pounce. They froze in this human totem, and as the music came to its ominous close, their overhead arms pressed slowly down, seeming to bring the descending curtain down with them, until it touched ground on the final note.[23]

At the other end of his range came *Pulcinella*. Balanchine did not like the old Diaghilev production—Massine and Picasso—and had made up his own based on commedia dell'arte, mixed with ideas he and Robbins threw together one afternoon, as Barbara Horgan took notes. Death and the human comedy were, as ever, the themes. Maybe they would begin with Pulcinella dying, and his skeleton would strike a Faustian bargain with the Devil to resurrect himself and do anything to stave off death, the Devil's due. It would be bawdy, full of cruelty and dirty jokes. Maybe Pulcinella would be thrown into the grave and his bones would fly out, or he would sell tickets to his own grave (with a sign pointing the way down) and mischievously shut any visitors in it. There could be transvestites and drag (for the Devil), a Mack Sennett chase,

Giotto's angels, an orgy of tangled spaghetti.[24] George and Jerry would play beggars in colorful rags and sneakers, two hams cracking each other up like an old vaudeville act. Rehearsals were chaotic and full of rowdy fun with Balanchine acting every role and Jerry at his comic best as they worked together or each took a part and split off into different corners of the room. Balanchine regaled the dancers with stories of how he had first heard Stravinsky's *Pulcinella* in Russia as a teenager and how the Soviet authorities had prohibited it. When the clock ran out, they threw this half-baked mess of a ballet up on stage and let it run on its own steam. The audience didn't always get it, but the dancers were having a blast.

By the time the festival came to a close on the seventh night, it was hard not to notice that George Balanchine's life had passed before them too, from *Pulcinella* to *Apollo, Orpheus, Agon,* and *Violin Concerto*. The final program featured *Choral Variations on Bach's "Vom Himmel Hoch"*—a ceremonial piece with children in white, dancers in white, and a processional—"He's preparing himself," Violette Verdy commented. It ended with the *Symphony of Psalms,* conducted by Robert Craft, but first George and Lincoln returned to the stage to say a few words and invite the audience to join them in a vodka toast to "Igor Fedorovitch friend of ours Stravinsky." As the singers took the stage, gaudily decked (as one critic put it) with full "chrome, tinsel and choir-robe dressing," the dancers sat informally on the floor around them, listening.[25] Only Balanchine was left standing, like an old general, at his usual first-wing post, watching the light-drenched stage as the singers climbed to Stravinsky's vocal heights.

Then: Russia itself.

On a bright day that September 1972, the company reassembled at the stage entrance to the State Theater with large suitcases and trunks crammed with tuna, peanut butter, popcorn, and blue jeans, ready to embark on the NYCB's second State Department-sponsored Russian tour.[26] This time, Balanchine went armed with *Violin Concerto,* which he had taken the trouble to clear with the Soviet authorities months before: he wanted Russia to see it.

But why? You might think the "bastard" Soviets would have no claim on his mind, but in the logic of exile, they still did. *Violin Concerto* was a profoundly Russian work—an icon—and it stood as proof of the path he and Stravinsky had taken out of the revolution; proof of Russia Abroad and the kingdoms they had made to counter Lenin's apostasies and the destruction of their homeland. He cared too because, in spite of himself, he still held a phantom imperial gold standard in his mind, as if performing this ballet on Russian soil would somehow affirm its accomplishment, but more than that, its place. It was his most Russian of Russian ballets, and when the company arrived in Moscow, he immediately arranged a special showing for the Bolshoi company and a few invited guests. It was a success, whatever that meant, and on performance nights you could find Soviet ballet's royalty—none of whom Balanchine entirely respected—crowded in the wings. It was like planting a flag on the moon: a Pyrrhic victory.

The USSR didn't roil him the way it had in 1962, even though the experience was more or less the same: poor food; plenty of surveillance; bugged hotel rooms (the dancers shouted into lamps and radiators: "More veggies!"); rickety planes with open holes serving rock candy and cigarettes; sick dancers; and sold-out shows (the six-thousand-seat Kremlin Palace of Congresses had an hours-long ticket line, with scalpers selling seven-ruble tickets for fifty rubles). Furtseva hosted a reception with skimpy food and higher-ups from Leonid Brezhnev's party apparatus, and in the streets, crowds of well-wishers reached out to touch the dancers as if they were strange animals or saints. Balanchine, who was reading Solzhenitsyn, seemed inured to it all, but the dancers were poorly informed and naïve. When one foolishly picked up a young man, the Soviet police arrived to search the theater and brutally beat this poor youth in front of them all before dragging him off in the back of a van. Shocked, Eddie Villella insisted on taking the next flight home; Balanchine just nodded at this show of naïveté and left him to make his own arrangements.[27]

Lincoln collected translations of much of the Soviet press, most of it bowing to Balanchine's greatness but finding his work coldly abstract and complaining that he used contemporary music but addressed no contemporary problems.[28] George ignored the criticism and avoided political confrontations, later explaining matter-of-factly: "They can't let people free, if they did it would have to be all free, free enterprise but they can't do that, it's socialism, the government controls, where do you start giving people freedom, where is that point, you can't, like Trotsky, always say: permanent revolution." The problem seemed to him obvious: "First you are revolutionary, and [then] proletariat becomes fat bourgeoisie, but we are born individuals, we want to have our little place."[29]

In Tbilisi, he and Karin went to dinner at Andrei's home. The run-down concrete apartment block where his brother lived had been scrubbed and spruced—and thoroughly bugged—in advance by the KGB. The small apartment, up a dank stairway, was crowded with tchotchkes and memorabilia, including pictures of George and Andrei's dead sister, Tamara, along with their dead mother's treasured icon of the Virgin Mary. So much distance had passed between them all since those childhood years, and George seemed at a loss when Andrei and his family presented him with a gift: Maria's gold brooch inlaid with small photos of each of her children.[30] Andrei announced that he was building a dacha and floridly described the plans but admitted it had been regrettably delayed. When George asked why delayed, Andrei replied simply, "No nails." This would be his last visit, George said.

On the final evening of performances in Tbilisi, crowds clamoring for tickets to the sold-out show grew so large that the police couldn't control them. In a state of high excitement, hundreds of people stormed the theater and crammed into every aisle and inch of the house to witness the performance. The police, faced with a possible riot and international scandal if they attempted to forcibly evacuate this sea of fans, let the performance proceed. The curtain call at the end turned into a vigil that went on for nearly an hour, with rhythmic clapping and chanting, until finally Balanchine came out and stood at the edge of the stage. He spread his arms and thanked them all, and when they still wouldn't go home, he invited them to New York: "Come see us, we will be there."[31] But his heart was not fully open during this Russian visit, and even the adulation of his father's native Georgia left him numb. His "legion of angels" had already won, and as the plane took off, he gently closed the door to Russia behind him. This time, for good.

The postscript was pitiable. True to his word, when the Soviet Georgian Dancers and Tbilisi Polyphonic Choir came to perform at Carnegie Hall two years later, Balanchine rented Le Poulailler restaurant and threw them a party. He wrote ironically to the booking agent through Barbara Horgan: "Please pass [the invitation] on to the powers that be, the 'Soviet' Georgians, the NKVD, the CIA, the 19th precinct, Clive Barnes and the Panovs." Still, he waxed sentimental about his Georgian roots, boasting to the press that "Georgians are warriors, but they are also elegant, generous, and temperamental. They are also just about the fastest moving people on earth—perhaps because they had to defend themselves against everybody for such a long time." He was holding on to his "home" by a thread of cliché. In his closet he even kept an old Georgian accordion, along with a full-fledged folk-costume, and a sketch of himself performing a Georgian warrior dance with a knife held in his teeth.[32]

As for his family, the denouement was sad, if predictable. When Andrei managed to get a visa to visit George in New York that same year, George welcomed him but turned a deaf ear to his pleas to introduce him and his music to the "famous Bernstein" in hope of a sensational concert tour in the West. (And when Andrei attempted to extend the visit for a week, his family back home bore the brunt: sudden visits by the KGB, questions, pressure, and veiled threats. He must not defect.) George faced it all with the blankness that was his only defense. He had nothing to say, so instead he took the wish list his nephew had sent him and piled his brother high with bits of Americana to take home: perfume, lipstick, silk dresses, toys, cowboy shirts, and wristwatches.[33] This was the last time he would see Andrei, another door that closed forever. He had his own life and his own angels.

Looking back from here, with Stravinsky and Russia gone and the Stravinsky Festival—his Russia—filling their place, one could see the scope of what Balanchine had accomplished. He had built, or "assembled," as he liked to say, a theater, a loyal troupe of extraordinary dancers, an audience, an orchestra, teams of designers, crews, a whole theatrical apparatus, and a vast body of work. But there was more to it, even, than that. George Balanchine had quietly established in midtown Manhattan, brick by brick, body by body, a "cathedral of dance," as he put it back in 1933 when he first arrived in America.

The NYCB was a dance company, but it was also his own private counter-revolution, a "realer than real" theatrical world, a phantasmagoria really, that stood against Communism and its supposed materialist paradise. Against capitalism and its supposed materialist paradise too, but less so, since in America at least, he had found his "little place."

The astonishing thing was that it all came from him. *Emanated* is true but too grand for this humble man, who pulled them all in with the matter-of-factness of a carpenter and the authority of a spiritual master. He made a whole new art out of *people*—women, really. Not just people he assembled but people he helped to make over years and decades, willful, eccentric, unpredictable individuals who depended entirely on his presence—and he on theirs—to make a fantasy of art. They all lived in this "little place" over which he presided. Which is why Balanchine dancers were famously nontransferable. They couldn't easily slot into another ballet company. Even Farrell was not Farrell out of his sight. He was the only one who knew how to coordinate all the people and parts of their great theatrical venture; and it was he who made sure that he wouldn't—couldn't—know what would happen once the curtain rose. Every night was like a controlled explosion, and the Stravinsky Festival was only a culmination of what he had been doing all his life. It could seem insular, and there were people, including Lincoln, who wanted him to work with other kinds of artists or composers, but that wasn't "what I like." Something inside him knew, with astonishingly little doubt, what he was doing, and he wouldn't budge. "You see, we are occupying in the world a little tiny spot. The rest is yours—do what you want."[34]

His overarching theme was service: "I feel seriously . . . that I am a servant, we all servants, destiny or god you could say, they send us all here and told you to be what you are and what I am, I am not so great or so proud, nothing, I am a servant or a waiter, and he said you are going to teach and to serve and make them dance. . . . And I know that there is nothing, no human on earth could oppose because THEY want me to do."[35]

It was a level of faith that led to a series of paradoxes. He was not an autocrat, even if he behaved autocratically. He was more like a monarchist, who felt a deep connection between God and the authority he had been given. But in life he simply demanded loyalty to the work that was done through him, and they demanded it of themselves too—or left. He was not a narcissist, and the NYCB was not a cult, except in the sense of cultic practices and a sacred space, which is why so many of them said things like "it felt like a religion." The entire endeavor was selfless—he made it, but not for himself, even though he was also certain of his own unique talent. Nor was he a Don Juan—love too was in service to dance—or even a man, really, as the people who knew him admitted and as he himself said many times. His detachment, which could be cruel, was a form of devotion, and it came at the cost of self-neglect too. He wasn't able to love, or fully to live, in the "normal" world. All of *that* was superfluous—pedestrian daily life, the surface, sleepwalking—and, above all, "You might be dead tomorrow." In some strange sense, he didn't really live his own life, which is why he could look so awkwardly airy and immaterial at times, even if he was also one of the most physically animated people alive. He existed to make dances, that's all. It was just who he was and what history had made him.

The philosophical and religious side of his mind mattered too, at least to him. He plotted his own religious course, cobbled together from Orthodoxy, but also from mysticism, Spinoza, Plato, Nietzsche, literature, astrology, and "what I like." It was a piecemeal metaphysics of his own making, and by accepting the fallenness of the body, he found a way to transcend it in dancing:

> It is impossible to explain certain things that are not related to regular life. You see, what we are trying to do . . . we try to explain certain things that are unexplainable. . . . We always want to know how much it weighs, what it costs, how should be done, and so forth. . . . But there is another thing which is very important that is not made of the material; it is made of something but it doesn't belong to this world, you see, the real world is not here, it is the spirit . . . beautiful. . . . Metaphysical is the real one.[36]

It was the "cloud in trousers"—or Quixote's "all spirit" to Sancho's "all body," as Auden had put it—and it constituted the defining fight and paradox of his dances and of his life.

Paradox, yes, but also truth. His dances were metaphysical, but they were never disembodied. He had moved past the Romantic ethereality of fairies, sylphs, and spirits and the binary of body and spirit that informed it. Even Balanchine's most spiritual dances made dancers physically dig into the ground, weight down—and up. They could roll through the foot connecting them to air and earth because they lived in both; they traveled through the flesh with the flesh. His dances were body *and* spirit, or even spirit *as* body. And, therefore, "ballet is woman" was woman as woman—the eternal feminine, but embodied, here and now.

His entire life was ballet. He didn't really care about anything else, except perhaps defying the USSR and honoring Mother Russia, which were related, after all, to his quest. The women he loved, the music he chose, the art he liked, the God he believed in, the friends he made, the dancers he worked with, the cooking, the carpentry, the ironing—all were in service to ballet. His focus was singular, but he had a brilliant and absorptive mind, with a musical and mathematical genius, and a keen sensuality—he really could see, hear, smell, taste, and feel more than most people, and in his dances, he expanded his audience's senses too. He had lived close to death, and dance was a way of defying death with music and a bodily life that he knew how to help his dancers achieve, if they would. He once told one of them, "You would never abandon things on earth, so that's why you don't get anywhere. The portals are open for you, but the passage is narrow."[37]

Don't forget beauty and entertainment. Pleasure in pattern and dance as a field of wildflowers, or a Botticelli painting or a night at the circus, were all part of his range. In pattern and intricacy of steps, Petipa was his greatest source, but the "floor" that they all stood on was music. "The music, I can't explain what it is, I mean, what's Webern. . . . So you have to try to paint time with body, to assemble somehow what's going on in sound. . . . Music is like aquarium . . . and the dancer is inside, it's all around you, it's like a fish goes through the water. . . . The music is the aquarium, and dancers are the fish, and everywhere they are touched."[38] Even if he went into the studio without particular steps or movements in mind, he always had a musical plan: "It is one thing to have music [but] what am I going to do with it? It is not so easy. Has to be a reason—a visual reason. Like probably a book—you have to start at the beginning and [know] how you end, and how it's going to happen, even if it's not a story."[39] How did he get there? "It's just inside of me. I have to feel that this little bundle is right and it represents to me beginning, middle, end and [it is] clear to me, very clear to me."[40] But even that didn't fully account for his greatest secret, which was to have made dance into its own musical score, tied to and moving in and out of a composer's musical score, in ways that the dancers felt and *did*, but didn't always know.[41] He gave them range. Move through the music, he might tell them, not always on it, and then catch it later; you are alive, the orchestra is alive, and there is give—and competition. And when the best of them arrived at those vistas that he had somehow provided but not ordained, where movement and music came together in a way that seemed to open out onto a fuller body and person, the audience rose with them.

He did ballet, yes, but it was a new kind of ballet that ranged far and wide from the base, and many of his dances, including many in the Stravinsky Festival, were made of steps that have no names and no past. It is often said that he made ballet abstract, or neoclassical, which is true but too narrow. He saw himself as "progressive"—all is new!—but he was also deeply conservative, a genius who borrowed from everything he knew and transcended it all. He picked and chose "what I like," from dance, music, art, light, and the sights, sounds, smell, taste, and feel of the changing world around him. "What I like" was an aesthetic, and it was an aesthetic above all of women, because women were beautiful and had more flexible bodies that could do more things. They were more sensitive instruments, easier for him to "wake up," and there was also eroticism to it.

We should remember too that when he started as a boy in St. Petersburg, ballet was still tied to the imperial court and had only recently, barely, been launched as a modern art. Balanchine grew up with the old ballet and old fashions—men in uniforms and women in corsets and long skirts, their bodies and legs hidden beneath piles of crinoline, silk, and lace. On the ballet stage, legs were tantalizingly revealed, but movement was still constrained by the tutu—a corset by another name, whose tight stays broadened the back, heightened the bust, and tapered the straight spine into a wasp waist with a tulle skirt flying out from the hips. Before Balanchine, the body was parceled and divided, upper from lower across the tutu's east-west demarcation line;

and right from left, across the north-south axis of the spine. Technique in the time of Petipa, who was still among Balanchine's greatest influences, was the artful stacking, balancing, and coordinating of the parts in symmetrical patterns through these axes. The body, always a perilous site of emotion and desire, was thus trained to stasis and harmony in dances as coordinated and well-oiled as the court itself.

Balanchine saw the violent breakdown of this hierarchical life of rules and manners, which had been ballet's and the body's mainstay. He *saw* broken bodies and gruesome death, the human form destroyed. But he also saw movement and speed, the motor car, steam trains, airplanes, factories, movies, and, above all, women—and legs—in view and in motion. More motion than ever before in human life. He started over, building with the sticks and bones of the old, ruined art and then with everything he picked up as he went along, and he picked up a lot. It mattered that he had not started with an image of a harmonious classical body—the war killed that. He was starting with the broken body, and over the years, he found a way to make this destroyed body whole, but it was a different whole from the parceled and stacked imperial form—it was impossible to go back.

The Balanchine body moved as one organic piece, head to toe—no parceling—and it could bend, contort, and even break without losing its beauty or form. It could transcend—and endure. It could be grotesque and tangled or out of joint or it could be beautifully patterned and harmonized across multiple bodily and spatial planes, but whatever the style or musical form—and here was the catch—this whole body had no clear axis, no tonal center. Its foundation stone—worse, its default—was chaos. The physical home, the positions of balance and return, had to be made and remade at every turn. Stability and perfection were death and had to be fought with sheer energy and the will to life, sent coursing through the body in dynamic opposites that might, just might, hold, thanks in large measure to music and immense physical energy. His dancers didn't stop, didn't pose, kept moving. To dance in that body was to know that you were on the edge, and it might all give way; holding it together was a complicated physics of energy and time, but also of anxiety. No dancer was alike, just as no human was alike, and he changed his dances all the time, tailored them to each individual.

It was a sea change, and it took a long time and constant vigilance to sustain. Even when he was away for a few months, their bodies began to blur as lethargy and convention set in. "Body is lazy, that's why you have me." This complete dependence between him and all of them is hard to fathom if we assume that art has a kind of autonomy—that it exists outside of its maker, like a painting or a written play or a score. Balanchine's dances were not like that. They were *live*, made for "these people, this music, here, now." Without him, the dancers didn't exist. Without them, his dances didn't exist—but no one could dance Balanchine without Balanchine. Other times, other people, other dances.[42]

Now was still now, and what happened next was surprising. He threw the throttle of his life into reverse. It was as if Stravinsky and this final Russian visit had set off some inner clock that sent him racing backward on a grand tour of his own imagination, and dances and music that had preoccupied him all his life rushed once again to the fore. It was a retrospective turn: he was almost seventy, and he was planning a Ravel festival, and a Tchaikovsky festival, and he wanted to do another Stravinsky festival too—all ways of marking his own retrospective life. None of this had anything to do with memorialization, an idea he despised. The point was more internal. He was still feeding on the material of his life, picking ideas and images from memory like found objects, and there were plenty left to gather. His horizons were naturally dimming, and he was taking stock: of people, places, music, events, and the great store of knowledge in his brain. "I have lived a long time," as he liked to say, and so,"What's the matter with now?" was met with the rejoinder of age: what about then?

THE END OF THE DANCE

Chapter 25

AGING

Variations pour une Porte et un Soupir (1974) was a Weimar-tinged ballet about a man swallowed up in a woman's vagina. It was a dance for Karin von Aroldingen and John Clifford to Pierre Henry's *Sonority* (1963), an electronic score in musique concrète style. Composed of the sounds of creaking doors and human sighs, the written score was all squiggles and points, and Gordon Boelzner showed Clifford how Balanchine had slyly connected the dots into an image of female genitalia. That was Karin: she was the "door" that wouldn't open to Clifford's "sigh." Like a Weimar cabaret dancer, with face painted white and wearing bright red lipstick and a short black wig, she was dressed in a white bodysuit belted with rhinestones, and her long silk skirt flooded the entire stage menacingly from the waist, its corners pulled like marionettes by stagehands in the wings. Clifford ("Cleeeford," as Balanchine called him) was old and lined in a gray bodysuit, with ratted, silver-streaked hair and black sunken eyes.

In the performance, Karin swelled her body or crawled on all fours circling her prey, as Clifford crept and loitered close to the floor, kneeling, twitching, begging, leaning against the forbidding "door," until finally a silhouette of a large spider walked across the white backdrop, and he collapsed in a death spasm as her voluptuous skirt engulfed him. Karin stepped coldly over his body and closed the door on her way out. The ballet produced bravos, boos—and walkouts: "I came to see ballet, not this shit," one man uttered as he fled up the aisle. Lincoln rushed backstage, thrilled at the Diaghilev-like scandal: "Isn't it wonderful?" He also saw it as "a tremendous and very frightening work," almost nihilistic: "The door is shut on our miserable sighs."[1]

A word about Karin. People sometimes think of her as an unlikely woman and dancer in Balanchine's life, and it is true that she was very different from any of the other dancers he had loved. She was not American, and she came with the nervous ambition and insecurity of her own family's scarred past. Her mother's father, from a well-to-do German textile family, had committed suicide during World War I, and his son had returned from the fighting crippled from the waist down. Karin's mother's first husband was killed in a plane crash, and her second husband, Karin's father, was a scientist who probably fought for the Wehrmacht and was killed in mysterious circumstances in Prague during World War II. Karin was raised mostly in divided Berlin, by strong women in hard times, partly in the Russian zone (where she witnessed "horrors"). Fantasy was a respite, and she hung on to moments like the year her mother arranged for Santa Claus to appear at the door with gifts for the children. Above all, she hung on to dancing, which gave order and joy to her otherwise chaotic life.

She trained seriously with Tatjana Gsovsky: a Moscow-born experimental dancer who, like Balanchine, had fled Russia for Weimar Berlin in the 1920s. Gsovsky's work was suffused with Russian and German expressionism, ballet, Isadora Duncan, Émile Jaques-Dalcroze, and Mary Wigman, and Karin got all of that in her training. She came to Balanchine through Lotte Lenya and Tatjana Gsovsky's 1960 production in Frankfurt of *The Seven Deadly Sins*: Karin danced Lenya's double. She had an awkward classical technique, but Balanchine invited her nonetheless—and she worked like a demon over the years, only half-successfully, to acquire a modicum of Balanchine precision. Her body was tight and blocky, with manly hands—not at all the ethereal type. Her most striking quality was her Central European sensibility—theatrical and athletic, with strains of Rudolf Laban's interwar

Freitanz and the weighted expressionism of Wigman. She could run and run through *Serenade* as if she were tearing barefoot through a field.

It wasn't so strange, really, that Balanchine was drawn to her. He had his own tangled German fate with his mother and his sister and the elusive Almedingens: von Aroldingen was not the same name (nor was it hers: she added the aristocratic "von"), but it was close enough. She liked to say that she was a descendant of the imperial Hohenzollern dynasty, so he gave her a photograph of himself as a younger man sitting pensively in his bathrobe, "a cloud in trousers." He wrote on the photo, addressing her as "Baronin Karin von Aroldingen Hannalure Elzingen, etc. etc. etc. etc." and signing off playfully as "Georg-Der-Erst, Mighty Mouse, etc. etc. etc. etc.": two orphans of the twentieth century joking about an imperial lineage neither possessed.[2] But Germany was real: the Germanic culture of his St. Petersburg upbringing; of his old nanny; of Weimar Berlin; and now of Hamburg, where he worked so often. Karin was on his route, his own German not-quite wife, and with her, he found himself in a comfortingly familiar language and culture.

Karin was as ruthless about dancing as any of the wives. When she married Morty in 1966, they went for a quick bite at Broadway Joe's after the ceremony so that she could be back on stage that night. The next day at the theater, Balanchine asked irritably, "Do you wash your husband's socks?," and when she got pregnant a few months later, she told no one and (by her own account) worked herself physically to the bone in hope of losing the baby. When that failed and Margo was born, Karin was back in class—thin as ever—in no time. Balanchine approvingly took notice: "Now I know that you are not the little Mrs. and mommy, you are a dancer."[3] Nothing mattered more to her than Balanchine and dancing, and with Suzanne gone, she stepped in.

Her relationship with Balanchine revolved around dancing, yes, but also around cooking and food—and plenty of alcohol—and around money and sex. She was acquisitive and nervous about money, couldn't get enough, and Balanchine indulged her every whim: Parisian fashions, jewelry, fine wines, restaurants, and elegant hotels. That was part of their arrangement, and they both enjoyed it, although as he aged, he also took to hiding rolls of cash in the closet of his apartment, where she wouldn't find them; cash was a gift he bestowed on many needy dancers, and that was strictly his province, not hers.[4] Some kind of sex was there; everyone knew it, although she would later deny it—protecting him, and herself, as they all did, from the inquisitive world. She teased fondly, "Du bist nur ein schmutziger alter Mann."[5] She was still young, with smooth skin and an ease of being, and he looked his age, body rounder and settled, if still physically expressive, with tufts of white hair flung far back on his deepening forehead and a balding patch at the back of the skull, artfully covered with thinning hair (he made regular visits to receive Harper Method scalp treatments). His eyes had grown more softly lit and kind.[6]

She took him to visit her family in Germany, and there are photos of them cooking with her mother and sister (Morty and Margo nowhere in sight), as well as in Paris dining with Morty and Margo, *à quatre*. George played his part and appeared at their door on Christmas bearing gifts and dressed as Santa, as in Karin's German fantasy Christmases and his *Nutcracker*. He gave Margo books—Hoffmann—and said he would dress her too when she was old enough. He composed a song for Karin with the lyricist Arthur Schwartz, an old Broadway hand from his musical-theater days, about an everlasting love that had "reached a lover's height, no others can ascend to it."[7] She lived for fairy-tale moments like her waltz with George in the princess of Monaco's ballroom, decorated with thousands of yellow roses of Texas flown in from Italy and arranged against a starry black-velvet sky, making her feel "like a supernatural being" in "my world without fear." But she could also be moody and maudlin, pouty and stubborn. She—they—drank a lot, and she even occasionally showed up for rehearsals and performances with alcohol under her breath. In his bizarre but playful list of "horse-blankets" for each of his coveted "stallions," he dubbed her "High-Lip-Sahne von Han(g)gover."

He lived between his home and sometimes hers and even purchased, in 1977, a small condominium across the way from Karin and Morty at 34 Canterbury Mews in Southampton. It was a new complex, built on twelve acres of dusty potato fields developed by a cheap Florida contractor—electric heat, no basement, freezing in the winter, rebates for units with no carpeting. It wasn't Weston, but it was good enough, and he immediately started gardening in the small plot of land around the modest one-bedroom unit: he planted weeping willows and roses of Sharon, put rugosa roses on the back terrace, and parked a potted hydrangea on the walkway out front. He bought a piano and glued a poster of Wonder Woman, full-length, in the bathroom, or was it Charlie's Angels in the bedroom?

George and Karin lived in his "Russian dacha," as friends called it, as if her other Morty-and-Margo life didn't exist. They would drive to the ocean together to watch the seagulls and stop at produce markets, and then he would open a bottle of chilled white wine and wash, for example, the beets for borscht. He grilled them in the oven, his secret recipe, and when they were done and peeled, he added double-strength beef broth, bay leaves, pepper, a pinch of sugar, and vinegar. Or Karin, Morty, and Margo would make a casserole across the way, while he ironed, played the piano, or disappeared into long rounds of solitaire.[8]

For Easter dinners, he engrossed himself in making a small altar with icons, candles, and photographs, including a black-and-white picture of his old childhood uncle as archbishop in full religious attire, with miter, satin, and gems. The food preparation was as involved as ever, and the dancers knew he or Karin might leave rehearsal early to tend a rising dough or batter. On the night, they laid the foldout tables in his apartment with fresh lilies and hyacinths—strong smells—as sacred choral music played on the tinny transistor radio. Once his guests arrived, dinner began with vodka and *zakuski* (appetizers), including the usual blinis with caviar and sour cream, or pâté de foie gras, followed by ham baked in rye dough, *kolbase* (spicy sausage), baked duck, veal roast with truffle gelée, and a salad of peas with Russian mustard and sour cream—all made from scratch in Balanchine's kitchen, and all laid out in an elegant buffet, with lots of wine. Then *kulich* and paskha and champagne. As the feast ended, in the wee morning hours, they all cracked colored eggs for good luck.[9]

Karin was his companion, but he was also intermittently courting Christine Redpath, a young beauty with flaming red hair he was drawn to; or Mara Lynn, a flamboyant Broadway pinup girl (married) who appeared at the theater wrapped in a black feather boa. There were others too, but he never let his feelings get out of hand, he told Jacques, patching over the loneliness inside: "I am free." More seriously, or at least enduringly, there was Pat Neary, the square-faced straight shooter who had left the company in a state of high pique during Suzanne's reign. Thanks to Balanchine's influence, she was now in Switzerland running the Ballet du Grand Théâtre de Genève (followed by the Ballett Zürich) and living there with her partner, Bob. In an almost comical arrangement that developed around this time, whenever George would come to work with her company, Bob would move out and Pat would remove every trace of his existence from their home, from razor blades to photos on the walls, and Balanchine would move in. When Balanchine left, Bob moved back in—until the next time. Everyone knew the charade, and Balanchine surely knew it too, but he didn't seem to mind. It was another convenient trio that brought a bit of warmth and sex, but the "other" man took care of the mundane husbandly duties and tiresome dramas of daily life. He was free.[10]

That year, Balanchine received a letter at the theater, which threw him around a more troubled corner of his past:

> Dear George,
>
> As wonderful as it is to watch your ballets, it is even more wonderful to dance them. Is this possible?
>
> Love, Suzi[11]

Since her departure, Farrell had been sending coyly insouciant letters to Balanchine, which he apparently did not answer. She continued through Barbara, assuring George delightedly that "we" are "infinitely happy," that she and Paul were practicing their Balanchine barre and would be of course forever Balanchine dancers, and that their cats (Top, Middle, and Bottom) would love to see him. She asked permission to dance *Meditation* with Béjart (and wrote that a later performance "will be for you. Love, Suzi").[12] The ballet was already hers, Barbara relayed as Balanchine's businesslike response, and she must have the documents, so she doesn't require permission. She and Paul returned for summers and sometimes showed up in Saratoga; "we" especially admired *Violin Concerto*, she wrote into the void, as she maneuvered through Jacques to get Balanchine's ear. But this new note was different: no mention of Paul. She had made her choice. Balanchine had won—sort of.

Privately, he agonized over whether to let her return to the company. He was still hurt, resentful—he hated even to drive past the Mayflower Hotel—where "*he*" had been with her (Barbara just groaned, "Enough!"), and he wouldn't go near St. Paul's Chapel. He complained bitterly to Jacques that he had given Suzanne diamonds and gifts, written poems, and composed music—a lovely waltz—and she just "took and took." She was a witch and only wanted to dance. If she wanted to come back, he told Davidova, she would have to *beg*—but when she did beg, if her note was begging, he relented. How could he deny her talent, not to mention his flat-out desire to be in her presence? She was a witch, but a witch he needed or couldn't resist. He arranged to meet her at his apartment, one hour, all business; Barbara would handle the details. Paul was not mentioned.[13]

On her first day back, Balanchine arrived for class through the back door of the studio ten minutes late, as usual. The room was crowded, and as he threaded his way through the dancers, he immediately took in the geography. The map of class is a display of company hierarchies: dancers have "favorite" places at the barre, strictly reserved on the basis of seniority and stature. When they leave the barre and move to the center of the room, favored dancers (they know who they are) come or are pulled to the front, and shy, insecure, or ashamed dancers—too fat, too out of shape, too whatever—slink to the rear. Men were usually at the back, second-class citizens in Balanchine's polity. That day, Suzanne, with her faded and fringed Russian shawl wrapped around her waist, had reclaimed her spot at the barre next to Jacques (quietly displacing, with unerring instinct, a rising young dancer). Around her stood a few old faces and a whole new younger generation for whom Farrell (at twenty-eight) was a walking legend. The air was thick as everyone waited to see how Balanchine would react. He froze for a moment, staring at them all, until Farrell broke rank and walked over to him with her quick stride, chin tucked over feelings, and gave him a perfunctory hug, which he vaguely returned. The pianist began.[14]

Their relationship would be strictly formal, an arrangement they both tacitly accepted. Suzanne would live her life with Paul outside the theater, and they both knew that Paul was still persona non grata. Balanchine would later help get him a job—in a faraway city. For her first performance, Balanchine cast Farrell in the role she had been scheduled to dance the night she left: the second-movement adagio of *Symphony in C*. It was a way of replaying the scenario as he wanted it. That evening the wings were packed with dancers craning to glimpse her entrance, and as the music began and she bourréed seamlessly onto the diagonal, escorted by Peter Martins, a gasp rose from the audience ("That's Pat Neary's mother," a senior corps dancer hissed jokingly on stage, breaking the tension). Otherwise, the performance proceeded as if she had never left and Paul had never existed. She even wore the pearl pendant Balanchine had given her, and he stood quietly in the first wing, watching. When it was over, Ronnie Bates pulled the edge of the curtain aside—unusual at the no-stars NYCB—and she slipped out onto the lip of the stage, alone, as New York welcomed her home. A friend enthused to Lincoln, who sat slumped in his seat in the first ring, "Isn't it wonderful she's back?" He just stared blankly: "It guarantees the next five years."[15]

Suzanne resumed her old roles, and Balanchine made Kay Mazzo and Patti McBride, and even Karin von Aroldingen, share her old parts, and their new ones too. This led to tensions, complaints, and fits. Patti was incensed when Balanchine put Suzanne into *her* role in *Who Cares?* and when she confronted him, he lashed out, "You were awful in it," which wasn't true, and she went home determined to quit the company, but they made up and carried on. In another case, he delayed reviving *Liebeslieder* because he didn't want to face Karin's ire when he returned Suzanne to her old role. But mostly he did what he wanted to do, noting defensively that they should stop complaining. Hadn't he provided enough for them all to dance? Suzanne was still Suzanne; she still moved him, and he still devoted himself to her extraordinary talent. As he told Jerry: "She's a terrific instrument, whatever you want she gives you, tremendous energy. . . . She is like some animal of the sea . . . a dolphin (turn up nose—cheeks—eyes gesture)—not human." But he didn't monopolize her, and even Jerry knew that he could finally use Suzanne in his own dances.[16]

Alone. That's how Balanchine imagined her. Even when she was partnered, she seemed alone—still the freest woman in the world. It began with *Tzigane* for the Ravel Festival, an exotic revel to the composer's 1924 Sonata for Violin and Cello, specially made for a virtuoso Hungarian violinist. It was pure Suzanne, alone on stage in a bewitching drama of her own contriving.

There were other dancers in the ballet, including her partner Peter Martins, but they went largely unnoticed. The role was a kind of truce, but it was also a dagger, and she knew it. Karin and Kay had *Violin Concerto;* she got *Tzigane,* a minor ballet full of theatrical tricks she had absorbed from Béjart. But then, less than a year later, he made for her a dance in *Chaconne,* from Gluck's opera *Orpheus and Eurydice.* He had staged the opera in 1936 at the Met; and again in 1963 for Liebermann's Hamburg State Opera. This time, however, he freely reordered the score, and added a new pas de deux for Farrell and Martins to Gluck's yearning Dance of the Blessed Spirits, which takes place in an imagined Elysian Fields. Balanchine made it one afternoon during an extra rehearsal squeezed in between matinee and evening performances. In forty minutes it was done, and the result was one of the most romantic pas de deux he—and Farrell—had ever made.

He wanted to make *Salomé* for Farrell too; on an old idea from Goleizovsky, he envisioned her dancing high on a tower with men clamoring far below. He began working on Oscar Wilde's scenario and Alban Berg's *Lulu Suite,* and Rouben Ter-Arutunian designed a set after the Russian artist Mikhail Vrubel—"a changeable-silk set inlaid with mirrors and blood," Lincoln reported. "George wants to call it THE SILVER CHARGER, but I don't think anyone would know what he means. It's not very Wildean-Beardsley; Greek-Orthodox Byzantine rather, or Armenian-Jewish."[17] *Salomé* was planned as part of a whole program of Viennese composers, but when they ran out of money, Balanchine dropped it and turned instead to *Vienna Waltzes* (1977). It was a lavish blockbuster, inconsequential except for the final waltz to Strauss's *Der Rosenkavalier* for Farrell.

"Who will I be with?" she asked him, noting that her usual partners had already been cast in earlier sections of the ballet. "You will be alone," he said, and he had her walk slowly from the downstage wing along the diagonal, back to the audience, in a white silk gown and long white gloves with a train of white flowing behind her. She was entering a ballroom, with black-crystal chandeliers and mirrored walls, that amplified her loneliness and recalled the deathly *La Valse.* She waltzed—with a phantom partner or, at moments, with a black-clad shadow, who appeared and disappeared from the wings along her way. Her waltz then multiplied and grew as the ballroom filled with couples, women in white silk gowns waltzing in a dizzying circular spectacle of a refracted nineteenth-century world. It was an extravaganza, and when Balanchine was asked why the elegant white gowns, designed by Karinska, required the most expensive Parisian silk, he responded matter-of-factly: "Because it moves. It's natural, made by worms. Nylon doesn't move, it's made by machines." And in a way, the ballet was not for Farrell at all, but for Karinska, who had just turned ninety. It would be her last ballet. Not long after the premiere, she collapsed in her apartment from a massive stroke that erased speech and memory.[18]

Age was gaining on them all. As Balanchine made *Vienna Waltzes,* he was still suffering from the lingering effects of sciatica that had landed him in the hospital in traction for six weeks the year before. In Saratoga that summer of 1977, the pain still flaring, he grimly sequestered himself in traction in his little cottage for hours a day, though that didn't stop him from cooking for the Leaches in their kitchen in his blue bathrobe—shoulder of veal with half a dozen sides "characteristically (if not monotonously) Georgian."[19] But there was no avoiding the fact that his body was getting slower, more staunch and thickened, and he felt tired, with ongoing and unexplained bouts of dizziness. The thickness may have been in part from the butter, which he slathered by the spoonful on everything—butter had saved him from TB, why not now?

He worried about impotence. Already an experienced consumer of Swiss clinics, he was taking serum injections from bulls' testicles and other virility potions,[20] and his visits to Florentine Karp, his old friend from the 1930s, were more and more frequent. A Polish Jew who had studied medicine in St. Petersburg before fleeing the Red Army for Paris and New York, she had treated Geva, Davidova, and a raft of émigrés. Balanchine spoke Russian with her, and she noted his accumulating ailments—arthritis, muscular neuralgia, hypertension, fatigue, dizziness, eczema—and administered Gerovital, a Romanian antiaging concoction, along with shots of B12, as well as "Berocca-C" (he called it "his Barocco") and even Ritalin and Valium. Like most women, she was a bit in love with him, and he often stayed for lunch, on fine china with silverware stamped by the Russian imperial house, at her home office on East Seventy-second Street, comfortingly hung with heavy Russian rugs and French art.[21] There were visits to psychics too, up dark staircases in old buildings, who read palms or performed various cures, but nothing seemed to help. He felt a slowing down inside and turned abruptly to say to Robbins one afternoon at the theater: "My father died at seventy-six. I have two more years left before—" and he took a dead man's pose, arms crossed over his chest.[22] Even Lincoln complained that George had become "so conscious of mortality that it has become demoralizing."[23]

Lincoln was aging too. In 1975 he had a heart attack followed by double-bypass surgery. As he recovered, Balanchine visited him at the hospital, saying little, the two trees still planted side by side on the same plot of land. Lincoln—ever insecure about George's respect for *him*—basked in George's presence. He never realized that the seemingly untouchable Balanchine too could feel, however occasionally, Maloross and in *his* shadow. Age was delivering other strikes to Lincoln as well: in 1973, W. H. Auden, "the strongest influence in my life since 1937," died at age sixty-six.[24] Eugenie Ouroussow, to whom Lincoln had entrusted the school in the war years, perished of a painful stomach cancer in 1975. Balanchine attended her funeral too, but when it was over, he said to Barbara glumly that funerals were not for him, and he wished to be cremated.[25]

In spite of aging, Lincoln was ever Lincoln: involved with one after another young man, usually an artist who would come to live with him on Gramercy Park, and perpetually in love, or lust, with this or that young male dancer, whom he would ply with books, ideas, and attentions, wanted or otherwise. Around this time he fixated on the Duell brothers, Danny and Joe. He dangled the idea of succession and sent books to the elder Danny to speed their education. "The books interest him, the giving was unwelcome," he noted, although there was also a poem called "Pulchinella Song, Opus 1" left in his papers, from "Daniel Duell"—light, naughty, erotic—all about "cock services" and other sexual antics.[26] More seriously, though, Lincoln was falling in love with Joe, whose immense talent and natural intelligence, along with his troubled family history and underlying fragility and bouts with mental illness, made him a natural Lincoln project. The young dancer and his girlfriend, the dancer Maria Calegari, were regular dinner guests at Gramercy Park, as Lincoln tried to provide the foundation he thought Joe might one day need to succeed Balanchine.

All of this was coming from the conspiratorial parts of Lincoln's mind, and he was constantly digging around to make his own secret artistic inroads into company life. A few years earlier, in 1973, he wrote a memorandum to one of his protégés, "NW" (probably Ned Wait, a young stage manager Lincoln had recruited), laying out thoughts and plans on how he and "NW" might protect languishing "dancers in crisis." That is, dancers who had been ignored or hurt by Balanchine's cruelly dismissive comments, "inserted like surgical needles, glancing, and almost too serious or hurtful to bear," and he wanted to "supplement, or circumvent Mr. B" to help these poor dancers, a project that seems to have gone exactly nowhere and for which he was singularly ill-equipped.[27] Turning to the inner mechanisms of the company, he offered more insight. "Unconsummated sexual energy," he wrote, had always been for Balanchine, "overtly and covertly . . . a tremendous tool, weapon or chisel," and dancers were drawn to the company because

> SOMETHING supra-normal moves them, however confused or unwilling, doubtful or hopeful, into our orbit. . . . What I am getting at is this: despite the crisis-situation with a constant percentage of the company, and however distressing and seemingly wasteful this is, our company is recruited from a certain part of the population capable of responding to vibrations emitted by Mr. B and his philosophy, or metaphysic. The fifteen or so dancers who variously constitute the heart of our company, have certain aims in mind differentiating them from other forms of competitive employment. This . . . adds up finally, to a kind of magnetic attraction to a very clear cut expression of physical perfection the basis of which is metaphysical.

It was this metaphysic—"a visible moral order"—that Lincoln saw himself "protecting." Mr. B's vision "of an angelic order . . . sent to minister Grace" was always "under attack, and the enemy is variously: party-politics, temporizing; easier, or more polite attitudes; popularism; gimmicks; vanity; bad-judgment; apathy; mortality. About some of these, something can be done; not all."[28]

And so Lincoln, that wounded elephant, powerful and ill at ease in equal measure, tended to his own injured parts and plotted his guerrilla incursions into the company he had cofounded but would never control. To most of the younger dancers, though, he was little more than a benign and eccentric giant who would walk into the studio unannounced in his dark suit and stand glaring at them or sit hunched at the front of the room intently watching. In an old habit, he would sometimes remove his large black shoes without quite knowing it and pad out in stocking feet.[29]

Lincoln meanwhile continued to occupy himself with the ever crisis-ridden finances of the company and school—power politicking, lunching with wealthy contacts, securing grants. In 1977 he handpicked and finally incorporated a board of directors, the NYCB's first. The call would come, as it did to Frederick Beinecke, who knew almost nothing about dance and was a mere acquaintance. Lincoln reached him one afternoon on a pay phone in Greece and urgently asked that Beinecke join the NYCB board. When he finally agreed, Lincoln invited him to the school, to the ballet, and to dinners at his home with Betty Cage and Mac Lowry.[30] Another recruit was Robert Gottlieb, editor in chief of Knopf and a Balanchine aficionado. Seeing that the whole enterprise was still being largely run by the small staff at "headquarters," Gottlieb got involved in scheduling and publicity, which he funneled through his Knopf office. Balanchine accepted this practical intervention, but for the most part, his approach to the board was dismissive. He advised Jacques, who was starting a new venture and needed a board, "A. don't go to meeting, B. do what you want, C. don't tell them till it's done, D. don't talk just listen and then go ahead and do what you feel is right."[31]

Lincoln similarly continued to spin out books on a wide range of subjects, among them, studies of Nijinsky, Nadelman, Augustus Saint-Gaudens's monument in Boston to black troops in the Civil War (to accompany an exhibition at the Met), and not least, a long and turgid article titled "Balanchine: A Fourth Dimension" (that began with Freud and passed by William James, Isaac Newton, and Marx on the way to Balanchine and "our millennial crisis").[32] He was still acting as company scribe and working on *Thirty Years: The New York City Ballet*, a history drawn from his personal diaries and earlier published accounts—part memory, part fiction, part commentary on his own part-fabricated story of how it all came to be.

His rituals with Balanchine meanwhile remained largely intact. He deposited books on literature, religion, and art on George's desk (e.g., on Kafka and Sufi poetry).[33] Together they were making "a codified series of laws for SAB"—"Caesar's laws," they called them; and Lincoln haggled with Jerry Robbins, seeing him alternately as the savior of the company and the scourge of their lives.[34] Jerry wrote in his journal after one of their dinners in these years of the "many things" they had discussed "about what I was doing & who I was & what my role was. He connected Jew-priest-rabbi-order, discipline & athlete all together. I came out wanting to get to work strongly. Good."[35] As for Lincoln's own inner "Jew-priest-rabbi-order, discipline," he limped along. He couldn't help hinting, for one, of his hopes in these years that George would *finally* produce the ballet they had been talking about for decades on the unlikely—and very Lincoln—theme of Audubon's *Birds of America,* to music by Morton Gould. "He never wanted to do *Birds of America,*" Jacques later recalled, "that's Lincoln stuffing it down his throat; he didn't like the music, and didn't like LK's idea to make a ballet with Lew Christensen tied to a stake naked . . . and B wanted . . . Audubon [to] be a Don Q kind of person, but LK was determined, and orchestrating everything, etc." So Balanchine dabbled and strung Lincoln along to the end, with no intention, they both knew, of ever producing the ballet.[36]

In 1976, however, he did do something that Lincoln loved. *Union Jack* was a full-company spectacle celebrating the Anglo-American alliance for the bicentennial year. The music, arranged by Hershy Kay (who had done *Stars and Stripes* too), was adapted from traditional British sources and included a Scottish tattoo, turn-of-the-century music-hall favorites, and sea songs, work chants, jigs, and drill orders from the Royal Navy. The decor by Ter-Arutunian featured kilts made by a tailor who supplied the Royal Canadian Mounted Police. The tailor sent swaths of plaid and velvet that Balanchine worked with in plotting the color patterns of the finale, which he mapped and color coded on a large sheet of paper before teaching it to the dancers. The ballet began with the Scottish tattoo—a sensational, slow, rhythmic procession of regiments filling the stage to drum variations—based on a tattoo Balanchine had witnessed in Edinburgh in 1952: "It's fantastic—200 pipers coming straight at you, the way they sway." No dancing, just a slow, deliberate march. At the end, the Union Jack unfurled against the backdrop as the full cast in navy uniform signaled with hand flags in marine semaphore, "God Save the Queen." Two days before the opening, Balanchine added cannon shots and a twenty-one-gun salute.[37]

It was a dance that would have done Lincoln's father proud, and Lincoln also delighted that this Independence Day tribute was made by a Jewish composer, an Armenian-born designer, and a Russian-born choreographer. He enthusiastically produced a small book to accompany the ballet. It was another Lincoln trilogy, based on the narrow political territory that he and George could agree on: *Union Jack* would be performed with *Stars and Stripes* and *Tricolore* (made a few years earlier for the French bicentennial) as part of a full evening "Entente Cordiale."[38]

A few months later, in the fall of 1977, Lincoln began once again to act strangely. His wife, Fidelma, was just recovering from a serious delusional breakdown, and in the strange logic of his overheated mind and their merged psychotic states, he succumbed to his own mad collapse. He thought he was Othello. He put a paper collar around a wooden sculpture in his living room and dripped blood on it. He took a picture of Abraham Lincoln and streaked that with blood too, a kind of delusional self-immolation, and he took a hammer to the delicate porcelain sculptures of an artist friend who was staying in his home. Finally, he showed up at the theater with his head shaved and wearing an old army uniform and started screaming at Balanchine, who stood stony faced, until guards and paramedics forcibly removed Lincoln from the theater during the intermission. As they escorted him out in lock grip, he turned to Barbara in a sad flash of clarity, "I'm sorry, honey."[39] With institutionalization, electrotherapy, and drugs, he soon recovered his sanity again, but who could really count on him now?

Still: he never left, always rode it out, always returned, and could be found days or weeks or months later planted backstage next to George or slumped in his first-ring seat. The theater was his home too, and his rage to keep it in these years was as epic as his endurance in making it. It was a curious balance. He had free rein and no authority, except in his proximity to Balanchine, a fact that left him forever pining to be closer still. The epilogue would contain a striking fact. In 1982 this Jew from Boston converted to Catholicism, in close consultation with Father William Lynch, the Jesuit priest he had known for decades. It was another step toward Balanchine. Lincoln even considered Russian Orthodoxy, but he couldn't understand Slavonic and settled instead for the pope.[40]

Even Robbins was aging, and in his case, aging involved an artistic crisis and reckoning, at least in his own mind, with Balanchine. In spite of his own enormous success, Jerry's admiration for Balanchine and what he took to be a kind of pure dance steadily consumed him. It all came to the fore in the agonies of making *Dybbuk*, to music by Bernstein, based on S. Ansky's Yiddish tale, which had been in the works for some two years before its premiere in 1974. Robbins had proposed *Dybbuk* to Balanchine back in the 1950s, but Balanchine had turned it down, largely because he didn't like Bernstein's music. Kirstein twisted the knife: why don't you offer it to the Israeli folk-dance troupe Inbal, he suggested—an idea, Jerry shot back, that was "about as valid" as Balanchine doing *Apollo* for Greek folk dancers. Come the 1970s, Balanchine still didn't like Bernstein's music, but the project went ahead anyway. Bernstein's score, when it was finally completed, was ambitious, for a full symphony orchestra, with sung Hebrew prayers and hidden mystical meanings tied to Kabbalah numerology and the Hebrew alphabet. Robbins talked to the dancers about fire and earth and told them to read Ansky. He began a fully narrative work with props, masks, hallucinations, magic circles, and Hasidic-style dances, but as he worked, he found himself stripping it all away: eliminating the story, characters, and rituals that had drawn him in the first place. Rehearsals were rocky—he was agitated, and he and Bernstein argued, as Jerry tried to arrive at some elusive Balanchine-like dance emotion, a suppressed version of the story that had almost no story at all—just dancing. (In a March 1976 journal entry, Jerry complained, "Lennie never learns; he fucks around with Christ, God & his country in each work, forgetting his best work came out of looking warmly at his life around him. . . . He sees himself a Sage, Prophet, Einstein—& all gets stuffed into symbols, fake statues, LARGE & IMPORTANT pieces. They come out hollow, sentimental.") The result was a lukewarm ballet that fell flat. Frustrated, Robbins cut the score even more, eviscerated any remaining narrative elements and retitled the ballet *The Dybbuk Variations*. By 1980 he had truncated the truncated version and retitled it again: *A Suite of Dances*.[41]

Part of his agony in these years had to do with John Murray Cuddihy's *The Ordeal of Civility: Freud, Marx, Lévi-Strauss, and the Jewish Struggle with Modernity*, which Jerry read a year after the opening of *Dybbuk*. The book inspired in him a kind of religious awakening, and he began to see ballet and Balanchine as part of a polite and genteel Christian culture that was "civilization'ing" his Jewishness—literally training the Jew out of him: "In what wondrous and monstrous ways would I move if I would dig down to my Jewish self."[42]

"We all try to 'speak' Balanchine," he later explained (referring to himself and other NYCB choreographers), but it doesn't work; "we all speak with the heavy accents of our natures—& only George can spin out the seamless flow of a natural native tongue." Trying to "do" a Balanchine-like work was "a futile effort—like trying to paint a Leonardo-like painting."[43]

In an effort to rediscover his Jewishness, and a more authentic voice, Robbins began attending Sabbath services and started work on a new autobiographical piece (which he would never finish) titled "The Jew Piece," later retitled "Poppa Piece." The problem of *Dybbuk*, he now saw, was the problem of Jerome Rabinowitz: "All the edifaces that I've erected to protect little Jerome Rabinowitz are collapsing—seem to have been wiped away in a few weeks." In the midst of this upheaval and the dispiriting experience of *Dybbuk*, he fell into a serious depression, exacerbated by romantic failures and a surfeit of psychotherapy, not to mention recreational drugs (mescaline, acid, mushrooms). In the summer of 1975, he reached a crisis point and at the advice of his doctor, who wanted to transition him onto the antidepressant Elavil, Jerry committed himself for three weeks to the mental ward at McLean Hospital in Belmont, Massachusetts, complete, he noted, a bit shocked, with "locks—passes—and crazies in the hall."[44] Soon after his release, he went on a tour with the company to Paris, where *Dances at a Gathering* and *Goldberg Variations*, two of his most pure-dance ballets, brought down the house. Maybe, he wrote in his journal, he would finally be able to "get up there with George—to feel secure enough to be even. Kill? Poppa?"[45]

The company was aging too, and the dancers who had joined Balanchine at the start were fading in the way that dancers do—cracks in appearance, wrinkled skin, a limb out of commission, joints seized up by sleep and barely oiled to life every morning with exhausting regimes of therapy and painful exercise. For someone like Jacques, or Francisco or Allegra (when she was there, which was rare) or Milly (who kept a small oxygen tank and a jar of honey backstage and finally retired in 1973), the black dogs of depression and gnawing self-doubt were not far behind, and anxiety naturally seeped and spread as their bodies refused to respond. Ballet paid no heed to aging, and these old soldiers found themselves left behind. For Jacques, who had been Balanchine's double and amanuensis for more than three decades, the shocking fact of his aching knees and stiff joints, worn down by years of dancing, was another kind of mirror. Barely middle-aged, he was fading as a dancer as Balanchine faded as a man, a crushing way of losing everything at the same time. Who would he be without their entwined lives? Would he even have a face to show to the world? Balanchine saw it, used it where he could, but he didn't have the energy or interest to bring along any but the most youthful talent rising from below.[46]

And what talent. The new dancers were younger and better trained, and, if anything, their youth captivated Balanchine ever more as he aged—he didn't mellow, didn't grow wiser, didn't forsake his desires. The older he got, it seemed, the more he wanted their love and attention. His relationship with Karin, or with Pat Neary or with any of the others, did nothing to quell his romantic appetite, and he did what he had always done: sent wine and perfume to dancers he admired, took them to dinner, made lewd comments (whispering "pussy" or "pussycat" under his breath to favorites). "I'm a man too, you know dear," but by now he was a *really* old man and his "wilding," as one of them put it, seemed to them dirty and weird, or something silly and pathetic. The old cycles were by then almost institutionalized, and the dancers were devoted and rebellious in all the predictable ways their predecessors had established: they worked to the bone, competed ruthlessly, gained weight and threw it angrily off in punishing diets, and obsessed over a kind of perfection he didn't even want. They also found boyfriends, dressed to the hilt, ornamented themselves lavishly, and accepted, rejected, and avoided his flirtations in confused cycles of ambition and pain. The mystery of what exactly he wanted continued to baffle them, but what they wanted was the same as it had always been: to dance.

It was an uncomfortable fact. As Balanchine aged and grew needier for them, they—his company—were sliding away from him. The company was bigger, more unwieldy, and the dancers were so young and so far away, fifty years—half a century—younger, and he seemed increasingly oblivious of their lives. The further they got, the less his Old World manners mattered and the more he tried to exert his will in hapless ways. The demands of carving their statues and making themselves into the tools of his art were hardening into something rigid and cultlike. Everything was the same, but more extreme, as he fought to control the levers of his art—and they fought to control the levers of their lives.

Imagine, for instance, the dressing room of the corps de ballet each morning, a windowless room that smelled of hot lights, with banks of mirrored tables spread with a phantasmagoria of beauty accoutrements: perfume, hair clips, hairnets, sprays, fresh flowers to tuck into a twist of hair, makeup, including mascara, oils, pancake, shiny and matte powder, and arrays of color and texture for eyes, neck, and every crevice of the face—all carefully discussed, compared, and applied like a mask. It was an atmosphere thick with femininity and artifice, as the dancers dressed their bodies in the latest French-cut leotards with flattering bust line and pink or black mesh tights (seam down the back), layered with matching or fashionably frayed leg warmers, pulled and arranged to hide an imperfection or show off a leg, just so. (Balanchine, who said he needed to see in order to teach, made them take their leg warmers off.) By evening, you could add the taste of pot brownies to this 1970s mix.

Toe shoes were their own preoccupation: handcrafted at great expense to specifications for each dancer by little old men somewhere in London, they would arrive by the dozens neatly packaged in tight plastic bags, stored and rationed by wardrobe from the "toe shoe room." Each pair then underwent a second making in the hands of the dancer: layers of shellac or glue poured or painted into the toe box for extra hardness, the shank ripped out or cut for increased flexibility, slippery satin carved off the tip of the toes for better traction, with ribbons and elastics hand sewn until the shoe fit flush to the foot, like a second skin. Some dancers even skipped the tights and wore their legs nude and pressed their bare feet into their shoes—closer contact, skin to floor. It was all part of the factory of their lives: like the makeup and perfume, toe shoes were worn out and daily discarded. It was a seventeenth-century theatricality, a crafted, almost-enameled exterior covering every inch of flesh. It was not an armor—who needs protection—it was actually who they were. Appearances—the surface, flatness, artifice, ephemera, the mystery of inside—were a kind of truth. The fact that they were flying in the face of popular fashions for transparency and their own informal T-shirt and blue-jeans generation didn't make them any less authentic. The pain involved in this increasingly baroque carving of their statues—the flat tummies and bathroom stalls turned over to laxatives, the Coke and cupcakes, the dieting, and the scrutiny of muscles and bodily shape, size, line, and proportion—could be as intense as ever as they tried to make themselves into human objets d'art.[47]

There were rebels, even—especially—among those who were most zealously ambitious in their desire to dance. Maria Calegari, who joined the company in 1974, was seventeen and from an Austrian and Italian family in Queens. She had a tall, Farrell-ish body—long and languid, but more bony and intense—with lush red hair. Balanchine had an eye on her from the start, Lincoln said, as a "possible replacement for Farrell," a kind of doubling, or by now tripling. He called her Germaine Greer, pulled her to the front in class, and quickly promoted her. She was naturally glamorous but deeply internal, with a flexible, hyperextended body and a fast-twitch, neurotic musculature that she seemed barely to control by sheer force of will. He flirted with her, but in rehearsals he was all business and pushed her to her limits. She veered: gained weight, fell out of favor, and finally confronted Balanchine in his office. Not for his behavior but what could she do to get her parts back? He lectured her, encouraged her, told her she had to work harder, more, more, more, and she cried and went off and did it—and her career took off.

Others left. Christine Redpath, full-bodied, a tomboy who could hold her own with the rough-talking stagehands, responded to his advances, went to dinner, received wine, worked hard on her dancing, and was given plum roles until she hit a brick wall inside. Then came the weight gain, depression, and anxiety. She retreated from dancing and had a flirtation with Baryshnikov—which didn't make Balanchine happy, but that of course was part of the point, another daughter gone to a son and a painful reminder of his own age. He lost interest, starved her of parts, until she finally left and joined Pat Neary's company of NYCB exiles in Switzerland.[48] Episodes such as this were another sign of the growing gap. What did he know about any of their lives, really? He was losing track—of their bodies, their strife, their desires and ambitions, their taste, their drinking, their politics, their very beings. Even their drugs were different: at a party one night at Balanchine's apartment, a few of the dancers surreptitiously arrived with cocaine. "Don't tell Balanchine, he thinks it's opium and doesn't like it," they whispered, as if he were some ancient relic. To Jacques, who was somewhere in between, Balanchine seemed more and more like the little father in Dostoyevsky's *The Brothers Karamazov* (or a figure from a Francis Ford Coppola film):

> He would get this father figure look and talk to me about god and religion . . . like the Godfather . . . the responsibility for the family, but in the end he couldn't know everything, so much was going on, and he didn't know it. . . . Like smoking in class, everyone doing it when he wasn't around, and he would say, isn't it great everyone has manners and no one is stealing or cheating and everyone loves each other and I would look at him, and it wasn't true.[49]

All of this mattered because his feel for the inner lives of the complicated human beings who *were* his dances was diminishing. The biggest problem he faced artistically was reaching them over this unbridgeable generational divide, which, in its way, became a new subject.

Consider Heather Watts. Long and wiry, with wide bony shoulders set uneasily on a spine misshapen by scoliosis, she had a jaunty, off-kilter gait, part attitude, part armor. She was one of a new "new breed": her father was a space engineer, and she was solidly American middle class—confident, insecure, spoiled, and about as far as you could get from the offbeat and orphaned Central European stock of the past. When she arrived at the school at age fifteen in 1968 on a Ford Foundation scholarship (another Diana Adams pick), she was wearing an embroidered Mexican top and white bell-bottoms from the army-navy store. Natasha Molostwoff greeted her from the last century in an elegant stretch-lace button-down shirt and cone bra and immediately informed this flower child from California that she would need a bra ("Get one"). Heather didn't and proved so disruptive and rebellious—late, lazy, drinking, smoking, men, mean-girl, anything she could fathom—that two years later, they threw her out. Balanchine didn't flinch and immediately took her into the company ("Where did you learn to do *that*?" he asked; "At your school," she replied).

"Audiences will not understand you," he told her, but he saw something he could use in her crooked spine and vexed vulnerabilities. For her, there were shoulders to stand on—and push aside. Even Suzanne, her idol in dancing, seemed old-fashioned in life with her zip-up boots and fur hats and the vampish way she wiped her lips. Heather threw her own hair into a ponytail—like the ones she saw in *Vogue* (and had grown up with on Barbie dolls)—and although she was in awe of Balanchine, he also seemed to her ancient and stodgily bourgeois. She wanted to drink cheap wine from bottles in Chinese restaurants—or scotch out of a glass in Paris, like Simone de Beauvoir—and couldn't fathom his penchant for Old World dining or crates of fine wine sent to dancers he coveted. Her life was somewhere between ballet girl and the Warholian drug-spliced avant-garde. Besides, she was protected: Peter Martins was her boyfriend, and Balanchine found that interesting, material he could work with.

He treated her as what she was: a rebellious adolescent child-woman. "That could be you," he said irritably one night in the wings, pointing to Patti McBride, "but you aren't even good enough to be in this company." Her lack of discipline infuriated him. When she didn't show up for a costume fitting, he pulled her angrily into his office, shaking as he unlocked the door, "Everybody waits for YOU! Mme Karinska waits for YOU!" He expelled her, pale-faced, back into the hallway, where "Horgie," who had heard it all, just rolled her eyes: "Oh stop acting like Sarah Bernhardt." In a full-cast rehearsal for Bizet, in which he had awarded "Hedder" a leading role, he spent nearly an hour making her humiliatingly repeat a simple piqué arabesque, again, again, again. No, no, no: don't bend your knee, just straight, plain, no ornament, no affect, and stop trying to be pretty, and above all stop trying to be Suzanne ("What—you want her flat-foot? Her husband? Her life? You really want to be like her?"). Finally, he cried out in exacerbation, "Don't do anything, just don't do anything!"

The thin black belt for the *Agon* costume had the full succession of dancers sewn on its inner side: Adams, Kent, Farrell, Mazzo, and now Watts. "Don't do anything" meant: Get out from under *that*. Forget all of them, forget all of that, don't act, no "fake soul," just do it, just be who you are, be "Hedder," NOW. She stared at him angrily through confused tears, fighting and acting out all the way as he tried to strip her theatrical notions and "fandom" (especially for Suzanne) and arrive at the unexpurgated Heather. The only way to make his aging dances live was for her and her generation to inhabit them with their bodies, their look, their style, and their kind of dancing—not some affected imitation of older dancers. Her horse-blanket? "Serica-belle-wattle," after an unknown land on the edge of the habitable world known for raw silk ("belle-wattle" spoke for itself). Her odd body—lightweight, intelligent, askew, full of self-doubt and fight—gave a new sharpness and poignancy to leotard ballets such as *Agon* and *Symphony in Three Movements*. She got it—wanted it—and loved it when she went to Paris as a guest artist with her *Agon* costume in a ziplock plastic bag. She was no old-fashioned ballerina laden with tutus and tulle: "We were different, we were Balanchine people."[50]

He was also preoccupied with Merrill Ashley (née Linda Michelle Merrill), a fresh-faced kid from Vermont with an almost too fierce ambition. She was Watts's opposite: obedient, disciplined, analytic—and obsessed with perfection. She had joined the company in 1967, and it looked like she might never make it out of the corps. "Too sweet, dear," Balanchine would say, wrinkling his nose, as he tried unsuccessfully year after year to wipe the plaster smile from her face and steer her over the "boring-border," as he put it, of perfection and technical prowess. Then things shifted: she pushed her technique so far that it unleashed her, and Balanchine started to see a woman who could help him reengineer the human body—and maybe reveal her soul. She could do things no one else could do, and she could do them with unprecedented speed and precision. In 1978 he made *Ballo della Regina* to Verdi's score for her and Ricky Weiss—another analytic mind—to see just how far he could push her physical breakthrough.

In *Ballo* he gave her some of the most difficult feats ever devised in the classical repertory, yet it wasn't bravura that emerged. It was a kind of muscular physics. The squareness and tension through her shoulders and face dissolved in her mercurial speed, legs slicing, as her torso and hips peeled open with ever more extreme torque and an épaulement that spiraled through her limbs and brought her once-studied anatomy to life. *Her* horse-blanket was "liane de mare liberum," referring to the philosopher Hugo Grotius's 1609 pamphlet on the freedom of the seas, and it was true that her expansive technique seemed to touch every shore. "My dancing machine," he called her, and when Weiss tore his Achilles on stage that fall during a performance of *Ballo* and had to limp into the wings, Ashley performed their difficult partnered steps alone and finished the ballet by herself. But there was a barb to Balanchine's compliments too: his "machine" had limited emotional range, and he tried to pull something more from her with the pensive *Ballade* in 1980, but it wasn't quite there. Then it was too late.[51]

Fast on the heels of *Ballo* came another high-speed breakthrough, *Kammermusik No. 2* (1978) to Hindemith's 1924 score, for Karin von Aroldingen and Colleen Neary with Sean Lavery, Adam Lüders, and a corps de ballet of eight men. Colleen (Pat's younger sister) was tall, and bold—all legs and a full figure. She had left the company in despair some months before, frustrated at being passed over in favor of Merrill and struggling with weight and insecurity. She returned with platinum-blond hair, and Balanchine said, Okay, but get your own hair back, not that blond fakery. As an incentive, he gave her *Kammermusik.* He positioned her next to Karin but a bit behind in space and time—"My little shadow," Karin called her (and gave her a small box to hold the shadow). The ballet was heady, mental, intellectual—"kammercomputer" they called it—a thrilling high-wire act in the spirit of *Agon* but more relentlessly paced, nervous and anarchic, tightly controlled, and full of canons and counterpoint. But the real engine of the ballet lay in the propulsive power of the men—all formidable dancers pushed to peak physical capacity. "When I first watched it," one dancer noted, "I thought, my god how clever is that, they are killing themselves, a billion steps for those women, and the men in the back are all you can see. An ironic tour de force."[52]

The men in the back were a new force. They were in the back of ballets, in the back of women, in the back of class—but now they were suddenly a thrilling presence. It was a fact of these late years that after decades of slim pickings and men whose bodies were ruined by wartime service or limited training, Balanchine finally had a cohort of sensational men, several of them Danes, all trained in a clean and precise style: Peter Martins had arrived in 1969 and was joined by Peter Schaufuss (very briefly), Adam Lüders (in 1975), Ib Andersen (in 1980)—those were the Danes. Helgi Tómasson had been with the company since 1970 and was Icelandic (and trained by Danes). Bart Cook, from Utah, joined in 1971 and became a principal dancer in 1979. None of these dancers was bravura in a princely or machismo style, and in spite of their classic good looks, they could seem almost androgynous.[53] There was something free about them, owing in part to a smooth, sleek style, technically hyperrefined, no edges, no drama—a different breed from that of the more theatrical d'Amboise, Moncion, and Villella. Martins had that princely physique, but by now, after years of pressure from Balanchine, he danced weight-down (high leaps deemphasized), and he was malleable and self-effacing. Andersen and Tómasson were lighter, freer, creatures of nature entirely without affect. Adam Lüders had that biblical name, and he was tall and internal, a sensitive dancer, almost too lyrical for his years, with a deep vulnerability. There was a hint of melancholy hesitation in his otherwise beautifully formed technique, and he was one of those rare dancers whose body conveyed mood and thought. Cook was soulful with a putty-like body and daring flexibility; he astonished even his fellow dancers in his performances of *The Four Temperaments* and *Square Dance*. The effect of these new men, taken together, on the NYCB was startling. "Ballet is woman" had to move over, and a new dimension of old work opened before our eyes. Balanchine's dancers had always been an essential life force, and as his own body continued to deteriorate, he would need these men more than ever.[54]

His health was slowing him down, and in 1972 he had befriended (and hired for the company) Dr. William Hamilton, a tall, Oklahoma-born orthopedic surgeon he had met through Misha Arshansky. "Beel" was admiring and a good listener. He also lived across the street from George, who would call impromptu to say, "Beel, maybe if you are not doing anything we could have dinner" and they would go out or cook something. Beel was always available to check in or offer health advice.[55] But in the battle between his body and the work he needed to do, he focused on the work. He was walking back down an old path, picking up old people and belongings he had left behind, and trying at the same time to provide for the dancers he had today. They were his children and needed him too, and he felt the peril his health posed for their future. Ever practical, he was making dances that would help them to survive—big ballets, spectacles that would sell tickets, but that "he liked" too.

He had already staged in 1974 the nineteenth-century French classic *Coppélia,* with music by Léo Delibes, with the help of Choura Danilova; they had danced it together as children at the Mariinsky. He saw it as a light family entertainment for Saratoga, but like *The Nutcracker,* it was based on a lurid story by Hoffmann, in this case *The Sandman,* about (as Balanchine put it) a "strange man [who] makes things." Coppelius was a diabolical man who secretly made a glassy-eyed automaton woman, whose beauty drove a would-be lover to suicidal madness. It pointed to Balanchine's oldest themes: mannequins and puppets, mute women with mysterious souls, and the cruel and obsessive predilections of human desire. He was similarly planning a new and darker *Sleeping Beauty* (he liked the eerie tale by Charles Perrault more than the sweetened old ballet), if Lincoln could only raise the money, and had already found a designer who could do tricks with projections and light—cheaper, more modern, a way of stripping down the stage without forgoing Mariinsky-style special effects.[56]

Don Quixote, on the other hand, was a problem. It was a clunky old production that no longer served its original purpose, which was Farrell. He wanted to be free—free to live, but also to die, and in these months, we can see Balanchine searching for ways to diminish once and for all this vital tie in his life. In the winter of 1978, he staged the ballet one last time and then retired it forever. By then *Quixote* was old, after all, and he had never quite gotten it right. He cast Adam Lüders as Quixote, the role he had first danced himself with Suzanne. Jacques still performed it too, but he was older now, and Adam was a new amanuensis, a younger double to take both his and Jacques's place. Balanchine taught him the ballet himself, a last chance to play out his old role. On the final night, after the long funeral scene, when Farrell draped herself over Quixote's dead body and the curtain fell, she stayed heavily on his chest for what seemed to Lüders like a very long time. Balanchine watched.[57]

One month later, on March 15, he suffered a heart attack.

Chapter 26

TIME TO GO!

He was at home alone. The heart attack was mild enough that he called Barbara, and she and Eddie rushed him to the NYU hospital, where his doctors thought it was serious enough to keep him for three weeks. In an ominous sign, while he was there, Nicky Nabokov was hospitalized a few blocks away for a routine procedure and died unexpectedly of heart failure. George received the news stoically and was not well enough to attend the funeral. He was in touch with Nicky's widow, Dominique, but what was there to say. It was Nicky's time to go, and he went, that's all.[1] But as George recovered at home and quietly tended to the rubber plants he was growing in mayonnaise jars, the seriousness of his own condition was difficult to ignore. His angina was getting worse, and as he slowly began to resume work, he seemed unsteady and frail. His vision was deteriorating, leading to cataract operations, and in the coming months he would suffer a painful episode with kidney stones. He pressed on, refusing to give in to any sign of decline. When his cardiologist strongly recommended that he retire, he got a new cardiologist.[2]

He had a new internist too. Like so many of the women he surrounded himself with, Edith Langner was of Central European (Polish and German) descent. She was initially a hard sell as a physician.[3] She didn't "look like" a doctor, he said—wrong casting: pretty, blond, and smart, with a glamorous office overlooking Central Park that looked more like an MGM studio than like the small chambers his doctors usually occupied. But she was a colleague of Dr. Hamilton's, and she was Barbara's doctor (Suzanne's too), part of the family, and once he accepted her expertise, he invited her to travel with the company and to stay in the little house in Saratoga with him and whomever else was there, another comforting medical and feminine presence (he chose her a perfume) as he faced his demise. Was she a little in love with him? Of course.[4]

Barbara pressed him to make a last will and testament, but he resisted. He didn't care a whit for posterity, he said; "I won't be there." It was part of his approach of almost deliberately erasing the traces of his life as he lived it. He wrote little, threw things away, moved many times and never established a permanent home, except in the theater, where he spent most of his time. Even his functional, "no style" apartment spoke of a man who wasn't fully there. His material possessions were few, and Barbara managed his finances to the end—he hardly knew or cared what he had, and his only indulgences were still distinctly ephemeral: perfumes, fine wine, elegant clothing, Old World hotels. Nor did he see his ballets as solid objects or assets, and he had always given them away free, "like butterflies," to other companies to perform as long as he judged the dancers good enough and the ballets could be staged by his trusted stagers. Besides, many of his ballets had been irretrievably forgotten and only a few captured on film—and with rare exceptions, he was unhappy with the result. "Those aren't my ballets," he quietly insisted. He seemed to like it that his fragile oeuvre was recorded only in the minds and bodies of his dancers and might one day disappear like a wayward spirit or a wisp of cloud. Like a life, really. Even if the dancers who came after he was gone correctly performed the steps of his dances, the ballets would be different: "Danced by dancers I don't know, that I haven't trained? . . . Those won't really be my ballets."[5] And if "those won't really be my ballets" was all that would be left, what did it even mean to make a will?

But the lawyer brought in by Horgan held a trump card. If you don't make a will, he finally explained to Balanchine, your dances may revert to your brother in the USSR as next of kin and could eventually end up in the hands of the Soviet state. There was no greater enemy in Balanchine's mind than Communist Russia, and it could be said that he had positioned his entire life, including his ballets, against it. As a committed player in the cultural Cold War, he wasn't about to lose this final round. He made the will.

It was a practical document: debts paid, duties dispensed, and as usual he didn't bother much with the past. Of his wives, only Tanny was mentioned, perhaps because the others had married well or were gainfully employed, and only 113 of some 425 known works were named—Horgan gave the lawyer a list of the dances kept by the company press office, and Balanchine seems to have divvied them up on the spot. The rest had been lost, and more would be forgotten in the years to come. A decade later, only 73 of the 113 would still remain in repertory. Copyright was another issue, but that was more easily dealt with. The law had changed in 1978, finally permitting choreographic works to be registered without a story or plot attached, and the astute Horgan had begun routinely registering copyright for Balanchine's works.[6]

The three primary legatees in the will were Barbara, Karin, and Tanny, the current women in his life. Barbara was there because she had always been there, his close personal assistant, companion, and trusted colleague for over two decades, and he knew she would need money and support. She had managed his life, so he left her to manage his death and made her his executor, by far the most powerful legacy in the will. Karin was there because she loved him now, and it was no accident that in addition to the rights to many of his greatest ballets, he left her the Sixty-seventh Street apartment, the home they had never quite shared since she already had a home with Morty and Margo. Tanny was the single greatest beneficiary: his guilt over leaving her—crippled—and his hasty Mexican divorce continued to haunt him. The alimony he paid annually was a support, but he knew that when he was gone, she would need whatever income the dances might generate.

The rest was cherry-picking, but deliberate cherry-picking. Balanchine gave Farrell the ballets that documented their failed love, not her extraordinary career: *Meditation, Don Quixote, Tzigane*.[7] Merrill Ashley got *Ballo della Regina*, probably because she was the only one who would ever have the technical capacity to dance it, and Patti McBride received a few token dances—she had danced a lot and been a loyal mainstay. Kay Mazzo was granted *Duo Concertant*, a work of elusive love from the Stravinsky Festival, as poignant and fragile as her dancing. He had already given Diana Adams *A Midsummer Night's Dream*, even though—or perhaps because—she had had a miscarriage and didn't perform the opening. Later he took the time to write a codicil (unbinding) to punish her for trying to collect on a performance of the ballet that he had personally licensed without fees. He would not, even at her behest, unnecessarily dirty his dances with money. To Rosemary Dunleavy, a ballet mistress who seemed to hold every step of every dance, machinelike, in her head (he called her R2-D2, not exactly a compliment), Balanchine gave *Le Tombeau de Couperin*, a ballet she had remembered when no one else could. Only three men made the final list: he nodded to Lincoln with only two early works, *Concerto Barocco* and *Orpheus*, and he awarded Eddie Bigelow, his Old Man Charlie since the 1940s, *The Four Temperaments* and *Ivesiana*. Betty Cage, who was still very much there, in spite of their cooling relations after she had taken Tanny's side in the divorce, received *Symphony in C*. He gestured to Jerome Robbins with *Pulcinella* and *Firebird*, dances they had made together in rare equanimity. Peter Martins, still an arriviste, got nothing (although Lincoln later coyly offered to give one of his to Peter, who politely declined). To his brother, Andrei, in the USSR, he left two gold watches, originally a gift to him from Lincoln.[8] When Andrei later found out, he was upset at this seemingly meager legacy, but perhaps he was wrong: the ballets were perishable, time went on.[9]

As for the NYCB and SAB, the institutions Balanchine and Kirstein had built up around Balanchine's talent, they got nothing at all. Balanchine did not think the NYCB would last any longer than his dances would last—even less. Without him, what would it be? When he was away for so much as a month, he said, the dancers lost their way and his dances deteriorated—why would his absence at death be any different? Besides, institutions had a way of melting into air; he had watched a whole Russian court crumble when the czar was deposed, and he didn't trust them. Each one of his past companies had disappeared into insolvency, and the NYCB was always teetering on the financial brink. Why should it survive his absence, and why should he even want it to or care? On a more basic level, the company, like the ballets, *was* the dancers—and dancers, not boards of directors, need to eat. So the dancers got whatever scraps might remain.

Yet with all the disclaimers and talk of butterflies and impermanence and a future he did not own, there were glimmers in these late years of a desire, "nevertheless," as he liked to say, to pin down a few of his dances. He had experimented in the past with dance-notation methods, all failed. A notator trained in Benesh, one of several existing systems, had worked with the company for a time, but Balanchine had found the results impractical. What could its inert figures meticulously recorded on a page really tell about his dances? A dancer could efficiently set a ballet using muscle memory, while a notation expert seemed to labor for hours over every position of an arm or leg. An expert in the system invented by Laban, Ann Hutchinson, had also notated a few of his ballets in the 1940s, but her future requests, made over years, met with skepticism. "Mr. Balanchine's feelings on Labanotation remain steadfast," Barbara wrote, finally annoyed at repeated inquiries, and she laid the issue of the ballets Hutchinson had already notated to rest with a written agreement: Balanchine owned the dances, and Hutchinson owned her Laban score. Balanchine couldn't use the score to mount his ballets without Hutchinson's permission, but Hutchinson couldn't reconstruct a ballet without Balanchine's permission. So there.[10]

Film and TV seemed more promising, in spite of the Breck shampoo debacle, and in 1973, soon after his last visit to Russia, Balanchine had impulsively accepted an invitation from Reiner Moritz, an ambitious German director and producer, to film fifteen of his ballets in Berlin. Moritz seemed serious, but the moment the company arrived, he and his team haughtily ignored Balanchine and started taking arty shots from the ceilings or sides, zooming in to catch an arm or a leg or a close-up of a swirling costume. They shot *Serenade* from every conceivable angle and then couldn't figure out how to reassemble the fragmented ballet, leaving Balanchine to piece it together from shards. Worst of all, they refused to let him into the editing room. He grew cranky and despondent and stood helplessly watching the monitors muttering, "Not my ballet." The mess of a result was eventually sold to ABC, and when it finally aired, Barbara at least made sure the dancers got paid.[11]

A few years later, he would make a last attempt. Merrill Brockway, a producer at PBS, was also a pianist, and although Balanchine was skeptical, he finally agreed to meet Brockway, who won him over by talking about music and promising artistic control. The shoots took place at a film studio in Nashville, and Brockway built a new floor for the dancers and worked closely with Balanchine. They shot from three cameras, each on isolated feed, and Balanchine was always in the control room. When something didn't work visually, he would say, "Don't worry, I fix," and rush down to the stage to reconfigure a dance, then rush back up, and say, "Roll camera." Don't you even want to tell me what you did, Brockway would ask, "No; roll camera," and they did. In the editing room, music was key: when Brockway cut on the downbeat, for instance, Balanchine said no, no, no—just before the breath, not on it.[12] Still, none of this was really a record or memorialization, and Balanchine had no interest in a definitive performance, whatever that might be. When Patti McBride made a mistake in *Rubies* and asked to reshoot it, he said, No, it is good enough; this is not *Giselle*, dear.[13]

Nothing he did was *Giselle*, and the moment he got the whiff of a dance aging into a "classic," he moved to change it or shake up the dancers to make sure they were still awake and in the moment. It could be a little thing, like shifting a phrase or adding a new step sequence into the mix at the very last moment, or (even) sticking his foot dangerously out onto the stage to make sure a dancer was alert. One night he whispered, "Do mistake waltz, dear," to Christine Redpath just before she went on stage—referring to the hilarious "mistake waltz" in a Robbins ballet in which a dancer mixes up all her steps, creating havoc through the ranks around her. Redpath's fellow dancers were appalled (What the hell were you doing out there?), but she just said, Mr. B told me to do it, and that was the end of that. When Jerry showed up for class one morning with a film crew, Balanchine said sardonically, "He's here for posterity," and began class by asking the gangly Dr. Hamilton, who happened to be in the room, to lie on the floor in his suit and perform entrechat quatre with his legs stuck up into the air.[14]

Then he shocked everyone by cutting the first and last sections of *Apollo* entirely, topping and tailing Stravinsky's score and sending critics and dancers into a flurry of confusion and recrimination. How could he cut Stravinsky's score? How could he take a knife to one of his own greatest works? He was nonplussed: "Van Gogh cut off his ear!"[15] He changed his ballets constantly, never set them in stone like a mausoleum, so why should *Apollo* be any different? These were other dancers and other times, and he no longer needed or liked the mimed birth and death scenes, which looked old and dated, so he stripped them out. The effect was striking: he had left out the life cycle, no birth, no death. It was both a fragment and a suspension, another move away from plot and toward memory. As for cutting a musical score: he had been parsing musical scores all of his life, mixing and matching movements or taking what he needed for theatrical effect and leaving the rest—like Stravinsky's nose: who needs it? Besides, no one was going to tell *him* what to do. "He rather behaves as if each day is his last," Lincoln reported to the dancer Marie Rambert. "He has been rehearsing a lot, and changing sacred steps so that the so-called critics are in a rage that they have to look at the changes and not recall what it *used* to be."[16] Erasing as he went.

In July 1978, a few months after his heart attack, he astonished even himself by hiring Mikhail Baryshnikov. Misha (as Balanchine fondly called him) had defected from the USSR in 1974 and was a Cold War superstar, but he was open and eager to move beyond the classical roles history assigned him. He was adventurous and had recently worked with Twyla Tharp on *Push Comes to Shove*, a dance to Haydn and ragtime that drew on everything from vaudeville and jazz to Tharp's own iconoclastic physical deconstructions. At first Balanchine wasn't sure about hiring a Russian star, but he knew Misha from the 1972 USSR trip, and they had met amicably again soon after Baryshnikov's arrival. Still, Balanchine worried: "It will destroy our dancers," he told Jerry, who was pushing for Misha to come; "OK, some of them are mediocre and middle but it holds together in our way. He'll have all the crazy people screaming for him and then writing letters because he isn't dancing every ballet on every night." It was a big decision, he said, "like picking Vice President."[17] But he was drawn to Misha, whose extraordinary artistry, modest composure, and impeccable St. Petersburg training were hard to resist.

Born in Latvia to Russian parents, Baryshnikov was also an exile and orphan of sorts. His adored mother had committed suicide when he was a child, and he had taken refuge from his cold and remote father at Balanchine's old Theater School in Leningrad, where he was taken in and formed by the great teacher Alexander Pushkin (who had also taken in and trained Nureyev). As a child, he had seen *Apollo* performed by Alicia Alonso's Cuban company and never forgotten the arresting movement and music, the sensuality and femininity—ballet and music as he had never before encountered them. He had attended every performance of the NYCB in Russia in 1972, and his admiration for Balanchine was among the reasons he had defected. Jerry pressed, and one afternoon, Balanchine called Misha on the phone and asked him to come to his apartment: "We can speak Russian," he said.

The appointment was set for 8:30 A.M., and Baryshnikov paced nervously outside for half an hour with coffee and cigarettes before ringing the bell dead on time. He found Balanchine in his sparsely decorated apartment with basic furniture, a Russian icon, a small transistor radio, and a photo of Mourka the cat propped on a table. Balanchine, he later recalled, was calmly ironing a shirt and surrounded by a mist of steam ("Where else can you get good results instantly? Nowhere!").[18] But really he too was nervous, and as he stopped to offer Baryshnikov a cup of tea, he noted that he was already on his third cup but had of course started first with hot water with lemon, since "that's how it should be done." He asked Baryshnikov if he ironed his shirts too, and Baryshnikov vaguely said yes (not really) but admitted he had "no method." So Balanchine showed him "how it should be done," starting at the cuff, moving to the sleeve, then the body, and ending with the collar (lots of steam). Did Misha like cats? No, he preferred dogs. "Too bad." Was he christened? Well, secretly, by his mother and grandmother, but he was unobservant. "That can change." They talked for some time, and Balanchine wanted to know everything about him, offering the kind of sweetness and caring he had for dancers he liked. I am old, he quietly warned Misha, who was undeterred. As for the contract, "We don't really have contracts, I prefer to keep these things simple," and that was that. Money was not discussed, and it was understood that the young dancer (who otherwise commanded high fees) would be paid according to the usual NYCB scale and listed alphabetically.[19]

It was too late. Balanchine's health was in free fall, and he just didn't have the energy to take full advantage of this vast new talent. Misha dove into the repertory and fought to master Balanchine's way of dancing, but the extreme, off-balance physicality and high-speed dynamics of the NYCB repertory took a harsh toll on his body. He could be moody and frustrated, and Balanchine tested him in all of the usual ways, especially by throwing him into roles at shockingly short notice with almost no rehearsal, or asking him to partner dancers he wasn't naturally drawn to. Misha withstood the whispers that "after all," he was not a Balanchine dancer, but Balanchine didn't care about any of that, and even Lincoln helped: forget about critics, they both said, and Balanchine doted on him, whenever he could muster enough energy to pay attention. He was interested, as he always was with a dancer he admired, in Misha being *Misha*—in what *he* would add to *Harlequinade* or *Agon* or the many other ballets he took on during his brief stay with the company. It was no accident that the changes and cuts in *Apollo* were first done for Misha, who had *arrived* classically pristine, as a fully formed Apollo, not as an untamed boy, yet he was also still young and wanted to learn.[20]

Russia was spread between them, and they grew close. Sometimes Balanchine called on the phone just to talk, usually about St. Petersburg—architecture, the Hermitage, Pushkin—and he once took twenty minutes to recite from memory, in Russian, Tatiana's famous letter from *Eugene Onegin* as Misha sat silently listening at the end of the line. Call me George, he insisted, but Misha stuck with Mr. B, as the dancers all called him. Balanchine invited the young dancer to Easter dinner at his home, as well as to dinner in Saratoga with the Leaches. "Misha . . . was so nervous he arrived early and downed two vodkas before Balanchine even got home," Dick Leach wrote in his diary that night. He added that the dancer was "surprisingly un-shy after the first glass of Stolichnaya [had] been Russianed down" and that he was "surprisingly fluent in English. Surprisingly, even brilliantly intellectual. Surprisingly helpful with the dishes." Balanchine had ordered three pounds of caviar and he made blinis and played the piano for them all.[21]

Mainly, Misha danced. He took on the vast repertory, and Balanchine worked with him on *Apollo* and *Harlequinade*, among many dances. Misha was around, watching and absorbing the ethos of the company, and he was amazed at its spontaneity, musicality, and abandon; Balanchine trusted him not to overdance, overact, and overplease and to follow his instincts as he found his way into the dynamics of the movement, he later reflected, "a way of letting the body speak without control."[22]

In the end, one of their most memorable collaborations came in *Prodigal Son*. This old and dated ballet, which Balanchine had long since professed to hate, became a deep encounter between them. It was a Russian ballet from the days of Diaghilev, Kochno, and Lifar, from Pushkin's story and Prokofiev's score. Balanchine even recorded a performance of the ballet with Brockway, and although he did not perform the role of the father for TV, he did dance it with Misha in rehearsals, some of which were recorded on film.[23]

The raw footage of these two Russians from opposite ends of the twentieth century rehearsing the son's journey home and into his father's arms was heartbreaking to watch. We see Balanchine lowering himself stiffly onto his knees as Misha stands by, visibly worried that this fragile man might hurt himself, but the next thing we know, Balanchine is on the floor playing Misha's part, curling into a fetal position, head clasped in his arms. They slip into Russian and Balanchine gestures, cajoles, and demonstrates and then gently pushes the young dancer this way and that to help him capture the movement. They take it from the top, with the music, and as Misha falls to his knees and begins the long journey across the stage, Balanchine falls to his knees too, and the old man and the boy are holding on to each other, inching along side by side. As these two sons arrive collapsed at the feet of the father, Balanchine, still in Misha's role, climbs into the father's stiffened arms, showing the son how to do it, where to place a shoulder, just how to lift a knee, like so. Misha tries it himself, and they are moving in and out of each other now, as dancers do, and Balanchine gently guides the son's body into the paternal cradle, pressing father and son together like clay. For a moment, Balanchine seems in possession of both roles as he takes the father's arm and guides it like a gesture of his own around the son and into the final protective embrace.

Then, fifteen months after they had started, with Balanchine's blessing, Misha took up an offer to direct American Ballet Theatre and was gone. But not gone: they still saw each other, and Balanchine (and Lincoln) told him to come back whenever he wished, but really, they all moved on.

With his angina attacks increasing and the end in sight, Balanchine circled back, like an animal to old territory, or a man who knows he will soon stand before God. He invited Suzanne to dinner at the Mayflower Hotel. It was an excruciating choice of locale. The Mayflower, scene of the crime, a place he had railed at and avoided for years because *she* had been there with *him*. The only account we have of this dinner is Farrell's, and she says Balanchine talked of the Bible, recited the Lord's Prayer in Latin, and spoke of temptation. "You know, I was wrong, I was an old man, and you were young. I should not have thought of you that way. You should have had your marriage." She took their dinner as an act of forgiveness, part of his "final summation." Soon after, he gave her a book: Mikhail Bulgakov's *The Master and Margarita*. She didn't read it ("I didn't need all of that information") but in her memoir, she summarized it as a romantic fairy tale "centered on the master, his unfinished novel, and a young married woman, Margarita, who he loved." They had been "tragically separated through nightmares often orchestrated by Satan himself" and were "finally united and resurrected in death, their 'home for eternity,' where he would complete his work and she would guard his sleep." It was a myth to live by, but had she read the novel, she would have found a more complicated interpretation of their dinner and of his gift.[24]

Bulgakov's novel, written in the cruel years of Stalin's Terror, was an upside-down, Faustian world of black magic and the absurd, a darkly satirical condemnation of Communism's satanic tricksters run wild and the theatrical antics of a police state. The Master is a Quixote-like sane madman, an author destroyed by his critics, who commits himself to an asylum. The story of the love between the Master and Margarita is indeed tangled up with the Master's unfinished novel (which is also Bulgakov's) and tells the story of Pontius Pilate and the crucifixion of Christ. But when the Master and Margarita are separated, it is Margarita who makes a Faustian pact with the Devil to find her lover, and it is the Devil, answering to Christ and to God, but also to fantasy and fiction, who reunites them and saves Margarita. He does it by giving her a magical cream that transforms her body, not unlike a dancer's, into a supernatural being: Margarita becomes a witch, a naked witch, in love with flying and the speed of her broomstick, and she soars, like the freest woman in the world, over the city and into the fifth dimension, gleefully welcoming guests from hell to Satan's Great Walpurgisnacht Ball, stark naked or draped in a black silk cape and nothing else.[25]

As for her beloved Master, his fate is sealed when the Devil informs him that Christ, "the hero you have invented," has finally read the Master's still-unfinished novel, and has asked the Devil to please "take the Master with you and grant him peace." And when our Devil responds, "But why aren't you taking him with you to the light?" the answer is clear: "He has not earned light, he has earned peace." And so the Master and Margarita remain in the Devil's charge: he poisons them, and when it is "*Time to Go!*" the earth cracks and falls away into a great apocalyptic scene, drawn from the book of Revelation, of sleek black horses and riders galloping from the vanishing city.[26] As they ride into the void, all their characters, their roles, their costumes, and their deceptions are swept from them, "unmasking all illusions," and they fly naked in their "true aspect."

They stop on the way to see poor Pontius Pilate, who has been suspended for nearly two millennia in a stone armchair on a flat summit in the moonlight. Unable to finish his own story or to walk the moon's beaconing path, he just talks madly to himself. The Master completes his novel on the spot—"You're free! He's waiting for you!"—and Pilate scampers up the moon path with his faithful dog, where he will eventually find Christ himself, who will relieve his guilt by the simple trick of assuring him that none of it ever happened. As the Devil guides the Master and Margarita to their "eternal home," the Master's own "anxious, needled memory begins to fade," and he feels himself set free by the pen of a poet, who is now writing his story, just as he wrote Pilate's. In the final reckoning of magicians and humans left on earth, where black cats roam and satanic nights are staged, tallied, and tried, the Master finally vanishes as if he too had never happened.[27]

We are left with the feeling that the only true thing is a great love—a Venus from the moon, a witch at the gate—and a life lived in another dimension, proof that everything is fiction and when it is "Time to Go!" the material world will break up and fall away into whatever fantasies we conspire to believe in. On stage, Farrell was like the Master's "secret wife"—secret because beneath her aloof and conventional exterior lay a wild and pagan witch that flew through his dances with an irreverent irony and womanly sensuality that did not elsewhere exist. But back in the pedestrian world of their lives, her spell had by now been broken, a fact illustrated by a thousand small incidents such as this one: when she and Jacques disagreed during a rehearsal about whether her steps should be performed center stage or off-center, Balanchine resolved the dispute with an ironic Bulgakov-like ploy, saying "It is off center, but for *you* we could move center over."[28]

It was almost time to go. He was getting too corporeal, too burdened by a body that was taking over his life. Alarmed at his growing dizziness and increasingly frequent attacks of angina, Dr. Langner and his cardiologists were pushing for an angiogram and had raised the possibility of a heart bypass. In spite of his suffering, he was reluctant to consider an operation. He had refused surgery for TB, after all, and was still standing. But his biggest problem with the whole idea was spiritual: he was afraid of interfering with God's plan. "When he says go, I go!" he said matter-of-factly, and assured Langner that the people from his past would all be waiting for him, gathered at a card table in the sky playing poker. He was reading around this time about "reverse time sense" and the idea that there might be "another world" in which people are born dead and get younger, so that when you arrive at birth, the cycle begins again. "Why not? Why should be the world only disintegrates?"[29] Conversations about the metaphysics of tampering with his heart—throwing God's dice—dragged dangerously on. An angiogram in March showed an urgent situation, and concerned by the delay, Dr. Hamilton ("Beel") arrived for a house call one afternoon to find George surrounded by icons and consulting with an old bearded Russian psychic, who was laying on hands and warning darkly that anesthesia might erase George's inner vision. But Balanchine also believed in science and progress—and he wanted to live.[30] Maybe God's plan *was* the bypass.

It was not that he was afraid of death. That had stalked him all his life, and he had found a way to be calm and embrace a kind of predestination that took the whole matter out of his hands. "I have a big army of angels standing, you know, opening the way. . . . Soon as he says that's enough for you, come back, and I will go back. . . . Usually people say [if] there is a god why couldn't I buy a house or buy a Cadillac. You're not going to get a Cadillac, it costs million dollars to keep it. . . . Or you want to marry somebody you think you are in love with, he says no, because it will be awful if you did. If you really got what you wanted, you will be running away and commit suicide but he knows in advance whatever you're going to do. To us it's a miracle because we didn't think its possible, but I believe it's possible because that's what they want; the curtain will go up and we are going to dance and something always will happen, until they decide that's enough. It's like they took Stravinsky away, it's finished, done, beautiful, you cannot do more than that, that's all we want you to do, and he went out and left us."

Besides, the dead were not so far off. "Tchaikovsky wants or Mendelssohn wants and he knows that you *like* him. It's not that you have to tell anybody, he knows if you like him or not, because you really have to like, you know people say I LOVE that way, I LOVE it, it's WONDERFUL. [But] you don't like anything, you really like yourself.... And if you are fake, they know you are fake." But if you are real, they help and preside: "It happens, for instance, not enough time, have to stage big ballet and people don't memorize, or somebody is sick, or everybody is sick and orchestra is not enough rehearsal, and we put together on the stage and doesn't work, and costumes are terrible, and blue tights, and its awful and we don't know what to do . . . and already at 6 pm in the evening it's still a mess—and in the evening it is great!"[31] How could he presume to intervene with *that*?

By May 1979 he couldn't get up, walk, or brush his teeth without excruciating pain, but still he held out. In June he drove with Karin and her daughter, Margo, to Southampton to rest before the summer Saratoga season. They stopped at a mall to buy sneakers for Margo, but Balanchine, who normally loved shopping, seemed tired and said he would wait in the car. Karin hurried to get him home, but after they reached his condo, she heard him on the phone to his doctor complaining of chest pains. She called Barbara, who called the hospital, and Karin put Balanchine and Margo back in the car and drove to the emergency room at New York Hospital, where Barbara was waiting. His doctors recommended immediate triple-bypass surgery, and he finally consented. On June 17 the surgery was successfully performed.[32] "We prayed quite a lot," Kirstein wrote to Richard Buckle, "and this seems to have worked."[33] Tanny sent a note too: "Dearest George, Just a scrawl to let you know I think and pray for you often.... God bless you. Moustapha says prayers for you to Allah as he is a Moslem cat. Love Tanny."[34]

When it was over, Dr. Langner came to visit and found Balanchine alert and hooked to the usual monitor charting his vital functions. As they talked, the monitor came disconnected, and instead of worrying about himself or calling for help (as she did), Balanchine calmly examined the device and said, "This is terribly designed, Ronnie Bates could do much better." Annoyed that he would miss the Saratoga season, he planned from his hospital bed an elaborate party in his absence at the Leaches', complete with caviar shipped from his favorite New York shop. His cardiac surgeon, Dr. Ephraim Glassman, promptly received a shipment of Dom Perignon, 1971.[35] It would take several months for Balanchine to recover, and although his energy and heart condition would improve, the surgery had done little to solve the underlying symptoms of a variant of mad cow disease that, unbeknownst to them all, was already ravaging his brain.

There is no evidence that he believed the surgery would save him. It was a way of buying time, his own little pact with the Devil to gain a moment to do the work he needed to do. He should have died before the surgery, but he didn't, just as he should have died of malnutrition or cholera in revolutionary Russia—or of TB in his Swiss sanitorium or somewhere in upstate New York from one of his attacks. It wasn't time to go yet. But he knew he would have to hurry.

As he recovered from the demon bypass, he was listening to Schumann, playing Schumann, reading Schumann. There was something urgent in his concentration, and Schumann bordered on an obsession, as he picked over scores and recordings, weighing pieces and interpretations. He talked to Karin about the German pianist Walter Gieseking's recording of the *Davidsbündlertänze*, a performance he admired for its intense feeling. It was not clear where all of this was going until one morning when Dr. Hamilton found him at home in his bathrobe sitting with the score to Schumann's *Davidsbündlertänze* spread messily before him. Balanchine hardly noticed the interruption. He was silently engrossed in the music, and preparing to stage a death.[36]

Davidsbündlertänze was composed for Schumann's beloved Clara after they secretly declared their everlasting devotion, against her father's angry refusal. She was eighteen, he was twenty-seven, and their ensuing romance of cloaked meetings, coded messages, and musical doppelgänger would finally end in joyous marriage. But not yet. *Davidsbündlertänze* was a hope and a vow: a series of dances for Clara full of "wedding thoughts." "My Clara," he wrote to her, "will know how to find the real meaning of those dances, for they are dedicated to her in a quite special sense." Among its loving clues was an excerpt from a mazurka that Clara had composed, and although the full score was largely in B minor, it began and ended in C major, Clara's key: "I sometimes feel as if my heart were crossed by a thousand narrow intersecting paths, along which my thoughts and feelings race up and down, and in and out, like human beings asking, Whither does this way lead? And that? And all the ways? And the answer is always the same, 'to Clara.' "[37]

The Davidsbünd, to which Clara also belonged, was an imaginary "secret society," he said, "which never existed save in the heart of its founder." Schumann invented its members, including Florestan and Eusebius, two sides of his personality: wild and mild, form and shadow, F-sharp and E-flat. Its purpose was to fight the "Philistines," those invaders from the sea who stood against everything Schumann believed in—like the "idiots" who had battled Balanchine all these years. Schumann assigned each of the eighteen *Davidsbündlertänze* to Florestan and Eusebius, marking their initials "E" and "F" in the score which, completing the circle, he dedicated to Goethe's grandson from "Florestan and Eusebius."[38]

Schumann was himself a kind of Balanchine doppelgänger: an admirer of Goethe, Hoffmann, Mendelssohn, and Bach and a man who loved puns, anagrams, doubles, and doubling and whose gnarled middle finger had ended his career as a pianist. He was a man too who had lived close to death and suffered illness, in his case syphilis—harsh retribution for his passionate sexuality (affairs with a servant and a prostitute) and the probable cause of his descent into suicidal madness and death. Above all, Schumann was an artist devoted to the eternal Clara, his Sophia, his Gretchen, his Margarita. In the *Davidsbündlertänze*, he assured his "Clarissima Cara, Cara Clarissima!" that F and E were not masked, as they had been in some past compositions: they were wearing their real faces.

Schumann had composed a wedding; Balanchine staged a funeral. The end, he said, would be a flood. Crashing ocean waves inundating the stage and sweeping away all before it. "I see a frozen landscape," he told Lincoln, "a ruined monastery and eight personages who inhabit ice, and at the end the sea rolls in like lava, only it's white ice and crystal."[39] When a film projection failed to achieve this cold and dramatic effect, Balanchine settled instead for a departure into blackness, and the small figure of a woman standing alone center stage, back to the audience, shoulders crumpled in grief, crying in the darkness.

The dances that would lead to this moment would not happen in a real place. There would be no ballroom or salon, only "a space in the past," he said, a stage stripped of scenery and time. He envisioned a "skeletal" set, but when that seemed too eerie, he and Rouben Ter-Arutunian draped the wings instead with long white silk curtains hung at an angle so that they discreetly closed off the stage from all sides. This made the ballet, perhaps not accidentally, very difficult to light, since side lighting was at best partial, leaving Ronnie to find a solution. The dancers were in a world of their own; they couldn't see into or out of the wings, and a wall of light blotted out the audience in front. There wasn't even an open cyclone-blue horizon stretching behind them, just a few blackened and knotted treelike hangings and the shimmering image of a watery cathedral building (Gordon Boelzner called it the "Karen Horney Clinic") suspended over a cold ocean, based on the lonely paintings of Caspar David Friedrich. Only the frosted stage lights—which would go black—gave the shimmering feeling of forever. The sole material object in this sparse and private world was a grand piano positioned in the downstage corner, with Gordon, in period dress, playing by heart. It was like dancing inside someone's mind.[40]

Balanchine drew his closest dancers around. They knew him so well that a mere gesture could bring forth whole streams of movement, no matter his unsteady balance and diminishing sight. There were no steps in this ballet, really, just the gossamer fragments of an almost-waltz, a turn, a run, a caress, and an embrace. Everything seemed to unfold spontaneously, full of immense feeling, yet made of nothing, nothing.[41] The four couples, in wispy chiffon pastels and an indication of a waistcoat, appeared and disappeared, beginning with Suzanne Farrell and Jacques d'Amboise and ending with Karin von Aroldingen and Adam Lüders. Heather Watts with Peter Martins and Kay Mazzo with Ib Andersen were the other sides of Schumann or love or both or neither.[42] Karin was Clara, he told her, and "you are Schumann," he said to Adam, who knew about the Davidsbünd and had read the love letters. This time, it was Karin—not Suzanne—who was dressed in white.

The music begins and ends with Clara—one key, one woman, one love—but Balanchine begins with Suzanne and ends with Karin—one key, two women, two loves. Suzanne's dance with Jacques, in Clara's opening C-major key, to the theme based on her mazurka, is full of impassioned feints and retreats, hands offered and withdrawn, fleeting changes of direction and missed encounters. Jacques shadows her, almost invisible, with a slight hand to the waist or a ghostlike lift to the side. As they rehearsed, Suzanne couldn't get her bearings. She felt lost and disoriented, and it didn't help that she had no sense of what the other couples were doing or where her little fragment with Jacques fit into the whole. Jacques was having his own problems: his shoulder was injured, and he couldn't lift his arm over his head; his corroded knees were painful, and his elegant body seemed to be deserting him. He was filled with self-doubt and felt strangely "slow stiff awkward blinking."[43] Yet when Suzanne told Balanchine that their dance seemed unfinished, "a mess of missed arms and legs," he just said that was exactly what he wanted and walked away.[44]

Karin and Adam performed the second dance, a gentle Austrian Ländler, a simple folk precursor to the waltz, played in the B-minor home key. They strolled on together arm in arm, her head resting on his shoulder, and their movements were slow, deliberate, and caring, like those of a loving couple cherishing a long embrace. Karin's later solo had the same feel, delicate, restrained, with moments of weeping—head bent, face cradled in hands—as she picked her way through fragments of movement like a mother tiptoeing silently through a sleeping baby's room. Heather and Peter were high-strung and nervous, and she constantly slipped away from his backward embraces. "Stop her, contain her, calm her," Balanchine quietly said. At one point, Peter fell stiffly to his knee, and Heather flung herself over his back from behind; Balanchine told her to stay there for a while, "just hold him, dear." Kay and Ib were a whirlwind of lyricism imbued, somehow, as she saw it, with "a bigger world, of living and knowing and loving and going."[45]

Suddenly, in a passionate musical moment, the stage darkened, and

Adam found himself alone in a wild and off-balance dance, hands flexed, body thrown awkwardly back, reaching, collapsing, whirling in a dizzying madness accompanied by flashing lights with wind machines billowing the white draperies. Soon, menacing deathlike figures intruded stiffly from the wings, like figments of Schumann's tormented mind: black-hooded scribes with giant quills and ledgers, Philistines from "the other side" come to torment Schumann ("Here comes Clive," Balanchine joked in rehearsals, referring to the critic Clive Barnes). "You have to be strange to do something great," Balanchine explained, and "I always like to get rid of these dark people who don't understand anything."[46] And he made them fade back into the wings, as Clara flew in to restore the light.

The end of the ballet mirrored the beginning, with a crucial switch. The Ländler returned as the penultimate dance: a note-for-note repeat of Karin and Adam's first dance in the B-minor home key, except that this time, Balanchine gave its lilting phrases to Suzanne and Jacques. Musically, as the scholar Charles Rosen has pointed out, it comes as a surprise, against convention, intruding like a memory or regret that flashes suddenly to mind without reason or explanation. At the end of this stolen moment, full of gentleness and longing, Suzanne and Jacques run forward and stop short, suspended at the edge of the stage, as if stunned by their own encounter and the limits it imposes. As she prepares to exit, he coils his body around her waist from below and lifts her under his bad shoulder with his whole body, as if she were part of himself, and carries her off in a low and long arch, facing nowhere. As they depart, Adam and Karin enter for the final dance in Clara's C-major key. All roads lead to Suzanne, but Karin has the last dance.

She leads Adam in, takes his hand, and puts it around her waist. The sky darkens and the cathedral is barely visible as she reminds her disoriented madman how to move with her. She bends her head, and he takes her arm, and they dance so softly, so quietly, hardly moving, together and apart, a shadow of themselves, until finally they stand face-to-face, with hands curled together like sleeping. The sky closes in around them as he gently bends to kiss her hand and turns to go, a huge man made small with grief in his shoulders. The stage darkens to black, and the piano softly, almost imperceptibly, strokes twelve middle Cs, like the chimes of a clock or a death knell. He turns to go, and the point of view suddenly shifts to him. He faces front, no mask, and Karin watches as he backs away, sucked toward the blackness of the vast ocean. He reaches for her as he disappears into a diminishing spotlight. She is left standing alone, back to the audience, in a thin cone of light. She slowly folds her head into her hand as the piano descends the register—going, gone, silence, curtain.

As Balanchine watched Adam sucked into whatever void awaited and saw Karin's shoulders slump across her wide bony back, he faced his most constant theme: the thin line, like the membrane of an eye, separating visible from invisible, life from death, here from there. Eurydice had been sucked into that void; the woman in *L'Errante,* living out the last ten seconds of her life, had been swallowed into a sheet of white silk fallen from the sky; even the old cloth wrapped like a vestment around the Prodigal Son served as a dividing line, as did the hands of the women in *Serenade* shielding their eyes from the moonlight, before passing finally into it. Only Quixote didn't need this filmy separation since he and Suzanne were already together in some liminal zone, where Diana had refused to go and Allegra wouldn't stay. This time, a secret had been revealed. His place, his first-wing perch, his view, was the view from everywhere—or nowhere—which meant that he could see inside them and outside himself and peel the orange with his eyes.

At the opening-night party, Lincoln went around with a long face saying it was Mr. B's death knell, and many of the dancers thought so too, although Balanchine naturally insisted it had nothing to do with his own life.[47] Jerry found it disturbingly suicidal, and it was true that in reality Schumann had tried to take his life by leaping into the ocean as he approached his final madness. Whatever its overtones, it was also Balanchine's way of bringing them all along, as he always had, this time to grief and mourning. It was not about "the guy who dies," really; it was about the woman who remains. "You know how to mourn," he said to Karin, it was in her Central European bones.

Grief was one thing, but there was no avoiding the banal business of illness and dying. He knew the degradations his poor body faced, but as the trick of the end of his life unfolded, it became clear that this time, there would be two endings, not one. Two bodies, like the two bodies of the king, and two deaths. He would have to live them both, and so must we. But the chronology was disrupted, as if someone had thrown the cards of fate and time into the air and they had fallen in their own order, an order imposed by God, or the opposing requirements of life and art. Life demanded its due. It would be the first death and final end, and it would proceed inexorably, ploddingly, of its own course. The second and real death would be a ballet. It was the only death he cared about, and it had to come first but be last. The demands of art, like Faust's bargain, were simple: he must have the final word.

So, in the last days afforded by the demon bypass, Balanchine would stage his own requiem, and then, like Quixote, or the man Alonso Quijano, he would die. But the only way to tell the story is in reverse, a little bow to Balanchine and his old practice of knowing the end before making the beginning of the dance.

Begin, then, with the mortal end.

Chapter 27

THE MORTAL END

He was resigned and knew he would have to play it out. That's what it was, playing it out, like a movie or a novel before his eyes that wasn't really him—"Not my ballets"—just the blur and tumble of his own dying. That was the astonishing thing about his personality, or his person. He didn't really care about his life, or his dying. That is, he lived it and cared while he did, but he was in some essential way detached from himself. He felt he had been put on earth to make dances, which contained their own world and a way to live—"Come with me"—and the Christlike role of the God-given artist. It could sound narcissistic, the kind of ego that eats a man alive, and it both was and really wasn't. The ego devoured the small earthly "guy who dies," but the artist was untouchable, an aspect of the divine. It was an old Romantic vision of genius, but with Balanchine it did not have the old melodramatic feel. It came more from a childlike innocence, just-born every time he stood in front of a score or a dancer he loved or the first wing of the theater at night. Innocent because as his body roughened with the grit and grime of daily life, the surfaces of his mind grew smoother than ever. He didn't want to "express himself"—that was anathema—and he didn't want his dancers to express themselves either. Why should they indulge in the dirt and pettiness of their own little lives? What did the trousers have to do with the cloud, really? He was fighting to lift them all, collectively, to another plane, into a supreme realm, but of course the only tools he had were the tools of strange and flawed human animals, himself included, now decaying.[1]

In the final months afforded by the demon bypass, he slowly gathered, you might say, his people and his ballets around. He made a new *Walpurgisnacht* from Gounod's *Faust* (1980), for Farrell, of course. He planned a magnificent Tchaikovsky Festival (1981), to which he contributed the only memorable dances.[2] The first was a restaging of his 1933 *Mozartiana*, for Farrell, again, this time dressed in a white tulle skirt with a layer of black, like a veil: "Black, but plain—like nothing, nothing," he said. Balanchine reordered Tchaikovsky's score, for his own dramatic effect, to start with the "Preghiera," a prayer for Farrell—alone—accompanied only by four small children. It began with a pose she recognized from a statue of the Virgin at the Church of the Blessed Sacrament on West Seventy-first Street, where she worshipped, and she recited the "*Ave verum corpus*" as she danced.[3] The rest of the ballet was fragmented and fitful, with movement, she later said, that seemed to build backward instead of forward. The second important dance he made for the festival was *Adagio Lamentoso*, from Tchaikovsky's Sixth (and last) Symphony. It would be his last fully conceived dance, and it would be performed only once. He aimed for a final Stravinsky Festival (1982), but by then his time was expiring, and he would be forced to leave it unfinished.

His life in the years leading up to his death in 1983 broke sequence and time in other ways too. It is hard to reconstruct and seemed to scatter into vignettes, little stories or vaudeville acts, a stuttering to a stop. It is a well-known effect, the experience of the late years as if they were already spooled into memories, loop-taped through the mind in anticipated loss or left floating in time. The events themselves were predictable—replays, really—but also erratic and urgent, like the needle of an old record player pushing at the edge of its last groove.

In 1980, for instance, just months after his bypass and the opening of *Robert Schumann's "Davidsbündlertänze,"* the dancers' union voted to strike. Unions were fundamentally Communist in his mind, and this fifth column in his midst was a betrayal he could not comprehend, coming as it did when his health was also breaking. They didn't know; they were young and self-absorbed, and even after his surgery, he seemed ageless, like some saint or god, in spite of his pale and unsteady appearance. When the union representatives told him of the strike that afternoon in his office, he "did a Sarah Bernhardt" (as he later put it) and angrily called them "pigs" and sharply told each one just how much money he had spent on their talent: "You owe me $14,000, and for you it is $18,000." He called a full company meeting and stood calmly at the front of the studio while they sat nervously on the floor around him listening as he recited the customary script: "Fine, if you want to strike, Lincoln and I will go elsewhere and make a new company in a day. This is the fifth company, and we will make the sixth." He asked for a full company vote—"I don't care if it is illegal. . . . Yes or no from a hundred and five!"—and he walked out. They voted to accept the contract.[4]

As if to make the point, he simultaneously announced a $30,000 contribution from the NYCB to an Italian earthquake-relief fund. The dancers felt betrayed—if the company was so poor, how could it afford *that* and not them, but Horgan assured them this money was coming directly from Balanchine's personal account. Still, it was an assertion of independence—the czar had spoken. Similarly, he went to the board that same year to ask them to raise money for another Stravinsky festival, but when he got there, he "went bonkers," Lincoln said, and told the shocked room that he wanted to raise money for bulletproof vests for the police. There ensued a visit to Mayor Ed Koch. Dressed to the nines in a Western-style shirt and suit jacket, Balanchine pulled up in a limousine with a confused board member in tow. She watched in amazement as Balanchine and Koch immediately fell into an involved conversation about food in Russia and Eastern Europe—caviar, blinis, schnapps—and the deal was done. Koch attended the performance (with blinis in the greenroom at intermission) and left early. Lincoln shrugged, "This is all Balanchine's politics, and maybe it is rather astute."[5]

There were high points. He found a new and extraordinary talent, the fifteen-year-old Darci Kistler from California, and pulled her up from the school and straight into principal roles—no time. The whole company stood crowded in the wings to watch this thrilling new marvel, who seemed to possess more life and physical intelligence than humanly possible. He told her, and anyone who else would listen, "Don't do anything!" Don't touch her, don't spoil her, don't fill her head with notions, she must be herself and just dance when he is gone.[6] Mel Tomlinson, who joined in 1981 from the Dance Theatre of Harlem, was his own story: long with a narrow and elegant frame, he was majestic and poised, masked by "tears of a cloud. . . . That's me," as he later put it. He had the silent physique of a man who had swallowed his past, lodged it behind the mask, like the local sayings he had ingested as a poor boy in the rural South: "An empty wagon makes a lot of noise, shhhh"; "A hit dog will holler, shhhh." His father had been incarcerated and was an alcoholic, and he had grown up with strong women at the height of the civil rights movement and ended up at Arthur Mitchell's DTH, which he left (in a dispute with Mitchell) to join Balanchine.

Several weeks before he was scheduled to begin as a member of the corps de ballet, Balanchine called: Do you know *Agon*? Yes, he had danced the lead role many times at DTH. Good, could you please be at the theater tomorrow to replace the injured Peter Martins and rehearse with "Hedder"? Meanwhile, Balanchine told Martins—who was not injured at all—"You are good, but you are not black." When Mel arrived, they ran through the ballet, and Balanchine instructed him not to be so careful with Heather. He wanted Mel to really throw her, push, pull, exert weight and tension—she was strong and wouldn't break, he said. Thirty minutes later, they were done. Mel would have a stage rehearsal with the full cast before opening night, Balanchine assured him—scant practice for a debut with the NYCB in a principal role, but Balanchine knew that the visual chemistry between the elegant, sinewy, and very black Tomlinson and the wiry, tensile, and very white Watts would be electric, and it was. To Tomlinson's disappointment, Balanchine was absent from the first wing during the performance, and the next day he appeared in Mr. B's office waving a review. Balanchine said quietly that he had not been well enough to come, but he knew how great Mel would be in the role.[7]

As for Peter Martins, who had already produced the promising and successful *Calcium Light Night*, Balanchine asked him to stage *The Magic Flute* for an SAB Workshop Performance.[8] It was the very ballet Balanchine had staged as a student at the former Imperial Theater School in a makeshift production in 1920 during the revolutionary years. A way, maybe, of setting Martins on his path.

There were melancholy low points too. He injured his knee, and Marika Molnar, the company's physical therapist, came to help. She was another new addition, hired to care for the dancers' injured bodies. She came through Dr. "Beel" Hamilton and in a sign of Balanchine's initial skepticism, she was given an old janitor's closet with a sink as an office. The dancers lined up around the hallway to see her and shrunk into the shadows whenever Mr. B turned the corner—no one wanted to be seen as injured, even though many of them were, but he did see—and see the good she was doing. He invited Marika to his office for schnapps, saying he thought she might need it. She was in. She was from a Catholic Hungarian family, and her mother had been a folk dancer and had her own little company back in Hungary before the family fled the Soviet tanks in 1956 for Austria. Marika was five and later remembered well this harrowing event in which they hid in cow manure in a truck in the dark of night and then ran when the guards in the lookout posts had turned away—an adventure for her as a kid, but the babies were given sleeping pills so that they wouldn't make a sound. When Marika came to Balanchine's home all those years later to help with his ailing knee, he ignored his pains and told her stories about his past instead until she quietly insisted, and then he just looked at her and said, Do you know how to waltz? And he took her into his wobbly embrace and waltzed backward to teach her; would that be sufficient exercise for his dying knee?[9]

He could be erratic. On another afternoon, John Taras was rehearsing a ballet on stage. Balanchine crossed the stage, leaning for balance on the wall, and stopped suddenly when he saw the dancers. He approached unsteadily and arranged them in a new formation. Confused, Taras asked which section of the ballet they were rehearsing this was for. Balanchine looked up surprised and said bluntly: "Flood," meaning *Noah and the Flood*, which hadn't been started yet. From then on, when the dancers didn't know what to do, they just said, "Flood."[10]

By 1982 his calendar, a book of days normally filled with artistic engagements, was crowded instead with neurologists, cardiologists, ophthalmologists, and ear, nose, and throat specialists—all working unsuccessfully to diagnose the increasingly severe and mysterious ailments afflicting him. He was being attacked where it mattered most: sight, sound, balance, and orientation in time. A dancer's instruments. He was beginning to see his ballets in double vision, and the stage seemed dim and far away. Ronnie Bates and the dancers stood mystified as he demanded brighter and brighter stage lights. Even the sound of music began intermittently to pain him—he flinched in rehearsals and threw his hands up over his ears, or stuffed balled-up bits of paper inside them to quell the noise.[11] The dancers noticed with alarm that at the theater, he was walking by holding on to the walls, and at her office, Dr. Langner saw red stains on his coat, picked up from her painted walls as he shuffled to the examining room, reluctant to ask for help and afraid he might fall. He needed a cane but leaned on an umbrella instead. At night, gunshots rang through his head, and he complained that soldiers fighting were keeping him awake, as if he were going mad.[12]

All around him, the question of succession was tense and swirling. He said little, committed to no one, made no public statement, and quietly demurred when the question was raised. Why should he care? He wouldn't be there, and "those won't really be my ballets." *That* was a battle for a future "now" he did not own, and they would have to fight it themselves. When the NYCB board chairman Orville Schell had pressed the topic over breakfast with Balanchine one morning in Saratoga, he got no response.[13] When Jacques, one of several contenders, who had along the way been promised the throne, raised it obliquely, Balanchine changed the subject and refused even to appoint d'Amboise ballet master. Suzanne thought for a fleeting moment that Paul might make a return, completing the Prodigal (or Oedipal) act, but she was as alone as ever in her fantasy.[14] John Taras, that capable old ballet master, thought he had a chance and lobbied through Lincoln, who kindly informed Taras that he had no idea of the titanic struggle at hand and didn't stand a chance. "The big battalions are the two chief choreographers, and Balanchine's express desires as interpreted by themselves. . . . I was barely considered in any of the discussions, and hardly figure in anyone's mind as far as the future goes."[15]

Lincoln, he was saying, should have had a say. It was *his* company too, after all, and whatever the complications of their relationship, he and Balanchine had existed side by side, tilling that same plot of land together for as long as anyone could remember. But now that Balanchine was dying, Lincoln's disorientation was extreme and he veered from the humiliating task of demanding a role and respect he no longer commanded, to depression, anger, irrational fits, and rages. He soothed funders anxious about giving money without a sense of the future ("George and I have to play politics, we need Jerry for the Jewish money, and the press and publicity value of him").[16] He lashed out at Jacques d'Amboise, an old favorite, calling him a traitor for running off to do Broadway and movies. He threw his weight behind Peter Martins, later changed his mind, and then changed it back again. No one knew what he really wanted, least of all him. For a moment, he thought he wanted Joe Duell, and for a moment, Duell thought he wanted it too. It was an old pattern: even while Lincoln was supporting Martins, he was also scheming darkly in his mind, cornering Joe at the theater or in the hallways, or pinning him to the wall with his manic focus and telling him *he* was the future. Others thought that Lincoln, or at least some part of Lincoln, wanted it himself.[17]

Jerome Robbins, by far the biggest of the "big battalions," had a special claim. His dances, after all, were a valuable and popular part of the NYCB repertory, and his own artistic life, seemingly so confident and independent, was also deeply bound to Balanchine. Faced with the abyss of Balanchine's momentous death looming before him, not to mention the churning institutional power vacuum, Jerry was feeling alternately defiant and angry; old and spent. He didn't want or need Balanchine's job but—ever prickly in matters of billing—he cringed at the mere thought of being associated with the novice heir apparent, Peter Martins. "In no way can I consider Peter an equal as choreographer," he testily wrote in a draft of a letter to the board, and he would have to be convinced and cajoled into playing his part.[18]

Really there was only one choice to take on the job of running the company on a daily basis, and it was Martins, "a very strong and silent Dane," as Lincoln called him; others noted more bluntly, "wood."[19] But with his square jaw, blond mane, and jaunty good looks, he nonetheless had a muscular ease and sex appeal that made him appear authoritative. He was as smooth as his dancing, and there were no chinks or glints of warmth in his personality; he seemed safe, his emotions under lock and key—an illusion, of course. Martins was by then already running much of the day-to-day operations of the company and wanted the job, badly, and he was working hard to secure the support of the board, of Lincoln, and of Barbara, Balanchine's soon-to-be executrix and a powerful ally. He had even published a book about himself that year. But what Martins really needed, or seems to have thought he needed, was legitimacy, which he never quite got.

When he asked, Balanchine apparently listened but held back. "At that point there was no response," Martins later admitted, and he never secured the master's blessing. Horgan, who was already on his side, swore Peter was "the one" and that Balanchine had been grooming him for years. She swears that Balanchine later called a deathbed meeting—"I was there!"—with Martins and two key board members, in which Balanchine told them, "It has to be Peter, Lincoln will destroy it." But at least one of the board members purportedly present later said there was no such meeting, and no one else seemed to know this meeting had taken place.[20] And if Balanchine did favor Martins, it may not have been for the reasons that Martins and his supporters later claimed. It is just as likely that Balanchine, in a final ironic twist, was looking to his successor to preside over the end of his dances: "Those won't really be my ballets."

If he was silent about the issue of succession, he couldn't resist making one thing perfectly clear: it could only be a man who loves women. It couldn't be either a woman or a homosexual, no matter that the only other choreographers he truly admired were Robbins and Ashton, both gay. His ballets, like his life, fell under a covenant: loving women. Everything about the NYCB was organized around the principle of the eternal feminine, so it is perhaps not surprising that, faced with the unfathomable idea of his own absence, all he could muster was that his dancers—his women—needed a man.[21]

He knew the end was approaching. That Easter he agreed to order some of the traditional pastries from a local bakery rather than laboriously making them himself. Easter night was rainy and blustery, and during the service at the Russian Orthodox Church, the wind blew out his candle three times in a row, a Trinity, until finally he said, "it's not supposed to be lit," and went on in darkness.[22] By then he could no longer easily stand, as he always had, tucked into the first wing during performances like a night watchman and was consigned instead to sitting uncomfortably on a small stool, which he hated. The stool soon appeared at rehearsals, and instead of dancing and indicating steps, he tried to explain the movements he couldn't do, an agonizing process that made it impossible to maintain his legendary patience and civility. He lashed out, forgot things, and seemed disoriented. One afternoon Robbins yelled at Ronnie Bates about a change in the program order, and Balanchine turned on Robbins angrily: "I changed it! I did it! This is what I want!" as the startled Robbins retreated. Another day, he found himself shouting at his baffled production staff: "Only I know what to do—nobody else knows anything!"[23] All true, but shocking to those accustomed to his lifelong humility and civility.

By June 1982 he was too dizzy to complete his dances for the Stravinsky Festival and had to leave them unfinished. Other hands took over his new productions of Stravinsky's *Noah and the Flood* and *Persephone*—an old project between Stravinsky and Gide that he had wanted in vain to choreograph in the 1930s. It was more ritual than dance, "like an Easter icon," he told an old dancer who observed that it had almost no steps or movement, and he told Kermit Love that *Persephone* was "a ceremony, really in a church. I'd like to do in Russian but we can't."[24] Balanchine had asked Vera Zorina ("Zora Verino," as the dancers called her) to narrate, but he was barely present for rehearsals, and she was cranky and imperious. The last dances officially ascribed to him, two solos for Suzanne to Stravinsky, would be more hers than his. He confided to Zorina, "I'm finished, I can't see anymore, I can't hear, and I walk like a drunken man."[25] That month, he gave Karin an eighteen-karat-gold enameled pendant with a seven-point diamond and gold lyre—a de facto wedding ring for the woman he would never quite have.[26] In August he was hospitalized for three nights for a cataract operation in his left eye, and ten days later, Jerry found him in his Southampton condominium playing the piano in jockey shorts, shirt hanging out, "hair astray, one eye black & very old & fragile looking—his Don Quixote come off the stage to visit him."[27]

His handwriting was growing unsteady, and he shakily recorded the phone numbers of his most trusted dancers and companions in large uncertain letters in his book and made a list of key numbers to keep handy: BARBARA, S.A.B., THEATER, STAGE, KARIN, KARIN'S SISTER (in German). His phone book was stuffed with scraps of illegible notes to himself, along with miscellaneous cards for various medical specialists and scattered well-wishing notes from dancers.[28] Nevertheless. In October he presided over the comedy of his own collapse in his plush room at the Watergate Hotel in Washington, D.C., with Karin, Barbara, and Marika all calling 911 in the wee hours of the morning (as a clueless security guard questioned this roomful of young women for possible prostitution). He even endured the ambulance back to New York, but only so far: when it got stuck in traffic on Sixty-seventh Street, he impatiently got out and walked waveringly home, horns honking, siren squealing, and Barbara flailing behind him. At home, he promptly dispatched the waiting nurse who had been hired by Barbara or Eddie: "What is she doing here?"[29]

He had a walker to get around the apartment but hated it, and at dinner when he couldn't get the food to his mouth and it dropped indecorously to the floor, he ground it angrily with his foot. Then came the fateful night when the candles—more candles—illuminating the icons in his home started a fire while he was in bed, and Morty and Karin rushed to put it out, before leaving him to sleep uneasily with the soldiers and their guns. A few days later, on November 4, 1982, he suffered the inevitable fall, the fractured ribs and wrist, and the trip to Roosevelt Hospital, where he would end his life. By then, ever practical, he had already signed over his power of attorney to Barbara, and his calendar diary, routinely updated in her neat hand, went blank.[30]

The hospital procession began. In his white hospital gown and blue robe, with his signature turquoise Native American bracelet on his left wrist, he sat in bed and grimly submitted to this last performance. It was Don Quixote on his deathbed, his loving Dulcinea at his side. Except that in life there was no Dulcinea: none of his five wives or the women he had loved were by his side to care for him now, and he complained sadly to Jacques that he wanted to go home and needed a wife.[31] Love, he wistfully noted, is greater than ballet. As the cast of characters, the men and women in his life, passed through like shadows of some past dance, it became evident that now they no longer mattered. He had taken care of them all, they said, taught them how to move, what to wear, what to eat, how to travel, how to dance, and how to *live*. For better and worse, he had governed their lives. But to him they were above all dancers, and Prospero-like, he still saw them as the stuff of ballets and the materials of art. The joys of reciprocity and intimacy were foreign to him—he was simply missing the whole middle emotional register, which meant he was missing friendship. It is hard not to see this as deliberate: he had locked it out, didn't want it—that way comes the deadening byt. It was a fact made painfully clear in the stark fluorescent hospital setting, far removed from the fantastical life on stage. George Balanchine didn't really have intimates.

Events moved quickly: his speech changed, and English gave way to his native Russian, transporting him back toward childhood. His sense of time collapsed, and he called the stage phone at the theater at all hours, asking his despairing dancers in Russian, French, and broken English what they were doing, or begging to talk to Karin. Karin was no Dulcinea, but she loved him at least. She was the wife he didn't have, the closest thing to a friend and lover, and although she had her own family responsibilities, she did come, often, bringing food, news, and a comforting maternal love. Morty, seeing the end, grew annoyed at Balanchine's constant calls to their home and put on an answering machine with his masculine voice firmly stating that no one was there. When Karin disappeared to Germany over Christmas, Balanchine called her mother's house day and night, and when she returned, he lay with his head resting in her lap, and she would stroke his brow and sing lieder in her native German, just like his old German nanny back in the Russia of his childhood.[32] He fixated on her, knew her footfall, forgot she had been there the moment she left, and called to berate her for ignoring him. Could she please come, now?[33]

They brought food, the only thing he had loved in life as much as women and dancing: Jacques and his wife, Carolyn, came with borscht from the Russian Tea Room, Zorina delivered wine and chocolates,[34] Dick and Kay Leach got his favorite hot cross buns from Mrs. London's bakery in Saratoga Springs,[35] and Eddie Villella arrived with Guinness Stout. Karin made the Georgian meatballs he loved and had taught her to cook, and a violinist from the orchestra who was Orthodox too brought holy water from the Russian Church uptown.[36] Misha brought spiced Georgian food, but by then Balanchine couldn't eat without choking, so he asked Misha to place a bit of the pasty *satsivi* onto his face, and Balanchine then smeared the walnuts, oils, and coriander into his skin and inhaled the scent lavishly as his face relaxed and the mask of pain fell momentarily away. Again, please.[37] Someone else brought the poster of Wonder Woman from Southampton and stuck it to the wall so that he could see it, and put a stash of slivovitz in the dresser drawers. He still had his favorite gold-coin watch, with its U.S.-dollar face, an icon of time and freedom, that he liked to proudly pull from his pocket to show admiring visitors.[38]

The parade included his ex-wives and most favored dancers, the musicians, his staff, and miscellaneous well-wishers or bottom-feeders looking for some final sign or drawn inexplicably by the spectacle of this mythic figure reduced to a mere shadow. Solomon Volkov, a new acquaintance with a knack for interviewing dying Russian artists (Shostakovich and later Joseph Brodsky and Nathan Milstein), came with his tape recorder and later produced a book that rings true (but he misplaced the tapes).[39] They all acted their parts, as people do with the dying, even those who thought they had been there but had not. Suzanne Farrell came and found mystical signs, even now, connecting his life to hers; her grandmother was sick on the floor below, and her cat Bottom—the one George had suggested she get—fell ill and died. She couldn't bear to see George this way, she said, and her visits trailed off. Ruthanna Boris came from afar wearing a Star of David, and when Balanchine reached out to touch it, she took it off and put it around his neck with his crucifix.[40]

Balanchine had never much cared for the niceties of social life, and his natural charm and sense of taste and propriety were fast deserting him. Only sex and eroticism—that final life force—seemed to interest him. He touched and admired the young women dancers who came to pay homage, tried to unbutton a shirt, stroked a leg, or asked them to dance around the room for him, which they did—a strange echo of their countless rehearsals together.[41] Could he even see their shade-like figures?

Soon he couldn't walk, and by December his lucid moments were diminishing. He was often barely coherent, unable to attend to his own toileting, crying, babbling in Russian, scratching and pulling his sheets over his head, or fingering the girly calendar left by a well-meaning visitor, or clutching the crucifix that hung from his neck on a thick gold chain.[42] Eventually he lost his speech entirely. His doctors watched helplessly, unable to understand or stem his rapid decline. They considered a brain biopsy, but decided against it—what good would it do to know more in the absence of known treatments? In lucid moments, Balanchine was still talking of Swiss clinics and longevity potions, and he reminisced with Danilova about his Magic Mountain retreat in the 1920s and told Tamara Geva, "Let's go to the country." The Russians at the school raised the possibility of taking him to the retirement community of the Tolstoy Foundation, but that went nowhere. In January several dancers had a birthday party for him in his hospital room full of the food he loved with balloons and fake gaiety, a performance marred only by his abrupt screaming fit of rage, and they left in a sad hush. Tanny visited in her wheelchair and said she wished they would feed him lots of butter so that he would die rather than suffer the humiliations of such an "undignified exit, with wail."[43]

Andrei Kramarevsky, the thick, muscular, and kindly Russian émigré that Balanchine had hired to teach at his school in 1975, provided rare relief. Together, they recited Russian poetry from memory at top voice (Pushkin, Griboyedov, Lermontov), and "Krammy" supported Balanchine's feeble limbs so that he could "walk" and carried him "like a rag doll" lovingly around the room and through the hospital halls.[44] Lincoln, presaging the power struggle to come, saw only a gloomy "coven of ghouls fluttering above George's bed . . . all waiting hopefully to cash in."[45] On cue, the board didn't wait, and on Wednesday, March 16, 1983, they announced the appointment of Peter Martins and Jerome Robbins as "ballet masters in chief."[46] Betty Cage bitterly noted that Balanchine was "not even dead yet," but the practical Horgan thought that Cage was "just angry" and didn't have an alternative. "Really, she didn't want anybody."[47] Lincoln didn't either, but he deeply resented this imperious and indecorous move by the board he had personally recruited. "They were hell-bent to do it now," he wrote to a friend; "Anyway, it's been done."[48] Balanchine wasn't informed, but he had foreseen it all in one of his legendary quips: "Après moi, le board."

As he retreated from the world, the trail of visitors thinned, and Balanchine's mind turned as if by instinct to his faith. He had fits of anxiety and fear and was haunted by visions of the Devil coming to get him. Barbara brought him a cross blessed by Pope Pius XII that a Jewish friend of hers had been given at the end of the war. Balanchine held it tightly to his chest, warding off evil: "Must believe, must believe," he whispered. "At that time he was out of his mind," Barbara later wistfully recalled, "but even so he wasn't willing to give up yet. That fucking Devil wasn't going to get him."[49] He hung on, as people do, unable to master this final loss.

The old Russians at the school found him a confessor, one Father Adrian Ouellette, a beautiful, bearded man with silky hair and a faintly exotic look, who agreed to prepare Balanchine for death.[50] An unlikely priest, Adrian was himself an outsider, an American from a broken and impoverished family in rural Massachusetts who had found his way to the Orthodox Church through Dominican nuns working with cancer patients and the ministrations of a White Russian priest. But above all, he had come to the faith through music. He had taught himself Russian, played the organ, sang, studied the musical tradition, and rose (and later fell) quickly in the ecclesiastical hierarchy.

He came daily in his robes and woolen skullcap with his portable Communion kit. He sat at the bedside, spread his cloth over the little hospital table, and carefully laid out the chalice and spoon. He poured from a plastic vial containing the Communion wine from that morning's liturgy, recited prayers to the angels, to St. George, and to other Balanchine favorites. He took Balanchine's confession: "Are you sure? Is there anything else?" He signed the cross, said the prayer of forgiveness, and administered Communion. Balanchine worked hard, Father Adrian later noted, to raise his frail arm to cross himself.[51] A friend came in February, through a snowstorm, and reflected in his diary that Balanchine was finally "facing away, like old generals do."[52]

Finally, starved of air by pneumonia, he was barely conscious. On April 30, alone in bed at night, he died.

Chapter 28

FUNERAL MARCH

It was a modest death, Lear stripped of worldly power and sound mind. Call me Georgi, he had always begged of the women he loved, wanting to be recognized as the simple man he felt like inside. But it was an epic death too because of the kingdom he had made and the world that was watching. Barbara Horgan got the call, and Lincoln Kirstein, Jerome Robbins, and Peter Martins were informed. The company had to be told, so at around 6 A.M. the staff started calling the dancers, and word quickly spread. The dancers—his dancers—did what they always did: they made their way to the theater. It was a Saturday, and they had two shows scheduled that day, matinee and evening. "Krammy" taught class, with Alla, the mystical Russian rehearsal pianist, in accompaniment, insisting with his own fierce physicality and commitment that they keep going, no matter the tears. They wandered into the familiar hallways, dazed, crying, hugging, and comforting each other in the wings. One dancer walked past the office Balanchine had shared with Jerry Robbins and saw Robbins sitting on a chair, limp and hunched, staring into space. She hugged him, thinking how much he looked like an orphan, but he hardly noticed.[1] Lincoln recorded the day blankly in his diary: "Balanchine died. Lazarus."[2] According to the Russian Orthodox calendar, this was the day of Lazarus's rising.

The world outside the company woke to the news too, and New Yorkers devoted to the NYCB made their way to the theater or gathered at SAB, where by chance the annual Workshop Performance showcasing new talent was taking place that day. The audiences in the lobby of the New York State Theater milled around, dazed, and strangers hugged each other and wept, an extraordinary scene of collective grief. Before the lights dimmed in the house, Lincoln Kirstein, all towering six feet three of him, hunched and glowering in his customary dark suit, stepped heavily in front of the curtain: "I don't have to tell you that Mr. B is with Mozart, Tchaikovsky, and Stravinsky. I do want to tell you how much he valued this audience, this marvelous audience, a big family. You kept us going 50 years and will another 50. One thing he didn't want was that this be interrupted. We will proceed. Think of yourselves as a coherent, supportive audience who understands the family that is about to perform here."[3]

Everyone that night was looking to Suzanne Farrell. At thirty-six she was still the company's most iconoclastic and physically intuitive dancer, and she saw herself as a widow of sorts. As she entered the stage to the opening notes of the lyrical second movement of Bizet's *Symphony in C*, in the role she had left and returned to, a role originally danced by Tanny that seemed to stretch across the women of Balanchine's American life, the house fell silent. "It was like a church," she later recalled,[4] and when it came to the fateful dive into a plunging arabesque at a heartbreakingly yearning phrase in the music, she seemed to reach the bottom of whatever feeling the audience shared. And if the public was overcome, so was she. At the end she couldn't quite bow. She stooped awkwardly and ran from the stage.[5]

As word spread across the country and around the world, Balanchine's small staff, exhausted and overwhelmed by the months of illness and grief and the new responsibilities suddenly thrust upon them, struggled to manage the response. Flowers, letters, telegrams, and phone calls flooded the theater: from the dancers, musicians, and stagehands; from Irving Berlin, Ray Bolger, Van Cliburn, the president of the American Federation of Musicians Local

802 (nevertheless!), Cartier, members of the board and major donors (foundations, individuals, past benefactors, Eddie Warburg, the Rockefeller family, and John Samuels, among others), and from representatives of the city, the state, and the boroughs and of Saratoga Springs, Kennedy Center, Lincoln Center, and dozens of smaller ballet companies that had looked to Balanchine as captain of the mother ship. There were notes from designers, wardrobe artists, and luminaries from Broadway, theater, and dance, including Maurice Béjart, Irina Baronova, Lew Christensen, Ruth Page, Robert Joffrey, and Merce Cunningham ("Dear Lincoln: just a word to convey my respects. So many years. It is a long and bedecked history. As always, my admiration for Mr. Balanchine and yourself. As ever, Merce"). President Ronald Reagan sent a personal note (he had awarded Balanchine the Presidential Medal of Freedom, in absentia, less than a month before). The State of New York passed a Resolution of Mourning, and Mayor Koch issued a formal statement of condolence and recognition. PBS marked the occasion with a panel and tribute to this extraordinary life. Finally, flowers and a telegram arrived from Andrei Balanchivadze from Tbilisi. He tried to come to New York for the funeral but could not get a visa, so instead Balanchine's Georgian family held their own services at the ancient Sioni Cathedral, which George had visited when he was there, and Andrei sent Georgian soil to New York to be scattered over his brother's grave.[6] Obituaries in print and on radio and TV datelined from New York to Texas and California and from Europe to Russia, Japan, India, and Australia.[7]

Balanchine's reach had been vast.

There was one final performance to prepare: the funeral. But before Balanchine's body could be sent on to the Russian Orthodox church on Ninety-third Street for the customary cleaning and prayers, the doctors at Roosevelt had a last medical procedure to perform. Carefully, methodically, they cut open the top of Balanchine's skull and surgically removed his brain. They fixed it in formalin and preserved forever this relic of the man. It was sent to a team of neurologists at Columbia University for analysis. Someone had to figure out what disease had killed George Balanchine.[8]

It took over a year for scientists to arrive at the conclusion that he had died of ataxic Creutzfeldt-Jakob disease (CJD), later commonly known (in another variant) as "mad cow disease." It was a condition barely understood at the time of his death, which may be why the diagnosis had been so elusive, although it was also true that the severity of Balanchine's clinical signs had been masked by his physical skills. The breakthrough work in discovering the disease was done by Dr. Stanley Prusiner in 1982 with the discovery of infectious proteins called prions, but the work was only fully accepted by the medical community long after Balanchine's death. There was no cure. Thin sections or layers cut from Balanchine's preserved brain treated and studied under a microscope revealed spongiform degeneration in the cerebellum along with numerous "kuru" plaques. It was the kuru that made Balanchine's case unusual, since these distinctive plaques had first been found among the Fore people of New Guinea—*kuru* was a word in the local language describing people mysteriously afflicted with a trembling state, severe loss of balance, memory loss, and eventual death. The Fore were cannibals whose women customarily ate the brains of the dead to give them eternal life. Because women were thought to have "higher" spiritual powers, they bore responsibility for this lineage.[9]

Years later, as the science improved, doctors returned to Balanchine's brain. Prusiner examined the samples and confirmed the CJD diagnosis, and others used material to successfully transmit Balanchine's CJD to a chimp, which suggests that the disease might indeed have been a transmissible form.[10] He could have gotten it from an injection containing human pituitary-gland extract ground from cadavers, still in use in the 1970s and 1980s, or perhaps from polluted food during the cruel revolutionary years. But it may still have been a "sporadic" case—a bolt from the sky: "Time to Go!" No one exactly knows, but rumors nonetheless persisted that Balanchine had died from his lifelong pursuit of youth and virility. If not, he was taken by chance or fate, another great theme in his life and dances. The probability of getting the disease in its sporadic form? One in a million.[11]

The ironies of the disease and the ongoing scientific interest in his brain would not have been lost on Balanchine, who once said when asked about the sources of his creativity, "It's Donovan's brain, dear," referring to the popular 1950s sci-fi book and film in which a dead man's still-living brain is surgically removed and wired to his doctor, who suddenly finds himself thinking the dead man's thoughts.[12] Not to mention echoes of the themes that filled his life: the spirituality of women, the fountain of youth, progress, science, potions, injections, balance, madness, memory, and not least, the dark-cloaked figure of fate.

In keeping with Russian Orthodox tradition, the funeral services began immediately. High-ranking authorities in the Church, however, were not sure they should happen at all. In their eyes, Balanchine was unredeemable. Orthodoxy allows only one marriage, maybe two, three *à la limite*, and Balanchine's four marriages and additional common-law wife—not to mention all the other women everyone knew he had loved, the rumors of sex, and the whispers of abortions—put him firmly outside Church bounds. He had not even bothered to seek the required blessing of the Church for his marriages and divorces. Worse still, they said, Balanchine had dedicated his life to mounting patently erotic dances that displayed scantily clad women on a public stage. As a matter of tradition and faith, Orthodox bishops and deacons are not supposed to attend the ballet, with its temptingly beautiful dancers, and Balanchine—it was undeniable—had hewn closely to a life of the flesh. He had even wanted to stage the sacrilege *Salomé*. What they failed to see, perhaps because this too was a kind of apostasy, was that he was a deeply mystical man who had drawn widely from any faith or philosophy that offered him insight or solace, including Sufism and Judaism, along with hybrid mystical varieties, such as Theosophy. But his commitment to his native Orthodoxy was firm, part of his commitment to Russia and the past, and it was also part of his ballets.

Like Balanchine, Father Adrian had little sympathy with the rigidly doctrinaire positions of the official Church. He insisted that Balanchine had repented and come to God and that his artistic practices had enriched so many lives. "He was like St. Nicholas, a wonderworker. And besides," he noted with sarcasm, "what do *you* know about him?" and "Who are *you* to cast stones?"[13] After difficult internal debate, the Church agreed to the requiem services on the stingy condition that high clergy not lead the service or bless it with too much attendance. This suited Father Adrian fine—he would personally lead the proceedings.[14]

Balanchine's church, or the church of his funeral services, was the Synodal Cathedral of the Sign, part of the Russian Orthodox Church Outside of Russia, which had been founded in Europe during the Russian Revolution as an outpost for émigrés, exiles, and other displaced persons. A stronghold of the White Russian aristocracy, its headquarters had moved to New York in the 1950s and acquired the elegant Baker mansion from the widow of George Baker, scion of American finance. The Baker ballroom became the Orthodox cathedral, and the old dining room served as an adjacent chapel. There was a Steinway, a sign of the Church's serious musical tradition and society past, and the congregation included princes, princesses, and high-ranking families from old Russia's ruling elite—Obolensky, Taneyev, Romanov, Ouroussow (including Balanchine's own Eugenie)—along with prominent American believers such as Yul Brenner and Vitali Ustinov. It was a fitting if not entirely welcoming destination for Balanchine, who was an exile but not a prince, and whose modest family of Georgian peasants and musicians made him an outsider to the White Russian aristocracy, a self-consciously elite society he both coveted and disdained.

The body. It had to be properly dressed. The ballet master John Taras—ever fastidious, devoted, useful—noticed Balanchine's unkempt appearance and took it upon himself to go to the choreographer's apartment and pick out the best suit he could find and bring it back to the church, along with one of the silk foulard scarves Balanchine liked to wear, elegantly knotted, and the Presidential Medal of Freedom—which Balanchine himself had never seen.[15]

The next day Taras brought an antique cross and laid it in Balanchine's hands and slipped another cross into the choreographer's suit pocket. Someone later placed under his wrist a small icon of St. George, his patron saint, taken perhaps from the collection of icons on his bedside table. Finally, the traditional scroll was draped over Balanchine's brow: "Holy God, Holy Mighty, Holy Immortal, have mercy on me." The body was now presentable: cleaned and dressed, with eyes closed and mouth set in a neutral masklike expression—an inanimate copy of Balanchine's customary calm. Barbara and

Eddie had chosen an Orthodox Jewish coffin, wooden with no metal, nothing fancy: Balanchine had always insisted he was a simple man and he hated "fancy" explanations of life and art, so why should his death be any different. On the day of the service, a Russian Orthodox funeral crown was laid on his head and a fresh red rose pinned to his lapel.[16] Gardenias and ivy decorated the coffin, and banks of flowers sent by his dancers piled up against the walls, like the ballets he always said were like flowers, beautiful and then gone, requiring no explanation.

The body mattered greatly, even lying there now, dead and without a brain. Unlike Roman Catholicism, which discounts the carcass and emphasizes the rising spirit, Russian Orthodoxy reveres the body too. "The best icon of God is man," the priest intones as he censes the congregation. Even in a fallen state, man can work through faith to become by degrees physically deified, and the devout are carefully watched after death to see if their bodies decay—an uncorrupted body is proof of saintliness. No one was expecting this of Balanchine, but seeing him there in this last pose, it was hard not to recall that the body had been the subject of his life. "The *soul* is *in* the body," as he had once explained, a bit defensively; "you have to be conscious of your body, you have to do something with it! *What* do you do? . . . [You] can entertain people. . . . We don't sin by dancing. We use our bodies like flowers in the field which are growing and beautiful."[17] Finally, on the Last Day, when the dead rise, Orthodox Christians say that God will bestow on each repentant soul a spiritualized body to serve him in the newly transfigured heavenly world. Both body and soul have a place in the afterlife, which Balanchine seemed to believe and not believe, even as he had devoted his life to dance and its ritual forms. Orthodoxy is best seen, smelt, and heard, rather than read: "Come and see" (John 1:46). It has even been argued within the faith that the body makes people higher, not lower, than the angels, a "synergy" of all of God's creation, material and spiritual, in one being. A people of the book, but also, in Balanchine's life, a people of the body.

For his dancers, all of this was connected to dancing. It is worth remembering, as Balanchine's body was prepared for the funeral march, the cleansing sweat and daily rituals of these dancers; the discipline, rote repetition, and self-denial; the fasting, chronic pain, and physical and emotional exhaustion—

all for the at times transporting experience of dancing one of Balanchine's glorious dances. They had given themselves to sensuality and metamorphoses, to making their bodies, and themselves, into something strange and not quite human—airy, flexible, mutable like clay. They were erotic, machines, angels, and fallen people—all at the same time. More seductive still, it was all so blissfully impersonal and free of the tiresome "I" and pedestrian problems of life. They were in service to some higher purpose—to Balanchine, art, God, who knew exactly what. "They love me for my ballets," as he had ironically observed, and it was true, even now.

The religious observations began on May 1. In keeping with Orthodox custom, the open coffin sat in the center of the ballroom cathedral from the moment the body arrived at the church until the requiem and burial on May 3. Services began that first evening at 8:00 with a private memorial for a few of Balanchine's closest associates, a quickly and somewhat haphazardly arranged group: "All of us went off to see Bal at the memorial," Jacques d'Amboise wrote in his diary as if he were running off to rehearsal, except that when he got there, "Bal" "looked like a solidified plaster replica—very tearful time.... Oh! I will be a long time adjusting to this."[18] There was a second service at 2:00 P.M. the following day, and the media arrived to film and photograph the ceremonies. On the morning of May 3, crowds arrived for the public service. They started coming at 8:30 for the 9:00 A.M. liturgical mass and 11:00 A.M. requiem service, and by midmorning more than a thousand people were crowded into the small cathedral or spilled out onto the ivy-covered balconies and into the stone courtyard and streets below. The church, officials admitted, had never been so well attended.

It was a warm and humid overcast day, and Lincoln Kirstein stood stoically in the courtyard receiving the mourners, his towering figure rooted to the spot. He had been standing by Balanchine since 1933, for most of his adult life, and he naturally assumed his position as the senior representative of the NYCB with his characteristic gravitas. It was barely a year since Kirstein had turned from Judaism to Catholicism, inching himself closer to Balanchine even in death.[19] With him stood Jerome Robbins and Peter Martins, like heads of family, or appointees in an apostolic succession of their own devising. Upstairs in the ballroom-cathedral, the coffin stood in the middle of the icon-laden room, where waltzing had once occurred, and a couple of photographers (one of them a former NYCB dancer), stood nervously waiting to document the event.[20] The mourners gathered around in a thick crowd. There are no pews in an Orthodox church, and the attendees are part of the service, on stage rather than watching, so they all stood shoulder to shoulder, each holding the requisite flickering taper candle. Only the wives stood apart, at the head of the coffin near the gilt iconostasis. They had each entered privately through a special passageway and taken their positions like figureheads on a ship's prow. It reminded one dancer of a Fellini film—all those wives in dark glasses, except that in reality there were no glasses, and they were all bare-eyed.[21]

The wives stood arrayed like the epochs of his life. He had "lived for a very long time," as he liked to say, through most of the twentieth century, and each of these women had accompanied him for part of the journey: Tamara Geva, Alexandra Danilova, Maria Tallchief, and Tanaquil Le Clercq. Only Vera Zorina was notably missing from the church that day. She was perhaps the wife Balanchine had loved most passionately, too passionately she later said, but she had never quite loved him back and sent white roses in her place.[22] The almost-wives were there too: Diana Adams, and of course Suzanne Farrell, who was escorted, as usual, by Eddie Bigelow. Farrell laid her own dozen white roses, tied with a wide blue ribbon, among the gardenias by the wall, and Karin von Aroldingen stood close by. Lucia Davidova was present with her perfectly smoothed coal-black hair and string of pearls, and Barbara Horgan and Betty Cage were there. Many of the mourners wept, but the wives all stood dry-eyed. There would be no wailing or unleashing of sentiment from them, just as there had been no wailing or unleashing of sentiment in his ballets. These were women with the restraint and poise their lives and profession had demanded, and they played their roles unflinchingly.[23]

The service was long—over two hours in Russian with incense and a full choir. The congregation, pressed tightly together, was perfectly still and silent. The heat from the candles, the smell of spiced incense and sweet flowers, the sweat and humidity, and the dim light and ritual chanting and endless incantations made it a physically draining experience. At least one person fainted, propped by the forested crowd, and the young dancers in particular appeared ashen—frail nymphs with long thin hair, wan, drained of color, shades in a mist of incense. The eulogy was delivered by Father Adrian, and His Grace Bishop Gregory deigned to deliver a few parting remarks in English. Gregory, alias George Grabbe, son of a Russian count who had fled the revolution, passed over Balanchine's momentous artistic life and piously dwelled on the facts that as a child George had joined the Church as an altar boy and that his relatives were clergymen "of high rank." Dick Leach noted in his diary: "The archbishop barely avoided caricature (which George would have enjoyed)." No matter: "The choir sang marvelously."[24] Tanny, who thought the priests were all Rasputins, watched with a sardonic glint and saw the dark humor in it all.

Finally, the moment came for the "Last Kiss." The formless crowd gradually made a line behind Father Adrian, and the procession past the coffin began, a choreography Balanchine himself had taught them in the funeral scene of *Don Quixote*. Back then, he had lain as if in a coffin on stage, arms crossed over his chest, just as he lay now, as the mourners all filed past and each in turn bent into the coffin to kiss his forehead and bid a final farewell. As she leaned to deliver her kiss, Farrell recognized the scroll draped across his brow just as it had been in the ballet. The final absolution was delivered, and the funeral cloth was drawn up over the coffin. The attendees all blew out their candles and placed them in the baskets provided. The coffin was closed, lifted on the shoulders of the pallbearers, and, led by Father Adrian and the wives, Balanchine was carried out of the ballroom and down the stairs into the courtyard, where the hearse awaited.

As the coffin reached the courtyard, one mourner noticed "that Mount Rushmore figure of Kirstein's began to quake. He sobbed mightily."[25] For Kirstein it must have felt like the end of an era—his era—and his collapsing face seemed to sum up the moment and all they had lost. Alexandra Danilova, looking frayed and emptied, with her heavy mascara and thinning hair, could be seen following the hearse alone down the middle of Park Avenue in a daze, trailing after Balanchine and the past they had shared as he disappeared in the distance.[26] Church officials, not knowing what to do with the unprecedented number of flowers that had been delivered to the church, set them all on the sidewalk like a giant bouquet, and they disappeared within minutes, mementos for the mourners. At Kirstein's special request, they held back Farrell's white roses for the burial, but in the confusion, someone took those too. In an inspired moment of theatrical improvisation, a woman backstage at the church quickly ordered an identical bunch from the local florist. He was out of long-stem whites but brought as many short-stem roses as he could find, and they were ceremonially placed on the coffin in the hearse.[27]

The burial was small—some were invited; others simply came; a few didn't even know it was happening. They drove to Sag Harbor's Oakland Cemetery in five black limousines. Barbara Horgan had chosen the spot based on her conversation with Balanchine after Eugenie Ouroussow's funeral in 1976. "Not for me," he had said, as they left the church. "Cremation." He didn't want to go to Venice, where Stravinsky and Diaghilev were both buried, he said; "it is damp, cold and Paris is worse—I got consumption there—better cremated." But the Russians—there were still several at the school who had known him for decades—were appalled and adamantly refused: the Orthodox Church does not allow cremation. On another occasion, Balanchine had told Robbins he wanted to be buried in Monaco: "There is where I started—there is where I want to end."[28] And in the hospital, he had told Hugo Fiorato that he didn't want to lie in Europe: "No, I am an American, I want to be buried in Sag Harbor, besides, it is near the railroad so if anyone wants to come see me it would be easy for them."[29] But Horgan didn't know about any of that.

When Balanchine was in the hospital, Horgan had driven around to different cemeteries on Long Island looking for a spot near his Southampton home, where he had enjoyed time with Karin and her family. He and Karin had once gone for lunch in Sag Harbor, and he had phoned Barbara to say that it was just like the South of France, a strange impression of this small nineteenth-century whaling town, with its quaint Americana. When Horgan came upon Oakland Cemetery, situated in the town, with its tranquil lawns and smell of the nearby sea, she called Tanny and Karin, and they agreed. There were more negotiations with the Russians since it was not consecrated ground, but a compromise was finally reached. The gravestone itself would be consecrated instead. Kirstein, in a final set design, ordered this last prop from the John Stevens Shop, one of the nation's oldest, which had also made memorial stones for John F. Kennedy and Tennessee Williams, among other American luminaries. Kirstein chose a durable Tennessee pink marble with hand-carved roman lettering and a simple arch shape, rather than a more ornate design inspired by Russian architecture. At its top the stone would show a Russian Orthodox cross, like the cross of St. Vladimir in the Church of the Transfiguration at Kizhi Pogost; then "George Balanchine, 1904–1983, Ballet Master"; and finally an engraved lyre. The stone was consecrated by Father Adrian and would be set in place in April of the following year.[30]

It was an odd resting place, this old nineteenth-century cemetery with whalers, local citizens, and a few other well-known artists and writers. This was not the celebrity burial ground farther north that housed Jackson Pollock and Willem de Kooning, among others, but a more modest retreat. Aside from a chance lunch, Sag Harbor and Oakland had nothing to do with Balanchine, really, and maybe that was the point. Alone and unmarried, an exile without children or family nearby, there was no natural place for him. He had no native soil, and this bucolic plot in the center of a small American town in a protected harbor on a spit of land jutting out into the Atlantic was about as close as he could come to being alone or sprinkled into the ocean itself. It was on America's farthest edge, looking out toward Europe: these were the two continents of his life and art. Russia was a vanished shore. Danilova, who was also alone, later joined him in the plot next door.

The limousines arrived. Storm clouds threatened but never burst, and Father Adrian led the services as each member of the small party threw a long-stem rose and a handful of dirt onto the coffin before it was lowered. Tanny clutched her flowers and leaned effortfully in her wheelchair, pitched at a dangerous angle, to toss her bouquet. Barbara and Karin, the last women in his life, threw the last roses into the grave, and as they all left, Karin's teenage daughter, Margo, stayed behind to pat the coffin as the gravediggers prepared to lower it into the earth. Jacques returned to have a private moment just in time to take Margo into his arms and lift her out of the way. As the funeral party drove out of the cemetery gates, they passed Suzanne Farrell, who had not been told when or where to go, arriving alone with Eddie Bigelow—late like the lost girl in *Serenade*. She found the coffin still visible, said some prayers, added her own white rose along with a handful of dirt, and went home. The others adjourned to eat and drink some of Balanchine's favorite foods at the home of friends Robert Fizdale and Arthur Gold: beluga caviar, orange cake, and plenty of vodka.

That night, Jacques d'Amboise wrote in his diary: "The day was extraordinary all those loving people because of a giant of Dance who really didn't care much for anybody."[31] It was a shocking statement, which was both true and not true. He did care, sometimes too much, but he drew the line at art. Which meant that in the end, in the bitter end, his life was not them but them on the stage. Love mattered more than ballet, but not in his life, or at least not in the life he had led.

Even if Balanchine was dead, the NYCB was not, and the company was by then a significant institution employing more than one hundred dancers, not to mention musicians, stagehands, and administrators. These were Balanchine's people, and he had been at the center of the entire NYCB enterprise from the start and deeply involved in the direction and daily running of the organization. He was never only an artist: he was also a company man, because a theater and making dancers was part of making dances. Everyone knew that the NYCB was openly, if quietly, autocratic—one man, one rule—and each and every individual who worked there, from principal dancers to stagehands, had felt the touch of Balanchine. "You can imagine what it is like," Kirstein wrote shortly after his death, "not to have an autocrat-tyrant-dictator. . . . We can call it the shift from autocracy to democracy, but this hardly explains it to those who for fifty years have gone on the assumption that there has been but one voice."[32] The effect on the dancers was immediate, and even Farrell "felt insecure in a way I never had before. . . . The theater was filled with dancers walking around, taking class, rehearsing, doing silly things, none of which seemed to make sense anymore."[33]

When Balanchine's will was revealed, the company faced a crisis. The ballets had all been willed to individual people, and the NYCB had received nothing at all. The company found itself stranded, with no clear right to perform any of Balanchine's dances. Members of the board were confused and outraged—"We didn't own one god damn Balanchine ballet," the then chair later recalled.[34] As legal counsel, Randal Craft was furious and led the board in a call to contest the will, arguing that the ballets belonged not to Balanchine himself, but to the company that had hired him. He orchestrated an overture to the wives in a vain attempt to elicit their support, but Barbara Horgan had their loyalty, more or less, and did not agree. His was a difficult claim, Craft later admitted, considering that Balanchine had founded the company and had barely been paid and had not even taken a salary until the Ford Foundation mandated it. But it did seem reasonable to Craft and others that the NYCB at least had an "implied right" to perform Balanchine's dances. The board was happy to pay. Tanny was offered $1 million for her rights and turned it sharply down—*her* dances were not for sale. Finally, someone on the board brought in an outside consultant from the legal firm Paul, Weiss, who warned them: you are threatening to sue Balanchine's heirs, including Tanny—who *will* be wheeled out in her wheelchair—not to mention Kirstein, cofounder of the company and a monumental cultural figure. If you bring a lawsuit, you will probably lose—and pay damages. The board capitulated. The estate controlled everything.[35]

Meanwhile, Barbara Horgan had hired Paul Epstein, a lawyer of Russian Jewish descent who had been going to the NYCB every night since the mid-1960s, "easily the greatest experience of my life." Kirstein, who at this point didn't like much of anything, found him "an aggressive (excuse me, Jewish) lawyer who has been trying to get on the NYCB Board for years. . . . He is 'impossible.'"[36] Epstein immediately realized that the problem was legal but that it was also and perhaps above all practical: If a company or an individual wanted to mount a ballet, who would they go to? Who would teach the ballets, and who would be paid and how? What if Karin or Barbara or any of the other legatees passed away or got sick? Then the company wanting to mount the ballet would have to go through the designated successors, who might not know or care. The tradition, which was really a genealogy, could be easily broken and the works scattered and made unavailable or lost—to the NYCB or anyone else. The lawyer who made the original will had advised Balanchine to put everything in trust, but he had refused. Too complicated. And what about Barbara? As executor, heir, and an employee of the NYCB, she was mired in conflicting interests. It was, as she later reflected, "a mess."[37]

The IRS got involved—taxes were owed, surely, but no one knew how much the ballets were worth. Balanchine had assumed they had no value, but the Feds disagreed and after years of wrangling finally decided that most of the dances would last about five years and that twelve of the greatest works might last fifteen years. On this somewhat arbitrary basis, they valued the repertory at $550,000, and the entire taxable estate at just over $1 million—a number which apparently included the Swiss bank account Balanchine had secretly kept "just in case" he needed to return to Europe unexpectedly, and which Barbara declared reluctantly, since she knew most of it would disappear in taxes.[38]

To fix the problem of the NYCB, Horgan and the trustees worked with Epstein to establish and administer a trust that would hold all the ballets and direct the income to the people Balanchine had designated in his will. All the legatees joined the trust in one way or another—some gave their inheritance outright, while others (such as Tanny, who still wanted to own her dances)—kept them but allowed the trust to help administer the rights and also willed the rights to or through the trust. The NYCB was given a five-year renewable license to perform all the ballets and granted exclusive rights to use Balanchine's name for fundraising. They could also prevent competing performances of any given Balanchine work by other troupes. Control was strictly centralized: ballet companies wishing to stage a work were required to work with a dancer assigned by the trust, and a group of repetiteurs was established to stage Balanchine's work around the world. Finally, Epstein helped to establish a protected trademark to prevent "just anyone" from mounting a dance. Through these clever legal mechanisms, the ballets acquired a brand-new lease on life—an afterlife that had nothing to do with Balanchine himself. Ironically, Horgan and the trustees found themselves at the head of a new priesthood, dedicated to guarding the Balanchine flame and maintaining the dances that he himself had declared extinct: "Not my ballets."

As it turned out, he wasn't quite right that the ballets didn't exist without him and his chosen dancers. They were like houses that could be filled and lived in by others. Or like a bed, to take one of his metaphors, that shapes to the body lying in it. They were the frame of the house, the skeleton of a butterfly, and how a dance would look, what it would be, the color, the character of the wood and floors, the pace and swoop of the wing, the trajectory of flight—that was up to future dancers. It looked one way with his dancers and would look radically another way with other dancers: "Not my ballets," but yes his ballets, nevertheless. As remnants of genius, they exist, fragile organisms, embattled and subject to human whim, reinvented or reincarnated until they might or might not be recognizable as—as what? Memory, fact, fate, some document in the sky? What could he leave—his nose? They are the cloud, the spirit, the perishable and immortal thing he left behind. And yet they survived under that little caveat, the insistent physical paradox that stood behind everything. The ballets only existed because of the dancers; but for the dancers, they only existed because of Mr. B and who he was, the life he had lived, and the eye and ear he cast over them nightly. Never underestimate the power of watching, for the watcher or the watched, or what can happen when the watcher is gone.

There was one last thing. His theater, his ballets, and his dancers were the ultimate exile: a whole invented world to replace the one he had lost. He had left Russia forever, but for all his Americana, he didn't really live anywhere. He made his own place from bits of the old world, and the shiny and dull pieces he picked up along the way. This is my small corner of the world, he kept saying; "we are born individuals, we want to have our little place,"[39] and his ballets were his little place with his dancers away from the "awful" people who killed and criticized and didn't understand anything. Where else could he live but there, in his own little place? And where else could he die?

Chapter 29

ADAGIO LAMENTOSO

It ended with a question. A little boy dressed in white appears holding a candle. A man asks him, "Tell me where this light comes from." The boy blows out the candle and replies, "If you tell me where this light went, I will tell you where it comes from." It was a Sufi parable, perhaps of Turkish origin, Balanchine said, implying not far from his Georgian roots.[1]

When the candle went out at the end of the ballet, Balanchine wanted the theater to go entirely black. Like the "black light" of bewilderment, the only true knowledge, described by some Sufi masters, when the visible world disappears and the Absolute or Divine, hidden in the darkness, comes to "light." Before the performance, Ronnie Bates and the crew rushed around covering every last source of light, from the illuminated exit signs to the thirty-watt bulb no one had noticed in the second-wing projection booth. The backstage work lights were similarly extinguished, and the stage cues even called for the orchestra lights to go black at the end. It was important. No light anywhere, please, nothing, nothing.[2]

Adagio Lamentoso was the last movement of the last symphony Tchaikovsky ever composed. He conducted its premiere nine days before his own tragic death from cholera, in 1893, at the age of fifty-three. Like many people at the time, Balanchine believed that Tchaikovsky had committed suicide because of persecution for his homosexuality, another artist driven to a mad act by a cruel and feckless society and "those dark people who don't understand anything."[3] Tchaikovsky had originally called this sixth and final symphony *Life!*, and he told his nephew, whom he loved passionately and to whom the symphony was dedicated, that he envisioned "a programmatic symphony, but with a program that shall remain a riddle to all—let them guess." He added, "Composing it I wept a lot." He envisioned four movements: "First movement—all upsurge, confidence, thirst for action. Must be short. (The finale is *death*—the result of destruction); 2nd movement is love; 3rd disappointment; 4th ends with a dying-out (also short)."[4]

In the end, Tchaikovsky found his own titles for his new symphony too programmatic, so he resorted to his brother's last-minute idea to call it the *Pathétique*. Balanchine, who said he was in touch with the dead Tchaikovsky, broke apart the movements, and like breaking bread or distributing the territories of a kingdom, he handed them to his closest collaborators. He omitted the first movement, with its references to the Russian Orthodox burial hymn for the dead, "Repose the Soul." This was not the moment to begin at the end, so he began instead with the second, the lyrical Allegro con Grazia, which he gave to Jerome Robbins, who made a beautiful *Serenade*-like bow to Balanchine. The third, Allegro Molto Vivace, with its energetic proclamations and full-throated joys, went to Robert Irving and the orchestra, who played it without dancers in front of a lowered curtain. The fourth, Adagio Lamentoso, was for Balanchine himself.[5]

Adagio Lamentoso didn't take much rehearsal. There were no steps, just gestures and bodies slumped and emptied in grief. There were no roles, no names, no curtain calls. Unusually, the dancers were not even listed in the program. It was performed only once, as the closing movement of the closing ballet on the closing night of the Tchaikovsky Festival in 1981, just as Balanchine's illness was overtaking him. Later, no one could quite remember these dances, or what they had all done that night. Even the lighting cues were not written out but hastily scribbled since they knew the ballet would not be repeated. It was as if the tissue of the ballet dissolved in their bodies as they performed it, leaving no trace—nothing, nothing.[6]

It was made from wisps of movement and memory. There were shadows of the monks from his uncle's investiture at the great Kazan Cathedral and of Goleizovsky's breathing cross in war-stricken revolutionary Petrograd. There were the seraphim of the Orthodox Church, which he had woven through *The Nutcracker* and into *Noah and the Flood* and *Don Quixote*. There was the innocent child, the mystical themes and parables, and Karin running like the wind and mourning like the Fates. And, of course, there was Tchaikovsky, who seemed to span all time and all Russias and had accompanied Balanchine from his youth to his first American dance and through to this, his final sojourn. Tchaikovsky's tremendous score brought them all together, the old dancers and the new, the ones who were there and the ones who were not, the women he had loved and the people who had come, and the stagehands responsible for putting out the lights. They were all his people, his animals, his spirit world, his life.

The dancers didn't know any of that, but everyone present backstage that night knew that this dance mattered greatly to him, that it was a ballet unlike any other ballet he had made, and they were part of it. As the dance ended and the curtain fell, a man called from the audience, "Vive Tchaikovsky!," but most people were hushed and astonished as they trailed out into the summer night. Robbins found the whole thing "heartbreaking in intent—& nearly corny in execution—& finally crushing."[7]

Adagio Lamentoso, with its crying musical peaks and mournful lows, like the rending of heaven and earth or the full baring of a human soul, opened on a dark and empty stage with six pools of light. The light was a special "no-color blue," so-called since it gave off only a cool white, no warmth. Three women—graces, fates, women of any kind—emerged from the back in pale blue-green flowing gowns, hair down and barefoot. They gestured to one another with the lilt of a body, the turn of a back, a fleeting embrace. No expression, no acting, pure bodily feeling, nothing else. They ran aimlessly apart and together, held on, and finally found themselves each alone, encircled in a pool of light, shoulders collapsed, heads hung sadly down.

The music swelled and pitched and a rush of new dancers in beige flowing garments flooded onto the stage, hands clasped in prayerful positions as they folded over themselves, doubled in grief, and fell to their knees, foreheads to the floor, hair spilled over their heads and arms outstretched, palms open to the steel-blue sky. A moment of pause before the music rose again, this time like a clearing, to herald a group of magnificent white angels, women harnessed to huge, diaphanous seraphim wings that glistened in a warm white light that streamed from the sides onto the moodily darkened stage. Each carried a single long-stem lily, and they glided in procession along the diagonals as the mourners whirled through and around them.

Next came a group in dark, hooded gowns, deep purples and reds, who joined this growing community of mourners and quietly took their places in the crowded midst of sunken women, as they formed a semicircle, hair and palms to the floor, or lost themselves moving through the ether, reaching for someone with fragile arms. People seemed to be everywhere, disappearing and reappearing, until the music fell down, down, down, and the women faded away, except for the three, each collapsed like a pile of soft flesh in her pool of light.

Then, monk-like black-cloaked men emerged and solemnly took the stage. A cross of light appeared on the floor, and the men prostrated themselves upon it, forming the dark mass of a living, breathing crucifix, shades of the breathing cross from Balanchine's youth. It heaved like the earth as the music slowly rose and fell, rose and fell, rose and fell.[8]

Finally, with the faint sound of the bassoon, a single bright light shone on a small boy in a white gown standing at the back corner of the darkened stage. Carrying a lit candle in both hands, the boy walked slowly across the back of the stage and turned to stand with his light at the head of the breathing cross. The music thinned and sank into a series of barely perceptible drum strokes, the beat of time, of a clock, of a heart. The cross stilled, and the earth closed. The lights went dark except for the single flame of the candle, and in a last breath, as the music ended, the boy in white blew out the candle. The theater plunged to black.

AUTHOR'S NOTE

Sometimes I feel as if I have been in pursuit of Balanchine my whole life. I grew up at the University of Chicago in an intense family of intellect and words, and dancing came to me like a revelation. It was blissfully free of words, a world of body and music that seemed to say things that words could not. I made my way to New York as a teenager in the mid-1970s and found myself immersed in Balanchine's Russian-émigré world in the years before his death. My audition at his school was in Russian, and my teachers included perfumed old dancers born in imperial St. Petersburg, such as Felia Doubrovska and Alexandra Danilova, who taught in wispy pastel chiffons, wore false eyelashes, and talked of the czar and Paris in the 1920s; or later émigrés such as the hobbled Helene Dudin (crippled, it was said, by the Soviets), Antonina Tumkovsky (Tumy), and Andrei Kramarevsky (Krammy). They were offset by the airy Muriel Stuart, who had danced with Pavlova; Stanley Williams, a quietly intellectual Dane; and Suki Schorer, a matter-of-fact American dancer who explained it all to us. I trained too with Joysanne Sidimus, Mimi Paul, and Melissa Hayden. I was invited by Suzanne Farrell, who taught advanced classes at the school, to spend a summer studying with her and Paul Mejia on their island in upstate New York and to her home near Lincoln Center (where I also met Romana); after I stopped dancing, we saw each other over the years, and I continued to learn from her more than I can say. These dancers are all characters in our story.

Meanwhile, at the school, I watched Balanchine rehearse, and snuck into performances nightly. I even took his ballet class once and participated as a student extra in *Adagio Lamentoso*, the late ballet about angels and death. I danced professionally with Maria Tallchief, Balanchine's third wife, and with his former dancers Francia Russell and Kent Stowell at the Pacific Northwest Ballet, where I had a chance to perform many Balanchine ballets myself. I went on to work closely with Jacques d'Amboise at his National Dance Institute, and I came to know other former NYCB dancers, who told me stories of *their* Mr. B. When Balanchine died, I was in New York and made the pilgrimage to the theater and attended the funeral service at the Russian Orthodox church.

Still, researching Balanchine for this book has been the greatest adventure and challenge of my professional life. I worked for over a decade, and he led me to archives across Russia, Europe, and the Americas and into vast areas of literature, music, and art: Sufism and mysticism, Plato, Galen, Spinoza, Goethe, Cervantes, and Hoffmann, to mention a few favorites, along with Pushkin, Tolstoy, Dostoyevsky, Gogol, Mayakovsky, Blok, and Bulgakov—and the Bible, always the Bible. I found myself immersed in art from icons and religious and Renaissance painting to Malevich, Beckmann, Dalí, Gross, Matisse, Picasso, Derain, and Tchelitchew—many of whom Balanchine knew and worked with. I learned about starvation, TB, polio, mad cow disease, and other ailments that afflicted his body and threatened his life. I went to St. Petersburg and retraced his childhood path and followed him to Georgia, the mythic land he claimed as his own but only laid eyes on in 1962 at the height of the Cold War. I met what family remains, found his mother's home, and stood by his father's grave; I traveled to the Gelati Monastery up a winding road high on a misty peak, where an old photo shows Balanchine gazing at the ancient frescoes, outlawed as objects of veneration by the Soviets in their anti-God fury. I went to the hospital in Copenhagen where he cared for his fifth wife, Tanaquil Le Clercq, after she was stricken with polio, and traversed the streets and canals of the city. I climbed the stairs of his apartment in Paris and dined at the hotel in Hamburg where he wept in debilitating rage over unrequited love. I went to theaters and Orthodox churches everywhere.

The cast of characters was huge, from the family he left in Russia, the towering roles played by Lincoln Kirstein and Jerome Robbins, his five wives and many loves, right down to the last stagehand at the theater. He seemed to stand at the apex of all their lives, and I spent hours reading letters and diaries—Igor Stravinsky, Vera Zorina, Tanny, Maria, Jerry, Betty Cage, Barbara Horgan, Jacques d'Amboise and other dancers, and, of course, Lincoln, inexhaustible Lincoln, whose diaries and vast correspondence are spread in archives across the country and occupied me for months at a time, an engrossing experience that often left me in tears at his intensity and faults, his pain and person. I even shadowed Balanchine's past biographers, poring over their notes and interviews and unraveling their paths into his life.

Music, Balanchine's holiest of holies, took me from Bach, Mozart, and Tchaikovsky through to Stravinsky, Hindemith, Ives, American jazz, and the experiments of Xenakis. His compositional sophistication in piecing together scores from a variety of musical sources made understanding his theatricality a fascinating and daunting task. All along the way, I consulted experts, read and listened voraciously, wondered at my ability to absorb the range of his experience, and more than once considered abandoning the project, certain I was not up to the task. Encountering Balanchine's mind was awe-inspiring. How could a single person encompass all that he did? And how could such a person be so humble? He was deeply flawed and human, but also genuinely otherworldly—not of this life, and he knew it.

Above all, I grew to know Balanchine through his dancers. Over years I interviewed nearly two hundred of them—a small sample of the many he worked with—and I can attest to the fact that Balanchine attracted and chose unusually eccentric and fascinating people. I was lucky. The society of his dancers was and remains forbiddingly tight-knit. One dancer circled her arms and clasped her hands in front of her to make the point: you are either in or out. I was a bit of both. I was the dancer who always had a yellow pad and the scholar and critic who had sat on both sides of the footlights and sifted through archives in search of the history of the art. It mattered that I had danced myself, and many of his dancers—not all—invited me into their homes, met with me in cafés, or came to my home, often repeatedly, and talked with me; shared diaries, photographs, home movies, and letters; and allowed me into their memories and experiences.

Finally, there were the dances. Beautiful, glamorous, glorious, strange, outrageous, at times gruesome. Some I knew well, and others were lost, but I did my best to capture what I could of them—or a few of them—in words. Not the dances themselves, of course, but the ideas I saw and felt, as well as some sense of what it might have been like to move that way. Balanchine was a watcher, and in my own small way, I was a watcher too. He was watching the world. I was watching him. Or, rather, I was watching his dancers who, in some alchemy of art, were also him. As he liked to point out, without them, the ballets don't exist, and nor does he. They called him "Mr. B."

ACKNOWLEDGMENTS

These acknowledgments are made with a full heart, but they cannot include the vast number of people who helped and shaped my sense of Balanchine and his world. In the decade, lifetime really, of research for this book, I would nonetheless like to formally thank a few people for all they have done to make *Mr. B* possible.

I begin with Barbara Horgan, Ellen Sorrin, and Nicole Cornell of The George Balanchine Trust; Nicholas Jenkins of the Lincoln Kirstein estate; and Christopher Pennington and Allen Greenberg of The Jerome Robbins Foundation/The Robbins Rights Trust, for their generous support and help with access to vital archival materials. I was also fortunate to meet Balanchine's remaining family, including Keti Balanchivadze and Tsiskari Balanchivadze in Tbilisi and Georges Mamoulia in Paris, who invited me into their homes and shared family stories and documents.

I have had the good fortune of research support along the way from the Dorothy and Lewis B. Cullman Center for Scholars and Writers, John Simon Guggenheim Memorial Foundation, Leon Levy Center for Biography, National Endowment for the Humanities, Charles H. Revson Foundation, and Ford Foundation.

Like all historians I am indebted to the archivists of the collections I used, especially at the Archive Centre, King's College, Cambridge; Beinecke Rare Book and Manuscript Library; Bibliothèque-Musée de l'Opéra National de Paris; Copenhagen City Archives; Harry Ransom Center; Kansas City Ballet Archives; NYCB Archives and Ballet Society Collections; New York Public Library; Paul Sacher Stiftung; and Roosevelt Warm Springs Archive. Special thanks to Linda Murray and her colleagues at the Jerome Robbins Dance Division of the New York Public Library for the Performing Arts and to Matthew Wittmann and everyone at Harvard University's Houghton Library, where the George Balanchine Archive resides.

I am also indebted to those who opened to me personal and family collections of letters, diaries, and papers—including Karin von Aroldingen; Merrill Ashley; Ketevan Balanchivadze; Anne Bass; John Benson; Hal Bigelow; Vida Brown; Gregory Cary; Jacques d'Amboise; John Day; Kate and Pamela Draper; Martin Duberman; Robert Gottlieb; Robert Greskovic; Barbara Horgan; Una Kai; Kim Kokich; Edith Langner; Bill, Lee, Rick, and Peter Leach; Vladimir Lehovich; Paul Mejia; Dominique Nabokov; Alexander Neubauer; Elise Paschen; Christine Redpath; Bentley Roton; Lynne Stetson; and Mark Taper.

I would like to offer special thanks to my Russian researcher, Ella Saginadze, a historian herself, who never tired of our quest for Balanchine in Russia and Georgia. I am also grateful to John Graham, Hiroaki Kuromiya, Georges Mamoulia, Erik Scott, Marci Shore, and Yuri Slezkine for help with archives in France, Russia, Georgia, Poland, and Ukraine. For translation from Russian, I depended on Anneta Greenlee, Anastassia Kostriukova, and Irina Klyagin; from Georgian, Nino Chimakadze; and from Danish, Dr. Christian Graugaard. Yanni Kotsonis introduced me to most of these wonderful Russian translators and researchers. My research assistant, Laura Quinton, who became in the years we worked together an impressive historian in her own right, was an invaluable help, and I relied on her judgment and sleuthing and her untiring work on the bibliography and endnotes. Along the way, I also had help from Emily Hoffman, Rachel Abrams, and Kate Kelley. Donald Donovan, Guilherme Recena Costa, Gabriel Silva, and Isabella

Cusano at Debevoise & Plimpton LLP provided vital pro bono services in uncovering CIA, FBI, and other government files.

I remain immensely grateful to the many dancers and colleagues who worked with Balanchine and spent hour upon hour with me sharing their thoughts and experiences. I owe special thanks to Karin von Aroldingen, Virginia Rich Barnett, Jacques d'Amboise, Carolyn George d'Amboise, Melissa Hayden, Una Kai, Lourdes Lopez, Patricia McBride Lousada, Arthur Mitchell, Maria Tallchief, and Mel Tomlinson, as well as to Robert Barnett, Maria Calegari, John Clifford, Bart Cook, Suzanne Farrell, Robert Gottlieb, Linda Hamilton, Allegra Kent, Adam Lüders, Conrad Ludlow, Paul Mejia, Marika Molnar, Susan Pillar, Francia Russell, Stephanie Saland, Suki Schorer, Perry Silvey, Lynne Stetson, Kent Stowell, Carol Sumner, Edward Villella, Barbara Walczak, and Ricky Weiss.

As ever, I owe much to my colleagues at the Center for Ballet and the Arts at New York University and to the university's provost, Katherine Fleming, for her loyal friendship and support. I am grateful in many ways to David Remnick at *The New Yorker*, and to my editor Leo Carey. The list of colleagues and friends, whose own work and help with contacts, expertise, research, and ongoing conversation over years, is long—among them are Joan Acocella, Alison Deegan Barry, Kathleen Begala, Kai Bird, Kim Brandstrup, Finn Brunton, Jonathan Burnham, Stephan Caras, Robert Caro, Mirjana Ciric, Stuart Coleman, Joy Connolly, Arlene Croce, Carys Davies, Leah Dickerman, Ilia Doronchenkov, Cheryl Effron, Oskar Eustis, William Forsythe, Julia Foulkes, Lynn Garafola, Donald Garrett, Barbara Graziosi, Michael Greenberg, Robert Greskovic, Julia Gruen, Saidiya V. Hartman, Jodi Hauptman, Connie Hochman, Brooke Holmes, Stephen Holmes, William Holste, Yves André Istel, Peter Kayafas, Daniel Kehlmann, Elizabeth Kendall, Judy Kinberg, Lori Klinger, Paul Kolnik, Jennifer Lake, Julian Lethbridge, Reynold Levy, Kathryn Lofton, Nicoletta Misler, Timothy Naftali, Tarik O'Regan, George Packer, Jed Perl, Claudia Roth Pierpont, Ross Posnock, Julia Randel, Michael A. Reynolds, Meryl Rosofsky, Debra Rose, Scott Rothkopf, Eugene Rusyn, Michael Sells, Diane Solway, Charles Stang, (the late) Jean Stein, Jean Strouse, Twyla Tharp, David Velleman,

Darren Walker, Stephen Walsh, Serapio Walton, Mariët Westermann, and Kara Yoo Leaman.

My debt is great to those who read and commented on the manuscript along the way: Sandra Bronfman, Alma Guillermoprieto, Moshe Halbertal, Alastair Macauley, Catherine Merridale, Akhil Sharma, and Leon Wieseltier. Catherine Oppenheimer read, critiqued, read again, and was the best of friends. I could not have written this book without the steady encouragement of Sarah Chalfant and Rebecca Nagel of the Wylie Agency. My thanks also extend to Alexandra Truitt and Jerry Marshall, who cleared photos. I send deep gratitude to David Ebershoff, my wonderful and wise editor, and to everyone at Random House, with special thanks to Plaegian Alexander, Maria Braeckel, Karen Fink, Michael Hoak, Loren Noveck, Darryl Oliver, and Andy Ward. In the UK, I am grateful to Granta, and especially to Laura Barber and Pru Rowlandson. Above all, my thanks go to Frederick Wiseman, who read, reread, and talked for hours, and without whom—well, without whom.

Finally, my marvelous children, Daniel and Nicholas Judt, grew into young men as I went, and they have been sharp commentators and editors, as well as the most gracious and loving of sons. *Mr. B* is dedicated to them.

SELECTED BIBLIOGRAPHY

ARCHIVES

Ailina Dance Archives, Savannah, Georgia
Archive Centre, King's College, Cambridge
Archive of Literature and Arts, Tbilisi
Archives of American Art, Smithsonian Institution, Washington, D.C.
Archives and Manuscript Department, A. A. Bakhrushin State Central Theatre Museum, Moscow
Archives Nationales, Paris
Archives de la Préfecture de Police, Paris
Archivio Fotografico, Fondazione La Scala, Milan
Beinecke Rare Book and Manuscript Library, Yale University, Connecticut (Beinecke)
Bibliothèque-Musée de l'Opéra National de Paris, Paris
Center for Creative Photography, Arizona
Central State Archive of Cinema and Photo Documents of Saint Petersburg, St. Petersburg
Central State Archive of Literature and Art of Saint Petersburg, St. Petersburg (TsGALI SPb)
Central State Archives of Saint Petersburg, St. Petersburg (TsGA SPb)
Central State Historical Archive, St. Petersburg (TsGIA SPb)
Copenhagen City Archives, Copenhagen
Danish National Archives, Copenhagen
Department of Literature and Art, Central Historical Archives of Georgia, Tbilisi
Department of Manuscripts, Russian National Library, St. Petersburg
Department of Manuscripts and Rare Books, St. Petersburg State Theatre Library, St. Petersburg
Department of Prints, National Library of Russia, St. Petersburg
Department of Russian Literature Abroad, Russian State Library, Moscow
Deutsche Oper Berlin, Berlin

Diakonissestiftelsen Archive, Copenhagen
Getty Research Institute, California
Harry Ransom Center, University of Texas at Austin, Texas (HRC)
Houghton Library, Harvard University, Massachusetts (Houghton)
House of the Russian Abroad Named After Alexander Solzhenitsyn, Moscow
Irving S. Gilmore Music Library, Yale University, Connecticut (YML)
Isamu Noguchi Archive, Noguchi Museum, New York
Jerome Robbins Dance Division, New York Public Library for the Performing Arts, New York (LPA)
Kansas City Ballet Archives, Tatiana Dokoudovska Library for Dance, Kansas
Kutaisi Central Archive, Kutaisi
Margaret Herrick Library, California
The Metropolitan Opera Archives, New York
Ministry of Internal Affairs Archive of Georgia, Gldani (in Tbilisi)
Ministry of Justice, Tbilisi
Municipal Archives, New York City Department of Records and Information Services, New York
The Museum of Modern Art Archives, New York
Music Division, Library of Congress, Washington, D.C. (LC)
The National Archives, Washington, D.C.
National Archives of Georgia, Tbilisi
National Records Center, U.S. Department of Homeland Security, Missouri
National Security Archive, Washington, D.C.
The Newberry Library, Illinois
New York City Ballet Archives, New Jersey (NYCB Archives)
Paul Sacher Stiftung, Basel
Peter Jay Sharp Special Collections, Lila Acheson Wallace Library, The Juilliard School, New York
Peterhof State Museum-Reserve, St. Petersburg
Rambert Archive, London
Rare Book and Manuscript Library, Columbia University, New York
The Record Library, St. Petersburg State Museum of Theatre and Music, St. Petersburg
Rockefeller Archive Center, New York
Roosevelt Warm Springs Institute for Rehabilitation Archives, Georgia
The Royal Library, Copenhagen
Royal Opera House Collections, London
The Royal Theater: Archives and Library, Copenhagen
Russian State Archive of Literature and Art, Moscow (RGALI)
Russian State Historical Archive, St. Petersburg (RGIA)
Savoy Hotel Archives, London
Slavic and East European Collections and Microform Reading Room, New York Public Library, New York
Smith College Archives, Massachusetts
Special Collections, University of Arkansas Libraries, Arkansas
Special Collections Research Center, Southern Illinois University, Illinois
State Archives of the Russian Federation, Moscow
State Museum of Georgian Theater, Music, Film and Choreography—Art Palace, Tbilisi
Tbilisi Historical Archive, Tbilisi
Weill-Lenya Research Center, Kurt Weill Foundation, New York

PERSONAL/FAMILY COLLECTIONS

Karin von Aroldingen
Merrill Ashley
Ketevan Balanchivadze
Evgeny Balashov
Anne Bass
John Benson
Eddie Bigelow
Ruthanna Boris
Vida Brown
Jacques d'Amboise
John Day
Robert Greskovic
Barbara Horgan
Una Kai
Edith Langner
Richard and Kay Leach
Vladimir Lehovich
Patricia McBride (Lousada)
Paul Mejia
Francisco Moncion
Dominique Nabokov
Sandy Neubauer
Christine Redpath
Lynne Stetson
Maria Tallchief
Bernard Taper
Roy Tobias
Daphne Vane
Heidi Vosseler

INTERVIEWS

Karin von Aroldingen
Merrill Ashley
Gillian Attfield
Michelle Audet
Debra Austin
Ketevan Balanchivadze
Tsiskari Balanchivadze
Vanusha Balanchivadze
Robert Barnett
Mikhail Baryshnikov
Anne Bass
Jeanne Hays Beaman
Frederick W. Beinecke
Toni Bentley
Hal Bigelow
Joyce Boelzner
Jean-Pierre Bonnefoux
Randall Bourscheidt
Merrill Brockway
Victoria Bromberg (Psihoyos)
Joy Williams Brown
Vida Brown
Mary T. Browne
Maria Calegari
Steven Caras
Dianne Chilgren
John Clifford
Janice Cohen (Adelson)
Stuart Coleman
William Coleman
Bart Cook
Randal Craft
Gail Crisa
Arlene Croce
Mary Sharp Cronson
Christopher d'Amboise
Jacques d'Amboise
D. Ronald Daniel
John Day
Marina De Brantes
Lisa De Ribere
Carole Deschamps
Sonny DeSoto
Carole Divet (Harting)
Kate Draper
Pamela Draper
Martin Duberman
Daniel Duell
William Earle
Paul Epstein
Renee Estópinal
Suzanne Farrell
Wilhelmina Frankfurt
Susan Freedman (Londoner)
Judith Friedman (Kupersmith)
Elissa Fuchs
Jeanne Fuchs
Judith Fugate
Vladimir Kirillovich Galitzine
Penelope Gates (Nyfenger)
Gene Gavin
Susan Gluck (Pappajohn)
Dwight Godwin
James Goldman
Robert Gottlieb
Gloria Govrin
Maxine Groffsky
William G. Hamilton
Peter Harvey
Melissa Hayden
Gale Hayman
David Hays
Linda Homek (Hamilton)
Barbara Horgan
Bea Howard
Charles Howard
Clinton Howard
David Howard
Lynne Howard
Peter Howard
Ann Inglis (Crowell)
Una Kai
Bel Kaufman
Allegra Kent
Judy Kinberg
Anna Kisselgoff
Winthrop Knowlton
Kim Kokich
Paul Kolnik
Andrei Kramarevsky
Edith Langner
Nancy Lassalle
Frank Lavoia
Chris Leach
Lee Leach
Peter Leach
Richard Leach
Olga Lehovich
Vladimir Lehovich
Sara Leland
Harvey Lichtenstein
Lourdes Lopez
Adam Lüders
Conrad Ludlow

Robert Maiorano
Georges Mamoulia
Kay Mazzo
Patricia McBride
Patricia McBride (Lousada)
Catherine McDavid Smith
Paul Mejia
Marlene Mesavage (DeSavino)
Barbara Milberg (Fisher)
Arthur Mitchell
Marika Molnar
Aidan Mooney
Richard Moredock
Catherine Morris (Leach)
Mark Morris
Mary Ellen Moylan
Dominique Nabokov
Ivan Nabokov
Jennifer Nairn-Smith
Colleen Neary
Sandy Neubauer
John Edward Niles
Catherine Oppenheimer
Tarik O'Regan
Adrian Ouellette (Father Adrian)
Francine Paino
Mimi Paul
Pamara Perry (Hangarter)
Delia Peters
Susan Pilarre
Stanley B. Prusiner
Malkhaz Purtskhvanidze
Charlotte Ray (Hammer)
Christine Redpath
Nanette Reedy (Quigley)
Nancy Reynolds
Virginia Rich (Barnett)
Theodore C. Rogers
Francia Russell
Francis Sackett
Paul Sackett
Stephanie Saland
Mack Schlefer
Suki Schorer
Ellen Shire
Joysanne Sidimus
Bettijane Sills
Robert B. Silvers
Perry Silvey
Victoria Simon
Jill Spalding
Marjorie Spohn
Zoya Staskevich (Jakowlew)
Jean Stein
Lynne Stetson
Faith Stewart-Gordon
Martin Stoner
Kent Stowell
Helen Strilec-Schatiloff
Carol Sumner
Martha Swope
Maria Tallchief
Mark Taper
Paul Taylor
Twyla Tharp
Ghislaine Thesmar
Jerry Thompson
Marcia Thompson
Mel Tomlinson
Maria Tucci
Hans Tuch
George Tucker
David Vaughan
Violette Verdy
Edward Villella
Anthony Vlatas (Father Menas)
Barbara Walczak
Serapio Walton
Heather Watts
Jonathan Watts
Barbara Weisberger
Ricky Weiss
Patricia Wilde
Robert Wilson
Damian Woetzel
Peter Wolff

RUSSIA (CHAPTERS 1 TO 4)

Primary

Alter, Robert. *The Hebrew Bible: A Translation with Commentary*. New York: W. W. Norton, 2019.

Babel, Isaac. *The Complete Works of Isaac Babel*. Edited by Nathalie Babel. Translated by Peter Constantine. Introduction by Cynthia Ozick. New York: W. W. Norton, 2002.

Balanchivadze, Andrey Melitonovich. *1905: Volume of Articles and Materials*. Tbilisi: Khelovneba, 1979.

Bely, Andrei. *Petersburg: A Novel in Eight Chapters*. Translated by David McDuff. Introduction by Adam Thirlwell. London: Penguin, 2011.

Berdyaev, Nicholas. *Dream and Reality: An Essay in Autobiography*. Translated by Katherine Lampert. London: Bles, 1950.

——. *The Russian Idea*. Boston: Beacon, 1962.

Blok, Aleksandr. *Blok: An Anthology of Essays and Memoirs*. Edited and translated by Lucy Vogel. Ann Arbor, MI: Ardis, 1982.

——. *Poems of Sophia*. Translated and edited by Boris Jakim. Kettering: Semantron, 2014.

——. *The Twelve: And Other Poems*. Translated by Jon Stallworthy and Peter France. New York: Oxford University Press, 1970.

Bocharov, Viktor, dir. *Zapozdavshaia prem'era (A Belated Premiere)*. Moskova: Kinokompania "Miris," 2003. DVD.

Chekov, Anton. *The Wife, and Other Stories*. Translated by Constance Garnett. New York: Macmillan, 1918.

Danilova, Alexandra. *Choura: The Memoirs of Alexandra Danilova*. New York: Fromm International, 1988.

Foster, John W. *Diplomatic Memoirs*. Vol 1. Boston: Houghton Mifflin, 1909.

Geva, Tamara. *Split Seconds: A Remembrance*. New York: Harper & Row, 1972.

Gogol, Nikolai. *Dead Souls*. Translated by Richard Pevear and Larissa Volokhonsky. New York: Vintage, 2011.

Gold, Arthur, and Robert Fizdale. *The Gold and Fizdale Cookbook*. New York: Random House, 1984.

Karsavina, Tamara. *Theatre Street: The Reminiscences of Tamara Karsavina*. London: Dance Books, 1981.

Le Clercq, Tanaquil. *The Ballet Cook Book*. New York: Stein and Day, 1966.

Lopukhov, Fedor. *Writings on Ballet and Music*. Edited and with an introduction by Stephanie Jordan. Translations by Dorinda Offord. Madison: University of Wisconsin Press, 2002.

Lunacharsky, Anatoly Vasilievich. *On Literature and Art*. Translated by Avril Pyman and Fainna Glagoleva. Moscow: Progress, 1973.

——. *Revolutionary Silhouettes*. Translated and edited by Michael Glenny. Introduction by Isaac Deutscher. New York: Hill and Wang, 1967.

Malevich, Kazimir. *Kazimir Malevich: The World as Objectlessness*. Texts by Simon Baier and Britta Tanja Dümpelmann. Basel: Kunstmuseum Basel, 2014.

Mariinsky Theater. *Vek Balanchivadze*. St. Petersburg: Aurora Design, 2004.

Mayakovsky, Vladimir. *The Bedbug and Selected Poetry*. Edited and with an introduction by Patricia Blake. Translated by Max Hayward and George Reavey. Bloomington: Indiana University Press, 1975.

——. *Vladimir Mayakovsky: Selected Poems*. Translated by James H. McGavran III. Evanston, IL: Northwestern University Press, 2013.

Meyerhold, V. E. *Meyerhold on Theatre*. Translated and edited by Edward Braun. New York: Hill and Wang, 1969.

Nietzsche, Friedrich Wilhelm. *The Birth of Tragedy and Other Writings*. Edited by Raymond Geuss and Ronald Speirs. Translated by Ronald Speirs. Cambridge: Cambridge University Press, 1999.

——. *Daybreak: Thoughts on the Prejudices of Morality*. Edited by Maudemarie Clark and Brian Leiter. Translated by R. J. Hollingdale. Cambridge: Cambridge University Press, 1997.

——. *On the Genealogy of Morality; and Other Writings*. Edited by Keith Ansell-Pearson. Translated by Carol Diethe. New York: Cambridge University Press, 1994.

Ouspensky, P. D. *Talks with a Devil*. Translated by Katya Petroff. Edited and introduced by J. G. Bennett. New York: Knopf, 1973.

Uspenskiĭ [Ouspensky], P. D. *Tertium Organum: The Third Canon of Thought: A Key to the Enigmas of the World*. Translated by Claude Bragdon. New York: Knopf, 1922.

Paléologue, Maurice. *An Ambassador's Memoirs*. Translated by F. A. Holt. 8 vols. New York: George H. Doran Company, 1924–25.

Pushkin, Aleksandr. *Boris Godunov and Other Dramatic Works*. Translated by James E. Falen. Introduction by Caryl Emerson. Oxford: Oxford University Press, 2007.

——. *The Captain's Daughter and The Negro of Peter the Great*. Translated and with an introduction by Rosemary Edmonds. London: N. Spearman, 1958.

——. *Eugene Onegin: A Novel in Verse*. Translated by Vladimir Nabokov. London: Routledge & Kegan Paul, 1964.

Rilke, Rainer Maria. *Stories of God.* Translated by M. D. Herter Norton. New York: W. W. Norton, 1963.

Solovyov, Vladimir. *Divine Sophia: The Wisdom Writings of Vladimir Solovyov*. Edited by Judith Deutsch Kornblatt. Translated by Boris Jakim, Judith Deutsch Kornblatt, and Laury Magnus. Ithaca, NY: Cornell University Press, 2009.

——. *The Meaning of Love*. Edited and with a revised translation by Thomas R. Beyer Jr. Introduction by Owen Barfield. New York: Inner Traditions, 1985.

Tracy, Robert, with Sharon DeLano. *Balanchine's Ballerinas: Conversations with the Muses*. New York: Linden Press/Simon & Schuster, 1983.

Turgenev, Ivan. *Fathers and Sons*. Translated by Peter Carson, with an introduction by Rosamund Bartlett and an afterword by Tatyana Tolstaya. London: Penguin, 2009.

Volynsky, Akim. *Ballet's Magic Kingdom: Selected Writings on Dance in Russia, 1911–1925*. Translated, edited, and with an introduction by Stanley J. Rabinowitz. New Haven, CT: Yale University Press, 2008.

Secondary

Abraham, Gerald. *Tchaikovsky: A Short Biography*. London: Duckworth, 1945.

Alexandrov, Vladimir E. *Nabokov's Otherworld*. Princeton, NJ: Princeton University Press, 1991.

Antonov, Sergei. *Bankrupts and Usurers of Imperial Russia: Debt, Property, and the Law in the Age of Dostoevsky and Tolstoy*. Cambridge, MA: Harvard University Press, 2016.

Baer, Nancy Van Norman, ed. *Theatre in Revolution: Russian Avant-Garde Stage Design, 1913–1935*. London: Thames and Hudson, 1991.

Ball, Alan M. *And Now My Soul Is Hardened: Abandoned Children in Soviet Russia, 1918–1930*. Berkeley: University of California Press, 1994.

Balzer, Harley D., ed. *Russia's Missing Middle Class: The Professions in Russian History*. Armonk, NY: M. E. Sharpe, 1996.

Barron, Stephanie, and Maurice Tuchman, eds. *The Avant-Garde in Russia, 1910–1930: New Perspectives*. Los Angeles: Los Angeles County Museum of Art, 1980.

Bartlett, Robert. *Why Can the Dead Do Such Great Things?: Saints and Worshippers from the Martyrs to the Reformation*. Princeton, NJ: Princeton University Press, 2013.

Bartlett, Rosamund, and Sarah Dadswell, eds. *Victory over the Sun: The World's First Futurist Opera*. Exeter, UK: University of Exeter Press, 2012.

Bisha, Robin, ed. *Russian Women, 1698–1917: Experience and Expression: An Anthology of Sources*. Bloomington: Indiana University Press, 2002.

Bowlt, John E. *The Silver Age: Russian Art of the Early Twentieth Century and the "World of Art" Group*. Newtonville, MA: Oriental Research Partners, 1982.

Boyd, Brian. *Vladimir Nabokov: The Russian Years*. Princeton, NJ: Princeton University Press, 1990.

Braun, Edward. *Meyerhold: A Revolution in Theater*. London: Methuen, 1995.

——. *The Theatre of Meyerhold: Revolution and the Modern Stage*. London: Methuen, 1986.

Brown, David. *Tchaikovsky: The Final Years, 1885–1893*. New York: W. W. Norton, 1991.

——. *Tchaikovsky: The Years of Wandering, 1878–1885*. New York: W. W. Norton, 1986.

Brumfield, William C., and Miloš M. Velimirović, eds. *Christianity and the Arts in Russia*. New York: Cambridge University Press, 1991.

Carlson, Maria. *No Religion Higher Than Truth: A History of the Theosophical Movement in Russia, 1875–1922*. Princeton, NJ: Princeton University Press, 1993.

Chamberlain, Lesley. *Lenin's Private War: The Voyage of the Philosophy Steamer and the Exile of the Intelligentsia*. New York: St. Martin's, 2006.

Clark, Katerina. *Petersburg: Crucible of Cultural Revolution*. Cambridge, MA: Harvard University Press, 1995.

D'Andrea, Jeanne, ed. *Kazimir Malevich, 1878–1935*. Los Angeles: Armand Hammer Museum of Art and Cultural Center, 1990.

De Waal, Thomas. *The Caucasus: An Introduction*. Oxford: Oxford University Press, 2010.

Dorontchenkov, Ilia, ed. *Russian and Soviet Views of Modern Western Art: 1890s to Mid-1930s*. Translated by Charles Rougle. Berkeley: University of California Press, 2009.

Engel, Barbara Alpern. *Mothers and Daughters: Women of the Intelligentsia in Nineteenth-Century Russia*. Cambridge: Cambridge University Press, 1983.

——. *Women in Russia, 1700–2000*. New York: Cambridge University Press, 2004.

Engelstein, Laura. *The Keys to Happiness: Sex and the Search for Modernity in Fin-De-Siècle Russia*. Ithaca, NY: Cornell University Press, 1992.

Figes, Orlando. *Natasha's Dance: A Cultural History of Russia*. New York: Metropolitan Books, 2002.

——. *A People's Tragedy: The Russian Revolution, 1891–1924*. New York: Viking, 1997.

Fitzpatrick, Sheila. *The Commissariat of Enlightenment: Soviet Organization of Education and the Arts under Lunacharsky, October 1917–1921*. Cambridge: Cambridge University Press, 1970.

——. *The Cultural Front: Power and Culture in Revolutionary Russia*. Ithaca, NY: Cornell University Press, 1992.

Frame, Murray. *School for Citizens: Theatre and Civil Society in Imperial Russia*. New Haven, CT: Yale University Press, 2006.

——. *The St. Petersburg Imperial Theaters: Stage and State in Revolutionary Russia, 1900–1920*. Jefferson, NC: McFarland, 2000.

Garafola, Lynn. *La Nijinska: Choreographer of the Modern*. New York: Oxford University Press, 2022.

Gasparov, Boris, Robert P. Hughes, and Irina Paperno, eds. *Cultural Mythologies of Russian Modernism: From the Golden Age to the Silver Age*. Berkeley: University of California Press, 1992.

Giroud, Vincent. *St. Petersburg: A Portrait of a Great City*. New Haven, CT: University Press of New England, 2003.

Gottlieb, Robert. *George Balanchine: The Ballet Maker*. New York: HarperCollins, 2004.

Gray, John. *The Immortalization Commission: Science and the Strange Quest to Cheat Death*. New York: Farrar, Straus and Giroux, 2011.

Homans, Jennifer. *Apollo's Angels: A History of Ballet*. New York: Random House, 2010.

Hosking, Geoffrey A. *Russia and the Russians: A History*. Cambridge, MA: Belknap, 2001.

Ivanov, S. A. *Holy Fools in Byzantium and Beyond*. Translated by Simon Franklin. New York: Oxford University Press, 2006.

Jakobson, Roman. *Language in Literature*. Edited by Krystyna Pomorska and Stephen Rudy. Cambridge, MA: Belknap, 1987.

Jangfeldt, Bengt. *Mayakovsky: A Biography*. Translated by Harry D. Watson. Chicago: University of Chicago Press, 2014.

Jones, Stephen F. *Socialism in Georgian Colors: The European Road to Social Democracy, 1883–1917*. Cambridge, MA: Harvard University Press, 2005.

Kelly, Aileen M. *Views from the Other Shore: Essays on Herzen, Chekhov, and Bakhtin.* New Haven, CT: Yale University Press, 1999.

Kendall, Elizabeth. *Balanchine and the Lost Muse: Revolution and the Making of a Choreographer*. New York: Oxford University Press, 2013.

Khuchua, Pavel. *Meliton Balanchivadze.* Tbilisi: Zarya Vostoka, 1952.

Kopp, Anatole. *Town and Revolution: Soviet Architecture and City Planning, 1917–1935.* New York: G. Braziller, 1970.

Kotkin, Stephen. *Stalin.* Vol. 1, *Paradoxes of Power, 1878–1928.* New York: Penguin, 2014.

Krasovskaya, Vera. *Vaganova: A Dance Journey from Petersburg to Leningrad.* Translated by Vera Siegel. Introduction by Lynn Garafola. Gainesville: University Press of Florida, 2005.

Law, Alma, and Mel Gordon. *Meyerhold, Eisenstein, and Biomechanics: Actor Training in Revolutionary Russia.* Jefferson, NC: McFarland, 1996.

Maguire, Henry. *The Icons of Their Bodies: Saints and Their Images in Byzantium.* Princeton, NJ: Princeton University Press, 1996.

Matich, Olga. *Erotic Utopia: The Decadent Imagination in Russia's Fin-De-Siècle.* Madison: University of Wisconsin Press, 2005.

——, ed. *Petersburg/Petersburg: Novel and City, 1900–1921.* Madison: University of Wisconsin Press, 2010.

Meinander, Henrik. *A History of Finland.* Translated by Tom Geddes. New York: Columbia University Press, 2011.

Meinertz, Alexander. *Vera Volkova.* Alton: Dance Books, 2007.

Merridale, Catherine. *Night of Stone: Death and Memory in Twentieth-Century Russia.* New York: Viking, 2001.

——. *Red Fortress: History and Illusion in the Kremlin.* New York: Henry Holt, 2013.

Milner-Gulland, Robin. *The Russians.* Oxford: Blackwell, 1997.

Misler, Nicoletta, ed. *In principio era il corpo: L'arte del movimento a Mosca negli anni '20.* Milan: Electra, 1999.

——. *The Russian Art of Movement, 1920–1930.* Turin: Umberto Allemandi, 2017.

Mitchell, Rebecca. *Nietzsche's Orphans: Music, Metaphysics, and the Twilight of the Russian Empire.* New Haven, CT: Yale University Press, 2015.

Nikolaev, A. B., D. A. Bazhanov, and A. A. Ivanov, eds. *The Russian Revolution of 1917: New Approaches and Views: Collection of Scientific Articles.* St. Petersburg: Rossiiskii gosudarstvennyi pedagogicheskii universitet im. A.I. Gertsena, 2016.

O'Connor, Timothy Edward. *The Politics of Soviet Culture: Anatolii Lunacharskii.* Ann Arbor, MI: UMI Research Press, 1983.

Olenina, Ana Hedberg. "Psychomotor Aesthetics: Conceptions of Gesture and Affect in Russian and American Modernity, 1910s–1920s." PhD diss., Harvard University, 2012.

Ometev, Boris, and John Stuart. *St. Petersburg: Portrait of an Imperial City.* New York: Vendome, 1990.

Ouspensky, Léonide, and Vladimir Lossky. *The Meaning of Icons.* Edited by Urs Graf-Verlag. Translated by G.E.H. Palmer and E. Kadloubovsky. Boston: Boston Book & Art Shop, 1969.

Pitches, Jonathan. *Vsevolod Meyerhold.* London: Routledge, 2003.

Poznansky, Alexander. *Tchaikovsky: The Quest for the Inner Man.* New York: Schirmer, 1991.

Pyman, Avril. *The Life of Aleksandr Blok.* Vol. 1–2. New York: Oxford University Press, 1979–80.

Rabinowitz, Stanley, ed. *And Then Came Dance: The Women Who Led Volynsky to Ballet's Magic Kingdom.* New York: Oxford University Press, 2019.

Rayfield, Donald. *Edge of Empires: A History of Georgia*. London: Reaktion, 2012.
Rieber, Alfred J. *Merchants and Entrepreneurs in Imperial Russia*. Chapel Hill: University of North Carolina Press, 1982.
Roné, Elvira. *Olga Preobrazhenskaya: A Portrait*. Translated and introduced by Fernau Hall. New York: M. Dekker, 1978.
Rosenthal, Bernice Glatzer, ed. *Nietzsche in Russia*. Princeton, NJ: Princeton University Press, 1986.
——, ed. *The Occult in Russian and Soviet Culture*. Ithaca, NY: Cornell University Press, 1997.
Ross, Janice. *Like a Bomb Going Off: Leonid Yakobson and Ballet as Resistance in Soviet Russia*. New Haven, CT: Yale University Press, 2015.
Rudnitsky, Konstantin. *Russian and Soviet Theatre: Tradition and the Avant-Garde*. London: Thames and Hudson, 1988.
Rzhevsky, Nicholas, ed. *The Cambridge Companion to Modern Russian Culture*. Cambridge: Cambridge University Press, 1998.
Scholl, Tim. *From Petipa to Balanchine: Classical Revival and the Modernization of Ballet*. New York: Routledge, 1994.
Schorske, Carl E. *Fin-de-Siècle Vienna: Politics and Culture*. New York: Vintage, 1980.
Schwartz, Boris. *Music and Musical Life in Soviet Russia, 1917–1970*. New York: W. W. Norton, 1973.
Scott, R. Erik. *Familiar Strangers: The Georgian Diaspora and the Evolution of Soviet Empire*. Oxford: Oxford University Press, 2016.
Singleton, Fred. *A Short History of Finland*. Cambridge: Cambridge University Press, 1989.
Sirotkina, Irina, and Roger Smith. *The Sixth Sense of the Avant-Garde: Dance, Kinaesthesia and the Arts in Revolutionary Russia*. London: Bloomsbury, 2017.
Slezkine, Yuri. *The House of Government: A Saga of the Russian Revolution*. Princeton, NJ: Princeton University Press, 2017.
Smith, Douglas. *Former People: The Final Days of the Russian Aristocracy*. New York: Farrar, Straus and Giroux, 2012.
Souritz, Elizabeth. *Soviet Choreographers in the 1920s*. Translated by Lynn Visson. Edited by Sally Banes. Durham, NC: Duke University Press, 1990.
Stanton, Leonard J. *The Optina Austyn Monastery in the Russian Literary Imagination: Iconic Vision in Works by Dostoevsky, Gogol, Tolstoy, and Others*. New York: P. Lang, 1995.
Stites, Richard. *The Women's Liberation Movement in Russia: Feminism, Nihilism, and Bolshevism, 1860–1930*. Princeton, NJ: Princeton University Press, 1991.
Suny, Ronald Grigor. *The Making of the Georgian Nation*. Bloomington: Indiana University Press, 1994.
Tait, A. L. *Lunacharsky: Poet of the Revolution, 1875–1907*. Birmingham, AL: University of Birmingham, 1984.
Taper, Bernard. *Balanchine: A Biography*. New York: Macmillan, 1974.
——. *Balanchine: A Biography*. 2nd ed. Berkeley: University of California Press, 1996.
Tassie, Gregor. *Yevgeny Mravinsky: The Noble Conductor*. Lanham, MD: Scarecrow, 2005.
Tsurtsumia, Rusudan, and Joseph Jordania, eds. *Echoes from Georgia: Seventeen Arguments on Georgian Polyphony*. Hauppauge, NY: Nova Science, 2010.
Twysden, A. E. *Alexandra Danilova*. London: C. W. Beaumont, 1945.
Volkov, Solomon. *Balanchine's Tchaikovsky: Interviews with George Balanchine*. Translated by Antonina W. Bouis. New York: Simon & Schuster, 1985.
Von Geldern, James. *Bolshevik Festivals, 1917–1920*. Berkeley: University of California Press, 1993.

Ware, Timothy. *The Orthodox Church*. Harmondsworth, UK: Penguin, 1963.
Weinberger, Eliot. *Angels and Saints*. New York: New Directions, 2020.
Wiley, Roland John. *Tchaikovsky*. Oxford: Clarendon, 1985.
———. *Tchaikovsky's Ballets: Swan Lake, Sleeping Beauty, Nutcracker*. Oxford: Clarendon, 2003.
Wirtschafter, Elisa Kimerling. *Social Identity in Imperial Russia*. Dekalb: Northern Illinois University Press, 1997.
Wood, Douglas Kellogg. *Men Against Time: Nicolas Berdyaev, T. S. Eliot, Aldous Huxley, & C. G. Jung*. Lawrence: University Press of Kansas, 1982.
Wortman, Richard S. *Scenarios of Power: Myth and Ceremony in Russian Monarchy*. Vol. 2, *From Alexander II to the Abdication of Nicholas II*. Princeton, NJ: Princeton University Press, 2000.
Young, Julian. *Friedrich Nietzsche: A Philosophical Biography*. Cambridge: Cambridge University Press, 2010.

RUSSIA ABROAD (CHAPTERS 5 TO 8)

Primary

Adam, Peter, dir. *Diaghilev: A Portrait*. Written and narrated by Tamara Geva. London: BBC TV, in association with RM Productions, Munich, 1979. Streaming video file, *MGZIC 9-496, LPA.
Athanassakis, Apostolos, ed. *The Homeric Hymns*. Baltimore, MD: Johns Hopkins University Press, 2020.
Balanchine, George, and Francis Mason. *101 Stories of the Great Ballets*. New York: Doubleday, 1975.
Baronova, Irina. *Irina: Ballet, Life, and Love*. Gainesville: University Press of Florida, 2005.
Bodenwieser, Gertrud. *The New Dance*. Edited and with a foreword by Marie Cuckson. Vaucluse, France: Rondo Studies, n.d.
Brooks, Virginia, dir. *Felia Doubrovska Remembered: From Diaghilev's Ballets Russes to Balanchine's School of American Ballet*. New York: Virginia Brooks Dance Films, 2008. DVD.
Clifford, John. *Balanchine's Apprentice: From Hollywood to New York and Back*. Gainesville: University Press of Florida, 2021.
Colin, Paul. *Josephine Baker and La Revue Nègre: Paul Colin's Lithographs of "Le tumulte noir" in Paris, 1927*. Introduction by Henry Louis Gates Jr. and Karen C. C. Dalton. New York: H. N. Abrams, 1998.
Croce, Arlene. *Going to the Dance*. New York: Knopf, 1982.
Duke, Vernon. *Passport to Paris*. Boston: Little, Brown, 1955.
Flanner, Janet. *Paris Was Yesterday, 1925–1939*. Edited by Irving Drutman. New York: Viking, 1972.
Garafola, Lynn, and Joan Acocella, eds. *André Levinson on Dance: Writings from Paris in the Twenties*. Hanover, CT: Wesleyan University Press, 1991.
Gropius, Walter, ed. *The Theater of the Bauhaus*. Translated by Arthur S. Wensinger. Middletown, CT: Wesleyan University Press, 1971.
Grosz, George. *The Autobiography of George Grosz: A Small Yes and a Big No*. New York: Allison & Busby, 1982.
Kandinsky, Wassily. *Concerning the Spiritual in Art*. Translated and with an introduction by Michael T. H. Sadler. New York: Dover, 1977.
Karlinsky, Simon, and Alfred Appel, eds. *The Bitter Air of Exile: Russian Writers in the West, 1922–1972*. Berkeley: University of California Press, 1977.

Kessler, Harry. *Berlin in Lights: The Diaries of Count Harry Kessler, 1918–1937*. Translated and edited by Charles Kessler. Introduction by Ian Buruma. New York: Grove, 1999.

Mann, Thomas. *The Magic Mountain*. Translated by John E. Woods. New York: Knopf, 1995.

Massine, Léonide. *My Life in Ballet*. Edited by Phyllis Hartnoll and Robert Rubens. New York: St. Martin's, 1968.

Milstein, Nathan, and Solomon Volkov. *From Russia to the West: The Musical Memoirs and Reminiscences of Nathan Milstein*. Translated by Antonina W. Bouis. New York: Henry Holt, 1990.

Nabokov, Nicolas. *Lectures on Russian Literature*. Boston: Mariner, 2017.

——. *Old Friends and New Music*. Boston: Little, Brown, 1951.

Nijinsky, Vaslav. *The Diary of Vaslav Nijinsky*. Translated by Kyril FitzLyon. Edited by Joan Acocella. New York: Farrar, Straus and Giroux, 1999.

Prokofiev, Sergey. *Sergey Prokofiev Diaries, 1924–1933: Prodigal Son*. Translated and annotated by Anthony Phillips. London: Faber and Faber, 2012.

Pushkin, Aleksandr. *The Collected Stories*. Translated by Paul Debreczeny. Introduction by John Bayley. London: Everyman's Library, 1999.

——. *The Queen of Spades and Other Stories*. Translated and introduced by Rosemary Edmonds. London: Penguin, 1962.

Rambert, Marie. *Quicksilver: The Autobiography of Marie Rambert*. London: Macmillan, 1972.

Remembering Mr. B: Master of Five Senses. New York: The George Balanchine Centennial, 2004.

Rist, Édouard. *La tuberculose*. Paris: Armand Colin, 1927.

Roth, Joseph. *What I Saw: Reports from Berlin, 1920–1933*. Translated and with an introduction by Michael Hofmann. New York: W. W. Norton, 2003.

——. *The White Cities: Reports from France, 1925–39*. Translated and with an introduction by Michael Hofmann. London: Granta Books, 2013.

Sokolova, Lydia. *Dancing for Diaghilev: The Memoirs of Lydia Sokolova*. Edited by Richard Buckle. New York: Macmillan, 1961.

Steinberg, Cobbett, ed. *The Dance Anthology*. New York: New American Library, 1980.

Stern, Fritz. *Five Germanys I Have Known*. New York: Farrar, Straus and Giroux, 2013.

Stravinsky, Igor. *Igor Stravinsky: An Autobiography*. New York: W. W. Norton, 1936.

Tyler, Parker. *The Divine Comedy of Pavel Tchelitchew: A Biography*. New York: Fleet, 1967.

Weill, Kurt. *Speak Low (When You Speak Love): The Letters of Kurt Weill and Lotte Lenya*. Edited and translated by Lys Symonette and Kim H. Kowalke. Berkeley: University of California Press, 1996.

Secondary

Baer, Nancy Van Norman. *Bronislava Nijinska: A Dancer's Legacy*. San Francisco: Fine Arts Museums of San Francisco, 1986.

Bardet, Jean-Pierre, Patrice Bourdelais, Pierre Guillaume, François Lebrun, and Claude Quetel. *Peurs et terreurs face à la contagion: Choléra, tuberculose, syphilis: XIXe–XXe siècles*. Paris: Fayard, 1988.

Barnes, David S. *The Making of a Social Disease: Tuberculosis in Nineteenth-Century France*. Berkeley: University of California Press, 1995.

Barré, Jean-Luc. *Jacques and Raïssa Maritain: Beggars for Heaven*. Translated by Bernard E. Doering. Notre Dame, IN: University of Notre Dame Press, 2005.

Bellow, Juliet. *Modernism on Stage: The Ballets Russes and the Parisian Avant-Garde*. Burlington, VT: Ashgate, 2012.

Bentley, Toni. *Costumes by Karinska*. New York: H. N. Abrams, 1995.
——. *Sisters of Salome*. New Haven, CT: Yale University Press, 2002.
Bergdoll, Barry, and Leah Dickerman, eds. *Bauhaus 1919–1933: Workshops for Modernity*. New York: Museum of Modern Art, 2009.
Buckle, Richard. *Diaghilev*. London: Weidenfeld and Nicolson, 1979.
——. *Nijinsky*. New York: Simon & Schuster, 1971.
Buckle, Richard, with John Taras. *George Balanchine, Ballet Master: A Biography*. New York: Random House, 1988.
Butler, Cornelia, and Catherine de Zegher. *On Line: Drawing Through the Twentieth Century*. New York: Museum of Modern Art, 2010.
Bynum, Helen. *Spitting Blood: The History of Tuberculosis*. Oxford: Oxford University Press, 2012.
Caws, Mary Ann, ed. *Surrealism*. London: Phaidon, 2004.
Chazin-Bennahum, Judith. *René Blum and the Ballets Russes: In Search of a Lost Life*. New York: Oxford University Press, 2011.
Chernow, Ron. *The Warburgs: The Twentieth-Century Odyssey of a Remarkable Jewish Family*. New York: Random House, 1993.
Coleby, Nicola, ed. *A Surreal Life: Edward James, 1907–1984*. Brighton, UK: Royal Pavilion, Libraries and Museums, 1998.
Dickerman, Leah, ed. *Inventing Abstraction, 1910–1925: How a Radical Idea Changed Modern Art*. New York: Museum of Modern Art, 2012.
Duberman, Martin B. *The Worlds of Lincoln Kirstein*. New York: Knopf, 2007.
Eksteins, Modris. *Rites of Spring: The Great War and the Birth of the Modern Age*. Boston: Houghton Mifflin, 1989.
Elswit, Kate. *Watching Weimar Dance*. New York: Oxford University Press, 2014.
Freedberg, David. *The Power of Images: Studies in the History and Theory of Response*. Chicago: University of Chicago Press, 1989.
Fussell, Paul. *The Great War and Modern Memory*. Introduction by Jay Winter. Oxford: Oxford University Press, 2013.
Garafola, Lynn. *Diaghilev's Ballets Russes*. New York: Oxford University Press, 1989.
——, ed. *Russian Movement Culture of the 1920s and 1930s: A Symposium Organized by Lynn Garafola and Catharine Theimer Nepomnyashchy, February 12–14, 2015*. New York: Columbia University, Harriman Institute, 2015.
Garafola, Lynn, and Nancy Van Norman Baer, eds. *The Ballets Russes and Its World*. New Haven, CT: Yale University Press, 1999.
García-Márquez, Vicente. *Massine: A Biography*. New York: Knopf, 1995.
Garelick, Rhonda K. *Electric Salome: Loie Fuller's Performance of Modernism*. Princeton, NJ: Princeton University Press, 2007.
——. *Mademoiselle: Coco Chanel and the Pulse of History*. New York: Random House, 2014.
Gay, Peter. *Weimar Culture: The Outsider as Insider*. New York: W. W. Norton, 2001.
George, Alys X. *The Naked Truth: Viennese Modernism and the Body*. Chicago: University of Chicago Press, 2020.
Geroulanos, Stefanos, and Todd Meyers, eds. *The Human Body in the Age of Catastrophe: Brittleness, Integration, Science, and the Great War*. Chicago: University of Chicago Press, 2018.
Giroud, Vincent. *Nicolas Nabokov: A Life in Freedom and Music*. Oxford: Oxford University Press, 2015.
Gold, Arthur, and Robert Fizdale. *Misia: The Life of Misia Sert*. New York: Knopf, 1980.

Golding, John. *Paths to the Absolute: Mondrian, Malevich, Kandinsky, Pollock, Newman, Rothko, and Still*. Princeton, NJ: Princeton University Press, 2000.

Gross, Kenneth. *Puppet: An Essay on Uncanny Life*. Chicago: University of Chicago Press, 2011.

Guest, Ann Hutchinson. *Labanotation*. New York: New Directions, 1954.

Heynickx, Rajesh, and Jan De Maeyer, eds. *Maritain Factor: Taking Religion into Interwar Modernism*. Leuven: Leuven University Press, 2010.

Hubbs, Joanna. *Mother Russia: The Feminine Myth in Russian Culture*. Bloomington: Indiana University Press, 1988.

Jelavich, Peter. *Berlin Cabaret*. Cambridge, MA: Harvard University Press, 1993.

Johnson, Paul, and Ethan Haimo, eds. *Stravinsky Retrospectives*. Lincoln: University of Nebraska Press, 1987.

Jordan, Stephanie. *Moving Music: Dialogues with Music in Twentieth-Century Ballet*. London: Dance Books, 2000.

Kavanagh, Julie. *Secret Muses: The Life of Frederick Ashton*. New York: Pantheon, 1996.

Laqueur, Walter. *Weimar: A Cultural History, 1918–1933*. New York: Putnam, 1974.

Lederman, Minna, ed. *Stravinsky in the Theatre*. New York: Da Capo, 1975.

Levenson, Thomas. *Einstein in Berlin*. New York: Bantam, 2003.

Lomas, David. *Narcissus Reflected: The Myth of Narcissus in Surrealist and Contemporary Art*. Edinburgh: Fruit Market Gallery, 2011.

Lynn, Kenneth Schuyler. *Charlie Chaplin and His Times*. New York: Simon & Schuster, 1997.

Mackrell, Judith. *Bloomsbury Ballerina: Lydia Lopokova, Imperial Dancer and Mrs John Maynard Keynes*. London: Weidenfeld & Nicolson, 2008.

Mazower, Mark. *Dark Continent: Europe's Twentieth Century*. New York: Vintage, 1998.

Mecham, Peggy. "Les Ballets 1933." PhD diss., New York University, 1993.

Mercer, Kobena. *Exiles, Diasporas, and Strangers*. Cambridge, MA: MIT Press, 2008.

Newhall, Mary Anne Santos. *Mary Wigman*. London: Routledge, 2009.

Partsch-Bergsohn, Isa, and Harold Bergsohn. *The Makers of Modern Dance in Germany: Rudolph Laban, Mary Wigman, Kurt Jooss*. Hightstown, NJ: Princeton Book Company, 2003.

Peukert, Detlev. *The Weimar Republic: The Crisis of Classical Modernity*. New York: Hill and Wang, 1992.

Rabinbach, Anson. *The Human Motor: Energy, Fatigue, and the Origins of Modernity*. Berkeley: University of California Press, 1992.

Raeff, Marc. *Russia Abroad: A Cultural History of the Russian Emigration, 1919–1939*. New York: Oxford University Press, 1990.

Richie, Alexandra. *Faust's Metropolis: A History of Berlin*. London: HarperCollins, 1998.

Robinson, Marc, ed. *Altogether Elsewhere: Writers on Exile*. San Diego: Harcourt Brace, 1994.

Rouault, George, and Jacques Maritain. *Rouault*. New York: Art Treasures of the World, 1954.

Sanders, Ronald. *The Days Grow Short: The Life and Music of Kurt Weill*. New York: Holt, Rinehart and Winston, 1980.

Scheijen, Sjeng. *Diaghilev: A Life*. New York: Oxford University Press, 2010.

Schorske, Carl E. *Fin-de-Siècle Vienna: Politics and Culture*. New York: Vintage Books, 1981.

Shead, Richard. *Ballets Russes*. New York: Knickerbocker, 1998.

Skidelsky, Robert. *John Maynard Keynes: The Economist as Saviour, 1920–1937*. Vol. 2. London: Macmillan, 1992.

Sontag, Susan. *Illness as Metaphor*. New York: Farrar, Straus and Giroux, 1978.

Sorley Walker, Kathrine. *De Basil's Ballets Russes*. New York: Atheneum, 1983.

Spurling, Hilary. *Matisse the Master: A Life of Henri Matisse, the Conquest of Colour, 1909-1954*. New York: Knopf, 2005.
Stach, Reiner. *Kafka: The Decisive Years*. Translated by Shelley Frisch. Orlando, FL: Harcourt, 2005.
Straus, Joseph N. *Remaking the Past: Musical Modernism and the Influence of the Tonal Tradition*. Cambridge, MA: Harvard University Press, 1990.
Styan, J. L. *Max Reinhardt*. Cambridge: Cambridge University Press, 1982.
Sutton, Tina. *The Making of Markova: Diaghilev's Baby Ballerina to Groundbreaking Icon*. New York: Pegasus, 2013.
Taruskin, Richard. *Defining Russia Musically: Historical and Hermeneutical Essays*. Princeton, NJ: Princeton University Press, 1997.
——. *Stravinsky and the Russian Traditions: A Biography of the Works Through Mavra*. 2 vols. Berkeley: University of California Press, 1996.
Tennant, Victoria. *Irina Baronova and the Ballets Russes de Monte Carlo*. Chicago: University of Chicago Press, 2014.
Toepfer, Karl Eric. *Empire of Ecstasy: Nudity and Movement in German Body Culture, 1910-1935*. Berkeley: University of California Press, 1997.
Van den Toorn, Pieter C. *The Music of Igor Stravinsky*. New Haven, CT: Yale University Press, 1983.
Walsh, Stephen. *Stravinsky: A Creative Spring: Russia and France, 1882-1934*. New York: Knopf, 1999.
Weitz, Eric D. *Weimar Germany: Promise and Tragedy*. Princeton, NJ: Princeton University Press, 2007.
White, Eric Walter. *Stravinsky: The Composer and His Works*. Berkeley: University of California Press, 1966.
Williams, Robert C. *Culture in Exile: Russian Émigrés in Germany, 1881-1941*. Ithaca, NY: Cornell University Press, 1972.
Wiser, William. *The Crazy Years: Paris in the Twenties*. New York: Atheneum, 1983.
Worringer, Wilhelm. *Abstraction and Empathy: A Contribution to the Psychology of Style*. Translated by Michael Bullock. Mansfield Centre, CT: Martino Fine Books, 2014.

AMERICA (CHAPTERS 9 TO 24)

Primary

A. Everett Austin, Jr.: A Director's Taste and Achievement. Hartford, CT: Wadsworth Atheneum, 1958.
Balanchine: New York City Ballet in Montreal. Vol. 2. Pleasantville, NY: Video Artists International, 2014. DVD.
Borges, Jorge Luis. *Other Inquisitions, 1937-1952*. Translated by Ruth L. C. Simms. Austin: University of Texas Press, 1964.
Brodsky, Joseph. *On Grief and Reason: Essays*. New York: Farrar, Straus and Giroux, 2020.
Burdick, Eugene, et al. *The Eighth Art: Twenty-three Views of Television Today*. New York: Holt, Rinehart and Winston, 1962.
Cage, John. *Silence: Lectures and Writings*. Middletown, CT: Wesleyan University Press, 1961.
Camus, Albert. *The Myth of Sisyphus, and Other Essays*. Translated by Justin O'Brien. New York: Vintage, 1991.
Cervantes, Miguel de. *Don Quixote*. Translated by Edith Grossman. Introduction by Harold Bloom. New York: Ecco, 2003.
Craft, Robert. *An Improbable Life: Memoirs*. Nashville: Vanderbilt University Press, 2002.
Croce, Arlene. *Afterimages*. New York: Knopf, 1977.

——. *Writing in the Dark, Dancing in "The New Yorker."* New York: Farrar, Straus and Giroux, 2000.

D'Amboise, Jacques. *I Was a Dancer: A Memoir*. New York: Knopf, 2011.

De Lauze, François. *Apologie de la danse*. Translated by Joan Wildeblood. London: Frederick Muller, 1952.

Denby, Edwin. *Dance Writings*. Edited by Robert Cornfield and William MacKay. New York: Knopf, 1986.

——. *Looking at the Dance*. New York: Horizon, 1949.

Eliot, T. S. *Sweeney Agonistes: Fragments of an Aristophanic Melodrama*. London: Faber & Faber, 1932.

Farrell, Suzanne, with Toni Bentley. *Holding On to the Air: An Autobiography*. New York: Summit Books, 1990.

Fromm, Erich. *The Art of Loving*. Introduction by Peter D. Kramer. Afterword by Rainer Funk. 1956. Reprint, New York: Harper Perennial Modern Classics, 2006.

Garis, Robert. *Following Balanchine*. New Haven, CT: Yale University Press, 1995.

Goethe, Johann Wolfgang von. *Faust, Part One*. Translated and with an introduction by David Luke. Oxford: Oxford University Press, 1987.

——. *Faust, Part Two*. Translated and with an introduction by David Luke. Oxford: Oxford University Press, 1994.

Gottlieb, Robert, ed. *Reading Dance: A Gathering of Memoirs, Reportage, Criticism, Profiles, Interviews, and Some Uncategorizable Extras*. New York: Pantheon, 2008.

Gray, Francine du Plessix. *Them: A Memoir of Parents*. New York: Penguin, 2005.

Hochman, Connie, dir. *In Balanchine's Classroom*. New York: Zeitgeist Films/Kino Lorber, 2021.

Hoffmann, E.T.A. *The Nutcracker and the Mouse King*. New York: Penguin, 2007.

James, William. *Writings, 1902–1910*. Edited by Bruce Kuklick. New York: Library of America, 1987.

Kent, Allegra. *Once a Dancer . . . : An Autobiography*. New York: St. Martin's, 1997.

Kirstein, Lincoln. *Ballet Alphabet, a Primer for Laymen*. New York: Kamin, 1939.

——. *The Book of the Dance: A Short History of Classic Theatrical Dancing*. Garden City, NY: Garden City Publishing, 1935.

——. *By with to & from: A Lincoln Kirstein Reader*. Edited by Nicholas Jenkins. New York: Farrar, Straus and Giroux, 1991.

——. *Mosaic: Memoirs*. New York: Farrar, Straus and Giroux, 1994.

——. *Movement and Metaphor: Four Centuries of Ballet*. New York: Praeger, 1970.

——. *Program Notes*. Edited by Randall Bourscheidt. New York: Eakins Press Foundation, 2009.

——. *Quarry: A Collection in Lieu of Memoirs*. Pasadena, CA: Twelvetrees, 1986.

——. *Rhymes of a PFC*. New York: New Directions, 1964.

——. *Thirty Years: Lincoln Kirstein's The New York City Ballet: Expanded to Include the Years 1973–1978, in Celebration of the Company's Thirtieth Anniversary*. New York: Knopf, 1978.

Kirstein, Lincoln, Jonathan Cott, and Edwin Denby. *Portrait of Mr. B: Photographs of George Balanchine*. New York: Viking, 1984.

Kirstein, Lincoln, and Muriel Stuart. *The Classic Ballet: Basic Technique and Terminology*. Preface by George Balanchine. New York: Knopf, 2004.

Le Clercq, Tanaquil. *Mourka: The Autobiography of a Cat*. New York: Stein and Day, 1965.

Lerman, Leo. *The Grand Surprise: The Journals of Leo Lerman*. Edited by Stephen Pascal. New York: Knopf, 2007.

Lithgow, John. *Drama: An Actor's Education.* New York: Harper, 2011.
Logan, Joshua. *Josh, My Up and Down, In and Out Life.* New York: Delacorte, 1976.
Lowry, W. M., ed. *The Performing Arts and American Society.* Englewood Cliffs, NJ: Prentice-Hall, 1978.
Lynes, George Platt. *Ballet.* Pasadena, CA: Twelvetrees, 1985.
——. *George Platt Lynes: Photographs, 1931–1955.* Introduction by Jack Woody. Pasadena, CA: Twelvetrees, 1981.
Magriel, Paul. *Chronicles of the American Dance: From the Shakers to Martha Graham.* New York: Henry Holt, 1948.
Martins, Peter, with Robert Cornfield. *Far from Denmark.* Boston: Little, Brown, 1982.
Mason, Francis, ed. *I Remember Balanchine: Recollections of the Ballet Master by Those Who Knew Him.* New York: Doubleday, 1991.
McCandless, Stanley. *A Method of Lighting the Stage.* New York: Theatre Arts Books, 1958.
Milberg Fisher, Barbara. *In Balanchine's Company: A Dancer's Memoir.* Middletown, CT: Wesleyan University Press, 2006.
Molière. *Don Juan and Other Plays.* Translated by George Graveley and Ian Maclean. Oxford: Oxford University Press, 2008.
Montassier, Gérard. *Le fait culturel.* Paris: Fayard, 1980.
Nabokov, Nicolas. *Bagázh: Memoirs of a Russian Cosmopolitan.* New York: Atheneum, 1975.
Ovid. *Ovid: Metamorphoses.* Translated by Rolfe Humphries. Bloomington: Indiana University Press, 1955.
Palmer, Tony, dir. *Stravinsky: Once at a Border . . .* New York: Pennebaker Hegedus Films, 2003. DVD.
Plato. *Phaedrus.* Translated by Christopher Rowe. New York: Penguin, 2005.
Plisetskaya, Maya. *I, Maya Plisetskaya.* Translated by Antonina W. Bouis. Foreword by Tim Scholl. New Haven, CT: Yale University Press, 2001.
Plotinus. *The Enneads.* Edited by Lloyd P. Gerson. Translated by George Boys-Stones, John M. Dillon, Lloyd P. Gerson, R.A.H. King, Andrew Smith, and James Wilberding. Cambridge: Cambridge University Press, 2018.
Robbins, Jerome. *Jerome Robbins, by Himself: Selections from His Letters, Journals, Drawings, Photographs, and an Unfinished Memoir.* Edited by Amanda Vaill. New York: Knopf, 2019.
Rosenthal, Jean, and Lael Wertenbaker. *The Magic of Light: The Craft and Career of Jean Rosenthal, Pioneer in Lighting for the Modern Stage.* Boston: Little, Brown, 1972.
Schorer, Suki, with Russell Lee. *Suki Schorer on Balanchine Technique.* New York: Knopf, 1999.
Sills, Bettijane. *Broadway, Balanchine, and Beyond: A Memoir.* Gainesville: University Press of Florida, 2019.
Spinoza, Benedictus de. *The Collected Works of Spinoza.* Edited and translated by Edwin Curley. Princeton, NJ: Princeton University Press, 1985–2016.
——. *The Essential Spinoza: Ethics and Related Writings.* Edited by Michael L. Morgan. Translated by Samuel Shirley. Indianapolis, IN: Hackett, 2006.
Stravinsky, Igor. *Poetics of Music in the Form of Six Lessons.* Translated by Arthur Knodel and Ingolf Dahl. Cambridge, MA: Harvard University Press, 1947.
——. *Stravinsky: Selected Correspondence.* Vol. 1. Translated and edited by Robert Craft. New York: Knopf, 1982–85.
Stravinsky, Igor, and Robert Craft. *Conversations with Igor Stravinsky.* Garden City, NY: Doubleday, 1959.
——. *Dialogues.* London: Faber Music, 1982.

——. *Dialogues and a Diary*. Garden City, NY: Doubleday, 1963.

——. *Memories and Commentaries*. Garden City, NY: Doubleday, 1960.

——. *Themes and Episodes*. New York: Knopf, 1966.

Stravinsky, Vera. *Dearest Bubushkin: The Correspondence of Vera and Igor Stravinsky, 1921-1954, with Excerpts from Vera Stravinsky's Diaries, 1922-1971*. Edited by Robert Craft. Translated by Lucia Davidova. New York: Thames and Hudson, 1985.

Stravinsky, Vera, and Robert Craft. *Stravinsky in Pictures and Documents*. New York: Simon & Schuster, 1978.

Tallchief, Maria, with Larry Kaplan. *Maria Tallchief: America's Prima Ballerina*. New York: Henry Holt, 1997.

Taylor, Paul. *Private Domain: An Autobiography*. Pittsburgh, PA: University of Pittsburgh Press, 1999.

Tomlinson, Mel, with Claudia Folts. *Beyond My Dreams*. Teaneck, NJ: TurningPointPress, 2018.

Turan, Kenneth, and Joseph Papp. *Free for All: Joe Papp, the Public, and the Greatest Theater Story Ever Told*. New York: Anchor, 2010.

Van Vechten, Carl, ed. *The Dance Writings of Carl Van Vechten*. Edited and with an introduction by Paul Padgette. New York: Dance Horizons, 1974.

Villella, Edward, with Larry Kaplan. *Prodigal Son: Dancing for Balanchine in a World of Pain and Magic*. New York: Simon & Schuster, 1992.

Zorina, Vera. *Zorina*. New York: Farrar, Straus and Giroux, 1986.

Secondary

Anderson, Jack. *The Nutcracker Ballet*. New York: Mayflower, 1979.

Ashton, Dore. *Noguchi East and West*. New York: Knopf, 1992.

Ballon, Hilary, and Kenneth T. Jackson, eds. *Robert Moses and the Modern City: The Transformation of New York*. New York: W. W. Norton, 2007.

Banes, Sally. *Dancing Women: Female Bodies on Stage*. New York: Routledge, 1998.

——. *Writing Dancing in the Age of Postmodernism*. Middletown, CT: Wesleyan University Press, 2011.

Barkan, Leonard. *The Gods Made Flesh: Metamorphosis and the Pursuit of Paganism*. New Haven, CT: Yale University Press, 1986.

——. *Nature's Work of Art: The Human Body as Image of the World*. New Haven, CT: Yale University Press, 1975.

Bender, Thomas. *New York Intellect: A History of Intellectual Life in New York City, from 1750 to the Beginnings of Our Own Time*. New York: Knopf, 1987.

Berg, A. Scott. *Goldwyn: A Biography*. New York: Knopf, 1989.

Bodensieck, Julius, ed. *Encyclopedia of the Lutheran Church*. Vol. 1. Minneapolis: Augsburg, 1965.

Boyd, Brian. *Vladimir Nabokov: The American Years*. Princeton, NJ: Princeton University Press, 1991.

Buckle, Richard, ed. *Katherine Dunham: Her Dancers, Singers, Musicians*. London: Ballet Publications, 1948.

Caro, Robert. *The Power Broker: Robert Moses and the Fall of New York*. New York: Vintage, 1975.

Caute, David. *The Dancer Defects: The Struggle for Cultural Supremacy During the Cold War*. Oxford: Oxford University Press, 2003.

Chilton, Karen. *Hazel Scott: The Pioneering Journey of a Jazz Pianist from Café Society to Hollywood to HUAC*. Ann Arbor: University of Michigan Press, 2008.

Chimènes, Myriam, ed. *La Vie musicale sous Vichy*. Brussels: Éditions Complexe, 2001.

Chujoy, Anatole. *The New York City Ballet*. New York: Knopf, 1953.

Clark, VèVè A., and Sara E. Johnson, eds. *Kaiso!: Writings by and about Katherine Dunham*. Madison: University of Wisconsin Press, 2005.

Coleman, Peter. *The Liberal Conspiracy: The Congress for Cultural Freedom and the Struggle for the Mind of Postwar Europe*. New York: Free Press, 1989.

Copeland, Roger, and Marshall Cohen, eds. *What Is Dance?: Readings in Theory and Criticism*. New York: Oxford University Press, 1983.

Croft, Clare. *Dancers as Diplomats: American Choreography in Cultural Exchange*. Oxford: Oxford University Press, 2015.

Das, Joanna Dee. *Katherine Dunham: Dance and the African Diaspora*. New York: Oxford University Press, 2017.

DeFrantz, Thomas F., ed. *Dancing Many Drums: Excavations in African American Dance*. Madison: University of Wisconsin Press, 2002.

Dickson, Gary. *The Children's Crusade: Medieval History, Modern Mythistory*. New York: Palgrave Macmillan, 2008.

Dreyfus, Laurence. *Bach and the Patterns of Invention*. Cambridge, MA: Harvard University Press, 2004.

Dunning, Jennifer. *"But First a School": The First Fifty Years of the School of American Ballet*. New York: Viking, 1985.

Emery, Lynne Fauley. *Black Dance: From 1619 to Today*. Princeton, NJ: Princeton Book Company, 1998.

Epstein, Jason, and Elizabeth Barlow. *East Hampton: A History and Guide*. New York: Random House, 1985.

Fong, Kevin. *Extreme Medicine: How Exploration Transformed Medicine in the Twentieth Century*. New York: Penguin, 2014.

Franko, Mark. *The Fascist Turn in the Dance of Serge Lifar: Interwar French Ballet and the German Occupation*. New York: Oxford University Press, 2020.

Friedman, Lawrence. *The Lives of Erich Fromm: Love's Prophet*. New York: Columbia University Press, 2013.

Friedman, Samantha, and Jodi Hauptman, eds. *Lincoln Kirstein's Modern*. New York: Museum of Modern Art, 2019.

Fursenko, Aleksandr, and Timothy Naftali. *One Hell of a Gamble: Khrushchev, Castro, and Kennedy, 1958–1964*. New York: W. W. Norton, 1997.

Gaddis, Eugene R. *Magician of the Modern: Chick Austin and the Transformation of the Arts in America*. New York: Knopf, 2000.

Gaines, Steven. *Philistines at the Hedgerow: Passion and Property in the Hamptons*. Boston: Little, Brown, 1998.

Garfias, Robert. *Gagaku: The Music and Dances of the Japanese Imperial Household*. New York: Theatre Art Books, 1959.

Garrett, Don, ed. *The Cambridge Companion to Spinoza*. Cambridge: Cambridge University Press, 1996.

———. *Nature and Necessity in Spinoza's Philosophy*. New York: Oxford University Press, 2018.

Goldner, Nancy. *Balanchine Variations*. Gainesville: University Press of Florida, 2008.

Gooch, Brad. *City Poet: The Life and Times of Frank O'Hara*. New York: Knopf, 1993.

Gordon, Linda. *The Moral Property of Women: A History of Birth Control in America*. Urbana: University of Illinois Press, 2002.

Gottschild, Brenda Dixon. *Digging the Africanist Presence in American Performance: Dance and Other Contexts*. Westport, CT: Greenwood, 1996.

Gray, John. *Feline Philosophy: Cats and the Meaning of Life*. London: Allen Lane, 2020.

Green, Martin, and John C. Swan. *The Triumph of Pierrot: The Commedia dell'arte and the Modern Imagination*. University Park: Pennsylvania State University Press, 1993.

Gruen, John. *The Private World of Ballet*. New York: Viking, 1975.

Guilbaut, Serge. *How New York Stole the Idea of Modern Art: Abstract Expressionism, Freedom, and the Cold War*. Translated by Arthur Goldhammer. Chicago: University of Chicago Press, 1983.

Hambourg, Maria Morris, and Jeff L. Rosenheim, eds. *Irving Penn: Centennial*. New York: Metropolitan Museum of Art, 2017.

Harley, James. *Xenakis: His Life in Music*. New York: Routledge, 2004.

Harrison, Helen, and Constance Ayers Denne, eds. *Hamptons Bohemia: Two Centuries of Artists and Writers on the Beach*. Foreword by Edward Albee. San Francisco: Chronicle, 2002.

Hatfield, Henry. *Goethe: A Critical Introduction*. Cambridge, MA: Harvard University Press, 1964.

Hatherley, Owen. *Landscapes of Communism: A History Through Buildings*. New York: New Press, 2015.

Heilbut, Anthony. *Exiled in Paradise: German Refugee Artists and Intellectuals in America, from the 1930s to the Present*. Berkeley: University of California Press, 1997.

Hill, Constance Valis. *Tap Dancing America: A Cultural History*. New York: Oxford University Press, 2010.

Hollander, Anne. *Seeing Through Clothes*. New York: Viking, 1978.

Holmes, Brooke. *The Symptom and the Subject: The Emergence of the Physical Body in Ancient Greece*. Princeton, NJ: Princeton University Press, 2010.

Horowitz, Joseph. *Artists in Exile: How Refugees from Twentieth-Century War and Revolution Transformed the American Performing Arts*. New York: Harper, 2008.

Hyland, William G. *Richard Rodgers*. New Haven, CT: Yale University Press, 1998.

Iversen, Hans Raun. *Rites of Ordination and Commitment in the Churches of the Nordic Countries: Theology and Terminology*. Copenhagen: Museum Tuscalanum Press, 2006.

Jackson, Kenneth T., and David S. Dunbar. *Empire City: New York Through the Centuries*. New York: Columbia University Press, 2002.

Joseph, Charles M. *Stravinsky and Balanchine: A Journey of Invention*. New Haven, CT: Yale University Press, 2002.

———. *Stravinsky's Ballets*. New Haven, CT: Yale University Press, 2011.

Jowitt, Deborah. *Jerome Robbins: His Life, His Theater, His Dance*. New York: Simon & Schuster, 2004.

Kalstone, David. *Five Temperaments: Elizabeth Bishop, Robert Lowell, James Merrill, Adrienne Rich, John Ashbery*. New York: Oxford University Press, 1977.

Kanstroom, Dan. *Deportation Nation: Outsiders in American History*. Cambridge, MA: Harvard University Press, 2007.

Kendall, Elizabeth. *Dancing: A Ford Foundation Report*. New York: Ford Foundation, 1983.

King, Terry. *Gregor Piatigorsky: The Life and Career of the Virtuoso Cellist*. Jefferson, NC: Mcfarland, 2010.

Knight, Amy. *Beria: Stalin's First Lieutenant*. Princeton, NJ: Princeton University Press, 1993.

Koerner, Joseph Leo. *Caspar David Friedrich and the Subject of Landscape*. New Haven, CT: Yale University Press, 1990.

Kosinski, Dorothy M. "The Image of Orpheus in Symbolist Art and Literature." PhD diss., New York University, 1985.

Kotkin, Stephen. *Stalin.* Vol. 2, *Waiting for Hitler, 1928–1941.* New York: Penguin, 2018.

Lamster, Mark. *The Man in the Glass House: Philip Johnson, Architect of the Modern Century.* New York: Little, Brown, 2018.

Laqueur, Thomas Walter. *Making Sex: Body and Gender from the Greeks to Freud.* Cambridge, MA: Harvard University Press, 1990.

——. *The Work of the Dead: A Cultural History of Mortal Remains.* Princeton, NJ: Princeton University Press, 2015.

Lawrence, Greg. *Dance with Demons: The Life of Jerome Robbins.* New York: Putnam, 2001.

Leaman, Kara Yoo. "Analyzing Music and Dance: Balanchine's Choreography to Tchaikovsky and the Choreomusical Score." PhD diss., Yale University, 2016.

Leddick, David. *George Platt Lynes, 1907–1955.* Foreword by Anatole Pohorilenko. New York: Taschen, 2000.

——. *Intimate Companions: A Triography of George Platt Lynes, Paul Cadmus, Lincoln Kirstein, and Their Circle.* New York: St. Martin's, 2000.

Lipsey, Roger. *Gurdjieff Reconsidered: The Life, the Teachings, the Legacy.* Boulder, CO: Shambhala, 2019.

——. *Hammarskjöld: A Life.* Ann Arbor: University of Michigan Press, 2013.

Lobenthal, Joel. *Wilde Times: Patricia Wilde, George Balanchine, and the Rise of New York City Ballet.* Lebanon, NH: ForeEdge, 2016.

Marías, Fernando, ed. *El Greco of Toledo: Painter of the Visible and the Invisible.* Madrid: El Viso, 2014.

Martin, Ralph G. *Lincoln Center for the Performing Arts.* Englewood Cliffs, NJ: Prentice-Hall, 1971.

McClary, Susan. *Feminine Endings: Music, Gender, and Sexuality.* Minneapolis: University of Minnesota Press, 2002.

McDaniel, Cadra Peterson. *American-Soviet Cultural Diplomacy: The Bolshoi Ballet's American Premiere.* Lanham, MD: Lexington, 2015.

Menand, Louis. *The Free World: Art and Thought in the Cold War.* New York: Farrar, Straus and Giroux, 2021.

Mendelson, Edward. *Early Auden.* New York: Viking, 1981.

——. *Later Auden.* New York: Farrar, Straus and Giroux, 1999.

Monk, Ray. *Ludwig Wittgenstein: The Duty of Genius.* New York: Free Press, 1990.

Mueller, John E. *Astaire Dancing: The Musical Films.* New York: Knopf, 1985.

Nash, George Harlan. *The Conservative Intellectual Movement in America since 1945.* New York: Basic Books, 1979.

Nicholas, Lynn. *The Rape of Europa: The Fate of Europe's Treasures in the Third Reich and the Second World War.* New York: Vintage, 1994.

Onslo-Ford, Gordon, ed. *Esteban Frances: 1913–1976.* Madrid: Dirección General de Patrimonio Cultural, Consejería de Educación y Cultura, 1997.

Orlov, Andrei A. *Dark Mirrors: Azazel and Satanael in Early Jewish Demonology.* Albany: State University of New York Press, 2011.

Oshinsky, David M. *Polio: An American Story.* Oxford: Oxford University Press, 2005.

Pagels, Elaine. *Adam, Eve, and the Serpent.* New York: Random House, 1988.

——. *Beyond Belief: The Secret Gospel of Thomas.* New York: Random House, 2003.

——. *The Gnostic Gospels.* London: Phoenix, 2006.

——. *Revelations: Visions, Prophecy, and Politics in the Book of Revelation.* New York: Viking Press, 2012.

Perl, Jed. *New Art City*. New York: Knopf, 2005.

Plaskin, Glenn. *Horowitz: A Biography of Vladimir Horowitz*. Translated by Gerald Fitzgerald. New York: W. Morrow, 1983.

Poggioli, Renato. *The Theory of the Avant-Garde*. Cambridge, MA: Belknap, 1981.

Posnock, Ross. *Renunciation: Acts of Abandonment by Writers, Philosophers, and Artists*. Cambridge, MA: Harvard University Press, 2016.

Prevots, Naima. *Dance for Export: Cultural Diplomacy and the Cold War*. Middletown, CT: Wesleyan University Press, 1999.

Prose, Francine. *The Lives of Muses: Nine Women and the Artists They Inspired*. New York: HarperCollins, 2002.

Protopopescu, Orel. *Dancing Past the Light: The Life of Tanaquil Le Clercq*. Gainesville: University Press of Florida, 2021.

Ramsey, Christopher, ed. *Tributes: Celebrating Fifty Years of New York City Ballet*. New York: W. Morrow, 1998.

Randel, Julia. "Dancing with Stravinsky: Balanchine, *Agon*, Movements for Piano and Orchestra, and the Language of Classical Ballet." PhD diss., Harvard University, 2004.

Raymond, Joad. *Milton's Angels: The Early-Modern Imagination*. Oxford: Oxford University Press, 2010.

Reed, Christopher. *Art and Homosexuality: A History of Ideas*. New York: Oxford University Press, 2011.

Reynolds, Nancy. *Repertory in Review: 40 Years of the New York City Ballet*. Introduction by Lincoln Kirstein. New York: Dial, 1977.

Reynolds, Nancy, and Malcolm McCormick. *No Fixed Points: Dance in the Twentieth Century*. New Haven, CT: Yale University Press, 2003.

Rich, Alan. *The Lincoln Center Story*. New York: Houghton Mifflin, 1984.

Richmond, Yale. *Cultural Exchange and the Cold War: Raising the Iron Curtain*. University Park: Pennsylvania State University Press, 2003.

Robinson, Harlow. *The Last Impresario: The Life, Times, and Legacy of Sol Hurok*. New York: Viking, 1994.

Robinson, Harlow. *Sergei Prokofiev: A Biography*. Boston: Northeastern University Press, 2002.

———. *Russians in Hollywood, Hollywood's Russians: Biography of an Image*. Boston: Northeastern University Press, 2007.

Rosen, Charles. *The Classical Style: Haydn, Mozart, Beethoven*. New York: W. W. Norton, 1997.

———. *The Romantic Generation*. Cambridge, MA: Harvard University Press, 1995.

Said, Edward. *Reflections on Exile and Other Essays*. Cambridge, MA: Harvard University Press, 2000.

Salmon, Shawn Connelly. "To the Land of the Future: A History of Intourist and Travel to the Soviet Union, 1929–1991." PhD diss., University of California, Berkeley, 2008.

Schmitz, Nancy Brooks. "A Profile of Catherine Littlefield, a Pioneer of American Ballet." EdD diss., Temple University, 1986.

Scholem, Gershom. *On the Kabbalah and Its Symbolism*. Translated by Ralph Manheim. Foreword by Bernard McGinn. New York: Schocken, 1996.

Seibert, Brian. *What the Eye Hears: A History of Tap Dancing*. New York: Farrar, Straus and Giroux, 2015.

Sherr, Laurence. "The Genesis of *Agon*: Stravinsky, Balanchine, and the New York City Ballet." DMA diss., University of Illinois at Urbana-Champaign, 1988.

Silk, M. S., and J. P. Stern. *Nietzsche on Tragedy*. Cambridge: Cambridge University Press, 1981.

Skeel, Sharon. *Catherine Littlefield: A Life in Dance*. New York: Oxford University Press, 2020.

Smith, Jane S. *Patenting the Sun: Polio and the Salk Vaccine*. New York: W. Morrow, 1990.

Sorrell, Walter, ed. *The Dance Has Many Faces*. Chicago: A Capella Books, 1992.

Sowell, Debra Hickenlooper. *The Christensen Brothers: An American Dance Epic*. New York: Routledge, 1998.

Stamelman, Richard. *Perfume: Joy, Scandal, Sin: A Cultural History of Fragrance from 1750 to the Present*. New York: Rizzoli, 2006.

Stang, Charles. *Our Divine Double*. Cambridge, MA: Harvard University Press, 2016.

Stansell, Christine. *American Moderns: Bohemian New York and the Creation of a New Century*. New York: Metropolitan Books, 2000.

Steichen, James. *Balanchine and Kirstein's American Enterprise*. New York: Oxford University Press, 2019.

Stein, Jean. *Edie: American Girl*. Edited with George Plimpton. New York: Grove, 1994.

Stevens, Mark, and Annalyn Swan. *De Kooning: An American Master*. New York: Knopf, 2004.

Stracky, Cathy, with Carol Craig. *Love All Around: The Romana Kryzanowska Biography*. Fort Wayne, IN: C & C Projects, 2019.

Straus, Joseph N. *Stravinsky's Late Music*. Cambridge: Cambridge University Press, 2001.

Taubman, William. *Khrushchev: The Man and His Era*. New York: W. W. Norton, 2003.

Teachout, Terry. *All in the Dances: A Brief Life of George Balanchine*. Orlando, FL: Harcourt, 2004.

Turner, Charles. "Xenakis in America." PhD diss., City University of New York, 2014.

Vaill, Amanda. *Somewhere: The Life of Jerome Robbins*. New York: Broadway Books, 2006.

Vendler, Helen. *A Life of Learning: Charles Homer Haskins Lecture for 2001*. New York: American Council of Learned Societies, 2001.

———. *Poets Thinking: Pope, Whitman, Dickinson, Yeats*. Cambridge, MA: Harvard University Press, 2004.

Walczak, Barbara, and Una Kai. *Balanchine the Teacher: Fundamentals That Shaped the First Generation of New York City Ballet Dancers*. Gainesville: University Press of Florida, 2008.

Walsh, Stephen. *Stravinsky: The Second Exile: France and America, 1934–1971*. New York: Knopf, 2006.

Warner, Marina. *Alone of All Her Sex: The Myth and Cult of the Virgin Mary*. Oxford: Oxford University Press, 2013.

———. *Phantasmagoria: Spirit Visions, Metaphors, and Media into the Twenty-First Century*. Oxford: Oxford University Press, 2006.

Washington, Peter. *Madame Blavatsky's Baboon: A History of the Mystics, Mediums, and Misfits Who Brought Spiritualism to America*. New York: Schocken, 1993.

Webb, James. *The Harmonious Circle: The Lives and Work of G. I. Gurdjieff, P. D. Ouspensky, and Their Followers*. Boston: Shambhala, 1987.

Weber, Nicholas Fox. *Patron Saints: Five Rebels Who Opened America to a New Art, 1928–1943*. New York: Knopf, 1992.

Williams, Bernard. *On Opera*. New Haven, CT: Yale University Press, 2006.

Wilson, Edmund. *The Thirties: From Notebooks and Diaries of the Period*. Edited with an introduction by Leon Edel. New York: Farrar, Straus and Giroux, 1980.

———. *The Twenties: From Notebooks and Diaries of the Period*. Edited with an introduction by Leon Edel. New York: Farrar, Straus and Giroux, 1975.

Yates, Frances A. *The French Academies of the Sixteenth Century*. New York: Routledge, 1988.

Young, Edgar B. *Lincoln Center, the Building of an Institution*. New York: New York University Press, 1980.

THE END OF THE DANCE (CHAPTERS 25 TO 29)

Primary

Bentley, Toni. *Winter Season: A Dancer's Journal*. New York: Random House, 1982.

Bulgakov, Mikhail. *The Master and Margarita*. Translated by Diana Burgin and Katherine Tiernan O'Connor. Annotations and Afterword by Ellendea Proffer. New York: Vintage, 1996.

——. *The Master and Margarita*. Translated by Richard Pevear and Larissa Volokhonsky. Introduction by Richard Pevear. New York: Penguin, 1997.

Gottlieb, Robert. *Avid Reader: A Life*. New York: Farrar, Straus and Giroux, 2016.

Kirstein, Lincoln, ed. *Union Jack: The New York City Ballet*. New York: Eakins, 1977.

Schumann, Robert. *The Letters of Robert Schumann*. Selected and edited by Karl Storck. Translated by Hannah Bryant. New York: B. Blom, 1971.

Secondary

Bednar, Gerald Joseph. "Faith as Imagination: The Contribution of William F. Lynch, S.J." PhD diss., Fordham University, 1990.

Brown, Malcolm Hamrick, ed. A *Shostakovich Casebook*. Bloomington: Indiana University Press, 2004.

Chernaik, Judith. *Schumann: The Faces and the Masks*. New York: Knopf, 2018.

Goldner, Nancy, ed. *The Stravinsky Festival of the New York City Ballet*. New York: Eakins Press, 1974.

Guest, Ann Hutchinson. *Dance Notation: The Process of Recording Movement on Paper*. London: Dance Books, 1984.

Hogan, Anne, ed. *Balanchine Then and Now*. Lewes, UK: Sylph Editions, 2008.

Jordan, Stephanie. *Stravinsky Dances: Re-visions Across a Century*. Alton, UK: Dance Books, 2007.

Kok, Roe-Min, and Laura Tunbridge, eds. *Rethinking Schumann*. New York: Oxford University Press, 2011.

Prusiner, Stanley B. *Madness and Memory: The Discovery of Prions—A New Biological Principle of Disease*. New Haven, CT: Yale University Press, 2014.

Rowland, Lewis P. *NINDS at 50: An Incomplete History Celebrating the Fiftieth Anniversary of the National Institution of Neurological Disorders and Stroke*. Bethesda, MD: U.S. Department of Health and Human Services, Public Health Service, National Institutes of Health, 2001.

Schimmel, Annemarie. *Mystical Dimensions of Islam*. Chapel Hill: University of North Carolina Press, 1975.

Sells, Michael A. *Mystical Languages of Unsaying*. Chicago: University of Chicago Press, 1994.

NOTES

Russian and Georgian archival and selected published sources have been translated for the author. A selected bibliography of Russian sources can be found at balletcenter.nyu.edu/MrB.

EPIGRAPH

1. George Balanchine speaking in *In Balanchine's Classroom,* directed by Connie Hochman (New York: Zeitgeist Films/Kino Lorber, 2021). The quote comes from a taped backstage conversation between Balanchine and his former dancer, then director and friend, Alfonso Cata. The tape was entrusted to Hochman by Cata's partner, the influential teacher Wilhelm Burmann. The last four lines come from WNET: *USA Dance: NYCB* (1965). With thanks to Connie Hochman.

INTRODUCTION: DEAD SOULS

1. George Balanchine, interview by John Gruen, Nov. 20, 1972, sound recording, *MGZTL 4-3110 JRC or *MGZTL 4-129, LPA.
2. Jacques d'Amboise Diary, July 8, 1965, courtesy of Jacques d'Amboise: "Sister Mary Mother the Breath" or "the breath."
3. Vernon Duke to Bernard Taper, Oct. 19, 1961, Taper Papers. This quote and others to come are from the papers of Bernard Taper, kindly shared with the author by his son, Mark Taper. They include letters, documents, and interviews (some recorded) with Balanchine and his dancers.
4. George Balanchine to Betty Cage, undated [c. 1962], RGI 1–10: Personal and Pro. Papers, Correspondence Balanchine-Mole, f. 180, John Taras Collection, NYCB Archives. Cage responded on Feb. 19, 1962: "I will tell Terry no. In fact, I will be delighted to tell Terry no."
5. W. H. Auden, quoted in Taper, *Balanchine,* 2nd ed., 5.

CHAPTER 1: HAPPY FAMILIES

1. Tamara: Metric book, Church of the Nativity on the Sands, 1902, f. 19, op. 127, d. 1317, 117–18, TsGIA SPb.

   Georgi: Metric book, Church of the Nativity on the Sands, 1904, f. 19, op. 127, d. 1586, 71–72, TsGIA SPb.

   Andrei: Metric book, Church of the Nativity on the Sands, 1905, f. 19, op. 127, d. 1672, 193–94, TsGIA SPb.

   Personal data of G. Balanchivadze (Ballet School), f. R-298, op. 2, d. 153, TsGALI SPb, includes the birth certificate, dated Apr. 18, 1906, and issued Jan. 23, 1920. I am grateful to Professors Michael Reynolds and Ekaterina Pravilova, both at Princeton University, for their help in interpreting these documents. Pavel Khuchua states that in 1900 Maria gave birth to Nina, who died as a baby, but so far research has been unable to locate birth or death records, and Khuchua offers no sources. Khuchua, *Meliton Balanchivadze.* The first four Russian chapters owe much to Elizabeth Kendall's groundbreaking *Balanchine and the Lost Muse.*
2. Kendall has shown that in the late 1930s, Meliton's Georgian wife, Gayane, petitioned the state to take Meliton's pension away from Maria, presumably after Meliton died in 1937. Gayane claimed that Meliton had continued to send money to her all his life. Kendall, *Balanchine and the Lost Muse,* 246.
3. George Balanchine, interview by Bernard Taper, 1961, Taper Tapes.
4. State peasants, unlike serfs, were free but obligated, through taxes and tithes, to a variety of local leaders and, after the Russian consolidation of power in the early nineteenth century, directly to the Russian state. Suny, *Making of the Georgian Nation,* 63–112.
5. Kutaisi Imereti Diocesan Chancellery, f. 21, op. 1, d. 18071, Kutaisi Central Archive: Imereti diocesan office for 1860–90 indicates that Anton and his wife, Ivlita, were state peasants. He died in 1889, and he had four children (Meliton, Ivan, Vasily, and Anna). In the Kutaisi Central Archive, we read of Khosia Balanchivadze, father of Otia (age fifty-four, who is too sick to take Communion that year), who married Anna Sekchina and gave birth to Kaikhosro (age twenty-five), a "monk widower" (Geri Kvrivi), and Niko (age sixteen). Of these three children, Kaikhosro Balanchivadze marries Tula Simonis, and they give birth to Anton Balanchivadze (age six). See also Kendall, *Balanchine and the Lost Muse,* 16, 246.
6. De Waal, *Caucasus,* 40.
7. Rayfield, *Edge of Empires;* Suny, *Making of the Georgian Nation;* De Waal, *Caucasus;* Jones, *Socialism in Georgian Colors.*
8. Kendall, *Balanchine and the Lost Muse,*16–22; Suny, *Making of the Georgian Nation,* 65; Meliton's school performance: f. 7, op. 1, d. 1090, Kutaisi Theological School, Kutaisi Central Archive; Vasiliy Balanchivadze, f. 789, op. 13, d. 158, RGIA (baptism); "This is my brother": Jacques d'Amboise, interview by the author, 2014.
9. Meliton Balanchivadze, personal file held at Tbilisi State Museum of Georgian Theater, Music, Film and Choreography; "Stone Sack": Kotkin, *Stalin,* vol. 1, 30–35; Suny, *Making of the Georgian Nation,* 130–43.
10. Kendall, *Balanchine and the Lost Muse,* 15–21; Khuchua, *Meliton Balanchivadze.* On Meliton's organizing of Georgian events, see f. 480, op. 2, d. 195, and f. 481, op. 1, d. 223, Tbilisi Historical Archive (XIX c.–1921). Meliton also became choirmaster for Lado Agniashvili's locally renowned choir, with its mix of folk traditions and Western musical styles. Tsurtsumia and Jordania, *Echoes from Georgia,* 39. I am grateful to John Graham for his expertise and help with the complexity of Georgian musical traditions.
11. Meliton Balanchivadze, St. Petersburg Conservatory of Music application, 1889, f. 361, op. 1, d. 187, TsGIA SPb.

12. Khuchua, *Meliton Balanchivadze*, 33–34; f. 481, op. 1, d. 223, Tbilisi Historical Archive, includes requests for permission to organize a concert to raise funds for the Society of Propagandizing Education Amongst Georgians in 1889; Vaso Balanchivadze, personal file held at State Museum of Georgian Theater, Music, Film and Choreography—Art Palace, Tbilisi.
13. Wortman, *Scenarios of Power*, 226.
14. Khuchua, *Meliton Balanchivadze*, 33–34.
15. George Balanchine, interview by Bernard Taper, 1961, Taper Tapes; Balanchivadze, *1905*.
16. Kendall, *Balanchine and the Lost Muse*, 32.
17. George Balanchine, interview by Bernard Taper, 1961, Taper Tapes.
18. Notes on interview with Andrei Melitonovich Balanchivadze, b. 18, f. Last Minute Interviews, Richard Buckle Papers, HRC; Natalia Alexeevna Almedingen, f. 2183, op. 1, d. 31, TsGIA SPb; Alexander and Alexey Almedingen, *Ves Petersburg*, 1907; Sofia Almedingen-Chumbadze, *Ves Petersburg*, 1913; Alexander Nikolaevich Almedingen, f. 126, op. 1, d. 3, TsGIA SPb; Pushkin House Archives, among others; Balzer, *Russia's Missing Middle Class*; Rieber, *Merchants and Entrepreneurs*; Wirtschafter, *Social Identity in Imperial Russia*; Figes, *Natasha's Dance*. With special thanks to Michael Reynolds and to Ekaterina Pravilova for their help with the Russian social landscape.
19. "Her family name": George Balanchine, interview by Bernard Taper, 1961, Taper Tapes; Oldenberg Institute: f. 467, TsGIA SPb, esp. op. 1, 45; Bisha, *Russian Women*; Engel, *Mothers and Daughters*; Meinertz, *Vera Volkova*, 200 (Volkova attended Smolny); Stites, *Women's Liberation Movement*; Foster, *Diplomatic Memoirs*; Sophie Kropotkin, "The Higher Education of Women in Russia," *Nineteenth Century* 43, no. 251 (1898): 117–34; "La Marquise de Fontenoy," *Chicago Tribune*, July 9, 1914, 6. A photo of the Oldenberg students is reproduced in Ometev and Stuart, *St. Petersburg*, 220–21. When Balanchine left Russia, he sent money to Nadezda for years, since his family told him she was an old maid. Andrei said she died poor and alone in the 1930s in Leningrad.
20. We do not know the precise scope of the lottery winnings—we know what we know through the Khuchua biography and the memories of Andrei Balanchivadze and of Balanchine himself. Balanchine said the ticket yielded one hundred thousand rubles and was Meliton's, but Kendall has shown that the property later purchased was in Maria's name, suggesting that the ticket and the money were hers: Kendall, *Balanchine and the Lost Muse*, 23. In Eugenie Ouroussow, "Notes on Balanchine: The Father," Taper Papers, Ouroussow says:

    > Fortune played a terrible trick on this unworldly man [Meliton]. Like almost everyone else in Russia in those days, he occasionally bought tickets for the national lottery. One day, in need of cash, he decided to sell his ticket. The bank clerk to whom he showed it told him that he had won 200,000 roubles—a fortune in those times. . . . Balanchivadze bought a smelting factory which failed and bought shares in several similar ventures. A few months later he was in jail for bankruptcy and debts. George didn't know this but remembers this period because everyone was sad and his mother often cried. She and the children went to live in a small Finnish town, neither city nor country. There they lived surrounded by snow. George didn't go to school, he studied at home. His best memories of that period are of piano lessons with his Russian mother.

21. Andrey Ukhov, "Preferences Toward Risk and Asset Prices: Evidence from Russian Lottery Bonds," working paper, Cornell University School of Hotel Administration, 2005;

Pavel Lizunov, "Russian Society and the Stock Exchange in the Late Nineteenth and Early Twentieth Centuries," *Russian Studies in History* 54, no. 2 (2015): 106–42; Antonov, *Bankrupts and Usurers of Imperial Russia.*

22. Chekhov tells the story of a couple who buy a ticket, and the thought of winning inspires an elaborate dream of happiness (a dacha!) that quickly unravels with greed, selfishness, more greed, and fighting over a future they don't yet have. The mere idea of the lottery ticket poisons their marriage and ruins their lives.
23. Meliton Antonovich Balanchivadze to Nikolai Mikhailovich Findeisen, 1907–1927, f. 816, op. 2, d. 1135, Department of Manuscripts, Russian National Library. Meliton reports on some of his wayward financial dealings in 1914, saying that he has lost his power-of-attorney documents and is waiting for Maria to sign.
24. The lore from the still-resentful Georgian side of the family filtered down to Georges Mamoulia, Apollon Balanchivadze's grandson, who says that Meliton had been involved with Maria, but had rushed back to Georgia and bribed a local priest to erase the record of his earlier marriage only so that he could marry her once she had won the lottery. Georges Mamoulia, interview by the author, Jan. 2018.
25. George Balanchine, interview by Bernard Taper, 1961, Taper Tapes. Other known addresses where the Balanchivadzes lived in these years:

    1902: Kirochnaya, 23
    1903: 4th Rozhdestvenskaya, 18-4
    1904: Baskov Pereulok, 23
    1907 or 1909: Suvorovsky Prospekt, 47

    Kendall, *Balanchine and the Lost Muse,* 247, 24, 28; T. N. Gorina, "Addresses of Georgy Balanchivadze in St. Petersburg-Petrograd," *Vestnik Akademii russkogo baleta imeni A.IA. Vaganova,* no. 1 (36), 2015, 14—Gorina says 1909 instead of 1907 for Suvorovsky Prospekt, citing official address books.
26. Kendall, *Balanchine and the Lost Muse,* 36, 249.
27. Meinander, *History of Finland.* I am grateful to Professor Meinander for kindly answering my questions.
28. Childhood photos held in the Ballet Society Collection, NYCB Archives.
29. Birth certificates: Kendall, *Balanchine and the Lost Muse,* 29–33.
30. Ouroussow, "Notes on Balanchine: The Father," Taper Papers.
31. Quoted in Kendall, *Balanchine and the Lost Muse,* 35.
32. Volkov, *Balanchine's Tchaikovsky,* 111–12. Volkov's earlier book on Shostakovich proved him an unreliable source, but much of what he writes of Balanchine rings true. He claims, however, to have misplaced the tapes and notes of his conversations with Balanchine; Keti Balanchivadze confirms that Andrei believed the Kresty story (Tsiskari and Ketevan Balanchivadze, interview by the author, Oct. 2017). The relevant Kresty Prison archives, including lists of inmates, were apparently destroyed in the revolutionary years.
33. Fiftieth birthday: Kendall, *Balanchine and the Lost Muse,* 34–35; rose: Taper, *Balanchine,* 27–28.

CHAPTER 2: ICONS OF CHILDHOOD

1. George Balanchine, interview by Bernard Taper, 1961, Taper Tapes.
2. Volkov, *Balanchine's Tchaikovsky,* 183.
3. R. Yuszczuk and B. Nicoloff, "An Interview with George Balanchine," *Orthodox Concern* 2, no. 4, 1967, 10–14.

4. Barbara Horgan has icons or images of St. George given to her by Balanchine; Anne Bass's personal collection also has an icon of St. George given to her by Kirstein, who said it belonged to Balanchine; see also RG10: Artifacts and memorabilia, NYCB Archives, including a box of icons carefully mounted for viewing and found sitting on Balanchine's bedroom table in his New York apartment at his death (according to Eddie Bigelow's archival label). They were shown to the author by Horgan:
   Top (handle) of a bishop's staff
   St. George
   St. Nicholas
   A "blessing" or memento, miniature image of the Crucifixion probably from a pilgrimage or a family heirloom
   A "blessing" or stone—probably also from a pilgrimage, as it is customary for Orthodox believers to collect dust or stones from the Holy Land or some other religious site or shrine
5. Ouspensky and Lossky, *Meaning of Icons;* Maguire, *Icons of Their Bodies;* Ware, *Orthodox Church.* Special thanks to William Holste, Ilia Doronchenkov, and Catherine Merridale; and to Father Adrian (Rev. Adrian Ouellette) and Father Menas (Anthony Vlatas), interviews by the author, Sept. 21 and Oct. 19, 2015.
6. Andrei Balanchivadze: Nona Lomidze, "My Brother—George Balanchine," translated by Nino Chimakadze, *Samshoblo (Motherland)* [journal] no. 4, Feb. 1990.
7. Notes on interview with Andrei Melitonovich Balanchivadze, b. 18, f. Last Minute Interviews, Richard Buckle Papers, HRC.
8. George Balanchine, interview by Bernard Taper, 1961, Taper Tapes.
9. Anna Kisselgoff, interview by the author, Sept. 9, 2016.
10. Sketch kindly shared with the author by Barbara Horgan.
11. Le Clercq, *Ballet Cook Book,* 57.
12. Le Clercq, *Ballet Cook Book,* 45–72; Gold and Fizdale, *Gold and Fizdale Cookbook.*
13. Ruthanna Boris, unpublished writings, kindly given to the author by Robert Gottlieb.
14. Lew Christensen and Gisella Caccialanza, interview by John Taras, 1984, sound recording, RG3/AV Materials, cassette tapes A-R, John Taras Collection, NYCB Archives; notes on interview with Lucia Davidova, fragment, Taper Papers.
15. George Balanchine, interview by Bernard Taper, 1961, Taper Tapes.
16. George Balanchine, interview by Bernard Taper, 1961, Taper Tapes; Meliton Antonovich Balanchivadze to Nikolai Mikhailovich Findeisen, 1907–27, f. 816, op. 2, d. 1135, Department of Manuscripts, Russian National Library.
17. George Balanchivadze, Imperial Theater School file no. 75: Balanchivadze Georgi, Aug. 9, 1913, RGIA.
18. Karsavina, *Theatre Street,* 49–50; Danilova, *Choura,* 14–15; Twysden, *Alexandra Danilova,* 20; George Balanchine, interview by Bernard Taper, 1961, Taper Tapes.
19. George Balanchivadze, Imperial Theater School file no. 75: Balanchivadze Georgi, Aug. 9, 1913, RGIA.
20. George Balanchine, interview by Bernard Taper, 1961, Taper Tapes.

CHAPTER 3: WAR AND PEACE

1. Paléologue, *Ambassador's Memoirs,* vol. 2, 242.
2. Wortman, *Scenarios of Power,* 501; Figes, *Natasha's Dance,* 201; Figes, *People's Tragedy,* 9, 25; Homans, *Apollo's Angels.*
3. Kendall, *Balanchine and the Lost Muse,* 48–49; P. N. Gordeev, "Petrograd Drama School

from March to August of 1917," in Nikolaev, Bazhanov, and Ivanov, *Russian Revolution of 1917*, 53–68.

4. Karsavina, *Theatre Street*, 88–89; Kendall, *Balanchine and the Lost Muse*, 51–52, 92 (from Kostrovitskaya); Volkov, *Balanchine's Tchaikovsky*, 190; Vasily Fastovich Pigulevsky, Archpriest, *A Letter to Sergei Fyodorovich Platonov*, July 20, 1905, f. 585, d. 3815, Department of Manuscripts, Russian National Library (nine children). See picture of the chapel in "Imperial Petersburg Theater School. The house church of the Holy Trinity, 1886–1892," 52441651 91612, Theater Museum SPb; Aleksei Fomkin, "Two Centuries of the Theater Church History," *Vestnik Akademii russkogo baleta imeni A.IA. Vaganova*, 2003.
5. Kendall, *Balanchine and the Lost Muse*, 73–74, 135; Gordeev, "Petrograd Drama School," 53–68.
6. Kendall, *Balanchine and the Lost Muse*, 50.
7. Merridale, *Night of Stone*.
8. Maria's passport documents from 1918 state that she also had an address in 1914 on the right bank of the Neva, no. 116, and in the Vyborgsky-Simbirsk in Petrograd, so the family may have still kept a St. Petersburg apartment. The family address given from 1915 was Bolshaia Moskovskaia 1–3, apartment 69, where the/an aunt(s) lived. Maria Balanchivadze personal file, f. 80, op. 22, d. 195, TsGA SPb; Maria Balanchivadze personal file, f. 80, op. 22, d. 195, TsGA SPb; portrait of Maria: Ketevan Machavariani Balanchivadze personal collection.
9. Kendall, *Balanchine and the Lost Muse*, 89–90; Balanchivadze family letters, private collection of Ketevan Machavariani Balanchivadze, and f. 236, Department of Literature and Art, Central Historical Archives of Georgia.
10. Kendall, *Balanchine and the Lost Muse*, 89; Roné, *Olga Preobrazhenskaya*, 89.
11. "Dancers are like animals" and "We spent a year": George Balanchine, interview by Phyllis Winifred Manchester, Mar. 20, 1975, sound recording, *MGZTC 3-291, LPA.
12. George Balanchine, interview by Bernard Taper, 1961, Taper Tapes; Kendall, *Balanchine and the Lost Muse*, 47.
13. "officers with spurs" and "monarchists, adherents of olden times": quoted in Frame, *St. Petersburg Imperial Theaters*, 78–79; Homans, *Apollo's Angels*, 250; Karsavina, *Theatre Street*, 143, 308.
14. See photos of the theater held at the St. Petersburg State Museum of Theatre and Music, St. Petersburg; Danilova, *Choura*, 28–29; Frame, *St. Petersburg Imperial Theaters*, 148.
15. George Balanchine, interview by Bernard Taper, 1961, Taper Tapes.
16. Frame, *St. Petersburg Imperial Theaters*, 21.
17. Yuri Slonimsky, "Balanchine: The Early Years," *Ballet Review* 5, no. 3 (1975–76): 6.
18. Kendall, *Balanchine and the Lost Muse*, 89.
19. Krasovskaya, *Vaganova*, 8; George Balanchine, interview by Jack Natkin, July 1974, sound recording, *MGZTL 4-1439, LPA.
20. George Balanchine, interview by Bernard Taper, 1961, Taper Tapes.
21. Gorina, "Addresses of Georgy Balanchivadze," 14; Anatoly Viltzak, "Everything I Remember" (Pages from the diary), *Ballet*, no. 4 (1993): 42–44.
22. Volkov, *Balanchine's Tchaikovsky*, 29.
23. Wiley, *Tchaikovsky's Ballets*, 258.
24. Poznansky, *Tchaikovsky*, 594.
25. Volkov, *Balanchine's Tchaikovsky*, 35.
26. Homans, *Apollo's Angels*, 294–95.
27. Quoted in Kendall, *Balanchine and the Lost Muse*, 92, from Vera Kostrovitskaya's unpublished memoir, document from Feb. 1917.

CHAPTER 4: A CLOUD IN TROUSERS

1. George Balanchine, interview by Bernard Taper, 1961, Taper Tapes. When Taper asked Balanchine how he knew the revolution had begun, he said simply, "They started to shoot." Kendall, *Balanchine and the Lost Muse;* Twysden, *Alexandra Danilova;* Merridale, *Red Fortress,* 291; Gordeev, "Petrograd Drama School," 53-68.
2. Taper, *Balanchine,* 46-48.
3. Balanchine quotes: George Balanchine, interview by Bernard Taper, 1961, Taper Tapes; Danilova, *Choura,* 47-50; catching rats in the basement: Milberg Fisher, *In Balanchine's Company,* 116.
4. Ometev and Stuart, *St. Petersburg;* Babel, "The Dead," in *Complete Works of Isaac Babel,* 495-96; Merridale, *Night of Stone,* 103-27; Ball, *And Now My Soul Is Hardened;* Paléologue, *Ambassador's Memoirs,* vol. 3, 226 (Rasputin); "please return": Figes, *People's Tragedy,* 777-81; Engel, *Women in Russia,*135-45. Images from the Museum of Political History, St. Petersburg, include several showing mass graves and funerals for the victims of the revolution, as well as Lenin and the Bolsheviks occupying Kschessinskaya's mansion.
5. Family letters: Letters from 1916, 1917, 1921, and undated, f. 326, s. 75-78, 80, 90, Department of Literature and Art, Central Historical Archives of Georgia. These and other family letters were made available to the author thanks to Keti Balanchivadze. Meliton Antonovich Balanchivadze to Nikolai Mikhailovich Findeisen, 1907-27, f. 816, op. 2, d. 1135, Department of Manuscripts, Russian National Library: Meliton says Maria came to Tiflis in 1922. On Finland: Meinander, *History of Finland;* Singleton, *Short History of Finland.* On Georgia: Scott, *Familiar Strangers;* Figes, *People's Tragedy,* 713-16; Nona Lomidze, "Andria Balanchivadze: My Brother—George Balanchine," *Samshoblo* (Motherland) [journal] no. 4, Feb. 1990 (translated from Georgian). On Nov. 9, 1918, Meliton wrote to the Georgian commission of national art requesting a larger space for his music school: Central Historical Archives of Georgia. Meliton survived the Bolshevik takeover and was elected to the Georgian Artists Union. See f. 5, op. 11, d. 1: Report of the General Meeting of Artists, Georgian Artists Union, Mar. 3, 1921, Archive of Literature and Arts, Tbilisi; Maria Balanchivadze, documents showing Maria's move back to Petrograd, Bolshaia Moskovskaia, 1-3, Apt. 69, from Vyborg in Oct. 1918, also proof of no criminal record; a letter dated Nov. 4, 1918, to the director of border crossings at Orsha or Kursk grants permission to her and son Georgi to cross the border and issues a passport, f. 80, op. 22, d. 195: Maria Balanchivadze, TsGA SPb.
6. Fitzpatrick, *Cultural Front,* 266.
7. Frame, *St. Petersburg Imperial Theaters,* 169-71; Paléologue, *Ambassador's Memoirs,* vol. 3, 229-30; Kendall, *Balanchine and the Lost Muse,*104 and 129; Fitzpatrick, *Commissariat of Enlightenment,* 266; Danilova, *Choura,* 47-48; "Instead of Preface," from Autograph Kostrovitskaia, R 157.1.19, TsGALI SPb; Tassie, *Yevgeny Mravinsky;* Twysden, *Alexandra Danilova.*
8. Homans, *Apollo's Angels,* 321-22; Lunacharsky quoted in Isaac Deutscher's introduction to Lunacharsky, *Revolutionary Silhouettes,* 13; "poet of the revolution": Fitzpatrick, *Commissariat of Enlightenment,* 3; "God is not yet born": quoted in Gray, *Immortalization Commission,* 142; Tait, *Lunacharsky.*
9. "pure landlord culture": Schwartz, *Music and Musical Life,* 12; "scientific mysticism": Fitzpatrick, *Commissariat of Enlightenment,* 5-7; Kendall, *Balanchine and the Lost Muse,* 123; George Balanchine, interview by Bernard Taper, 1961, Taper Tapes, including Balanchine's own memories of Lunacharsky and his familiarity with Lunacharsky's ideas.
10. Jakobson, *Language in Literature,* 285.

11. On *Orpheus*, see Braun, *Meyerhold.* 114–17; on *Masquerade*, see Rudnitsky, *Russian and Soviet Theatre*, 23.
12. Jangfeldt, *Mayakovsky*, 157-58; Von Geldern, *Bolshevik Festivals*, 63-71; Slonimsky, "Balanchine," 1-64.
13. Quoted in Rudnitsky, *Russian and Soviet Theatre*, 61.
14. Rudnitsky, *Russian and Soviet Theatre*, 91.
15. Law and Gordon, *Meyerhold, Eisenstein, and Biomechanics*; Braun, *Theatre of Meyerhold*; Pitches, *Vsevolod Meyerhold*.
16. "Walking almanac": Slonimsky, "Balanchine," 22; on Griffith: Kendall, *Balanchine and the Lost Muse*, 133; "Instead of Preface," from Autograph Kostrovitskaia, R 157.1.19, TsGALI SPb; Peter Gusev to Yuri Slonimsky, Memories of George Balanchine and the Petrograd Theater School, 1952–75, f. 22, op. 4, d. 48, Department of Manuscripts and Rare Books, St. Petersburg State Theatre Library.
17. "roar of the collapse": Blok, *The Twelve*, 35–36; "I see angels' wings": Blok quoted by Kornei Chukovsky, excerpts from "A. A. Blok: The Man," in *Blok: An Anthology of Essays and Memoirs*, 72-82.
18. "Byt is motionless" and other quotes on byt: Jakobson, *Language in Literature*, 278; "Soon there will be no more death"and "how can bodiless," which is from the poem "Man": Jakobson, 287.
19. Rosenthal, *Occult in Russian and Soviet Culture*; Rosenthal, *Nietzsche in Russia;* Matich, *Erotic Utopia*; Nietzsche, *On the Genealogy of Morality*; Nietzsche, *Birth of Tragedy*; Young, *Friedrich Nietzsche*; Alexandrov, *Nabokov's Otherworld*; Solovyov, *Divine Sophia*; Solovyov, *Meaning of Love*; Carlson, *No Religion Higher Than Truth*; Uspenskiĭ [Ouspensky], *Tertium Organum*; Ouspensky, *Talks with a Devil*; Webb, *Harmonious Circle*; Washington, *Madame Blavatsky's Baboon*; Wood, *Men Against Time*; Berdyaev, *Russian Idea*; Berdyaev, *Dream and Reality*; Kelly, *Views from the Other Shore*.
20. Slonimsky, "Balanchine," 1-64; Vera Kostrovitskaya, "Memories about Studying in the Ballet School," unpublished manuscript, f. 22, op. 5, d. 8, 9, 10, 20, Department of Manuscripts and Rare Books, St. Petersburg State Theatre Library; Kendall, *Balanchine and the Lost Muse*, 159.
21. Kendall, *Balanchine and the Lost Muse*, 134; George Balanchine, interview by Bernard Taper, 1961, Taper Tapes.
22. Slonimsky, "Balanchine," 22-23.
23. Vera Kostrovitskaya's remarks on Slonimsky's memoirs, manuscript, 1970s, f. 22, op. 5, d. 16, Department of Manuscripts and Rare Books, St. Petersburg State Theatre Library (Shiryaev); Rudnitsky, *Russian and Soviet Theatre*, 87.
24. Rudnitsky, *Russian and Soviet Theatre*, 87; Vera Kostrovitskaya, "First Acquaintance," Memories about V. V. Dmitriev and B. M. Erbstein, unpublished manuscript with editions, 1970s, f. 22, op. 5, d. 12, Department of Manuscripts and Rare Books, St. Petersburg State Theatre Library. Dmitriev went on to a successful career and won the Stalin Prize; Erbstein was later arrested and sent to the Gulag—he was freed after Stalin's death and committed suicide sometime in the Khrushchev era. See Inna Sklyarevskaya, "Balanchine in Petrograd: The Take Off," in Mariinsky Theater, *Vek Balanchivadze*; on Shiryaev: Bocharov, *Belated Premiere*; Anna Kisselgoff, "Pioneering Russian Films Show Ballet Master's Wit," *New York Times*, Jan. 14, 2005.
25. Vera Kostrovitskaya, "Pages of Memories," *Dancing Times*, Mar. 1985 (Leningrad Choreographic School), f. 157, op. 1, d. 30, TsGALI (Sollertinsky); Grove Music Online, s.v. "Sollertinsky, Ivan Ivanovich," by L. M. Butir, revised by Larisa Georgievna Danko,

Jan. 20, 2001, doi.org/10.1093/gmo/9781561592630.article.26150; Kendall, *Balanchine and the Lost Muse,* 115–71.

26. Tamara Geva in Tracy and DeLano, *Balanchine's Ballerinas,* 30. Geva recalled performing this dance, but the ballet was made for Olga Mungalova.
27. Rubenstein's Romance in E-flat Major, op. 44, no. 1, for voice and piano, performed by violin and piano. See www.balanchine.org for a list of works. None of Balanchine's early ballets survived; all we have are fragments of memory from Geva, Kostrovitskaya, and others who were there.
28. Olga Matich, "The Poetics of Disgust: To Eat and Die in Petersburg," in Matich, *Petersburg/Petersburg,* 69–70.
29. School of American Ballet Workshop, May 1981.
30. Kendall, *Balanchine and the Lost Muse,* 139–40.
31. Von Geldern, *Bolshevik Festivals,* 199–207.
32. Geva, *Split Seconds,* 291–95; Tamara Geva, interview by Bernard Taper, Sept. 24, 1960, Taper Papers; Kendall, *Balanchine and the Lost Muse,* 209; marriage record book, Central District of Petrograd, record 1008, f. P 6143, op. 2, d. 1113, sheet 19, vol. 19, TsGA SPb. The marriage registration shows their address as Grafskii Pereulok, 5, Apt. 9. Meliton Antonovich Balanchivadze to Nikolai Mikhailovich Findeisen, 1907–27, f. 816, op. 2, d. 1135, Department of Manuscripts, Russian National Library.
33. A certificate dated Dec. 22, 1923: Personal data of G. Balanchivadze (Theater, 1921–24), file no. 211, TsGALI SPb; Slonimsky, "Balanchine," 38; George Balanchine, interview by Bernard Taper, 1961, Taper Tapes:

    > I wanted to be a dashing kind of a man on stage, leaping and turning, and something like that; I didn't want to be at all [a noble dancer], frankly, at that time I didn't like classical dancing, man's dancing, matter of fact, I appreciate that it was clean, but I didn't have much desire to look at it. I wanted it to have more character, like what now I hate. . . . And that's what shows you, when you are primitive you would like to have that kind of a soup, vermicelli, noodle, dripping here, you see, and that's what I used to like.

34. Kendall, *Balanchine and the Lost Muse,* 150.
35. Rudnitsky, *Russian and Soviet Theatre,* 97–98; Nicoletta Misler, "Designing Gestures in the Laboratory of Dance," in Baer, *Theatre in Revolution,* 156–76; Misler, *Russian Art of Movement,* further quoting Foregger: "The body of the dancer which subdivides time and space provides us with a well defined plastic design, a kind of plastic melody," 343; Kendall, *Balanchine and the Lost Muse,* 198–99.
36. "desanctify": Misler, *Russian Art of Movement,* 344; "Slow!": Rudnitsky, *Russian and Soviet Theatre,* 94–95.
37. Kendall, *Balanchine and the Lost Muse,* 181.
38. "Suprematism": George Balanchine, interview by Bernard Taper, 1961, Taper Tapes; *Black Square*: Kendall, *Balanchine and the Lost Muse,* 177; Lopukhov, *Writings on Ballet,* 69–101; Souritz, *Soviet Choreographers,* 266–77; D'Andrea, *Kazimir Malevich,* 166–67; Peter Gusev to Yuri Slonimsky, Memories of George Balanchine and the Petrograd Theater School, 1952–75, f. 22, op. 4, d. 48, Department of Manuscripts and Rare Books, St. Petersburg State Theatre Library.
39. Bartlett and Dadswell, *Victory over the Sun,* 5.
40. "not belong solely to the earth": quoted in D'Andrea, *Kazimir Malevich,* 167; Malevich, *Kazimir Malevich;* Gray, *Immortalization Commission,* 161–62.

41. Lopukhov, *Writings on Ballet; Theatre Magazine,* Dec. 11, 1923 (cover photo); George Balanchivadze, "The Non-Commissioned Officer's Widow, or How A. L. Volinsky Whipped Himself," *Theatre Magazine,* Dec. 25, 1923.
42. Salomé, Richard Buckle Papers, HRC; Danilova, *Choura,* 58–59. See Misler, *Russian Art of Movement,* 90–120, 196–250. In 1922, for example, Yurii Ars presented *Evenings of the Denuded Body,* Lev Lukin [Saks] presented *Evenings of the Liberated Body,* and Goleizovsky's company performed Debussy's *Faun* in Boris Erdman's costumes of miniskirts and *caches-sexes,* 96, 289. Salomé was a favored theme at the time and was performed by Zinadia Tarkhovskaia bare breasted as part of Goleizovsky's Chamber Ballet performances at the Hermitage Theater in August 1922, 199.
43. Souritz, *Soviet Choreographers,* 175–76; Elizabeth Souritz, "The Young Balanchine in Russia," *Ballet Review* 18, no. 2 (1990): 66–71; Sally Banes, "Goleizovsky's Manifestos: The Old and the New: Letters about Ballet," *Ballet Review* 11, no. 3 (1983): 64–76; Misler, "Designing Gestures"; Misler, *In principio era il corpo;* Sirotkina and Smith, *Sixth Sense;* improvisation: Slonimsky, "Balanchine," 46.
44. Mikhail Mikhailov, "My Classmate: George Balanchivadze," *Dance News,* Mar.–May 1967; Nina Stukolkina, "Young Ballet," *Sovetskii balet* (1987): 53–56; Kendall, *Balanchine and the Lost Muse,* 186–93; Taper, *Balanchine,* 61; "[moving] ballet from its dead point": Mikhailov, "My Classmate."
45. Frédéric Chopin's Piano Sonata in B-flat Minor, op. 35, no. 1, second movement.
46. "changing from the mourners": Geva, *Split Seconds,* 300; Tracy and DeLano, *Balanchine's Ballerinas,* 30; Gottlieb, *George Balanchine,* 24; Homans, *Apollo's Angels,* 326.
47. Vera Kostrovitskaya, "Piece of Memories about G. Balanchivadze's Production of *Funeral March* and of the 2nd Shakespeare's Sonnets," unpublished manuscript, with Kostrovitskaya and Slonimsky's editions, 1970s, f. 22, op. 5, d. 11, Department of Manuscripts and Rare Books, St. Petersburg State Theatre Library.
48. "a solid evening of theatrical vulgarity": Volynsky, 1923, quoted in Souritz, *Soviet Choreographers,* 75; "All is new!": Slonimsky, "Balanchine," 52, 60–61.
49. Mikhail Kuzmin, "About Eugen the Unfortunate," *Ezhenedel'nik,* Dec. 11, 1923 (State Art Library, Moscow). For reviews, see *Zhizn' iskusstva, Petrograd.* 1924, no. 15, 8–9; *Zhizn' iskusstva, Petrograd.* 1923, no. 51, 9; some extracts from Soviet periodicals concerning union, "the Young Ballet," and G. Balanchivadze, 1925, manuscript with editions, f. 22, op. 5, d. 418, Department of Manuscripts and Rare Books, St. Petersburg State Theatre Library.
50. Blok, *The Twelve;* Vogel, *Alexander Blok;* Sirotkina and Smith, *Sixth Sense,* 65–80; Olenina, "Psychomotor Aesthetics." On the Institute of the Living Word, see Sirotkina and Smith, *Sixth Sense.* I am also grateful to Professor Olenina for sharing her insights and research into the Institute of the Living Word. On the ballet *The Twelve,* see especially Nina Stukolkina, "Young Ballet," 53–56; Lunacharsky, *On Literature and Art* (esp. Lunacharsky's essay on Blok); Misler, *In principio era il corpo* and *Russian Art of Movement.*
51. Twysden, *Alexandra Danilova,* 47; Danilova, *Choura,* 59.
52. George Balanchine, interview by Bernard Taper, 1961, Taper Tapes. Balanchine later recalled the *Sacre du Printemps* request and denial. On *Pulcinella*: Kendall, *Balanchine and the Lost Muse,* 212.
53. Decree issued by the Moscow Soviet on August 26, 1924; Misler, *Russian Art of Movement,* 113.
54. Dmitriev had two co-administrators on the contract, but they later appear to drop out and do not figure in the July 7 contract signed in Stettin.
55. Kendall, *Balanchine and the Lost Muse,* 213–43, gives a detailed account of Ivanova's

death and the aftermath; Danilova, *Choura*, 59-62; Geva, *Split Seconds*, 308-19; George Balanchine, interview by Bernard Taper, 1961, Taper Tapes, in which Balanchine talks of Ivanova's "murder"; Volkov, *Balanchine's Tchaikovsky*, 146-47.

56. Chamberlain, *Lenin's Private War*; Geva, *Split Seconds*, 320-23.
57. Tamara Geva, interview by Nancy Reynolds, May 4, 1976, sound recording, *MGZTL 4-1860, LPA. In the recording, Geva reminisced about her father, who had many agents and collected from all over Europe. During World War II, she received a telegram telling her that he was killed by a bomb.
58. "beautiful bread": Taper, *Balanchine*, 74; Danilova, *Choura*, 63; contracts: copies are held in the George Balanchine Archive, MS Thr 411 (2807), Houghton; correspondence with the theater from Balanchivadze and Efimov (together), and Danilova (separately): personal data of G. Balanchivadze (Theater, 1921-24), file no. 211 and f. R-260, op. 3, d. 925 and 1133, TsGALI SPb.
59. "The Cloud in Pants: A Tetraptych," in *Vladimir Mayakovsky: Selected Poems*.
60. Mayakovsky's suicide note can be found in full in Jangfeldt, *Mayakovsky*, 547-48. The final lines read:

    As they say—
      "The game is over"
    love's boat
    has smashed against the reef of the everyday.
    I'm quits with life
    And there is no reason
    To keep a record of pains
      Cares and quarrels
    Be happy,
    Vladimir Mayakovsky

RUSSIA ABROAD

1. Clifford, *Balanchine's Apprentice*, 3, and interviews by the author, Aug. 2 and 3, 2014.
2. The number of fleeing Russians given by historians depends in part on date-span: Figes, *Natasha's Dance*, 528, 544, estimates that three million departed between 1917 and 1929; Mazower, *Dark Continent*, 1-80, gives the number as one million in the immediate aftermath of the revolution. The other numbers are Mazower's and are only a small part of a vast picture he paints of disruption, movement, and loss in these years. See also De Waal, *Caucasus*, 57; dancers' stories emerged from dozens of interviews and research into family histories.

CHAPTER 5: WEIMAR CULTURE

1. Geva, *Split Seconds*, 324-30; Danilova, *Choura*, 63-66; "Berlin is freezing": Roth, *What I Saw*, 17; Levenson, *Einstein in Berlin*; Weitz, *Weimar Germany*.
2. *Berlin, Symphony of a Great City*, directed by Walter Ruttmann (Chatsworth, CA: Image Entertainment, 1999); *People on a Sunday*, directed by Robert Siodmak (New York: Criterion Collection, 2011).
3. Richie, *Faust's Metropolis*, 334; Raeff, *Russia Abroad*; "Charlottograd": quoted in Marion Kant, "The Russians in Berlin, 1920-1945," in Garafola, *Russian Movement Culture*, 73-79; Williams, *Culture in Exile*; Chamberlain, *Lenin's Private War*, 205-9; Figes, *Natasha's Dance*, 525-86.
4. George Balanchine, quoted by Alexander Bland in *The Observer*, Sept. 23, 1979.
5. "Tiflis pixie": Duke, *Passport to Paris*, 296; Barbara Horgan, interview by the author,

Nov. 23, 2012. On his lack of education on European art, see also the interview with George Balanchine in Peter Adam, dir., *Diaghilev: A Portrait.*

6. Elswit, *Watching Weimar Dance*, 79; Jelavich, *Berlin Cabaret*, 176, 181 (Roth quote).
7. "André Levinson on Balanchine, 1925-1933," translated by John Goodman, *Ballet Review* 46, no. 1 (2018): 79-122.
8. Elswit, *Watching Weimar Dance*; Richie, *Faust's Metropolis*; George, *Naked Truth.*
9. Bodenwieser, *New Dance.*
10. Elswit, *Watching Weimar Dance*, 18, 68-75; Toepfer, *Empire of Ecstasy*; Bodenwieser, *New Dance.*
11. Kandinsky, *Concerning the Spiritual in Art*, 28-29, 63.
12. "simulating aphasia": Leah Dickerman, "Inventing Abstraction," in Dickerman, *Inventing Abstraction*, 16; Schorske, *Fin-de-Siècle Vienna*, 345-65.
13. Jack Anderson, "Who was Gret Palucca?" *New York Times*, Aug. 15, 1993; Worringer, *Abstraction and Empathy*; "the visible trace of the invisible": Butler and de Zegher, *On Line*, 154.
14. Butler and de Zegher, *On Line*, 148-204 ("trace forms," 155); Sirotkina and Smith, *Sixth Sense*, 45-65; Weitz, *Weimar Germany*, 345-51.
15. "art is shit": Laqueur, *Weimar*, 119; "nullity": Hans Arp quoted in Dickerman, *Inventing Abstraction*, 52.
16. Newhall, *Mary Wigman*; Partsch-Bergsohn and Bergsohn, *Makers of Modern Dance.*
17. Lincoln Kirstein Diary, Jan. 28, 1931, (S) *MGZMD 123, Lincoln Kirstein Papers, LPA:

    > To see Mary Wigman, the German dancer . . . whom I decided instantly to dislike. Mary Wigman has been universally advertised, 'Not a dancer but a priestess.' She has an ugly body, and hideous costumes. . . . Shiny stuff with great pieces cut out of them in arbitrary places to ruin any flow of line. She has a certain kind of aggressive masculine strength. She can stick her diaphragm out so she seems to have two pairs of breasts. Her dancing is a triumph of awkward transitions and a few good ideas developed only as static gestures. Her subject matter is ecstasy, bliss, despair, etc., consequently the only possible climax is always exhaustion, a monotonous lack of ability to sustain an impression and a repetition based on an unsatisfactory system of gestures proving conclusively the great superiority of the ballet technique over hers. A ballet of this would be insufferable.

18. Stern, *Five Germanys I Have Known*, 71; Laqueur, *Weimar*, 172-81.
19. Lothar Schreyer, a Bauhaus "master," quoted in Laqueur, *Weimar*, 177.
20. Laqueur, *Weimar*, 174-80; Oskar Schlemmer, "Man and Art Figure," in Gropius, *Theater of the Bauhaus.*
21. "What I want to show": quoted in Gay, *Weimar Culture*, 105-7; "half-clothed me": Michael Kimmelman, "Chuckling Darkly at Disaster," *New York Times*, June 27, 2003.
22. Richie, *Faust's Metropolis*, 345; Styan, *Max Reinhardt*; Jelavich, *Berlin Cabaret*; Elswit, *Watching Weimar Dance*; "You know about Reinhardt?!": John Clifford, interview by author, Aug. 2 and 3, 2014.
23. Danilova, Geva, Buckle, Scheijen, and Taper give varying accounts.

CHAPTER 6: BIG SERGE

1. Garafola and Baer, *Ballets Russes*; Buckle, *Diaghilev*; Garafola, *Diaghilev's Ballets Russes*; Scheijen, *Diaghilev*; Bellow, *Modernism on Stage.*
2. Quoted in Bowlt, *Silver Age*, 169.
3. Quoted in Buckle, *Diaghilev*, 135.

4. Anna Pavlova, for example, left the Ballets Russes shortly after its first season to form her own touring company and spent the rest of her life performing around the world.
5. Spurling, *Matisse*, 230.
6. Quoted in Figes, *Natasha's Dance*, 276.
7. Quoted in Buckle, *Diaghilev*, 162.
8. Buckle, *Diaghilev*, 253–55 ("shaken like an earthquake": 253); Eksteins, *Rites of Spring*, 9–54.
9. Quoted in Nijinsky, *Diary of Vaslav Nijinsky*, xx, and Buckle, *Nijinsky*, 495.
10. Nijinsky, *Diary of Vaslav Nijinsky*, xx; Buckle, *Nijinsky*, 495.
11. Misia Sert told Count Harry Kessler of Diaghilev's difficulties arranging an entry permit from the French government to return to Paris from Spain. When the permit finally came through, she came to Spain to accompany him back to France. Just before they crossed the border, she asked if he had anything at all suspicious with him, and he produced a wad of letters, including two from Mata Hari, who had just been arrested for espionage, which Sert hastily destroyed. Kessler, *Berlin in Lights*, 273.
12. Sokolova, *Dancing for Diaghilev*, 242.
13. "automatized" and "machinery": Drue Fergison, "Bringing *Les Noces* to the Stage," in Garafola and Baer, *Ballets Russes*, 187; Taruskin, *Defining Russia Musically*, 400; "resemble the saints": Buckle, *Diaghilev*, 411–12; Garafola, *La Nijinska*, esp. chapters 5–7.
14. Garafola, *Diaghilev's Ballets Russes*, 112–31, and *La Nijinska*, 149–94 (the ballet must be "an article of fashion," 172; "on a beach," 171); Danilova, *Choura*, 135–36; Duke, *Passport to Paris*, 135, 140.
15. Scheijen, *Diaghilev*, 393–95. With thanks to Lynn Garafola.
16. Gold and Fizdale, *Misia;* Garelick, *Mademoiselle*, 163; Anka Muhlstein, "The Cut of Coco," *New York Review of Books*, Oct. 9, 2014. According to her friend Denise Mayer, Misia once ended up in jail for drug use; Mayer's husband got her out. See Kochno, b. 17, f. 1, Gold and Fizdale Collection, Peter Jay Sharp Special Collections. In these years, Misia, along with Coco Chanel, was among Diaghilev's primary patrons and constant companions. Chanel, an orphan who grew up in poverty, was by then presiding over an empire of luxurious "poor girl" fashion and perfume. She and Misia had a symbiotic and erotically charged relationship, and their glamorous and giddy lives were a sign of the decadence animating them all. It was not uncommon to see Misia, in a Chanel dress with long strings of pearls knotted at the waist, sitting in a café calmly lifting her skirt to inject her thigh with morphine. Meanwhile, they both wrote checks and sidled close, finding in Diaghilev and his Ballets Russes what many people seemed to find there: a higher purpose.
17. Interview with George Balanchine in Peter Adam's *Diaghilev: A Portrait;* Boris Kochno, Préface & trad. française des notes autobiog. de Serge Diaghilev, Fonds Kochno, pièce 122, Bibliothèque-Musée de l'Opéra National de Paris (suits, voice, and manner); Kochno, b. 17, f. 1, Gold and Fizdale Collection, Peter Jay Sharp Special Collections; Giroud, *Nicolas Nabokov*, 13; Skidelsky, *John Maynard Keynes*, 99.
18. Danilova, *Choura*, 66; Gold and Fizdale, *Misia*, 246–48.
19. Danilova, *Choura*, 69.
20. When Balanchine registered at a local police station in Paris in 1931, his carte d'identité was stamped Georges Balanchin. On name change: Buckle and Taras, *George Balanchine, Ballet Master*, 32. Balanchine was officially fired from the State Academic Theaters on Sept. 26, 1924, retroactive to Sept. 8, when he was supposed to return and didn't. Personal data of G. Balanchinvadze (Theatre 1921–24), file no. 211, pp. 4–5, TsGALI SPb.
21. Quoted in Shead, *Ballets Russes*, 119; Homans, *Apollo's Angels*, 356.
22. Interview with George Balanchine in Peter Adam's *Diaghilev: A Portrait*.

23. Slonimsky, "Balanchine," 52, 60–61.
24. "Balanchine: Demigod of the Dance," *Newsweek,* May 4, 1964.
25. Scheijen, *Diaghilev,* 400; Kirstein, *By with to & from,* 210–11.
26. Interview with George Balanchine in Peter Adam's *Diaghilev: A Portrait.*
27. Jerome Robbins and George Balanchine, interview by Rosemarie Tauris, June 19, 1972, sound recording, *MGZTL 4-3065, LPA.
28. Danilova, *Choura,* 105.
29. George Balanchine to Serge Diaghilev, Sept. 25, 1925, George Balanchine, Misc. Correspondence, (S) *MGZM-Res. Bal G., LPA.
30. "as fragile as Venetian glass" and "the kick of a horse": Agnes de Mille quoted in Sutton, *Making of Markova,* 13; interview with Ninette de Valois in Adam's *Diaghilev: A Portrait* (Markova memorized her new name); Garafola, *La Nijinska,* 191–93, notes that by one account, the meeting at Astafieva's studio was also a kind of second audition for Balanchine as choreographer.
31. Alicia Markova, interview by John Taras, Sept. 3, 1983, RG3/AV Materials, John Taras Collection, NYCB Archives; Spurling, *Matisse,* 481; notes on interview with Tamara Geva, Sept. 24, 1960, Taper Papers; stepping in for Markova: interview with George Balanchine in Adam's *Diaghilev: A Portrait;* Twysden, *Alexandra Danilova,* 72–74. Reports conflict over whether Matisse was there or not. Spurling says Matisse was not involved, but Markova insists that he was there.
32. "dancing for the Grand Inquisitor": Danilova, *Choura,* 77, 137; Sokolova, *Dancing for Diaghilev,* 60, 141; "always twisted": Mackrell, *Bloomsbury Ballerina,* 424.
33. Notes on interviews with George Balanchine, Balanchine Book: Notes on Tapes and Interviews, b. 45, Richard Buckle Papers, HRC.
34. Sokolova, *Dancing for Diaghilev,* 211.
35. Soulima Stravinsky, interviewed by Thor E. Wood, Feb. 3 and 5, 1977, and Jan. 14, 1978, transcript, *MGZMT 5-563, LPA, 79.
36. Milstein and Volkov, *From Russia to the West,* 240.
37. George Balanchine to Serge Diaghilev, Sept. 26, 1927, George Balanchine, Misc. Correspondence, (S) *MGZM-Res. Bal G, LPA.
38. Kirstein Diary, July 16, 1934, LPA; interview with Alexandra Danilova, 1962, Taper Papers; George Balanchine to Serge Diaghilev instructing him to please send all salary and advances, etc., for himself, Danilova, Efimov, and Geva to Dmitriev from Dec. 11, 1924, until the end of their contract on July 1, 1925: b. 3, fol.: Balanchine, George, Letters, 1931–32, MS Thr 465 (92), S. L. Grigoriev Papers, Houghton.
39. Interview with Alexandra Danilova, 1962, Taper Papers; Danilova, *Choura,* 85; b. 16, fol.: Danilova, Richard Buckle Papers, HRC; Geva, *Split Seconds,* 335; notes on interview with George Balanchine, Feb. 14, 1961, Taper Papers; Kirstein Diary, Feb. 14, 1935, LPA.
40. Vernon Duke to Bernard Taper, Oct. 19, 1961, Taper Papers; Jacques d'Amboise, interview by the author, May 21, 2018.
41. Dominique Nabokov, interview by the author, May 9, 2013.
42. Interview with Natasha Nabokov, Jan. 29, 1963, Taper Papers.
43. Milstein and Volkov, *From Russia to the West,* 245–56.
44. Interview with Natasha Nabokov, Jan. 29, 1963, Taper Papers.
45. Duke, *Passport to Paris,* 178–79; four-handed piano: Boris Kochno, interview by Radio France, May 1981, sound recording, *MGZTL 4-1282, LPA.
46. Vernon Duke to Bernard Taper, Oct. 19, 1961, Taper Papers.

47. Danilova, *Choura,* 85–86.
48. "Valse Pestchinka," 1928: Balanchine compositions, b. 55, f. 3, MS Thr 411 (2188), George Balanchine Archive, Houghton.
49. Duke, *Passport to Paris,* 296.
50. Garafola, *Diaghilev's Ballets Russes,* 266.
51. Balanchine to Diaghilev, Sept. 26, 1925, Fonds Kochno, pièce 5, Bibliothèque-Musée de l'Opéra National de Paris.
52. Garafola, *Diaghilev's Ballets Russes,* 268; notes on interviews with George Balanchine, Balanchine Book: Notes on Tapes and Interviews, b. 45, Richard Buckle Papers, HRC.
53. Colin, *Josephine Baker,* xxiii.
54. "grimly fascinated": Vernon Duke to Bernard Taper, Oct. 19, 1961, Taper Papers; Caws, *Surrealism,* 16–29; Barbara Horgan, interview by the author, Oct. 24, 2018. Balanchine owned a Max Beckmann painting that ended up in Zorina's possession after they separated; he eventually gave the Dalí drawings to Karin von Aroldingen, and they are now held at Harvard's Houghton Library in the Balanchine Archive.
55. Photographs: *Jack in the Box,* Ballet Society Collection, NYCB Archives; Wiser, *Crazy Years,* 135–42.
56. Photos of Balanchine as Snowball: "Costume for Snowball, Roof Lyceum Theatre, London, 1926," RG8-34, Ballet Society Collection, NYCB Archives; Banes, *Writing Dancing.*
57. Garafola, *Diaghilev's Ballets Russes,* 138–39.
58. Bellow, *Modernism on Stage,* 213–17.
59. "Adler": collection of the author.

CHAPTER 7: APOLLO

1. Walsh, *Stravinsky: A Creative Spring,* 379, 431–33, 467–69; Giroud, *Nicolas Nabokov,* 61–64, 81; Heynickx and De Maeyer, *Maritain Factor,* esp. Stephen Schloesser, "The Rise of a Mystic Modernism: Maritain and the Sacrificed Generation of the Twenties," 28, 40; Barré, *Jacques and Raïssa Maritain.*
2. Rosemary Edmonds, "Introduction," in Pushkin, *Queen of Spades,* 12–14.
3. Walsh, *Stravinsky: A Creative Spring,* 431–33.
4. "fake Ukrainian": Milstein and Volkov, *From Russia to the West,* 242; the ballet was originally commissioned by Elizabeth Sprague Coolidge, and the world premiere was at the Library of Congress in Washington, D.C., staged by Adolf Bolm.
5. Buckle, *Diaghilev,* 494.
6. George Balanchine, "The Dance Element in Stravinsky's Music," in Steinberg, *Dance Anthology,* 150–51.
7. "What he is doing is magnificent": quoted in Nabokov, *Old Friends,* 83; Garelick, *Mademoiselle,* 173; Croce, *Going to the Dance,* 116–17; Lincoln Kirstein, "The Diaghilev Period," in *By with to & from,* 125.
8. Quoted in Walsh, *Stravinsky: A Creative Spring,* 468.
9. Stravinsky, *Igor Stravinsky,* 99–100.
10. Walsh, *Stravinsky: A Creative Spring,* 429. Stravinsky's politics also veered toward order, but as Walsh documents, it was above all his anti-Semitism that sustained his views. He openly courted Mussolini from at least 1926, and he performed in Hitler's Germany until the late 1930s. See also Walsh, *Stravinsky: The Second Exile,* 82–84.
11. Balanchine notebook: collection of the author.
12. George Balanchine on the making of *Apollo,* quoted by Alexander Bland in *The Observer,*

Sept. 23, 1979; Reynolds, *Repertory in Review,* 46–50; Julia Randel, "Un-voicing Orpheus: The Powers of Music in Stravinsky and Balanchine's 'Greek' Ballets," *Opera Quarterly* 29, no. 2 (2013): 109–45. With special thanks to Heather Watts.

13. Taper, *Balanchine,* 91; Danilova, *Choura,* 88–89; O. A. Trefilova and I. A. Rozanov, "Professor of Surgery at the University of Moscow I. P. Aleksinsky: His Life and Work in Russia and in Emigration," in *History of Medicine* 1, no. 4 (2014): 45–58. Aleksinsky had impeccable émigré credentials: he had served in the czar's military hospitals during the war and fled the Bolsheviks with General Pyotr Wrangel in one of the final evacuations from the Crimea. Aleksinsky was Orthodox, anti-Bolshevik, stateless, and an active member of Russia Abroad.
14. Scheijen, *Diaghilev,* 423–25.
15. Another source for the ballet was Pushkin's story "The Stationmaster." Reynolds, *Repertory in Review,* 102–7; Aleksandr Pushkin, "The Stationmaster," in Pushkin, *Collected Stories;* Yuszczuk and Nicoloff, "An Interview with George Balanchine," 10–14.
16. Prokofiev, *Sergey Prokofiev Diaries,* 792 (on Matisse); "Bachiness": Taruskin, *Stravinsky,* 1618; Reynolds, *Repertory in Review,* 102–7; Yuszczuk and Nicoloff, "An Interview with George Balanchine," 10–14.
17. Scheijen, *Diaghilev,* 426, 432, drawing on Prokofiev's diaries, which record the intense interest Diaghilev took in the ballet; Prokofiev, *Sergey Prokofiev Diaries,* 729–850; Anna Kisselgoff, "Dance: Prodigal Son by City Ballet," *New York Times,* Apr. 16, 1986. Kisselgoff says that Kochno told her in the 1980s that the story was biblical, not from Pushkin at all; Balanchine and Mason's *101 Stories of the Great Ballets* also says that the story is biblical; Kirstein, *Program Notes,* 100: in his 1971 notes for *Prodigal Son,* Kirstein said that Balanchine worked from a "peasant woodblock picture" illustrating the story. If there was a source for the look and feel of Rouault's designs for *Prodigal Son,* it lay in the artist's devastatingly expressionist landscape *My Sweet Homeland, What Has Become of You?* (1927), part of his *Miserere* series bearing witness to the shattered bodies and dislocated lives strewn across the twentieth-century horizon.
18. Prokofiev, *Sergey Prokofiev Diaries,* 827–29.
19. "protoplasm" and "There's no sex to them": Reynolds, *Repertory in Review,* 102–7; "[He] wanted a real garden": quoted in Harlow, *Prokofiev,* 229.
20. "inhuman contortions": *Daily Mail,* July 2, 1929; Agnes de Mille, "Balanchine's Choreography (1930)," *Dance Index,* Mar. 1945, 32–35.
21. Villella, *Prodigal Son,* 83; notes by Merrill Brockway accompanying *Choreography by Balanchine, Parts 1-4,* directed by Merrill Brockway and Emile Ardolino, (Thirteen/WNET; New York: Nonesuch Records, 2004); Freedberg, *Power of Images;* Hubbs, *Mother Russia,* 28–30; Brooks, *Felia Doubrovska Remembered;* Damian Woetzel, conversation with the author, Oct. 17, 2018 ("So Fritz Lang"); b. 18, fol.: My Talks with Balanchine in 1974 and after Don Q in 1967, Richard Buckle Papers, HRC.
22. Buckle, *Diaghilev,* 523.
23. Dossier d'oeuvre: *Prodigal Son,* Bibliothèque-Musée de l'Opéra National de Paris. The picture is dated 1929. Later, after Lifar had double-crossed him, Balanchine claimed to have given Lifar a hard time in rehearsals: "Here you stand straight . . . very straight, and fall on your back." Lifar hesitated and turned to Diaghilev, exclaiming that this would hurt his back, but Balanchine said he persisted, telling Lifar that he would show him, and he turned and fell backward like a plank onto his back. "I had to do it once," Balanchine explained, "but he had to do it every night." Barbara Milberg Fisher in *Remembering Mr. B,* 73.
24. Notes by Merrill Brockway accompanying *Choreography by Balanchine.* See "267. Prodigal Son," Balanchine Catalogue, The George Balanchine Foundation, accessed via

balanchine.org; Reynolds, *Repertory in Review*; Jacques d'Amboise, interview by the author (and email), Oct. 20, 2018.

25. When Barbara Milberg Fisher asked why the father wasn't kinder, Balanchine replied: "No. Father does not move. He is like God. Boy must come to *him*." Milberg Fisher, *In Balanchine's Company*, 57.
26. B. 18, fol.: My Talks with Balanchine in 1974 and after Don Q in 1967, Richard Buckle Papers, HRC.
27. Mackrell, *Bloomsbury Ballerina*, 304–8; Skidelsky, *John Maynard Keynes*, 339; the Papers of John Maynard Keynes, King's College Archive Centre: Keynes to his mother, Aug. 20, 1929 (JMK/PP/45/168/10), and efforts to bring Fedor Lopokov to Britain (JMK; the Papers of Lydia Lopokova, King's College Archive Centre: correspondence concerning *Dark Red Roses*, 1929 (LLK/1/1).
28. In another perfect detail, according to a guide at the church, its walls contain a secret passage to the roof where secret bells can be rung by priests, as if the sound came spontaneously from God.
29. Gold and Fizdale, *Misia*, 260; "The Diaghilev Period," in Kirstein, *By with to & from*, 103; Scheijen, *Diaghilev*, 439–40; Garelick, *Mademoiselle*, 180–216; Duberman, *Worlds of Lincoln Kirstein*, 65–66. Contrary to Scheijen, Garafola, *La Nijinska*, 272, says that, according to a letter from Ernest Ansermet to Stravinsky, Diaghilev died alone.
30. Duberman, *Worlds of Lincoln Kirstein*, 65–66, 636.

CHAPTER 8: MAGIC MOUNTAIN

1. B. 18, fol.: My Talks with Balanchine in 1974 and after Don Q in 1967, Richard Buckle Papers, HRC.
2. Taper, *Balanchine*, 124–47; Buckle, *George Balanchine*, 54–55.
3. Balanchine notebook, collection of the author.
4. Rist, *La tuberculose*; Sontag, *Illness as Metaphor*; Bynum, *Spitting Blood*; "horizontals": Mann, *Magic Mountain*, 71; Stach, *Kafka*; Barnes, *Making of a Social Disease*; Jean-Pierre Bardet, "Malades et sanatoriums dans l'entre-deux-guerres," in Bardet, Bourdelais, Guillaume, Lebrun, and Quetel, *Peurs et terreurs*, 218–35; Balanchine to Kochno, in Buckle, *George Balanchine*, 55; Balanchine to Kochno, from the Grand Hotel du Mont Blanc, Passy (Hte Savoie), b. 3, MS Thr 465 (92), S. L. Grigoriev Papers, Houghton.
5. Kirstein Diary, July 12 and 20, 1934, LPA; Balanchine's scarred left lung did eventually collapse, of its own accord.
6. Notes for 1929–33 and phone conversation with Dr. E. J. Langner, undated, Taper Papers; "rather sad" and other quotes are from Buckle, *George Balanchine*, 55, and letters sent from the Grand Hotel du Mont Blanc, Passy (Hte Savoie): b. 3, MS Thr 465 (92), S. L. Grigoriev Papers, Houghton.
7. Buckle, *George Balanchine*, 55; Taper, *Balanchine*, 127–28, for a varying account.
8. "I did not plan," as well as quotes from the following paragraph: Balanchine to Kochno, b. 3, MS Thr 465 (92), S. L. Grigoriev Papers, Houghton.
9. Balanchine to Kochno, from London's Red Court Hotel, Russell Square, b. 3, MS Thr 465 (92), S. L. Grigoriev Papers, Houghton; Duke, *Passport to Paris*, 178–79 (Berlitz).
10. The Papers of John Maynard Keynes, King's College Archive Centre: efforts to bring Fedor Lopokov to Britain (JMK/PP/45/207); the Papers of Lydia Lopokova, King's College Archive Centre: notification of Balanchine's Labor Permit, procured by Keynes (LLK/1/1).
11. Danilova, *Choura*, 85–109; interview with Alexandra Danilova, 1960s, Taper Papers; notes on interview with George Balanchine, Feb. 14, 1961, Taper Papers; notes from 1985

interview, b. 16, fol.: Danilova, Richard Buckle Papers, HRC; private conversations with the author over the years from the 1970s until Danilova's death.

12. Chazin-Bennahum, *René Blum*.
13. Tennant, *Irina Baronova;* Baronova, *Irina;* Tamara Toumanova, interview by John Taras, 1983, sound recordings, cassette tapes A-R, RG3/AV Materials, John Taras Collection, NYCB Archives; Jennifer Dunning, "Tatiana Riabouchinska, 83, Ballerina and Disney Model," *New York Times,* Sept. 3, 2000. Irina Baronova was born in St. Petersburg to a high-ranking family, but during the revolution, her father, a banker with a post in the imperial navy, was shot, and her brother was killed. She was smuggled by her mother over the border into Romania and a childhood of poverty and hardship, which finally led them to Paris. Tatiana Riabouchinska's father was an imperial banker too, and in 1917 the family was placed under house arrest, but loyal servants helped them escape. As for Tamara Toumanova, she was born in a cattle wagon in 1919 as her father, an army colonel, fled and the family headed for Shanghai and eventually Paris.
14. "A ghostly assembly": A. V. Coton, quoted in Chazin-Bennahum, *René Blum,* 121; "bent sadly," pet rabbit, and gifts: Tamara Toumanova, interview by John Taras, 1983, RG3/AV Materials, John Taras Collection, NYCB Archives; Baronova, *Irina;* Tennant, *Irina Baronova;* Taper, *Balanchine,* 134–41; Lincoln Kirstein to Muriel Draper, July 13, 1933, b. 5, f. 154, YCAL MSS 49, Muriel Draper Papers, Beinecke, with thanks to Lynn Garafola; kindergarten: Boris Kochno, interview by Radio France, May 1981, sound recording, *MGZTL 4-1282, LPA.
15. Bentley, *Costumes by Karinska,* 10–28; Barbara Karinska, interview by Natalie Kamendrowsky, 1974, transcript, *MGZTC 3-1782, LPA.
16. Sorley Walker, *De Basil's Ballets Russes,* 51, 165–79.
17. Quoted in Buckle, *George Balanchine,* 59–60.
18. Diana Gould Menuhin, "Dancing for Balanchine: 1933," *Ballet Review* 16, no. 3 (1988): 35–42; Mecham, "Les Ballets 1933," 60.
19. Lomas, *Narcissus Reflected.* 46; Stella Beddoe, "Edward James and Les Ballets 1933," in Coleby, *Surreal Life,* 41–48.
20. Sanders, *Days Grow Short;* Mecham, "Les Ballets 1933"; Weill, *Speak Low.*
21. Menuhin, "Dancing for Balanchine: 1933," 37.
22. Weill, *Speak Low,* 82.
23. Edward James to Drew, Mar. 1, 1965, correspondence, *Seven Deadly Sins,* Weill-Lenya Research Center; Taper Papers.
24. Kim H. Kowalke, "Seven Degrees of Separation: Music, Text, Image, and Gesture in *The Seven Deadly Sins,*" *South Atlantic Quarterly* 104, no. 1 (2005): 7–62, esp. 14, 2; Kim H. Kowalke, "A Tale of Seven Cities: A Chronicle of the Sins," *On the Next Wave* 3, no. 1-2 (October 1985): 20–25; Brigid Doherty, "Test and Gestus in Brecht and Benjamin," *MLN* 115, no. 3 (2000): 442–81.
25. Kirstein Diary, June 7, 1933, LPA.
26. Mecham, "Les Ballets 1933"; Danilova, *Choura,* 158–59; Ruthanna Boris, unpublished writings, courtesy of Robert Gottlieb; Giroud, *Nicolas Nabokov,* 105; Natalia Nabokov, interview by John Taras and Richard Buckle, John Taras Collection, NYCB Archives; Lincoln Kirstein to Muriel Draper, June 11, 1933, b. 5, f. 154, Muriel Draper Papers, Beinecke.
27. Florentine Karp to John Niles (a Karp relative), interview by the author, Aug. 28, 2016, although reviews do not mention these protests.
28. Weill, *Speak Low,* 90. Edwin Denby, who would become one of the most important and

devoted writers on Balanchine's work, was in the audience too—he had just fled Germany and by 1935 would be in America.

29. "Les Ballets 1933 progressive": Kirstein Diary, June 9, 1933, LPA; "We agreed that Balanchine": Kirstein Diary, June 24, 1933, LPA; "ecstasy": Kirstein Diary, June 9, 1933, LPA.
30. Kirstein Diary, June 15, 1933, LPA.
31. Kirstein Diary, June 7, 1933, LPA.
32. looked exhausted and a bit ill: Kirstein Diary, July 8, 1933, LPA; "his magnificent instrument": Kirstein Diary, July 3, 1933, LPA; Flanner, *Paris Was Yesterday*.
33. All quotes and this account of Kirstein's meeting with Balanchine come from Kirstein Diary, July 11 and 16, 1933, LPA; "brought up during the Revolution" can be found in Lincoln Kirstein to Muriel Draper, July 13 and 18, 1933, b. 5, f. 154, Muriel Draper Papers, Beinecke. In Kirstein's letter to Mools on July 13, he elaborated: "I mean to put Balanchine at the head of the school and develop the training according to Nijinsky's plan for a trained dancer's body: i.e. the whole body. I would like to have the benefit of the Gurdgieff exercises, but the design will be mainly according to the classical tradition."
34. Balanchine's immigration visa to the United States, issued by the U.S. Consulate General Montreal, reproduces his French carte d'identité, no. 11267, issued on Oct. 22, 1931, valid until May 1, 1934.

CHAPTER 9: LINCOLN

1. Kirstein, *Quarry*, 68.
2. Duberman, *Worlds of Lincoln Kirstein*, 4. Duberman reports that during the surgery, sweat glands were removed, leaving scar tissue. It is not entirely clear what exactly the small knot of flesh was, but it may have been scar tissue or remaining skin. Kirstein apparently suffered from castration nightmares for years to come.
3. Quoted in Lerman, *Grand Surprise*, 361.
4. Duberman, *Worlds of Lincoln Kirstein*, 1–22; see also the Kirstein Diaries, 1922–23 and 1927, b. 2, f. 8 and 10, (S) *MGZMD 123, Lincoln Kirstein Papers, LPA.
5. Barbara Horgan, interview by the author.
6. Kirstein, *Quarry*, 68.
7. Kirstein Diaries, 1922–23 and 1927, b. 2, f. 8 and 10, (S) *MGZMD 123, Lincoln Kirstein Papers, LPA.
8. Duberman, *Worlds of Lincoln Kirstein*, 3–22; on family history, also see Lincoln Kirstein to Richard Buckle, July 30, 1983, b. R15115, Richard Buckle Papers, HRC.
9. Kirstein, *Mosaic*, 39; Nancy Reynolds, "In His Image: Diaghilev and Lincoln Kirstein," in Garafola and Baer, *Ballets Russes*, 291–311.
10. In the 1930s he was working on a novel called *The Leader*, about the rise of an American Hitler; Kirstein Diary, Aug. 28, 1933, LPA (among many references). After the war he published a poetry collection, *Rhymes of a PFC*.
11. Kirstein, *Quarry*, 13.
12. Lincoln would edit (and Louis would largely fund) *Hound and Horn* until 1934, when he gave it up to focus on Balanchine and ballet; "Ditch and Bugle": Robert B. Silvers, interview by the author, Sept. 16, 2015.
13. See Duberman, *Worlds of Lincoln Kirstein*; Weber, *Patron Saints*; Gaddis, *Magician of the Modern*.
14. Homans, *Apollo's Angels*, 458.
15. Kirstein (like Balanchine himself) did not like *Prodigal Son*, with its "semi-satirical ac-

cents" that "had the same undesirable effect as an over-elaborate image in a poem." Kirstein, *By with to & from*, 20.

16. Kirstein, *By with to & from*, 5, 16, 21.
17. The Kirstein diaries, dating from 1919 to 1937 (not inclusive), are held at the Jerome Robbins Dance Division, New York Public Library for the Performing Arts (LPA). The diaries I draw on are located in the Lincoln Kirstein Papers, c. 1913–94, (S) *MGZMD 123: b. 2, f. 1, 1922–23; b. 2, f. 10, 1927; b. 3, 1930–31; b. 4, f. 18, 1932–33; b. 4, f. 20, 1933–34; b. 4, f. 22, 1934; b. 5, f. 25, 1934–37. Lincoln later excerpted the diaries in his own writings; he also created shorthand edited typescripts, and at least one other editor worked on some of these typescripts too. The quotes from the diaries are taken from the original handwritten books.
18. In July 1983, soon after Balanchine's death, Kirstein wrote two corrective letters to his "dear Dicky": Lincoln Kirstein to Richard Buckle, July 11 and 30, 1983, fol.: Kirstein to Buckle, 1962–73, Richard Buckle Papers, HRC.

> Please understand this, once and for all.
>
> I'm not going to answer your letters about my details in much detail; you are writing the fucking book; not me. I don't care what you do; or if it ever appears, or what it says. I won't read it when it's printed, and as I told . . . [your publisher], I am not collaborating on it in any way, except to hand you the elementary diaries.
>
> As far as I'm concerned, the past is but a dog to its vomit. I want to forget the early days, Balanchine and HOW IT ALL CAME TO BE. I am 76 and I am not going to spend what energy I have left making some sort of grave-marker for myself.
>
> You seem to think I'm some sort of visionary who conceived of a Great Institution in a blinding Pauline dream and was ever faithful to my Ideal. Quite au contraire; it was one step at a time all the way. I was no visionary, but merely a sly fellow playing at an exciting game. I was never very ambitious for the company or for myself; nor was George. We were too occupied for some forty years in practical day to day survival.
>
> It would be a relief, one day, to read a book which is supposedly the history of a great institution, close of quotes, which is not burnished in shit. That is why I let you have the diary. But to compress a real and constant anxiety; three nervous-breakdowns, bankruptcies, etc. in what MacRae [the publisher] thinks is saleable is, oddly enough, not very appetizing.
>
> Which, dear Dicky, is why I refused to do the whole thing myself, and that is why essentially, I don't give a fuck what you or anyone else does or says.
>
> As usual, Lincoln.

19. Villella, *Prodigal Son*, 59.
20. Kirstein Diary, June 9 and 24, 1933, LPA.
21. Kirstein Diary, June 9, 1933, LPA.
22. Kirstein Diary, June 7, 1933, LPA.
23. Kirstein Diary, June 19, 1933, LPA.
24. Kirstein Diary, July 16, 1933, LPA.
25. Kirstein Diary, June 3, 1933, LPA.
26. Kirstein Diary, Oct. 6, 1932, LPA.
27. Duberman, *Worlds of Lincoln Kirstein*, 511.
28. See especially, Kirstein Diary, Aug. 31, 1933, and May 6 and 16, 1934, LPA; Lamster, *Man in the Glass House*.
29. Duberman, *Worlds of Lincoln Kirstein*, 234–35. Johnson's flirtation at Harvard with the

openly anti-Semitic Lowells (wealthy, powerful, with a long history at Harvard; Abbot Laurence Lowell served as the university president from 1909 to 1933), who were still fighting to exclude Jews from the university, was especially galling to Lincoln's father, Louis, who had taken a leading role in opposing them. Lincoln's colleague Nancy Lassalle later noted to the author that "Lincoln didn't seem like a Jew": Nancy Lassalle, interview by the author, Jan. 7, 2012, and Nov. 18, 2012.

30. Lincoln Kirstein to Mina Curtiss, July 15, 1949, MS Thr 1045, Lincoln Kirstein Correspondence, Houghton.
31. Lincoln Kirstein to Richard Buckle, letter on the history of his family, fol.: Kirstein to Buckle, 1962–73, Richard Buckle Papers, HRC; "heretic": Kirstein, *Quarry*, 71.
32. Kirstein, *Mosaic*, 130–55; Lipsey, *Gurdjieff Reconsidered.* 113–45.
33. Kirstein Diary, Feb. 11, 1931, LPA; on Gurdjieff and nihilism, see Duberman, *Worlds of Lincoln Kirstein*, 95.
34. Kirstein Diary, Dec. 3, 1932, LPA.
35. Kirstein Diary, Nov. 15, 1932, LPA.
36. Kirstein Diary, Dec. 3, 1932, LPA.
37. Kirstein Diary, Mar. 29, 1931, LPA.
38. Duberman, *Worlds of Lincoln Kirstein*, 113–17.
39. Kirstein Diary, May 19, 1933, LPA; Duberman, *Worlds of Lincoln Kirstein*, 142–43.
40. Kirstein Diary, Nov. 15, 1932, LPA.
41. Kirstein Diary, June 19, 1933, LPA.
42. *Lincoln Kirstein's Modern* exhibition, Museum of Modern Art, New York City, 2020.
43. Lincoln Kirstein, "Dancing in Films," *New Theatre*, Sept. 1936, 11–13.
44. Kirstein Diary, Oct. 11, 1932, LPA.
45. Kirstein Diary, May 12, 1933, LPA; Duberman, *Worlds of Lincoln Kirstein*, 223.
46. Kirstein Diary, Jan. 28, 1931, LPA.
47. Gaddis, *Magician of the Modern*, 39.
48. Kirstein Diary, May 12 and 14, 1933, LPA; see also Gaddis, *Magician of the Modern.*
49. Lincoln Kirstein to Muriel Draper, July 13, 1933, b. 5, f. 155, Muriel Draper Papers, Beinecke.
50. The letter, which is held at the Wadsworth Atheneum archives, is partially reproduced in Gaddis, *Magician of the Modern*, 199–203; "My God!": Gaddis, 203–4; Kirstein to Draper, July 13, 1933, b. 5, f. 154, Muriel Draper Papers, Beinecke.
51. Gaddis, *Magician of the Modern*, 212.
52. Balanchine cabled his emphatic response: "PRESENCE DIMITRIEV EST NECESSAIRE." Duberman, *Worlds of Lincoln Kirstein*, 189.
53. Duberman, *Worlds of Lincoln Kirstein*, 199; stuff whatever costumes: Lincoln Kirstein to George Balanchine, Sept. 6, 1933, b. 19, MS Thr 411 (973), George Balanchine Archive, Houghton.
54. Lincoln Kirstein to Chick Austin, Aug. 16 and Aug. 11, 1933, quoted in Gaddis, *Magician of the Modern*, 210.
55. Aug. 12, 1933, cable quoted in Gaddis, *Magician of the Modern*, 212.
56. Kirstein Diary, Sept. 17, 1933, LPA.
57. Kirstein Diary, Oct. 11, 1933, LPA.
58. Kirstein Diary, Oct. 14, 1933, LPA.

CHAPTER 10: NEW YORK

1. New York, Passenger and Crew Lists (including Castle Garden and Ellis Island), 1820–1957, roll T715, 1897–1957, 5001–600, roll 5405, accessed via Ancestry.com.

2. Kirstein Diary, Oct. 19, 1933, LPA; Gaddis, *Magician of the Modern*, 215–18.
3. Gaddis, *Magician of the Modern*, 218, from *Hartford Courant*, Oct. 20, 1933.
4. Kirstein Diary, Oct. 20, 1933, LPA.
5. Kirstein Diary, Oct. 22, 1933, LPA.
6. Kirstein Diary, Oct. 22, 1933, LPA.
7. See Dunning, *"But First a School"*; also see annual brochures and other information, School of American Ballet, New York [clippings], *MGZRC 53, LPA.
8. Lincoln is working on Balanchine and Dmitriev's immigration by late Oct. 1933. Kirstein Diary, Oct. 26 and Nov. 4, 1933, LPA; George Balanchine immigration papers, U.S. Citizenship and Immigration Services, Department of Homeland Security, National Records Center. On U.S. immigration and deportation policies, see Mae Ngai, "The Strange Career of the Illegal Alien: Immigration Restriction and Deportation Policy in the United States, 1921–1965," *Law and History Review* 21, no. 1 (2003): 69–107; Kanstroom, *Deportation Nation*, esp. chap. 5.
9. Silas Spitzer, "Brahms, Borscht and Ballet," *Holiday*, Feb. 19, 1959.
10. Kirstein Diary, Sept. 7, 1934, LPA.
11. Kirstein Diary, Mar. 11, 1934, LPA.
12. Kirstein Diary, Nov. 8, 1933, LPA.
13. Kirstein Diary, Oct. 30, 1933, LPA; Kirstein Diary, Nov. 8, 1933, LPA.
14. Kirstein Diary, Oct. 29, 1933, LPA.
15. Kirstein Diary, Oct. 26, 1933, LPA.
16. Autograph Manuscripts, undated, b. 55, MS Thr 411 (2189), George Balanchine Archive, Houghton; Leaman, "Analyzing Music and Dance," 6.
17. Milstein and Volkov, *From Russia to the West*, 250–51.
18. Dominique Nabokov, interview by the author, Nov. 22, 2015; Peter Wolff, interview by the author, Apr. 23, 2014; Jean Stein, interview by the author, Dec. 4, 2015; William Lord Coleman, interview by the author, Dec. 8, 2015; Craft, *Improbable Life*, 126; "Icons in New Surroundings," *Arts and Decoration*, Sept. 1934. Records accessed via Ancestry.com:
—Davidova's 1927 U.S. naturalization papers say that she was born in 1900 in Constantinople and married to Karp of the Turkish Republic, b. 1896. They reside at the Embassy Hotel, 116 West Fifty-sixth Street, and she has been resident in the United States continuously for five years, having arrived on the Lapland in 1922. Her profession is "actress."
—The 1938 London Aeroplane Club Aviator's Certificate (Arlington House, Arlington Street W.1. Davidova, Lucia, Mme.) gives her citizenship as American and birthplace as Constantinople, Turkey, in 1903. It includes a picture of her wrapped in a fur stole.
—According to the 1940 U.S. Federal Census, she is Turkish-born, not married, not working ("no profession"), and thirty-eight years old; her highest education grade is eight, and she is a "lodger" in a rented home at 11 East Seventy-seventh Street in the household of Victor Sospice, who was French, and his German wife and their son.
19. "Patent-leather eyes" was Robert Craft's description. Jean Stein, interview by the author, Dec. 4, 2015; Lucia Davidova, outtakes in Tony Palmer's film *Stravinsky: Once at a Border.*
20. Dominique Nabokov, interview by the author, Nov. 22, 2015.
21. Notes on interview with Lucia Davidova, fragment, Taper Papers; Lucia Davidova London Aeroplane Club Aviator's Certificate, 1938, accessed via Ancestry.com.
22. Kapa Davidov, né Garabed Tavitian; his 1928 application for U.S. naturalization lists his birthplace as Constantinople, Turkey; other travel documents list his nationality as Armenian (accessed via Ancestry.com). See also the profile of Davidov in *The New Yorker*, July 17, 1948.

23. Kirstein Diary, Nov. 1, 1933, LPA.
24. Kirstein Diary, Nov. 7, 1933, LPA.
25. Kirstein Diary, Oct. 22, 1933, LPA.
26. Kirstein Diary, May 20, 1934, LPA.
27. Kirstein Diary, Oct. 18, 1933, LPA.
28. Kirstein Diary, Oct. 30, 1933, LPA.
29. This narrative is drawn from Kirstein Diary, Nov. 11 and 12, 1933, LPA.
30. Kirstein Diary, Nov. 17, 1933, LPA.
31. Kirstein Diary, Dec. 2 and 3, 1933, LPA; song Balanchine later composed and dedicated to Lincoln and Ashfield: Compositions, b. 55, f. 1, MS Thr 411 (2188), George Balanchine Archive, Houghton.
32. Ruthanna Boris, unpublished memoir, courtesy of Robert Gottlieb.
33. I am grateful to Vladimir Lehovich (Ouroussow's son) for inviting me into his home and sharing family documents and letters, along with his own memories, including his unpublished "Crimean Notes: A Glimpse into Family Matters." Vladimir Lehovich, interviews by the author, Sept. 2, 2015; Feb. 6 and Mar. 17, 2016; Olga Lehovich (Ouroussow's daughter), interview by the author, May 8, 2016; fol. 31: Ouroussow, Eugenie, RG 1-4; Bio Files A-Taras (A), John Taras Collection, NYCB Archives, includes a newspaper article by Nancy Randolph, undated, reporting on the wedding of Princess Eugenie Ouroussow and Dimitry Lehovich at the Russian Church of Christ the Savior, 121st Street and Madison Avenue, attended by Grand Duchess Marie (daughter of Czar Alexander II) and Prince Obolensky, among other White Russian luminaries; "The final task of the perfect art": "The World of Doctor Zhivago," undated, b. 9, f. 6, Slav. Reserve 09-393, Dmitri and Eugenie Lehovich Collection, 1906–1995, New York Public Library—typescript for Ouroussow's book-length essay on Pasternak and the Russian symbolists, which included chapters on the New Testament, Berdyaev, Blok, and Soloviev; Dunning, *"But First a School,"* 56.
34. Barbara Horgan, interview by the author.
35. Jacques d'Amboise, interview by the author, July 6, 2018; Molostwoff's passport said she was of Russian birth, but both d'Amboise and Vladimir Lehovich remember her being of Armenian origin. She married in an Armenian church. She joined SAB in 1938. See Dunning, *"But First a School,"* 56; Olga Lehovich, interview by the author, May 8, 2016; Natasha Molostwoff, interview by John Taras, Oct. 12, 1984, RG3/AV Materials, John Taras Collection, NYCB Archives. Catherine McDavid Smith (Nathalie Gleboff's daughter) also recalled Molostwoff; interview by the author, Aug. 21, 2015.
36. Catherine McDavid Smith, interview by the author, Aug. 21, 2015; Anna Kisselgoff, "Nathalie Gleboff, Director of School of American Ballet, Dies at 88," *New York Times*, Oct. 8, 2007.
37. Olga Lehovich, interview by the author, May 8, 2016.
38. Folder on the 1930s, School of American Ballet, New York [clippings], LPA.
39. Barbara Weisberger, interview by the author, Sept. 23, 2013; Ruthanna Boris, unpublished writings, courtesy of Robert Gottlieb; on Holly Howard: Clinton, Charles, David, Peter, Bea Howard, and Lynne Howard Couser, interviews by the author, May–July 2019; on Kathryn Mullowny: Richmond Campbell (son), interview by the author, May 8, 2019; on Lew Christensen and Gisella Caccialanza: interview by John Taras, 1984, RG3/AV Materials, John Taras Collection, NYCB Archives; on Lew Christensen: d'Amboise, *I Was a Dancer,* 112; Jennifer Dunning, "Lew Christensen Dies at 75; Lead Dancer for Balanchine," *New York Times,* Oct. 10, 1984. (Gisella Caccialanza was an Italian dancer, trained by Cecchetti, who worked with Balanchine in the 1930s and 1940s. She was a

founding member of the American Ballet and of Ballet Society, and she also performed with Balanchine in Hollywood. She married Lew Christensen in 1941, and they left New York in 1951.)

40. Dunning, *"But First a School,"* 55.
41. Schmitz, "Profile of Catherine Littlefield," esp. 23 (drinking, swearing, smoking), 75–77 (docks, etc.).
42. Quoted in d'Amboise, *I Was a Dancer,* 76.
43. Francisco Moncion, interview by Peter Conway, Apr. and May 1979, transcript, *MGZMT 5-959, LPA; d'Amboise, *I Was a Dancer,* 70–76.
44. Kirstein Diary, Apr. 14, 1934, LPA.
45. See b. 2, undated folder, School of American Ballet, New York [clippings], LPA, for a copy of the School of American Ballet (Division of Theatrical Sciences) list of Kirstein's lectures.
46. "Russian Composer-Pianist," *Los Angeles Times,* Sept. 28, 1919; Mikeshina, Ariadna [clippings], *MGZR (Mikeshina, Ariadna), LPA.
47. Elise Reiman, interview by John Taras, Dec. 14, 1983, RG3/AV Materials, John Taras Collection, NYCB Archives.
48. John Day (son of Daphne Vane), interview by the author, May 25, 2019.
49. Kirstein Diary, Oct. 27, 1934, LPA; Kirstein Diary, May 11, 1943, LPA.
50. Kirstein Diary, Dec. 21, 1934, LPA.
51. Kirstein Diary, Jan. 24, 1934, LPA.
52. Kirstein Diary, Feb. 28 and Mar. 20, 1934, LPA.
53. I am grateful to Kate and Pamela Draper for sharing their memories and their trove of family photos, letters, and documents, including letters from Balanchine to their mother, Heidi Vosseler; Kate and Pamela Draper, interview by the author, Feb. 9, 2019.
54. Kirstein Diary, July 15, 1934, LPA.
55. Kirstein Diary, Apr. 17 (*Serenade*) and Oct. 13 ("brothel"), 1934, LPA.
56. Kirstein Diary, Oct. 22, 1933, LPA.
57. Kirstein Diary, Nov. 18 and Oct. 19 and 23, 1933, LPA. Lincoln and the Warburgs suggested Ernest Bloch, the Swiss composer of the sacred service *Avodath Hakodesh,* but nothing came of it.
58. Kirstein Diary, Jan. 15 and 23, 1933, LPA.
59. Kirstein Diary, Aug. 30, 1934, LPA.
60. Kirstein Diary, Aug. 18 and Oct. 14, 1934, LPA; Lynn Garafola, "Lincoln Kirstein: Man of the People," in Friedman and Hauptman, *Lincoln Kirstein's Modern,* 29–35.
61. Kirstein Diary, Dec. 2, 1933, LPA.
62. Kirstein Diary, Mar. 14, 1934, LPA.
63. Kirstein Diary, Apr. 5, 1934, LPA.
64. Ruthanna Boris, "Serenade," in Gottlieb, *Reading Dance,* 1063–69.
65. Eddie Warburg, Balanchine's early patron, later said it was he who asked Balanchine to soften the Heil pose: Alastair Macaulay, "Serenade: Evolutionary Changes," *Ballet Review* 44, no. 4 (2016), 86 (from Kirstein, *Thirty Years,* 39–40); another dancer said that Balanchine joked, "I invented before Hitler" (Una Kai to author, letter from May 2014);"give it a Heil Hitler," Karin von Aroldingen, unpublished memoir, courtesy of von Aroldingen.
66. Kirstein Diary, Jan. 25–Dec. 4, 1934, b. 5, f. 22, (S) *MGZMD 123, Lincoln Kirstein Papers, LPA.
67. Ghislaine Thesmar, interview by the author, May 13, 2014.
68. On *Serenade,* see Macaulay, "Serenade," 74–119; Boris, "Serenade," in Gottlieb, *Reading*

Dance, 1063–69; letters from George Balanchine and Lincoln Kirstein to George Antheil, b. 1 and b. 2, George Antheil Papers, 1919–1959, Rare Book and Manuscript Library, Columbia University. In 1934 Balanchine asked the composer George Antheil to arrange the music, and although he eventually did, the first Warburg performance was probably from a simple piano reduction. Kirstein later wrote angrily and dismissively to Antheil and severed relations. Kirstein Diary, Feb. 27, 1935: "Antheil's orchestration of Serenade was so bad, so full of Antheilism's, it can't be used. Cd. 'Serenade' be . . . abandoned: No!" I am grateful also to Simon Morrison for his thoughts and research on Antheil.

69. Kirstein Diary, Mar. 22, 1934, LPA.
70. Kirstein Diary, May 28, 1934, LPA.
71. "more or less fruitlessly": Kirstein Diary, June 6, 1934, LPA; Abercrombie's: Kirstein Diary, June 8, 1934, LPA; "Bal. changes things": Kirstein Diary, June 7, 1934, LPA.
72. Kirstein Diary, June 9, 1934, LPA. With thanks to Alastair Macaulay for sharing insights and his own transcriptions of the diary.
73. Abraham, *Tchaikovsky*, 90; Brown, *Tchaikovsky*, 120.
74. Quoting the dancer Leda Anchutina: Reynolds, *Repertory in Review*, 36.
75. Taper, *Balanchine*, 169.
76. Taper, *Balanchine*, 172.
77. Ruthanna Boris, who was in the original cast, later recalled asking Balanchine how he arrived at the pose of the dark angel over the man's (Charles Laskey's) back. George impishly responded, "You know, Lasky, he is very near-sight. I thought he does not see, so, maybe more comfortable if eyes have cover and Kathryn looks where to go." Boris, "Serenade," in Gottlieb, *Reading Dance*, 1069.
78. Raymond, *Milton's Angels*, 293: Pseudo-Dionysius describes angels as "clear and spotless mirrors." Angels, it was thought, could sense without organs—they just know.
79. Balanchine to Colleen Neary, quoted in Macaulay, "Serenade," 91.
80. Heather Watts, interview by the author, Mar. 22, 2016; Victoria Simon, interview by the author, Apr. 7, 2015.
81. *Serenade* became a lifelong project, and Balanchine kept it close to him, like a talisman, at key moments throughout his life: he would stage it at the Paris Opera just after World War II, in 1947, and it would feature in the founding season of the NYCB in 1948. When Balanchine's company toured the USSR in 1962 at the height of the Cuban Missile Crisis, the seventeen dancers would stand in their opening pose tensely waiting for the audience response. And during the Tchaikovsky Festival at the NYCB in 1981, two years before his own death, *Serenade* would be present too. It was there at his American beginning, and it was there at his end.
82. Kirstein Diary, Nov. 25, 1934, LPA.
83. In the years to come, Balanchine would make important revisions in the choreography, costumes, sets, and music. He would add, cut, and rearrange well into the 1960s, when *Serenade* finally settled into the "text" that we know today—although even then Balanchine continued to adjust and rehearse the ballet personally until he was too old and sick to continue. From the 1970s, for example, the three principal women in the "Elegy" danced with luxurious flowing hair, increasing the eroticism and femininity of the dance. This was a final improvised moment, probably added when one of the dancers' hair accidentally came unpinned and fell loose in rehearsal (like a Clairol commercial, Balanchine noted). The lighting was simple. The opening preset was the lit cyclone-blue backdrop, and there were only three cues—at the very beginning, when women broke their hands at the wrist; when a woman fell; and from the 1970s, when the boys lifted the girl onto the final diagonal.

CHAPTER 11: TIME OF TROUBLES

1. For Kirstein's account of the events, see Kirstein Diary, July 12–21, 1934, LPA. In a letter from Dr. F. René Murad, a practicing Austrian émigré physician at Mount Kisco and Northern Westchester Hospital, to Lawrence K. Altman of *The New York Times,* on May 8, 1984, Murad recalls the incident in 1933 when he was called to the scene of Balanchine's collapse; letter courtesy of Dr. Edith Langner.
2. Louis Berman (1893–1946) was the author of *The Glands Regulating Personality: A Study of the Glands of Internal Secretion in Relation to the Types of Human Nature;* Kirstein Diary, June 21, 1934, LPA: Balanchine "has fallen in love with a diet prescribed by the gland-specialist Louis Berman to achieve a more favorable parathyroid and adrenal condition and to put calcium into his lungs."
3. Letter from George Balanchine to Heidi Vosseler on hospital stationery, undated, courtesy of Pamela and Kate Draper.
4. Kirstein Diary, July 20, 1934, LPA; the doctors Balanchine consulted in the coming months included Dr. George G. Ornstein (a Romanian-Jewish émigré, U.S. Army Medical Corps, professor of medicine at Columbia University and an expert on TB) and Dr. Miron Silberstein (an Odessa-born, Munich-trained, Jewish émigré physician who was the National Surgeon of the Army and Navy Union and known in arts circles), as well as Dr. Irving Clark and Dr. Foster Kennedy. A chest X-ray taken much later (1975) showed the "well known narrowing of the left side of the chest with thickened pleura and many large calcifications in the upper left lung, all consequences of the old disease. The heart is drawn over to the left side. The right lung is clear with only a few small calcifications in the right upper lung of no consequence." Letter from Peter de Nesnera, MD, May 29, 1975, b. 70, MS Thr 411 (2416), George Balanchine Archive, Houghton.
5. Letter from Balanchine to Vosseler, courtesy of Pamela and Kate Draper.
6. Kirstein Diary, July 21–Aug. 18, 1934, LPA; articles and advertisements on Cranker: *New York Times,* Nov. 19, 1933, Apr. 1 and 29, 1934, and May 2, 1934; *Altoona Mirror,* May 6, 1938; Ida Jean Kain, "Exercise Needed by Paralytic," *Atlanta Constitution,* Apr. 26, 1937; *Newark Advocate,* Mar. 11, 1937.
7. Letters from George Balanchine to Heidi Vosseler on hospital and Cranker Health Camp stationery, undated, courtesy of Pamela and Kate Draper.
8. Kirstein Diary, July 21–Aug. 18, 1934, LPA; on Kopeikine, see Kirstein Diary, Aug. 18, 1934, LPA.
9. Kirstein Diary, Apr. 24, 1936, LPA.
10. Kirstein, *Book of the Dance,* 321.
11. Lincoln Kirstein, "Revolutionary Ballet Forms," *New Theatre,* Oct. 1934, 13–14.
12. Kirstein Diary, Feb. 14, 1935, LPA.
13. Miscellaneous notes for interview with Balanchine about Tchelitchew, Parker Tyler Papers (uncatalogued), HRC; see also Kirstein Diary, Nov. 17 and 24, 1934, LPA.
14. "something without L'amour": Kirstein Diary, Nov. 13, 1934, LPA; "I told him": Kirstein Diary, Oct. 20, 1934, LPA.
15. Kirstein Diary, Oct. 20, 1934, LPA.
16. Kirstein Diary, Jan. 28, 1934, LPA.
17. Kirstein Diary, Jan. 27 and 28 and Feb. 15, 1934, LPA.
18. Hauptmann had been tried and convicted for the kidnapping and murder of the Lindbergh baby a few months before.
19. Paul Hindemith to Gertrud Hindemith, Apr. 12 and 27, b. 23, f. 362, 1940, MSS 47, Paul Hindemith Collection, YML.

20. George Balanchine to William Boyce, 1934, b. 19, MS Thr 411 (1014), George Balanchine Archive, Houghton.
21. Duke, *Passport to Paris,* 369.
22. Kirstein Diary, Nov. 13, 1934, LPA.
23. Kirstein Diary, Aug. 6, 1935, LPA.
24. American Ballet program, Merovitch tour, 1935, microfilm, Paul Sacher Stiftung; Alexander Merovitch naturalization records, accessed via Ancestry.com; "Matzoh-King": Kirstein Diary, Oct. 15, 1935, LPA.
25. Steichen, *Balanchine and Kirstein's American Enterprise,* 96–102.
26. On Merovitch, see Walsh, *Stravinsky: The Second Exile,* 4; Plaskin, *Horowitz,* 161–203, 171; and King, *Gregor Piatigorsky,* 89; the George Balanchine interview by Phyllis Winifred Manchester (Mar. 20, 1975, *MGZTC 3-291, LPA) includes a discussion of Manischewitz and Merovitch. On the tour generally and "psychic shock," see Kirstein Diary, Oct. 15–25, 1935.
27. Kirstein Diary, Jan. 17, 1936, LPA: "He says if nothing happens at the Met he will go back to Russia and do something there as all of his friends and father are in important positions."
28. He knew it from Diaghilev's production too.
29. Miscellaneous notes for interview with Balanchine about Tchelitchew, Parker Tyler Papers (uncatalogued), HRC; Kirstein Diary, Nov. 17 and 24, 1934, LPA.
30. Kirstein Diary, Oct. 20 and Nov. 13, 1934, LPA.
31. Elissa Fuchs, interview by the author, Mar. 14, 2014. Fuchs staged her own version of the opera in the late 1930s and sought Balanchine's advice; Kirstein to Johnson, Jan. 23, 1935, Edward Johnson Correspondence, 1935–36, Metropolitan Opera Archives. See also Lynes's photos of Daphne Vane in the role of Eurydice. Tchelitchew also painted Vane's portrait—otherworldly—around this time.
32. "Travesty": *World Telegram,* May 23, 1936; "Elysian Fields" and "in the usual": review from illegible clipping 1936, all held in the Metropolitan Opera Archives, fol. "Orfeo ed Eurydice, 1935–36," see also Edward Johnson Correspondence, 1935–36, and an untitled file with correspondence, including letters by Kirstein, Metropolitan Opera Archives; also, Kirstein Diary, Apr. 24, 1936, LPA; Kirstein Diary, May 25, 1936, LPA.
33. Kirstein wrote in his diary (Dec. 10, 1936) that an immigration agent was investigating Balanchine's private life and that George was fearful of possible deportation: "The denunciation said syphilis and making passes at the boys as well." An extensive archival search for an INS deportation or investigation file yielded nothing—apparently any such files at the local field level would have been destroyed. My thanks to Debevoise and Plimpton for tirelessly conducting this search. On deportation policy: Ngai, "Strange Career." Clinton, Charles, David, Peter, and Bea Howard, and Lynne Howard Couser, interviews by the author, May–July 2019.
34. The dancer Barbara Weisberger remembered rumors that Holly Howard had five abortions (Barbara Weisberger, interview by the author, Sept. 23, 2013). The dancer Gisella Caccialanza later also confirmed rumors of pregnancy and threats of deportation, and said, "We'd go over to her mother's apt, it was real dark, and we had come to the conclusion it was a den, and we had all that going on." John Taras noted: "They say—no proof—Holly is running a whore-house in Boston. Everybody said she became a whore and it was because of him" (Lew Christensen and Gisella Caccialanza, interview by John Taras, 1984, sound recording, RG3/AV Materials, John Taras Collection, NYCB Archives). In his diary Kirstein said Howard had had four abortions (Nov. 27, 1936) and that George had been seeing

her—often with her mother, Lois—at least since January 1935 (Jan. 12 and Apr. 16, 1935). Holly Howard died in 1968 or 1969 (according to records accessed via Ancestry.com); the dancer Yvonne Patterson's photo of her was from 1936: snapshots, American Ballet Tour, 1936, (S) *MGZMD 259, Yvonne Patterson and William Dollar Papers, LPA; Clinton, Charles, David, Peter, and Bea Howard and Lynne Howard Couser, interviews by the author, May through July 2019.

35. Elissa Fuchs, interview by the author, Mar. 14, 2014; Reynolds, *Repertory in Review,* 45–46; Steichen, *Balanchine and Kirstein's American Enterprise,* 117–23; "being in prison," quoted in Steichen, *Balanchine and Kirstein's American Enterprise,* 177; fol. "Orfeo ed Eurydice, 1935-36," and fol. "Edward Johnson, Correspondence, American Ballet, Balanchine, 1935-36," Metropolitan Opera Archives, contains the letter dated March 19, 1938, relieving Balanchine and the American Ballet Theatre of their duties at the Met. See also Balanchine's strongly worded note (with Lincoln's help?) directed at the Met: (S) *MGZM-Res. Bal G, George Balanchine, Misc. Correspondence, LPA.
36. Walker Evans photographs of Ballet Caravan: Ballet Caravan, b. 22, f. 224, (S) *MGZMD 123, Lincoln Kirstein Papers, LPA.
37. Dunning, *"But First a School,"* 85–86. Dmitriev left in June 1940; Balanchine told Jacques d'Amboise that he sent Dmitriev money even in the 1940s if he had some from a Broadway show or film; d'Amboise, *I Was a Dancer,* 118.
38. George Balanchine Ballet Inc., Jan. 1938: Tax Returns; George Balanchine Ballet Inc., 1938–40, b. 81, MS Thr 411 (2431), George Balanchine Archive, Houghton.
39. On Ballet Theatre, see Balanchine, George, b. 7, f. 488-89, (S) *MGZMD 49, American Ballet Theatre Records, 1936-67, LPA. Richard Pleasant to Dwight Deere Wiman (Broadway producer and Balanchine's agent), Sept. 8, 1939: Pleasant says he is very sorry Balanchine will not be a founding member of Ballet Theatre. The door is still open to Balanchine and to Miss Zorina "the welcome mat out." Pleasant hints that a Balanchine ballet would of course be a wonderful addition to their repertory.
40. Lincoln Kirstein to Richard Buckle, July 30, 1983, fol.: Kirstein to Buckle, 1962–73, Richard Buckle Papers, HRC.
41. "free man": b. 15, f. 1401–1402, (S) *MGZMD 48, Records of the Ballet Russe de Monte Carlo, LPA; Balanchine, George, b. 7, f. 488–489, (S) *MGZMD 49, American Ballet Theatre Records, 1936-67, LPA, esp. the series of telegrams from J. Alden Talbot to Ellen Bywater (both Ballet Theatre) from Feb. 15, 1944, to Feb. 26, 1944, over a contract that Balanchine "refuses to sign . . . Balanchine impossible . . . says he is free man and cannot place himself in position to be sued. He suggested dropping the whole thing. I told him he could not back out now." For Hollywood: Memoirs, undated, f. 67, Eddie Albert Papers, Margaret Herrick Library; Contracts, f. 7, Paramount Pictures production records, Margaret Herrick Library; Balanchine, George, f. 115, Paramount Pictures contract summaries, Margaret Herrick Library.
42. George Balanchine to Vera Zorina, Nov. 1937 (from 513 North Camden Drive, Beverly Hills), Collection of Letters from George Balanchine to Vera Zorina, ML30.27e.B35 no. 1, LC.
43. Barbara Horgan, interview by the author, Sept. 3, 2014; Robinson, *Russians in Hollywood.* 132.
44. Notes on interview with Natasha Nabokov, Jan. 29, 1963, Taper Papers.

CHAPTER 12: ZORINA

1. George Balanchine's condolence letter to Maria at Meliton's death (telegram in Russian), State Museum of Georgian Theater, Music, Film and Choreography—Art Palace, Tbilisi.

2. George Balanchine to Meliton, "Congrats 50th Anniversary Career," 193? [1934], State Museum of Georgian Theater, Music, Film and Choreography—Art Palace, Tbilisi.
3. Meliton Balanchivadze to George Balanchine, Aug. 20, 1936, b. 2, MS Thr 411 (116), George Balanchine Archive, Houghton.
4. Balanchine to Zorina, Nov. 1937; Balanchine to Zorina, Mar. 27, 1941, LC.
5. Massine's wife at the time was the Russian dancer Eugenia Delarova, who later married a wealthy man and was a friend and supporter of Balanchine and the NYCB.
6. Letters and notes to Vera Zorina from Léonide Massine, 1935 and undated, b. 37, MS Thr 632 (574), Vera Zorina Papers, Houghton; Zorina, *Zorina*; Vera Zorina, interview by John Gruen, Oct. 19, 1972, transcript, *MGZMT 3-209, LPA; García-Márquez, *Massine*, 239–42.
7. Edwin Denby in *The New York Sun*, Oct. 1936, quoted in García-Márquez, *Massine*, 25.
8. García-Márquez, *Massine*, 307.
9. Berg, *Goldwyn*, 298–306; George Balanchine, "The Ballet and the Film: The Making of the Goldwyn Follies," *Dance Herald*, Apr. 1938, 1, 7–8; Taper, *Balanchine*, 177–201; "Georgie": b. 39, f. 6, Gold and Fizdale Collection, Peter Jay Sharp Special Collections.
10. Buckle, *Balanchine*, 120. Buckle reproduces the letter to his mother, in English, undated: the letter says "a few days" after his marriage, so probably Dec. 1938.
11. Duke, *Passport to Paris*, 351–58; Zorina, *Zorina*, 187; John Day (son), interview by the author, May 25, 2019. Day senior fell in love with Daphne Vane.
12. George Balanchine, interview by Jonathan Cott, summer 1978, sound recording, *MGZTL 4-2685, discs 1–3, LPA.
13. Balanchine to Zorina, June 14, 1944. On June 21, Balanchine wrote further to Zorina, "I hope you are resting and gaining some weight." Letters from George Balanchine to Vera Zorina, LC.
14. Zorina, *Zorina*, 200–25 ("like a gesture": 200).
15. Balanchine's letters to Zorina are divided into two collections: Letters from George Balanchine to Vera Zorina, ML30.27e.B35 no. 1, LC; Letters to Vera Zorina from George Balanchine, 1938–43, b. 2, MS Thr 632 (55), Vera Zorina Papers, Houghton. Most are in the Library of Congress collection.
16. Balanchine to Zorina, Dec. 12, 1937, LC.
17. Balanchine to Zorina, undated (probably winter 1937), LC.
18. Balanchine to Zorina, Nov. 23, 1937, and undated, LC.
19. Notes on interview with Natasha Nabokov, Jan. 29, 1963, Taper Papers.
20. George Balanchine to Vera Zorina, Sept. 1938, b. 2, MS Thr 632 (55), Vera Zorina Papers, Houghton.
21. George Balanchine and Eva B. Hartwig, license no. 1055, New York City Municipal Archives, Borough: Staten Island, vol. 1, 211, Marriage License Indexes, 1907–1938, accessed via Ancestry.com.
22. Zorina, *Zorina*, 230.
23. Balanchine, George, photograph no. 12, State Museum of Georgian Theater, Music, Film and Choreography—Art Palace, Tbilisi.
24. Notes on interview with Richard Rodgers, Taper Papers.
25. Balanchine to Zorina, Apr. 20, 1939, LC.
26. Zorina, *Zorina*, 245–46; Vernon Duke to Bernard Taper, Oct. 19, 1961, Taper Papers (Duke notes that Balanchine spent more than he had and got into trouble with a jeweler on Fifth Avenue when he could not pay his bills); Duke, *Passport to Paris*, 400; notes on interview with Natasha Nabokov, Jan. 29, 1963, Taper Papers; on the missing front door, see *St. Louis Post-Dispatch*, Nov. 16, 1941.

27. Notes on interview with Lucia Davidova, Taper Papers. Davidova says that Balanchine was always competitive with Massine and that Zorina was a low point in his life. Zorina and her mother too were "mercenary," and Balanchine was weak and still tubercular, and they didn't even give him a decent meal.
28. Popular Balanchine Dossiers, 1927–2004, (S) *MGZMD 146, LPA: *On Your Toes compiled by Lynn Garafola*, b. 9–13; *Ziegfeld Follies of 1936 compiled by Beth Genné*, b. 8; *Great Lady compiled by Barbara Palfy*, b. 17; *I Married an Angel compiled by Marilyn Hunt*, b. 18; *Babes in Arms compiled by Constance Valis Hill*, b. 14; *Cabin in the Sky compiled by Constance Valis Hill*, b. 20–21.
29. Notes on interview with Richard Rodgers, Taper Papers.
30. *On Your Toes compiled by Lynn Garafola*, b. 9–13, LPA; "Stupid": Vernon Duke to Bernard Taper, Oct. 11, 1961, Taper Papers.
31. Hyland, *Richard Rodgers*, 119; Logan, *Josh*, 122–24; *I Married An Angel compiled by Marilyn Hunt*, b. 18, LPA.
32. Duke, *Passport to Paris*, 374.
33. Songs: autograph manuscripts, manuscript photocopies, printed, undated, b. 56, MS Thr 411 (2194), George Balanchine Archive, Houghton:

    > Last night I dremt that you and I why did you come to make me cry how come and why we ever met so now I'm lost and can't forget again I'm waiting for the next night for you put out my candle light in darkness sink in to your eyes like never ending heavens—stary skies third night again has now descended but love for you yet ever ended oh lonely heart why should I rove be gone mirage I won't regret I've left no tears for lonely nights to wet why not then die—but die with you in Love let me die in love.

    Fol. 11, "When Without You I Feel So Lonely":

    > When without you I feel so lonely when with you I feel divine I want your love to be mine only come and live with me and be mine if you love me so tell me soon you are the sun and silver moon if you are sun then burn me fast or shining bride be mine at last. Your golden founten hair grandeur your eyes are velvet deep blue purr like frozen hills bears thy boosom white snow on whose like rose tops petals pink grow when without you I feel so lonely when whith you I feel divine I want your love to be mine only why not I forever be thine.

34. Fred Danieli recalled that during *On Your Toes*: "Balanchine was fascinated with American rhythms. Absolutely loved tap. Tried to learn it." Danieli quoted in Banes, *Writing Dancing*, 60; also see *Ziegfeld Follies of 1936 compiled by Beth Genné*, b. 8, LPA.
35. *On Your Toes* was originally proposed to Astaire, but he turned it down. "Reminiscences of Richard Rodgers, 1968," interview by Kenneth W. Leish, transcript, Columbia Center for Oral History, Columbia University, 156–60; *On Your Toes compiled by Lynn Garafola*, b. 9–13, LPA.
36. Seibert, *What the Eye Hears*, including 200; *Babes in Arms compiled by Constance Valis Hill*, b. 14, LPA.
37. Quoted in Mueller, *Astaire Dancing*, 3, from Ivan Nabokov and Elizabeth Carmichael, "Balanchine: An Interview," *Horizon*, Jan. 1961, 44–56.
38. Seibert, *What the Eye Hears*, 241.
39. Seibert, *What the Eye Hears*, esp. 244–48; Hill, *Tap Dancing America*.

40. Buckle, *Katherine Dunham; Cabin in the Sky compiled by Constance Valis Hill,* b. 14, LPA.
41. On *Cabin in the Sky,* see George Balanchine, interview by William Stott and an unidentified woman, July 7, 1977, C2644, HRC; "Bally": Constance Valis Hill, "*Cabin in the Sky*: Katherine Dunham's and George Balanchine's Afro Americana" (paper presented at the American Studies Association Conference, Detroit, MI, Oct. 13, 2000); Duke, *Passport to Paris,* 391–93; *Cabin in the Sky compiled by Constance Valis Hill,* b. 20–21, LPA; notes on conversation with Balanchine, undated (c. 1961), Taper Papers; Banes, *Writing Dancing,* 53–69. The premiere of *Cabin in the Sky* took place on Oct. 25, 1940.
42. Letters to Vera Zorina from George Balanchine, 1938–43, b. 2, MS Thr 632 (55), Vera Zorina Papers, Houghton: Balanchine writes from the Hotel Wellington, Seventh Avenue at Fifty-fifth Street, to Mrs. George Balanchine, 120 East End Avenue, undated (author's note: undated, but see "pity" reference in the next letter postmarked Dec. 11, 1940, dating it to around this time). We don't know exactly when Balanchine left, but by December 1940, Zorina is living at 120 East End Avenue, and he was writing to her from the Hotel Wellington; in his letters dated and postmarked Dec. 11 and 13, he tries to explain why he left. As early as May 24, 1940, Lincoln wrote to his associate Frances Hawkins, reporting that Balanchine and Zorina were getting divorced: RG3: Dir. and Execs. Correspondence and Subject Files: Lincoln Kirstein, no. 5310, Ballet Society Collection, NYCB Archives.
43. Balanchine to Zorina, Dec. 13, 1940 (postmark), LC.
44. Balanchine to Zorina, Dec. 11 and 13, 1940, LC.
45. Balanchine to Zorina, Dec. 13, 1940, LC.
46. Balanchine to Zorina, undated (from Ruxton Hotel), LC.
47. Letters from George Balanchine to Vera Zorina, ML30.27e.B35 no. 1, LC; George Balanchine to Vera Zorina, May 29, 1937, to July 25, 1944, b. 2, MS Thr 632, Vera Zorina Papers, Houghton.
48. Balanchine to Zorina, Mar. 10 and 22, 1941, LC; Balanchine to Zorina, Mar. 15, 1941, b. 2, MS Thr 632, Vera Zorina Papers, Houghton.
49. Balanchine to Zorina, Mar. 15, 1941 (written from Park Chambers to Mrs. George Balanchine, 120 East End Avenue), b. 2, MS Thr 632, Vera Zorina Papers, Houghton.
50. Balanchine to Zorina, Mar. 25, [1941] (2 A.M., Park Chambers, no envelope), LC.
51. Balanchine to Zorina, Mar. 22, 25, and 27, 1941, LC.
52. Ruthanna Boris, unpublished writings, courtesy of Robert Gottlieb.
53. On his having borrowed money from Hart, see Notes, c. 1961, Taper Papers.
54. Interview with Betty Cage and Natasha Molostwoff, Balanchine Book: Notes on Tapes and Interviews, b. 45, Richard Buckle Papers, HRC. The fire was reported in the *New York Herald Tribune* on Apr. 1, 1941; on Davidova's thinking Balanchine was suicidal, see Natasha Molostwoff, interview by John Taras, Oct. 12, 1984, sound recording, RG2/AV materials, John Taras Collection, NYCB Archives; notes on interview with Lucia Davidova, Taper Papers. In the same interview, Taras remembered Balanchine crying over a meal at Tony's Restaurant.
55. On the negotiations, see b. 28, f. 2775–2777, (S) *MGZMD 48, Records of the Ballet Russe de Monte Carlo, LPA.
56. Balanchine to Zorina, Nov. 21, 1942, LC.
57. Joseph, *Stravinsky and Balanchine.* The elephant ballet, to Stravinsky's *Circus Polka,* was on Apr. 9, 1942.
58. Balanchine to Zorina, Aug. 2, 1943, b. 2, MS Thr 632 (55), Vera Zorina Papers, Houghton.

59. Balanchine to Zorina, June 4, 1944 (from the Biltmore Hotel, Los Angeles, to Mrs. Vera Zorina, Ritz Tower), 1944, LC.
60. Zorina, *Zorina,* 284.
61. Zorina, *Zorina,* 297. Divorce proceedings and papers filed Jan. 17, 1946, in the Second Judicial District Court of the State of Nevada, Washoe County; separation of property formally agreed Nov. 8, 1945.
62. Interview with George Balanchine, Jan. 24 [1961?], Taper Papers; on the house, which Zorina gave to her mother, see the notes on the interview with Natasha Nabokov, Taper Papers.
63. Kirstein says that between rehearsals for *Cabin in the Sky* and *Balustrade,* Balanchine made *Concerto Barocco,* later presented in South America. Ballet Society, b. 22, f. 223, Lincoln Kirstein Papers, (S) *MGZMD 123, LPA.

CHAPTER 13: BALANCHINE'S WAR

1. Kirstein notes in the report of the director for the year ending June 30, 1941, that Balanchine began a "workshop course" on "stage practice" for the advanced students of the Professional Division; *School of American Ballet* catalogue, 1937, fol. 1930s, School of American Ballet, New York [clippings], LPA.
2. James Steichen, "Balanchine's 'Bach Ballet' and the Dances of Rodgers and Hart's *On Your Toes,*" *Journal of Musicology* 35, no. 2 (2018): 267–93. Steichen also points out that Balanchine later bequeathed *Concerto Barocco* to Lincoln in his will, perhaps in recognition of Lincoln's role in helping it happen. In the concentric circles of their lives, as Balanchine returned to Bach in 1941, Draper married Heidi Vosseler.
3. *Concerto Barocco* had a preview performance at the Kaye Playhouse in New York in 1941, but the premiere took place at the Theatro Municipal in Rio de Janeiro in 1941. On Berman's costumes, see John Martin, "The Dance: Open Season," *New York Times,* Sept. 9, 1945; see also the review the following day, Sept. 10, 1945.
4. Lynes was doing publicity for Boosey & Hawkes. For a list of photographs and dates for dancers to be photographed, see fol. 3102, RG6: Antecedents, South American Tour Administration, 1941, Ballet Society Collection, NYCB Archives. Leddick, *Intimate Companions;* George Platt Lynes, 1950–52, b. 16, f. 225, Lincoln Kirstein Papers, (S) *MGZMD 97, LPA; Francisco Moncion, interview by John Taras, sound recording, RG3/AV Materials, John Taras Collection, NYCB Archives. When Taras asked Moncion when the nude Lynes photos were taken, he said that Balanchine was interested in mood photographs of dancers and "trying to reproduce the male-female thing."
5. I owe the expression, and more, to conversations with the late Anne Hollander, and to her book, *Seeing Through Clothes.*
6. Edwin Denby, "The Ballet: A Balanchine Masterpiece," *New York Herald Tribune* (undated, but appears to b. 1945); Dreyfus, *Bach;* Chilton, *Hazel Scott;* Steichen, "Balanchine's 'Bach Ballet.'"
7. George Balanchine, interview by Time Abroad, recorded by Brinkerhoff, c. 1941. Thanks to Serapio Walton, who played me a digitized version of this old recording. The text Balanchine reads was perhaps written by Lincoln, but at the end he speaks extemporaneously about his own work.
8. Fol. 26: Marie Jeanne, RG1-4 Bio Files A-Taras (A), John Taras Collection, NYCB Archives. Taras recounting rehearsals he had seen of the original.
9. Kara Yoo Leaman, "Musical Techniques in Balanchine's Jazzy Bach Ballet," *Journal of Music Theory* 65, no. 1 (2021): 139–69, and Leaman, "Analyzing Music and Dance." An

example of the complexity of Balanchine's use of music can be seen in Leaman's analysis of a single passage ("Musical Techniques," 31–32):

> Balanchine's use of 5s and 4s alternates with Bach's own use of fives and fours in this passage, mmm. 123–37 (the climax with its two surrounding ritornellos). . . . At first, Balanchine pairs his 5s with Bach's 4s in the first tonic ritornello. When Balanchine takes the 4s, he does so over Bach's harmonic progressions that are driven primarily by descending-fifth root motions, a different kind of 5, but one that would have been familiar to Balanchine through his musical training. When Bach's ritornello takes back the 4s, Balanchine pairs it with a combination of 5s and 4s. Keeping in mind that the music continues to express 3/4 meter through 6s and 2s, and that the base suggests 3s against which Balanchine's second group expresses 3s with rotated accents, . . . we see the variety and density of Balanchine's metric manipulations in the movement's climax and its surroundings.

10. Barbara Walczak, interview by the author, Aug. 2017.
11. As early as 1939, Lincoln was writing to George proposing that they resume their work together and giving him artistic carte blanche. After years on the road touring the United States and begging his reluctant father for infusions of cash to support his fledgling Ballet Caravan, Lincoln had realized, again, that he needed George. Lincoln Kirstein to George Balanchine, May 20, 1939, f. 5308, Lincoln Kirstein Correspondence, RG3: Dir. and Execs. Correspondence and Subject Files, Ballet Society Collection, NYCB Archives.
12. Kirstein did send reports to Nelson: see Duberman, *Worlds of Lincoln Kirstein,* 359. The reports are held in the Rockefeller Archive Center; Kirstein's FBI file shows the agency's efforts to figure out exactly why he was in South America in the first place, noting that he was "definitely not on a mission for the War Department or for any other governmental agency. However, the Coordinator of Inter-American Affairs has to pass upon his trip." The documents note that Kirstein was interviewed on Sept. 9, 1942, in the lobby of the Pan Am offices in Panama, concerning "the pro-Nazi sentiments of one [name redacted], a Brazilian, then serving with the Brazilian Army." Kirstein's known left-wing sentiments and activities from at least 1938 were a subject of ongoing investigation by the FBI.
13. Fol. 3102, RG6: Antecedents, South American Tour Administration, 1941, Ballet Society Collection, NYCB Archives; Duberman, *Worlds of Lincoln Kirstein,* 359–69. On June 6, 1941, Balanchine and the dancers departed from Argentina, bound for Rio; Kirstein joined them a week later.
14. Lincoln Kirstein to Rose Stein Kirstein, Aug. 4 [1941], f. 5, MS Thr 1045, Lincoln Kirstein Correspondence, Houghton.
15. Lincoln Kirstein to Frances Hawkins, undated (from the Hotel Crillon in Santiago), series 3: Correspondence with Frances Hawkins, 1941–44, b. 2, Lincoln Kirstein Correspondence and Notes, Museum of Modern Art Archives. See also Lincoln Kirstein to Rose Stein Kirstein, f. 5, MS Thr 1045, Lincoln Kirstein Correspondence, Houghton.
16. RG3: Dir. and Execs. Correspondence and Subject Files, 5833: Kirstein, Louis and South American Tour of American Ballet Caravan, May 29, 1941–Sept. 21, 1942, Ballet Society Collection, NYCB Archives—including Aug. 18, 1941, letter from Lincoln to his parents.
17. Barbara Horgan, interview by the author, Feb. 24, 2014. Ironically, Aalto was perhaps best known for his design of a Finnish TB sanatorium.
18. MoMA to George Balanchine, Feb. 23, 1942, b. 25, MS Thr 411 (1280), George Balanchine Archive, Houghton—the letter thanks him for his gift.
19. War Years, b. 20, Richard Buckle Papers, HRC; on the "Happiness" packages, sent in

1945 through the relief agency Continental Forwarders, see Charitable Donations, 1942–1969, b. 105, f. 1, and May–June correspondence, Tolstoy Foundation (U.S.), 1945, b. 39, MS Thr 411 (2771) and (1911), George Balanchine Archive, Houghton.

20. Membership cards, undated, b. 110, MS Thr 411 (2813), George Balanchine Archive, Houghton: including Balanchine's Registration certificate for the Selective Service, dated Feb. 15, 1942, and his subsequent "notice of Classification" (order no. 11837) by the local board, Sept. 21, 1943 (card notes the "small scar on right cheek").
21. On Feb. 23, 1943, Lincoln was inducted into the army at Fort Dix. Duberman, *Worlds of Lincoln Kirstein*, 382–86.
22. "Concerts Help Charity; Kreisler Recital Will Aid War Fund—American Friends Service to Gain," *New York Times*, Mar. 21, 1943; "Funds for Starving; Receipts of 'Crucifixion of Christ' Will Be Nucleus of Relief for Children," *New York Times*, Apr. 4, 1943. The Met was rented to Stokowski for $1,000; the premiere was on Apr. 9, 1943. "Benefit Concert for Starving Children, 1943" (at the Metropolitan Opera House in New York City), American Friends Service Committee, www.afsc.org/document/benefit-concert-starving-children-1943.
23. "Museum of Modern Art Opens Exhibition of Therese Bonney's War History Written with the Lens," Dec. 11, 1940, Museum of Modern Art, www.moma.org/momaorg/shared/pdfs/docs/press_archives/654/releases/MOMA_1940_0085_1940-12-10_401210-76.pdf.
24. "C'était ciel": Kirstein Diary, Dec. 18, 1934, LPA; "J. S. in Manhattan," *Time*, Apr. 1943, 49; Robert Badger, "Stokowski Conducts Miracle Play," *New York World-Telegram*, Apr. 10, 1943; "the veil of the temple": Benefit Concert for Starving Children, 1943, www.afsc.org/document/benefit-concert-starving-children-1943.
25. Kirstein's editor's note in the first issue of *Dance Index*, 1942–49 (New York: Arno Press).
26. Donald Windham to Bud, Feb. 27, 1945, b. 16, fol.: Donald Windham letters, 1944–45, YCAL MSS 424, Donald Windham and Sandy Campbell Papers, Beinecke.
27. Lincoln Kirstein, "Ballet Master's Belief," in Kirstein, Cott, and Denby, *Portrait of Mr. B*, 203.
28. I am grateful to Don Garrett, Moshe Halbertal, and Leon Wieseltier for help with Spinoza's thought in relation to Balanchine's scattershot notes. See Garrett, *Cambridge Companion to Spinoza;* Garrett, *Nature and Necessity;* Spinoza, *Essential Spinoza;* and Spinoza, *Collected Works*.
29. Yuszczuk and Nicoloff, "An Interview with George Balanchine," 10–14. Balanchine also made arrangements to visit Roman Yuszczuk at St. Vladimir's Seminary in Tuckahoe, New York. Correspondence with Roman Yuszczuk, 1967, b. 41, MS Thr 411 (2108), George Balanchine Archive, Houghton.
30. This particular fragment is typed, presumably in conversation with the editor, Windham, who has written in the margins: "No!"
31. "Notes on Choreography and Teaching by George Balanchine," undated, b. 110, MS Thr 411 (2814), George Balanchine Archive, Houghton. The article drawn from Balanchine's notes was published in *Dance Index*, Feb.–Mar. 1945.
32. Goethe, *Faust, Part Two*, 169–70.
33. Goethe, *Faust, Part One*; Goethe, *Faust, Part Two*; "Eros: first cause of it all": Goethe, *Faust, Part Two*, line 8479; see also David Luke's introduction to Goethe, *Faust, Part Two*, xxxi; Hatfield, *Goethe*.
34. Goethe, *Faust, Part Two*, 39.
35. Goethe, *Faust, Part Two*, 52.
36. Goethe, *Faust, Part Two*, 238–39; the angels explain, on 234: "He who strives on and lives

to strive / Can earn redemption still. / And now that love itself looks down / To favor him with grace, / The blessed host with songs may crown / Him welcome to this place."

37. Goethe, *Faust, Part Two,* 239 (the final lines: "Das Unbeschreibliche, / Hier ist's getan; / Das Ewig-Weibliche / Zieht uns hinan").
38. The Prayer to the Holy Cross of the Lord in Balanchine's hand in Russian on Savoy Hotel stationery, undated, but probably around 1945, when the "Notes on Choreography and Teaching by George Balanchine" were written. Savoy stationery is difficult to date precisely, but telephone numbers date to the war or early postwar years, although it is not clear how or why Balanchine had stationery from this London hotel. Hotel records held at the archive of the Savoy show that he did stay there, but later; it is possible someone gave him the stationery, we just don't know. I am grateful to Susan Scott for her help in tracing Balanchine's visits (in a note in the 1960s, the maids recorded that he took the hangers!). The prayer was filed with "Notes on Choreography and Teaching by George Balanchine," b. 110, MS Thr 411 (2814), George Balanchine Archive, Houghton. With thanks to Marina Warner and to her book *Alone of All Her Sex;* Hubbs, *Mother Russia.*
39. Performed on Jan. 22, 1946.
40. Smith, *Patenting the Sun;* Oshinsky, *Polio.*
41. On *Resurgence,* see Basil O'Connor to George Balanchine, Jan. 30, 1946, b. 26, MS Thr 411 (1310), George Balanchine Archive, Houghton: O'Connor thanks Balanchine for his "superlatively moving and impressive contribution to the 1946 March of Dimes Fashion Show. Both the conception and the execution of your ballet interpreted the story of the fight against infantile paralysis as only an art medium can."
42. Tallchief, *Maria Tallchief.*
43. Maria Tallchief Diary, Sept. 4, 1944, courtesy of Elise Paschen.
44. Tallchief, *Maria Tallchief,* 51–59.
45. Eddie Bigelow photographs, courtesy of Hal Bigelow.
46. Notes on George Balanchine interview, Feb. 14, 1961, Taper Tapes.

CHAPTER 14: LINCOLN'S WAR

1. Duberman, *Worlds of Lincoln Kirstein,* 383–84.
2. Lincoln Kirstein to Eugenie Ouroussow, Oct. 8, 1943, Vladimir Lehovich personal collection.
3. Lincoln Kirstein to Mina Kirstein Curtiss, undated (from Fort Belvoir), b. 3, f. 20, MS Thr 1045 (10), Lincoln Kirstein Correspondence, Houghton.
4. Quoted in Duberman, *Worlds of Lincoln Kirstein,* 387; Lincoln Kirstein to Sandy Campbell, Sept. 21, 1943, b. 11, fol.: Kirstein, Lincoln/Isherwood, Donald Windham and Sandy Campbell Papers, Beinecke.
5. Series 3, b. 2, Lincoln Kirstein Correspondence and Notes, MoMA Archives.
6. Lincoln Kirstein to Sandy Campbell, Apr. 4, 1943, b. 11, fol.: Kirstein, Lincoln/Isherwood, Donald Windham and Sandy Campbell Papers, Beinecke.
7. Letter dated Nov. 9 [1944?], series 3, b. 2, Lincoln Kirstein Correspondence and Notes, MoMA Archives: "I am a kind of Max Allentuck [vaudeville manager] for the local outfit, soothe embarrassments, iron out petty difficulties with the prefecture, see [clean?] (oilcloth only) muzzle for the colonel's gun, and generally storm pill-boxes and do valuable historical monumental and architectural work of all sorts."
8. Lincoln Kirstein to Margaret Marshall, Apr. 24, 1945, b. 8, f. 90, (S) *MGZMD 123, Lincoln Kirstein Papers, LPA.
9. Kirstein ("Goosie") to "Grooslie" (probably Fidelma Cadmus), May 13 and 22, 1945, and others, War Letters, (S) *MGZMD 123, Lincoln Kirstein Papers, LPA.

10. Duberman, *Worlds of Lincoln Kirstein*, 385–404; Nicholas, *Rape of Europa*, esp. 337, 346–48; Lincoln's own accounts include "War Uncovers a Ghost of Gothic Fresco," *Art News*, May 1–14, 1945; "Monuments of Old Germany," *The Nation*, Sept. 1, 1945; "A Visit to Der Stuermer," *The Nation*, June 30, 1945; and "The Quest of the Golden Lamb," *Town and Country*, Sept. 1945; War Letters, (S) *MGZMD 123, Lincoln Kirstein Papers, LPA. Kirstein immortalized some of the Hungen and other documents in poems called "Scraps" and "The Chosen," in Kirstein, *Rhymes of a PFC*, 175.
11. Lincoln Kirstein to Mina Kirstein Curtiss, b. 3, f. 10, MS Thr 1045 (10), Lincoln Kirstein Correspondence, Houghton.
12. "Groozlir" (Lincoln Kirstein) to "Grouslie" (Fidelma Cadmus), May 22, 1945, War Letters, (S) *MGZMD 123, Lincoln Kirstein Papers, LPA.
13. Lincoln Kirstein to Margaret Marshall, Apr. 24, 1945, b. 8, f. 90, (S) *MGZMD 123, Lincoln Kirstein Papers, LPA. Margaret Marshall was the literary editor of *The Nation*.
14. Kirstein, *Thirty Years*, 88–89; Sowell, *Christensen Brothers*, 229–32.
15. The SAB logo had been a modern Vitruvian man since the 1930s; Kirstein and Stuart, *Classic Ballet*, 184: "At the moment, when representational art has declined into subjective expressionism, and its chief former subject, the human body in space, has been atomized into rhetorical calligraphy, the academic dance is a fortress of its familiar if forgotten dignity. To it future painters and sculptors may one day return for instruction in its wide plastic use."
16. On wartime "company" life, see, for example, Lincoln Kirstein to Mina Curtiss ("Goosie"), Oct. 31, 1944, b. 3, MS Thr 104 (10), Lincoln Kirstein Correspondence, Houghton.
17. Ballet Society Year Book, 1946–47, and School of American Ballet catalogue, 1947, fol.: 1940s–1960s, School of American Ballet, New York [clippings], LPA.
18. McNeil Lowry, "Conversations with Kirstein—I," *New Yorker*, Dec. 15, 1986, 44–80.
19. Lincoln Kirstein to Virgil Thomson, Aug. 11, 1946, b. 29/57, f. 19, MSS 29, MSS 29A, Virgil Thomson Papers, YML; "native dances": Ballet Society announcement enclosed.
20. For correspondence and scenario for *The Children's Crusade*, see b. 4, f. 136, and b. 23, f. 362, Paul Hindemith Collection, YML. See also Dickson, *Children's Crusade*.
21. Paul Hindemith to Gertrud Hindemith, Apr. 27, 1940, b. 4, f. 137, Paul Hindemith Collection, YML. Hindemith broke with Massine in 1940. For Balanchine's 1937 correspondence with Hindemith, see Hindemith, Paul, 1937, b. 16, MS Thr 411 (812), George Balanchine Archive, Houghton; "his $250 'bucks' on the table": Paul Hindemith to Ernest Voigt, Oct. 1940, b. 4, f. 160, Paul Hindemith Collection, YML.
22. Milstein and Volkov, *From Russia to the West*; Vernon Duke to Bernard Taper, Oct. 19, 1961, Taper Papers; Tallchief, *Maria Tallchief*, 58–59.
23. Paul Hindemith to Willy Strecker, May 30, 1941, b. 4, f. 160, Paul Hindemith Collection, YML.
24. Todd Bolender coaching "Phlegmatic" variation from *The Four Temperaments*, Sept. 15, 1997, video recording, *MGZIA 4-7185, LPA; Friedman and Hauptman, *Lincoln Kirstein's Modern*. On *Cave of Sleep* and Tchelitchew, see Elizabeth Sawyer, "In the Teeth of the Evidence: Hindemith and Balanchine," *Dance Now*, Winter 2002–2003.
25. On Seligmann's elaborate costumes, Francisco Moncion, interview by Peter Conway, Apr. and May 1979, transcript, *MGZMT 5-959, LPA; "pumpkin hats": d'Amboise, interview by the author, June 26, 2018; Tchelitchew: Todd Bolender, tape, Balanchine Book: Notes on Tapes and Interviews, b. 45, Richard Buckle Papers, HRC. Critics complained of Seligmann's "elaborate museum pieces . . . which pretty thoroughly stifled" the dance: John Martin, "The Dance: Progress; Ballet Society Adventure Starts Off Well," *New York Times*, Feb. 16, 1947.

26. George Platt Lynes, photographs of "Phlegmatic" variation, *The Four Temperaments*, b. 9, f. 5, Todd Bolender Collection, Kansas City Ballet Archives.
27. Holmes, *Symptom and the Subject*.
28. Todd Bolender to Una Kai, Feb. 3, 2004, Una Kai Papers, Ailina Dance Archives.
29. Todd Bolender, interview by John Taras, sound recording, RG3/AV Materials, John Taras Collection, NYCB Archives.
30. Arlene Croce, writing in *The New Yorker*, on Dec. 8, 1975, captured the martial aspect in the ballet's finale: "After a silence in which nobody moves, the great finale begins its inexorable massed attack. All the parts the ballet is made of are now seen at once in a spectacle of grand-scale assimilation. Apotheosis. We see a succession of sky-sweeping lifts; we see a runway lined by a chorus of grands battements turned to the four points of the compass. The lifts travel down the runway and out as the curtain falls."
31. Lincoln Kirstein to Lucia Chase, Nov. 14, 1946, f. 3846-3847, (S) *MGZMD 49, American Ballet Theatre Records, LPA.
32. Lincoln Kirstein, interview by Bernard Taper, Apr. 6 [probably c. 1962], Taper Papers.
33. Maria Tallchief told one of her students that Balanchine was so modest that "I never saw him Naked!" Paul Mejia, interview by the author, July 26, 2015; Tallchief, *Maria Tallchief*, 115 (toilet), 87–90, 102–5.
34. "Dear Mashka!": George Balanchine to Maria Tallchief, courtesy of Elise Paschen; Jill Spalding, interview by the author, Aug. 10, 2017.
35. On Maria's preference for poker, see d'Amboise, *I Was a Dancer*, 269; Natasha Molostwoff, interview by John Taras, Oct. 12, 1984, sound recording, RG3/AV Materials, John Taras Collection, NYCB Archives.
36. B. 16, fol.: Davidova,Richard Buckle Papers, HRC; sewing: Natasha Molostwoff, interview by John Taras, Oct. 12, 1984, sound recording, RG3/AV Materials, John Taras Collection, NYCB Archives; mopping floors: Lucia Davidova, in Mason, *I Remember Balanchine*, 133.
37. B. 16, fol.: Davidova, Richard Buckle Papers, HRC; Davidova in Mason, *I Remember Balanchine*, 133.
38. Le Clercq, *Ballet Cook Book*.
39. Tallchief, *Maria Tallchief*, 116–20.
40. George Balanchine to Maria Tallchief, 1947 (from the Grand Hotel, Paris), courtesy of Elise Paschen.
41. B. 16, fol.: Tallchief, Richard Buckle Papers, HRC.
42. Dossier d'artiste: Balanchine, Bibliothèque-Musée de l'Opéra National de Paris: selected press from 1947, including *Franc-Tireur*, Oct. 2, 1947; *L'Intransigeant*, July 30, 1947.
43. Kirstein Diary, Apr. 9, 1935, b. 5, f. 25, (S) *MGZMD 123, Lincoln Kirstein Papers, LPA; Lincoln Kirstein to Virgil Thomson, Nov. 9, 1944, and Feb. 3, 1945, b. 29/57, f. 19, Virgil Thomson Papers, YML; Mark Franko, "Serge Lifar and the Question of Collaboration with the German Authorities under the Occupation of Paris (1940–1949)," *Dance Research* 35, no. 2 (2017), 109; Sandrine Grandgambe, "La Réunion des Théâtres Lyriques Nationaux," in Chimènes, *La Vie musicale*, 109–26.
44. Dossier d'artiste: Balanchine, fol. Opéra Press, 1947, Bibliothèque-Musée de l'Opéra National de Paris: see 1947 press release from Hirsch—a speech he gave at a press conference to thank George, Maria, and Tamara Toumanova for coming. The life of a dancer is already hard, and then came the occupation, which had demoralized the company; Balanchine and Toumanova and Tallchief created a new "atmosphere" and the dancers rose to the occasion—this is the moment, Hirsch said, when the Paris Opera has shown, once again, that it is first in the world.

45. "We gave *Apollo*" and following: George Balanchine to Lincoln Kirstein, Apr. 17, 1947, and May 8, 1947, f. 5351, RG 3: Dir. and Execs. Correspondence and Subject Files, Ballet Society Collection, NYCB Archives; John Taras to Lincoln Kirstein, June 29, 1947, b. 9, f. 143, (S) *MGZMD 123, Lincoln Kirstein Papers, LPA: "Balanchine is counting the days till New York and the food situation is appalling. London by comparison is a Paradise. Reception at the [Paris] Opera House has been bad for both Balanchine and Toumanova and they are all very unhappy."
46. Correspondence: 1946 Rainer, Michael (on *The Four Temperaments*), f. 5465, RG 3: Dir. and Execs. Correspondence and Subject Files, Ballet Society Collection, NYCB Archives. Rainer also tried to arrange for NYC schoolchildren to attend a dress rehearsal free of charge, with union approval.
47. George Kirstein to Lincoln Kirstein, Mar. 12, 1947, b. 8, f. 86, (S) *MGZMD 123, Lincoln Kirstein Papers, LPA, details Kirstein's financial situation as of 1946:

    $39,000 in his personal account, available to him "by picking up the telephone." George advises Lincoln not to spend it on Ballet Society. If he needs money, take a loan against father or mother's estate, George suggests.

    $53,000 in irrevocable trust—only interest available to him in his lifetime.

    15,400 SHARES of Federated generation an income of approx. $22,000 annually.

    See also Duberman, *Worlds of Lincoln Kirstein,* 417–25. In 1950 Kirstein writes to Betty Cage that he had given over $250,000 in the past fifteen years: Lincoln Kirstein to Betty Cage, Aug. 25, 1950, b. 2, f. 26, (S) *MGZMD 97, Lincoln Kirstein Papers, LPA.
48. Lincoln Kirstein to Virgil Thomson, Sept .12, 1947, b. 29/57, f. 19, Virgil Thomson Papers, YML.
49. Joseph, *Stravinsky's Ballets,* 156–66.
50. "colt-angel": Lincoln Kirstein to Mina Kirstein Curtiss, Apr. 30, 1948, b. 3, MS Thr 1045 (10), Lincoln Kirstein Correspondence, Houghton; "shrieked": Kirstein referred to the performance with *Orpheus,* on Apr. 28, 1948. The first performance of *Symphony in C* was Mar. 22, 1948.
51. Quoted in Joseph, *Stravinsky and Balanchine,* 193.
52. Joseph, *Stravinsky and Balanchine,* 205.
53. Interview with Robert Craft, outtakes in Palmer, *Stravinsky*; Stravinsky was meticulous about measuring time.
54. Joseph, *Stravinsky's Ballets,* 158.
55. Relations between Kirstein and Noguchi were tense over money, and Lincoln wrote a sharply worded letter in Apr. 1948, after the designs were done, saying that he had no desire to ever work with Noguchi again. Nonetheless, Noguchi's lyre, in fact and image, had a long life at the NYCB and became the company's totem image, printed on posters and letterhead. See *Lyre for Orpheus,* 1948, by unknown photographer, cabinet 1, drawer 3, file 00277, The Noguchi Museum; Lincoln Kirstein to Isamu Noguchi, May 29, 1948, cabinet 8, drawer 3, file 015, MS_COR_037_013, The Noguchi Museum; Ashton, *Noguchi East and West.*
56. Jean Rosenthal, "The Dance: Pattern of Light," *New York Times,* July 29, 1951; Winthrop Sargeant, "Please, Darling, Bring Three to Seven," *New Yorker,* Feb. 4, 1956, 33–59; Rosenthal and Wertenbaker, *Magic of Light.*
57. Interview with Stravinsky, *Los Angeles Times,* Sept. 21, 1947, quoted in Stravinsky, *Stravinsky,* vol. 1, 267.
58. Rilke, Cocteau, and Anouilh also added angels to their renditions of Orpheus; see Kosin-

ski, "Image of Orpheus," 198, 370. Kosinski quotes Noguchi, 373: "There is a joy in seeing sculpture come to life on the stage in its own world of timeless time. . . . Theater is a ceremonial, the performance is a rite. Sculpture in daily life should or could be like this. In the meantime, the theater gives me its poetic, exalted equivalent."

59. *Ovid: Metamorphoses*, lines 59–60.
60. Joseph, *Stravinsky and Balanchine*, 208.
61. Lincoln Kirstein to Mina Kirstein Curtis, Apr. 30, 1948, b. 3, MS Thr 1045 (10), Lincoln Kirstein Correspondence, Houghton.
62. Duberman, *Worlds of Lincoln Kirstein*, 437–41.
63. Lincoln Kirstein statement upon Baum's death, City Center of Music and Drama, 1948–77, b. 7, MS Thr 411 (367), George Balanchine Archive, Houghton.
64. Morton Baum, "History of the New York City Ballet," unpublished manuscript, undated, b. 19, f. 10, *LPA MSS 1992-001, Morton Baum Papers, LPA; City Center, 1952, b. 1, f. 9, Morton Baum Papers, LPA; Kirstein, *Thirty Years*, 105.
65. Betty Cage to George Balanchine, Mar. 10, 1952, and Balanchine's response, f. 180: Balanchine/Betty Cage Correspondence, RG1-10: Personal and Pro. Papers, Correspondence Balanchine-Mole, John Taras Collection, NYCB Archives.
66. An AGMA dancer's contract from 1953, for example, showed rehearsal weeks paid at $62.50 per week, and performance weeks in New York City paid at $125 to $135 per week; a rehearsal week in Italy came to $90, and nine performance weeks in Europe were paid at $90. The dancers always had "layoff" weeks when they were not paid at all, and they collected unemployment when they could. Courtesy of Vida Brown personal collection. Baum, "History of the New York City Ballet," loosely sketched the losses and gains for each season as follows:

    Oct. 1948: loss $47,000
    Jan. 1949: loss $7,500; 64 percent attendance
    Nov. 1949: loss $32,500 (three new works)
    Feb. 1950: loss $16,000
    London 1950: loss $50,000
    Chicago spring 1950: loss $20,000
    Fall 1950: loss $12,000
    Spring 1951: profit $10,000
    June 1951: loss $12,800
    Sept. 1951: profit $1,500
    Nov. 1951: loss $23,300
    Spring 1952: loss $48,000
    Europe tour 1952: loss $41,000
    Fall 1952: profit $40,000

67. Lincoln Kirstein to Mina Kirstein Curtiss ("Goosie"), b. 3, MS Thr 1045 (10), Lincoln Kirstein Correspondence, Houghton.
68. George Balanchine to Lincoln Kirstein, Aug. 4, 1942, b. 10, f. 171, *MGZMD 97, Lincoln Kirstein Papers, LPA.
69. Baum, "History of the New York City Ballet."
70. Kirstein was all the while being watched by the FBI, which noted, for example, in a summary report dated Mar. 16, 1955, that he had spoken on Oct. 26, 1947, at a conference of Cultural Freedom and Civil Liberties sponsored by the Arts, Sciences, and Professions Division of the Progressive Citizens of America. The California Committee on Un-American Activities, Reports, 1947 and 1948, the report said, has cited Progressive Citizens of America as a "new and broader Communist front for the entire United States"

formed in Sept. 1946, at the direction of "Communist steering committees" from the "Communist-dominated National Citizens Political Action Committee" and the "Independent Citizens committee of the Arts, Sciences and Professions [*redacted*]." The report also says that a "confidential informant of known reliability" had sent a letterhead of People's Songs, Inc., of New York City, showing Kirstein as a member of the board of sponsors, and that "The California Committee of Un-American Activities Reported in 1948 that People's Songs was a Communist front." See the Lincoln Kirstein files, Federal Bureau of Investigation, Rockefeller Archive Center (with thanks to Lynn Garafola and Eric Foner).

CHAPTER 15: COMPANY

1. "Headquarters": Betty Cage, Balanchine Book: Notes on Tapes and Interviews, b. 45, Richard Buckle Papers, HRC; "at once labor negotiator": Lincoln Kirstein quoted in Jennifer Dunning, "Betty Cage, 82, Quiet Force Behind City Ballet," *New York Times*, Dec. 26, 1999; on Cage's book about tai chi, see Virginia Lee Warren, "Mighty Clever, These Chinese Exercises That Don't Make You Sweat," *New York Times*, Nov. 4, 1971.
2. U.S. Federal Census Records from 1919, 1920, 1930, and 1940 for Herold Cage and Harriet Pettis, accessed via Ancestry.com; in the census of 1930, Herold Cage was listed as "White"; in 1940 he was listed as "Negro." In both censuses, his wife and children, including Betty, were listed as "Negro."
3. Barbara Horgan, interviews by the author, Apr. 28, 2012; Aug. 9, 2013; Nov. 12, 2012; and Oct. 2, 2016. She did leave briefly before the tour to the USSR, but when Balanchine called her soon after his return and asked her to be his personal assistant, she accepted immediately.
4. Hal Bigelow, interview by the author, Aug. 8, 2015; Eddie Bigelow personal papers, courtesy of Hal Bigelow, including diaries, photos, letters, and notes. In the 1960s Eddie disappeared for several months to sail the Atlantic with a couple of friends: "If this doesn't blow some of the mustiness out of my soul, nothing will." And as if to keep the high winds at his back upon his return, he eventually moved into a boat in the Seventy-ninth Street Boat Basin. See also Una Kai, interviews by the author, Feb. 27, Mar. 3, and Apr. 9, 2014; Una Kai unpublished memoir, courtesy of Una Kai; "eyes are like oysters": Robert Gottlieb, interview by the author, Nov. 29, 2012; "Big and low": Dominique Nabokov, interview by the author, Jan. 28, 2015.
5. When Balanchine read the first edition of Taper's biography, he said, Say more about the dancers. The list is long and includes in the upcoming years many dancers of Central and East European descent, perhaps because their parents were more familiar with ballet, which held a high place in Russia and Europe—for example, Joysanne Sidimus (Russian and Polish Jews), John Clifford (Lithuanian and Greek), Paul Mejia (Russian), Mimi Paul (Russian Jews from Odessa and Swiss French), Carol Sumner (Lithuanian), Victoria Simon (Russian and Austro-Hungarian Jews), Stephanie Saland (Polish, Lithuanian, and Russian Jews), Bettijane Sills (Polish Jews), Ricky Weiss (Russian and Polish Jews), Susan Freedman (Russian Jews), Judith Friedman (Russian and Polish Jews), Elissa Fuchs (Polish, French, German, and Viennese Jews), Kay Mazzo (Italian and Yugoslavian), John Prinz (Austro-Hungarian), Jean Rosenthal (Romanian Jews), Kevin Tyler (born Arkady Tkatchenko, Russian), John Taras (Ukrainian), Rouben Ter-Arutunian (Armenian), Marika Molnar (company physical therapist, Hungarian), and Anna Kisselgoff (chief dance critic of *The New York Times*, Russian Jews).
6. Barbara Walczak, interviews by the author, Mar. 13, 2013; Nov. 23, 2015; and Feb. 14, 2018; among others.

7. Barbara Milberg Fisher, interview by the author, Oct. 8, 2013; Milberg Fisher, *In Balanchine's Company*.
8. Patricia McBride Lousada, interview by the author, May 6, 2013; private correspondence with Tanaquil Le Clercq, courtesy of Patricia McBride Lousada.
9. Una Kai, interviews by the author; Una Kai unpublished memoir, courtesy of Una Kai.
10. Unpublished memoir, b. 1, Janet Reed Papers, 1916–2000, (S) *MGZMD 379, LPA. In 1949 Reed joined NYCB, where she danced until 1958 and then was its ballet mistress until 1961; Janet Reed, interview by John Taras, Oct. 31, 1983, sound recording, RG3/AV Materials, John Taras Collection, NYCB Archives.
11. Patricia Wilde, interview by the author, Dec. 6, 2013; Lobenthal, *Wilde Times*.
12. Pamara Hangarter, interview by the author, Aug. 8, 2015.
13. Melissa Hayden, interview by the author, May 21, 2005, as well as many conversations with Hayden, who was the author's teacher and a personal friend; Melissa Hayden Papers, MS Thr 499, Houghton; Allegra Kent, interview by the author, Nov. 5, 2018; Jacques d'Amboise, interviews by and conversations with the author; Stuart Coleman, interview by the author, July 15, 2015, and conversations.
14. On Adams's always cold and wet hands, Jonathan Watts, interview by the author, Sept. 12, 2014; Barbara Horgan, interview by the author, June 12, 2012; Barbara Walczak, interview by the author, Feb. 6, 2015; Diana Adams, interview by John Taras, 1984, sound recording, RG3/AV Materials, John Taras Collection, NYCB Archives; Dossier de compagnie: NYCB press materials, 1956, Bibliothèque-Musée de l'Opéra National de Paris; David Vaughan (husband of Adams's daughter Georgina), interview by the author, Apr. 11, 2016. U.S. census and other records accessed via Ancestry.com show Adams's father was an English teacher born in Georgia in 1901; her mother was also from Georgia, born in 1901. Adams was raised in Tennessee. See correspondence with Diana Adams, b. 1, f. 2, (S) *MGZMD 257, Hugh Laing and Antony Tudor Papers, LPA.
15. Tanaquil Le Clercq to Edith Le Clercq, undated (from Paris, 1947–48?), b. 4, f. 92, RGI Personal and Family Papers, Tanaquil Le Clercq Collection, NYCB Archives; Joel Lobenthal, "Tanaquil Le Clercq," *Ballet Review* 12, no. 3 (1984): 74–86; Protopopescu, *Dancing Past the Light*.
16. Allegra Kent, interviews by the author, Nov. 22, 2012, and Feb. 6, 2015; Kent, *Once a Dancer*; Barbara Horgan, interview by the author, and quoted in Mason, *I Remember Balanchine*, 381. Kent entered the company as an apprentice.
17. Robert Barnett, interviews by the author, Mar. 7, 2013; Sept. 6, 2015; and Sept. 7, 2015.
18. Interview with Billy Weslow, archives for the film *In Balanchine's Classroom*, shared with the author by Connie Hochman.
19. Francisco Moncion, interviews by Peter Conway, 1979, and Lee Edward Stern, 1980, *MGZT 5-959 and *MGZTC 3-1299, LPA; Francisco Moncion, interview by John Taras, sound recording, RG3/AV Materials, John Taras Collection, NYCB Archives; Francisco Moncion personal papers, courtesy of Gregory Cary; "royal family": Jonathan Watts (Leech), interview by the author, Sept. 12, 2014.
20. Todd Bolender, interview by John Taras, sound recording, RG3/AV Materials, John Taras Collection, NYCB Archives; miscellaneous papers, Todd Bolender Collection, Kansas City Ballet Archives—esp. the unfinished manuscript for a memoir, "Backstage at the Ballet," b. 15, f. 15/1.
21. Jonathan Watts, interview by the author, Sept. 12, 2014.
22. D'Amboise, *I Was a Dancer*, 272.
23. James L. Hicks, "Police Say Janitor Has Confessed," *Afro-American*, Mar. 21, 1953; "Janitor Hacks Numbers Racketeer to Pieces," *Jet*, Mar. 26, 1953; "Police Hold Janitor in Torso

Case: Harlem Man Accused in Gruesome Rackets Murder, Butchery," *Hartford Courant*, Mar. 11, 1953; U.S. Federal Census Records, 1900–1940, accessed via Ancestry.com.

24. The show had a book and lyrics by Truman Capote, with music (and lyrics) by Harold Arlen, and Balanchine was responsible for the choreography—until he resigned because of an angry artistic dispute with the director, Peter Brook. See Le Clercq, Tanaquil, 1951–98 and undated, b. 101–103, (S) *MGZMD 182, Jerome Robbins Personal Papers, LPA; letter in Edith Le Clercq's handwriting, undated (1956), b. 101, f. 10, (S) *MGZMD 182; Jerome Robbins (Personal Papers, LPA) mentions Tanny remembering being in Philly while George was doing *House of Flowers* and that no one in the hotel was talking to each other, and George "kept telling me that Peter Brook had ruined the show. I am sure that Peter was telling his wife ditto."
25. Arthur Mitchell, interview by the author, July 3, 2013.
26. Arthur Mitchell, interview by the author, July 3, 2013. The outburst was confirmed in Lynn Garafola's exhibition, although I could find no press confirmation of it.
27. Arthur Mitchell, interview by the author, July 3, 2013; Allen Hughes, "Without Regard for Color," *New York Times*, Feb. 21, 1965. Soon after Mitchell joined the company, Balanchine stopped company class and asked his new dancer to point his toe, harder, harder, harder. As Arthur tried, Balanchine broke the tension by saying, "Or else I will send you back to Little Rock!": Milberg Fisher, *In Balanchine's Company*, 149–53.
28. Arthur Mitchell, interview by the author, July 3, 2013; Catharine Hughes, "Poet in Motion," *Ebony*, Oct. 1968; Lynn Garafola, "Timeline: Arthur Mitchell's Performing Career," *Arthur Mitchell: Harlem's Ballet Trailblazer*, Columbia University, 2018, exhibitions.library.columbia.edu/exhibits/show/mitchell/arthur-mitchell-artist/timeline.
29. Betty Cage to Lincoln Kirstein, June 2, 1952, b. 10, f. 168, (S) *MGZMD 97, Lincoln Kirstein Papers, LPA.
30. Rosenthal and Wertenbaker, *Magic of Light*; Winthrop Sargeant, "Please, Darling, Bring Three to Seven," *New Yorker*, Feb. 4, 1956, 33–59. Jean Rosenthal to George Balanchine, Oct. 15, 1957, b. 33, MS Thr 411 (1603), George Balanchine Archive, Houghton. Perry Silvey, interview by the author, Feb. 2, 2021.
31. D'Amboise later said (*I Was a Dancer*, 209) that he knew very well that Balanchine could be petty, jealous, and vengeful, but faced with the evidence, "I would want to deny it, walk away, tuck any criticism of him in the bottom of the drawer and forget it."

CHAPTER 16: DISCIPLINING THE BODY

1. Sobatka, quoted in Una Kai, unpublished memoir.
2. Patricia Wilde, interview by the author, Nov. 6, 2013.
3. Barbara Walczak, interview by the author, Mar. 11, 2021.
4. Patricia McBride, interview by the author, Nov. 6, 2013.
5. Judith Friedman in *Remembering Mr. B*, 38.
6. On Balanchine's classes, see miscellaneous papers, Todd Bolender Collection, Kansas City Ballet Archives—esp. the unfinished manuscript for a memoir, "Backstage at the Ballet," b. 15, f. 15/1; Barbara Walczak, interviews by the author, Mar. 13, Apr. 30, and May 15, 2013; Walczak and Kai, *Balanchine the Teacher*; Roy Tobias Tapes, courtesy of Patricia McBride Lousada. These very moving tapes were made when Tobias was dying from a neurodegenerative disorder, and he made them to document his time at the NYCB in the 1950s, with special attention to classes. See also the accounts by Allegra Kent, Jacques d'Amboise, Francisco Moncion, Karin von Aroldingen, Judith Friedman, and Jean-Pierre Bonnefoux in *Remembering Mr. B*, 26, 38, 48 ("rattlesnake's head" and others).

7. Francia Russell, interview by the author, Aug. 6, 2013; Jonathan Watts, interview by the author, Jan. 31, 2020; Joysanne Sidimus in *Remembering Mr. B*, 79; "You know what it's like?": Linda H. Hamilton and George Stricker, "Balanchine's Children," *Medical Problems of Performing Artists* 4, no. 4 (1989): 143–47.
8. Sketch can be found in RGI 3 AV Materials, Tanaquil Le Clercq Collection, NYCB Archives: Sketch of foot positioning for fifth position drawn by George Balanchine, © The George Balanchine Trust, courtesy of the NYCB Archives.
9. Walczak and Kai, *Balanchine the Teacher*, 232.
10. Courtesy of Barbara Horgan, who saved this relic from, she says, the 1950s.
11. Bettijane Sills, interview by the author, Mar. 6, 2016.
12. Milberg Fisher, *In Balanchine's Company*, 89.
13. It was Lincoln's T. S. Eliot: "Poetry is not a turning loose of emotion, but an escape from emotion; it is not the expression of personality, but an escape from personality."
14. Walczak and Kai, *Balanchine the Teacher*, 30.
15. Plato, *Phaedrus*, 252 D7; "working on your statue" and "wholly yourself," are from Plotinus (referring to Plato), "On Beauty," in *Enneads*, 1.6.9, 91–103.
16. Barkan, *Gods Made Flesh*, 5. Barkan describes a kind of Ovidian metamorphosis

    > in which morality wars with beauty and is often submerged by it . . . the amours of the gods are destructive but beautiful; the talents of the girl are sacrilegious but magnificent; the fate of the girl is degradation but also eternal life as an artist. Metamorphosis is both punishment and reward, morality and beauty. It is a fact of nature, but at the same time it describes a complicated aesthetics, a seamless web of changing narrative and a structure that takes us from crime (mortal presumption) to punishment (animal transformation) via a route that undoes the power of that punishment.

17. D'Amboise, *I Was a Dancer*, 271.
18. George's "Limericks about Dancers," a small notebook held in an anonymous private collection shared with the author, among them: "Here comes young girl from Toronto / She could not say she didn't want to / to man with good figure / for whom she was Igor / But lost him to Cuban bell cunto" ("Melissa Hayden, Youskevitch, Alonso"); drawing in the author's collection.
19. Lynne Stetson, interview by the author, May 11, 2016.
20. Collection of the author.
21. Barbara Walczak, interview by the author, June 27, 2019.
22. Janet Reed, interview by John Taras, sound recording, RG3/AV Materials, John Taras Collection, NYCB Archives.
23. Robert Barnett, interview by the author, Mar. 7, 2013, remembers Balanchine lashing out at Allegra; Kent, *Once a Dancer*, 81, remembers his stony silence.
24. Diana Adams, interview by John Taras, sound recording, RG3/AV Materials, John Taras Collection, NYCB Archives.
25. Barbara Walczak, interview by the author, Mar. 13, 2013, and subsequent conversations over nine years.
26. Bettijane Sills in *Remembering Mr. B*, 50; d'Amboise, *I Was a Dancer*, 267–69.
27. On oil lamps and heaven: Wilhelmina Frankfurter, interview by the author, June 17, 2013; "Ballet is artifice": Lynne Stetson, interview by the author, May 11, 2016.
28. Patricia Wilde, interview by the author, Dec. 6, 2013; d'Amboise, *I Was a Dancer*, 267–69, and personal communication.

29. Suki Schorer in *Remembering Mr. B*, 25.
30. When Francia Russell married the dancer Kent Stowell and had a child in the 1960s, she had already stopped dancing and was teaching and transitioning to ballet mistress; she knew very well that there was no place for her son in the theater and kept that part of her life at home. Francia Russell and Kent Stowell, interview by the author, Aug. 6, 2013.
31. Carolyn George (later Carolyn George d'Amboise) quoted in d'Amboise, *I Was a Dancer*, 208-9.
32. D'Amboise, *I Was a Dancer*, 291.
33. Judith Friedman, interview by the author, Jan. 29, 2015. Friedman was at the school from 1949 and joined the company in 1957.
34. Homans, *Apollo's Angels*, 470.
35. Edward Mendelson, interview by the author, Oct. 21, 2015.
36. Patricia Neary in *Remembering Mr. B*, 75.
37. Jonathan Cott, "Two Talks with George Balanchine," in Kirstein, Cott, and Denby, *Portrait of Mr. B*, 145.
38. Milberg Fisher, *In Balanchine's Company*, 38.
39. Diana Adams, interview by John Taras, 1984, sound recording, RG3/AV Materials, John Taras Collection, NYCB Archives.
40. Janet Reed, interview by John Taras, sound recording, RG3/AV Materials, John Taras Collection, NYCB Archives. Balanchine similarly scoffed at pretentious "idiot" critics clinging to traditions they did not understand. At a conference in London in the 1950s, he listened while a group of notables objected that he had betrayed the "traditional" Russian *Swan Lake* by rechoreographing it. Well, he dryly explained, when the ballet was first performed in Europe, Diaghilev asked *me* to change it, so what *you* think was the original was really *mine*, and what you are seeing now in my choreography is the original! When good reviews came in, he just shrugged and said he must be doing something wrong to have approval from such people.
41. Milberg Fisher, *In Balanchine's Company*, 65-67, 85-87; RGI 7: personal and family papers translations through writings, f. 192, Tanaquil Le Clercq Collection, NYCB Archives.
42. Betty Cage to Lincoln Kirstein, May 13 and 20, 1952 , b. 10, f. 168, Lincoln Kirstein Papers, *MGZMD 97, LPA.
43. Interview with George Balanchine in *L'Express*, Apr. 2, 1973:

    Comment composez-vous un ballet? Vous écoutez et réécoutez la musique?

    Non, je ne l'écoute pas, je la regard. Je lis la partition—c'est ainsi qu'on comprend la musique.

    (How do you compose a ballet? [Do] you listen and relisten to the music?

    I don't listen, I look, I read the score—that is the way I understand the music.)
44. Mason, *I Remember Balanchine*, 308.
45. Leaman, "Analyzing Music and Dance," 115, 201-3. Building on the seminal work of Stephanie Jordan and Charles M. Joseph, Kara Yoo Leaman invented a "choreomusical score," which she uses, with the help of video of dances, to show Balanchine's work as a "visual musician."
46. Leaman, "Analyzing Music and Dance," 46, provides a good summary of this research.
47. D'Amboise, *I Was a Dancer*, 276.
48. Milberg Fisher, *In Balanchine's Company*, 16.
49. An Italian mystic quoted in William James, "The Varieties of Religious Experience," in James, *Writings, 1902-1910*, 245.
50. Berdyaev, *Russian Idea*, 230, 245.

51. George Balanchine speaks at a National Press Club program held in his honor, hosted by Gigi Yellen and broadcast by National Public Radio, Feb. 1. 1977, sound recording, *MGZTL 4-3313, LPA.

CHAPTER 17: TANNY AND JERRY

1. "Music: New Wings for Firebird," *Time*, Dec. 12, 1949.
2. Robinson, *Last Impresario*.
3. Tallchief, *Maria Tallchief*, 124.
4. Lincoln Kirstein to Richard Buckle, Dec. 2, 1949, fol.: Kirstein to Buckle: 1949–59, Richard Buckle Papers, HRC.
5. Joysanne Sidimus, interview by the author, Feb. 20, 2020.
6. "Music: New Wings for Firebird," *Time*, Dec. 12, 1949.
7. B. 20, Envelope: 1951–52, Richard Buckle Papers, HRC, includes an undated note from Chagall saying ironically that he has heard about Balanchine's *Firebird* and regrets not working with him on it. An irritated follow-up notes his admiration for Balanchine and ends by suggesting sarcastically that the choreographer might dignify him with a response; correspondence with Marc Chagall, 1951–70, b. 6, MS Thr 411 (344), George Balanchine Archive, Houghton (in Russian); Reynolds, *Repertory in Review*, 96; d'Amboise, *I Was a Dancer*, 92; Milberg Fisher, *In Balanchine's Company*, 46; Una Kai, unpublished memoir.
8. Lincoln Kirstein to Mina Kirstein Curtiss, July 2 and 18 and Aug. 9, 1950, b. 3, MS Thr 1045 (10), Lincoln Kirstein Correspondence, Houghton; press from 1950 tour, b. 31, Richard Buckle Papers, HRC; Tanaquil Le Clercq Scrapbooks, 1950–65, *ZBD-361, microfilm, LPA.
9. The annulment papers (courtesy of Elise Paschen, dated Aug. 22, 1951; filed Aug. 23, 1951) name Elizabeth M. Balanchine as the plaintiff and George Balanchine as the defendant (attorney L. Arnold Weissberger is for the plaintiff; the second attorney is blank) but don't name the complaint; however, they say that Balanchine was given time to respond and failed to do so; Vida Brown, interview by the author, Apr. 3, 2013.
10. Tanaquil Le Clercq, interview by Charles Engell France, 1974, streaming audio file, LPA.
11. Later, in the early 1950s, George and Tanny staged a shopping trip to the Dior Boutique in Paris for State Department purposes: "Balanchine's at Dior," *Photographs of Marshall Plan Programs, Exhibits, and Personnel*, identifier: 20010982, record group 286, National Archives; these photographs and other modeling events can be found in f. 371, RG3/AV Materials, Tanaquil Le Clercq Collection, NYCB Archives.
12. Tanaquil Le Clercq by Cecil Beaton, Condé Nast, f. 397, RGI 7: personal and family papers, Tanaquil Le Clercq Collection, NYCB Archives.
13. Irving Penn to Tanaquil Le Clercq, 1948–49, b. 4, f. 149, RGI: personal and family papers, Biographical Files, Tanaquil Le Clercq Collection, NYCB Archives; Hambourg and Rosenheim, *Irving Penn*. Penn liked to place his subjects in a tightly angled corner he had designed, a claustrophobic "roomette"or stage with bare, dark walls that enclosed his subjects in an intimate but confining space. Penn captured a generation of postwar artists in his sharply confined spaces, including Georgia O'Keeffe, Charles James, Elsa Schiaparelli, George Grosz, Jerome Robbins, Igor Stravinsky, Truman Capote, Marcel Duchamp, Le Corbusier, Alfred Hitchcock, Peter Ustinov, and W. H. Auden.
14. Letters to Tanaquil Le Clercq, 1957-65, MS Thr 411, George Balanchine Archive, Houghton.
15. Fire Island. 1950s, George Balanchine at Natasha Molostwoff's "shack" and other photographs: RG3/AV Materials, Tanaquil Le Clercq Collection, NYCB Archives.

16. Patricia McBride Lousada, interview by the author, May 6, 2013.
17. George Balanchine to Tanaquil Le Clercq, f. 182, RGI 7: personal and family papers, Tanaquil Le Clercq Collection, NYCB Archives.
18. Vaill, *Somewhere,* 154; Jowitt, *Jerome Robbins,* 144; "Working with Balanchine: A Conversation with Jerome Robbins," interview by Ellen Sorrin, Mar. 3, 1993, sound recording, *MGZTL 4-3090, LPA. It is not clear if Balanchine called Robbins or if someone from the company relayed the message.
19. Lincoln Kirstein to Richard Buckle, Oct. 29, 1949, fol.: Kirstein to Buckle: 1949–59, Richard Buckle Papers, HRC; "ballet in dungarees": Jowitt, *Jerome Robbins,* 100.
20. Lawrence, *Dance with Demons,* 4.
21. Jowitt, *Jerome Robbins,* 16.
22. Jowitt, *Jerome Robbins,* 167.
23. Jowitt, *Jerome Robbins,* 118.
24. Vaill, *Somewhere,* 167.
25. Quoted in Lawrence, *Dance with Demons,* 254.
26. Robbins, *Jerome Robbins,* 1–14, from "The Jew Piece," Jan. 1975.
27. Quoted in Jowitt, *Jerome Robbins,* 49.
28. Jowitt, *Jerome Robbins,* 97–98. Robbins had adapted "Robyns" and other variants as a stage name over the years, but this was a legal change of name. In a sign of their own ambivalence and ambition for their son, his parents went along, becoming Harry and Lena Robbins.
29. Jowitt, *Jerome Robbins,* 424, from a 1975 journal entry.
30. George Balanchine to Tanaquil Le Clercq, undated (1952), f. 1, MS Thr 411, George Balanchine Archive, Houghton.
31. On Nora Kaye, see Richard Buckle Papers, HRC; Duberman, *Worlds of Lincoln Kirstein,* 475.
32. Cunningham's *The Seasons* was in rep briefly until early 1949 (in 1966 he returned to stage *Summerspace* from 1958, but Balanchine thought the music was uninteresting); David Vaughan interview with the author, Mar. 16, 2017. Lincoln approached de Mille (on behalf of himself and Balanchine, he said) in June 1951, and then backed out in Sept. 1952 for financial reasons, he told her: Lincoln Kirstein to Agnes de Mille, *MGZMD 37-650, Agnes de Mille Papers, LPA.
33. Lincoln Kirstein to Mina Kirstein Curtiss, Feb. 13, 1950, b. 3, bMs Thr 1045, Lincoln Kirstein Correspondence, Houghton.
34. George Balanchine to Betty Cage, 1957 (from Copenhagen), RGI 1-10: Personal and Pro. Papers, Correspondence Balanchine-Mole, f. 167, John Taras Collection, NYCB Archives.
35. Duberman, *Worlds of Lincoln Kirstein,* 488–89.
36. When Jerry made a ballet in which the woman fell to her knees before a man, Balanchine said quietly in the wings, "Should be opposite." Mikhail Baryshnikov, interview by the author, Oct. 5, 2021.
37. B. 3, f. 10–25, MS Thr 1045, Lincoln Kirstein Correspondence, Houghton.
38. Collection of cards that come with flower deliveries, Tanaquil Le Clercq Collection, NYCB Archives.
39. In the merry-go-round of Jerry's love life, he was in love with her too, and they were even for a moment engaged to be married (it fell through).
40. Lincoln Kirstein to Jerome Robbins, July 16, 1951, b. 99, (S) *MGZMD 182, Jerome Robbins Personal Papers, LPA.
41. Jacques d'Amboise, interview by the author, May 21, 2012; d'Amboise, *I Was a Dancer,* 209.

42. "a fatefully inescapable whirlpool": quoted in Baer, *Bronislava Nijinska*, 60; "We are dancing": quoted in Reynolds, *Repertory in Review*, 117–19. Bronislava Nijinska had done her own choreography to this music in the 1930s.
43. Francisco Moncion, interview by John Taras, sound recording, RG3/AV Materials, John Taras Collection, NYCB Archives.
44. *La Valse* was forever associated with Tanaquil Le Clercq. When she was stricken with polio in 1956, it dropped from the repertory. When it was later revived for Patricia McBride and others, it was doubly haunting: suffused with new dramatic interpretation *and* the memory of Le Clercq.
45. Jerome Robbins to Tanaquil Le Clercq, Sept. 25 (from Florence, 1951?), b. 4, f. 153, RGI: personal and family papers, Biographical Files, Tanaquil Le Clercq Collection, NYCB Archives.
46. Lincoln Kirstein to Jerome Robbins, Sept. 6, 1951, b. 99, *MGZMD 182, Jerome Robbins Personal Papers, LPA.
47. Fol. 153, b. 4, RGI: personal and family papers, Biographical Files, Tanaquil Le Clercq Collection, NYCB Archives.
48. "Working with Balanchine: A Conversation with Jerome Robbins," interview by Ellen Sorrin, Mar. 3, 1993, sound recording, *MGZTL 4-3090, LPA. Tanaquil Le Clercq wrote to Robbins about Balanchine's comic ballet *À la Françaix* that it was "dreadful—not very funny, vulgar, slapstick—embarrassing" and that "the idea of Maria stripping off a Sylphide tutu and revealing a sexy body clad in coral swimsuit, is a little much for me." Tanaquil Le Clercq to Jerome Robbins, Sept. 1, 1951, b. 101, f. 8, (S) *MGZMD 182, Jerome Robbins Personal Papers, LPA.
49. Jerome Robbins to Robert Fizdale, undated (probably 1952), b. 87, f. 16, (S) *MGZMD 182, Jerome Robbins Personal Papers, LPA.
50. She would be part of his comic ballet *The Concert* in 1956, and by that time George was in control enough to enjoy it—he even stepped in one night, adding his own comic performance.
51. Una Kai, unpublished memoir. Kai was married to Eddie Bigelow and was there and confirms that she was the only one of Tanny's friends, and they retreated to the bedroom for a while to take a break from the Russians.
52. Lincoln Kirstein to Richard Buckle, Jan. 2, 1952 (but he means 1953), fol.: Kirstein to Buckle: 1949–59, Richard Buckle Papers, HRC.
53. George to Andrei, undated (early 1950s), f. 326, s. 91, Department of Literature and Art, Central Historical Archives of Georgia. This note is in George's hand, in Russian.
54. George Balanchine to Tanaquil Le Clercq, with drawings, undated, f. 6, MS Thr 411, George Balanchine Archive, Houghton; RG3/AV Materials: Photographs, Tanaquil Le Clercq Collection, NYCB Archives.
55. Robert Barnett in *Remembering Mr. B*, 8; Jonathan Watts, interview by the author, Sept. 12, 2014.
56. Lincoln Kirstein letter, Jan. 26, 1953, f. 20, MS Thr 1045, Lincoln Kirstein Correspondence, Houghton.
57. Barbara Horgan, interview by the author, June 23, 2015. Horgan says that at "headquarters" they didn't worry about CIA funding: "We saw it as part of the Marshall Plan." Giroud, *Nicolas Nabokov*, 250–69. George was slated to do a new *Sacre du Printemps* with Picasso, but it fell through.
58. Barbara Horgan, unpublished letters to her mother and father, 1953, courtesy of Barbara Horgan.
59. 1954 Report, b. 1, f. 11, *LPA MSS 1992-001, Morton Baum Papers, LPA.

60. Betty Cage to Lincoln Kirstein, Sept. 1, 1952, b. 10, f. 171, Lincoln Kirstein Papers, (S) *MGZMD 97, LPA.
61. 1954 Report, b. 1, f. 11, *LPA MSS 1992-001, Morton Baum Papers, LPA.
62. Lincoln Kirstein to Betty Cage, Aug. 18, 1952, b. 10, f. 171, Lincoln Kirstein Papers, (S) *MGZMD 97, LPA.
63. George Balanchine to Dwight D. Eisenhower, Oct. 1, 1952, b. 40, MS Thr 411 (2051), George Balanchine Archive, Houghton. Villella, *Prodigal Son,* 42: Balanchine told Villella, "In politics, it's Eisenhower, in sports it's Mickey Mantle, in ballet it's Woman."
64. Betty Cage to Lincoln Kirstein, undated (probably 1952), b. 10, f. 169, Lincoln Kirstein Papers, (S) *MGZMD 97, LPA: "George says that television comics, etc. do not supply a good fairy tale of any scope at all for a child's fantasy or imagination. They must be brought to the ballet."
65. George Balanchine to Lincoln Kirstein, Aug. 4, 1952, from London, typed by Betty Cage, who noted that she typed it verbatim—George wanted it in his words, "at least for you, who know him well," b. 10, f. 181, Lincoln Kirstein Papers, (S) *MGZMD 97, LPA. In another letter George wrote to Betty Cage, "As I am always saying 'don't rush' or only rush when you are catching 'the flees.'" Betty Cage, Balanchine Book: Notes on Tapes and Interviews, b. 45, Richard Buckle Papers, HRC.
66. Charles Boultenhouse, "New York, 1952: Metamorphoses," *Ballet Review* 23, no. 1 (1995): 29–31; shed costumes: Una Kai, interview by the author, Apr. 9, 2014.
67. Lincoln Kirstein to Richard Buckle, Sept. 22, Oct. 22, and Nov. 22, 1952, fol.: Kirstein to Buckle: 1949–59, Richard Buckle Papers, HRC; Todd Bolender, Balanchine Book: Notes on Tapes and Interviews, b. 45, Richard Buckle Papers, HRC; Paul Hindemith to Willy Strecker, Nov. 28, 1952, b. 5, f. 177, Paul Hindemith Collection, YML; Reynolds, *Repertory in Review,* 142–43.
68. Walsh, *Stravinsky: The Second Exile,* 239, 282–84.
69. "Reflections on 'The Rake,'" *Opera News,* Feb. 1953.
70. Walsh, *Stravinsky: The Second Exile,* 266–79; Olin Downes, "Rake's Progress Has US Premiere," *New York Times,* Feb. 15, 1953.
71. Rosenthal and Wertenbaker, *Magic of Light.*
72. Milberg Fisher, *In Balanchine's Company,* 99; Reynolds, *Repertory in Review,* 152; Edwin Denby, "Opus 34," in Gottlieb, *Reading Dance,* 202–6; Rosenthal and Wertenbaker, *Magic of Light;* "pail of cold filth": Una Kai, interview by the author, Apr. 9, 2014; Anne Crowell Inglis, interview by the author, Apr. 9, 2014; Aidan Mooney and Bill Earle, interview by the author, June 24, 2015; Allegra Kent, interview by the author, Feb. 6, 2015; Francisco Moncion, Apr. and May 1979, transcript, *MGZMT 5-959, LPA; Kirstein said of the music, "Balanchine has done a hideous new Schoenberg twelve tone no. which is like the noise of a parrots beak on a blackboard in the middle of a night of massacre." Lincoln Kirstein to Richard Buckle, Jan. 19, 1954, fol.: Kirstein to Buckle, 1949–59, Richard Buckle Papers, HRC; d'Amboise, *I Was a Dancer,* 207.
73. Allegra Kent, interview by the author, Feb. 6, 2015; Kent, *Once a Dancer,* 71–78.
74. On *Don Juan* (never performed, unfinished): "Don Juan: The Making of a Ballet," b. 22, f. 228, (S) *MGZMD 123, Lincoln Kirstein Papers, LPA; d'Amboise Diary, Apr. 29, 1969: "Met Breath at Plaza on way home. He went on about Morton Baum and doing Don Juan for Hugh that he gave it up but I should do it and so on."
75. Balanchine's *Nutcracker* was not the first American *Nutcracker.* In 1944 William Christensen staged the ballet for the San Francisco Ballet, inspired in part by memories of Russian émigrés settled in the area.

76. Volkov, *Balanchine's Tchaikovsky,* 183, 179; photo of an early production of the ballet showing the angels can be found in the Melissa Hayden Papers, Houghton.
77. Hoffmann, *Nutcracker and the Mouse King,* 8.
78. The tree, at least in its State Theater days, weighed 2,500 pounds and went up from a hole in the floor on a cabled pinrail with an arbor balance. Frank Lavoia, interview by the author, Sept. 30, 2016.
79. Reynolds, *Repertory in Review,* 153–58; Edwin Denby quoted in Anderson, *Nutcracker Ballet,* 128; Taper, *Balanchine,* 22–23; Milberg Fisher, *In Balanchine's Company,* 114–16; interview with Betty Cage, undated, Taper Papers (40K and 90K); "a smasharoo": Lincoln Kirstein to Mina Kirstein Curtiss, Oct. 10, 1954, b. 3, f. 20, MS Thr 1045 (10), Lincoln Kirstein Correspondence, Houghton; Tanaquil Le Clercq, interview by Marian Horosko for WNCN, Fall 1963, sound recording, *MGZTI 4-60, LPA.
80. Duberman, *Worlds of Lincoln Kirstein,* 511–12; Bednar, "Faith as Imagination."
81. Volkov, *Balanchine's Tchaikovsky,* 160.
82. Tallchief, *Maria Tallchief,* 158.
83. John Martin, "A Dancer Yesterday, a Ballerina Today," *New York Times,* Feb. 28, 1952; with thanks to Barbara Walczak for sharing her unpublished writings on Tanny's performance in *Swan Lake.*
84. Martin, "A Dancer Yesterday."

CHAPTER 18: AGON

1. Jacques d'Amboise in *Afternoon of a Faun: Tanaquil Le Clercq,* directed by Nancy Buirski (New York: Kino Lorber, 2014); Allegra Kent, interview by the author, Feb. 6, 2015; Oshinsky, *Polio,* 255; Smith, *Patenting the Sun.*
2. Walsh, *Stravinsky: The Second Exile,* 348, 354; Stravinsky remained in the hospital for five weeks, until November 17.
3. Arlene Croce, "The Spelling of Agon," *New Yorker,* July 12, 1993; Milberg Fisher, *In Balanchine's Company,* 138–44 (tarot cards).
4. Medical record of Tanaquil Balanchine, Department of Medicine, 1956, with thanks to Dr. Christian Graugaard for his translation, Diakonissestiftelsen Archives (the Diakonissestiftelsen still exists today); Medical Record of Tanaquil Balanchine, Blegdamshospitalet, Epidemihospitalet, Copenhagen City Archives; Liselotte Malmgart, "The Historical Development of Diaconal Consecration Rites in Denmark," in Iversen, *Rites of Ordination,* 205; "Deaconess," in Bodensieck, *Encyclopedia of the Lutheran Church,* 659–64; on polio and its treatment, Fong, *Extreme Medicine.*
5. Jerome Robbins to Tanaquil Le Clercq, Nov. 13, 1956; Jerome Robbins to George Balanchine, Nov. 13, 1956; Edith Le Clercq to Jerome Robbins (thanking him for the orchids, another gift), undated, b. 101, f. 9, (S) *MGZMD 182, Jerome Robbins Personal Papers, LPA; Vida Brown, interview by the author, Apr. 3, 2013; Una Kai, Ann Crowell Ingles, Patricia Wilde, Barbara Milberg Fisher, Robert Barnett, and Virginia Rich, group interview by the author, Sept. 6, 2015; Barbara Horgan, interview by the author, Mar. 16, 2016. There is understandable memory confusion over the precise sequence and timing of events surrounding Le Clercq's illness.
6. Diana Adams letters, Richard Buckle to John Taras, July 30, 1984, f. 197, John Taras Collection, NYCB Archives; Diana Adams, interview by John Taras, sound recording, RG3/AV Materials, John Taras Collection, NYCB Archives.
7. Notes on interview with Lucia Davidova, Mar. 6, 1961/62, Taper Papers.
8. Tanaquil Le Clercq to "dear dear Robert Escoffier" (in her very weak and childish hand),

undated (1957), f. 4, (S) *MGZMD 108, Letters to Robert Fizdale and Arthur Gold, LPA.

9. "large gooey": Tanaquil Le Clercq (in Edith's hand) to Jerome Robbins, Nov. 25, 1956, b. 101, f. 9, (S) *MGZMD 182, Jerome Robbins Personal Papers, LPA; Edith Le Clercq to Betty Cage, Dec. 22, 1956, RG1-10: Personal and Pro. Papers, Correspondence Balanchine-Mole, f. 177, John Taras Collection, NYCB Archives (exercise, health); Medical Record of Tanaquil Balanchine, Blegdamshospitalet, Epidemihospitalet, Copenhagen City Archives; Miss Bang et al., Tanaquil Le Clercq (in Edith's hand) to Jerome Robbins, Nov. 27, 1956, b. 101, f. 9, Jerome Robbins Personal Papers, LPA.
10. On exercises, the American embassy, and "plumpy," see Edith Le Clercq to Betty Cage, Feb. 1, 6, and undated. 1957, f. 177, John Taras Collection, NYCB Archives; on Velveeta, see Tanaquil Le Clercq to Robert Escoffier, undated (1957), f. 4, (S) *MGZMD 108, Letters to Robert Fizdale and Arthur Gold, LPA; "chained": Tanaquil Le Clercq to Jerome Robbins, Jan. 27, 1957, b. 10, f. 13, (S) *MGZMD 182, Jerome Robbins Personal Papers, LPA; Tanaquil Le Clercq to Jerome Robbins, Jan. 7, 1957, b. 101, f. 11, Jerome Robbins Personal Papers, LPA; "I would *almost* say": Tanaquil Le Clercq to Jerome Robbins, Jan. 27, 1957, b. 101, f. 13, Jerome Robbins Personal Papers, LPA.
11. "We are always on the beach": Tanaquil Le Clercq (in her very shaky left hand in large letters) to Jerome Robbins, undated, b. 102, f. 7, Jerome Robbins Personal Papers, LPA; "call *Jeree*": Tanaquil Le Clercq to Jerome Robbins, postmarked Feb. 19, 1957, b. 101, f. 2, Jerome Robbins Personal Papers, LPA.
12. Edith Le Clercq to Betty Cage, Dec. 22, 1956, RG1-10: Personal and Pro. Papers, Correspondence Balanchine-Mole, f. 177, John Taras Collection, NYCB Archives.
13. Edith Le Clercq to Betty Cage, Feb. 1, 6, and undated. 1957, RG1-10: Personal and Pro. Papers, Correspondence Balanchine-Mole, f. 177, John Taras Collection, NYCB Archives.
14. Tanaquil Le Clercq (in Edith's hand) to Robert Fizdale and Arthur Gold, Jan. 7, 1957, and undated, f. 4 and 5, Letters to Robert Fizdale and Arthur Gold, (S) *MGZMD 108, LPA.
15. Tanaquil Le Clercq to Jerome Robbins, Jan. 22, 1957, b. 101, f. 11, Jerome Robbins Personal Papers, LPA.
16. Tanaquil Le Clercq (in Edith's hand) to Jerome Robbins, postmarked Nov. 25, 1957, b. 101, f. 9, Jerome Robbins Personal Papers, LPA.
17. Tanaquil Le Clercq to Jerome Robbins, postmarked Jan. 27, 1957, b. 101, f. 13, Jerome Robbins Personal Papers, LPA.
18. Edith Le Clercq to Lincoln Kirstein, undated (1957), f. 167, John Taras Collection, NYCB Archives.
19. George Balanchine to Betty Cage, undated (likely Jan. or Feb. 1957), RG1-10: Personal and Pro. Papers, Correspondence Balanchine-Mole, John Taras Collection, NYCB Archives.
20. Tanaquil Le Clercq to Robert Fizdale, Feb. 13, 1957, f. 5, Letters to Robert Fizdale and Arthur Gold, (S) *MGZMD 108, LPA.
21. Tanaquil Le Clercq to Jerome Robbins, Mar. 12, 1957, b.101–103, f. 3, Jerome Robbins Personal Papers, LPA.
22. Tanaquil Le Clercq to Jerome Robbins, Mar. 1957, b. 102, f. 3, Jerome Robbins Personal Papers, LPA.
23. Edith Le Clercq to Betty Cage, Feb. 6, 28, and undated, 1957, f. 177 and 178, and SAS correspondence about the flight from Copenhagen to New York, f. 178, John Taras Collection, NYCB Archives; Conversations with Betty Cage, 1982, Balanchine Book: Notes

on Tapes and Interviews, b. 45, Richard Buckle Papers, HRC (confirms Polio Foundation payment).

24. Records show that she was in Warm Springs from Apr. 28 until Nov. 22.
25. Tanaquil Le Clercq medical records, including Admitting Report, Apr. 28, 1957, and Medical Social Progress Notes, and a copy of the summary from D. Henry H. Jordan, MD, at Lenox Hill, Roosevelt Warm Springs Institute for Rehabilitation Archives.
26. Tanaquil Le Clercq to Jerome Robbins, May 2 and 6, 1957, b. 102, f. 4, Jerome Robbins Personal Papers, LPA; Warm Springs, GA, undated, f. 2, Letters to Robert Fizdale and Arthur Gold, (S) *MGZMD 108, LPA.
27. Patricia McBride Lousada in *Afternoon of a Faun: Tanaquil Le Clercq*.
28. George Balanchine to Tanaquil Le Clercq, postmarked May 6, 1957, f. 2, MS Thr 411, George Balanchine Archive, Houghton.
29. Tanaquil Le Clercq to Jerome Robbins, postmarked Sept. 16, 1957, b. 102, f. 5, Jerome Robbins Personal Papers, LPA.
30. Notes on a conversation with George Balanchine, Jan. 1961 or 1962, Taper Papers; letters between George Balanchine and R. Raymound Couirault (Paris), Correspondence: Tanaquil Le Clercq, b. 20, MS Thr 411 (1031), George Balanchine Archive, Houghton. Couirault had developed a new treatment for polio. Balanchine wrote in 1961 to ask if the doctor might please send the treatment directly from France (it was too expensive at the Pharmacie Française in New York City) so that he could administer it to his wife.
31. Notes on a conversation with George Balanchine, Jan. 1961 or 1962, Taper Papers.
32. Pilates's disciple Carola Trier was also one of Tanny's therapists at Lenox Hill and also worked extensively with many dancers (including the author).
33. Tanaquil Le Clercq to Jerome Robbins, July 5, 1957, b. 101–103, Jerome Robbins Personal Papers, LPA; Tanaquil Le Clercq to Robert Fizdale and Arthur Gold, Aug. 1957, Letters to Robert Fizdale and Arthur Gold, LPA; Fromm, *The Art of Loving*.
34. Tanaquil Le Clercq to Jerome Robbins, Feb. 25, 1957, b. 101–103, Jerome Robbins Personal Papers, LPA.
35. Notes on interview with Lucia Davidova, Mar. 3, 1961 (or 1962), Taper Papers; Barbara Horgan, interview by the author, Mar. 16, 2016; Apartment leases, 1964–69, b. 70, MS Thr 411 (2415), George Balanchine Archive, Houghton: includes lease at the Apthorp, Mar. 10, 1958–Mar. 31, 1960, 390 West End Avenue, Apt. 6A, rent $225/month, and says that Balanchine moved from his previous residence at 41 East Seventy-fifth Street.
36. On the Chinese cook, Tanaquil Le Clercq to Robert Fizdale ("Dear Zino"), undated (1957), f. 4, Letters to Robert Fizdale and Arthur Gold, (S) *MGZMD 108, LPA; on Tanny's range of motion: Barbara Horgan, interview by the author, Mar. 16, 2016; on the Audubon eagle and clocks: Taper, *Balanchine*, 243.
37. Letters from George Balanchine to Tanaquil Le Clercq, May–Aug. 1957 and undated, f. 2, MS Thr 411, George Balanchine Archive, Houghton; Vespa shed: Tanaquil Le Clercq to Robert Fizdale, July 15, 1957, f. 4, Letters to Robert Fizdale and Arthur Gold, LPA.
38. Tanaquil Le Clercq to Jerome Robbins, postmarked July 1957, b. 102, f. 5, Jerome Robbins Personal Papers, LPA.
39. Lincoln Kirstein correspondence with Igor Stravinsky, July 15, 1947; Apr. 29, 1948; and Nov. 28, 1949, MF 96.1, Igor Stravinsky Collection, Paul Sacher Stiftung. "*?—" comes from the 1949 correspondence.
40. Betty Cage to Lincoln Kirstein, undated (from Genoa, 1953), b. 10, f. 175, (S) *MGZMD 97, Lincoln Kirstein Papers, LPA: "[George] does not want to [do] a Stravinsky Festival. He says no one will come. I agree."

41. Stravinsky, *Stravinsky,* vol. 1; Lincoln Kirstein correspondence with Igor Stravinsky, Nov. 28, 1949; Feb. 16 and 19, 1951; and Nov. 28, 1951 (Terpsichore); Aug. 26, 28, 29, and 31, 1953; and Sept. 9, 1953, Igor Stravinsky Collection, Paul Sacher Stiftung.
42. Igor Stravinsky to Lincoln Kirstein, Sept. 9, 1953, Igor Stravinsky Collection, Paul Sacher Stiftung; see also Joseph, *Stravinsky's Ballets,* 175.
43. "beautiful part of mathematics": Mersenne quoted in Yates, *The French Academies of the Sixteenth Century,* 285; "Christian Orpheuses": Yates, 64.
44. De Lauze, *Apologie de la danse,* 17. The atonal aspects of the score were developed later, in 1957.
45. Walsh, *Stravinsky: The Second Exile,* 321.
46. Palmer, *Stravinsky;* Walsh, *Stravinsky: A Creative Spring,* 250, and Walsh, *Stravinsky: The Second Exile,* 170.
47. Vera's diary entries are reproduced in Stravinsky, *Dearest Bubushkin.* Stephen Walsh says that Craft mistranslated, embellished, and made up many of the entries and that his record is unreliable. The cheesecake reference must be taken with a grain of salt.
48. Joseph, *Stravinsky's Ballets,* 273.
49. Joseph, *Stravinsky and Balanchine,* 247–49; Joseph, *Stravinsky's Ballets,* 170–89; *Agon*: MF 213, score and sketches, Igor Stravinsky Collection, Paul Sacher Stiftung.
50. Igor Stravinsky to Lincoln Kirstein, Aug. 13, 1954, Igor Stravinsky Collection, Paul Sacher Stiftung.
51. Nietzsche, "Homer on Competition," in *On the Genealogy of Morality,* 193; Nietzsche, *Birth of Tragedy;* Silk and Stern, *Nietzsche on Tragedy;* Young, *Friedrich Nietzsche,* 304–7, 330–38.
52. Lincoln thought that the title was influenced by T. S. Eliot, and he also later pointed to ideas about agonism in Poggioli, *Theory of the Avant-Garde;* Kirstein, *Movement and Metaphor,* 242–43.
53. Joseph, *Stravinsky and Balanchine,* 247–49.
54. Stravinsky and Craft, *Conversations with Stravinsky,* 23.
55. Walsh, *Stravinsky: The Second Exile,* 360.
56. Joseph, *Stravinsky's Ballets,* 188.
57. Diana Adams, interview by John Taras, 1984, sound recording, RG3/AV Materials, John Taras Collection, NYCB Archives.
58. Arthur Mitchell, interview by the author, July 3, 2013; Melissa Hayden, interview by the author, May 21, 2005; Barbara Walczak, interviews by the author, Feb. 6, 2015, and Feb. 5, 2020; Francia Russell, interviews by the author, Aug. 6, 2013, and Feb. 6, 2020; Jonathan Watts, interview by the author, Jan. 31, 2020; Reynolds, *Repertory in Review,* 182; Milberg Fisher, *In Balanchine's Company,* 153–70; Leigh Witchel, "Four Decades of Agon," *Ballet Review* 25, no. 3 (1997): 52–78.
59. Melissa Hayden, interview by the author, May 21, 2005.
60. Francia Russell, interview by the author, Feb. 6, 2020.
61. Ann Hutchinson did make a Labanotation score, but neither Balanchine nor the dancers knew how to read it.
62. Deni Lamont as told to Heather Watts: Heather Watts, interview by the author, Sept. 18, 2014.
63. Photos of these rehearsals taken by Martha Swope are reproduced in part in Taper, *Balanchine,* 263–73.
64. Martha Swope, interview by the author, Sept. 19, 2013; Taper describes the scene in his biography: Taper, *Balanchine,* viii.

65. Milberg Fisher, *In Balanchine's Company*, 161.
66. Igor Stravinsky to Pierre Souvtchinsky, Nov. 16, 1957, quoted in Walsh, *Stravinsky: The Second Exile*, 374.
67. Walsh, *Stravinsky: The Second Exile*, 373–74.
68. Western Union Telegram from Igor Stravinsky, Nov. 27, 1957, f. 1, *MGZM-Res (S), George Balanchine, Misc. Correspondence, LPA: "To you to whom I dedicate Agon. Am sending today my heartiest wishes for a great success your beautiful composition highly deserves. I am in thought with you. Stravinsky."
69. Taper, *Balanchine*, viii.
70. Tanaquil Le Clercq Medical Record: Functional Evaluation, Nov. 22, 1956, Roosevelt Warm Springs Institute for Rehabilitation Archives.
71. Correspondence with the National Foundation for Infantile Paralysis (March of Dimes), b. 26, MS Thr 411 (1310), George Balanchine Archive, Houghton. Betty Cage wrote to the foundation on Nov. 21, 1957, noting that the March of Dimes had bought the entire house for the performance on Nov. 27 at a cost of $6,500.
72. Adjustments to tempos continued in the years to come when Stravinsky worked with Balanchine and conductor Robert Irving. William James Lawson, "Robert Irving: A Personal Memoir," *Ballet Review* 41, no. 4 (2013): 69.
73. Barbara Walczak, interviews by the author, Feb. 5, 2015, and Feb. 5, 2020; Francia Russell, interview by the author, Feb. 6, 2020.
74. Interviews with George Balanchine and members of the New York City Ballet, by Jac Venza for the National Educational Television network, 1964, sound recording, *MGZTC 3-24, LPA:

    Balanchine: Musically it is complicated you have to analyze in advance what it is all about this music, what kind of a sound it is and why it was written that way. Well, somebody must do that and in this case I did it, and I also have a friend. . . . Music is always, even if it is commissioned, it is always written first. And when the music comes, we will try to put dancing to it.

    Venza: What did you and Stravinsky begin with?

    Balanchine: To have some dancing, numbers, a competition. . . . I said let's do a series of dances, and he told me he has the idea to do French, old type of French dances, bransles, etc., court dancing, but mostly you don't hear that, partly it is tonal, partly it is not. Each number starts with exactly the same music. It is twelve tone it is not harmonic, it is inharmonic, twelve notes, and it starts with twelve dancers and then all the ways it can be divided, one and two, four and four and so forth, if you will find another division, I think we found every possible division of twelve.

75. Jonathan Watts, interview by the author, Jan. 31, 2020.
76. Jennifer Dunning, "Nananne Porcher, 78, Lighting Designer," *New York Times*, June 23, 2001; Rosenthal and Wertenbaker, *Magic of Light*; Winthrop Sargeant, "Please, Darling, Bring Three to Seven," *New Yorker*, Feb. 4, 1956, 33–59.
77. Reynolds, *Repertory*, 182.
78. Denby, "Three Sides of *Agon*," in Denby, *Dance Writings*, 461.
79. Stephanie Jordan, "Agon: A Musical/Choreographic Analysis," *Dance Research Journal* 25, no. 2 (1991): 1–12; Randel, "Dancing with Stravinsky"; Tarik O'Regan, interview by the author, Nov. 22, 2015.
80. The final swivel turning their backs to the audience may have been added later. It is not performed on the 1960 Montreal tape, but Stravinsky did note it in his 1957 published

score: "The female dancers leave the stage. The male dancers take their position as at the beginning—back to the audience." *Agon*: MF 213, Igor Stravinsky Collection, Paul Sacher Stiftung. Jonathan Watts recalls freezing and looking away from the audience, no backward swivel on the opening night; interview by the author, Sept. 12, 2014.

81. Telegrams after the opening of *Agon*: MF 137.1, Igor Stravinsky Collection, Paul Sacher Stiftung; correspondence with Soulima Stravinsky, including Western Union telegram dated Nov. 29, 1957, MF 107, Igor Stravinsky Collection, Paul Sacher Stiftung.
82. Lincoln Kirstein to Igor Stravinsky, Dec. 9, 1957, reproduced in Stravinsky, *Stravinsky*, vol. 1.
83. Gooch, *City Poet*, 343 (O'Hara took the *Guernica* comparison from the painter John Button, who was there too); on Duchamp: Denby, "Three Sides of *Agon*," in Denby, *Dance Writings*, 459.
84. John Martin, "Ballet: Four of a Kind," *New York Times*, Dec. 2, 1957.
85. Betty Cage to George Balanchine, Aug. 17, 1955, RG1-10: Personal and Pro. Papers, Correspondence Balanchine-Mole, f. 180, John Taras Collection, NYCB Archives.
86. Martin, "Ballet: Four of a Kind," *New York Times*, Dec. 2, 1957; Balanchine had been planning to strip *Apollo* for some time: in 1954 Kirstein reported that Balanchine was reimagining Apollo and that he envisioned it "done with stark simplicity for Jacques d'Amboise and will be a revelation." Quoted in Stravinsky, *Stravinsky*, 289.
87. *Ohne warum* (without why), a phrase from the German mystic Angelus Silesius, was a concept echoed by (among others) Emerson, Wittgenstein, and Balanchine. See Arlene Croce, "Balanchine Said," *New Yorker*, Jan. 26, 2009; Posnock, *Renunciation*, 1-66.
88. Walsh, *Stravinsky: The Second Exile*, 374–75.
89. Lincoln Kirstein to Igor Stravinsky, Aug. 24, 1953, in Stravinsky, *Stravinsky*, 289.
90. "A Word from George Balanchine," *Playbill*, Dec. 1957, *MGZEA Agon (Balanchine), LPA.
91. Caute, *Dancer Defects*, 48–49. Publicly announced in September 1956, this IBM computer would be proudly exhibited at the American pavilion in the Brussels World's Fair in 1958 and in Moscow at the American National Exposition in 1959. RAMAC stood for "Random Access Memory-AC" (in tech-speak) and was later marketed as "Random Access Method of Accounting and Control." "RAMAC: The First Magnetic Hard Disc," accessed via www.ibm.com/ibm/history/ibm100/us/en/icons/ramac/.
92. The Russian obsession with Nietzsche, especially in the early years of the twentieth century, is perhaps best described by Nicolas Berdyaev in *The Russian Idea*. This was the Nietzsche of religious themes: "Nietzsche was accepted as a mystic and a prophet," and symbolism in Russia, he explained, was a search for spiritual order and a turn to mysticism. It was an "inward revolution," a dawn, a future day, a rising sun. All of this was tied up in these Russian minds both with the coming new era of the Holy Spirit and with the occult. The basic theme, Berdyaev says, of early-twentieth-century Russian thought is the theme of the divine in the cosmos, of cosmic divine transfiguration, of the divine in man. Berdyaev, *Russian Idea*, 230, 245.
93. *Balanchine: New York City Ballet in Montreal*, vol. 2—including Balanchine introducing *Agon* (telecast Mar. 10, 1960).
94. Quoted in Young, *Friedrich Nietzsche*, 321, from the preface to *The Gay Science*. Nietzsche goes on (326–27): "For most people, the intellect is an awkward, gloomy, creaking machine that is hard to start; when they want to work with the machine . . . they call it 'taking matters *seriously*' . . . and where laughter and gaiety are to be found [they suppose that] thinking is good for nothing—that is the prejudice of this serious beast against all 'gay science.' Well then, let us prove it a prejudice."

95. Arlene Croce, "The Spelling of Agon," *New Yorker,* July 12, 1993; Melissa Hayden, interview by the author, May 21, 2001; Melissa Hayden's notes on *Agon,* Melissa Hayden Papers, Houghton (uncatalogued).
96. Croce, "The Spelling of Agon."
97. Interviews with George Balanchine and members of the New York City Ballet, by Jac Venza for the National Educational Television network, LPA.
98. Rev. 1:11.
99. Scholem, *On the Kabbalah,* 30.
100. *Balanchine: New York City Ballet in Montreal,* vol. 2.
101. For Balanchine, this was a practical matter. An older dancer's name would simply disappear from the casting lists, replaced by someone younger and more promising. Performing less is a kind of slow poison for a dancer, who becomes nervous, insecure, out of shape—until finally, she gives up. In more urgent cases, the news would be delivered in a pink slip, but Balanchine increasingly relied on Betty, and later Barbara, to field the emotional consequences. "We don't want Mounsey any more," he wrote to Betty in 1958, and "I hope Barnett and his wife will live happily in Atlanta for ever after! . . . Walczak was always very nice . . . [but] I don't see any future." Gone. George Balanchine to Betty Cage, May 7, 1958, b. 6, MS Thr 411 (304), George Balanchine Archive, Houghton.
102. Lincoln Kirstein to Donald Richie, Sept. 24, 1958, quoted in Duberman, *Worlds of Lincoln Kirstein,* 533; Kirstein to Betty Cage, July 11, 1958, quoted in Buckle, *Balanchine,* 214: "Balanchine wants to get through the winter as well as possible, and in the summer start from scratch with a small company and six new ballets, a la Ballet Caravan, which we feel we can book, and then enlarge the group to a company like 1947 at the Center, but there will be the difference of a repertory and ten years of work."
103. "There is no second performance. They're all first performances," Balanchine told Barzin, quoted in Mason, *I Remember Balanchine,* 248.

CHAPTER 19: COLD WAR

1. Prevots, *Dance for Export,* 74; passport issued Feb. 4, 1960, with a visa to the USSR, b. 110, MS Thr 411 (2815), George Balanchine Archive, Houghton.
2. Homans, *Apollo's Angels,* 373, from *New York Times,* Sept. 20, 1959.
3. "retardative and uncreative": Kirstein quoting Balanchine, Lincoln Kirstein to Hans Tuch, Sept. 29, 1963, b. 10, f. 165, (S) *MGZMD 97, Lincoln Kirstein Papers, LPA; "Soviet garbage": d'Amboise, *I Was a Dancer,* 241.
4. Taper, *Balanchine,* 273–74.
5. Jacques d'Amboise, interview by the author, Jan. 27, 2008.
6. "If I Were President": b. 30, Thr 411 (1407), George Balanchine Archive, Houghton, and copy of the speech and Balanchine's letter to Jackie Kennedy, July 18, 1961, Taper Papers; "America's Faerie Queene": unidentified film clip from 1962, with thanks to Serapio Walton; letter to Jackie, Homans, *Apollo's Angels,* 514. Further cementing Balanchine's romance with the Kennedys, on Jan. 20, 1962, NYCB danced *Stars and Stripes* at Kennedy's Second Anniversary Inaugural Celebration.
7. Letter dated Sept. 18, 1961, b. 40, MS Thr 411 (2051), George Balanchine Archive, Houghton.
8. Leach fought in the Pacific with the navy during World War II and went on to direct the Aspen Institute, where he founded the Aspen Music Center; he worked with Nelson Rockefeller on the founding of Lincoln Center, where he directed programming under its first president, General Maxwell D. Taylor, until President Johnson called Taylor to service in Vietnam.

9. Lincoln Kirstein, Notes of the Formation of a National Program of Ballet Education, Grant 05900465 to Ballet Society, Inc., Ford Foundation. (Note that the nonprofit entity was still technically called Ballet Society.)
10. Interview with George Balanchine in Kendall, *Dancing*, 68.
11. See George Balanchine correspondence with Ford Foundation, undated, b. 12, MS Thr 411 (625), George Balanchine Archive, Houghton. This document is undated, probably 1962 or 1963, and may have been a draft; another version edits out some of the key phrases.
12. Cable from Lincoln Kirstein to Max Isenberg, Mar. 28, 1962, Bureau of Educational and Cultural Affairs Historical Collection, University of Arkansas.
13. Sol Hurok was involved in negotiating the tour, and he needed the NYCB to agree to go before he could get the Bolshoi, so he worked tirelessly behind the scenes on both sides to bring about an agreement.
14. Duberman, *Worlds of Lincoln Kirstein*, 551; Lincoln Kirstein to Richard Buckle, Apr. 18, 1962, Richard Buckle Papers, HRC.
15. Lincoln Kirstein to Richard Buckle, May 15, 1962, Richard Buckle Papers, HRC.
16. George Balanchine speaks at a National Press Club program held in his honor, Feb. 1, 1977, sound recording, *MGZTL 4-3313 JRC, LPA.
17. "1962 NYCB Tour," f. 2329, op. 8, d. 2320, USSR Ministry of Culture, RGALI.
18. Una Kai, interview by the author, Apr. 9, 2014.
19. "Calculated vulgarity": quoted in Reynolds, *Repertory in Review*, 188; "Is it as innocent as it seems?": John Martin, "All Four of Balanchine's New Ballets Score High—Events of the Week," *New York Times*, Feb. 2, 1958. The company also performed *Stars and Stripes* at Nelson Rockefeller's inauguration as governor of New York.
20. In another key, in 1959 Balanchine made *Native Dancers*, a sly play on the name of Alfred G. Vanderbilt's racehorse Native Dancer. The horse was a TV celebrity and made the cover of *Time* in 1954. Balanchine liked to think of dancers as horses. You are writing the biography of a racehorse, he told Taper; "a racehorse doesn't keep a diary." Taper, *Balanchine*, x.
21. Prevots, *Dance for Export*, 3; Croft, *Dancers as Diplomats*; Richmond, *Cultural Exchange and the Cold War*, 179–80. It was not just the Soviets who were suspicious. Even conservatives on the American Right were wary of abstraction in painting, which they linked to leftist artists. When U.S. organizers worked with MoMA to prepare an art exhibition for the American National Exhibition in Moscow in 1959, they insisted on limiting abstract paintings to only 10 percent of the show. Ironically, one U.S. senator even branded abstraction in art as a "sinister conspiracy conceived in the black heart of Russia."
22. Maria Balanchivadze death certificate, Feb. 11, 1959, at age eighty-four, held in Tbilisi: Georgia's SSR (Soviet Socialist Republic), Ministry of Justice, Department of Acts on Citizens' Condition, Vake district, "Record of Death Act" no. 218, February 28, 1959 (with thanks to Ekaterine Diasamidze); Andrei Balanchivadze cable (from Tbilisi) to Western Union, Mar. 6, 1959, b. 2, MS Thr 411 (115), George Balanchine Archive, Houghton. George receives it on Mar. 10. Andrei doesn't know where to send the cable—"Try 131 West 55th" the cable notes.
23. Duberman, *Worlds of Lincoln Kirstein*, 533.
24. Balanchine's half of *Episodes* was composed of Symphony (op. 21, 1928), Five Pieces for Orchestra (op. 10, 1911–13), Concerto (op. 24, 1934), Variations (op. 30, 1940), and ricercars (in six voices, from Bach's *Musical Offering*, 1935); "Do what you do": David Hays, interview by the author, Jan. 31, 2014.
25. Symphony, op. 21, transcription for piano by George Balanchine, b. 60, MS Thr 411

(2235), George Balanchine Archive, Houghton. There are notes on the choreography in the score: a staff was added between the treble and bass clefs, and in this staff, Balanchine transcribes phrases from the other two staffs, along with notes such as "walking back"; "boys walking turns"; "girls arab[esque]"; "arab[esque] turns"; "pas de bour in succession (5+4+5)"; "J walk away"; "boys walk away"; "hitchkick"; the top of the score notes: V=Violette, J=Jonathan. In the "Variationen," there are again two staffs, and he has written in the middle space. We don't know if these notes were made before or after the choreography was done.

26. D'Amboise, *I Was a Dancer,* 203; d'Amboise, interview by the author, Aug. 10, 2011. Balanchine sardonically told Bernard Taper that maybe he should have a program note for the "idiots" to instruct them; "there is nothing funny about this ballet so please do not annoy your neighbors by laughing." Notes on *Episodes,* conversation with George Balanchine, undated, Taper Papers; Misler, *In principio era il corpo,* 159, image 339.
27. Paul Taylor, interview by John Gruen for WNCN-FM, New York, Jan. 5, 1976, *MGZTC 3-315, LPA; Paul Taylor, interview by Anita Page for WFCR, Amherst, MA, Nov. 15, 1967, *MGZTC 3-34, LPA; "Geek" and "were being sharply jerked around": Taylor, *Private Domain,* 90–91; Paul Taylor, interview by the author, Feb. 3, 2014.
28. "like being in church": Lynne Stetson, interview by the author, May 27, 2016; Kent, *Once a Dancer,* 133–34; critics quoted in Reynolds, *Repertory in Review,* 195–98.
29. Francisco Moncion, interview by Peter Conway, Apr. and Mar. 1979, transcript, *MGZT 5-959, LPA.
30. John Martin, "Ballet: Season's Novelty," *New York Times,* Mar. 23, 1961; and "The Dance: Synthetics," *New York Times,* Apr. 9, 1961; Denby, *Dance Writings,* 470–71.
31. "Review of *Electronics,*" b. 25, f. 35, (S) *MGZMD 182, Jerome Robbins Personal Papers, LPA. With thanks to Amanda Vaill for bringing this document to my attention.
32. *Seven Deadly Sins*: Una Kai, interview by the author, Apr. 9, 2014; Carol Sumner, interview by the author, Dec. 5, 2015; Peter Harvey, interview by the author, Feb. 6, 2015; Robert Maiorano, interview by the author, June 13, 2004; *Seven Deadly Sins* documents and photographs, Weill-Lenya Research Center; *Seven Deadly Sins* images, NYCB Archives; Kent, *Once a Dancer,* 113–17; Allegra Kent, interviews by the author, Nov. 22, 2012, and Sept. 2, 2015; Bertolt Brecht, W. H. Auden, Chester Kallman, and Eric Bentley, "The Seven Deadly Sins of the Lower Middle Class: Ballet Cantata," *Tulane Drama Review* 6, no. 1 (1961): 123–29; Rouben Ter-Arutunian, interview by Joan Kramer, Aug. 23 and 26, Sept. 8, 9, 21, and 22, and Oct. 12 and 13, 1976, sound disc, LPA; Reynolds, *Repertory in Review.* See also Paul Thek's painting *Seven Deadly Sins,* of Kent and Lenya under the cape, courtesy of Peter Harvey. The production was featured in *Life* with photos by Gordon Parks, Dec. 22, 1958.
33. Edward Villella, interview by the author, November 5, 2014; Villella, *Prodigal Son.*
34. When someone asked him what the ballet "meant," Balanchine deflected: "Very simple. Poet comes back to life. Marries somnambulist. They move to Scarsdale, nice house, five children. She cooks—*aw*-ful, heavy quiches," b. 38, f. 6, Gold and Fizdale Collection, Peter Jay Sharp Special Collections; Danilova, *Choura,* 159–60; Kent, *Once a Dancer*; correspondence with Allegra Kent, b. 18, MS Thr 411 (959), George Balanchine Archive, Houghton; "The main point": George Balanchine to John Taras, Mar. 1 (1957, from Hotel d'Angleterre in Copenhagen) (written by Edith Le Clercq and signed by Balanchine), f. 155, John Taras Collection, NYCB Archives.
35. Betty Cage to Liebermann, Nov. 30, 1960, b. 15, MS Thr 411 (753), George Balanchine Archive, Houghton; Sara Leland, interview by the author, Dec. 6, 2014; Ricky Weiss, in-

terview by the author, Sept. 8, 2015; Karin von Aroldingen, interview by the author, Nov. 8, 2012; David Hays, interview by the author, Jan. 21, 2014. When asked at the time to mount *Liebeslieder* for another troupe, Balanchine admitted it was impossible. No one (including him) knew it, he said; each dancer knew only her part, and there were in any case no steps. On later changes to the sets, see Howard Moss, "Balanchine after Balanchine," *New York Review of Books*, July 19, 1984.

36. Mendelssohn's overture and incidental music were not enough for an evening-length ballet, so Balanchine wove in other Mendelssohn excerpts, which seemed to mirror the distinct worlds of Shakespeare's play: antiquity in the overture from *Athalie;* the supernatural fairy worlds in the overture to *Die schöne Melusine*, a German fairytale, and in *Die erste Walpurgisnacht*, inspired by Goethe. For the wedding celebration, Balanchine chose *Die Heimkehr aus der Fremde*, composed as an occasional piece in celebration of Mendelssohn's parents' silver wedding anniversary, and the love pas de deux came from the simple and moving String Symphony no. 9, composed by Mendelssohn in a lyrical, self-reflective style when he was just fourteen.
37. Quoted in Reynolds, *Repertory in Review*, 126.
38. Quotes from Jonathan Cott, "Two Talks with George Balanchine," in Kirstein, Cott, and Denby, *Portrait of Mr. B*, 133–45. Shakespeare's text continues, "I will get Peter Quince to write a ballet of this dream. It shall be called 'Bottom's Dream,' because it hath no bottom; and I will sing it in the latter end of our play, before the Duke"; *Midsummer Night's Dream*, act 4, scene 1, lines 203–16.
39. Pagels, *Revelations*, 22–35.
40. Rouben Ter-Arutunian, interviews by Joan Kramer, Aug. 23 and 26, Sept. 8, 9, 21, and 22, and Oct. 12 and 13, 1976, sound recording, *MGZTL 4-382, LPA.
41. *Noah and the Flood*, June 14, 1962, CBS TV, video recording, *MGZIA 4-2535, LPA; Interviews, 1977–80, b. 110, MS Thr 411 (2812), George Balanchine Archive, Houghton; Personal Correspondence, 710-39: *The Flood;* MF 95.1, MF 139, Igor Stravinsky Collection, Paul Sacher Stiftung; "Working Notes for 'The Flood,'" reproduced in Stravinsky and Craft, *Dialogues; Noah and the Flood.* 1962, RG8 A-V Materials, NYCB Archives; Walsh, *Stravinsky: The Second Exile*, 409–59; d'Amboise, *I Was a Dancer*, 278–79.
42. "It's a pyramid": Bernard Taper, "Television and Ballet," in Burdick et al., *Eighth Art;* Transcription of interview with George Balanchine for "Television in Ballet," Taper Papers; "*Noah and the Flood* was ghastly": Lincoln Kirstein to Richard Buckle, June 15, 1962, Richard Buckle Papers, HRC.

CHAPTER 20: USSR

1. On the poster: Joysanne Sidimus, interview by the author, Feb. 20, 2020; Kent, *Once a Dancer*, 161; Karin von Aroldingen, unpublished memoir.
2. Taper, *Balanchine*, 273–89; Buckle, *Balanchine*, 234–37; 1962 photographs, NYCB Archives; photographs, Georgia 1962, MS Thr 411 (2439), George Balanchine Archive, Houghton; photographs of George Balanchine and Andrei Balanchivadze, State Museum of Georgian Theater, Music, Film and Choreography—Art Palace, Tbilisi; Ketevan Balanchivadze, private collection of photos; photos including Balanchine with Furtseva, 3068-3-1769 л15, RGALI.
3. Ketevan Balanchivadze, interview by the author, Oct. 2017; "a nice puddle duck": Eugenie Ouroussow to Vladimir Lehovich quoting Lincoln, in Vladimir Lehovich personal collection.
4. Interview with George Balanchine, Nov. 12, 1962, Taper Papers; Andrei's Western Union

cable from Tbilisi, Mar. 6, 1959, b. 2, MS Thr 411 (115), George Balanchine Archive, Houghton. The following account also draws on interviews with, among others, Arthur Mitchell, Melissa Hayden, Bettijane Sills, Victoria Simon, Conrad Ludlow, Allegra Kent, Robert Maiorano, Suzanne Farrell, Jacques d'Amboise, Joysanne Sidimus, Francia Russell, Kent Stowell, Gloria Govrin, Sally Leland, Kay Mazzo, Mimi Paul, Suki Schorer, Carol Sumner, Violette Verdy, Edward Villella, and Hans Tuch.

5. Kirstein, "Cultural Confrontation," unpublished manuscript, b. 11, f. 177, (S) *MGZMD 97, Lincoln Kirstein Papers, LPA.
6. Letter to Lydia, Oct. 16, 1962, Francisco Moncion personal papers; d'Amboise, *I Was a Dancer,* 236–37; Joysanne Sidimus, interview by the author, Feb. 20, 2020; Russia, 1962, b. 16, Richard Buckle Papers, HRC; Salmon, "To the Land of the Future"; Hatherley, *Landscapes of Communism;* Mr. and Mrs. George Macomber, "Moscow During the Crisis—I: Quiet Metropolis Without Tension," *Boston Globe,* Dec. 2, 1962; Frank Starr, "Hospitality Pops Up in Moscow," *Chicago Tribune,* May 21, 1967.
7. Mina Curtiss to Fidelma Cadmus, Oct. 10, 1962, b. 7, f. 49, (S) *MGZMD 123, Lincoln Kirstein Papers, LPA; "Cultural Confrontation," b. 11, f. 177, (S) *MGZMD 97, Lincoln Kirstein Papers, LPA.
8. Merridale, *Red Fortress,* 346–48; Taubman, *Khrushchev,* 515–52; Joysanne Sidimus, interview by the author, Feb. 20, 2020.
9. "Shock Waves in Moscow," *Time,* Oct. 19, 1962, reporting on the tour, which was covered across the United States; John Martin, *New York Times,* Oct. 10 and 22, 1962, and Nov. 9, 13, and 22, 1962; footage of an interview with Balanchine, Lepeshinskaya, and Kirstein, YouTube video, accessed Sept. 22, 2021, www.youtube.com/watch?v=jL8gWIwZzxY#t=81; Nancy Reynolds, "The Red Curtain: Balanchine's Critical Reception in the Soviet Union," in *Proceedings of the Society of Dance History Scholars* (Pennington, NJ: Society of Dance History Scholars, 1992), 56–57; Balanchine, George, clippings, 1926–1960s, b. 2, 3, 4, (S) *MGZR-Res., Balanchine, LPA, including a range of national press coverage of the 1962 tour; Russian press (translated) including, among others, Album of A. E. Diner, Tour in the USSR, printed clippings from newspapers and magazines, 1962–1964, f. 2337, inventory 2, item 204, RGALI.
10. Eugenie Ouroussow to Vladimir Lehovich, Nov. 23, 1962, Vladimir Lehovich personal collection.
11. Hans (Tommy) Tuch, interview by the author, Feb. 8, 2013.
12. Eugenie Ouroussow to Vladimir Lehovich, Nov. 23, 1962, Vladimir Lehovich personal collection.
13. Duberman, *Worlds of Lincoln Kirstein,* 553; Taper, *Balanchine,* 284–86; "A little green devil": Shaun O'Brien to Richard Buckle, b. 16, f. 1962 Russia, Richard Buckle Papers, HRC; "Impossible to describe": George Balanchine to Tanaquil Le Clercq, b. 1, f. 3, MS Thr 411, George Balanchine Archive, Houghton.
14. On the Cuban Missile Crisis, see: miscellaneous notes from the tour, Francisco Moncion personal papers; d'Amboise Diary, Oct. 17–Nov. 1, 1962; Robert Maiorano, interview by the author, June 13, 2004; Betty Cage to Eugene Tanner, Feb. 2, 1962, f. 175, RGI 1-10, Personal and Pro. Papers, Correspondence Balanchine-Mole, John Taras Collection, NYCB Archives; Interview with Betty Cage, b. 16, f. 1962 Russia, Richard Buckle Papers, HRC; d'Amboise, *I Was a Dancer;* "Cultural Confrontation," b. 11, f. 177, (S) *MGZMD 97, Lincoln Kirstein Papers, LPA; Taubman, *Khrushchev;* Fursenko and Naftali, *One Hell of a Gamble;* William F. Scott, "The Face of Moscow in the Missile Crisis: Observations of the Attachées in the Soviet Union in the Fall of '62," Declassified CIA report, ARC 7282817, from "Studies in Intelligence," 1955–1992, Record Group 263,

National Archives; Jason Mullins, "Embassy Moscow: A Diplomatic Perspective of the Cuban Missile Crisis," *Georgetown Security Studies Review*, Dec. 10, 2013, georgetownsecuritystudiesreview.org/2013/12/10/embassy-moscow-a-diplomatic-perspective-of-the-cuban-missile-crisis/; President's Intelligence Checklist for October 27, 1962, issued by the Central Intelligence Agency (declassified in part, sanitized copy approved for release, 2015/07/23), reported that the NYCB was playing to packed houses and that intelligence from "many Soviet quarters" indicated that the company was having "a deep impact in Soviet intellectual circles." The United States went to DEFCON 2 on Oct. 24, 1962. With thanks to Timothy Naftali.

15. D'Amboise, *I Was a Dancer*, 246; "Triumphant NYCB" and "Balanchine Talks to Russia About His Artistic Credo," *Dance News*, Dec. 1962; Ministry of Culture files on the 1962 New York City Ballet Tour, f. 2329, op. 8, d. 2320, RGALI; "Cultural Confrontation," b. 11, f. 177, (S) *MGZMD 97, Lincoln Kirstein Papers, LPA.
16. Taper, *Balanchine*, 285–86; typed notes on interviews with Natasha Molostwoff and Eugenie Ouroussow, Dec. 10, 1962, Taper Papers; interviews with George Balanchine, Nov. 12 and Dec. 10, 1962, Taper Papers.
17. Notes on Russia chapter from interview with George Balanchine, Taper Papers.
18. Interview with George Balanchine, Dec. 10, 1962, Taper Papers.
19. Interview with George Balanchine, Dec. 10, 1962, Taper Papers. When Lopokov died in 1973, Balanchine cabled the Kirov Theater expressing condolences and saying that he would "always be grateful for his encouraging support in the beginning of my choreographic adventure." Lopokov, Fedor, b. 21, MS Thr 411 (1091), George Balanchine Archive, Houghton. Balanchine also sent this telegram to the Fedor Lopokov Jubilee Commission Conservatory Teatralnia Ploshad 3 Leningrad, undated:

    > It is with great pleasure that I send you this greeting from myself and from my company stop I wish to tell you how much I appreciated you during my first feeble attempt to choreography your friendly advice assisted me greatly and I want to send you my sincerest congratulations with my wishes that you go on forever as we need people like you. My young dancers know you were the first one to show that symphonies could be used for dance and they join me now in sending you our best wishes and respect. George Balanchine, NYCB Company.

20. Buckle, *Balanchine*, 241, from Kirstein, *Thirty Years*, 177–78; Taper, *Balanchine*, 286–88.
21. Taper, *Balanchine*, 288.
22. Joysanne Sidimus, interview by the author, Feb. 20, 2020.
23. D'Amboise Diary, Oct. 31 and Nov. 6, 1962.
24. "a kind of crucifixion": quoted in Duberman, *Worlds of Lincoln Kirstein*, 553; d'Amboise Diary, Oct. 27, 1962; "Lincoln said he needs to get out for a while," said Betty Cage to Gene Tanner, Nov. 2, 1962, f. 175–74, John Taras Collection, NYCB Archives.
25. Figes, *Natasha's Dance*, 554–56; Walsh, *Stravinsky: The Second Exile*, 470–72; Stephen Spender to Nicolas Nabokov, Oct. 3, 1961, b. 2, f. 41, Nicolas Nabokov Papers, Beinecke:

    > I do not think you should bother about these old men making fools of themselves. Stravinsky . . . is just the Russian Bertrand Russell. They obviously will do anything to get their names in the newspapers and there is no use in trying to argue with them at this stage. You might be writing your own work. Even if you do stop him, it will probably be used against you that you did and you will appear in Volume XII of Bob's [Craft's] memoirs as the true Reactionary who stopped Stravinsky being buried in the Kremlin. Still I suppose I am no more capable of stopping you than you are of stopping Stravinsky.

26. Family letters, Keti Balanchivadze personal papers; Keti and Tsiskari Balanchivadze interviews, interviews by the author, Tbilisi, Nov. 2017; Kendall, *Balanchine and the Lost Muse*, 248, makes the suggestion, based on family interviews, that Tamara may have died on a train trying to get back to Georgia; George Balanchine, interview by Bernard Taper, 1961, Taper Tapes: Balanchine says that Andrei told him that Tamara died in Leningrad during the siege.
27. Balanchivadze, Apollon, Tbilisi Police File, Political Administration, case no. 64220, Indictment of Citizen Balanchivadze Apollon Melitonovich, 12, IX, 1928; Balanchivadze, Apollon, police file, f. 102, 1913, op. 243, d. 134, State Archives of the Russian Federation.
28. Maria Balanchivadze to Andrei Balanchivadze, Apr. 20, 1930, and undated, and Tamara Balanchivadze to Maria Balanchivadze, Aug. 17, 1931, Keti Balanchivadze personal collection; Keti Balanchivadze, interviews by the author, Nov. 8 and 11, 2017; interviews by the author with locals in Maria's old building and neighborhood, Nov. 9, 2017.
29. "Although almost everything has been destroyed," she wrote to Andrei on Easter in 1930, "I listened to the chants during the whole Holy week. . . . The believers were given their freedom"; Keti Balanchivadze personal collection.
30. Keti Balanchivadze, interviews by the author, Nov. 8 and 11, 2017; we visited the cemetery together.
31. Notes on interview with Natasha Molostwoff, b. 16, f. 1962 Russia, Richard Buckle Papers, HRC.
32. Rayfield, *Edge of Empires*, 352; Kotkin, *Stalin*, vol. 2, 507.
33. Rayfield, *Edge of Empires*, 353; Kotkin, *Stalin*, vol. 2, 501–14, 1010–11; Scott, *Familiar Strangers*; Knight, *Beria*, 74–87.
34. Kotkin, *Stalin*, vol. 2, 1010.
35. Keti Balanchivadze, interviews by the author, Nov. 8 and 11, 2017; Merab Kezevadze (Director of the Kutaisi Central Archive), interview by the author, Nov. 9, 2017; Malkhaz Porskhvanidze (interview by the author, Nov. 9, 2017) worked at the Kutaisi Pantheon and talked about his father, who he said was a theater director who was at the George Balanchine dinner, along with other friends from their theater circle, and spoke of rumors, unsubstantiated, of Meliton's murder; Khuchua, *Meliton Balanchivadze*, says he was buried in the fence of the oldest temple of Bagrat. Irakli Balanchivadze was arrested and shot in late 1937 or early 1938. Irakli Balanchivadze biography accessed via National Parliamentary Library of Georgia, www.nplg.gov.ge/gwdict/index.php?a=term&d=26&t=201; Meliton Balanchivadze's official biography, Biographical Dictionary of Georgia, accessed via www.nplg.gov.ge/bios/ka/00003513/; commission for the organization of the funeral of the People's Artist M. A. Balanchivadze: *Zarya Vostoka* (Dawn of the East), Tbilisi, Nov. 24, 1937, no. 269 and 270. I am grateful to Erik Scott, Georges Mamoulia, Hiroaki Kuromiya, and Keti Balanchivadze for their help and expertise.
36. Notes on conversation with Natasha Molostwoff and Eugenie Ouroussow, Dec. 10, 1962, Taper Papers; notes on interview with Natasha Molostwoff, b. 16, f. 1962 Russia, Richard Buckle Papers, HRC; photographs, Georgia 1962, MS Thr 411 (2439), George Balanchine Archive, Houghton. In the coming years, long after Balanchine's visit, someone, sometime, for some reason, added a small sculpted head of Meliton to the corner of this gray stone monument, and leaned a modest plaque next to the piano keys with the composer's birth and death dates incorrectly inscribed—another careless fact.
37. Photographs, Georgia 1962, MS Thr 411 (2439), George Balanchine Archive, Houghton; George Balanchine photographs, State Museum of Georgian Theater, Music, Film and Choreography—Art Palace, Tbilisi.
38. Vanusha Balanchivadze (interview by the author, Nov. 9, 2017) said that he and his cousin

Tamaz were at the location (if not at the table) of the George Balanchine *supra* as boys, and that Tamaz's father Bidzina Balanchivadze hosted the *supra* at his home on Javakhishvili Street in Kutaisi.

39. D'Amboise Diary, Nov. 24, 1962; Maria Tallchief also believed he was born in Georgia, as did Karin von Aroldingen.
40. Notes on conversation with Natasha Molostwoff and Eugenie Ouroussow, Dec. 10, 1962, Taper Papers; notes on interview with Natasha Molostwoff, b. 16, f. 1962 Russia, Richard Buckle Papers, HRC.
41. D'Amboise Diary, Nov. 23, 1962; Jacques d'Amboise, interview by the author, Oct. 10, 2013; miscellaneous notes on Russia, 1962, Francisco Moncion personal papers; photographs, Georgia 1962, MS Thr 411 (2439), George Balanchine Archive, Houghton.
42. Tbilisi crowds: photographs, Georgia 1962, MS Thr 411 (2439), George Balanchine Archive, Houghton; memorandum from Mr. Tuch to Boerner and Siscoe, Dec. 3, 1962, b. 73, f. 28, Bureau of Educational and Cultural Affairs Historical Collection, University of Arkansas.
43. D'Amboise, *I Was a Dancer*, 265, and interview by the author, Oct. 10, 2013.
44. Interview with George Balanchine, Dec. 10, 1962, Taper Papers.
45. Lincoln Kirstein to Richard Buckle, June 15, 1962, Richard Buckle Papers, HRC: "Balanchine is doing groundwork for 2 whoppers; a Don Quixote in which he will, well, er—dance, the Don himself." Balanchine had been in conversations with Nicolas Nabokov since the 1930s about a new production of *Quixote*.

CHAPTER 21: MASTER BUILDER

1. George Balanchine note to Mac Lowry upon his retirement in 1974, b. 12, MS Thr 411 (625), George Balanchine Archive, Houghton.
2. Barbara Horgan, interviews by the author, June 23, 2015, and Mar. 16, 2016.
3. Eugenie Ouroussow to Vladimir Lehovich, Apr. 15, 1962, Vladimir Lehovich personal collection. Lehovich, Eugenie, b. 2, f. 24, Dmitry and Eugenie Lehovich Collection, Slav. Reserve 09-393, New York Public Library.
4. Vespa, 1952, b. 106, MS Thr 411 (2778), George Balanchine Archive, Houghton.
5. Ford Foundation correspondence, b. 12, MS Thr 411 (625), George Balanchine Archive, Houghton.
6. Letter from Tanaquil Le Clercq, undated (1962, from Hamburg before arriving in Russia), f. 14, (S) *MGZMD 108, Letters to Robert Fizdale and Arthur Gold, LPA:

   Sat morning.

   [....] George called from Hamburg. I was hoping that he would feel better. Tired but well, I don't know what it is. He said he felt "nervous and jittery." That's not like GB then he again said he had to go to California to "make money" Baum doesn't pay me anything you know, he said. This is also not like George. I think perhaps physically he is tired so Baum and money and his age upset him—whereas if you're okay they don't bother you. He said everyone "wants something." He couldn't find papers or records that he wanted before he left.... And it got him down. Every criticism about Midsummer Night's Dream seemed to "get him" and there were plenty. He said he was nervous about spending so much money. Then he went to a City Center meeting. Baum said "couldn't you make it just one act?" It's not very interesting etc. etc. and Dr White from the opera said it was lovely "but the music—now now you don't really think Mendelssohn is a good composer." He said if only it had had music by Richard Strauss—then that would have been really perfect. George said he screamed at him "you go to Hell"—All this nagging and picking at him. Then Baum!! Well you know George lives on the royalties of his ballets—so he asked Betty this year to ask Baum for a small salary—I mean George is there doing everything morning noon and night, it would take about 3 people on salary to do what he does—without—he teaches for free—no fee for a ballet (just royalties) Rehearses for nothing etc. etc. So what do you think Baum suggested!! A little salary—and that they should pay George no royalties—not one ballet would he get money for, City Center would have them all. —Well I think this hurt George just terribly—he and Baum have been together for about 25 years—I could just cry—No I could just kill them. Love T

7. Approximately $74 million today.
8. Report of the President to the Board of Directors of the Juilliard School, Nov. 1963 (including Nov. 8, 1963: Board Trustee Minutes 2, School of American Ballet, further report of discussions), Juilliard School; John Taras and Eugenie Ouroussow, interview by Marian Horosko and Alvin H. Reiss for WYNC, 1965, sound recording, *MGZTL 4-1883, LPA. Balanchine saw the Juilliard alliance as a way to possibly provide students interested in choreography a serious musical education—which never quite happened.
9. Balanchine's statement upon receipt of the Ford Foundation grant, b. 12, MS Thr 411 (625), George Balanchine Archive, Houghton.
10. Kendall, *Dancing*; Ford Foundation press release, Dec. 16, 1963, b. 12, MS Thr 411, George Balanchine Archive, Houghton. The other companies that received support under the grant were San Francisco Ballet ($644,000), Boston Ballet ($144,000), Houston Ballet ($173,000), Pennsylvania Ballet ($295,000), National Ballet (D.C.) ($400,000), and Utah Ballet ($175,000). The Joffrey had received $2 million from Rebekah Harkness in 1962, but the money fell through a year later, which left the company in dire straits. Boston, San Francisco, Pennsylvania, and Utah were run by strong Balanchine supporters.
11. Eugenie Ouroussow to Vladimir Lehovich, Dec. 22, 1963, Vladimir Lehovich personal collection; Lincoln Kirstein ran hot and cold toward Graham, but mainly cold. He wrote to Marie Rambert, July 29, 1976, Rambert Archive: "[Graham] represents everything I hate: the vaunted Ego; female domination on a basis of castration: the I, I, I: the Me Me Me. La Graham; O.K. Leave her to heaven; I certainly never want to see her again in this life. She is part of the Great Nature that is, for me, Negative Energy; the sullen sodden earth; not the province of AIR, which is where you and I flourish."
12. Lincoln Kirstein to Jerome Robbins, Jan. 11, 1963, b. 99, f. 4, (S) *MGZMD 182, Jerome Robbins Personal Papers, LPA.
13. George Balanchine, interview by Bernard Taper, undated (early 1970s), Taper Tapes.
14. They would share the State Theater with Richard Rogers's Music Theater of Lincoln Center and later with the New York City Opera.
15. Julia Foulkes, "The Other West Side Story: Urbanization and the Arts Meet at Lincoln Center," *Amerikastudien* 52, no. 2 (2007): 227–47; Ballon and Jackson, *Robert Moses*, 279–89. The Vivian Beaumont Theater was completed in 1965; Juilliard and Damrosch in 1969. The Lincoln Square Title 1 project also included buildings for Fordham University, the American Red Cross, PS 199, and Lincoln Towers (a luxury high-rise).
16. Kinescope of CBS TV live telecast of opening night ceremonies at the New York State Theater, Apr. 23, 1964, DVD, *MGZIDVD 5-3206, LPA. The performance also included *Allegro Brillante*. On Apr. 29, for the opening of Lincoln Center, Balanchine made a ditty called "Clarinade," with music by Morton Gould composed for Benny Goodman. Goodman (Tanny said) thought "his mother [might] be Georgian, a name like Grusniki or Groozinka." Postcard from Tanaquil Le Clercq, postmarked Feb. 18, 1962, f. 11, (S)

*MGZMD 108, Letters to Robert Fizdale and Arthur Gold, LPA; on Lincoln Kirstein and Nelson Rockefeller, see Duberman, *Worlds of Lincoln Kirstein,* 520.

17. Robert Moses, "Remarks on the Groundbreaking of Lincoln Square," in Jackson and Dunbar, *Empire City,* 736–38.
18. Duberman, *Worlds of Lincoln Kirstein,* 559; funding numbers: *Newsweek,* May 4, 1964; Milton Esterow, "State's Theater Opens at Center," *New York Times,* Apr. 24, 1964; Ballon and Jackson, *Robert Moses,* 279–89; Caro, *Power Broker*; Martin, *Lincoln Center*; Young, *Lincoln Center*; Foulkes, "Other West Side Story."
19. Lamster, *Man in the Glass House,* 289–301; *Newsweek,* May 4, 1964; Young, *Lincoln Center,* 13–59; Venice and "marvel of cut-crystal": Letter from Tanaquil Le Clercq, undated, f. 11, (S) *MGZMD 108, Letters to Robert Fizdale and Arthur Gold, LPA; headlights: Jerome Robbins to Richard Buckle, Apr. 22, 1964, b. 50, Richard Buckle Papers, HRC.
20. Jerome Robbins to Richard Buckle, Apr. 22, 1964, b. 50, Richard Buckle Papers, HRC; mauve linoleum: Barbara Horgan to Egon Seefehlner, 1969, b. 10, MS Thr 411 (494), George Balanchine Archive, Houghton.
21. Letter from Tanaquil Le Clercq, postmarked Feb. 18, 1964, f. 11, (S) *MGZMD 108, Letters to Robert Fizdale and Arthur Gold, LPA.
22. Karel Shimoff in *Remembering Mr. B,* 78.
23. Duberman, *Worlds of Lincoln Kirstein,* 559; Lamster, *Man in the Glass House,* 289–301.
24. Lincoln Kirstein to Richard Buckle, Oct. 4, 1964, Richard Buckle Papers, HRC; Lincoln Kirstein to Richard Buckle, Aug. 4, 1964, Richard Buckle Papers, HRC: "They are trying to get Lucia Chase or Mrs. Kean's company or anybody including the Het Needrland Balet to replace us; while I foresaw this, it is nevertheless rather a blow."
25. "Your associates": Lincoln Kirstein to John D. Rockefeller (through his office), July 1959; "I doubt": Lincoln Kirstein to Van Vechten, undated, in Duberman, *Worlds of Lincoln Kirstein,* 552, 559; Lincoln Center vs. City Center, 1961–64, b. 10, f. 11, *LPA MSS 1992-001, Morton Baum Papers, LPA; William Bender, "Now the Ballet Is Pulling Out," *New York Herald Tribune,* Dec. 12, 1964. In a companion article on the same page, Murray Kempton said that Lincoln Center was a real estate endeavor having nothing to do with culture—the sign of a "dead civilization." As Lincoln later put it, "Elite is a word to be fought for," and dancers must claim their right to belong to a "legitimate elite alongside ball players, brain surgeons, or brokers": Lincoln Kirstein, "The Performing Arts and Our Egregious Elite," in Lowry, *Performing Arts,* 196–97.
26. Lincoln Center vs. City Center, 1961–64, b. 10, f. 11, *LPA MSS 1992-001, Morton Baum Papers, LPA, including correspondence between Schuman (Lincoln Center) and Newbold Morris (City Center), and press release for the morning papers, dated Jan. 11, 1965; W. McNeil Lowry, "Conversations with Kirstein—I," *New Yorker,* Dec. 15, 1986, 44–80, and "Conversations with Kirstein—II," *New Yorker,* Dec. 22, 1986, 37–63.
27. Although he later complained that it was a mere "toy" Mariinsky: Lowry, "Conversations with Lincoln Kirstein—I."
28. Correspondence with Mark and Ruth Schorer, 1968–78, b. 35, MS Thr 411 (1680), George Balanchine Archive, Houghton.
29. Richard Moredock, interview by the author, Mar. 2, 2016; Richard Moredock and Merrill Ashley, interview by the author, Apr. 12, 2016; Susan Pillar, interview by the author, Feb. 6, 2016; Carol Sumner, interview by the author, Dec. 5, 2015; Barbara Horgan, interview by the author, Sept. 3, 2014; Lynne Stetson Diary, 1963–70, private collection, July 7, 1969: "Renee described Gordon's room at the Adelphi Hotel to me. He has a huge giant-sized cross made of lilies and some praying hands that light up. In the city his apart-

ment has a bleeding finger on the sink, an arm on the kitchen wall, a huge fish in his bathtub that he removes when he uses it, no chairs except for a dentist's chair, and metal flowers all over the place. An elephant foot and a collection of masks."

30. Tanaquil Le Clercq to Robert Fizdale, postmarked Oct. 3, 1958, f. 6, (S) *MGZMD 108, Letters to Robert Fizdale and Arthur Gold, LPA.
31. With thanks to Rick, Chris, Peter, and Lee Leach for showing me River Run and sharing family archives, including the diaries of Dick Leach; local Saratoga Springs press, including Robert L. Sammons, "Artistic Renaissance at Saratoga Springs," *Town and Country*, July 1966, 79; Duane La Flesche, "The $4 Million Wink . . . 5 Years Later," *Knickerbocker News*, July 9, 1966; *Saturday Review*, July 30, 1966; *Performing Arts Saratoga*, 1966; note from Kay Leach to Richard Buckle and interview with Kay Leach, Balanchine Book: Notes on Tapes and Interviews, b. 45, Richard Buckle Papers, HRC.
32. George Balanchine/Barbara Horgan to James Doolittle, May 1964, James Doolittle to George Balanchine, May 21, 1964, and George Balanchine to James Doolittle, June 11, 1965, b. 21, MS Thr 411 (1095), George Balanchine Archive, Houghton.
33. Letter from Barbara Horgan to her mother, Sept. 13, 1963, courtesy of Barbara Horgan. Horgan learned her limits: when she once tried to influence Balanchine about a dancer at the school, he turned icy and left the room. She called to apologize, and he listened and curtly said okay and hung up. Barbara Horgan, interview by the author, Nov. 12, 2012.
34. Buckle, *Balanchine*, 196–97; Morton Baum, unpublished notes for "A History of the New York City Ballet," b. 19, f. 10, *LPA MSS 1992-001, Morton Baum Papers, LPA; *New York Herald Tribune*, Nov. 4, 1959, announcing lend-lease ballets. That year, Balanchine sent an angry letter to the State Department saying that he did not mean for them to send a letter to *all* opera houses offering his dances free! He needed more control. Apologies followed from the State Department: United States, Dept. of State, 1959–78, b. 39, MS Thr 411 (1043), George Balanchine Archive, Houghton.
35. Correspondence with Leonid Davidovich Leonidoff, 1952–79, b. 20, MS Thr 411 (1043), George Balanchine Archive, Houghton.
36. Other examples:

    Correspondence with Royal Opera House Covent Garden, 1949–88, b. 34, MS Thr 411 (1612), George Balanchine Archive, Houghton.

    1962: Horgan conducted a long correspondence about costumes for *Prodigal* and *Serenade* with the Royal Opera House in London, specifying that they "must be the same as ours."

    On Nov. 27, 1972, Horgan wrote explaining that for *Agon* and *4Ts* costumes were easy—a leotard is a leotard, get some and go, she said. *Prodigal* costumes were shipped from US, with correspondence showing lots of hassle and the details of shipping. When no bald heads arrived, Horgan wrote—surely you can buy some rubber heads at a theatrical store in London.

    Correspondence with Marie Rambert, 1960–61, b. 32, MS Thr 411 (1535), George Balanchine Archive, Houghton:

    arrangements for *Night Shadow* at the Ballet Rambert. Balanchine offered the ballet with no fee, but insisted Rambert must pay Taras his $250 fee to set the ballet.
37. Correspondence with Deutsche Oper Berlin, 1965–89, b. 10, MS Thr 411 (494), George Balanchine Archive, Houghton.
38. George Balanchine Archive, Houghton; George Balanchine Correspondence, bMS Thr 411 (1043); Leonidoff Correspondence, 1952–79, Letters from Horgan, May 1966. He repeats this no and adds *Liebeslieder* to the list on Sept. 27, 1966 (although he had already said no in 1960, per correspondence between Betty Cage and Liebermann, Oct. 14 and

Nov. 30, 1960). Two years later, Barbara Horgan writes to Flemming Flindt at the Royal Danish Ballet on Feb. 12, 1968, to say that Balanchine is sorry but he can't send *Liebeslieder* because nobody knows it and he would have to bring the eight dancers (bMS Thr 411 Kongelige Teater Denmark, 1950–88 [986]). Balanchine does finally give *Liebeslieder* to Vienna in 1976 (Horgan to Leonidoff, May 5, 1976). At one point in 1966, Horgan wrote to Leonidoff to say that they were shorthanded on stagers since "all of our 'ladies' are either pregnant or will have just given birth (Francia Russell and Victoria Simon) and Una wants less and less to travel because of her little girl."

39. For example, d'Amboise Diary, Apr. 17 and Sept. 4, 1964; "mooshy": Charles Engell France, "A Conversation with John Clifford," *Ballet Review* 4, no. 1 (1971): 3–33; John Clifford, interview by the author, Aug. 2, 2014.
40. Travel Itineraries, 1964–78, b. 106, MS Thr 411 (2777), George Balanchine Archive, Houghton.
41. Eugenie Ouroussow to Vladimir Lehovich, Jan. 1965, Vladimir Lehovich personal collection.
42. Francia Russell, interview by the author, Aug. 3, 2013.
43. This dinner in 1958 is one of many descriptions of meals and food in Tanny's letters: Letters from Tanaquil Le Clercq, 1958, 1960, and undated, f. 6, 7, and 10, (S) *MGZMD 108, Letters to Robert Fizdale and Arthur Gold, LPA. In another example of George and the domesticity of their lives, Tanny related this incident in 1960:

> We are going through a "home improvement" week, before rehearsals start—WELL GB saw these lovely brass, standing lamps at Gimbels. We talked it over, decided they were a MUST and the next day off he went armed with a blank check (we have no charge at Gimbels). He got down there, picked out the lamps and made out his $16- check—the salesman asked him for his identification "Don't have any" he replied "oh surely sir, drivers license perhaps?" cooed the clerk—and here I hate to say it—our man told a whopper "don't have a car" he said "no car?" said the clerk "no" said GB "do <u>you</u> have a car?" "Well no" said the clerk "Blue Cross perhaps" but of <u>course</u> said GB "you don't think I carry it around do you?" He proceeded to tell the clerk, and a grey haired lady that this was a free country you weren't obliged to carry around things proving who you are—in France you sneeze and they ask you for your Carte d'identite—George says when he finished there was a little group around him—I'll bet—the floor manager was called and George told him that he George was trusting Gimbels with a 160 dollars—the lamps were to be sent in a week. "How do I know you don't take my check and don't send lamps?" he then told them suppose he could identify himself and the check bounces? What good is that. The result seems to be that Gimbels gave IN. GB arrived home very late—all flustered—and I have asked my mother to open a charge.

44. Jeanne Fuchs, interview by the author, Mar. 14, 2014; Richard Clurman, interview by Bernard Taper, June 9, 1984, microcassette, Taper Tapes.
45. Letter from Tanaquil Le Clercq, 1958, f. 8, (S) *MGZMD 108, Letters to Robert Fizdale and Arthur Gold, LPA.
46. Letter from Tanaquil Le Clercq, 1958, f. 6, (S) *MGZMD 108, Letters to Robert Fizdale and Arthur Gold, LPA.
47. Tanaquil Le Clercq Papers, NYCB Archives; Gray, *Feline Philosophy*.
48. B. 16, fol.: Davidova, Richard Buckle Papers, HRC: Buckle notes on a scrap of paper, "Lucia in dreadful hotel in Paris with GB when suicidal over Diana," and notes from meet-

ing with Lucia Davidova, Nov. 30, 1984; Todd Bolender, tape and notes on conversations with Betty Cage, May 1982; Balanchine Book: Notes on Tapes and Interviews, b. 45, Richard Buckle Papers, HRC, and d'Amboise Diary, June 19, 1974, also report a conversation with Balanchine relaying the Canada story and miscarriage of his child.

49. D'Amboise Diary, Jan. 29, 1963.
50. Violette Verdy, interview by the author, Nov. 1, 2013.
51. Interviews with George Balanchine and members of the New York City Ballet, by Jac Venza for the National Educational Television network, 1964, sound recording, *MGZTC 3-24, LPA.
52. D'Amboise Diary, Feb. 17, 1983.
53. Wardrobe master Leslie (Ducky) Copeland, born in Featherstone, Yorkshire, served in the Royal Navy and joined NYCB around 1958. See Richard F. Shepard, "About New York," *New York Times*, Nov. 27, 1979; "played sugar daddy": d'Amboise Diary, Mar. 16, 1963.
54. Patricia McBride, interview by the author, Nov. 6, 2013: "We were so used to touching him and smelling him and his perfume—he wore what my mom wore—Coty Emeraude, just a touch—light because he is a man. He had a shelf of bottles of Guerlin etcetera, and he would wear them. Sensual."
55. Una Kai, multiple interviews by and correspondence with the author in 2014; Cynthia Kai, interview by the author, Feb. 15, 2021.
56. He did give one dancer he was intimate with a performance or two of the lead in *Stars*, for example, and another got a moment in *Rubies*, but these were small token gifts that did not make a career.
57. Violette Verdy, interview by the author, Nov. 1, 2013.
58. Marjorie Bresler in *Remembering Mr. B*, 9.
59. Karel Shimoff in *Remembering Mr. B*, 78.
60. Lipsey, *Hammarskjöld*, xiii: "We cannot mould the world as masters of the material thing. Columbus did not reach the East Indies. But we can influence the development of the world from within as a spiritual thing"—he said, speaking to an audience in New York in Sept. 1953. Michael Ignatieff, "The Faith of a Hero," *New York Review of Books*, Nov. 7, 2013; "Gagaku," *Dance Observer*, Aug.-Sept. 1959, 103; Garfias, *Gagaku*. Hammarskjöld had already introduced Kirstein and Balanchine to the Swedish choreographer Birgit Cullberg, a student of Kurt Jooss and Central European expressionist dance, who staged her *Medea* on the NYCB in 1958.
61. She warmed up before class: Francia Russell, interview by the author, Aug. 3, 2013; her big toe: Frederick Wiseman, interview by the author, July 28, 2020.
62. Kent, *Once a Dancer*, 179.
63. Villella, *Prodigal Son*, 135–37; Kent, *Once a Dancer*, 177–83; Rolf Liebermann to George Balanchine, Dec. 22, 1969, b. 15, MS Thr 411 (753), George Balanchine Archive, Houghton: Liebermann wants *Bugaku*, but Balanchine says no via Horgan: "This is a very special ballet one which Mr. Balanchine is not eager to be produced outside of his own company." In a later letter to Sonia Arova, Horgan notes that Balanchine "is very particular about this ballet." Barbara Horgan to Sonia Arova, Jan. 8, 1970, MS Thr 411 (753), George Balanchine Archive, Houghton.
64. Farrell, *Holding On to the Air*, 76.
65. Kent, *Once a Dancer*, 177–83.
66. D'Amboise Diary, Mar. 1 and 12, 1963.
67. D'Amboise Diary, Mar. 27, 1963.
68. Farrell, *Holding On to the Air*, 103, 18–106.
69. Farrell, *Holding On to the Air*, 11–13.

70. "more than usual corn": Lincoln Kirstein to Richard Buckle, Dec. 10, 1963, Richard Buckle Papers, HRC; "Yes, it is emotions": George Balanchine and members of the New York City Ballet, interviewed by Jac Venza for the National Educational Television program *The American Arts*, sound recording, *MGZTC 3-24, LPA.
71. *Playboy, Tanny's Time, National Geographic*, all dated Jan. 1963, RG3/AV Materials, photographs, Tanaquil Le Clercq Collection, NYCB Archives.
72. "little Jerry": Barbara Horgan, interview by the author, Mar. 6, 2013; Francia Russell and Kent Stowell, interview by the author, Aug. 6, 2013; Lincoln Kirstein to Rouben Ter-Arutunian, June 15, 1964, f. 5, (S) *MGZM-Res. Kir L., LPA; postcard from Tanaquil Le Clercq, postmarked June 17, 1964, f. 11, (S) *MGZMD 108, Letters to Robert Fizdale and Arthur Gold, LPA; Lincoln Kirstein to Jerome Robbins, July 14, 1964, b. 99, f. 4, (S) *MGZMD 182, Jerome Robbins Personal Papers, LPA. Insurance, b. 78, MS Thr 411 (2422), George Balanchine Archive, Houghton: on Oct. 7, 1964, Balanchine, through Horgan, officially withdrew claims for disability pay because of palsy (July 10, 1964) and loss of part of forefinger (June 12, 1964).
73. Lincoln Kirstein to Richard Buckle, June 15, 1962, Richard Buckle Papers, HRC.

CHAPTER 22: DON QUIXOTE

1. Farrell, *Holding On to the Air*, 107, 106–23.
2. Quoted in Balanchine and Mason, *101 Stories*, 120.
3. Balanchine arrived back in New York City on Dec. 2 or 3: d'Amboise Diary. Score commissioned Dec. 7: Giroud, *Nicolas Nabokov*, 361.
4. Letters dated Mar. 30 and Apr. 8, 1964, series 1, Personal Correspondence (1962–66): Balanchine, George, Nicolas Nabokov Papers, HRC; "Don't worry": George Balanchine to Nicolas Nabokov, Apr. 1, 1965, b. 1, f. 30, GEN MS 1154, Nicolas Nabokov Papers, Beinecke. The commission is dated Dec. 7, 1962. For the orchestration, Nabokov wanted to work from Tchaikovsky's *Sleeping Beauty* but had to pass the orchestration to a colleague, Fernand Quattrocchi: Giroud, *Nicolas Nabokov*, 361; "Don Quichotte; ballet en 3 actes. Libretto par Nicolas Nabokov et Georges Balanchine," London, New York, Édition M.P. Belaieff, 1966, *MSI, LPA; Nicolas Nabokov in *Playbill*, Jan. 1973.
5. Farrell, *Holding On to the Air*, 110–12; Suzanne Farrell, interviews by the author, Feb. 14, 2017, Mar. 17 and Sept. 11, 2016.
6. Le Clercq, *Ballet Cook Book*, 68.
7. Nicolas Nabokov to Robert Irving, Apr. 14, 1965, b. 4, f. 66–67, GEN MSS 1154, Nicolas Nabokov Papers, Beinecke: Nabokov wrote apologetically to Irving about the orchestral additions, explaining: "Thereupon I asked him whether your orchestra had normally three trumpets and three trombones to which he said to me 'absolutely.' "
8. Barbara Horgan, interview by the author, Mar. 6, 2013.
9. Farrell, *Holding On to the Air*, 112–13.
10. D'Amboise, *I Was a Dancer*, 286.
11. Farrell, *Holding On to the Air*, 115; "Everything a man does": "Mr. B Talks about Ballet," *Life*, June 11, 1965.
12. Eugene Berman had been in talks with Nicky and George to design the ballet in the 1950s, but Balanchine decided against Berman, to his angry disappointment; Onslo-Ford, *Esteban Frances*.
13. "fairy talk": Barbara Horgan, interview by the author, Sept. 3, 2014; Veronica Horwell, "Kermit Love," *The Guardian*, June 26, 2008; and Dennis Hevesi, "Kermit Love, Costume Creator, Dies at 91," *New York Times*, June 24, 2008.
14. Arshansky was from Moscow and had survived the revolution, he said, because of an icon

of St. Nicholas hung from his neck. He bought a house in a Russian-émigré community near Augusta, Maine, inspired by an icon of St. Nicholas in one of the town's Russian Orthodox churches. The town also had a Russian bakery and a restaurant, and you could purchase handmade Russian boots. Arshansky called his house Elysian Fields, and it was musty and filled with relics and old delicate china, and he made dinners for visitors with lamb marinated for a week. Balanchine later visited and for a moment considered buying property nearby. "Town Was Once Home to 400 Russian Refugees," *Los Angeles Times*, Jan. 20, 1985; Stetson Diary.

15. Frank Lavoia, interview by the author, Sept. 30, 2016.
16. The program notes were edited by Nancy Lassalle: *Don Quixote*, undated, b. 4, f. 68, GEN MSS 1154, Nicolas Nabokov Papers, Beinecke.
17. "Balanchine Returns in New Ballet," *Chicago Tribune*, May 28, 1965.
18. *Don Quixote: Unedited Footage*, May 27, 1965, video recording, *MGZIDVD 5-2996, discs 1–5, LPA.
19. Christopher d'Amboise, interview by the author, Dec. 5, 2014. These children included Jacques's son Christopher d'Amboise and the young Judy Fugate (as the damsel in distress). Both later became principal dancers with the company.
20. "Don Quichotte; ballet en 3 actes. Libretto par Nicolas Nabokov et Georges Balanchine."
21. Farrell, *Holding On to the Air*, 101, 116, 124.
22. D'Amboise, *I Was a Dancer*, 287.
23. Yuszczuk and Nicoloff, "An Interview with George Balanchine," 10–14.
24. Balanchine and Mason, *101 Stories*, 120; see also the notes from Frances Mason for an article with comment by George Balanchine about *Don Quixote*, b. 4, f. 66–67, GEN MSS 1154, Nicolas Nabokov Papers, Beinecke, and "Don Quichotte; ballet en 3 actes. Libretto par Nicolas Nabokov et Georges Balanchine."
25. Cervantes, *Don Quixote*, 937.
26. Farrell, *Holding On to the Air*, 121.
27. Farrell, *Holding On to the Air*, 122–23.
28. "paralyzed by success": Michael Steinberg, "Don Quixote," *Boston Globe*, May 31, 1965; "horror": Clive Barnes, "Balanchine—1975 and Beyond," *New York Times*, Oct. 17, 1965; "And Suzi": Farrell, *Holding On to the Air*, 124.
29. Borges ("Partial Enchantments of the *Quixote*," in *Other Inquisitions*, 43–46) captured a spirit that lived in Balanchine's production too: "Why does it make us uneasy to know that the map is within the map and the thousand and one nights are within the book of *A Thousand and One Nights*? Why does it disquiet us to know that Don Quixote is a reader of the *Quixote*, and Hamlet is a spectator of *Hamlet*? I believe I have found the answer: those inversions suggest that if the characters in a story can be readers or spectators, then we, their readers or spectators, can be fictitious."

CHAPTER 23: THE ALABASTER PRINCESS

1. D'Amboise Diary, Sept. 16, 1965. The following is based on interviews with Farrell and her own account in *Holding On to the Air* and on interviews with Paul Mejia and other dancers and company people.
2. D'Amboise Diary, July 12, 1967; Francisco Moncion, interviewed by Peter Conway, 1979, transcript, *MGZMT 5-959, LPA; Francisco Moncion personal papers, courtesy of Gregory Cary.
3. Ricky Weiss, interviews by the author, June 1, 2005, and July 10, 2015; Mimi Paul: Merrill Ashley, interview by the author, May 21, 2012; "Who would ever have believed": Carolyn George, quoted in d'Amboise, *I Was a Dancer*, 283.

4. Farrell, *Holding On to the Air,* 136.
5. Farrell, *Holding On to the Air,* 87.
6. Farrell, *Holding On to the Air,* 183.
7. D'Amboise Diary, Feb. 17, 1966.
8. Dominique Nabokov, interview by the author, Nov. 22, 2015.
9. Farrell, *Holding On to the Air,* 160. Farrell refers to an erotic poem in her autobiography but doesn't reveal it. This one—which may be a different poem—is in Balanchine's hand and held in his papers; Songs: autograph manuscripts, f. 2, b. 56, MS Thr 411 (2194), George Balanchine Archive, Houghton. Another version, also in his hand: "Lazy Suzi DON'T be so choozy / Lay your body next to me / turn your dishes offer your kishess / Suzan Lazy make me crazy / what a pleasure to be at leisure when my Suzy turns for me / time to spare for / to pray [?] for / not a care for / have no flare for."
10. Farrell, *Holding On to the Air,* 159.
11. "sounded expensive": quoted in Reynolds, *Repertory in Review,* 247. With thanks to Claude Arpels for his memories and help with archival access.
12. Balanchine originally wanted to include *Sapphires,* set to Schoenberg—and Weimar—but the blue was hard to light on stage, so he dropped it.
13. "Show me" and "You are going forever": Mimi Paul, interview by the author, Apr. 21, 2014; "I just accepted it": Patricia McBride, interview by the author, Nov. 6, 2013; "the Irish policeman": Conrad Ludlow, interview by the author, July 27, 2014. In another example of Balanchine's off-color humor, around this time the company hosted a group of West Point cadets backstage, and as Pat spun multiple pirouettes one morning in class, Balanchine commented wryly that if she wasn't careful, she would "screw herself into the ground"; John Clifford, interview by the author, Aug. 3, 2014.
14. Peter Harvey, interview by the author, Feb. 6, 2015. For a detailed description of how the set was made, see Peter Harvey, "Designing for George Balanchine: Diaries of Ballet Productions, Part One: Brahms-Schoenberg Quartet, Jewels, Chaconne and Elegie on Dance in America," *Dance Chronicle* 20, no. 2 (1997): 121–72.
15. D'Amboise Diary, June 22, 1967; Jeanne Fuchs, interview by the author, Aug. 20, 2020; Barbara Horgan, interview by the author, Feb. 24, 2014.
16. Balanchine signed the lease for 142 West End Avenue, Apt. 26R, on Apr. 24 for May 1 [1967]: Apartment leases, 1946–69, b. 70, MS Thr 411 (2415), George Balanchine Archive, Houghton; Barbara Horgan, interview by the author, Feb. 24, 2014; *Les intermittences du coeur* (The Fickleness of the Heart), 1950, is now held at the Wadsworth Atheneum.
17. City Center life, medical, and retirement plans, 1969–83, b. 78, MS Thr 411 (2422), George Balanchine Archive, Houghton.
18. Balanchine and Romana were both in New York in early 1947, approximately nine months before Paul was born. They were both married, and there is no evidence of an affair, but she was there—which added fuel to the rumor mill's fire.
19. Paul Mejia, interviews by the author, Sept. 26 and 27, 2015, and July 24, 2016; Paul Mejia family photos and paintings; a local newspaper obituary for Roman calls him "last of the moujiks" with a photo in traditional Russian dress, Paul Mejia personal collection; Paul Mejia, interviewed by Kyra Lynn Kaptzan for WNYU-FM, Nov. 28, 1970, sound recording, *MGZTC 3-1970, LPA; Stracky, *Love All Around.*
20. Gold and Fizdale notes, b. 39, f. 6, Gold and Fizdale Collection, Peter Jay Sharp Special Collections; "Teach him": Paul Mejia, interviews by the author, Sept. 26 and 27, 2015, and July 24, 2016.

21. George Wehner Scores, 1936–66, JPB 06-68, LPA; Paul Mejia, interviews by the author, Sept. 26 and 27, 2015, and July 24, 2016.
22. Sari's portrait of Wehner ended up decades later on the wall of Mary T. Browne, a psychic Farrell and others consulted after Balanchine's death. Mary T. Browne, interview/session with the author, July 19, 2016 (portraits are in her apartment on Horatio Street in New York).
23. Paul Mejia, interviews by the author, Sept. 26 and 27, 2015, and July 24, 2016.
24. D'Amboise Diary, May 9, 1967: "Bal has taken Tony [Blum] out of *Agon* for Edinburg but has him doing it here for Boston. Paul Mejia to go to Edinburgh instead. Bal started out of the blue attacking Tony ect [*sic*] 'a fairy interior decorator' ruining my choreography ect. He is preparing himself and his guilt for what he has done—so that he can say I have a right to do it. Bullshit . . . Shaun said rumor Susanne and B married."
25. Farrell, *Holding On to the Air*, 179–85; interviews by the author with Suzanne Farrell, Paul Mejia, Gail Crisa, Barbara Horgan, Ricky Weiss, John Clifford, Robert Maiorano, Richard Moredock, Delia Peters, Lynne Stetson, and Jacques d'Amboise, among others.
26. Mimi Paul, interview by the author, Apr. 21, 2014; Gloria Govrin, interview by the author, Apr. 16, 2013. Balanchine signed a letter to Lucia Chase in 1968 asking if Chase might have room for Mimi Paul, saying he couldn't afford her: Balanchine, George, b. 7, f. 489, (S) *MGZMD 49, American Ballet Theatre Records, LPA; Joel Lobenthal, "A Conversation with John Prinz," *Ballet Review* 44, no. 3 (2016): 32–37; "Things are falling apart": Suzanne Farrell, interview by the author, Feb. 14, 2017.
27. Baum died on Feb. 7, 1968, age sixty-two. Betty Cage had a heart attack in May that year and recovered. Kirstein was released on September 22, 1967, and lived mostly at home for the next year, organizing photos for his book *Movement and Metaphor*. Duberman, *Worlds of Lincoln Kirstein*, 570; Lithgow, "Three Lincolns," in Lithgow, *Drama*; Maria Tucci, interview by the author, Sept. 1, 2015.
28. "don't bring garbage": d'Amboise Diary, Jan. 31, 1971; hairstyles: Lynne Stetson, interview by the author, May 27, 2016.
29. "You see": George Balanchine, interview by John Gruen, Nov. 20, 1972, sound recording, *MGZTL 4-3110 JRC or *MGZTL 4-129, LPA; John Gruen, "This Man Can Turn a Woman into a Star: George Balanchine," *Vogue*, Mar. 1, 1972; "CURSE NOT": Stetson Diary, Nov. 18, 1968.
30. Stetson Diary, Oct. 1968 and Nov. 18, 1968.
31. Stetson Diary, Oct. 7, 1965.
32. Ricky Weiss, interview by the author, June 1, 2005; Robert Maiorano, interview by the author, Dec. 12, 2015; Jennifer Nairn-Smith, for one, was fired with a letter, interview by the author, October 4, 2015. The dancers nicknamed one of their colleagues who performed on LSD (and was later also fired) "crystal-foot": Stetson Diary, May 20, 1969.
33. D'Amboise Diary, Aug. 26, 1965.
34. Gloria Govrin, interview by the author, Apr. 16, 2013; Ricky Weiss, interviews by the author, June 1, 2005, and Sept. 8, 2015.
35. Tape of Balanchine's class, May 29, 1976, with Gordon Boelzner at piano, Merrill Ashley personal collection; Francia Russell, interview by the author, Aug. 6, 2013; Jonathan Watts, interview by the author, Jan. 31, 2020.
36. "Leif Ørnberg," *Danskefilm.dk*, danskefilm.dk/skuespiller.php?id=3602; pictures of his arrest at gunpoint are held in the Royal Library, Copenhagen.
37. Scot J. Paltrow, "Peter Martins, Off Balance: In the Wake of Last Summer's Wife-Beating Scandal, Can the New York City Ballet's Artistic Director Get Back on His Toes?," *Los*

Angeles Times, Dec. 6, 1992; Martins, *Far from Denmark* (a book that some dancers called "far from the truth").

38. Stetson Diary, Apr. 5, 1970.
39. Balanchine let them all know where he stood: when Wilde retired, he cruelly left her farewell performance early. D'Amboise Diary, Oct. 31, 1965: "The 'Breath' left after pas de deux—snuck off like a naughty boy—what a rat (remember this Jacques!)."
40. Quoted in Farrell, *Holding On to the Air*, 163.
41. On Xenakis, see Turner, "Xenakis in America," 65–74; Site officiel Iannis Xenakis, accessed via www.iannis-xenakis.org; Xenakis, Iannis, b. 41, MS Thr (2093), George Balanchine Archive, Houghton; Oxford Music Online, s.v. "Iannis Xenakis," by Peter Hoffman, Jan. 20, 2001, accessed via www.oxfordmusiconline.com; *The Poème Electronique*, accessed via www.cirma.unito.it/vep/event.html.
42. Site officiel Iannis Xenakis, www.iannis-xenakis.org; autobiographical sketch from Montassier, *Le fait culturel*.
43. "lost cities": "Balanchine Lights Up the Sky," *Wall Street Journal*, Jan. 23, 1968, 16; "as mercury breaks" and other quotes: Reynolds, *Repertory in Review*, 251–53; Harley, *Xenakis*, 8–13; Donald Henahan, "How One Man Defines Man," *New York Times*, Mar. 17, 1968, D19; Oxford Music Online, "Iannis Xenakis"; Tom Service, "A Guide to Iannis Xenakis' Music," *The Guardian*, Apr. 23, 2013; Turner, "Xenakis in America."
44. "swimming around": Farrell, *Holding On to the Air*, 150; "Crazy sounds": Farrell quoted in Reynolds, *Repertory in Review*, 253; "bomb the audience": Lincoln Kirstein to Richard Buckle, June 22 and July 3, 1968, Richard Buckle Papers, HRC.
45. Nanette Reedy, interview by the author, July 12, 2016. Farrell reconstructed *Pithoprakta* for her own company of dancers in 2007, and the author spoke to her about it at length.
46. Quoted in Reynolds, *Repertory in Review*, 251–53. Clive Barnes noted in *The New York Times* ("Shape, Pulse and a Ballet," Feb. 4, 1968) that rather than the "psychedelic firework displays of our time," Balanchine gives us "a glass of cold water."
47. Lincoln Kirstein to the sculptor Astrid Zydower, Dec. 20, 1967, in Duberman, *Worlds of Lincoln Kirstein*, 570. There were plans for another Xenakis ballet, but when the composer sent the score, Balanchine said he had to hear it and could not know what it sounded like from just the score; Xenakis was eventually paid and the whole thing dropped. Correspondence with Iannis Xenakis, b. 41, MS Thr (2093), George Balanchine Archive, Houghton.
48. *Agon* interview with Xenakis and Balanchine, June 24, 1973, *En Scenes*, accessed via fresques.ina.fr/en-scenes/fiche-media/Scenes00967/agon-balanchine-et-xenakis.html:

> **Balanchine:** Music is time, like the world, and whether it is beautiful or not that's another thing, but first of all, it is time, you must be on time, punctual. Composer is architect of time, and then we are . . . The music is the floor for us.
>
> **Xenakis:** When I look at what you do, I also see an architecture of time, it exists in and of itself, another architecture than the music, it is too modest what you say . . .
>
> **Balanchine:** Yes, if you have a beautiful bed, and you lie in the bed, and your body takes a shape [he softens as if lying in the bed, taking its luxurious shape].

49. Robert Maiorano, interview by the author, Dec. 12, 2015; correspondence with Henry Kissinger, b. 19, MS Thr 411 (975), George Balanchine Archive, Houghton. Balanchine invited Kissinger with Nicky and Isaiah Berlin to a performance of *Don Quixote*, promising that if Kissinger came, he would honor him by performing the title role himself. In 1980 Kissinger acted as chairman of a committee to raise $13 million for NYCB. A press release notes that Kissinger is a fan of the company and of Balanchine. In 1982 Balanchine sent a

personal cable after Kissinger's heart surgery, dated February 20, 1982: "Congratulations, you will live a long time now. Best wishes from another triple-coronary by-pass success. George Balanchine." D'Amboise Diary, Aug. 15, 1973: "At nite heard end of Nixon speech. Breath in Kaye Von Ding dressing room he went on after about how glorious N was and good for him Bomb[ing?] Cambodia ect—I disagreed with him heatedly and walked away."

50. Walsh, *Stravinsky: The Second Exile*, 540.
51. Lincoln Kirstein to Richard Buckle, Apr. 18, 1968, f. Kirstein to Buckle, 1962–73, Richard Buckle Papers, HRC. Stravinsky had wanted to add an instrumental prelude specially for Balanchine's production, but he didn't manage to complete it. Taruskin (*Stravinsky and the Russian Traditions*, vol. 2) describes the ways in which Stravinsky arrived at an "atonal tonality" imbued with a deeply Russian sensibility—a sound recalling at moments *Sacre* or *Les Noces*. This "atonal tonality" provided no single axis around which symmetries could be constructed; instead there was a kind of changing axis around which Stravinsky arranged intervals. That is, Stravinsky was willing to lose the center, but he reconstructed it each time—only to lose it again. He was less interested in what Taruskin calls serialism's "strict intervallic order" (1673); instead Stravinsky built new static, vertical chords and harmonies that chased the center, which was itself a moving target. Nicolas Nabokov put it this way: "Toward the very end of Stravinsky's life something changed. He wrote a piece, his last grand piece of music, the *Requiem Canticles*. Though in it he used the novel devices of serial technique, he somehow overpowered them. It was immediately, instinctively, totally lovable to me. I was able without any effort to penetrate into the essence of its tragic beauty. I was as fully taken and shaken by it as I used to be in the thirties and forties by every new composition of Stravinsky" (quoted in Taruskin, *Stravinsky*, 1649).
52. Delia Peters, interview by the author, Oct. 6, 2020.
53. Eugenie Ouroussow to Vladimir Lehovich, Sept. 15, 1963, and Jan. 28, 1965, Vladimir Lehovich personal collection.
54. "They never stay" and following quotes: George Balanchine on the Dance Theatre of Harlem, interview by John Gruen, May 29, 1971, sound recording, *MGZTL 4-128, LPA.
55. A point I owe to Amanda Vaill.
56. Francisco Moncion, interview by Peter Conway, 1979, transcript, *MGZT 5-959, LPA.
57. Melissa Hayden, interview by the author, May 21, 2005.
58. Mel Tomlinson, interview by the author, Sept. 6, 2015.
59. George Balanchine on the Dance Theatre of Harlem, interview by John Gruen, May 29, 1971, sound recording, *MGZTL 4-128, LPA.
60. Gloria Govrin, interview by the author, Apr. 16, 2013.
61. Farrell, *Holding On to the Air*, 182–83.
62. He had danced Fokine's version of Thamar back in 1925 with Diaghilev, and now he wanted to do his own—closer to the poem—but Lincoln couldn't find his way to funding it. Thamar was also, of course, the subject of Meliton's opera. Lincoln Kirstein to Richard Buckle, June 22, 1968, Richard Buckle Papers, HRC: "We are deeply interested in Thamar. Is it in a condition that it could be hung. . . . Whether to reproduce it, redesign it (with Ter-Aroutunian who is a sort of Georgian too)"; Lincoln Kirstein to Richard Buckle, July 3, 1968, Richard Buckle Papers, HRC: "I spoke firmly and finally with Balanchine. He wants THAMAR, but . . . we are hard up since Morton Baum died and I have small funds until September. . . . Balanchine does not want to spend more the $5000 for the scenery, if in good condition. If in poor condition we can repair a certain amount. There is the alternative of Rouben Ter-Aroutunian doing it. . . . Balanchine's TAMAR will be closer to Pushkin [Lermontov?] than Fokine's was."

63. El Paso, Texas, records do not show the divorce, which suggests that it may have been arranged across the border; "nice": quoted in Vaill, *Somewhere*, 405.
64. George Balanchine, "Love Is a Simple Thing," Carnegie Hall Recording Co., Feb. 15, 1969 (5:50).
65. "You're better than this": Barbara Horgan, interview by the author, Feb. 24, 2014; Travel itineraries, 1964–78, MS Thr 411 (2777), George Balanchine Archive, Houghton; Dominique Nabokov, interview by the author, Nov. 22, 2015; Lincoln Kirstein to Fidelma Cadmus ("Goosie"), Apr. 1, 1969, b. 8, f. 85, (S) *MGZMD 123, Lincoln Kirstein Papers, LPA.
66. Autograph manuscripts, b. 56, f. 9, MS Thr 411 (2194), George Balanchine Archive, Houghton. Balanchine later retranscribed "Silver Night" on notepaper and then as a score with music.
67. "She's a witch" and "garbage": d'Amboise Diary, June 15, 1974, and Apr. 29, 1969; "I am Zeus": Stetson Diary, May 1, 1969; "Inca Finka": Violette Verdy, interview by the author, Nov. 1, 2013.
68. "We felt like flower children": Ricky Weiss, interview by the author, June 1, 2005; Jerome Robbins, "Jerome Robbins Discusses Dances at a Gathering with Edwin Denby," *Dance Magazine*, July 1969, 47–55. I owe much to Vaill, *Somewhere*, for the events to come.
69. There are varying accounts of exactly what happened that night; this one is based on interviews with many of those who were there, along with accounts in biographies, diaries, and memoirs. "How dare he": George Balanchine, interview by John Gruen, Nov. 20, 1972, LPA; "he is like a scorpion": John Clifford, interview by the author, Aug. 2, 2014.
70. Clive Barnes, *New York Times*, May 23, 1969; Jowitt, *Jerome Robbins*, 386–87. To put an end to speculation about what the ballet meant, Robbins wrote a statement in 1971, published the following year in *Ballet Review*, that slyly mimicked Yvonne Rainer's "NO Manifesto" of 1965:

    THERE ARE NO STORIES TO ANY OF THE DANCES IN "DAAG"
    THERE ARE NO PLOTS AND NO ROLES.
    THE DANCERS ARE THEMSELVES DANCING
    WITH EACH OTHER TO THAT MUSIC IN
    THAT SPACE.
    Thank you very much.

71. Lincoln Kirstein to Jerome Robbins, June 1, 1969, and undated, b. 99, f. 4, (S) *MGZMD 182, Jerome Robbins Personal Papers, LPA.
72. D'Amboise Diary, July 17, 1970; George Balanchine, interview by John Gruen, Nov. 20, 1972, LPA; John Gruen, "This Man Can Turn a Woman into a Star: George Balanchine," *Vogue*, Mar. 1, 1972; Suzanne Farrell and Paul Mejia, interview by John Gruen, Nov. 3, 1972, sound recording, *MGZTL 4-151, LPA.
73. After Balanchine's death, Paul and Suzanne eventually divorced. Roman Mejia (Paul's son by a different wife), is currently a soloist with the NYCB—like the returned ghost of Paul in a final revenge, or vindication, of Balanchine.
74. See esp. Irving Penn contact sheet, 1971, shared with the author by Robert Greskovic. One of the printed photographs is held by the National Portrait Gallery, Smithsonian Institution; gift of Irving Penn.
75. Lincoln Kirstein to Jerome Robbins, June 1, 1969, b. 99, f. 4, (S) *MGZMD 182, Jerome Robbins Personal Papers, LPA.
76. Kay's grandfather was Rubenstein's (and Rachmaninoff's) agent, and the piano had been chosen for Kay by Rubenstein himself at the Steinway store on Fifty-seventh Street in New York. Balanchine also later composed a song specially for Kay. Rick Leach, interview by

the author, Aug. 12, 2015; Kay Leach, handwritten notes to Richard Buckle, courtesy of Chris Leach; Peter, Lee, and Chris Leach, interviews by the author, Aug. 8, 2015.

77. Lease signed on July 16, 1969, for two years (Aug. 1, 1969, to July 31, 1971) for 27 West Sixty-seventh St., Apt. 9RE and W (five rooms and two baths); rate: $362.65/month; bills sent to NYCB at the theater. Barbara Horgan handled all of this. Apartment Leases, 1964–69, MS Thr 411 (2417), George Balanchine Archive, Houghton.
78. Milstein and Volkov, *From Russia to the West*, 265; Jill Spalding Milstein, interview by the author, Aug. 8, 2017.
79. Paul and Francis Sackett, interview by the author, Feb. 25, 2020.
80. Delia Peters, interview by the author, Mar. 31, 2016.
81. Letter from Barbara Horgan to her mother, Oct. 10, 1969, courtesy of Horgan, who also wrote: "By the by, Miss von Ding has just rented herself a small apartment, and I guess will leave husband and probably baby. Very spice, no? Hum, never a dull moment"; on Karin and Morty, interviews by the author with Karin von Aroldingen and Barbara Horgan, among others, and Jacques d'Amboise, interview by Bernard Taper, Nov. 7, 1983, Taper Tapes.
82. "It was very touching": Lincoln Kirstein to Marie Rambert, May 1, 1971, Rambert Archive; "Stravinsky was only one": b. 18, fol.: Craft, Richard Buckle Papers, HRC; Walsh, *Stravinsky: The Second Exile*, 561. Adding to his sense of instability, a few weeks later (in May) Betty Cage suffered a heart attack: Barbara Horgan to Alfonso Cata, June 12, 1971, b. 14, MS Thr 411 (722), George Balanchine Archive, Houghton.
83. Reynolds, *Repertory in Review*, 280; Clive Barnes, "Balanchine—Has He Become Trivial?," *New York Times*, quoted in Jowitt, *Jerome Robbins*, 403.
84. Barbara Horgan to Francia Russell, June 15, 1971, b. 34, MS Thr (1622), George Balanchine Archive, Houghton.
85. "Because you see" and "Ninety-nine percent": George Balanchine, interview by John Gruen, Mar. 1, 1972, sound recording, *MGZTL 4-127, LPA; "He's not a man": Karin von Aroldingen to Bernard Taper, personal microcassette notes, Taper Papers.

CHAPTER 24: A LEGION OF ANGELS

1. Quoted in Goldner, *Stravinsky Festival*, 14.
2. Goldner, *Stravinsky Festival;* George Balanchine, interview by Jonathan Cott, 1978, sound recording, *MGZTL 4-2685, LPA. A substantial part of this interview was transcribed and included in Kirstein, Cott, and Denby, *Portrait of Mr. B.*
3. Jerome Robbins and George Balanchine, interview by Rosemarie Tauris, June 19, 1972, sound recording, *MGZTL 4-3065 JRC, LPA.
4. Barbara Horgan, interview by the author, June 23, 2015.
5. Richard Clurman, interview by Bernard Taper, 1984, Taper Tapes.
6. Quoted in Goldner, *Stravinsky Festival*, 15.
7. "I danced [*Sacre*]": Jerome Robbins and George Balanchine, interview by Rosemarie Tauris, June 19, 1972, sound recording, *MGZTL 4-3065 JRC, LPA; George Balanchine, interview by Jonathan Cott, 1978, sound recording, *MGZTL 4-2685, LPA.
8. Stephanie Jordan, "Divertimento from *Le Baiser de la Fée*: Ghost Stories," in Hogan, *Balanchine*, 33–41.
9. George Balanchine, interview by Jonathan Cott, 1978, sound recording, *MGZTL 4-2685, LPA; interview with George Balanchine in *L'Express*, Apr. 2, 1973.
10. Goldner, *Stravinsky Festival*, 229–46; "You discuss": Barbara Horgan, interview by the author, Sept. 3, 2014.
11. Kay Mazzo, interview by the author, July 13, 2015.

12. John Clifford, interview by the author, Aug. 3, 2014.
13. Jerome Robbins to Robert Fizdale, 1972, b. 88, f. 12, (S) *MGZMD 182, Jerome Robbins Personal Papers, LPA.
14. "In all my experience": Jerome Robbins and George Balanchine, interview by Rosemarie Tauris, June 19, 1972, sound recording, *MGZTL 4-3065, LPA; "The short order cooks": Jerome Robbins to Robert Fizdale, Mar. 31, 1972, b. 88, f. 2, (S) *MGZMD 182, Jerome Robbins Personal Papers, LPA; Normandy landing: Lincoln Kirstein quoted in Goldner, *Stravinsky Festival*, 51.
15. D'Amboise Diary, June 3, 1972. Jacques concluded, "B believes he is mystical—special, superior, and god endowed, cannot fail and cannot be wrong."
16. Letter from Tanaquil Le Clercq, 1970s, f. 13, (S) *MGZMD 108; letters to Robert Fizdale and Arthur Gold, LPA.
17. "looking like a lost rhino," "woodchuckish," and "I mean you felt privileged": Letter from Tanaquil Le Clercq, 1970s, f. 13, (S) *MGZMD 108, Letters to Robert Fizdale and Arthur Gold, LPA; d'Amboise Diary, June 18, 1972, also noted: "JP Bonnefous Kaye—PM and Von Ding (she was the least)" and "I can't get over—the dancers were super"; "We don't listen to them": John Clifford, interview by the author, Aug. 2, 2014.
18. Karin von Aroldingen, unpublished memoir.
19. Interview with George Balanchine, early 1970s, Taper Papers.
20. For an analysis of the musical score, see Jordan, *Stravinsky Dances*. With thanks to Heather Watts for her insights.
21. Quoted in Stravinsky and Craft, *Dialogues and a Diary*, 83–84.
22. "We were one animal" and "I felt like": Heather Watts, interview by the author, Nov. 11, 2014.
23. George Balanchine, interview by Jonathan Cott, 1978, sound recording, *MGZTL 4-2685, LPA: "In *Symphony in Three Movements* there is a second movement little piece like Balinese, like Oriental, like a church, he liked the Balinese, this little bit of orientalism, yes, he liked it, he was like a Turk himself, I made special pas de deux it is like a prayer. . . . If you listen to that part."
24. Notes taken by Barbara Horgan during meetings between Jerome Robbins and George Balanchine on *Pulcinella*, with possible ideas while listening to music together, b. 59, f. 2–7, (S) *MGZMD 182, Jerome Robbins Personal Papers, LPA; Anna Kisselgoff, *New York Times*, June 23, 1972; Jerome Robbins and George Balanchine, interview by Rosemarie Tauris, June 19, 1972, sound recording, *MGZTL 4-3065, LPA.
25. "He's preparing himself": Violette Verdy, interview by the author, Nov. 1, 2013; "chrome, tinsel": David Hamilton, *The Nation*, review reprinted in Goldner, *Stravinsky Festival*, 220.
26. Kay Leach, handwritten notes for Richard Buckle, drawn from her diary entries of July 22 and 27, 1972. Found in a book in her house and shared with the author by the Leach family.
27. Merrill Ashley Diary, 1972, Russia; Christine Redpath, home movies 1972–78, and interview by the author, Dec. 2, 2018; Deborah Austin, interview by the author, Sept. 9, 2015; NYCB 1972 Tour Reviews, b. 10, f. 163, (S) *MGZMD 97, Lincoln Kirstein Papers, LPA; documents on the tour of the New York City Ballet (USA) in the USSR in 1972 (plan, reports, correspondence), f. 3162, op. 1, d. 1564, RGALI.
28. Reviews (1952–72), b. 10, f. 163, (S) *MGZMD 97, Lincoln Kirstein Papers, LPA.
29. George Balanchine, interviews with Bernard Taper, 1973, Taper Tapes.
30. Keti Balanchivadze, interviews by the author, Nov. 8 and 11, 2017.
31. George Balanchine, interviews with Bernard Taper, 1973, Taper Tapes; Karin von Aroldingen, unpublished memoir.

32. Letter from Horgan [?] to the Georgian dancers' agent, Sept. 19, 1974, b. 37, MS Thr 411 (1779), George Balanchine Archive, Houghton.
33. Keti Balanchivadze, interviews by the author, Nov. 8 and 11, 2017; two letters from Andrei Balanchivadze to G. Balanchine, c. 1972 (one with a recipe for *satsivi* and one from Amiran), with a list (in Russian) of presents he would like to receive, courtesy of Robert Greskovic personal collection.
34. George Balanchine, interview by John Gruen, 1972, sound recording, *MGZTL 4-3110 JRC or *MGZTL 4-129, LPA.
35. George Balanchine, interview by Bernard Taper, mid-1970s, Taper.
36. George Balanchine, interview by John Gruen, 1972, sound recording, *MGZTL 4-3110 JRC or *MGZTL 4-129, LPA.
37. George Balanchine (speaking to Alfonso Cata) in Hochman's film *In Balanchine's Classroom.*
38. George Balanchine, interview by Jonathan Cott, 1978, sound recording, *MGZTL 4-2685, LPA.
39. George Balanchine, interview by Bernard Taper, mid-1970s, Taper Tapes.
40. George Balanchine, interview by Jonathan Cott, 1978, sound recording, *MGZTL 4-2685, LPA.
41. Among others who noted this achievement: interview with Xenakis and Balanchine, June 24, 1973, *En Scenes,* accessed via http://fresques.ina.fr/en-scenes/fiche-media/Scenes00967/agon-balanchine-et-xenakis.html.
42. George Balanchine, interview by Bernard Taper, 1973, Taper Tapes.

CHAPTER 25: AGING

1. Barbara Horgan, interview by the author, Apr. 28, 2012; John Clifford, interview by the author, Oct. 4, 2015; Karin von Aroldingen, unpublished memoir, and interviews by the author, June 1, 2012, and Dec. 13, 2015; *Variations pour une Porte et un Soupir,* rehearsal in practice room with Gordon Boelzner, videotaped by Jerome Robbins, c. 20 minutes, 1974, NYCB Archives; "a tremendous and very frightening work": Lincoln Kirstein to Marie Rambert, Jan. 4, 1974, quoted in Duberman, *Worlds of Lincoln Kirstein,* 581.
2. Shared with the author by von Aroldingen.
3. Karin von Aroldingen, unpublished memoir.
4. On Nov. 15, 1982, he would write her a check for $10,000, for what we don't know. Checkbooks, 1968–82, 2420, b. 77, f. 14, MS Thr 411 (2420), George Balanchine Archive, Houghton.
5. This was a fond intimacy overheard after a dinner and conveyed by one of the dancers in an interview by the author, Aug. 8, 2018.
6. Receipts for scalp treatments, on and off from 1969: Bills, b. 73, f. 1, MS Thr 411 (2418), George Balanchine Archive, Houghton.
7. George Balanchine, "The World Is Turning Fast," 1982; songs: autograph manuscripts, manuscript photocopies, printed, undated, b. 56, f. 12, MS Thr 411 (2194), George Balanchine Archive, Houghton. "Dedicated to Karin" is printed above the title of the song.
8. "Russian dacha": b. 39, f. 6, Gold and Fizdale Collection, Peter Jay Sharp Special Collections; Bills, 1964–82, b. 73, f. 10, MS Thr 411 (2418), George Balanchine Archive, Houghton; on his cooking, see Karin von Aroldingen, unpublished memoir; on Southampton, see Barbara Horgan, interview by the author, July 7, 2016; George Tucker (property manager), interview by the author. 34 Canterbury Mews, Southampton, Suffolk County, NY, Court of Record, Deed of Purchase (subject to purchase mortgage of $46,350), dated Sept. 23, 1977.

9. Karin von Aroldingen, unpublished memoir; Dominique Nabokov, interview by the author and photographs, courtesy of Nabokov.
10. D'Amboise Diary, Jan. 2, 1976; Barbara Horgan, interview by the author, Mar. 6, 2013; John Clifford, interview by the author, June 3, 2014; Christine Redpath, interview by the author, June 2, 2016.
11. Farrell, *Holding On to the Air*, 212.
12. Suzanne Farrell to George Balanchine, Nov. 7, 1973, b. 11, MS Thr 411 (583), George Balanchine Archive, Houghton.
13. D'Amboise Diary, June 15, 1974: "Went talked with Bal at great length on his love of Susanne and Zorina and breaking up. 'Susanne was a witch' never give presents let girl give presents to you—when you worship them you lose them—they will not like you they will take take. How I gave diamonds gifts to Susanne wrote poems composed music—a lovely waltz—she took and took—ambition—only wants to dance"; d'Amboise Diary, Dec. 10, 1979: "I walk the Breath to Dorchester—He is wise—we talked of love, greed, Farrell, etc., Pushkin, witches"; d'Amboise Diary, Apr. 18, 1981: "We talked of LOVE and the WITCH in some women. How we still love them."
14. Barbara Horgan wrote to Farrell: "I told him about your arrival, and he said 'fine, fine, fine.' So I guess everything is 'fine, fine, fine.'" Letter dated Oct. 11, 1974, b. 11, MS Thr (583), George Balanchine Archive, Houghton.
15. Suzanne Farrell, interview by the author, Feb. 14, 2017; "That's Pat Neary's mother": Delia Peters, interview by the author, Mar. 31, 2016; pearl pendant: Lourdes Lopez, interview by the author, July 12, 2013; Barbara Horgan, interviews by the author, Mar. 16, 2016, and Oct. 24, 2018; Dianne Chilgren, interview by the author, Sept. 23, 2015; Gail Crisa, interview by the author, Jan. 28, 2017; Maria Calegari, interview by the author, Apr. 9, 2016; correspondence with Suzanne Farrell, b. 11, MS Thr (583), George Balanchine Archive, Houghton; "Isn't it wonderful": Gottlieb, *Avid Reader*, 249. See also Anna Kisselgoff, "Ballet: Miss Farrell Returns in Triumph," *New York Times*, Jan. 18, 1975; "Horgan to Taper," Jan. 2 phone call [undated, probably after 1983], Taper Tapes; microcassette notes on dinner with Jacques d'Amboise, Taper Papers; fol.: Davidova, 1985, and Buckle's notes and letter dated Oct. 30 (year not included), b. 16, Richard Buckle Papers, HRC; notes on interview with Suzanne Farrell, 1983, Taper Tapes.
16. *Who Cares?*: notes on interview with Patricia McBride, July 14, 1983, Taper Tapes; "She's a terrific instrument": Farrell, Suzanne, b. 87, f. 11, (S) *MGZMD 182, Jerome Robbins Personal Papers, LPA, including a page of notes detailing Balanchine's thoughts on Suzanne c. 1975.
17. Barbara Horgan, interview by the author, Oct. 24, 2018; Lincoln Kirstein to Richard Buckle, Sept. 1, 1977, Richard Buckle Papers, HRC.
18. Suzanne Farrell, interview by the author, Feb. 14, 2017; Farrell, *Holding On to the Air*, 234; Bentley, *Costumes by Karinska*. Farrell's phantom waltz partner was Jean-Pierre Bonnefoux, until he was injured and momentarily replaced by her old Béjart partner, Jorge Donn, who happened to be in town.
19. Richard Leach Diary, July 26, 1976, courtesy of the Leach family.
20. Jacques d'Amboise, interview by the author, June 26, 2018.
21. Travel documents accessed via Ancestry.com show Florentine Karp (1885–1987) as being born in Lodz, and entering the United States with her husband (?), Nissen Karp. She is identified as a doctor, age fifty, who is "of the Hebrew race," speaks English and Russian, has "undetermined" citizenship, and has left Le Havre on the SS *Paris* for New York on Apr. 29, 1936; Susan Heller Anderson and David W. Dunlap, "Caviar and Birthday Cake," *New York Times*, June 22, 1985; John Niles (Karp's great-nephew), interview by

the author, Aug. 28, 2016; see Bills, 1964–82, b. 73, f. 4–10, MS Thr 411 (2418), George Balanchine Archive, Houghton, including receipts from Dr. F. Karp. In January 1975, she added 5 mg of Ritalin and 5 mg of Valium. "Berocca-C" and "his Barocco": William Hamilton, interview by the author, Sept. 17, 2015.

22. "My father died": quoted in Vaill, *Somewhere*, 465.
23. Lincoln Kirstein to Richard Buckle, Jan. 26, 1977, Richard Buckle Papers, HRC.
24. W. H. Auden, quoted in Duberman, *Worlds of Lincoln Kirstein*, 580.
25. Barbara Horgan, interview by the author, Aug. 8, 2013.
26. Letter from 1976, b. 4, fol. 64: Danny and Joe Duell, *MGZMD 97, Lincoln Kirstein Papers, LPA.
27. Lincoln Kirstein Memo to "NW" on NYCB, 1973, b. 4, f. 154, (S) *MGZMD 97, Lincoln Kirstein Papers, LPA. Kirstein's estimates in this document of the "dancers in crisis" he hoped to help could be crushing: Lynda Yourth, for example, was an "incurable masochist. . . . What is to be done in this (not very important) case? Nothing"; Frank Ohman, once one of Lincoln's great white hopes, was now deemed "invincibly stupid"; and Allegra Kent had sadly "made every mistake in the Book of Life. . . . Her situation is desperate." For John Clifford, he expressed contempt ("Actually he thinks he's Shirley Temple"). As for Ronnie Bates, he was "very close" to Mr. B but "more of a mechanic and a man who has settled for what he thinks he is grateful for . . . (he's a simple character)."
28. Kirstein Memo to "NW" on NYCB, 1973, b. 4, f. 154, (S) *MGZMD 97, Lincoln Kirstein Papers, LPA.
29. Jacques d'Amboise, interview by the author, June 26, 2018.
30. Frederick Beinecke, interview by the author, Feb. 2, 2015.
31. D'Amboise Diary, Sept. 23, 1981.
32. Lincoln Kirstein, "(Balanchine)," f. 4, and "Balanchine: a fourth dimension," f. 6, (S) *MGZM-Res. Kir L, Lincoln Kirstein Letter and Writings, LPA.
33. Lincoln Kirstein to Richard Buckle, July 30, 1983, Richard Buckle Papers, HRC.
34. D'Amboise Diary, July 31, 1979.
35. Jerome Robbins journal entry, Nov. 1971, quoted in Jowitt, *Jerome Robbins*, 411.
36. Jacques d'Amboise, interview by Bernard Taper, Nov. 7, 1983, Taper Tapes: Jacques added, "We must do this—because of Lincoln. Way out to appease Lincoln."
37. Anna Kisselgoff, *New York Times*, May 13, 1976.
38. Reynolds, *Repertory in Review*, 332–36; Arlene Croce, *New Yorker*, May 31, 1976; Union Jack, b. 10, f. 157, (S) *MGZMD 97, Lincoln Kirstein Papers, LPA; Anna Kisselgoff, *New York Times*, May 13, 1976; Rouben Ter-Arutunian, interview by Joan Kramer, Aug. 23 and 26, 1976, Sept. 8, 9, 21, and 22, 1976, and Oct. 12 and 13, 1976, sound disc, *MGZTL 4-382, LPA; Kirstein, *Union Jack*.
39. Duberman, *Worlds of Lincoln Kirstein*, 591–93; Linda Hamilton, interview by the author, Nov. 7, 2015; Barbara Horgan, interview by the author, Mar. 16, 2016.
40. Gottlieb, *Avid Reader*; Lincoln Kirstein to Marie Rambert, Nov. 30, 1977, Rambert Archive; Duberman, *Worlds of Lincoln Kirstein*, 509; Gillian Attfield, interview by the author, Dec. 11, 2015.
41. Vaill, *Somewhere*, 442–44; Jowitt, *Jerome Robbins*, 420–31.
42. Notes: Poppa Piece, b. 3, f. 1, (S) *MGZMD 182, Jerome Robbins Personal Papers, LPA; Jowitt, *Jerome Robbins*, 424; original handwritten personal notes, 1976 and 1990, b. 3, f. 1-2, (S) *MGZMD 182, Jerome Robbins Personal Papers, LPA.
43. Journals, "Bodrum July-84," 1984, b. 21, f. 10, (S) *MGZMD 182, Jerome Robbins Personal Papers, LPA.
44. Jowitt, *Jerome Robbins*, 428–30; Notes: Recent revival of Balanchine's *Symphonie Con-*

certante, 1983, b. 3, f. 5, (S) *MGZMD 182, Jerome Robbins Personal Papers, LPA; "All the edifaces" and "locks": Vaill, *Somewhere*, 453.

45. Quoted in Vaill, *Somewhere*, 461.
46. Francisco Moncion Diary, 1974–80, personal collection; d'Amboise Diary, 1974–80; Melissa Hayden, interview by the author, May 21, 2005; Christine Redpath, interview by the author, June 2, 2016. Before a performance, Melissa Hayden liked to do barre work with a Woolworth's mirror propped on a ladder, and when she came off stage and things had gone well, she might say, "Honey, now that was dancing."
47. Bentley, *Winter Season*, esp. the introduction; author's memory.
48. George Balanchine's Personal Checkbooks, 1968–82, b. 77, MS Thr (2420), George Balanchine Archive, Houghton: fol. 9: Jan. 17, 1979, Christine Redpath, $1,500; fol. 10: Aug. 8, 1979–Aug. 30, 1979, Christine Redpath Loan, $1,000, and Oct. 15, 1979, Christine Redpath Loan, $1,000.
49. Jacques d'Amboise, interview by Bernard Taper, Nov. 7, 1983, Taper Tapes.
50. Heather Watts, interviews by the author, July 1, 2013; Nov. 5, 12, 14, 18, and 19, 2014; Apr. 26 and June 8, 2016; and Feb. 13, 2018.
51. Merrill Ashley, interviews by the author, Sept. 13, 2012, Feb. 6 and Apr. 12, 2016, and Mar. 3, 2018; Ricky Weiss, interview by the author, June 1, 2005; d'Amboise Diary, Nov. 14, 1978; Jacques d'Amboise, interview by the author, June 1, 2011.
52. Christine Redpath, interview by the author, June 2, 2016; Colleen Neary, interview by the author, Oct. 5, 2015; Adam Lüders, interviews by the author, Aug. 18, 2014, and Nov. 8, 2018; Karin von Aroldingen, interviews by the author, June 1 and Nov. 18, 2012, and Dec. 13, 2015.
53. Balanchine also set up a special class for boys in the school with Stanley Williams. Lincoln noted his "abruptly manifested" interest in training boys. Duberman, *Worlds of Lincoln Kirstein*, 596.
54. Mel Tomlinson, interview by the author, Aug. 1 and Sept. 6, 2015; Tomlinson, *Beyond My Dreams*.
55. William Hamilton, interview by the author, Sept. 15, 2015; Clay Risen, "William G. Hamilton, Doctor to Dancers, Is Dead at 90," *New York Times*, Apr. 13, 2022.
56. George Balanchine, interview by Jack Natkin, July 1974, sound recording, *MGZTL 4-1439, LPA, on *Coppélia*; Lincoln Kirstein to Marie Rambert, June 1, 1974, Rambert Archive; Christine Redpath, home movies, 1972–78, including rehearsals of *Coppélia* with Balanchine; Lincoln Kirstein to Richard Buckle, Aug. 18, 1975, Richard Buckle Papers, HRC: "Balanchine is very well and full of plans for big ballets, if and when we can find money. He is now speaking of a SLEEPING BEAUTY since he has found a designer who thinks he can do tricks with projections which really work, and we can have a good visual production without heavy built pieces"; Perrault's *Sleeping Beauty*: Balanchine Book: Notes on Tapes and Interviews, b. 45, Richard Buckle Papers, HRC.
57. Farrell, *Holding On to the Air*; Adam Lüders, interview by the author, Aug. 8, 2018; Christine Redpath, home movies, 1976, including Balanchine rehearsing Farrell and d'Amboise in *Don Quixote*.

CHAPTER 26: TIME TO GO!

1. Giroud, *Nicolas Nabokov*, 405; Dominique Nabokov, interview by the author, 2021.
2. Edith Langner, interview by the author, Mar. 14, 2014; notes on interview with and letter from Edith Langner, Jan. 4, 1983, Taper Papers; Travel Itineraries, 1964–78, b. 106, MS

Thr 411 (2777), George Balanchine Archive, Houghton; rubber plants: Bernard Taper, "Balanchine's Will," *Ballet Review* 23, no. 2 (1995): 29.

3. Desk calendars, b. 109, MS Thr 411 (2810), George Balanchine Archive, Houghton: Langner was the first appointment on his calendar, Nov. 1, 1978. (The author was a patient of Dr. Langner in the 1970s.)
4. D'Amboise Diary, Sept. 6, 1980: "The Doc lady of Bal [Edith Langner] joined us for dinner, she is very very bright personable and says all the right things—claims to b. 36."
5. Taper, "Balanchine's Will," 29–36; Barbara Horgan, interview by the author, Dec. 11, 2015. Horgan went to Randal R. Craft Jr., a Lincoln recruit to the board, who recommended Theodore M. Sysol.
6. Taper, "Balanchine's Will," 29–36; Bills, 1964–82, b. 73, f. 10, MS Thr 411 (2418), George Balanchine Archive, Houghton. Bills from Haight, Gardner, Poor and Havens, the firm that consulted on Balanchine's last will and testament, show meetings from Mar. 23, 1977, through May 25, 1978. The will was dated May 25, 1978, and executed on June 25, 1978, before the required witnesses. Copyright, Checkbooks, 1968–82, b. 77, f. 11–12 and 14, MS Thr 411 (2420), George Balanchine Archive, Houghton:
   July 1, 1980: Register of copyrights (10 ballets) $100
   July 23, 1980: Register of copyrights (8 ballets) $80
   Dec. 2, 1981: Register of copyrights (4 ballets) $40
   Dec. 7, 1981: Register of copyrights (*Nutcracker*) $10
   Dec. 10, 1981: Register of copyrights (*Coppélia*) $10
   Nov. 17, 1982: Register of copyrights (*Mozartiana, La Valse*) $20
7. Balanchine had already given *Meditation* to Farrell some years before.
8. The will was complex and specified, for example, foreign and domestic rights. Its implications played out over the years to come and have been simplified here to emphasize the personal and emotional thrust; on Andrei's reaction, see Keti Balanchivadze, interviews by the author, Nov. 8 and 11, 2017.
9. Eglevsky's widow was also named for three minor works.
10. The Benesh expert was Jurg Lanzrein; Guest, *Dance Notation.* The choreographer Hanya Holm took her dances for *Kiss Me, Kate,* recorded in Labanotation by Ann Hutchinson, to the copyright office and was granted copyright. Balanchine did the same with a "similarly notated script" of *Symphony in C* but it was first rejected because it had no story and then later, after a fake story was added, was accepted. Correspondence with Ann Hutchinson Guest, 1964–84, b. 15, MS Thr 411 (739), George Balanchine Archive, Houghton; John Martin, "The Dance: Copyright, Hanya Holm's Works Are First to be Registered," *New York Times,* Mar. 30, 1952.
11. Author interviews with Barbara Horgan, Pat Neary, Christine Redpath, Ricky Weiss, Merrill Ashley, and John Clifford, among others; Charles Engell France, "A Conversation with John Clifford," 3–33; Barbara Horgan to Jerome Robbins, Sept. 30, 1973 (from Park Hotel, Meinekestr., Berlin), b. 94, f. 2, (S) *MGZMD 182, Jerome Robbins Personal Papers, LPA.
12. Merrill Brockway, interview by the author, Jan. 29, 2013; Judy Kinberg, interview by the author, Oct. 10, 2018.
13. Balanchine would also work with Brockway's colleague Emile Ardolino on a film production of his ballet *Porte et un soupir,* to music by Ravel. Archival filming of performances was against union rules until 1981.
14. "Do mistake waltz": Christine Redpath, interview by the author, June 2, 2016; "He's here for posterity": Heather Watts, interview by the author, Nov. 14, 2014.

15. Jacques d'Amboise, interview by the author, June 26, 2018.
16. Lincoln Kirstein to Marie Rambert, 1980, quoted in Duberman, *Worlds of Lincoln Kirstein,* 596. The cuts to *Apollo* were made in 1979.
17. Quoted in Vaill, *Somewhere,* 465.
18. Kay Mazzo in *Remembering Mr. B,* 70.
19. Linda Winer, "Baryshnikov's Leap Changes Ballet World," *Chicago Tribune,* May 7, 1978; Mikhail Baryshnikov in *Remembering Mr. B,* 60, and interview by the author, Oct. 5, 2021, and several subsequent conversations by phone.
20. Anna Kisselgoff, "Ballet: A Cut Apollo," *New York Times,* May 3, 1979.
21. Pushkin, b. 18: M. Baryshnikov, Richard Buckle Papers, HRC; Richard Leach Diary, July 19, 1978; Peter, Lee, and Chris Leach, interview by the author, August 8, 2015 (at River Run). I am grateful to the Leaches for sharing scrapbooks, diaries, letters, and memories, as well as showing me the home and the cottage where Balanchine stayed.
22. Mikhail Baryshnikov, interview by the author, Nov. 26, 2021.
23. "Dance in America: Balanchine—*Prodigal* Rehearsal," 1977 [later?], video recording, *MGZIDF 29, Mikhail Baryshnikov Archives, LPA; *Prodigal Son,* Main Hall Rehearsal with Karin von Aroldingen, Mikhail Baryshnikov, and George Balanchine, 1978, film, 28 minutes, courtesy of Serapio Walton.
24. Farrell, *Holding On to the Air,* 241–42; "I didn't need": Suzanne Farrell, interview by the author, Feb. 14, 2017.
25. Balanchine restaged the *Walpurgisnacht Ballet* from Gounod's *Faust,* which he had originally made in 1975 at the Paris Opera, on Suzanne Farrell and the NYCB in 1980.
26. Bulgakov, *Master and Margarita* (Burgin and Tiernan O'Connor trans.), 308. Richard Pevear and Larissa Volokhonsky translate this as "It's Time!"
27. "You're free!": Bulgakov, *Master and Margarita* (Pevear and Volokhonsky, trans.), 382; "anxious, needled memory": Bulgakov, 384.
28. Jacques d'Amboise, interview by the author, May 19, 2012.
29. George Balanchine, interview by Jonathan Cott, 1978, sound recording, *MGZTL 4-2685, LPA.
30. William Hamilton, interview by the author, Sept. 17, 2015; Edith Langner, interviews by the author, Mar. 14, 2014, Apr. 22, 2015, and Oct. 19, 2016; notes on an interview with and letter from Edith Langner, Jan. 4, 1983, Taper Papers.
31. George Balanchine, interview by Bernard Taper, early 1970s, Taper Tapes.
32. Desk calendars, 1974–82, b. 109, MS Thr 411 (2810), George Balanchine Archive, Houghton: Balanchine's schedule at the time, meticulously kept by Horgan, indicates an extended hospital stay: June 7–July 4, 1979, NYU/H [Hospital]; July 5–11, NYUH-CCU; July 12–15, NYUH; and on July 15, home. Taper gives the surgery date as June 19.
33. Lincoln Kirstein to Richard Buckle, June 21, 1979, Richard Buckle Papers, HRC.
34. Tanaquil Le Clercq to George Balanchine, undated, b. 20, MS Thr 411 (1031), George Balanchine Archive, Houghton.
35. Shipment to Ephraim Glassman ordered on July 3, 1979: Bills, 1964–82, b. 73, f. 11, MS Thr 411 (2418), George Balanchine Archive, Houghton.
36. William Hamilton to the author, Oct. 30, 2016.
37. "wedding thoughts": Chernaik, *Schumann,* 85, 252; "My Clara" and "I sometimes feel": Schumann, *Letters of Robert Schumann,* 181 (letter dated Feb. 6, 1938).
38. Wayne Heisler Jr., "Choreographing Schumann," in Kok and Tunbridge, *Rethinking Schumann,* 341.
39. Lincoln Kirstein to Marie Rambert, Apr. 8, 1980, Rambert Archive.
40. "a space in the past": Anna Kisselgoff, "Schumann Ballet's Ideas Revealed by Balanchine,"

New York Times, June 28, 1980, 19; "Karen Horney Clinic": Perry Silvey, interview by the author, Feb. 14, 2021.

41. Rouben Ter-Arutunian, interview by Joan Kramer, Aug. 23 and 26, Sept. 8, 9, 21, and 22, and Oct. 12 and 13, 1976; sound disc, *MGZTL 4-382, LPA:

    > I find it interesting to be able to present the stage space, which is a given space after all the dimensions once the curtain goes up are given, we know them. . . . But I always wish to suggest that there is a beyond, that it leads to an escape of an indetermined distance, to break the form, break the limits of that stage and create a mystery that you don't know where it comes from and you don't know what it is. I hope that a project Balanchine has in mind will materialize and I hope to be able to present a solution with this color, which I think it demands.

42. Kay Mazzo was pregnant and soon replaced by Sally Leland, a dancer of feeling and freedom. When she protested that he might need someone with a stronger technique, he took her head in his hands and assured her that the others were too young and inexperienced; "it needs *you.*" Sally Leland, interview by the author, Apr. 6, 2014.
43. D'Amboise Diary, May 14, 1980.
44. Farrell, *Holding On to the Air,* 248–49.
45. "Stop her": Heather Watts, interview by the author, Oct. 16, 2014; "a bigger world": Kay Mazzo, interview by the author, July 13, 2015.
46. "Here comes Clive": Heather Watts, interview by the author, Oct. 16, 2014; "You have to be strange" and "I always like": interview with George Balanchine by Kisselgoff: "Schumann Ballet's Ideas," *New York Times,* June 28, 1980, 19; Jacques d'Amboise, interview by the author, 2014.
47. D'Amboise Diary, June 19, 1980.

CHAPTER 27: THE MORTAL END

1. Several dancers told me about Balanchine's Christ imagery, which Jacques d'Amboise also recorded repeatedly in his diary in these years.
2. Arlene Croce, "Tchaikovsky," *New Yorker,* June 29, 1981, 386–87, points out that the festival began with an orchestral medley, no dancers, largely consisting of pieces about death: the cantilena over Juliet's bier from *Romeo and Juliet*, Lise's aria from *Pique Dame* as she stands over the canal ready to throw herself to her death, Lensky's aria before the duel in *Onegin.*
3. The music was Tchaikovsky (Suite no. 4, op. 61 [*Mozartiana*], 1887, which was based on Mozart's Gigue in G Major [K. 574]; Minuet in D Major [K. 355]; the motet in *Ave verum corpus* [K. 618]; and *10 Variations on "Les hommes pieusement" from "La rencontre imprévue" by Gluck* [K. 455]) (see balanchine.org); Volkov, *Balanchine's Tchaikovsky,* 112–13; Farrell, *Holding On to the Air,* 253–56; Suzanne Farrell, interview by the author, Mar. 17, 2016, and Feb. 14, 2017; Maria Calegari, interview by the author, Apr. 23, 2017.
4. "I don't care if it is illegal" and a full account can be found in Bentley, *Winter Season;* Taper, *Balanchine,* 375–77; Paul Boos in *Remembering Mr. B,* 65; d'Amboise Diary, Dec. 22, 1980:

    > At Union meeting vote turned down the management contract 25 to 23, then another vote 26 to 18 to empower the committee to strike. 2 week deadline. Bal when he heard in Betty's office with 3 members of union and the committee there called them all PIGS—I talked to him later. He said he did a "Sarah Bernhardt" Flo owes me 14,000, 18,000 from others etc etc SAB Scholarships and he went on its his co his ballets the B[oard] of Directors exist for him—he would have a meeting of all dancers (he refused to accept the vote of the few) and tell them to vote freely and if they wanted to to go—He would form another co.

5. Winthrop Knowlton, interview by the author, Apr. 1, 2015; Barbara Horgan, interview by the author, Sept. 3, 2014; Lincoln Kirstein to Richard Buckle, May 14, 1980, Richard Buckle Papers, HRC: "Balanchine went bonkers and contributed our opening-night receipts to buy bullet-proof vests for the City police. The Mayor came, thanked him (us), and left before being detained by much of the program; today we are having a free program for school-children. This is all Balanchine's politics, and maybe it is rather astute."
6. On Darci Kistler, see especially d'Amboise Diary, Nov. 14, 1982, as well as author's personal observations and interviews with dancers.
7. Mel Tomlinson, interview by the author, Aug. 1 and Sept. 6, 2015.
8. Performance date May 9, 1981—the author was in these rehearsals; Kendall, *Balanchine and the Lost Muse*, 5–7, 141–42.
9. Marika Molnar, interview by the author, Dec. 20, 2015.
10. Heather Watts, interview by the author, Jan. 28, 2021.
11. Jacques d'Amboise, interview by the author, May 22, 2012.
12. Umbrella: notes on interview with Carolyn George d'Amboise, May 1983, cassette, Taper Tapes; soldiers: Barbara Horgan, interview by the author, Mar. 16, 2016; on Balanchine's declining health: Barbara Horgan and Bernard Taper, undated (c. 1983/84), Taper Tapes; William Hamilton, interview by the author, Sept. 17, 2015; Edith J. Langner, interviews by the author, Mar. 14, 2014, Apr. 22, 2015, Nov. 19, 2016, and May 9, 2018; Jacques d'Amboise, interview by the author, June 26, 2018; desk calendars, 1974–82, b. 109, MS Thr 411 (2810), George Balanchine Archive, Houghton.
13. Barbara Horgan, interview by the author, Dec. 11, 2015; Gillian Attfield, interview by the author, Dec. 11, 2015; Robert Gottlieb, "Balanchine's Dream," *Vanity Fair*, Dec. 1998, 270–97; Schell in Saratoga: Buckle, *Balanchine*, 312–27.
14. D'Amboise Diary, Apr. 5, 1983.
15. Lincoln Kirstein to Richard Buckle, Mar. 25, 1983, Richard Buckle Papers, HRC.
16. D'Amboise, *I Was a Dancer*, 319.
17. Duberman, *Worlds of Lincoln Kirstein*, 601–3; d'Amboise, *I Was a Dancer*, 339–40; Gillian Attfield, interview by the author, Dec. 11, 2015. Attfield claimed she had proof of Lincoln's ambition but did not surrender it.
18. Quoted in Jowitt, *Jerome Robbins*, 462.
19. Lincoln Kirstein to Richard Buckle, Mar. 25, 1983, Richard Buckle Papers, HRC.
20. "At that point": Martins quoted in Taper interview with Peter Martins, 1983, Taper Papers; "I was there!": Barbara Horgan, interview by the author, Dec. 11, 2015; one of the board members: Gillian Attfield, interview by the author, Dec. 11, 2015 (the other board member was Orville Schell, deceased); no one else seemed to know: for example, Schell said he had pushed Balanchine in Saratoga the summer before, to no avail, Buckle, *Balanchine*, 312–27.
21. D'Amboise Diary, Jan. 28, 1982; Karin von Aroldingen, interview by the author, Dec. 13, 2015.
22. Taper, *Balanchine*, 381.
23. Small stool: Linda Hamilton, interview by the author, Oct. 8, 2015; "I changed it!": Vaill, *Somewhere*, 475; "Only I know what to do": Zorina, *Zorina*, 299.
24. John Taras finished *Persephone*; "like an Easter icon": Jonathan Watts, interview by the author, Sept. 12, 2014; Kermit Love sent Richard Buckle sketches that Balanchine had made for the ballet: "I am enclosing a xerox of the two drawings George did in a meeting with me, to suggest the positioning for scenes, dancers, and singers in *Persephone*. As you probably know, this was the last major work that George conceived, and it was a labor of love for both of us." Balanchine's drawings are messy, including large groupings indicated

in squiggly lines, not figures, with a huge figure at the center wearing flowing robes. One of Kermit's own drawings shows a huge winged creature low to the ground, wing spanning the whole stage. Kermit Love, Balanchine Book: Notes on Tapes and Interviews, b. 45, and b. 18, fol.: Kermit, July 21, 1986, Richard Buckle Papers, HRC; Mel Tomlinson, interview by the author, Sept. 6, 2015.

25. Zorina, *Zorina*, 300.
26. There is a June 17, 1982, receipt for a June 9 delivery: Bills, 1964–82, b. 73, f. 14, MS Thr 411 (2418), George Balanchine Archive, Houghton.
27. The cataract operation took place on Aug. 16, 1982. In a journal entry on Aug. 24, 1982 (in Vaill, *Somewhere*, 481), Jerome Robbins quotes Balanchine as saying, "My legs won't hold me up—no muscle—some performers work from a chair—not me—I must show them"; Jowitt, *Jerome Robbins*, 457–58.
28. Phone book, undated, b. 110, MS Thr 411 (2816), George Balanchine Archive, Houghton. Stuffed into the back of the phone book, along with other notes, were two cards, one that had arrived with flowers—"To our dear Mr. B. With all of our love, Your Girls, Diana, Catherine, Wilhelmina, Renee, Jeiu [*illegible*]"—and a small white card: "So Happy to know your fine! Much Love, Maria and Buzz." The phone book also includes a loose, stained, rose-colored paper fragment in someone else's hand: "I, that orgastic self glorification the ravenous raging self of erotic fantasy and adolescent day dreams of power when talent and moral intelligence fail them."
29. Marika Molnar, interview by the author, Dec. 20, 2015; Barbara Horgan, interview by the author, Nov. 30, 2016; Karin von Aroldingen, unpublished memoir.
30. Bills, 1982, b. 73, f. 14, MS Thr 411 (2418), George Balanchine Archive, Houghton: Morgan Guaranty Trust Co., where Balanchine had an account, signed power of attorney to Barbara, in addition to his accountant, Albert Ziegler, who already had it, on October 29, 1982; desk calendars, 1974–84, b. 109, MS Thr (2810), George Balanchine Archive, Houghton.
31. D'Amboise Diary, Dec. 1, 1982; notes on interview with Carolyn George d'Amboise, May 1983, cassette, Taper Tapes.
32. Jacques d'Amboise, interview by the author, May 22, 2012.
33. Barbara Horgan and Bernard Taper, undated (c. 1983/84), Taper Tapes; Barbara Horgan, interviews by the author, Aug. 12, 2013, and June 23, 2015; Merrill Ashley, interview by the author, Feb. 6, 2016; d'Amboise Diary, Dec. 30, 1982; Karin von Aroldingen, unpublished memoir.
34. Natalia Nabokov, interview by John Taras and Richard Buckle, John Taras Collection, NYCB Archives.
35. Richard Leach Diary, Feb. 6, 1983.
36. Helen Schatiloff, interview by the author, Feb. 27, 2017.
37. *Remembering Mr. B*, 30; Mikhail Baryshnikov, interview by the author, Nov. 5, 2021.
38. Barbara Horgan, interview by the author, July 7, 2016; Richard Moredock, interview by the author, Mar. 2, 2016; Wilhelmina Frankfurt, interview by the author, Apr. 6, 2016.
39. Volkov's Shostakovich book claims to contain pages the composer approved in writing, but scholars have shown that they were all previously published—and misrepresented by Volkov as verbatim conversations *with him*. See Brown, *Shostakovich Casebook*.
40. Jacques d'Amboise, interview by the author, May 22, 2012; Barbara Horgan, interview by the author, n.d.; Buckle, *Balanchine*, 312–27, especially 316.
41. Wilhemina Frankfurt, interview by the author, June 17, 2013, and Apr. 6, 2016; Linda Hamilton, interview by the author, Nov. 7, 2015; Judith Friedman, interview by the author, Jan. 29, 2015, among others.

42. Calendar: d'Amboise Diary, Dec. 26, 1983; crucifix: Zorina, *Zorina*, 301–2; Rev. Adrian Ouellette, interview by the author, Sept. 21, 2015. After Balanchine's death, Horgan gave this cross to Father Adrian, and he wears it with his own cross.
43. D'Amboise Diary, Dec. 26, 30, and 31, 1982, Jan. 1 and 12, 1983, and Mar. 31, 1983; Swiss clinics: Danilova, *Choura;* Barbara Horgan, c. 1983/84, Taper Tapes; "undignified exit": Letter from Tanaquil Le Clercq to Pat Lousada, courtesy of Lousada; Prusiner, *Madness and Memory*.
44. D'Amboise Diary, Jan. 30, 1983; Andrei Kramarevsky, interview by the author, Feb. 4, 2016.
45. Lincoln Kirstein to Richard Buckle, Apr. 20, 1983, Richard Buckle Papers, HRC.
46. Press releases, 1983, b. 110, MS Thr 411 (2817), George Balanchine Archive, Houghton.
47. Barbara Horgan, interview by the author, Dec. 11, 2015.
48. Lincoln Kirstein to Richard Buckle, Mar. 25, 1983, Richard Buckle Papers, HRC. See also Duberman, *Worlds of Lincoln Kirstein*, 586–610.
49. Horgan, interview by the author, June 23, 2015.
50. Balanchine may also have met him at Doubrovska's funeral in 1980; letter from Lincoln Kirstein to Anne and Sid Bass, Dec. 20, 1982, courtesy of Anne Bass.
51. Rev. Adrian Ouellette, interview by the author, Oct. 19, 2015.
52. Richard Leach Diary, Feb. 6, 1983.

CHAPTER 28: FUNERAL MARCH

1. Andrei Kramarevsky, interview by the author, Feb. 4, 2016; Delia Peters, interview by the author, Mar. 13, 2016.
2. Engagement calendar/diaries, b. 6, f. 31, (S) *MGZMD 123, Lincoln Kirstein Papers, LPA.
3. Jennifer Dunning, "Performance Pays Tribute to Balanchine," *New York Times,* May 1, 1983; the author was present.
4. Farrell, *Holding On to the Air,* 266.
5. Heather Watts, interview by the author, June 8, 2016.
6. Keti Balanchivadze, interview by the author, Nov. 11, 2017.
7. Sympathy notes, f. 1–4, b. 108, and funeral service, May 2, 1983, b. 108, MS Thr 411 (2803) and (2797), George Balanchine Archive, Houghton.
8. When Balanchine's relatives in Georgia found out in the early 1990s that the brain had been removed, they were furious. Shouldn't the family have been consulted? Did "they" have the right to desanctify the body, just like that? Why did it matter what he died of? Keti Balanchivadze, interviews by the author, Nov. 8 and 11, 2017.
9. Prusiner, *Madness and Memory;* Stanley B. Prusiner, interview by the author, Oct. 21, 2016.
10. Rowland, *NINDS at 50,* 201; with thanks to the late Dr. Rowland for his insights.
11. Dr. James E. Goldman, interview by the author, Jan. 30, 2017.
12. Wilhelmina Frankfurt, interview by the author, Apr. 6, 2016.
13. Rev. Adrian Ouellette, interview by the author, Sept. 21, 2015.
14. Prince Vladimir Kirillovich Galitzine, warden of the Synodal Cathedral of the Sign, interview by the author, Mar. 5, 2017, and several phone conversations.
15. Awards, 1966–83, f. 2, b. 105, MS Thr 411 (2769), George Balanchine Archive, Houghton: Presidential Medal of Freedom, including an Apr. 13 letter from Ronald Reagan about the medal, accepted on Balanchine's behalf by Farrell, thanking Balanchine for "the wonderful books which Miss Farrell brought me on your behalf"; also telegrams an-

nouncing the award dated Feb. 25, 1983, and later inviting Balanchine to a luncheon for the Medal of Freedom recipients at the White House, by the southwest gate: "Mr. George Balanchine will please present this card at the Southwest gate The White House. Not Transferable."

16. Buckle, *Balanchine*, 312–25; Anna Kisselgoff, "Dance View: The Soviets Acknowledge Balanchine's Place in Ballet," *New York Times*, July 22, 1984; death photos taken by John Taras, John Taras Collection, NYCB Archives.
17. Yuszczuk and Nicoloff, "An Interview with George Balanchine," 10–14.
18. D'Amboise Diary, May 1, 1983.
19. Duberman, *Worlds of Lincoln Kirstein*, 599.
20. Steven Caras, interview by the author, June 4, 2021.
21. Debra Austin, interview by the author, Sept. 9, 2015.
22. Barbara Horgan, interview by the author, Sept. 3, 2014.
23. Randall Bourscheidt, interview by the author, May 13, 2015; Jennifer Dunning, "Friends Crowd Church for Balanchine Funeral," *New York Times*, May 4, 1983; Aidan Mooney, interview by the author, June 24, 2015.
24. Richard Leach Diary, May 3, 1983.
25. Buckle, *Balanchine*, 325.
26. Anne Bass, interview by the author, Dec. 3, 2012.
27. Helen Strilec Schatiloff, interview by the author, Mar. 5, 2017; Vladimir Kirillovich Galitzine, interview by the author, Mar. 5, 2017.
28. Jerome Robbins journal entry, Nov. 1971, quoted in Jowitt, *Jerome Robbins*, 457–58.
29. Notes on interview with Hugo Fiorato, June 16, 1983, Taper Papers.
30. Barbara Horgan to John Benson, Jan. 23, 1984, and May 23, 1983, courtesy of John Benson; John Benson interview by the author, Mar. 14, 2017; Kendall, *Balanchine and the Lost Muse*, 44; documents, b. 109, MS Thr 411 (2800), George Balanchine Archive, Houghton.
31. D'Amboise Diary, May 3, 1983; d'Amboise, *I Was a Dancer*, 356–57.
32. Lincoln Kirstein to Anne and Sid Bass, Dec. 20, 1982, courtesy of Anne Bass.
33. Farrell, *Holding On to the Air*, 266.
34. Ted Rogers, interview by the author, Feb. 8, 2015.
35. Randal Craft, interview by the author, Apr. 4, 2017; Daniel Daniels, interview by the author. The outside consultant was Colleen McMahon, see her essay, "Choreography and Copyright," *Art & the Law* 3, no. 8 (1978), 1–2.
36. Taper, "Balanchine's Will," 36; Paul Epstein, interview by the author, Oct. 16 and 20, and Nov. 14, 2014; Lincoln Kirstein to Anne and Sid Bass, May 18, 1983, courtesy of Anne Bass: "The legal condition of Balanchine's legacy in choreographic works is simply something with which the IRS has never had to deal."
37. Barbara Horgan, interview by the author, Mar. 7, 2017; Randal Craft, interview by the author, Apr. 4, 2017.
38. Barbara Horgan, interview by the author, Dec. 11, 2015; Taper, "Balanchine's Will," 33–36.
39. George Balanchine, interview by Bernard Taper, 1973, Taper Tapes.

CHAPTER 29: ADAGIO LAMENTOSO

1. "Tell me where this light comes from": Anna Kisselgoff, "City Ballet: 'Pathétique' with Balanchine 'Adagio,'" *New York Times*, June 16, 1981; Schimmel, *Mystical Dimensions*, 144. With thanks to Michael Sells for his help in understanding the parable: the sheikh who

interrogated the boy in this story is Junayd of Baghdad, one of the most famous early Islamic mystics, many of whom were schooled by humble people, in some cases, a young woman maidservant.

2. Paul Kolnik, interview by the author, Aug. 20, 2015.
3. Interview with George Balanchine by Kisselgoff, "Schumann Ballet's Ideas," *New York Times*, June 28, 1980, 19; Jacques d'Amboise, interviews by the author, 2011–18.
4. Wiley, *Tchaikovsky*, 345.
5. Some critics also see in the first movement, and in the *Adagio Lamentoso*, rhythmic references to the sixth ode from the Canon of the Orthodox memorial service. Wiley, *Tchaikovsky*, 430:

    Where are the passions of this earth?
    Where are the dreamings of the moment?
    Where is the gold and silver? Where is the host of servants? And fame?
    All is dust, all is ashes, all is a shadow.

6. By some accounts, the ballet was performed twice, although the first time was almost certainly a dress rehearsal, when a sliver of light seeped in at the end. With this ballet, Balanchine could not compromise, so for the premiere on the closing night of the Tchaikovsky Festival, the theater was checked and double-checked to extinguish even the smallest source of light.
7. Jerome Robbins journal entry, 1981, quoted in Jowitt, *Jerome Robbins*, 451; Heather Watts, interview by the author, June 8, 2016; Carol Divet, interview by the author, July 27, 2016; Cathy Morris, interview by the author, Feb. 1, 2021; Paul Kolnik, interview by the author, Aug. 20, 2015; Anna Kisselgoff, interview by the author, Sept. 9, 2016; Renee Estópinal, Wilhelmina Frankfurt, Marjory Spohn, Cathy "Cate" Morris, and Susan Gluck, interviews by the author, June 17, 2013; Adam Lüders, interview by the author, Nov. 8, 2018; Frank Lavoia, interview by the author, Sept. 30, 2016; Stephanie Saland, interview by the author, Jan. 22, 2021; Judith Fugate, interview by the author, Jan. 23, 2021; Richard Roud,"Where Angels Feared Not at All to Tread," *The Guardian*, July 2, 1981, 10; Claudia Roth Pierpont, "Balanchine's Romanticism," *Ballet Review* 12, no. 2 (1984): 7–17; Kisselgoff, "City Ballet," *New York Times*, June 16, 1981; Poznansky, *Tchaikovsky*; Richard Taruskin, "Pathetic Symphonist," *New Republic*, Feb. 6, 1995; Volkov, *Balanchine's Tchaikovsky*, 226; Buckle, *Balanchine*, 309; Wiley, *Tchaikovsky*; Symphony no. 6 ("Pathétique") performance on stage by the NYCB on the final evening of its Tchaikovsky Festival, June 14, 1981, electronic resource, *MGZIDF 7032, LPA.
8. An effect achieved by the men beneath it doing push-ups. At the end of the dance, the orchestra lights remained up until the candle went out—music, light, and life extinguished at the same moment in time.

CREDITS AND PERMISSIONS

Grateful acknowledgment is made to the following for permission to use the following materials:

Christopher d'Amboise on behalf of the Estate of Jacques d'Amboise: Excerpts from published and unpublished writings of Jacques d'Amboise, including, but not limited to, letters, interviews, and notes. Used by permission of Christopher d'Amboise on behalf of the Estate of Jacques d'Amboise.

The George Balanchine Trust: Excerpts from published and unpublished writings of George Balanchine, including, but not limited to, letters, interviews, and notes, © The George Balanchine Trust. BALANCHINE is a trademark of The George Balanchine Trust. Used by permission of The George Balanchine Trust.

The New York Public Library for the Performing Arts: Excerpts from published and unpublished writings of Lincoln Kirstein, including, but not limited to, letters, interviews, and notes, contained in the Lincoln Kirstein papers housed at the Jerome Robbins Dance Division, The New York Public Library for the Performing Arts.

The Robbins Rights Trust: Excerpts from published and unpublished writings of Jerome Robbins, including, but not limited to, letters, interviews, and notes, copyright © Jerome Robbins. Used by permission of The Robbins Rights Trust.

PHOTO INSERT 1

Page 1: Top: © St. Petersburg State Museum of Theatre and Music. **Center:** Courtesy of Art Palace of Georgia. **Bottom:** Courtesy of Ketevan Balanchivadze. **Page 2: Top:** © St. Petersburg State Museum of Theatre and Music. BALANCHINE is a trademark of The George Balanchine Trust. **Center:** With the permission of Richard Buckle, Esq. CBE. Harry Ransom Center, The University of Texas at Austin. **Bottom:** Courtesy of Ketevan Balanchivadze. BALANCHINE is a trademark of The George Balanchine Trust. **Page 3: Top, center, and bottom:** © St. Petersburg State Museum of Theatre and Music. **Page 4: Top and bottom:** © St. Petersburg State Museum of Theatre and Music. **Center:** © The State Museum of Political History of Russia. **Page 5: Top:** © St. Petersburg State Museum of Theatre and Music. BALANCHINE is a trademark of The George Balanchine Trust. **Center:** © St. Petersburg State Museum of Theatre and Music. **Bottom:** From the private archive of the family of K. Ya. Goleizovsky. Photo Courtesy of Dr. Nicoletta Misler. **Page 6: Top:** *Étude*, Choreography by George Balanchine, © The George Balanchine Trust. Courtesy New York City Ballet Archives. BALANCHINE is a trademark of The George Balanchine Trust. **Center:** Courtesy of Robert Greskovic. BALANCHINE is a trademark of The George Balanchine Trust. **Bottom:** Library of Congress, Music Division. **Page 7: Top:** Courtesy New York City Ballet Archives. BALANCHINE is a trademark of The George Balanchine Trust. **Center:** *La Chatte,* Choreography by George Balanchine, © The George Balanchine Trust. Courtesy New York City Ballet Archives. **Bottom:** *Jack in the Box*, Choreography by George Balanchine, © The George Balanchine Trust. © Man Ray 2015 Trust / Artists Rights Society (ARS), NY / ADAGP, Paris 2022. Courtesy New York City Ballet Archives. **Page 8: Top:** *Apollon Musagète,* Choreography by George Balanchine, © The George Balanchine Trust. Photo by Sasha/Hulton Archive/ Getty Images. **Center:** *L'Errante*, Choreography by George Balanchine, © The George Balanchine Trust. Courtesy New York City Ballet Archives. **Bottom left:** *Mozartiana,* Choreography by George Balanchine, © The George Balanchine Trust. Bibliothèque-Musée de l'Opéra National de Paris, Bibliothèque nationale de France. **Bottom right:** Private Collection © The Lucian Freud Archive. All Rights Reserved 2022/Bridgeman Images. **Page 9: Top:** Courtesy New York City Ballet Archives. BALANCHINE is a trademark of The George Balanchine Trust. **Center:** Alfred Eisenstaedt/The LIFE Picture Collection/Shutterstock. BALANCHINE is a trademark of The George Balanchine Trust. **Bottom:** Henri Cartier-Bresson © Fondation Henri Cartier-Bresson/Magnum Photos. BALANCHINE is a trademark of The George Balanchine Trust. **Page 10: Top:** *Serenade,* Choreography by George Balanchine, © The George Balanchine Trust. MS Thr 411 (2471), Harvard Theatre Collection, Houghton Library, Harvard University. **Center right:** Photo by Carl Van Vechten, © Van Vechten Trust. Carl Van Vechten Papers. **Center left:** Yale Collection of American Literature, Beinecke Rare Book and Manuscript Library used with permission of The George Platt Lynes Estate. Courtesy New York City Ballet Archives. **Bottom:** MS Thr 632 (55), Harvard Theatre Collection, Houghton Library, Harvard University. BALANCHINE is a trademark of The George Balanchine Trust. **Page 11: Top left:** Everett Collection. **Top right:** Everett Collection. BALANCHINE is a trademark of The George Balanchine Trust. **Bottom left:** © *Cabin in the Sky,* 1940, 2022. Collection Center for Creative Photography, University of Arizona © The Heirs of W. Eugene Smith. BALANCHINE is a trademark of The George Balanchine Trust. **Bottom right:** Photo by George Konig/Keystone Features/Getty Images. **Page 12: Top:** Used with permission of The George Platt Lynes Estate. Donald Windham and Sandy Campbell Papers. Yale Collection of American Literature, Beinecke Rare Book and Manuscript Library. BALANCHINE is a trademark of The George Balanchine Trust. **Center:** Jerome Robbins Dance Division, The New York Public Library for the Performing Arts. **Bottom:** *The Four Temperaments,* Choreography by George Balanchine, © The George Balanchine Trust. Photo by Carl Van Vechten, © Van Vechten Trust. Jerome Robbins Dance Division, The New York Public Library for the Performing Arts. **Page 13: Top left:** AP Photo/John Rooney. BALANCHINE is a trademark of The George Balanchine Trust. **Top right:** *Orpheus,* Choreography by George Balanchine, © The George Balanchine Trust. Photo by Roger-Viollet via Getty Images. **Bottom left:** *Orpheus,* Choreography by George Balanchine, © The George Balanchine Trust. Courtesy New York City Ballet Archives. **Bottom right:** *Firebird,* Choreography by George Balanchine, © The George Balanchine Trust. Used with permission of The George Platt Lynes Estate. Jerome Robbins Dance Division, The New York Public Library for the Performing Arts. **Page 14: Top left:** Photo by Ernst Haas/Getty Images. BALANCHINE is a trademark of The George Balanchine Trust. **Top right:** Courtesy New York City Ballet Archives. BALANCHINE is a trademark of The George Balanchine Trust. **Bottom left:** Courtesy New York City Ballet Archives. **Bottom right:** Courtesy of Barbara Horgan. BALANCHINE is a trademark of The George Balanchine Trust. **Page 15: Top:** Courtesy New York City Ballet Archives. Photo by Martha Swope © The New York Public Library for the Performing Arts. BALANCHINE is a trademark of The George Balanchine Trust. **Center:** Photo by Martha Swope © The New York Public Library for the Performing Arts. **Bottom:** Photo by Tanaquil Le Clercq. Courtesy New York City Ballet Archives. **Page 16: Top:** *La Valse,* Choreography by George Balanchine, © The George Balanchine Trust. Courtesy New York City Ballet Archives. **Center:** With the permission of Richard Buckle, Esq. CBE. Harry Ransom Center, The University of Texas at Austin. BALANCHINE is a trademark of The George Balanchine Trust. **Bottom:** Photo John Taras. Courtesy New York City Ballet Archives. BALANCHINE is a trademark of The George Balanchine Trust.

PHOTO INSERT 2

Page 1: Top, center, bottom: Courtesy New York City Ballet Archives. BALANCHINE is a trademark of The George Balanchine Trust. **Page 2: Top, center, bottom:** Photo by Tanaquil Le Clercq. Courtesy New York City Ballet Archives. BALANCHINE is a trademark of The George Balanchine Trust. **Page 3: Top:** Photo © Fred Melton. Jerome Robbins Dance Division, The New York Public Library for the Performing Arts. BALANCHINE is a trademark of The George Balanchine Trust. **Center:** Gordon Parks/The LIFE Picture Collection/Shutterstock. BALANCHINE is a trademark of The George Balanchine Trust. **Bottom:** Used with permission of The George Platt Lynes Estate. **Page 4: Top left:** Photo by Carl Van Vechten, © Van Vechten Trust. Jerome Robbins Dance Division, The New York Public Library for the Performing Arts. **Top right:** Collection of the author. BALANCHINE is a trademark of The George Balanchine Trust. **Bottom:** *Agon,* Choreography by George Balanchine, © The George Balanchine Trust. Photo by Martha Swope © The New York Public Library for the Performing Arts. **Page 5: Top:** *Apollo,* Choreography by George Balanchine, © The George Balanchine Trust. Photo © Carolyn George. Jerome Robbins Dance Division, The New York Public Library for the Performing Arts. **Center:** *Stars and Stripes,* Choreography by George Balanchine, © The George Balanchine Trust. Gjon Mili/The LIFE Picture Collection/Shutterstock. **Bottom:** *The Seven Deadly Sins,* Choreography by George Balanchine, © The George Balanchine Trust. Gordon Parks/The LIFE Picture Collection/Shutterstock. **Page 6: Top left:** *Episodes,* Choreography by George Balanchine, © The George Balanchine Trust. Photo by Martha Swope © The New York Public Library for the Performing Arts. **Top right:** © Bakhrushin Theatre Museum, Moscow. **Bottom:** Courtesy New York City Ballet Archives. Photo by Martha Swope © The New York Public Library for the Performing Arts. BALANCHINE is a trademark of The George Balanchine Trust. **Page 7: Top:** Courtesy New York City Ballet Archives. Photo by Martha Swope © The New York Public Library for the Performing Arts. BALANCHINE is a trademark of The George Balanchine Trust. **Bottom left:** *A Midsummer Night's Dream,* Choreography by George Balanchine, © The George Balanchine Trust. Courtesy New York City Ballet Archives. **Bottom right:** *Prodigal Son,* Choreography by George Balanchine, © The George Balanchine Trust. Photo by Martha Swope © The New York Public Library for the Performing Arts. **Page 8: Top:** *Electronics,* Choreography by George Balanchine, © The George Balanchine Trust. Courtesy New York City Ballet Archives. **Center:** Courtesy New York City Ballet Archives. BALANCHINE is a trademark of The George Balanchine Trust. **Bottom:** © St. Petersburg State Museum of Theatre and Music. BALANCHINE is a trademark of The George Balanchine Trust. **Page 9: Top:** Courtesy New York City Ballet Archives. BALANCHINE is a trademark of The George Balanchine

Trust. **Center:** Courtesy of Art Palace of Georgia. BALANCHINE is a trademark of The George Balanchine Trust. **Bottom:** MS Thr 411 (2439), Harvard Theatre Collection, Houghton Library, Harvard University. BALANCHINE is a trademark of The George Balanchine Trust. **Page 10: Top:** Photographer: Fred Fehl. Photo courtesy of Gabriel Pinski. BALANCHINE is a trademark of The George Balanchine Trust. **Center:** *Don Quixote,* Choreography by George Balanchine, © The George Balanchine Trust. Jerome Robbins Dance Division, The New York Public Library for the Performing Arts. BALANCHINE is a trademark of The George Balanchine Trust. **Bottom:** Photo by Martha Swope © The New York Public Library for the Performing Arts. BALANCHINE is a trademark of The George Balanchine Trust. **Page 11: Top:** Photo by Paul Slade/Paris Match via Getty Images. BALANCHINE is a trademark of The George Balanchine Trust. **Bottom:** Gjon Mili/The LIFE Picture Collection/Shutterstock. BALANCHINE is a trademark of The George Balanchine Trust. **Page 12: Top:** Photo by Martha Swope © The New York Public Library for the Performing Arts. BALANCHINE is a trademark of The George Balanchine Trust. **Center:** George Balanchine, New York, 1971—contact sheet © The Irving Penn Foundation. BALANCHINE is a trademark of The George Balanchine Trust. **Bottom:** *Serenade,* Choreography by George Balanchine, © The George Balanchine Trust. Courtesy of Nolan T'Sani. **Page 13: Top left, top right:** Photo by Martha Swope © The New York Public Library for the Performing Arts. BALANCHINE is a trademark of The George Balanchine Trust. **Center:** *Violin Concerto,* Choreography by George Balanchine, © The George Balanchine Trust. Photo © Carolyn George. Jerome Robbins Dance Division, The New York Public Library for the Performing Arts. **Bottom:** *Symphony in Three Movements,* Choreography by George Balanchine, © The George Balanchine Trust. Photo by Martha Swope © The New York Public Library for the Performing Arts. **Page 14: Top left:** *Vienna Waltzes,* Choreography by George Balanchine, © The George Balanchine Trust. Courtesy New York City Ballet Archives. BALANCHINE is a trademark of The George Balanchine Trust. **Top right:** *Prodigal Son,* Choreography by George Balanchine, © The George Balanchine Trust. Photo by Martha Swope © The New York Public Library for the Performing Arts. **Bottom left:** *Ballo della Regina,* Choreography by George Balanchine, © The George Balanchine Trust. © Steven Caras, all rights reserved. **Center right:** *Agon,* Choreography by George Balanchine, © The George Balanchine Trust. Photo by Martha Swope © The New York Public Library for the Performing Arts. **Page 15: Top left:** Photo by Martha Swope © The New York Public Library for the Performing Arts. BALANCHINE is a trademark of The George Balanchine Trust. **Top right, center right:** Photo © Carolyn George. Jerome Robbins Dance Division, The New York Public Library for the Performing Arts. BALANCHINE is a trademark of The George Balanchine Trust. **Bottom left:** © Steven Caras, all rights reserved. BALANCHINE is a trademark of The George Balanchine Trust. **Bottom right:** *Robert Schumann's "Davidsbündlertänze,"* Choreography by George Balanchine, © The George Balanchine Trust. © Steven Caras, all rights reserved. **Page 16: Top left:** Courtesy New York City Ballet Archives. Photo by Martha Swope © The New York Public Library for the Performing Arts. BALANCHINE is a trademark of The George Balanchine Trust. **Top right:** Newberry Library, Chicago (The Lars Luick Papers). **Bottom:** *Adagio Lamentoso,* Choreography by George Balanchine, © The George Balanchine Trust. © Paul Kolnik.

INDEX

Page numbers of illustrations appear in italics.

ABOUT THE AUTHOR

JENNIFER HOMANS is the dance critic for *The New Yorker*. Her widely acclaimed *Apollo's Angels: A History of Ballet* was a bestseller and named one of the ten best books of the year by *The New York Times Book Review*. Trained in dance at George Balanchine's School of American Ballet, she performed professionally with the Pacific Northwest Ballet. She earned her BA at Columbia University and her PhD in modern European history at New York University, where she is a scholar in residence and the founding director of the Center for Ballet and the Arts.